MW01007016

# HISTORICAL DICTIONARY

The historical dictionaries present essential information on a broad range of subjects, including American and world history, art, business, cities, countries, cultures, customs, film, global conflicts, international relations, literature, music, philosophy, religion, sports, and theater. Written by experts, all contain highly informative introductory essays on the topic and detailed chronologies that, in some cases, cover vast historical time periods but still manage to heavily feature more recent events.

Brief A–Z entries describe the main people, events, politics, social issues, institutions, and policies that make the topic unique, and entries are cross-referenced for ease of browsing. Extensive bibliographies are divided into several general subject areas, providing excellent access points for students, researchers, and anyone wanting to know more. Additionally, maps, photographs, and appendixes of supplemental information aid high school and college students doing term papers or introductory research projects. In short, the historical dictionaries are the perfect starting point for anyone looking to research in these fields.

# HISTORICAL DICTIONARIES OF RELIGIONS, PHILOSOPHIES, AND MOVEMENTS

**Jon Woronoff, Series Editor**

# Historical Dictionary of Medieval Philosophy and Theology

## *Second Edition*

Stephen F. Brown
Juan Carlos Flores

ROWMAN & LITTLEFIELD
Lanham • Boulder • New York • London

Published by Rowman & Littlefield
A wholly owned subsidary of The Rowman & Littlefield Publishing Group, Inc.
4501 Forbes Boulevard, Suite 200, Lanham, Maryland 20706
www.rowman.com

Unit A, Whitacre Mews, 26-34 Stannary Street, London SE11 4AB

British Library Cataloguing in Publication Information Available

**Library of Congress Cataloging-in-Publication Data**

Names: Brown, Stephen F., author. | Flores, Juan Carlos, 1970–, author.
Title: Historical dictionary of medieval philosophy and theology / Stephen F. Brown, Juan Carlos
    Flores.
Description: Second edition. | Lanham : Rowman & Littlefield, 2018. | Series: Historical dictionaries
    of religions, philosophies, and movements | Includes bibliographical references.
Identifiers: LCCN 2018002878 (print) | LCCN 2018005525 (ebook) | ISBN 9781538114315 (elec-
    tronic) | ISBN 9781538114308 | ISBN 9781538114308¬q(hardcover : alk. paper)
Subjects: LCSH: Philosophy, Medieval—Dictionaries. | Theology—History—Middle Ages,
    600–1500—Dictionaries. | Philosophy—Dictionaries.
Classification: LCC B721 (ebook) | LCC B721 .B77 2018 (print) | DDC 189.03—dc23
LC record available at https://lccn.loc.gov/2018002878

Printed in the United States of America

*To Jack, Faith, Grace, Lucy, Nicolás, and Alex—*

*If you want to see far and wide, stand on the shoulders of giants.*

# Contents

# Editor's Foreword

This latest volume to the Historical Dictionaries of Religions, Philosophies, and Movements series focuses on the philosophy of the Middle Ages, but this is a philosophy so intertwined with religion that it also includes theology. Although covering mainly Christianity and the West, it also touches on Judaism and Islam and their centers in Europe and includes information on the great Greek philosophers Plato and Aristotle. Although relegated to the past, medieval philosophy and theology can be used to address present-day problems.

This second revised and expanded edition of *Historical Dictionary of Medieval Philosophy and Theology* contains a dictionary section with brief entries on important philosophers and thinkers of the period, such as Anselm, Thomas Aquinas, Peter Abelard, John Duns Scotus, and William of Ockham, but also their predecessors, such as Augustine, Plato, Aristotle, Avicenna, and Averroes. Other entries describe major concepts and issues, institutions and organizations, and conflicts and other events. A chronology and introduction provide a time line and an overview, appendixes contain reference material, and an extensive bibliography lists a variety of works for further research.

Given the unusually large span of time and amount of information in this book, it is fortunate that its two authors combine a broad range of backgrounds and interests. Stephen F. Brown is American, and Juan Carlos Flores was born in San Salvador, although both pursued their doctoral studies at the University of Louvain in Belgium. They obtained their doctorates in philosophy and also have extensive theological backgrounds. Dr. Brown completed his undergraduate studies at St. Bonaventure University and has taught in the Theology Department of Boston College for almost four decades. Dr. Flores did his doctoral dissertation on the doctrine of the Trinity and Henry of Ghent and is professor at the University of Detroit Mercy. Both have written extensively and are editors of medieval Latin philosophical and theological texts.

Jon Woronoff
Series Editor

# Reader's Notes

Medieval names in library catalogs or book indexes generally begin with the first name, so if you were looking for Peter Damian or Peter Lombard, you would look under Peter. This book follows that standard, but there are many Peters, Johns, and Williams. Some are more widely known by their last name, and many readers might not even know their first name. For example, the first entry in this dictionary is ABELARD, PETER, since most people have heard of Abelard. In fact, so many are familiar with that name that they might believe Abelard was his sole name.

An even more complex situation arises in the case of the names of Jewish and Muslim authors, as they have native names and also Latin names. To many non-Jewish or non-Muslim people, the only name they might know is the Latin (and English) form. For example, Averroes is the Latin name for the Arab philosopher Ibn Rushd, which could also be listed under RUSHD, IBN.

In this book, we have followed the general rule of listing authors under their first names. However, when someone's second name is used more often in the literature than their first name, or when the dominant use in the English-speaking world is the Latin form of a Jewish or Arabic author's name, we have gone with the more usual name. We have tried, however, to provide the alternative name as a cross-reference. For example, AVERROES is the main entry, but there is also a RUSHD, IBN *see* reference.

In the bibliography, we have tried to provide English translations of the primary writings of authors and the secondary writings about their lives and teachings in the same order as in the dictionary. Usually, secondary writings will indicate authors who are written about in the book or article titles. Whether they do or do not, we have indicated the subject of the book or article in parentheses at the end of the listing.

# Preface

*The Middle Ages* and *Medieval* were not originally purely temporal terms signifying the period between the ancient and modern worlds. They were pejorative expressions, much like the phrase *the Dark Ages*. What we call the Middle Ages was first viewed as a period of low intellectual achievement compared to the high philosophical and literary accomplishments of the Greco-Roman world that preceded it and the technological advances and philosophical and theological alternatives of the modern world that followed.

The negative judgment regarding medieval intellectual life is perhaps best captured in the closing paragraph of W. T. Stace's *A Critical History of Greek Philosophy*: "Philosophy is founded upon reason. It is the effort to comprehend, to understand, to grasp the reality of things intellectually. Therefore it cannot admit anything higher than reason. To exalt intuition, ecstasy, or rapture, above thought—this is death to philosophy. Philosophy, in making such an admission, lets out its own life-blood, which is thought. In Neo-Platonism, therefore, ancient philosophy commits suicide. This is the end. The place of philosophy is taken henceforth by religion. Christianity triumphs, and sweeps away all independent thought from its path. There is no more philosophy now till a new spirit of enquiry and wonder is breathed into man at the Renaissance and the Reformation. Then the new era begins, and gives birth to a new philosophic impulse, under the influence of which we are still living. But to reach that new era of philosophy, the human spirit had first to pass through the arid wastes of Scholasticism."

We hope that this volume will challenge to some degree this evaluation. While this book is not a history of medieval philosophy or theology but rather a historical dictionary, we have attempted to include within it a description of the important persons, events, and concepts that shaped medieval philosophy and theology. Perhaps surprisingly for some, this is not exclusively a dictionary of Christian philosophers and theologians. Arabian and Jewish thinkers played an important role in the history of medieval philosophy and theology—both within their own cultural and religious worlds as well as, and perhaps even more so, in the Christian world. The medieval world of philosophy and theology is a multicultural world. The medieval philosophical and theological endeavor was one of great interplay among authors from the three great religious traditions, who adopted, adapted, and shared the philosophical riches of the classical world and the religious resources of the biblical heritage.

In relation to the temporal context of this volume, we might clarify another point: among the authors, events, and concepts we include in this volume are some that certainly are not counted as medieval. Plato, Aristotle, Cicero, and Seneca lived centuries before the medieval period. The biblical revelation, on which the medieval conceptions of the created world were mainly based, was complete and already richly examined and interpreted when medievals studied it. Contemplation and friendship were discussed long before they were treated by medieval thinkers. Yet these ancient and biblical authors, events, and concepts were of the utmost importance to medieval philosophers and theologians. They are presented here in terms of their influence in the medieval era.

In compiling this book, we have depended on a large variety of primary and secondary sources. In a special way, we want to acknowledge our indebtedness to *The New Catholic Encyclopedia* (2002), *The Dictionary of the Middle Ages*, *The Columbia History of Western Philosophy*, *Dictionnaire de la Théologie Catholique*, *Dictionnaire de la Spiritualité*, and *Lexicon für Theologie und Kirche*. We have also depended on a number of other dictionaries and histories of philosophy and theology, most notably, E. Gilson, *History of Christian Philosophy in the Middle Ages*; A. Maurer, *Medieval Philosophy*; J. Marenbon, ed., *Medieval Philosophy*; J. J. E. Gracia and T. B. Noone, eds., *A Companion to Philosophy in the Middle Ages*; Y. Congar, *A History of Theology*; B. Hägglund, *History of Theology*; P. W. Carey and J. T. Lienhard, eds., *Biographical Dictionary of Christian Theologians*; J. Pelikan, *The Growth of Medieval Theology*; and M. L. Colish, *Medieval Foundations of the Western Intellectual Tradition*. The sources of the first edition of this work were printed works. Here in this second edition, our search for bibliography has been assisted by electronic sources, in particular the *Stanford Encyclopedia of Philosophy*.

# Acronyms and Abbreviations

| | |
|---|---|
| A | first column of a page |
| B | second column of a page |
| BL. | Blessed |
| c. | *capitulum* (chapter) |
| ca. | circa (about) |
| d. | died |
| ed. | edited by |
| ep. | *epistola* (letter) |
| fl. | flourished |
| *HCPMA* | (*History of Christian Philosophy in the Middle Ages*) |
| lect. | *lectio* (reading) |
| *LG* | *Lumen Gentium* (*Encyclical Letter: Light of the World*) |
| n. | *numerus* (paragraph number) |
| O. Cart. | Ordo Cartusiensis (Carthusians) |
| O. Cist. | Ordo Cisterciensium (Cistercians) |
| O.E.S.A. | Ordo Eremitarum Sancti Augustini (Order of the Hermits of St. Augustine) |
| O.F.M. | Ordo Fratrum Minorum (Franciscans) |
| O.P. | Ordo Praedicatorum (Dominicans) |
| O.S.B. | Ordo Sancti Benedicti (Benedictines) |
| p. | page |
| PG | Patrologia Graeca (Greek Patrology) |
| PL | Patrologia Latina (Latin Patrology) |
| St. | Saint |
| trans. | translated by |

# Chronology

**500 (ca.)** Dionysius the Pseudo-Areopagite, writings of.

**525 (ca.)** Boethius died.

**529** Justinian closes Platonic school at Athens; John Philoponus, *On the Eternity of the World*.

**532 (ca.)** Athenian philosophers establish a school at Harran.

**538 (ca.)** Simplicius writing commentaries at Harran.

**562** Cassiodorus, *Institutiones*.

**570** Muhammad born.

**575 (ca.)** John Philoponus died.

**590–604** Gregory the Great, pope.

**597** Augustine of Canterbury arrives in England.

**633** Isidore of Seville died.

**662** Maximus the Confessor died.

**711–712** Muslim conquest of Spain.

**735** Venerable Bede died.

**754 (ca.)** John Damascene died.

**762** Baghdad becomes capital of 'Abbasid caliphate.

**800** Charlemagne crowned emperor.

**804** Alcuin died.

**834** Fredegisus died.

**850–851** Eriugena, *On Predestination*.

**860 (ca.)** Ratramnus of Corbie, *De anima ad Odonem*.

**861–866** Eriugena, *Periphyseon*.

**867 (ca.)** Gottschalk of Orbais died.

**868** Ratramnus of Corbie died.

**870 (ca.)** Al-Kindi died.

**871 (ca.)** Eriugena died.

**893–908 (ca.)** Remigius of Auxerre expounds Martianus Capella and Boethius.

**925** Al-Razi died.

**942** Saadiah Gaon died.

**950** Al-Farabi died.

**953** Costa ben Luca died.

**1037** Avicenna died.

**1050** Ratramnus's positions on the Eucharist condemned at Synod of Vercelli.

**1057/8** Ibn Gabirol (Avicebron) died.

**1072** Peter Damian died.

**1076** Anselm, *Monologion*.

**1077–1078** Anselm, *Proslogion*.

**1092** Roscelin accused of tritheism.

**1093 (ca.)** Al-Ghazali, *The Incoherence of Philosophers*.

**1109** Anselm died.

**1116 (ca.)** Abelard, *Dialectica*.

**1120** Abelard, *Theologia "Summi boni"* (treats the Trinity).

**1121** Abelard's Trinitarian views condemned at Council of Soissons.

**1122** William of Champeaux died.

**1125 (ca.)** Roscelin died.

**1138** Abelard, *Ethics*.

**1142** Hugh of Saint-Victor died.

**1142 (ca.)** Abelard died.

**1153** Bernard of Clairvaux died.

**1160** Peter Lombard died.

**1160 (ca.)** John of Salisbury, *Metalogicon*.

**1173** Richard of Saint-Victor died.

**1180** Maimonides, *Mishneh Torah*; John of Salisbury died.

**1190** Maimonides, *Guide of the Perplexed*.

**1198** Averroes died.

**1200** First charter of University of Paris.

**1204** Maimonides died.

**1210** Aristotle's natural philosophy forbidden at Paris Arts Faculty.

**1214** First known charter of Oxford University; David of Dinant died.

**1221** St. Dominic died.

**1226** St. Francis died.

**1245** Alexander of Hales died.

**1249** William of Auvergne died.

**1253** Grosseteste died.

**1260–1270 (ca.)** William of Moerbeke, Latin translations of Aristotle.

**1264** Aquinas, *Summa contra Gentiles*.

**1267** Aquinas, *Summa theologiae*; Roger Bacon, *Opus maius*.

**1268** Bacon, *Opus minus* and *Opus tertium*.

**1270** Bishop Tempier condemns 13 propositions at Paris.

**1274** Aquinas died; Bonaventure died.

**1277** Bishop Tempier condemns 219 propositions at Paris; Peter of Spain died.

**1280** Albert the Great died.

**1284** Siger of Brabant died.

**1292** Roger Bacon died.

**1293** Henry of Ghent died.

**1308** John Duns Scotus died.

**1317–1327** Gersonides, *Wars of the Lord*.

**1321** Dante died.

**1322** Peter Aureoli died.

**1328** Meister Eckhart died.

**1334** Durandus died.

**1342** Marsilius of Padua died.

**1344** Gersonides died; Walter Chatton died.

**1347** William of Ockham died.

**1349** Thomas Bradwardine died; Robert Holcot died.

**1354** Turks occupy Gallipoli, reaching Europe.

**1358** Adam Wodeham died; Gregory of Rimini died.

**1361** Beginning of second wave of Black Death.

**1384** John Wycliffe died.

**1410** Hasdai Crescas died.

**1420** Pierre d'Ailly died.

**1429** John Gerson died; Paul of Venice died.

**1531** Niccolò Machiavelli, *The Prince*.

**1548** Francisco Suárez born.

**1596** René Descartes born.

**1597** Francisco Suárez, *Disputationes metaphysicae*.

**1599** Petrus Fonseca died.

**1605** Francis Bacon, *The Advancement of Learning*.

**1612** Suárez, *De legibus*.

**1617** Suárez died.

# Introduction

Medieval philosophy is an outgrowth and continuation of ancient philosophy. Plato, Aristotle, the Stoics, and the Neoplatonists formulated philosophical insights that, in the medieval period together with revelation, yielded a number of outstanding well-ordered visions of reality. "Scientifically well ordered" is a predominant characteristic of medieval philosophy and theology, especially in its more mature phases. This is certainly not true of Plato's dialogues taken either severally or as a whole. Though truer of Aristotle, his extant writings still left certain fundamental issues open for intense debate, development, and resolution. Moreover, his *First Philosophy*, which we now call the *Metaphysics* (the treatise that comes closest to presenting his fundamental science of reality), is a posthumous compilation of his different insights into first and dependent causes and the unified character of general reality, rather than, as medieval thinkers would later aspire to achieve, an integrated science of this subject. Nevertheless, Plato and Aristotle, the primary philosophical sources for medieval thinkers, in their various inquiries do adhere consistently to discernible methodologies that greatly informed the fundamental frameworks of medieval outlooks. Choosing between the Platonic and Aristotelian approaches as starting points for a philosophy became for medievals, as for many even today, a basic decision, one with far-reaching consequences. Though sharing enough to be synthesized by some into one vision, most subsequent philosophers understood the irreducible fundamental differences of these two perennial approaches. It forced them to choose as a starting point either one or the other.

Plato's basic insight is that the mind's assessment of sense experience appeals to sources only seen, however obliquely, with the mind's eye. When we judge, for example, one thing to be better than another, we appeal to a standard of goodness. This standard cannot appear to us through the senses. If it did, it would not really be the true standard, for then we would still be able to judge it itself in relation to other things, necessitating a higher norm in accord with an invisible standard of goodness. Though we appeal to goodness as a standard of judgment, we do not understand goodness itself perfectly, and we experience much difficulty when trying to give a scientific account of it. However, forms such as goodness are each understood as one unchanging essence. If goodness were somehow many or were of different types, it would need to be judged to be a good thing, and that by which it

1

would be so judged would then be goodness itself. The soul that judges by means of these perfect forms possesses, therefore, some knowledge of an unchanging measure, however imperfect that knowledge may be.

True knowledge, properly speaking, can only be of unchanging things, since they alone can yield unwavering truth and provide a norm for judging changing realities. Of changing things, namely sensible things, we can only have opinion, not true knowledge. Man's access to unchanging realities that transcend the sensible world is evidence, for Plato, of the preexistence of the soul. The soul must have lived in a world of unchanging realities before its birth into its present earthly existence. The access to unchanging realities is not explainable in terms of our present sense experiences, which are of changing things. Yet, some knowledge of unchanging realities is now present to us. So, it can only be present to us as something we remember from our pre-earthly life. These basic insights pervade Plato's dialogues, and they provide keys to the further developments of his thought. We cannot here spell out all these developments that are found in his many dialogues, but we can indicate two general consequences of his developed thought (refer to the section "Plato in the Medieval World"). First, the sensible world, as a copy of a truer intelligible reality, owes its character and order to an ultimate source or cause that produced the orderly world we inhabit out of the desire to give of itself, that is, to share its goodness and wisdom. Secondly, the soul, above all a lover of true reality, thirsts for a return to this ultimate source, which is the ground of life, knowledge, and reality.

The central tenets of Aristotle's philosophy likewise depend on his starting point, which is his account of change. Even in the *Metaphysics*, dealing with topics to be studied after all others, he begins by addressing change as that which first presents itself as a subject for philosophical questioning. The fact of something *new* coming into being, the most evident of phenomena, must be explained, not explained away, as Aristotle feels his predecessors had done. Plato's unchanging forms, understood by Aristotle as causes separate from changing things, fail by their very definition as unchanging realities to account for change. The same applies to those philosophers who, like Parmenides and Melissus, posit only one principle of being. These thinkers are caught in the following dilemma: either something comes from being or from nonbeing. If from the former, then it already was, and therefore does not come to be. If from the latter, then nothing ever would come to be. Either way, there is no real change, in the sense of something truly new coming into being. On the other hand, claiming that all reality is in flux or is always changing, as Heraclitus and his followers seem to convey, destroys all intelligibility in nature, as there remains no fixed ground for our judgments. When we would speak of anything, it already has passed away or ceased to be. Learning from the failures of earlier natural philosophers to explain change or how something new can come into reality, Aristotle finally arrived at an account of change that was based on three principles: two contraries, and an underlying subject. Every type of change is the actualization of a potency.

This portrait of change is dealt with more fully in our entry on Aristotelianism. Suffice it to say here that in this account Aristotle discovers the immanent forms governing and dictating the goals of all processes, including the human soul as the form of the body. He also discovers the eternal nature of change, the eternal character of the universe that includes it, and the eternal existence of the ultimate cause of all change and motion, the first Unmoved Mover. This First Cause, which is pure actuality, governs all things as the ultimate end that each thing approaches through the limited actualization of its form. As natural forms are immanent, the sensible world is not a copy of higher unchanging forms and does not owe its orderly patterns to a Creator. The Unmoved Mover is not an efficient cause. It is complete in itself and has no relation on its part to other things. However, other things are all related to it. They want either consciously or unconsciously to be complete just as the Prime Mover is complete. They do not want to be the Prime Mover, since they do not have the nature or essence of the Prime Mover. However, they do want to be complete according to their natures. Men, for instance, by having a human form or nature, want to be as fully human as they can be. In this way, but at their own level, they try to imitate the Prime Mover, aiming at becoming complete, but complete as human beings. Their immanent form, the human soul, aims them in that direction.

The immanence of forms not only is the key to Aristotle's philosophy of human activity; indeed it is the key to the activities of all things, whose forms make them the kind of things they are and lead them to do the things they do. The immanence of forms also means that human knowledge of them is abstractive: the intellect knows these forms when it draws them out of the sensible particulars in which the forms are found. We do not arrive at the knowledge of universal principles through recollection of universal transcendent realities we encountered in some previous life. Finally, as the human soul itself is an immanent form, its goal is actualization according to its nature, a nature that is fulfilled chiefly through growth in knowledge and moral virtue. When Aristotle says, "All men by nature desire to know," he is not simply giving a description. He is declaring that it is the very nature of man that he wants to know the things that lead to the highest human happiness. Only in pursuing such objects will he be fulfilled as a human being.

More than Plato and Aristotle, the Neoplatonists, particularly Plotinus and Proclus, do provide explicit philosophical systems, basically syntheses of Platonic and Aristotelian thought. These syntheses, which served as examples for medieval philosophical and theological systems, essentially subordinated Aristotelianism to Platonism: the sensible reality adequately described by Aristotle depends on the more fundamental reality discerned from Plato's writings. Plato's ultimate source is to be understood as the One, from which all things emanate (through necessary stages bridging spiritual and material reality) and to which all things seek to return. In general, medieval thinkers try to move beyond the necessity embedded in this conception, with its concomitant theses, in their pursuit of an intelligible account of the God of revelation who freely created the world.

While "scientifically well ordered" is the characteristic style of medieval speculation, God oriented is its central tendency. Understanding the most worthy objects of knowledge, namely, God and his works, is the chief task. The resources for this task are reason and revelation. The scientific character of medieval philosophy and theology largely stems from the conviction of the fundamental compatibility of these two sources. The truth is one. How can two contradictories both be true? Revealed truth is therefore compatible with rational truth. The truth of reason found in the texts of the philosophical tradition must be gathered and synthesized. Such philosophical syntheses in their turn must themselves be examined and judged in relation to the truth of revelation. This attitude is what generated competing philosophical and theological visions. The philosophies of Plato, Aristotle, and their followers are viewed by medieval thinkers as great intellectual inheritances, since these philosophers concluded, on the basis of reason, truths about God and the world that were often consonant with and illustrative of truths affirmed by revelation. However, the great Greek thinkers did not say all that could be said about God. Nor were they free from erroneous judgments. Some of their conclusions stood in need of revision. Inspired by the teachings of revelation and their conviction of the one divine source of the truths found in creation and in revelation, medieval thinkers drew further intelligibility from studying the philosophical tradition and the world they experienced, and they formulated well-ordered versions of this intelligibility. These syntheses are neither classical nor modern, but properly medieval, though dependent on classical sources.

To the extent that the wisdom of the classical philosophical tradition is still relevant today, medieval philosophy and theology continue to have something to offer us. To realize this more fully, medieval thought needs to be studied, understood, and appreciated in terms of its own richness, not according to how it agrees with our present-day ways of thinking. To the extent that solidly based, well-ordered thought can still be one of the aspirations of our life of reason, medieval philosophy and theology provide some of history's best models. How this desire for a well-thought-out, unified view of reality cannot be an aspiration today is difficult to see. It challenges many contemporary trends that use reason more for the destruction of argument and reasoned discourse, substituting the celebration of personality, or limiting all worth in terms of immediate practical ends. Such trends toward disorder have always existed. The desire to find the fundamental order of reality, as it presents itself in experience and well-informed tradition, remains the purest aspiration of reason, the core of our being. Furthermore, medieval thinkers, in their quest for God, whose presence they found in the proper ordering of the soul and in the beauty of the world, provided some of the most thorough reflections on the spiritual dimensions of reality—reflections that are still relevant in our own present-day search for the meaning of our human existence. In addition, the fruits of their concern for rigor and clarity provide us with some of the best examples of intellectual analysis.

## VARIETY WITHIN MEDIEVAL PHILOSOPHY AND THEOLOGY

The medieval period is the longest of the traditional historical periods of philosophy and theology. Encompassing three rich religious traditions, there is within it also great diversity. Above, an attempt was made to establish that the defining feature of medieval philosophy and theology is its well-ordered character. The well-ordered nature of medieval thought in no way implies a lack of diversity in medieval attempts to harmonize the various classical philosophies with the revealed texts of the sacred Scriptures. The Arabic philosophers, Avicenna and Averroes, for instance, both deal seriously with Aristotle. Avicenna, however, is very much inspired by Neoplatonism, and he reads Aristotle's texts from a metaphysical perspective that is more conformed to the Neoplatonic tradition. He thus deals with being and its attributes, as well as with God as the cause of being.

Averroes sets aside this metaphysical approach to reality and attempts to return to a purer, in the sense of a less Neoplatonic, approach to Aristotle. He accentuates Aristotle's natural philosophy and pays attention to its focus on motion. His analysis of motion leads him to attend to the immanent causes of changing things as well as to the transcendent immovable causes, among which the First or Prime Mover is the highest. Avicenna and Averroes thus present us with two different forms of Aristotelianism. In the Christian world, St. Bonaventure also attends to Aristotle. Yet, his particular view of reality gathers its impetus from the Platonic tradition, above all from the writings of St. Augustine. Although St. Bonaventure incorporates many Aristotelian elements into his vision of things, he subordinates them to the Christian approach to truth found in the Augustinian tradition. His approach to God stresses introspection: an analysis of cognition, judgment, and volition at different levels possesses the symbolic character of sensible things, the soul as the higher place where these things reveal a truer meaning, and God as the ultimate source of meaning and the Creator of the soul and of all sensible reality.

## OVERVIEW OF THE MEDIEVAL INTELLECTUAL WORLD

The above samples of the different ways in which medieval philosophers and theologians read Aristotle are only a hint of the rich diversity found in the writings of the medieval authors from the three religious traditions examined here. In the remainder of this introduction, we attempt to present an overview of the world of medieval philosophy and theology to help the reader better locate the authors, events, and concepts presented in the Dictionary that follows. This overview aims to provide the context for a fuller understanding of the descriptions given in the particular items treated in the present volume.

Essentially, medieval philosophers and theologians depended on revelation and reason as their sources. For them, revelation was the word of God found in their sacred Scriptures. Jews, Christians, and Muslims are described as having this in common: they are "people of the Book." Jews are guided by the Hebrew Scriptures. These same Scriptures are called the Old Testament by Christians, who have added the Scriptures of the New Testament to their canon of books revealed by God. Muslims also accept the Old and New Testaments as divinely revealed and consider Moses and Christ as prophets. They interpret these Scriptures according to the later revelation to their prophet, Mohammad, that they believe is found in the Koran.

Respect for teachers was strong in all three traditions. For the Jewish people, this respect was inspired by the words of Daniel (12:3): "Those who are wise shall shine like the brightness of the sky, and those who lead many to righteousness, like the stars for ever and ever." Similarly, St. Paul (2 Timothy 3:16) encouraged Christians to reflect on their sacred books with the words, "All Scripture is inspired by God and is useful for teaching, for reproof, for correction, and for training in righteousness." Ghazali, in *Ihya ulum al-din* (*The Revival of Religious Sciences*, trans. N. A. Faris, 2), speaks for Muslims: "The guides for the road [straight path to God] are the learned men who are heirs of the Prophet. . . . I have therefore deemed it important to engage in writing this book to revive the science of religion, to bring to light the exemplary lives of the departed imams, and to show what branches of knowledge the prophets and the virtuous fathers regard as useful." In their studies, along with the Scriptures, the medievals also used the resources of reason. Reason for them often concretely took the form of a book, since the chief representatives of natural reason were the philosophers whose writings strongly influenced human efforts to understand the world and the meaning of life. For Moses Maimonides, a leading medieval Jewish thinker, the principal representative of reason was Aristotle. The same could be said for the Islamic author Averroes and for the Christian theologian Thomas Aquinas. For others in the same three traditions, the chief voice of reason came from the Neoplatonists: Plotinus and Proclus for the 11th-century Jewish philosopher Avicebron; Denis the Areopagite for the ninth-century Christian author John Scotus Eriugena; and Proclus and the Neoplatonic Alexandrian commentators, especially John Philoponus, for the ninth-century Muslim writer al-Kindi. In their efforts to come to an understanding of God's wisdom, or the Book of Life, the Jewish, Christian, and Muslim authors used both books, revelation, or the Book of Scripture, and reason, or the Book of Nature.

These different religious traditions viewed revelation and reason in various ways. The Jewish and Muslim traditions tended to view the Scriptures predominantly as a collection of laws for guiding their actions as the people of God. The Christian tradition certainly adhered to the moral precepts, such as the Ten Commandments, but it also viewed God's revelation as presenting essential elements of belief or faith. Christian doctrines, such as the Trinity of persons in God and the twofold nature of Christ, as God and man, required justification and meaningful clarification, as well as defenses when attacked. How could God be both one and three? How could Christ be both God and man? In less complicated ways, Judaism and Islam, though religions of law, are also religions of faith, and they also had need of theologies: they too had to provide justifications, clarifications, and defenses for beliefs concerning the nature and attributes of God, the character of creation, and the instruments of divine providence. All three religious traditions viewed God as the author of all things and thus of revelation and of true reason. Al-Kindi, in his *Metaphysics* or *On First Philosophy*, expressed well the attitude that justified the use of all God-given sources in the search for truth: "We ought not to be ashamed of appreciating the truth and of acquiring it wherever it comes from, even if it comes from races distant and nations different from us. For the seeker of truth nothing takes precedence over the truth, and there is no disparagement of the truth, nor belittling either of him who speaks it or of him who conveys it" (ed. Abu Ridah, c. 1, p. 103, 4–8; trans. A. Ivry, p. 58).

## FAITH AND REASON

Although medieval thinkers within all three religious traditions could justify the use of reason in their attempts to understand God's revelation to them, by affirming that God is the author of the Book of Scripture and the Book of Nature and that any conflict between the two books could only be apparent, the medieval Christian authors provide many more explicit reflections on conflicts between faith and reason. Medieval Muslim writers interpreted their Scriptures within the tradition of the heirs to the Prophet. Their Jewish counterparts followed in the footsteps of the interpreters of their Law. Christian theologians took their lead from the early Church Fathers, in whose writings the battle between faith and reason had already been waged. Tertullian, in the late second and early third centuries, underscored the conflict in his famous set of rhetorical questions: "What has Athens to do with Jerusalem? What concord is there between the Academy and the Church? What between heretics and Christians?" (*Prescription against Heretics*, c. 7). For Tertullian, philosophy of every type was the source of heresy, not the source of truth. On the other hand, Clement of Alexandria, at roughly the same time in the Greek world, took a much more positive view of philosophy in his *Stromata* or *Miscellanies*, c. 5: "God is the cause of all good things; but of some primarily, as of the Old and the New Testament; and of others by consequence, as philosophy. Perchance, too, philosophy was given to the Greeks directly and primarily, till the Lord should call the Greeks. For this was a schoolmaster to bring the Hellenic mind, as the law, the Hebrews, to Christ. Philosophy, therefore, was a preparation, paving the way for him who is perfected in Christ."

These citations from Tertullian and Clement of Alexandria stand for negative and positive views toward philosophy within the tradition of the Christian Fathers of the Church. Similar attitudes can be found among medieval Jewish and Muslim authors. In general, however, some reconciliation of faith and reason was achieved in the intellectual worlds of all three religions. The dominant and more nuanced Christian attitude is expressed by the words of St. Augustine in *On Christian Doctrine* (II, 42): "But just as poor as the store of gold and silver and garments which the people of Israel brought with them out of Egypt was in comparison with the riches which they afterwards attained at Jerusalem, . . . so poor is all the useful knowledge which is gathered from the books of the heathen when compared with the knowledge of Holy Scripture. For whatever man may have learnt from other sources, if it is hurtful, it is there condemned; if it is useful, it is therein contained. And while every man may find there all that he has learnt of useful things elsewhere, he will find there in much greater abundance things that are to be found nowhere else, but can be learnt only in the wonderful sublimity and wonderful simplicity of the Scriptures." Basically, for Augustine, all the traditional Greek and Roman liberal arts (grammar, rhetoric, dialectic, arithmetic, geometry, astronomy, and music) could be helpful, indeed even necessary, for understanding the Scriptures. Yet, he always stressed that they must be at the service of the divinely revealed truth.

## TERMS *THEOLOGY* AND *PHILOSOPHY*

It is important here to clarify the meaning of words like *theology* and *philosophy*, since they will be words often used and employed in different senses.

*Theology* is not a biblical word, and its use was avoided especially in the Latin West. Tertullian in *Ad nationes* reported a distinction presented by the Roman author Varro (d. 27 B.C.) distinguishing three types of theology: one that presented the gods of the poets; another, the gods of the philosophers; and a third, the gods of the city. In this Varronian tradition, *theology* signifies one of these three explanations of the gods. It thus was a term that was usually avoided by Tertullian and other Latin Christian writers. For Augustine, also, the term *theology* had these Varronian meanings, and he criticizes each of them in Book VI of *The City of God.* Even when he praises the Platonists for presenting God as transcending the soul and as the creator of the world, he calls them "knowers of God" (*Dei cognitores*) rather than "theologians" (*theologi*).

It seems that in the Latin West it is not before Peter Abelard that we find *theology* used for a summa of Christian teachings. In his *Commentary on Romans*, Abelard refers a number of times to a *Theologia*, as when he says, "But the solutions to these proposed questions we will leave to the examination that will take place in our *Theology.*" This use of the term, however, seems to die out with the death of Abelard.

It returns again in the 13th century with Albert the Great, who seems to have Aristotle in mind when he employs it. For Aristotle, in his *Metaphysics*, which ends with the treatment of the First Mover (or God), speaks of his treatise as being "theological." All the more, believes Albert, should Christians, who study the true God revealed in the Scriptures, be able to call their study of the divine revelation in the Scriptures theological. Yet even here one must be cautious. In the mid-13th century, Richard Rufus, in the prologue to his *Commentary on the Sentences of Peter Lombard*, will limit the meaning of *theology* to the Scriptures themselves and will not apply the term to any human study of the realities revealed through the Scriptures: "This commentary does not seem to be necessary, since this summa is not theology itself, nor any part of it. Theology is the divine Scriptures complete in themselves and perfect without this or any other summa. Rather such summae are partial clarifications of some of the things which are said in an obscure way in the Scriptures, and are therefore useful and are things added to help us."

At the beginning of the 14th century at Paris, the Dominican Durandus of Saint-Pourçain, as will be seen later, declared that when we ask, "Is theology science?" the term *theology* can mean "the Scriptures themselves" or "the study whereby the things handed down in the Scriptures are defended and clarified by using sources that are better known to us" or "the study that deduces further things from the sayings of the Scriptures in a way that conclusions are deduced from premises." In short, in the medieval period, the term *theology* will have a variety of meanings.

The transmission of the Greek term *philosophia*, philosophy or love of wisdom, in the Latin tradition also shows its many meanings. The origin of the term is attributed to Pythagoras, who did not want to surrender to the pretense of being "wise" but preferred to describe himself as a philosopher or "lover of wisdom." In the Roman world, Cicero called philosophy the mother of the arts. Seneca was more technical, and he offered a division of philosophy, according to a Stoic-Platonic model, into rational philosophy (logic), natural philosophy (physics), and moral philosophy (ethics). An alternative division, that of Aristotle, was gleaned from a search of his works by Boethius and consisted of logic, theoretical philosophy (physics, mathematics, and "first philosophy" or theology), practical philosophy (ethics, politics, and economics), and poetical philosophy. The Stoic-Platonic and Aristotelian schemas were both divisions of philosophy in its strict or technical sense.

In a more common meaning, *philosophy* was taken to stand for all learning and thus included among its parts the classical liberal arts mentioned above. It could also refer to the different sects of philosophy (in the strict sense), as, for instance, when Cicero speaks in his *De oratore* (*On the Orator*) of "the proper function of the two philosophies," that is, of the Academics (the followers of Plato) and the Peripatetics (the disciples of Aristotle).

In contrast with the term *theology*, the word *philosophy* is found in the Bible, where it is used once by St. Paul (Colossians 2:8): "Beware that you are not deceived by philosophy!" Paul's warning according to medieval Christian authors should be read in terms of the specification made by the Letter of James (3:15), which warns against wisdom from below or earthly wisdom. In chapter 7 of his *Prescription against Heretics*, cited above, Tertullian used *philosophy* in this sense when he attacked those who attempted "to produce a mottled Christianity of Stoic, Platonic, and dialectical composition."

Other early Christian authors took a different approach. They had studied philosophy before converting to Christianity and saw the benefits it could provide as they searched for truth and for understanding and attempted to strengthen their faith and the faith of others. In his *Confessions*, Augustine praised Cicero's *Hortensius* as an instrument of God that led him beyond the materialist trap of the Manichean philosophy. In his *On Christian Teaching*, he urged caution when studying pagan learning, but one of the main purposes of this work was to argue how philosophy (in the general sense that included the seven liberal arts and many other disciplines) could help in our understanding of sacred Scripture. He even went on to suggest that his Christian readers study philosophy in its more technical sense, advising them to "read the Platonists." In such exhortations, he was only advocating what he and many other Greek and Latin Fathers of the Church had in fact done. Augustine contrasted the "philosophy of this world," "Academic philosophy," "the philosophy of the Gentiles," and "worldly philosophy" with "Christian philosophy," "our philosophy," "true and sacred philosophy," and "the most true philosophy," describing thereby the difference between pagan and Christian ways of life and truth and even calling Christian faith "philosophy."

Through the works of Cassiodorus and Isidore of Seville that deal with the liberal arts, philosophy, in the sense of the general pagan knowledge as employed in Augustine's program of Christian education, was passed down to the Carolingian world. In his *On Grammar*, Alcuin, Charlemagne's educational leader, wrote of the trivium and quadrivium as "the seven steps of philosophy" that are necessary to lead the mind to "the heights of sacred Scripture" (PL 101:853–54).

Augustine's contrast between "worldly philosophy" and "Christian philosophy" carried over into the concrete when the term *philosopher* was used. In a sermon on the feast of St. Augustine, Peter Comestor employed this term to describe Augustine himself, as he provided a portrait of St. Monica, Augustine's mother, asking God that "He might make her son be a Catholic rather than a philosopher." The same author used the title "philosopher" to describe Horace, a poet attached to "worldly" rather than "heavenly" wisdom. The students of Peter Abelard also referred to him as "a philosopher," but in a very different and affirming sense: because he was a person who tried to satisfy students' requests for reasons that would support the mysteries of faith proclaimed in the Bible.

## "PHILOSOPHY" IN 13TH-CENTURY EUROPE

The Augustinian "philosophy" program itself continued up to the 13th century (and beyond), with the liberal arts and certain elements of the Stoic and Platonist philosophies that had been assimilated into it helping to direct the mind to the heights of sacred Scripture. In the new universities, founded in the late 12th and early 13th centuries, the curriculum of the Arts Faculty served a preparatory function, providing students with the liberal arts, tools they needed for their later work in the studies of Scripture, law, and medicine. The principal component in this preparatory program of studies that might be considered philosophy in the technical sense was dialectic or logic. During these years of preparatory studies in dialectic, the Old Logic (the *Isagoge* or *Introduction* of Porphyry and *The Categories* and *On Interpretation* of Aristotle, with Boethius's commentaries) and the New Logic (Aristotle's *Prior Analytics*, *Posterior Analytics*, *Topics*, and *Sophistical Refutations*, translated in the 12th century) were the core of the logic curriculum.

During and after these introductory studies, students could learn indirectly the philosophies of the Stoics and Platonists that had been assimilated into the commentaries, questions, and disputations they followed. Philosophy in its strict technical sense, however, only gradually gained a stronger foothold in the universities. This additional philosophical learning only came with the translations of Aristotle's nonlogical works (such as *The Physics*, *On the Soul*, *Metaphysics*, *On the Heavens*, and *Nicomachean Ethics*) and the Greek and Arabic commentaries on them that were translated in the late 12th century and throughout much of the 13th. It was at this point that medieval Christians directly encountered the very real challenge presented by a "pure" philosopher, Aristotle, to their inherited Christian worldview. During the first half of the 13th century, the public reading of Aristotle's works in courses was frequently prohibited, but in 1255 at Paris these works became part of the official curriculum. In effect, from this time on, the Faculty of Arts gradually became a faculty focused mainly on Aristotelian philosophy.

The condemnation in 1277 of certain propositions alleged to be taught in the Faculty of Arts at Paris reveals how the arrival of Aristotle's purely pagan view of reality could challenge the dominant Christian view that had been passed down through the teachings of the Church Fathers, especially through the works of St. Augustine. Was it possible to employ Aristotle's philosophy as a handmaid or servant of Scripture without respecting it on its own terms? Was it possible to take Aristotle most seriously and not have to adapt in a significant way the traditional Christian vision of reality? The seriousness of the challenge is evident if we pay attention to the condemned statements that deal with philosophy:

1. That there is no more excellent state than to give one's self to philosophy.
2. That the wise men of the world are only the philosophers.
3. That there is no question that can be dealt with through reason that the philosopher should not dispute and definitively settle, because reasons are gathered from things.

Such claims and the reaction to them at the University of Paris reveal well the serious effect the arrival of Aristotle's philosophy had on the universities. In reality, the universities for the most part developed their curriculum in the Arts Faculty and the Theology Faculty as a response to this Aristotelian challenge. The thrust of the third proposition listed above reveals the condemned claim that from a certain interpretation of Aristotle's works, the intelligible content of reality was exhausted by the natural abilities of a philosopher. Articles of the Christian faith, such as the Trinity and the Incarnation, had no intelligibility from this radical Aristotelian perspective. They were simply articles of faith, statements to be blindly believed. The claims implied in this proposition were a denial of the meaning and truth-value of all the articles of the Christian faith, a rejection of the meaningfulness of the Septuagint text of Isaiah the prophet (Isaiah 7:9): "Unless you believe, you shall not understand," and a dismissal of theology as "Faith seeking under-standing," the motto of the tradition flowing from St. Augustine through St. Anselm.

Here we have clear evidence that a certain approach to Aristotle's philoso-phy was viewed as a challenge to the intelligible character of Christian belief. Yet we also have similar evidence that at the University of Paris, Aristotelian philosophical argument had gained a real hearing and was for many, in different ways, a respected discipline despite the problems to which the condemnations pointed. There was a saying in the earlier years of the 13th-century universities that "one should never get gray hair in the Arts Faculty." This was a way of characterizing the preparatory character of the Arts faculty when its curriculum was mainly centered on the seven liberal arts. In these circumstances, masters of arts should want eventually to move on to the higher, more challenging, faculties of Scripture, law, and medicine. When the Arts Faculty gradually became an Aristotelian philosophy enclave, some of the teachers wanted to stay. They thought, or at least were deemed to think, that philosophy dealt with reality and that theology was a matter of pure belief, empty of intelligibility, or that Scripture and theology put into simple and imaginative language the truths that were more literally and sub-tly expressed by the philosophers. This view, however, was certainly not a stance that dominated. For most members of the Arts Faculty and all mem-bers of the Theology Faculty at this time, Aristotelian philosophy was a handmaid to theology. Among these, some judged that it could be a better handmaid when a knowledge of it was developed in as strong a way as possible and on its own terms. Others, such as Peter John Olivi, saw this push for a stronger role of philosophy as an effort to idolize Aristotle, turning him into "a god of this world."

## PARALLELS IN JUDAISM AND ISLAM

Among Muslims and Jews in Islamic lands, where the educated language for both was Arabic, the usual terms for *philosophy* and *theology*, namely *falsa-fah* (*falasifa*: philosophers) and *kalam* respectively, also had different mean-ings. In the case of *falsafah*, depending on the context, it could have broad and narrow senses, meaning either secular learning or a type or sect of philosophy. At times, *falsafah* is used for any natural knowledge or for general teachings, such as the disciplines of the liberal arts, obtained from "foreign" sources. At other times, it signifies the teachings of the technical philosophers, and in these cases, the meaning can vary according to each "philosopher" or "theologian" and the claims of his doctrine. Moreover, depending on the context and user, *falsafah* could be seen either favorably or unfavorably. Ghazali, for instance, can be viewed as antiphilosophical, when in reality he was not opposed to technical philosophy as such but rather challenged the philosophical approaches of those who in an uncritical way accepted too readily certain Greek philosophical positions, especially some of the Aristotelian theses concerning the natural world, such as affirming that God knows only universals, not particulars, or maintaining that the world is eternal.

Even after *kalam*, literally "word" or "speech," came to mean in intellectual circles theology as a scientific study, different approaches to *kalam* emerged, each with its own method and purpose. *Kalam*, a term that could be translated as "dialectical theology," had its origins in the Muslim world, especially among the Mu'tazilites. Perhaps the real import of *kalam* can best be gained from its use by Saadiah Gaon, the Jewish author who wrote in Arabic in the 10th century. His *Book of Doctrines and Beliefs* is his effort to strengthen and correct the beliefs of his fellow Jews by clarifying the collection of foundational Jewish beliefs. He provides a detailed discussion of the attributes of God that includes a denunciation of the Christian Trinity and defends with four Aristotelian-type arguments creation ex nihilo, as he opposes Aristotle's theory of the eternity of the world.

In sum, the main conflicts between philosophy and theology in all three religious traditions were similar and reach their highest intensity when *philosophy* is taken in its strictest senses, referring to the philosophy of the Platonists in the earlier medieval conflicts and to the philosophy of Aristotle when his nonlogical works were translated into Arabic and Latin.

## MEDIEVAL JUSTIFICATIONS FOR THE USE OF PHILOSOPHY

Clement of Alexandria, in the opening chapter of his *Stromata*, provided the analogy that justified the respect medieval Christians gave to the guidance passed down by the Fathers of the Church: "It is a good thing, I reckon, to leave to posterity good children. This is the case with children of our bodies. But words are the progeny of the soul. Hence we call those who have instructed us, fathers." Whether they were called "the heirs of the Prophet," "the interpreters of the Law," or "the Fathers of the Church," the ancients were respected guides to the teachings of the Scriptures. When Peter Abelard was criticized by St. Bernard of Clairvaux and William of Saint-Thierry for using pagan authors as authorities, he then instinctively turned to the Fathers of the Church for his justification. He argued that he was simply following the Patristic tradition. His first appeal was to St. Jerome, who in his *Letter to Magnus*, countering at an earlier time the challenge of his use of pagan sources, claimed,

And as if this were not enough, that leader of the Christian army [St. Paul], that unvanquished pleader for the cause of Christ, skillfully turns a chance inscription into a proof of the faith. For he had learned from the true David to wrench the sword of the enemy out of his hand and with his own blade to cut off the head of the arrogant Goliath. He had read in Deuteronomy the command given by the voice of the Lord that when a captive woman had had her head shaved, her eyebrows and all her hair cut off, and her nails pared, she might then be taken to wife. Is it surprising that I too, admiring the fairness of her form and the grace of her eloquence, desire to make that secular wisdom which is my captive and my handmaid, a matron of the true Israel? Or that shaving off and cutting away all in her that is dead, whether this be idolatry, pleasure, error, or lust, I take her to myself clean and pure and beget by her servants for the Lord of the Sabbath? My efforts promote the advantage of Christ's family, my so-called defilement with an alien increases the number of my fellow-servants.

Abelard later could, and did, enlist, among others, the voices of Cyprian, Hilary, Eusebius, and Gregory the Great, and he invoked again Jerome's image of the handmaid to illustrate the servant character of philosophy, the class name for all pagan learning, including philosophy properly so called.

Jewish and Muslim authors fought parallel battles concerning the use of philosophy. Moses Maimonides, for example, in his *Treatise on Logic*, refereed the debate between the superiority of logic over grammar, portraying logic as a universal grammar and distinguishing between generally accepted religious opinions and traditions and universally and necessarily valid ones. His *Guide of the Perplexed*, dealing with the traditional Jewish teachings, became one of medieval Judaism's most studied and controversial works. In his treatment of the problem of the relation between faith and reason, Maimonides was influenced strongly by the Islamic philosopher Al-Farabi, who provided a contrasting treatment of philosophical logic and the grammar of ordinary language. In effect, the extended result of this debate for Al-Farabi was that religion is essentially the popular expression of philosophy communicated to nonphilosophical believers by prophets. Al-Farabi's position was influential among several of the philosophically inclined, such as Avicenna, Averroes, and Maimonides, who nuanced and adapted it within their own systems. Their attitudes toward reason and revelation, however, were found unacceptable by many Jewish and Muslim theologians or interpreters of the divine law.

## BEGINNING AND DEVELOPMENT OF MEDIEVAL ARABIAN AND JEWISH PHILOSOPHY AND THEOLOGY

Philosophy began and flourished in the medieval Islamic world before it developed in the Jewish or Christian communities. The study of Aristotle started with Alkindi in the ninth century at Baghdad. He had translations of Aristotle's *Metaphysics* and *On the Heavens* made and also did the same for some of Proclus's writings. This translation effort was continued at the Christian school in Baghdad attended by Al-Farabi in the first half of the 10th century. There he studied under the Christians Ibn Haylan and Abu Bishr Matta. The latter translated the *Poetics* and the *Posterior Analytics* of Aristotle into Arabic. The *Posterior Analytics* dealt with demonstrative science and set up the rules for accepting universal and necessary truths. According to its canons, truths based on any authority, whether divine or human, are not demonstrative. Christian students were not permitted to study the *Posterior Analytics*, but Al-Farabi was so allowed. Over a hundred works were attributed to him by medieval biographers: on logic, the philosophy of language, metaphysics, the philosophy of man, and politics. Although he was preceded by Alkindi, Al-Farabi must be given the premier place in the beginnings of Islamic philosophy. His first main influence was on Avicenna, an 11th-century author who must be rated as one of the greatest thinkers in the history of philosophy. His summaries of Aristotle's philosophy were authoritative, even though, under the influence of the Koran and Plotinus, they went beyond Aristotle's teachings themselves.

In reaction to the philosophical-theological amalgam of Avicenna, the 12th-century Spanish Moor Averroes, in Cordova, attempted to remove the accretions made to Aristotle's philosophy by his Arabic predecessors and to recover it in all its rational purity. His commentaries on Aristotle's many philosophical works were paragraph-by-paragraph explanations of what Aristotle held, seemingly assuming an identity between what Aristotle taught and philosophy itself. Besides his opposition to Avicenna's mixture of Aristotle with foreign contributions from the Koran and Plotinus, Averroes also fought the theologians. Averroes's attack was focused on Ghazali's *The Incoherence of the Philosophers*, which was a theological attempt to show the falsity of Aristotelian and Neoplatonic teachings as found primarily in Avicenna, such as the eternity and necessity of the world and other doctrines that, to Ghazali, conflicted with the teachings of the Koran. In his *Incoherence of the Incoherence*, Averroes attempted to refute the argument of Ghazali as he attacked the theologians who unhappily, according to him, mixed faith and reason: unable to reach demonstrative knowledge and the unity of truth it alone ensures, the different schools of *kalam*, dialectically departing from distinct authoritative principles according to their interpretation of the Koran, divided Islam into doctrinal sects.

The Jewish philosophical and theological world was closely linked to the Arabian intellectual tradition. The writings of these Jewish authors were originally in Arabic, though many were later translated into Hebrew (and Latin). These writings also manifested the dialectical style found in the works of Islamic *kalam*. Saadiah Gaon, the 10th-century Egyptian expert in Jewish law and Hebrew grammar, and the translator into Arabic and commentator on many biblical books, introduced, as already indicated, dialectical theology into the medieval Jewish community. The challenges his community faced were both internal and external. From within there was a great deal of perplexity due to the Karaites, Jews who rejected the authority of the oral rabbinical tradition and accentuated the role of rational judgment in regard to their religion. From without were the difficulties arising from the religious rivalries originating from Muslims and Christians and from the philosophical teachings of the Platonists and Aristotle. Philosophy became for Saadiah a necessary instrument in facing these perplexities. In his biblical commentaries, and especially in his *Book of Doctrines and Beliefs*, he employs his knowledge of the Platonic and Aristotelian philosophies to clarify and strengthen the doctrines handed down in the Jewish community to transform basic faith into rational belief. In the 11th century, Avicebron, in *The Source of Life*, continued this form of *kalam*, placing technical philosophy at the service of belief.

In the 12th century, Maimonides, born in Cordova and educated in philosophy by Arabian teachers, sought to reconcile Aristotelianism and Judaism in his *Guide of the Perplexed*. The *Guide*, Maimonides tells the reader, is meant to help those who are perplexed with seeming contradictions between secular knowledge and the letter of Jewish revelation. Strongly influenced by Al-Farabi in his view of the relations between religious doctrines and philosophy, as already noted above, he developed a vision of the reconciliation of faith and reason that drew him high respect in certain philosophical and theological circles and condemnation in others. The 14th-century Jewish writer Gersonides, adhering to Aristotelian philosophy more extensively and explicitly than Maimonides, brought the tensions between philosophy in its Aristotelian dimensions and Jewish beliefs to a high point in Europe. Many found his interpretation of the truths of revealed religion insufficient or superficial. In fact, his approach even elicited negative reactions against philosophy as such in Jewish circles.

## BEGINNINGS OF "PHILOSOPHY" AND "THEOLOGY" IN THE LATIN WEST

The beginning of medieval philosophy and theology in the Latin West might be placed at the time of the return of the classical liberal arts education to the European continent under Charlemagne. The liberal arts were transported to England when Gregory the Great sent Augustine of Canterbury as a missionary to bring Christian life and faith there in the late sixth century. The arts flourished at the cathedral school of York, as well as at the monastic schools of Malmesbury and Yarrow. Alcuin, who had been well trained at York, led the educational reform at Charlemagne's palace school and revived the school system of western Europe that had been destroyed by the invading barbarians. Alcuin himself, while a philosopher only in the sense of knowing and loving classical literature, was not a *philosophus* in the technical sense of the term. He was complemented, however, in the proper philosophical arena by an Irishman, John Scotus Eriugena, who translated the works of Dionysius the Pseudo-Areopagite, a mysterious author who was associated with and given the reverence due to the Dionysius converted by St. Paul at the Athenian Areopagus. In reality, Dionysius was strongly influenced by Proclus and must have lived around 500. Eriugena translated his works and the clarifications given to them by Maximus the Confessor in his *Ambigua*. John Scotus Eriugena also produced his own original philosophical treatise, *On the Division of Nature*.

The works of Dionysius the Pseudo-Areopagite did not bring knowledge of the Platonist philosophy to the Latin West for the first time. It had already been incorporated into the writings of St. Augustine and Boethius. However, with the translations of Dionysius's works, Platonist philosophy arrived with different dimensions and with the presumed authoritative support of St. Paul. The use of his works by St. John Damascene, the last of the Greek Fathers, added further respect to Dionysius's philosophy. The medieval Latin West had only sparse translations of the works of Plato himself, but the Platonic tradition was very present, mainly through the Platonism assimilated by the Fathers of the Church and the texts of the Pseudo-Areopagite and his glossators, Maximus the Confessor and Anastasius the Librarian, and later through the commentaries on Dionysius's works by Hugh of Saint-Victor and some of his successors at this famous Augustinian monastery.

Knowledge of Aristotle's philosophy was limited to some of his logical works and the general introduction to them written by Porphyry. Boethius provided the trusted translations of Aristotle's *Categories* and *On Interpretations* and multiple commentaries on these treatises that preserved the traditional understandings of them by Aristotelian and Platonist commentators. The presence of Stoic philosophy, especially in its moral teachings, was felt in the writings of Cicero and Seneca. For the most part, however, classical philosophers were known in the assimilated and adjusted forms represented by the early Christian authors who had dealt with them directly.

## BIRTH OF MEDIEVAL CHRISTIAN THEOLOGY

The early medieval Christian theological world, in discussions over problems related to the Trinity, divine omnipotence, predestination, and the Eucharist, was characterized by efforts to retrieve the Patristic teachings. The difficulties and contentions that arose often grew out of grammatical concerns and logical consistencies, demanding precision relating to the principal liberal arts of grammar and dialectic. A significant change came with St. Anselm in the 11th and Peter Abelard in the 12th century.

Anselm searched for a deeper understanding of the mysteries of the faith, such as the Trinity and the redemptive Incarnation, often going beyond the issues of grammar and dialectic. He treaded ground that was new in his era, though he believed it was well justified in the Patristic tradition. This appeal to a Patristic tradition is clear from the preface to his *Monologion*:

> Having gone back over it many times, I have not been able to find anything I said in it that is not in agreement with what the Catholic Fathers say, and especially with what is said in the writings of Saint Augustine. For this reason, if it seems to anyone that what I have said in this work is startlingly new or not in accord with the truth, I ask him not to denounce me right away as a rash proclaimer of novelties or as a bold defender of falsehood. First, let him diligently examine the books *On the Trinity* written by the aforementioned Saint Augustine. Then let him judge my work, measuring it by his teaching.

Anselm's *Cur Deus Homo* likewise is prefaced with a letter to Pope Urban II that begins with a justification for his different approach to the study of man's Redemption:

> Even though after the time of the Apostles many of our holy Fathers and Doctors say a great number of things, and indeed things of great weight, concerning our faith, they do this so that they might refute the foolishness of unbelievers and soften the hardness of their hearts. They also do so to nourish those who, with their hearts already cleansed with faith, take delight in understanding what they believe—an understanding that we should pursue once we have accepted our faith as certain. And even though we cannot hope either in our time or in the future to equal them in the contemplation of the truth, still I do not judge it objectionable if, established in the faith, we propose to apply ourselves to an investigation of its nature.

Abelard, shortly thereafter, had objections raised against his manner of approaching theological issues. He was well known for his dialectical method, presented most explicitly in his *Sic and Non* (*Yes and No*). This work was a training text for students, teaching them different ways of reconciling apparently conflicting Scriptural and Patristic authorities. The preface to this work suggests various possible ways of harmonizing the discordant citations. The difficulties may be due to scribal errors in transcription, a translator's mistake, or a failure to realize the nature of the audience to which the text was addressed, since authors often chose not to express themselves with technical precision but opted for simpler explanations that might help people who could not grasp exact language to come to some understanding. One must also be aware when reading conflicting statements that the meaning of a word may vary or that an author may have changed his mind in a later work. After presenting these and other principles for solving conflicting statements, Abelard, in the principal body of the work, posed actual yes and no, or pro and contra, statements on various issues as practice cases. He did not provide the answers but left the students to work them out for themselves.

In other works of Peter, we find actual doctrinal positions that were challenged by some of his contemporaries, especially William of Saint-Thierry and St. Bernard of Clairvaux, as heretical. Some other positions he held, for example, regarding the necessity of God creating the best possible world, while not viewed as heretical, were challenged by contemporaries and hotly debated even up to the time of Thomas Aquinas.

## METHODS OF STUDY

### The *Lectio*

The pro and con approach to study found in Abelard's *Sic et Non* treatise provides the occasion to underscore the procedures of education that guided studies in the liberal arts, philosophy proper, and the reading of Scripture or theology. These procedures were reading (*lectio*), questioning (*quaestio*), and disputing (*disputatio*). Each of these exercises has a long history. The *lectio* or reading exercise already had classic phases at the time of Varro, shortly before the time of Christ. The first stage of the *lectio* was reading in the narrow and simple sense of reading aloud. The next level of *lectio* involved analysis of the text: looking at its plan, its faults and achievements, its originality, etc. A commentary, which included definitions, etymologies, and explanations of figures of speech and rhetorical techniques, came next. This more extended exercise of reading was capped off with a judgment. This judgment generally was based on aesthetic appreciations. However, in the world of St. Augustine and earlier Christian authors, judgments concerning particular biblical texts were made in terms of the rule of faith and would measure whether or not the interpretation increased the love of God and neighbor.

The nature and purpose of the *lectio* developed as the years went by. Robert of Melun, a pupil and sometime critic of Abelard, attacks readers who limit *lectio* to the recitation of biblical texts or to the recitation and glosses on them. Robert wanted more from the lector (reader): "What else do we look for in a *lectio* than the *understanding* of the text, which is called its meaning?" For him, as for Abelard, *lectio* means all the activities that lead up to "understanding." "What is known, if the meaning is not known, or what is taught if the meaning is not unfolded?"

The lector routinely focused on traditionally respected texts. The *lectio* for teachers of grammar was centered on the texts of Donatus and Priscian; the *lectio* for the teachers of rhetoric concentrated on the texts attributed to Cicero and Quintilian. The *lectio* for the dialecticians centered on Porphyry's *Isagoge* (*Introduction*), Aristotle's *Categories* and *On Interpretation*, and Boethius's commentaries on them. The *lectio* for theology was the biblical text. These were the authoritative texts. The glosses providing definitions, etymologies, etc. came from those who offered special help. For the Bible, in particular, the authorities were Jerome, Ambrose, Augustine, Hilary, Basil, Gregory the Great, John Chrysostom, etc. The philosophical authorities were Aristotle, Cicero, Boethius, Plato, Chalcidius, Marius Victorinus, Macrobius, and Dionysius the Pseudo-Areopagite. The chief characteristics of the *lectio* were that it was authoritative, based on respected interpreters, and assimilative, passing on the riches carried by a wise tradition. The lector was a teacher whose expertise was to know and pass on the authoritative teachings of the liberal arts, of the philosophers, and of the Bible, that is, any of the ancient authorities who might help the scholar or apprentice to learn more about the authoritative texts.

## The *Quaestio*

The medieval *quaestio* exercise developed when readers like Abelard, Robert of Melun, and others went beyond recitation and glosses and attempted to discover the meaning of the texts they studied. When, for instance, they examined the biblical texts, they found that the understanding of different Patristic authorities varied. When the authorities were in conflict, they had to evaluate the authorities and provide reasons why one gave a better explanation than another. The arguments of the authorities began to become more central to the interpretation of a biblical text than the authoritative weight of their names. This was not a new event; it had gone on in the Patristic period itself. Abelard and Robert of Melun claimed to follow the Fathers in their procedures.

Robert of Melun accentuates the point that these new forms of questions "sometimes arise because of a doubt; sometimes, however, they arise because of the need to teach." Some questions, that is, are real, spontaneous, and natural; others are raised for methodological reasons. The latter type of *quaestio* is even posed concerning materials where no real doubt exists: "Does God exist?" "Is the soul spiritual?" "Are parents to be honored?" They are asked because the teacher is seeking a deeper understanding on his own part and on the part of the scholars. He does not really doubt that God exists or that the soul is spiritual. He often asks such questions because he wants to have stronger reasons for affirming God's existence or the soul's spirituality.

A further characteristic of the *quaestio* is that only certain kinds of questions tend to go beyond seeking information to pursue understanding. Gilbert of Poitiers describes the type of question that leads to understanding: "A *quaestio* arises from an affirmation and its contradictory negation. When one part of a contradiction seems to be true and the other part seems to have no arguments supporting its truth, or when neither one side nor the other seems to have supporting arguments for their truth, . . . then the contradiction is not a *quaestio*. It is only when both sides of the contradictories seem to have arguments for their side that there is a *quaestio*."

This type of question forced the lector to try through dialectics to find a ground for reconciling the opposed authoritative statements. The attempt to do so became successful for the person posing the question when he provided the reasons for his preference. In giving reasons for his determination of the matter under question, he himself then became an authority and was thus tranformed into a *magister* or master. The introduction of this form of *quaestio* as the method of inquiry thereby altered the study of the Bible. It became a rational form of knowledge. The masters, at the palace, monastic, and cathedral schools, who established themselves as authorities of lasting influence begot schools and began to command in their age a respect that had previously only been accorded to the Fathers of the Church.

## The *Disputatio*

The new type of question at first was tied to the text it studied to arrive at a deeper understanding of it. It examined, for example, the biblical text and raised questions as they would naturally arise while reading the Scriptural text in its order of presentation. The *magistri*, however, as they became more sure of the natural path of their rational efforts to understand better, began to see the need to introduce a logical order to replace the textual order of questions suggested by a biblical narrative. The exercise of the new logically ordered collection of questions took the name *disputatio* as its title. The results of these disputations were gathered together to form a summa, that is, a *summa quaestionum*.

The *disputatio* itself also evolved. For example, when Odo of Soissons taught at Paris around 1164, his *quaestiones* were separated from the *lectio* inasmuch as they were entertained at a different session from the reading of Scripture. The themes, however, of these separated *quaestiones* still arose from the Scriptural text. By the time of Simon of Tournai (around 1201), the separation of the *quaestiones disputatae* from the *lectiones* was complete. The *disputatio* had become a work of a separate rational discipline. It still dealt with the issues raised by the biblical text, but it was no longer the exegesis of the Scriptural text. It was a rationally organized treatise involving many questions dealing with a common subject matter.

## NEOPLATONIC INFLUENCES ON TWELFTH-CENTURY THEOLOGY

Certainly the most influential tradition in theology was that of St. Augustine. His nuanced views of God's inner triune life, of the divine origin of all creation, of the soul and of God as the true object of its hunger, of peace as the tranquility of the divine order of reality, of the role of divine illumination in the processes of man's knowledge, of the nature of true wisdom and earthly science—all these were passed down in Augustine's *City of God*, *The Trinity*, *The Confessions*, *On Christian Doctrine*, and his many sermons, letters, and doctrinal and moral treatises. No other Father of the Church, only God's Scriptures, had such authority.

Boethius, though a translator of and commentator on Aristotle's logical works, had strong influence in certain circles. His theological treatises, however, strongly depended on Proclus and to a lesser degree on Porphyry. His theological tractates (*On the Trinity*, *On the Catholic Faith*, *Against Eutyches*, and the *De hebdomadibus*), although not as famous as his *Consolation of Philosophy*, were commented on by Thierry of Chartres, Gilbert of Poitiers, and Clarembald of Arras, Gilbert's corrector and the successor of Anselm of Laon.

As already mentioned, translations of the works of Dionysius the Pseudo-Areopagite (*The Divine Names*, *The Mystical Theology*, *The Celestial Hierarchy*, and *The Ecclesiastical Hierarchy*), along with his Greek commentators and expositors, brought further distinctions of Christian Neoplatonic philosophy and theology to the medieval Latin world. This was especially true at the monastery of Saint-Victor, where Hugh's and Richard's commentaries on Dionysius, following in the tradition of John Scotus Eriugena and John the Saracen, led the way, and they were followed up at Saint-Victor as late as the time of Thomas Gallus in the 13th century. Nor was this influence of Neoplatonism at Saint-Victor limited to Dionysius and commentaries on his works. The doctrinal treatises of Hugh, and even more explicitly those of Richard, carried a variety of Neoplatonic influences, even if indirectly, from Porphyry and Proclus.

## DEVELOPMENT OF SCHOLASTIC THEOLOGY IN THE TWELFTH CENTURY

In the discussions of *lectio*, *quaestio*, and *disputatio*, it should have become clear that these traditional methods of study had developed in significant new ways. Anselm of Canterbury and Peter Abelard were asking questions aimed at deepening the understanding of the articles of the Christian creed. Furthermore, even those who ignored Anselm and those who criticized Abelard were organizing their study of the Bible into summae, or collections of questions following a logical order of integration. Schools that ignored the new rational or "understanding" approach to the study of Scripture had trouble competing for students. The school of Laon lost its influence, and the school of Saint-Victor, despite its strengths, eventually lost out to the cathedral school at Paris.

Among the logically ordered collections of questions related to the truths of the Christian faith, the most respected 12th-century *summa quaestionum* was what came to be called the *Sentences* of Peter Lombard. This work, in four books, drew many marginal commentaries to its various copies, and even those who developed their own separate summae often followed Lombard's manner of organization. Peter was so respected that he gained the title *magister* or master. It was by this honorific title that he is referred to in the hundreds of commentaries written on his *Sentences* up to the 17th century.

The principal text in regard to Scriptural teaching in the 12th century was the Bible itself. Many of the commentaries on Scripture were done according to the model of moral interpretation, especially guided by the *Moralia on Job* of Gregory the Great and the medieval moral tradition following him. More complicated discussions of doctrinal issues, such as the Trinity, the Incarnation, and other truths of the Christian Bible, were set aside for later disputations in afternoon sessions. It was only in the 13th century, under Alexander of Hales at the University of Paris and Richard Fishacre at the University of Oxford, that the *Sentences* of Peter Lombard were made an official textbook and moved to the morning hours to help deal with "the difficult doctrinal questions." The *Historia Scholastica* (*Scholastic History*) of Peter Comestor was also introduced at Paris as an official text to help give a narrative overview of the whole of biblical history while individual biblical texts were being studied.

# DEVELOPMENTS IN THE ARTS FACULTY IN THE 13TH CENTURY

The *universitas magistrorum et studentium* or "community of masters and students" that formed the nascent University of Paris at the turn of the 13th century had inherited a serious collection of texts that were authoritative in all the areas of the ancient liberal arts. A new inheritance, however, was arriving from centers of translation, such as the one in Toledo, where Gerard of Cremona, Dominic Gundissalinus, and John ibn Daud were busy providing new texts of Aristotle or ones attributed to him, along with a strong collection of commentaries on these Aristotelian works. Boethius had earlier translated some of the logical works of Aristotle and written commentaries on them. The new translations, even if they were better, did not replace the long-standing Boethian texts of Aristotle's Old Logic: the *Isagoge* of Porphyry and the *Categories* and *On Interpretations*. The New Logic brought new translations of the *Prior Analytics* and *Topics*, replacing earlier translations attributed by some to Boethius. Using Greek and Arabic texts, translators such as James of Venice improved on the text of the *Sophistical Refutations* and presented for the first time the *Posterior Analytics*.

Due in large part to the translating efforts of Gerard of Cremona, a number of the nonlogical works of Aristotle also became available. He translated the *Physics, On Generation, On the Heavens*, and the first three books of *On the Meteors* from the Arabic, and these were joined by the efforts of Henricus Aristippus, based on a Greek text, for Book IV of *On the Meteors* and *On Generation*. Anonymous translations from the Greek of the *Physics, On the Soul*, and books I through IV of the *Metaphysics* also appeared before the beginning of the 13th century. These texts of Aristotle had been available centuries before in the Arabic world and had drawn commentaries on them from Avicenna and Averroes, who helped people of the Muslim world deal with conflicts between the Koran and Aristotle's philosophy. It is this collection of texts and the Arabic commentaries associated with Aristotle's "natural philosophy" that at the beginning of the 13th century presented in the Latin West an increasingly real challenge to the traditional Christian vision of reality that had been based in a significant way on the theological vision of St. Augustine.

In 1210, along with the condemnation of heretical teachings by David of Dinant, the decree marking that condemnation also asserted, "Neither may the books of Aristotle concerning natural philosophy, nor the comments on them, be read publicly or in secret at Paris, and this shall be forbidden under penalty of excommunication." Five years later, the new statutes of the university repeated the prohibition. A cautious approach to Aristotle's natural philosophy can also be found in Pope Gregory IX's letter to the masters of theology in 1228, warning them to keep philosophy in its position as a handmaid to their own study and to avoid adulterating the divine message of the Scriptures by succumbing to the imaginings of the philosophers. Gradually, however, the complex Aristotelian corpus entered the curriculum in Paris. The 1255 statutes show that, in effect, the Arts Faculty had changed from a curriculum centered on the liberal arts that Augustine championed in *On Christian Doctrine* to a faculty where the principal study, at least at an introductory level, was the philosophy of Aristotle.

In reality, the statutes of 1255 gave such a short period of time for the study of each of the texts of Aristotle required for graduation that the level of study was quite rudimentary. The study of the texts of Aristotle was done in summary fashion, not by an elaborate commentary or any added series of questions. We find the more extensive and profound commentaries, such as those of St. Thomas on the *Nicomachean Ethics*, *On the Soul*, *Physics*, and the *Metaphysics*, only later. From the sermons of St. Bonaventure in the late 1260s and the condemnations of 1270 and 1277, however, we can chart the advance of Aristotle's philosophy in the Arts Faculty and discover the fundamental conflicts between Aristotle's philosophy, especially as expounded by Averroes, and the traditional Christian positions concerning the creation of the world, the nature of the human intellect, God's knowledge of the world, and his providence that guides it.

The intensity of the conflict in the Arts Faculty waned at the end of the 13th century. Debates over interpretations of Aristotle's texts continued to take place in the Arts Faculty. Realistic and nominalistic views of his categories and the application of them throughout his works on natural philosophy competed. It came to the point that there were just a few fundamental ways of reading his texts, and the disagreements began to find fixed forms and traditions. Staying in the Arts Faculty in the late 13th century not only might indicate a general interest in the philosophy of Aristotle; it could also hint at a primary allegiance to his teachings. Aristotle's philosophy for some was a way of life that might set itself up against the Christian way of life. So, wanting to stay in the Arts Faculty might seem to entail a commitment to a philosophy considered to be the sole intellectual pursuit that dealt with reality.

Matters had changed by the turn of the century. If Walter Burley can be taken as an early 14th-century example, a choice between either being a philosopher or being a theologian had disappeared. One could be, and indeed most were, both. Throughout most of his academic life, from 1300 to 1337, Burley wrote on the logic and physics of Aristotle and never seemed to be charged with the suspicion that he thought theology, which he studied at Paris in the second decade of the century, was based on a faith that had no intellectual content. In the 14th century and thereafter, the university Arts Faculty at Paris and Oxford had become a center for studying Aristotle's philosophy, and most often for studying it philosophically. The latter expression *philosophically* needs explanation. At the time of Thomas Aquinas in the last half of the 13th century, some radical Aristotelians, when they ran into difficulties with church authorities, attempted to justify themselves by saying they were only proceeding "philosophically," by which they meant that they were merely reciting what Aristotle said. For Thomas Aquinas himself and most other medieval authors of the late 13th and succeeding centuries, "studying philosophically" meant rather that the members of the Arts Faculty were judging whether or not Aristotle's positions corresponded to reality. In other words, they were asking, Is what Aristotle says true?

## DEVELOPMENTS IN THE THEOLOGY FACULTY FROM THE 13TH CENTURY ONWARD

In the prologue to his *Summa aurea* (*Golden Summa*), William of Auxerre, writing around 1230, summarized under three headings the various tasks that theologians have undertaken throughout the centuries. They have provided arguments that increase and strengthen the faith of Christian believers; they have defended by the use of arguments the faith of the Christian community against heretics; and, finally, they have led some unbelievers through arguments to accept the faith of the Church. Arguments, for William then, are important for a theologian to fulfill his offices. Yet the arguments are not the theologian's principal center of gravity. A theologian is primarily a person of faith. Faith itself, he insists, is an illumination of the mind that helps the believer to see God and divine things. He notes that "the more one's soul is illumined by faith and then enlightened by the arguments he considers, the more a believer sees not just that something is as he believes it to be, but *how* it is as he believes it to be, and *why* it is as he believes it to be." In effect, William is here pointing to a fourth task for the theologian, the role indicated by St. Anselm: simply to understand. This, he continues, is what Isaiah (7:9) was speaking about when he said, "Unless you have believed, you shall not understand."

Twenty-some years later, when Thomas Aquinas was studying and teaching theology, the Arts Faculty, as we have seen, was on its way toward becoming an Aristotelian philosophy faculty. The general approach to theology enunciated by William of Auxerre, and followed by many other Parisian masters, encountered a dramatically different philosophic atmosphere in which it needed to develop. The very word *theology* was coming into use, and it was taking on an association found in Aristotle's *Metaphysics*. Aristotle's *Metaphysics*, at least in its last book, was theology in the sense of being a science that dealt with the divine realities. Christian revelation also dealt with the divine realities. Could such Christian teaching in any legitimate way be a science like Aristotle's "theological science"? It is a question Thomas posed at the very beginning of his *Summa theologiae*: Can sacred teaching be a science? His answer was not a flat-out yes or no.

Aquinas knew that Aristotle himself had made a distinction about "science" in the *Posterior Analytics*. Sciences could be of two kinds: a simple science that could stand on its own, justifying its own principles or starting points, and a subalternated science, like optics, that received some of its basic principles from another science, a simple science, such as from geometry, which deals with lines. Aristotle considered optics to be a science not in the stronger simple sense of the term, but rather in a subalternated sense. It depended on geometry, then developed its own conclusions concerning particular kinds of lines that demanded further special considerations, lines of vision.

Theology, for Aquinas, is a subalternated science. It borrows some of its premises or principles from the simple science that God and the blessed have of the divine realities and that have been revealed in the Scriptures. It then draws further insights and conclusions regarding these truths with the assistance of the things we know naturally. Theology is not a simple science, but it is a true, subalternated science, that is, a science subalternated to the knowledge of God and the blessed. Aquinas developed his science of theology according to this pattern that he sensed an Aristotelian would respect. An Aristotelian presumably would respect it not primarily because it was Aristotelian but because it is our natural way of claiming to know divine things that are manifested in a twofold way: in the natural world of creation and in the biblical revelation.

Not all who were well trained in Aristotle's philosophy accepted Thomas's view of the nature of theology. For Godfrey of Fontaines, Aquinas certainly was a man to be respected. Godfrey even argued, in *Quodlibet XII* (1296 or 1297), that certain propositions that were associated with Aquinas and condemned at Paris in 1277 by Bishop Stephen Tempier should no longer be condemned in the sense that Thomas Aquinas meant them. Godfrey asked Nicholas Bar, the bishop of Paris at the time, to correct some of the propositions condemned by his predecessor for the following reason: "The condemnation of such articles impedes students in their search for knowledge, since these condemnations keep them away from one [namely, Thomas] who deserves to have applied to him the Lord's words in Matthew's Gospel: 'You are the salt of the earth.' In fact, the teachings of all the other doctors are corrected by Thomas's teaching, and when Thomas is used as a corrector their teachings are given more taste and spice."

This respect for Aquinas is not a late development. Godfrey's student notebook, preserved in the Bibliothèque Nationale of Paris, contains in his own hand the earliest and perhaps the most accurate copy we have of Aquinas's *De aeternitate mundi* (*On the Eternity of the World*). Godfrey's extant

*Quodlibeta* (*Quodlibets*) and *Quaestiones ordinariae* (*Ordinary Questions*) manifest Thomas's continual presence as a respected partner in debate. Respect and familiarity, however, are not identical with agreement. Godfrey can be, at the same time, one of Thomas's strongest critics. Godfrey's criticism is a critique that seems, generally speaking, to claim that Thomas has bent Aristotle far too much to make him fit the Christian vision of reality. This is certainly the case when Godfrey discusses the nature of theology in q. 10 of *Quodlibet IV* (1287).

For Godfrey, Thomas basically misses the point in his appeal to Aristotle's model of a subalternated science to defend his scientific claim. The fundamental point to keep in mind is that science, in Aristotle's portrait of it, deals with evidence. If you have evidence, you can have science; if you do not, you cannot have science. Godfrey thus declares that science is a stable quality we develop in the soul that possesses both the certitude of evidence and the certitude of conviction. If the kind of theology linked to the Scriptures were truly a science, then its conclusions would have both these forms of certitude, that is, they would have both the certitude of evidence and the certitude of conviction. This, however, is not the case. What we find in theology are conclusions that are certain. However, when they are based on premises that are certain but not evident, as they are in the case of theological premises obtained purely from biblical revelation, then they have the certitude of conviction based on faith alone. For sure, the conclusions of theology that are based on the certitude of divine revelation are more solid than even the most probable of human opinions, since the latter lack both the certainty of evidence and the certainty of conviction. Insistently, Godfrey asks what benefit does it bring to a theologian, who in this life would like to gain the certitude of evidence, that the revealed premises he begins with are evident to God and the blessed? We might perhaps be able to speak of theology as science for God or the blessed, but can we justifiably speak of our human theology as scientific knowledge? Godfrey responds in the negative. We still do not have the certitude of evidence that is required for our knowledge to be scientific.

Of course, theologians have spoken of their studies as science since the time of the Fathers of the Church. In doing so, Godfrey would argue, they must have meant *science* in some less proper or imperfect sense, not in a sense that would claim that we have evidence in any experiential way of the revealed principles of the Christian faith. So, when theology is declared to be a science, the kind of evidence that a theologian may claim must be such that the excellence of the objects of Christian faith is respected and the weakness of the theologian's knowledge of such elevated objects is acknowledged. In short, it must be "science of the faith." *Science* is used here in a different sense than the proper sense that Aristotle gives to it. *Science* here is also a relational or comparative term: in comparison to the simple believer, a theologian has science. It is much more evident to one trained in theology than to the untrained believer that when he hears one of the articles of the Creed, for example, "He rose from the dead," it is Christ, both God and man, who rose from the dead, and he knows how this may be possible or he can at least explain how it is not impossible and thus show that Christian beliefs are not irrational. The simple believer cannot do this. So, there are some kinds of knowledge that the theologian possesses beyond the capacities of the person of simple faith.

For Godfrey, a theologian operates in the enigmatic manner that St. Paul ascribes to all believers: "We see now through a mirror in a dark manner" (1 Corinthians 13:14). The theologian has some kind of evidence, but it is not the type that takes away faith. Because of the lack of proportion that exists between the highest revealed truths and the theologian's intellect, the theologian's grasp of evidence is not like his grasp of the principles of other sciences. Still, it is enough to justify the use of the term *science* in some broad sense to describe his knowledge. Theologians, as believers in the realities of the faith and sharers to some degree through divine revelation and their studies in some knowledge of them, participate now in the science which they will later enjoy in the light of glory. In the present life, they have a foretaste of that future knowledge when they are first assisted and enlightened by faith, an imperfect light when compared to the blessed's light of glory, and then employ their sense knowledge and natural abilities to understand the revealed realities that they still do not see face-to-face.

Although a critic of Aquinas, Godfrey's view of the scientific status of theology is closer to Aquinas's than it is to that of his contemporary opponent, the other prominent critic of Aquinas, Henry of Ghent. Henry's approach to the subject is, at its core, Augustinian, unlike Aquinas's and Godfrey's, though it addresses Aristotle extensively. Seeking to restore the illumination theology of Bonaventure and Augustine, Henry stresses that God is the light ultimately sustaining all degrees and types of intellectual vision and that He can grant some theologians, like Augustine, some evidence of his revelation, such as His triune nature. He supports this attitude with a highly developed theory of knowledge that subordinates Aristotelian to Augustinian tenets. In this life, this theological evidence remains, compared to that of God and the blessed, imperfect. As an unclear glimpse of what God and the blessed see perfectly, this evidence, unlike other types of scientific evidence, does not by definition exclude belief but rather is strengthened by both natural reason and faith. However, this theological evidence, being of God Himself, who is simply first, cannot be obtained through a prior science, since God does not know by the kind of deductive process that is characteristic of science.

Theology does not borrow its principles from a higher science in any Aristotelian meaning of science in the *Posterior Analytics*. Thus, it does not fit Aristotle's model of subalternation. Those who want to make it fit, like

Aquinas and Godfrey, are poor students of Aristotle. Subalternation takes place when a science knows the *why* (*propter quid*) about which another science merely knows the *that* (*quia*). But the principles of theology concern what is absolutely first, and the *propter quid* can only be known through what is prior; therefore theology cannot be subalternate to any science. This is so even if God and the blessed know clearly and by vision what theologians know more obscurely and with assistance of faith. This is a distinction of degrees of cognitive clarity and not the subalternation that Aristotle had in mind. In fact, human theological wisdom, insofar as it grounds the truth of subalternate sciences through a discursive knowledge of what is prior to them, may be said to approach the definition of *propter quid* more than divine science, which is immediate, not discursive. Thus, Henry's strict adherence to Aristotle's text permits him to distinguish theology as a wisdom beyond any wisdom Aristotle had in mind, while at the same time showing how all other sciences are subordinate to theology. Henry's approach received strong criticism from Godfrey and others who sought to approach theology as an Aristotelian science. On the other hand, it breathed new life into the Augustinian approach, influencing both Scholastics and mystics.

## DECLARATIVE AND DEDUCTIVE THEOLOGY

After the time of Godfrey and other critics of Aquinas, especially Henry of Ghent, theology seemed to take one of two paths. The main approach was the method of deductive theology. The center of attention in this procedure is on the truths of the faith with an eye to drawing out further insights, conclusions, and applications of these basic teachings. The habit or ability that one develops with this form of theology is deductive. The focus is on what further truths are involved in or can be deduced from the basic Christian truths, that is, from the articles of the Creed. The second and less embraced approach is the method of defensive or declarative theology. In this arena, the theologian centers his attention on the articles of the Creed in themselves and attempts to explain, to defend, and to provide analogies that might clarify or make us see better the most fundamental Christian truths.

Peter Aureoli (d. 1322), a Franciscan theologian whose career flourished in the second decade of the 14th century, became the great defender at Paris of this so-called less common form of theology. He did not speak of theology in terms of "science" but rather in terms of "wisdom." And he interpreted "wisdom," according to Book VI of Aristotle's *Nicomachean Ethics*, as a combination of "science" and "intellect." Peter Aureoli thus distinguished the deductive or scientific approach to theology from the declarative or premise-oriented theology that focused on the first principles or fundamental starting points of theology (i.e., the Creed). His theology primarily concentrated on the premises or articles of the faith in themselves and not on the principles or premises as sources of further conclusions. It is helpful to remember that Aquinas, in his *Exposition on the "De Trinitate" of Boethius,* had said that Aristotle defended his first principles by showing that to deny them led to self-contradiction and that he attempted to give analogies or examples that would confirm these first principles. This is what Peter Aureoli considered the primary task of the theologian: to explain key theological terms so that the articles of faith were understood as clearly as possible, to defend the articles of the faith against heretics, and to find suitable analogies to confirm these articles.

Peter was not primarily interested in extending the domain of Christian theology; he was principally concerned with finding ways of nourishing the faith of believers and confirming the main articles of the faith. These articles of the faith thus became the center of attention. Explaining the terms connected with a trinitarian God or with a divine Mediator was one of the principal chores of the theologian. Another task was to develop the facility for answering the challenges of heretical thinkers concerning these truths. A further challenge was to discover the most suitable examples or analogies to illustrate as adequately as possible the faith content of the Church's belief or creed concerning the Trinity, Incarnation, or the other articles of the Creed.

Aureoli defended this declarative approach to the study of theology by appealing to St. Augustine and claiming that his *De Trinitate* was a sure illustration of the clarification of theological terms, of the separation of true doctrine from heretical teachings, and of the search for sturdier analogies of the mystery of the triune God. In following the example of Augustine, the theologian develops a habit that is distinct from the habit of faith. It is a declarative habit, not a faith habit (which the theologian has in common with all believers). It does not cause faith; it brings understanding to a faith that is already firm.

In the 1340s, an Augustinian Hermit, Gregory of Rimini, commented on the *Sentences* of Lombard at Paris and opposed the declarative theology of Peter Aureoli. According to Gregory, a theologian does not principally search for analogies drawn from the natural world. He does not principally go to other sciences, other teachings, or probable propositions. His principal effort is to understand the Scriptures. He advances the knowledge of the faith by extending its explicit domain. Theology is deductive. It draws out what follows necessarily from the truths contained formally in sacred Scripture. The theologian's ability is not really distinct from that of the simple believer. He principally develops a faith habit. The difference is that his faith habit is one that holds more explicitly what the ordinary believer holds implicitly. All believers accept whatever God has revealed; a theologian is able to make explicit what most believers hold implicitly because of their trust in the First

Truth who is the guarantee of the Christian faith. In his advice to Peter Aureoli and other declarative theologians, Gregory instructs them to go back to Augustine and reread his texts. They have gotten it all wrong:

> But it is established that every such element of knowledge either is expressly contained in sacred Scripture or is deducible from what is contained there. Otherwise, the Scriptures would not suffice for our salvation and for the defense of our faith, etc. Yet, Augustine, in the last chapter of Book II of *On Christian Teaching* tells us that the Scriptures do suffice, when he says: "Whatever a man might learn outside of Scripture, if it is harmful, it is condemned in the Sacred Writings; if it is useful, then it is already found there."

In short, theology is primarily about faith. Dependence on other sources is accidental or secondary, not essential or primary. As believers, Gregory argued, we do not accept something as true because of a probable argument supporting it; we accept it because it is divinely revealed. Theologians have as their main task to manifest what is divinely revealed, not to search for nonessential arguments to bolster the faith.

## A NECESSARY MARRIAGE

Although Peter Aureoli and Gregory of Rimini had their followers, many theologians saw the need for both approaches to theology. Peter of Candia, who lectured on the *Sentences* of Lombard at Paris in 1378–1380, criticized both authors to the degree that they stressed only one side of the theological challenge. For Peter of Candia, both approaches were necessary and legitimate. We can consider the divine revelation as containing explicit truths, or we can consider it as providing principles that can be further understood by being made more explicit. We cannot think of declarative and deductive theology as though they are two distinct opposed theologies. We should rather speak of them as two legitimate and necessary theological habits or abilities that should be developed by all well-balanced theologians.

Not all truths of the faith are explicitly contained in the Scriptures: that is why the Fathers of the Church and the Councils had to make them explicit. In doing so, they practiced deductive theology. Still, not all doctrines are clear in themselves. At times, when dealing with the Trinity, words such as *person*, *nature*, and *substance* need to be defined. Distortions coming from heretical teachings need to be corrected. And even though we accept God's revelation because of the gift of faith, still arguments confirm and strengthen our faith. Faith is fundamental. We do not accept revealed truths because of the arguments presented. Yet, the arguments are not useless. That is why St.

Augustine encouraged his readers to pursue "that knowledge by which our most wholesome faith, which leads to true happiness, is begotten, nourished, defended, and strengthened."

Faith is a gift or grace, but it is also helped by good example, by preaching, by argument, and many other human efforts. God can and does give his gifts through human instruments. As Aquinas put it, "science begets and nourishes faith by way of external persuasion . . . , but the chief proper cause of faith is that which moves man inwardly to assent." God uses human instruments, such as preachers and teachers, to beget, nourish, defend, and strengthen faith. Yet such instruments are not sufficient on their own to produce faith. If they were, then every competent preacher would be effective in leading his listeners to affirm the faith, and every able teacher would be successful in his efforts to defend and strengthen the faith. Theology in none of its forms provides the evidence for the assent of faith. The affirmations to revealed truth are based on the gift of faith. Peter of Candia poses his question concerning the nature of theology in these precise terms: "Does the intellect of human beings here in this world acquire through theological study evident knowledge of revealed truths?" And his formal answer is, "Through theological study only declarative and faith-extending habits are developed, and through these developed abilities no evident knowledge of the articles of the faith is acquired." This statement well summarizes the efforts of medieval theologians to explain what they hoped to attain in their classes of theology and the habits they hoped to develop there.

## DISSATISFACTIONS WITH UNIVERSITY PHILOSOPHY AND THEOLOGY

Throughout this introductory essay, mention has been made of disagreements among Muslim, Jewish, and Christian teachers about the inroads of "foreign elements" from outside cultures or conflicts from within over authors who are helpful or orthodox and ones who are harmful, schismatic, or heretical. Different developments, especially developments in methods, such as the *lectio*, the *quaestio*, and the *disputatio*, have been indicated. There were also discussions of developments in the types of schools—those associated with the king's or emperor's household, those surrounding a monastery, or those attached to a cathedral—and the birth of the university, which was not a collection of buildings but rather "a community of masters and scholars." Hidden among the descriptions of these various structures of purposes, faith loyalties, methods, and locations are further causes of tension that need some consideration.

Some of these tensions have already been hinted at when, for example, mention was made of the attitude of mind of some radical Aristotelian thinkers who, whether Muslim, Jewish, or Christian, seemed to hold, without any less faith than someone who held the opposite, that *kalam* or dialectical theology was not really an intellectual discipline. Similar compartmentalizing attitudes of mind also showed up in *Quodlibet* disputations at the University of Paris in the 1270s, when the question "Must a person have faith in order to be a theologian?" arose. Or the importance of deductive and declarative theology might be questioned by an Oxford faculty member who seems to prefer preaching to asking *quaestiones* when he ends many of his lectures on the *Sentences* of Peter Lombard with a practical sermon. There are, to push the point, throughout the course of the history of medieval philosophy and theology many tensions and many challenges that are just part of the realities of people having limited time or limited interests, various challenges and various abilities.

There is, however, one tension that seems more dramatic and important. It is a tension that in germ appeared early in the history of Christianity. It can be found in Patristic times when Augustine warned that Christians should not study useless and curious subjects that do not beget, nourish, defend, and strengthen the Christian faith. It was a tension later manifested in the medieval debates over the speculative or practical goals of the study of theology. In the late 14th and early 15th centuries, it was formulated in the question "Does one study to increase one's knowledge of God and his creation or to foster a greater love of God and neighbor?" Such a question expresses the tension manifested in Jean Gerson's sermon *Against the Curiosity of Scholars*, when he criticized the followers of the Franciscans John Duns Scotus and William of Ockham, who had lost the "simplicity of heart" spirit of study manifested in St. Bonaventure's *The Journey of the Mind into God*. Gerson declared, "I cannot bring myself to appreciate the way the Franciscans, having dismissed this great teacher, have turned to I know not what novelties and are prepared to fight tooth and nail for them."

It is also evident in the very practice of the 15th-century Carthusian Denys Ryckel, who, in his *Commentary on the Sentences of Peter Lombard*, totally ignores the theologians of the 14th century and retrieves the earlier, and what he considers the more wholesome, spiritual approach to theology found in the writings of William of Auxerre, St. Bonaventure, St. Thomas Aquinas, and Henry of Ghent. To a great extent the study of university philosophy and theology was also criticized by those who followed the mystical elements of Albert the Great's writings and who favored the Neoplatonic tradition: Berthold of Moosburg, Johannes Tauler, Heinrich Suso, and Jan van Ruysbroeck. Certainly, studies in the Arts and Theology Faculties of the universities continued in the 14th and 15th centuries and even flourished. Often these faculties were developed along particular lines or schools: realists and nominalists; Thomists, Scotists, and Ockhamists. The multiplication of universities in these centuries bears witness to a continued life for medieval philosophy and theology, despite the criticisms of those who saw the various approaches of these particular schools as competing forms of the sin of curiosity.

## MODERN CRITICISMS OF MEDIEVAL PHILOSOPHY AND THEOLOGY

The Scientific Revolution of the 16th and 17th centuries influenced specifically modern conceptions of man and the universe that shared a rejection of the medieval and classical outlook. The new paradigm of scientific explanation—the mathematical law applied to empirical phenomena—had proved increasingly successful. The final victory of this new science was Isaac Newton's universal law of gravitation, accounting for the motion of all bodies, earthly and heavenly. Even though the success of the new science related to bodies, such as the confirmation of Nicolaus Copernicus's heliocentric theory, it also influenced the explanation of other dimensions of existence. And even though the new science focused mainly on *how* things occur (in mathematical terms), while medieval science focused mainly on the purpose or *why* of things, the new emphasis replaced, more than supplemented, the old. Insofar as the question *why* fell outside the new explanatory boundaries, it came to be seen by many as unscientific. Rather, mechanistic explanations began to dominate.

For the medieval mind, on the other hand, why something happens cannot be divorced from how it happens, since the end always governs the means. To Thomas Aquinas, the notion of law, for instance the natural law (which grounds his ethics), is through and through teleological: man is inclined to virtue because this is the best fulfillment of his rational nature. Immanuel Kant's morals offer a telling contrast to Aquinas's medieval approach. Kant, in his very search for human freedom and autonomy, presupposes a mechanistic view of the world: "Thus a kingdom of ends is possible only on the analogy of a kingdom of nature; yet the former is possible only through maxims, i.e., self imposed rules, while the latter is possible only through laws of efficient causes necessitated from without. . . . nature as a whole is viewed as a machine." (*Grounding for the Metaphysics of Morals*, 2:438, trans. J. W. Ellington, Hackett edition). In other words, Kant's categorical imperative is meant as a (self-determined and thus free) law analogous to the (necessary) law of nature. Yet Kant still wants his imperative to be as necessary, universal, and compelling as the mechanistic laws of nature. Moreover, he wants the moral agent to focus on the purely formal aspect of the action—the capacity of the action to become a universal law—rather than on the proper ends of man's nature considered as a whole.

The growing influence of the new science presupposed at least some acceptance of its fundamental premise: reality is primarily what is reducible to mathematical laws, namely bodies. This premise is manifested most saliently in the modern assumption, found, for example, in Galileo, Thomas Hobbes, and John Locke: external bodies possess "objective" or primary reality, while the mind of the perceiver is a more "subjective" or secondary reality. This distinction has metaphysical and moral ramifications. Concerning metaphysics, with spiritual dimensions relegated to the "subjective," material reality becomes the primary criterion and reference point. René Descartes's search for certitude in the human subject itself presupposes the characteristic modern break between the objective and subjective realms. Concerning morals, with teleology relegated to the past, emphasis is placed either on the practical benefits of human endeavor, as in Francis Bacon, or on abstract principles, as in Kant.

These remarks on the Scientific Revolution and its ensuing influence on philosophy are not meant as a resolution of choice between the modern and the medieval outlooks. They are meant simply to point out that modern philosophy, like medieval philosophy, also rests on basic assumptions about man and the universe. They are also meant to point out that the success of the new science pertained to an area of reality, namely material reality, specifically to an aspect of material reality, namely how it works. The question of the extent to which modern science applies to the rest of reality is open for debate. So too is the question of the relative strengths of medieval and modern philosophy.

However, other factors aside from the Scientific Revolution, such as new political and economic realities, contributed to the modern rejection of the medieval outlook. This historical period cannot be discussed fully here, but some of the philosophical views that voice this rejection can be pointed out. It is possible to trace various elements of medieval philosophy and theology and indicate their survival in the writings of modern authors. This effort has already been made in the case of Descartes with the attempts at establishing his dependence on various Jesuit sources, especially Francisco Suárez's *Disputationes* and the Suárezian manuals used at La Flèche, the Jesuit school where Descartes began his philosophical studies. Nonetheless, despite certain limited inheritances from medieval philosophy and theology, the predominant attitude among modern authors in regard to their medieval predecessors is one of rejection.

This stance of rejection holds for many areas of thought. It is most evident in *The Prince* written by Niccolò Machiavelli in 1513. In chapter 15, Machiavelli criticizes the whole orientation of classical and medieval political and moral philosophy:

> For many authors have constructed imaginary republics and principalities that have never existed in practice and never could; for the gap between how people actually behave and how they ought to behave is so great that anyone who ignores everyday reality in order to live up to an ideal will soon discover he has been taught how to destroy himself, not how to preserve himself. For anyone who wants to act the part of a good man in all circumstances will bring about his own ruin, for those he has to deal with will not all be good. So it is necessary for a ruler, if he wants to hold on to power, to learn how not to be good, and know when it is and when it is not necessary to use this knowledge.

The Greek word for virtue or human excellence, *arete*, was translated into Latin as *virtus*. *Virtutes* (virtues) for ancient and medieval philosophers were the characteristics or habits human beings had to develop to become excellent human beings. For Machiavelli, *virtue* took on a new meaning: the Italian *virtù* for him meant "learning how not to be good, and knowing when it is and when it is not necessary to use this knowledge." Machiavelli's *virtù* is more aptly translated as *cunning*.

Thomas Hobbes followed Machiavelli's negative view of the nature of human beings in *The Citizen*:

> The greatest part of those men who have written aught concerning commonwealths [he contends] either suppose, or require us, or beg of us to believe that man is a creature born fit for society. The Greeks call him "a political animal"; and on this foundation they so build up the doctrine of civil society, as if for the preservation of peace, and the government of mankind, there were nothing else necessary than that men should agree to make certain covenants and conditions together, which they themselves should then call laws.

For Hobbes, this is a false conception of man's nature, which is basically selfish. The positive view of man, according to Hobbes, also provides the wrong key to his character: man's strongest control is fear. His behavior, in reality, is controlled by actual force or by the fear of force, not by reason or a desire to fulfill an ideal image he has of himself. Classical and medieval education is useless and ineffective from Hobbes's perspective.

In his *Leviathan*, Hobbes brings forward another criticism, challenging the whole classical and medieval view of life's meaning. There is no ultimate *eudaimonia* (happiness); that is, there is no final goal that gives human life its real meaning. There is, in brief, no ultimate human good to be pursued; there are only the actual, finite goals we aim at each day: eating a good meal, having a comfortable home, enjoying good health, visiting a particular vacation spot, and saving money for more such enjoyments in old age. There is no ultimate meaning to human life, only proximate satisfactions of our appetites. Francis Bacon, in *The Great Instauration*, endorsed a view of science that well fit this philosophical vision of Hobbes. Bacon ridiculed the various medieval followers of Aristotle: "Philosophy and the intellectual sciences stand like statues, worshipped and celebrated, but not moved or advanced. Nay, they sometimes flourish most in the hands of the first author, and afterwards degenerate."

He argued that "the wisdom derived from the Greeks is but like the boy-hood of knowledge, and has the characteristic properties of boys: it can talk but it cannot generate, for it is fruitful of controversies but barren of works." He argued the case against the Aristotelian and medieval ideals of knowledge in favor of pursuing "inventions that may in some degree subdue and over-come the necessities and miseries of humanity." For Bacon, the true ends of knowledge are the benefits it brings to the material dimensions of man's earthly life.

In the realm of religion, modern critics were also forceful opponents of medieval Scholasticism. Martin Luther, in his *Disputation against Scholastic Theology*, argued against what he presented as the common opinion: that no man can become a theologian without Aristotle. He claimed that, on the contrary, "no one can become a theologian unless he becomes one without Aristotle," and that "the whole Aristotle is to theology as darkness is to light." He considered "the entire *Ethics* of Aristotle to be the worst enemy of grace."

In their views of ethics and politics, in their portraits of man's nature, in their considerations of life's purpose, in their presuppositions concerning true religion, the early modern authors were very critical of the direction and accomplishments of medieval developments in philosophy and theology. Later modern philosophers and theologians who disagreed with these early authors of modernity did not, however, choose to return to the perspectives of classical or medieval sources. They rather argued for new forms of mod-ern ways of thinking. Kant, for example, disagreed with the pessimistic view of man presented by Hobbes but also criticized the optimistic view offered by Jean-Jacques Rousseau. Instead of recovering an earlier view of man's nature, however, he chose instead to avoid the battle over man's nature. He decided to anchor his ethics and politics not in nature, but in pure reason, that is, the pursuit of rational self-consistency that would never make any act morally obligatory unless it could become a universal rational law. In his judgment, this approach to morality avoids foisting our opinions about some-thing being right and wrong on others. It limits us from turning our desires into moral demands. It leaves outside the discussion of morals particular conceptions of what a man is or ought to be. Man can only obligate himself and others to what rational beings can be obligated to perform in terms of their rational self-consistency.

In considering the goals of science, the early modern view of Bacon was to find inventions that might alleviate man's sufferings and satisfy his temporal needs. Rousseau criticized this view of the purpose of science in concrete ways by asking what are man's real needs? He argued against artificial needs created by a society that has pulled many human lives into a vortex of artificial desires. Yet he never thought of asking the classical and medieval question: What is man's ultimate desire or what is the most fulfilling form of human life?

One strong component of recent modern thought, accented particularly by Georg Wilhelm Friedrich Hegel, is that nature is no longer a dominant characteristic of reality. The ruling category is history. We are ever progressing. Progress is not only the law of ever-improving technology; it is the law of human history. We as human beings are becoming ever freer by overcoming the obstacles to human progress. We are not as prejudiced as our forefathers. We no longer live in local ghettoes. We are becoming cosmopolitan, multicultural, a global village. The rallying cry is "Keep marching forward."

The modern critics of early modernity are true critics of the early moderns. Yet they have not escaped their basic presuppositions. In effect, Kant, Rousseau, and Hegel represent a second wave of modernity, and both waves are fundamentally at odds with classical and medieval thought. They portray the medieval world as passé, outdated, archaic.

## STUDY OF MEDIEVAL PHILOSOPHY AND THEOLOGY TODAY

It might be objected that some modern researchers have returned to the study of the classical philosophies of Greece and Rome and that there are many who are interested in the philosophies of Plato, Aristotle, Plotinus, and Proclus. This objection might be confirmed by the observation that there have also been restorations of the study of medieval philosophies and theologies, especially through the endorsements of Pope Leo XIII's encyclical letter *Aeterni Patris* (*On the Restoration of Christian Philosophy*) in 1879 and the more recent 1978 encyclical of Pope John Paul II, *Fides et Ratio* (*Faith and Reason*). Certainly, these and other efforts have turned attention once again to classical and medieval thought. Often, however, this interest has been almost purely historical: the philosophies and theologies of the ancients and medievals are appreciated in the same way that any archeological remains are honored. In some instances, nonetheless, medieval philosophies and theologies have been studied as manifestations of timeless truth. Is what they teach true or false, wise or unwise, reasonable or unreasonable? Before such questions can be answered, there is a prior requirement: we have to understand the medieval authors on their own terms. We have to enter their well-forgotten world and see if we can understand things the way they saw them. We have to bracket our own modern categories and frames of reference. Do the ancients and medievals have anything to teach us? Are truth, wisdom, and reason time-bound categories? Or can we learn from people who thought differently, and even perhaps more richly, than we do ourselves at the present time? We hope the rest of this volume will put our readers at the beginning of the path to answering such questions.

# A

**ABELARD, PETER (1079–ca. 1142).** A philosopher, theologian, spiritual guide, writer, preacher, and hymnist, Peter Abelard was born at Le Pallet, near Nantes. He studied **dialectic** under **Roscelin** of Compiègne, a **nominalist**, and **William of Champeaux**, an extreme **realist**. As a dialectician, Abelard disagreed with the claim of Roscelin that **universals** were only spoken words. Around 1112, he turned to the study of **theology**, working under and then resisting the direction of **Anselm of Laon**. He began to teach at the cathedral school of Notre Dame around 1113 and drew students from many nations. At Paris, he became involved with Heloise, the niece of Fulbert, a canon of the cathedral. When Fulbert had him castrated in 1118, Peter retired to the seclusion of the monastery of Saint-Denis, and Heloise entered a convent. Retreating later to a smaller monastery dependent on Saint-Denis, Abelard wrote his *Theologia "Summi boni"* (*Theology beginning with "Of the Highest Good"*), a book that was attacked both by Roscelin and by students of Anselm of Laon. In 1121, his book was condemned at the Council of Soissons. A year later, when he raised the ire of his fellow monks by contesting the authenticity of the abbey's claim to have been founded by St. Denis, Abelard received permission from Suger, the abbot of Saint-Denis, to leave the abbey.

He established an oratory that he named Le Paraclet and established a school there. When Heloise and her companions were expelled from their Argenteuil convent, which was taken over by Saint-Denis, Abelard offered them Le Paraclet as their home. He wrote a rule for the convent there and prepared more than 140 hymns for the nuns to use in the celebration of their liturgies. At the same time, Peter worked on his *Sic et Non* (*Yes and No*), a training textbook for students of theology, and also on his *Theologia Christiana* (*Christian Theology*). During the 1130s, he wrote a new version of his theology entitled *Theologia "Scholarium"* (a theology that begins with the words "At the request of our students"); a commentary on St. Paul's Epistle to the Romans; and his ethical treatise, *Scito te ipsum* (*Know Thyself*). His theological works raised objections from **William of Saint-Thierry** and **Bernard of Clairvaux**, which led to Peter's condemnation by the Council of

Sens in 1140. While at Cluny on his way to Rome to appeal to Pope Innocent II, he found out that the pope had already confirmed the condemnation of the council. He accepted his punishment, becoming a monk at Cluny under Peter the Venerable and refraining from public teaching. He died in approximately 1142 at the priory of St. Marcel near Chalon-sur-Saône, where Peter the Venerable sent him for care. Refer to the introduction, "Methods of Study."

**ABRAHAM IBN DAUD OR AVENDUTH (ca. 1110–1180).** This Jewish scholar is famous as a translator who worked in Toledo with Dominicus Gundissalinus in translating Arabic works into Castilian, while Gundissalinus translated them from Castilian into Latin. This is especially the case in regard to a number of the works of **Avicenna**. However, he is perhaps even more appreciated as a philosopher insofar as he made the first influential attempt before **Maimonides** to integrate Aristotle (as presented by **Al-Farabi** and Avicenna) with Jewish thought. He borrowed from earlier Jewish thinkers, such as **Saadiah Gaon** and **Judah Halevi**, whom he also criticized, and **Abraham ibn Ezra** and **Bahya ibn Paquda**, whom he praised for their philosophical support on some points.

Ibn Daud's two main works are *Sefer ha-Quabbalah* (*The Book of Tradition*) and *Ha-Emunah ha-Ranah* (*The Exalted Faith*). The first focuses on human and Jewish history, but most especially on the history and survival of rabbinic Judaism. The second stresses the harmony between revelation and reason by providing the philosophical truths of Avicenna's form of **Aristotelianism** and citing Scripture passages that confirm these philosophic truths, as well as intermingling Scripture and philosophical teachings to support one another.

**ABRAHAM IBN EZRA (ca. 1093–1167).** Born in Tudela, Spain, Abraham is a well-respected thinker in the history of Jewish thought. He produced widely read texts in several fields, such as poetry, grammar, biblical **exegesis**, mathematics, astronomy, astrology, and **Neoplatonic** philosophy. In his work, one finds the confluence of *kalam* and a variety of philosophical elements and sources. Scholars are still assessing the relative unity among his ideas and writings. The influence of **Saadiah Gaon** is notable, as well as that of the old rabbinical treatise *Sefer Yetzira* (*Book of Formation*). In addition, Abraham's treatment of different levels of reality in terms of mathematical properties associates him with the Pythagorean tradition. He also kept a friendly relationship with **Judah Halevi** and is well known for his extensive travels in North Africa and Europe. Abraham died in Calahorra, Spain.

**ABU MA'SHAR OR ALBUMASAR (787–886).** A native of Balkh (in Khorasan) who worked in Baghdad, Abu Ma'shar al-Balkhi Ja'Far ibn Muhammad was a contemporary and intellectual adversary of **Al-Kindi**, who influenced him, particularly in metaphysics. Like Al-Kindi, his general philosophical framework is **Neoplatonic**: all emanates from and seeks to return to the One. Albumasar, however, had strong astrological interests, devoting much energy to the account of the influence of the heavens on the human sphere. In his account, he drew significantly from **Aristotelian** cosmology and scientific methodology, as well as from **Ptolemaic astronomy**. His general worldview was also inspired by a great variety of traditions and sources, e.g., Syrian, Indian and Iranian. In the Latin West, Albumasar was influential in the development of science, particularly astronomy. Treated as an authority in astronomy, along with Aristotle, his views were appropriated and developed by thinkers such as **Roger Bacon** and **Albert the Great**. His major work, *Kitab al-mudhal al-kabir* (*The Book of the Great Introduction to Astronomy*), was first introduced into the Latin world in abbreviated form through **Adelard of Bath**'s *Ysagoge minor* (first decades of the 12th century). Then John of Seville (in 1133) and Herman of Carinthia (in 1140) provided full translations. His *Kitab alquiranat* (*The Book of Conjunctions*), relating astrology to history, was also influential among medieval thinkers. Albumasar died in Al-Wasit (in Iraq).

**ACCIDENT.** An accident, in philosophical language, is the general classification used by **Aristotle** to speak about all forms of reality that are not substances. Substances are things that can stand on their own: a man, a mountain, the sun, etc. A man may be short and fat, mountains may be high and bare, and the sun is hidden at night. These many descriptions of a man, a certain mountain, and the sun are accidental, describing something that does not have to belong to the substances that now have these accidents, which do not stand on their own like substances. Literally, a substance means "something that stands under." Substances stand under the accidents that belong to them. Different medieval philosophers and theologians explain the character of certain accidents in different ways. For example, if someone is described as tall, this for a certain philosopher would not be a description of a characteristic that really belongs to the so-called tall person. If this tall person moved into a room with giant-sized basketball players, he would not be tall in this new context. Tallness is a relative term that is used to describe the height of someone in relation to others in the room or context. When he moves into a room with basketball players, he does not lose a real quality of tallness. Nothing in him has changed. So, tallness is a relative term, not a term that expresses an absolute characteristic that is in the person described as tall. These discussions or debates are carried on particularly between philosophers who are called **nominalists** and **realists**. *See also* ANALOGY.

**ADAM MARSH (ca. 1210–1259).** Born near Bath, Adam took his arts degree under **Robert Grosseteste** and also studied theology under him until Grosseteste became bishop of Lincoln in 1235. Adam joined the **Franciscans** at Worcester ca. 1233 and became the first Franciscan regent master at Oxford. He lectured on theology to the friars from 1247 to 1253. He continued his close relationship with Grosseteste and was an advisor to him at the First Council of Lyons in 1245. He collaborated with Robert on a concordance of sacred Scripture and the Fathers of the Church, wrote a commentary on the *Six Days of Creation* (*Hexaëmeron*), and probably authored the *Question concerning the Ebb and Flow of the Tide* that was formerly attributed to Grosseteste. Fittingly, he is buried next to Grosseteste at Lincoln Cathedral.

**ADAM OF BUCKFIELD (ca. 1220–ca. 1285).** Adam became a master of arts at Oxford in 1243. It is presumed that he never became a master of theology, since all the works ascribed to him are called "notes" or "glosses" on **Aristotle**'s books on natural philosophy. **Adam Marsh**, his teacher in ancient and Arabian natural philosophy, recommended him highly to **Robert Grosseteste** in 1249 for a rectorship at Iver in Buckingshire. Fifteen years later (1264), he was a canon at Lincoln Cathedral, seemingly no longer associated with the University of Oxford. Although he cites **Avicenna** and **Ghazali**, he follows **Averroes**'s manner of providing literal expositions of each paragraph of Aristotle's texts. In his commentary on Book I of Aristotle's *De anima*, he adds to the literal exposition a *quaestio*. This procedure anticipates the method found in many commentaries later in the 13th and succeeding centuries: a literal explanation followed by questions related to the deeper meanings found in the text. Despite his close dependence on Averroes for his method of explaining philosophical texts, however, Adam still holds to the more **Platonist** tradition of a plurality of forms in material substances.

**ADAM OF SAINT-VICTOR (ca. 1110–ca. 1180).** Born in Brittany, Adam was a liturgical poet and canon regular at the Abbey of Saint-Victor at Paris (founded in 1110). He entered the abbey ca. 1130, around the same time as his contemporary **Andrew of Saint-Victor**. Adam was a student of **Hugh of Saint-Victor**, the mystical theologian. More than for his theology, however, Adam is best known for his composition of approximately 45 sequences, rhythmic pieces that follow the Alleluia in the Mass. Adam perfected Sequence poetry and is reputedly the master of its final form. This genre was developed in the late 11th or early 12th century and was practiced at Saint-Victor even before Adam's time. To some extent, in both form and content, Adam's poetry reflects his theological attitudes. Like his teacher Hugh and other Victorines, such as **Richard of Saint-Victor**, Adam's theological ideas are quite **Augustinian**, as shown by his poem on mankind, *Haeres peccati* (*Heir of Sin*) (PL 196:1422). His emphasis on alliteration and play on words reflects the use of **allegory** in biblical **exegesis**, when the visible is understood as both revealing and concealing the invisible.

**ADAM WODEHAM (ca. 1298–1358).** Author of the prologue to **William of Ockham**'s *Summa logicae*, Wodeham was a careful and respected text scholar and an acknowledged interpreter of the philosophy and theology of **John Duns Scotus** and William of Ockham. In effect, he helped establish their reputations through his masterful representation of their positions. A commentator on **Peter Lombard**'s *Sentences* three times—at London, Norwich, and Oxford—Wodeham was also respected in his own right. He influenced the Augustinian theologian **Gregory of Rimini** more than did either Duns Scotus or Ockham. He also was a major authority for the Cistercian **John of Mirecourt** and the Augustinian **Alphonsus Vargas**. Even later, in the 1380s, he was still cited by **Pierre d'Ailly** and **Peter of Candia**. In 1512, John Mair (Major), the famous Scottish theologian and historian, provided an abbreviated version of the first edition of Wodeham's Oxford *Commentary on the Sentences* made in the late 13th century by **Henry Totting of Oyta**.

**ADELARD OF BATH (ca. 1070–ca. 1146).** A **Benedictine**, Adelard was educated at Tours, taught at Laon, and then traveled in the Arabian cultural worlds of Sicily and Spain. His *Natural Questions* were his most influential work, giving to medieval learning in England, especially through **Alexander Nequam**, its focus on natural philosophy and mathematics. His earlier letter to his nephew, titled *De eodem et diverso* (*On the Same and the Different*), is most renowned for its treatment of universals. Using an Arabic text, he was the first (ca. 1120) to translate Euclid's *Elements*. He also translated a number of works of Greco-Arabic science, including *An Introduction to Astronomy* and *An Introduction to the Quadrivium*. As an author, he produced *On Birds*, *On Falconry*, *Rules for the Abacus*, and *Function of the Astrolabe*.

**AEGIDIUS.** *See* GILES OF ROME (AEGIDIUS ROMANUS) (ca. 1245–1316).

**AELRED (ETHELRED) OF RIEVAULX, ST. (ca. 1110–1167).** He joined the **Cistercians** at Rievaulx in 1134. After serving as novice master in 1142–1143, he was named abbot of the Rievaulx foundation at Revesby. In 1147, he became abbot of Rievaulx, the most flourishing Cistercian abbey in England. His writings, *The Mirror of Charity*, *On the Soul*, and especially *On*

*Spiritual Friendship*, earned him the title "Bernard of the North." He also wrote *A Rule of Life for a Recluse* for his sister and two historical works: *The Life of Edward the Confessor* and *Genealogy of the Kings of England*.

**ALAN OF LILLE (ALANUS DE INSULIS) (ca. 1116–1202).** His traditional title, *Doctor Universalis* (Teacher with Universal Talents), well captures his abilities: Scripture commentator, philosopher, preacher, hymnist, poet, and theologian. Born in the northern French town of Lille, Alan studied under **Gilbert of Poitiers** in the early 1240s and taught at Paris for more than a decade (1257–1270), and then at Montpellier from 1271 to 1285. His **summa** begins with the words "*Quoniam hominess*" (Since men . . .) and is complemented by his *Disputed Questions*. His most cited theological work is his *Regulae de sacra scriptura* (*Rules of Sacred Scripture*), which is a collection of traditional and original principles of **theology** along with their explanations. One of his more famous rules is "Deus est sphaera intelligibilis cuius centrum ubique, circumferentia nusquam" (God is an intelligible sphere whose center is everywhere and whose circumference is nowhere). From **Boethius**'s *Consolation of Philosophy* and Bernard Silvestris's *Cosmography*, Alan gains much of the inspiration for his famous theological treatise, *De planctu naturae* (*Nature's Lament*), and the nine-book theological poem *Anticlaudianus* (*The Good and Perfect Man*), both of which were written during his years at Montpellier. Alan retired to the **Cistercian** monastery of Cîteaux, where he died in 1202.

**ALBERT OF SAXONY (ca. 1316–1390).** Albert became a master of arts at Paris in 1351 and remained in that role until 1362. During his stay at Paris, he also at times served as rector of the **university**. In 1362, he entered the service of Pope Urban V at Avignon. Within a few years (1365), he had convinced the pope to establish the University of Vienna, where he served as the first rector. In 1366, he was named the bishop of Halberstadt, an office he held until his death in 1390. Albert wrote a number of commentaries on **Aristotle**'s works: *Posterior Analytics*, *On the Soul*, *Physics*, *On the Heavens*, and *On Generation and Corruption*. Often his commentaries followed the works of **John Buridan** and **Nicholas Oresme**, though he shows some independence from them on questions devoted to the infinite and the eternity of the world. His *Treatise on Proportions* was very much dependent on **Thomas Bradwardine** and **Nicholas of Oresme**. In reality, because he was frequently published in the early 16th century, he became more famous than his sources and even was responsible for spreading their renown. The *Commentary on the Nicomachean Ethics* attributed to him runs close to the path of the realist **Walter Burley**, whereas his dependence on **William of Ockham** in logic has often gained him the tag "**nominalist**." This apparent conflict has led to a challenge against the authenticity of his *Ethics* commentary. Among Albert's works are also some practice exercises in logic: *On Insolubles*, *On Obligations*, and *On Sophisms*.

**ALBERT THE GREAT (ca. 1200–1280).** Albertus Magnus, or Albert the Great, was born near Ulm, Germany, in the town of Lauingen. While studying law at Padua, he was invited by Jordan of Saxony, the successor of St. Dominic as head of the Order of Preachers, to join the young fraternity. Quite likely he did his novitiate at Cologne, where he also studied theology. He taught at various **Dominican** *studia* (Hildesheim, Freiburg im Breisgau, Regensburg, and Strasbourg) before going to Paris around 1241 to become a master of theology. As a bachelor in **theology**, he lectured *cursorie* on the **Bible**, responded at disputations, and commented on the *Sentences* of **Peter Lombard** (1243–1245). As *magister actu regens* (regent master), he held one of the two Dominican chairs in the Faculty of Theology at Paris until the end of the academic year 1248. He then left Paris for Cologne, where he was charged with establishing a *studium generale* (university-level school for the whole of the Dominican order).

During his time at Paris, Albert wrote his commentaries on **Dionysius the Pseudo-Areopagite**, but he turned in a different direction when he arrived at Cologne: he developed a plan for commenting on all the works of **Aristotle**. He did not choose to do a detailed exposition but used paraphrases to map out Aristotle's thought. These paraphrases followed the order of the text, presented its contents, recast its main points, and provided support for it with additional arguments. In his efforts to improve on the Aristotelian corpus, thereby going beyond paraphrasing and dealing with the philosophical issues raised by the text, he appealed to the writings of Cicero and **Boethius** and to the new translations from the Arabic of the texts and commentaries of **Avicenna**, **Al-Farabi**, **Al-Gazel**, and **Averroes**. Due to his vast erudition and his incorporation of extensive post-Aristotelian experiences and experiments, Albert gained the title of *Doctor Magnus*. Refer to appendix 1 and to the introduction, "Developments in the Theology Faculty from the 13th Century Onward."

**ALCHER OF CLAIRVAUX (fl. 2ND HALF OF 12TH CENTURY).** Alcher was a member of the **Cistercian** order at the Abbey of Clairvaux (ca. 1150–1275), initiated by **Bernard of Clairvaux**. He wrote one of the most influential **monastic** works on the **soul**, the compilation titled *De spiritu et anima* (*Concerning Spirit and Soul*), which provided thinkers of the 13th century with a great number of sources on the subject. The sources include **Augustine**, **Boethius**, **Macrobius**, **Hugh of Saint-Victor**, Cassiodorus, and **Isidore of Seville**. Alcher, in this work, also stressed the reflection of the

**Trinity** in the soul. The fact that this work was attributed to Augustine contributed to its popularity. By the time of **Thomas Aquinas**, however, this attribution was already denied. The work was supposedly a response to the *Letter on the Soul*, an important treatise addressed to Alcher by his fellow Cistercian **Isaac of Stella**. Alcher is also known for his treatise *De diligendo Deo* (*On the Enjoyment of God*).

**ALCUIN (ca. 735–804).** Probably a native of York, England, this theologian and educator contributed significantly to the Carolingian Renaissance, especially in the formation of **schools** and the revival of classical learning, particularly the **liberal arts**. As a child, he entered the cathedral school at York, and he took over the direction of the school after his master, Aelbert, became archbishop of York. After meeting Charlemagne in 781, he was invited to the emperor's court as master of the palace school, which moved as the royal residence changed. Alcuin was assigned a number of important roles by Charlemagne, including leadership in Charlemagne's educational reforms. Prominent in ecclesiastical affairs, he also became abbot of St. Martin's at Tours. The educational efforts of Alcuin and his followers paved the way for the growth of the schools and the eventual formation of the **university** in the late 12th century, the setting for the great intellectual achievements of the Middle Ages and beyond. His chief work is the *Didascalicon*, a collection (largely a compilation of older sources) serving as school texts in the seven liberal arts. He also wrote theological works that exhibit some knowledge of philosophy, such as his *Belief in the Holy and Undivided Trinity*. Alcuin also had a number of students who continued his project, such as Rhabanus Maurus, the author of the influential treatise *On the Education of Clerics*.

**ALEXANDER NEQUAM OR NECKHAM (1157–1217).** Alexander seemingly obtained his name from his petition to start a monastery school at St. Albans. The abbot answered the request by saying, "If you are good, you may come; if you are wicked (*nequam*), certainly not (*nequaquam*)." He came and ironically received the name "Nequam." He taught **theology** at Oxford before entering the Augustinian monastery at Cirencester sometime between 1197 and 1202. He became abbot there in 1212. Alexander attended the Fourth Lateran Council in 1215 and died in England shortly after his return. He is buried in the Cathedral of Worcester.

His most renowned works are in the liberal arts: *De nominibus utensilium* (*Concerning the Names of Utensils*) and *Corrugationes Promethei* (*The Wrinkles of Prometheus*). His fame in regard to **Aristotelian** philosophy is mainly due to his *De naturis rerum* (*On the Nature of Things*), a work that indicates his familiarity with the logic of Aristotle and the titles of a number of his works, such as the *Ethica vetus* (the old translation of the *Ethics*).

Some of his knowledge of Aristotle's view of the **soul** is derived from **John Blund**'s *Tractatus de anima* (*The Treatise on the Soul*). His acquaintance with Aristotle regarding others of his teachings could well be derived from the *Aphorismi* (*Aphorisms*) of Orso, the medical writer from Salerno.

Alexander's theological teachings may be found in his incomplete *Speculum speculationum* (*Mirror of Reflections*), a work of four books that deals with God and the **Trinity** in Books I and II; creation, **angels**, and the soul in Book III; and **grace** and free will in Book IV. Both **Anselm of Canterbury** and **Anselm of Laon** play a strong part, along with the Fathers of the Church, in his treatment of God and the Trinity. The treatment of the soul shows the influence of **Avicenna**'s *De anima*, especially in the employment of Avicenna's technical vocabulary. However, Alexander's treatment of **freedom** in Book IV shows his departure from Avicenna. Alexander is the earliest of the Oxford theologians and was quoted at Oxford throughout the 13th and 14th centuries.

**ALEXANDER OF HALES (ca. 1185–1245).** Alexander, called the *Doctor Irrefragibilis* (Irrefutable Teacher) and *Doctor doctorum* (Teacher of Teachers), was a secular master who became a **Franciscan** and thus gave the Franciscans their first chair in theology at Paris. While still a secular master, he wrote *Glossa in quattuor libros Sententiarum Petri Lombardi* (*A Gloss on the Four Books of the "Sentences" of Peter Lombard*). This work was especially important, since it was the first time that a book different from the Scriptures was used as a textbook at the ordinary hours reserved for the study of the **Bible**. (Alexander did not provide a reason for doing so, but a decade later the Dominican **Richard Fishacre** offered an explanation for this innovation.) Alexander also began a **summa** that received the title *Summa fratris Alexandri* (*The Summa of Brother Alexander*), which was completed by William of Melitona (Middleton) by order of Pope Alexander IV. William completed the work by incorporating into Alexander's corpus materials of his own, materials from his teacher's *Glossa in quattuor libros Sententiarum*, Alexander's *Disputed Questions*, treatises of **John of La Rochelle** and **Odo Rigaud**, and compatible elements from earlier and contemporary authors (**Praepositinus, William of Auxerre**, and **Philip the Chancellor**). His title *Doctor doctorum* is derived from his influence on three great Franciscan masters who were students of Alexander at the University of Paris: **St. Bonaventure**, John of Rupella, and Odo Rigaud.

**ALFARABI.** *See* FARABI, AL- (AL-FARABI) (ca. 870–ca. 950).

**ALGAZEL.** *See* GHAZALI, AL-, OR ALGAZEL (1059–1111).

**ALHACEN OR AL-HASAN (965–ca. 1040).** A native of Basra, Abu Ali al-Hasan ibn al-Hasan ibn al-Haytham, known in the Latin West as Alhacen, is best known for his contributions to the mathematical and natural sciences, especially **optics**. In his optics, he draws from **Aristotelian** physics, Euclidean and Ptolemaic mathematics, and Galenic science. His *De aspectibus* (also known as *Perspectiva*) had enormous influence in Europe, particularly through **Roger Bacon**. Al-Hasan died in Cairo.

**ALKINDI.** *See* KINDI, AL- (ALKINDI) (d. ca. 870).

**ALLEGORY.** In general, allegory (from the Greek, meaning "to speak something other") is a literary device to express imaginatively something that is difficult to grasp. For example, in *The Republic*, **Plato** speaks of men as prisoners in a cave who are bound in a way that only allows them to see what is reflected on a wall in front of them. Behind them, other men carry statues in front of a fire, and these statues throw shadows on the wall. There are many levels of meaning to this allegory. The everyday realities men encounter are like the shadows on the wall of the cave. At first, the men do not know of the fire, the statues, those carrying them, or that the shadows they see are produced by these unknown realities. Later, a few men escape, and after a difficult adjustment, they realize that their first way of experiencing things was controlled by the new things they now see. Of course, some of these men who escaped the world of shadows might escape again and discover that even the statues that produce the shadows are not really real but as statues are copies of higher realities. One aspect of allegory is that we may keep climbing to new, higher, and more enriched levels of understanding.

Philosophers like Plato read the stories of poets such as Homer and Hesiod from a philosophical or rational perspective. They criticized the poets' portraits of the gods and heroes as imaginative productions that were equivalent to shadows on the wall of Plato's cave. The philosophers' gods and heroes were not the poets' gods and heroes but were rationally discovered realities that were perhaps captivatingly but certainly unsuitably presented in Homer's *Iliad* and *Odyssey* and Hesiod's *Works and Days*.

When the Jewish Scriptures were translated into the Greek Septuagint during the Diaspora of the Jewish people in Alexandria, the portraits and stories of their God and their ancestors were treated by the philosophers there in much the same manner as they had criticized the Greek poets. The philosophers saw the Old Testament God as preferring the Jews without adequate reason and treating their neighbors vindictively. Jewish authors, such as Philo Judaeus, had to respond to these charges and did so by showing a nonsurface meaning to the stories of Scripture. For example, he took one of the great heroes of the Old Testament, Abraham, and showed that the story of

Abraham was the story of all men, a wayfarer on his way to the promised land, searching and struggling along the way, attempting at times to reach it on his own and realizing that there is his own way and God's way to get there, and finally consenting to do the will of God, no matter what it demands. In similar fashion, reading the stories of the Bible in allegorical ways, he attempted to show the wisdom of the sacred books.

Christians, with the Old and New Testaments, ran into the same criticisms of their extended story by the philosophers. The **Fathers of the Church**, especially in dealing with the stories of the Old Testament that might scandalize believers or provoke ridicule from adversaries, used allegorical interpretation to overcome such difficulties. Someone who might be shocked or horrified that God asked Abraham to sacrifice his son Isaac might gain a different sense of such a sacrifice if he realized that in the case of Jesus, God the Father was willing to sacrifice his own Son. The parallel between the sacrifice of Isaac and the sacrifice of Christ, the one an allegorical type of the other, adequately quieted the designs of Marcion and his followers, who wanted to abandon any ties between the Old and New Testaments, the God of the Old Testament and the God of the New Testament, God the Creator and God the Redeemer of all men.

The Fathers did not follow the Greek philosophers who completely abandoned their inherited mythology. They realized that many of the contents of the Old and New Testament were to be accepted literally and historically, while also having further or allegorical meanings. **St. Augustine**, in his work, *On Christian Teaching*, distinguishes between the words of Scripture that indicate literally what is necessary for salvation and the words of Scripture that urge us on to see deeper truths that can only be reached by gaining further understanding of what is said in the sacred texts. The first truths are the Scriptural declarations that are to be accepted by all believers. The other truths are those to be pursued by theologians, attempting to deepen their knowledge of God and His wisdom by using their special God-given talents to "render an account of the faith that is in them" (1 Peter 3:15). They do so by pursuing the many levels of meaning found in the Scriptures, traditionally presented in the Patristic and medieval Christian world as the four senses of Scripture: the literal or historical, the allegorical or spiritual, the moral or tropological, and the **anagogical** or mystical. *See also* EXEGESIS.

**ALPHONSUS VARGAS OF TOLEDO (ca. 1300–1366). A Hermit of St. Augustine**, Alphonsus lectured on the *Sentences* at Paris in 1344–1345, following on the heels of his fellow Augustinian, **Gregory of Rimini**. Like Gregory at Paris, Alphonsus also concentrated on the thought of English theologians. This shows a change of direction in the Parisian approach to the study of theology in the 1330s and 1340s, which previously had limited contemporary sources almost exclusively to authors who had studied in Paris. Alphonsus refers to his fellow Augustinian **Giles of Rome** as *Doctor noster* (Our Doctor), but the character of the thinking of this "second school" of Augustinian Hermits (Gregory and Alphonsus) is very different from that of the earlier 13th-century Augustinian school of Giles. Alphonsus became master of theology in either 1346 or 1347 and left Paris to teach at one of the Augustinian houses of study. He was named bishop of Badajoz by Pope Innocent VI in 1353. A year later, he was transferred to the See of Osma. He became archbishop of Toledo in 1361 and died in that city in 1366.

**AL-RAZI (ca. 865–ca. 925).** The Persian Abu Bakr Muhammad ibn Zakaria al-Razi, called Rhazes in Latin, appears in the chronology of philosophers in Islam as the second significant figure (the first is **Al-Kindi**). He drew amply from Hellenistic sources, such as Galen. The influence of his work is primarily in the field of medicine, and several of his texts were translated into Latin. He is known for his defense of **Plato** against what he saw as **Aristotle**'s corruption of philosophy, as well as for his own denial of divine revelation. To Al-Razi, God's justice would not favor any particular group through special revelation. Rather, philosophy as a way of life is the medicine of the **soul**, since the universal way to God and the good life is through the use of the intellect. Al-Razi also propounded atomist explanations of matter and held, according to his interpretation of Plato's *Timaeus*, that the world was created from eternal matter. These positions, against the chief medieval project of synthesizing reason and revelation, as well as against the immense influence of Aristotle, are quite remarkable and clearly explain his unpopularity among contemporaries. Only a few of his properly philosophic writings survive, such as *The Spiritual Medicine* and *The Philosophical Life*.

**AMALRIC OF BÈNE (MID-12TH CENTURY–ca. 1206).** Born at Bène, near Chartres, Amalric became, after first studying arts at Paris, a master of theology at the same university. Together with **David of Dinant**, Amalric as well as his followers, the so-called Amalricians, were condemned at the Council of Paris in 1210 and at the Fourth Lateral Council in 1215. The Amalricians disappeared soon thereafter. Since we have no writings by Amalric himself, what can be conjectured about his doctrines comes from documents that condemn them, often associating his teachings with those of his followers. This situation should give us pause when assessing Amalric himself.

Amalric and David of Dinant were both condemned as pantheists: they did not distinguish sufficiently between God and creatures so as to preserve the clear Christian teaching concerning the transcendence of God. For Amalric, God is the form of the universe. He is present in all things in quite a literal sense. Christ is physically present in the actual universe, as he is also in the bread and wine of the Eucharist. Moreover, the Holy Spirit is in all human **souls** to the degree that all souls are divine and perfect and, therefore, wholly good agents. The only one excluded from this ubiquity is God the Father. Amalric's views largely stem, apparently, from misinterpretations of **John Scotus Eriugena**, **Aristotle**, and Scripture. Thus, Amalric was judged as undermining the Trinity's transcendence and as confusing good and evil. Amalric generated a significant following, and there seem to be connections between his views and subsequent popular heresies of the period, such as the Free Spirit heretics of the latter part of the 13th century.

**ANAGOGY.** The anagogical sense of sacred Scripture is one of the spiritual senses of Scripture. The Greek *anagogia* means "a leading upward," and *anagogy* is tied to all the biblical passages that treat of heaven or eternal goods. **Dionysius the Pseudo-Areopagite** employed the term to designate the spiritual sense that always elevates the mind of the reader toward high and sublime realities. Anagogical understandings are found in the Old Testament: in the Book of Tobias (c. 13), the city of Jerusalem, the capital of the Kingdom of Judah, is understood anagogically as the eternal, heavenly kingdom that God has prepared for his chosen ones. The Epistle to the Hebrews (c. 7) in the New Testament understands the priesthood of Melchisedech as pointing anagogically to the priesthood of Christ, who offers an eternal sacrifice in heaven. Medieval exegetes often follow these leads in the Scriptures to find other earthly types and figures that speak to them spiritually of heavenly realities.

**ANALOGY.** Both philosophers and theologians argue by analogy when they use one thing to argue to another. This logical procedure is a way of going from something that is better known to get a grasp of something that is less known. **Aristotle**, for example, when he wanted to show how there could be one science, first philosophy, that dealt with all things despite the differences among them, picked as his analogy the case of medicine, which could deal with many different kinds of things, for example, the health found in a man; the diet, which is different from a man's health but which helps to keep him healthy; and a urine sample, which is different from a man's health but which is a sign of good or bad health in the man. Despite the differences between health, diet, and a urine sample, they are all in some way related to the health of the man, so medicine studies all of them. Similarly, realities are different: some are substances, while others, such as the color, height, and weight of a substance, are not substances themselves but **accidents**. Yet accidents are the accidents of substances, so they are connected. If we could tie every accident to a substance, and every substance to some primary substance on which individual substances depend, then we could arrive at linking all reality together. When we do this, we have the way of uniting all things and of having a science that deals with all things. Analogy becomes a very important way of arguing in philosophy and theology to try to lead people from things they understand or know better to things that they do not understand and about which they know less. Of course, some analogies are more plausible than others, so a whole theory of analogy and the different kinds of analogies developed as part of philosophical and theological training in the **Arts Faculty** and the **Theology** Faculty.

**ANDREW OF SAINT-VICTOR (ca. 1110–1175).** A native of England, Andrew is known principally as an exegete of sacred Scripture. He entered the Abbey of Saint-Victor at Paris in 1130, around the same time as his contemporary **Adam of Saint-Victor**, and like Adam he studied under **Hugh of Saint-Victor**. In addition to being a canon regular at Saint-Victor, he was during two periods abbot of a daughter house of Saint-Victor, namely Wigmore Abbey in Herefordshire, England. In 1147 Andrew went to Wigmore as its first abbot. He returned to Saint-Victor ca. 1154–1155, and afterward, ca. 1161–1163, he went back to Wigmore as abbot until his death. Andrew was quite original in both scholarly interest and approach. With little attraction to the fields of theological speculation and natural science, he devoted himself intensely and almost exclusively to a rather neglected study that had been but one of the concerns of his master Hugh: the historical and literal sense of the sacred text. He thus distinguishes himself sharply from his contemporary and peer **Richard of Saint-Victor**, a great intellectual force at Saint-Victor, who developed the spiritual and speculative aspect of Hugh's exegesis. In pursuing his goal, Andrew manifests an original critical approach as well as uncommon scholarly skills, most notably by his knowledge of languages that permitted him to bypass translations.

As an exegete, Andrew preferred neither to gloss nor to comment on whole texts, but to expound upon select passages of special significance or difficulty, considering only what he thought necessary for the understanding of the letter. His main Christian sources are Patristic commentaries, among which St. Jerome's stand out, and the **gloss**. Andrew also seriously investigated and drew from Jewish sources. As is to be expected, Andrew relies both on his master Hugh as well as on traditional authorities. However, his main criterion for **exegesis** is ultimately his critical approach to research. He does not hesitate to disagree openly with anyone, be it Hugh, **Augustine**, or Jerome, in his search for textual truth. In this search, Andrew favors common sense, having a preference for natural over supernatural explanations for solving difficulties. Andrew's pioneering stress on the fundamental importance of literal exegesis in biblical scholarship influenced later medieval exegetes such as **Peter Comestor**, **Peter the Chanter**, **Stephen Langton**, **Hugh of Saint-Cher**, and **Nicholas of Lyra**. *See also* ORDERS (RELIGIOUS).

**ANGELS.** This English term is derived from the Greek *angelos*, which means "messenger." In the Scriptural tradition of Jewish, Christian, and Islamic revelation, the word for angel is also related to the notion of messenger, namely the Hebrew *malakh*, the Latin *angelus*, and the Arabic *mala'ika*. Thus, angels are seen as intermediaries between God and human beings. They are not seen necessarily as superior to human beings, although in many instances they are. Generally, angels are portrayed as God's messengers (e.g., in prophecy), agents, or attendants, as beings that minister toward the fulfillment of God's will. However, there are also fallen angels or devils; their leader is Satan or Lucifer, who endeavors to frustrate God's will and to entice human beings to do likewise.

In medieval philosophy and theology, angels are treated systematically in the area known as angelology, the account of angels. In **Jewish philosophy and theology**, as well as in the **Cabala**, one finds various accounts of angels, among which those of Philo of Alexandria, **Saadiah Gaon**, **Judah Halevi**, **Salomon ibn Gabirol**, Abraham ibn Ezra, **Moses Maimonides**, and Abraham ibn Daud are noteworthy. In Christianity, one of the most fundamental texts in the development of angelology was *On the Celestial Hierarchy* (*De coelesti Hierarchia*) by the sixth-century **Neoplatonic** author known as **Dionysius the Pseudo-Areopagite**. Here three levels of angelic choirs are described, and only the lowest level is seen as interacting with human beings. This Greek work was influential in medieval Latin thought, chiefly through the translation of **John Scotus Eriugena**. **Peter Lombard** developed the angelology of this work, and so did the various **Scholastics** who commented on Lombard's *Sentences* (a standard text at **universities**). In this tradition, **Thomas Aquinas** and **Duns Scotus** provided two classic alternative accounts of angels, the former viewing them as incorporeal and the latter as corporeal. Other influences in medieval Christian accounts of angels were the **Fathers of the Church**, such as **Augustine** and Origen, who generally spoke of angels as created corporeal beings. In Islamic philosophy (*falsafah*), as in Jewish philosophy, it was common to identify angels with the intelligences of the **Aristotelian** and Neoplatonic traditions, namely the immaterial movers (of the heavenly bodies), which depend on the First Mover or God. The accounts of **Al-Farabi**, **Avicenna**, and **Averroes** were especially important both in Islam and in Jewish and Christian philosophy. Islamic theology (*kalam*) and mysticism (**Sufism**) also yielded various accounts of angels as beings that functioned as intermediaries between God and human beings.

In the various medieval accounts of angels, and depending on the philosophical and theological framework governing a given angelology, one finds divergent views concerning basic questions about them (both within and across traditions), such as their created status, their (corporeal/incorporeal) nature, their rank in regard to human beings, their roles as God's ministers, and the senses in which Scriptural passages mentioning angels are to be interpreted. The constant factor is the very attempt to account for angels as a part of revelation.

**ANSELM OF CANTERBURY, ST. (1033–1109).** Born in Aosta in 1033, in 1060 Anselm entered the Norman abbey of Bec, where he studied under **Lanfranc**. He was elected abbot in 1078, succeeding the abbey's founder. In 1093, he was named to succeed Lanfranc as archbishop of Canterbury, but there were continued disputes with the kings over the appointment. After reaching agreement in 1106, he had to face further contention with the archbishop of York over primacy. He died in 1109, was canonized probably in 1163, and was declared a **Doctor of the Church** in 1720.

Anselm is a very different student of Christian doctrine than his medieval predecessors. One can sense this change in Anselm's justificatory preface at the beginning of his *Monologion* and in his cover letter to Pope Urban II concerning *Cur Deus Homo* (*Why the God-Man*), cited in the introduction under "The Birth of Medieval Christian Theology." However, as he explains in these notices, he believes that he is continuing what **St. Augustine** and the other **Fathers of the Church** were doing, not just collecting and arranging their authoritative statements. Anselm indicates his theological goal: "I do not judge it objectionable if, established in the faith, we propose to apply ourselves to an investigation of its nature."

Anselm's project is to bring understanding to the truths of the faith, and to do so as the Fathers had done, with the hope of perhaps taking this understanding a step further. The *Monologion* and *Proslogion* attempt to lead us to a deeper understanding of God. Anselm provides a new nominal definition of God: "That beyond which nothing greater can be conceived." It is not enough to prove that God is a being who is wise, since there may be many wise beings. God has to be of a wisdom than which none greater can be conceived. Anselm argues that a being greater than which none can be conceived has to exist really and not just as a thought, for if he only existed in our thought, then we could conceive of a being who would be greater, namely, a being of this kind that actually exists. In his *Cur Deus Homo* (*Why the God-Man*), Anselm extends his pursuit further, seeking a greater understanding of the mysteries of the Incarnation and Redemption of the God-Man. In his *De libertate arbitrii* (*On the Freedom of the Will*) and *De Concordia praescientiae et praedestinationis et gratiae Dei cum libero artibrio* (*On the Harmony of Foreknowledge, Predestination, and the Grace of God with Free Will*),

Anselm searches for insight into how to reconcile God's omniscience and predestination with human freedom. Repeating a theme he developed at the Council of Bari in 1098, he wrote his *De processione Spiritus Sancti* (*On the Procession of the Holy Spirit*) in 1102, a treatise arguing that the Holy Spirit proceeds from both the Father and the Son.

Anselm is known primarily as a theological writer, although one might classify his *De Grammatico* (*On the Grammarian*), a work on logic and grammar, as a philosophical treatise, since it is an introduction to dialectics as a preparation for studying theological issues. In this work, he examines whether *grammarian* primarily signifies a man who knows grammar, the grammar that is known by the man, or the having of the knowledge of grammar by a man. Discussions of this type will later lead to the developments in logic that focus on the signification and supposition of terms. In all, his systematic treatises, letters, meditations, and prayers fill five tall volumes in the modern Latin edition. Refer to the introduction.

**ANSELM OF LAON (ca. 1050–1117).** Born in Laon, Anselm studied under **Lanfranc** at the monastery of Bec. After short sojourns in Paris and Chartres, he directed the famous school of Laon with his brother Raoul. Anselm became known as "the teacher of teachers," since among his students he counted **Gilbert of Poitiers**, **William of Champeaux**, and **Peter Abelard**. Abelard criticized him for senile forgetfulness, but he was in his mature days a respected teacher and glossator on the Epistles of St. Paul and the Psalter. He leaned more toward the moral reading of Scripture in the tradition of Gregory the Great, and he was praised more for his knowledge of the comments of the **Fathers of the Church** than for his depth of understanding. Quite likely the contrast in the approaches of Anselm and Abelard to the study of the Scriptures is best captured in **Robert of Melun**'s *Sententiae* (*Sentences*). For Robert (and Abelard), it is not enough to pass on the Patristic authorities: "What is known, if the meaning is not known, or what is taught if the meaning is not unfolded? Neither is anything learned if the meaning continues to be totally unknown." Despite the criticisms of Abelard and Robert of Melun, Anselm was one of the best **lectors** of the 12th century (refer to the introduction, "Methods of Study").

**ANTONIUS ANDREAS (ca. 1280–ca. 1335).** His most-used Scholastic title, *Scotellus* (Little Scotus), tells much of the story of this **Franciscan** from the Spanish province of Aragon. He studied under **Duns Scotus** during the years 1302–1307, when the Subtle Doctor lectured at Paris. It was during this period that Scotus had most influenced and successfully gathered the first members of his school. Antonius, along with **James of Ascoli**, William of Alnwick, **John of Bassolis**, and **Hugh of Newcastle**, were the first Scotists.

Antonius through his writings, many published in the late 1400s, had a great deal of influence in the development of Scotism. He was such a strong follower of Scotus that the *Commentary on the Sentences* attributed to him is now under challenge, since in this work the author disagrees with Scotus concerning the principle of individuation. On the other hand, the *Quaestiones de anima* (*Questions on the Soul*) attributed to Scotus, but suspected to be the work of Antonius, have been restored to Scotus himself as the rightful author.

**AQUINAS, THOMAS.** *See* THOMAS AQUINAS (1225–1274).

**ARIANISM.** This is a fourth-century **heresy** regarding the Christian teaching that there are three persons in God. Arius (ca. 250–326), a priest in Alexandria, denied the divinity of Christ, who in Christian teaching is the Son of God and the Second Person of the Trinity, and the doctrine of three persons in God. He was attacked by St. Anthanasius and later by the Cappadocian fathers, Basil the Great, Gregory Nazianzus, and Gregory of Nyssa (*see* FATHERS OF THE CHURCH). The heresy of Arianism was condemned officially at the Council of Constantinople in 381, when this second general council of the Church reaffirmed the Nicene Creed, which was approved at the first general or ecumenical council of the Church held at Nicaea in 325.

**ARISTOTELIANISM.** Platonism and Aristotelianism, the philosophies of **Plato** and his student Aristotle (384 or 383–322 B.C.) as used, interpreted, and transformed, are the two chief philosophic currents in the Middle Ages. A native of the Greek colony of Stagira, Aristotle was known in the Middle Ages simply and officially as the Philosopher. His were the most influential philosophic writings of the period, where commentaries of Aristotle surpass in quantity any other philosophic genre. His extensive writings include the following chief texts. On **logic** and language, he wrote the *Organon* (six treatises on **dialectic**), the *Rhetoric*, and the *Poetics*. The *Physics*, *On the Heavens*, *On Generation and Corruption*, *Meteorology*, and *On the Soul* deal with aspects of natural philosophy. His moral philosophy is found in the *Nicomachean Ethics*, *Eudemian Ethics*, and *Magna Moralia*, while his thoughts on the state are found in his *Politics*. The *Metaphysics* treats "things after physics," dealing with topics presupposing the study of physics (natural philosophy), such as immaterial **substances** and the divisions and attributes proper to being as such. In logic, Aristotle's authority was practically undisputed, providing Jewish, Christian, and **Islamic** thinkers with a structure that served as the instrument for sound thinking and for the acquisition of knowledge in the different subjects. Concerning Aristotle's works on the **nature** of things, even though medieval thinkers had to reinterpret or correct what they saw as lacking in a philosophy without reference to revelation, Aristotle provided a great deal of the framework for medieval conceptions of God, the world, and humanity. His conclusion that the world is eternal, his cryptic remarks concerning the immortal aspect of the human **soul**, and his view that rational speculation is man's proper end were especially controversial. Still, some of the outstanding medieval thinkers, such as **Avicenna**, **Maimonides**, and **Aquinas**, saw in Aristotle's thought more than in other philosophies the truer and more compelling rational principles, reconcilable after some adjustments with the infallible truth of revelation.

A major difference between the development of Islamic thought (including **Jewish philosophy** in Islamic lands) and Christian thought is that the former had access to the majority of Aristotle's works by the ninth century (*see FALSAFAH, AL-*), while the Christians did not gain full access until the 13th century (including the *Politics*, which was not available previously to medieval Jews and Muslims). In the 13th century, Christians also received important Islamic and Jewish works. At Toledo, scholars such as **Gerard of Cremona**, **Dominic Gundissalinus**, and John Avendauth in the 12th century, and **Michael Scot** and Hermann the German in the 13th century, translated into Latin important Greek and Arabic texts. The Latin translations of **James of Venice** in the 12th century and, especially, those of **William of Moerbeke** (1215–1285) at Paris proved fundamental to the Christian assimilation of philosophy (**Thomas Aquinas**, for example, used Moerbeke's translations). Before this time, Christians possessed only Aristotle's works in dialectic (for their transmission, *see* DIALECTICS). The reception of the totality of Aristotle's corpus in the Christian West stimulated a philosophical revolution and high point in medieval Christian philosophy at the emerging European **universities**. A brief sketch of Aristotle's thought and of its general role in medieval philosophy follows.

A basic teaching of Plato is that knowledge is a recollection of what he calls eternal forms. Things of our experience are not fully knowable because of their fleetingness. Only their permanent models, of which changing things remind us, yield unwavering or true knowledge. Changing things possess only partial reality to the extent that they are copies of true reality, that is, to the degree that they "participate" in the forms. A central focus of Plato's writings involves a description of the significance and manifestation of the forms, as well as the life facilitating their knowledge. This is the chief goal of the soul, which is above all a lover of wisdom. Though very much influenced by Plato's philosophy, Aristotle departs from different principles that give his philosophy a distinctive character. Aristotle took seriously the question of change, that is, the question of how something *new* comes into being. Aristotle interpreted Plato's forms as existing separately from empirical reality, and thus as unable to explain change; as an explanatory device, participation to

Aristotle is an empty metaphor (*Metaphysics* I, 9, 991b, 19–23). Equally deficient are the extreme positions of Heraclitus and Parmenides. Heraclitus, stressing the changing aspect of all things, made knowledge, which requires some permanent referent, impossible. Parmenides, stressing the self-same character of the real, went too far in denying the reality of change altogether.

Drawing from preceding natural philosophers, Aristotle's own account of change is based on three principles, two contraries and an underlying subject (*Physics* I, 7). These principles apply whether a thing comes to be without qualification or with qualification. For example, a man comes to be musical from being unmusical. In this type of change, the man is the underlying subject that goes from one contrary state, unmusical, to another, musical. He does not come into existence as a man. He already exists as a man. Rather, while remaining a man, he receives a new quality (musical) and, as it were, loses an old quality (unmusical). In the case of a man, coming or ceasing to be without qualification would be generation and death respectively. This type of change is also explained in terms of three principles. For here too an underlying subject goes from being in a condition to its contrary. In the case of human generation, a given biological material that is not a specific person, but which has the potential to become that specific person, becomes that person through generation. Every change, therefore, consists of a subject, of a condition that the subject acquires, and of a condition that the subject loses in virtue of the aforementioned acquisition.

Aristotle's doctrine of actuality and potentiality is intimately tied to this account (*Physics* I, 8, 191b, 27–29). For his account of change amounts to saying that the underlying subject is in potency to the contrary state, and change is the actualization of this potency (*Physics* III, 1, 201a, 10–14). This in turn means that natural forms exist only in matter. These forms are the states acquired by different material subjects. This in turn implies that matter is the principle of individuation: things belonging to a species are many individuals because their shared form is educed from many material subjects which are in potency to the shared form. Individuality comes from matter, not form. Form, being of itself one, brings unity along with actuality to matter; it makes matter into what it is. But a form is always the form of a composite, and thus the form is multiplied because of its existence in material subjects. The substances we experience, such as rocks, trees, and cats, are composites of matter and form and are actual insofar as form gives reality to matter. Of Aristotle's four causes, form and matter are the two causes that constitute a thing intrinsically; the efficient and final causes point to the origin and destination of a thing, respectively (*Physics* II, 3). Knowledge will therefore have to be explained in terms of intellectual abstraction, as natural forms only exist in matter. To grasp them, we must abstract or draw out the form from the matter with which it is united. The **soul**, itself the form of a body (*De anima* II, 1), has no access to transcendent forms, as Plato had claimed.

Since forms exist only in individuals, they are only potentially intelligible. They only become actually intelligible when the matter is set aside by the intellect and we grasp the form in its **universal** character. This book we perceive here and now, for example, is actually visible, but only potentially intelligible in that we only know the universal nature of a book when we in some way see with the eye of the mind the commonality among all books as books. To be made actually intelligible as universals, the intellect needs to strip these forms from their material conditions. The intellect is not only passive as receptive of these universals, but an active principle that extracts forms from matter (*De anima* III, 4–5). Since all reduction of potency to act must be in virtue of a prior act, an actualizing principle of understanding, the so-called agent intellect, is posited by Aristotle to explain how any potential understanding becomes actual in human individuals. This agent intellect, a pure actuality, is said to be the only immortal aspect of the soul (*De anima* III, 5), although its nature and its kind of immortality remain a question for later thinkers.

Aristotle's doctrine of the four causes, which he uses to explain all things, whether of nature or art, whether in motion or motionless, acquires special significance, and perhaps its original significance, in regard to the substantial change of natural things. Any substance, whether natural or artificial, is a composite of matter and form, the two intrinsic causes. In regard to the causes, there are two important differences between artificial and natural things. First, in artificial things the efficient cause is of a different order than the effect. The maker of a bicycle is not another bicycle but a human being. In natural things, on the other hand, the efficient cause is of the same order as the effect: trees generate trees and dogs, dogs. Second, in artificial things, the final cause is distinct from the formal cause. The final cause of a bicycle, its use or riding, is distinct from the form or shape of the bicycle. In natural things, on the other hand, the final cause is linked to the formal cause. For their end or purpose is actualization according to form. Unlike a bicycle, which does not become a more full-fledged bicycle by riding, a child becomes an adult by living. The end or purpose of a child, or of any other natural thing, is actualization according to form. Natural things, especially living things, possess their goals within—their forms are inherent principles of motion that tend toward their proper goals (*Physics* II, 1). This is the basis of Aristotle's theology: not only art but also nature acts for the sake of an end.

These two differences between artificial and living things presuppose the deeper distinction between the two. The form of an artificial thing is its intelligible shape, governing some material principle. The form of a living thing is not its shape, but the cause of its shape, growth and activity. Form in this latter sense is a type of life proper to a given species. The form of a dog, for example, is the life of the dog. This is the principle by which the dog grows, barks, sleeps, acts, and so on. It is ultimately also the cause of the shape of the dog; when the dog dies, his shape will disintegrate. Form here, as in artificial things, plays the role of actualizing matter. But form in this case is much more than shape: form as a type of life actualizes matter in the sense of being its immanent principle of action and development.

Still, living things are composites of form and matter, soul and body. For all living things are individuals generated through substantial change. This means that they are the result of an underlying subject's acquisition of form through generation. Growth and development are the actualization of the subject's potency. Accordingly, souls, just as any other natural forms, exist only in and as material subjects. The soul, the principle of actuality of a composite, is not an individual of itself but a constitutive principle of an individual. These material subjects come to be and pass away; only their species persist through a succession of individuals (*De anima* II, 4, 415b, 3–8).

For Aristotle, any motion or change presupposes a prior as well as a subsequent motion or change. For motion is when a subject, that is already actual as subject, goes from a potential to an actual state. But the subject came into being, and coming into being is a motion, and so another subject is presupposed in this latter motion. And this second subject came into being, and so a third subject is presupposed that itself came into being and required a fourth, and so on. What holds in the order of generation also holds in the order of perishing, since perishing, like generation, is a motion. The eternity of motion implies the eternity of the universe, as well as that of its ultimate cause, the first Unmoved Mover, which moves and orders all as a final cause, as that for the sake of which all ultimately move. Without such a mover, itself unmoved, there would be an infinite regress of motions—an impossibility. Without this first cause, there would be nothing to ground the eternal process of motion and change (*Physics* VII, 5, 256a, 3–25; VIII, 6, 258b, 10–, 259a, 3–; VIII, 6, 258b, 10–, 259a, 14). This final cause, as eternal and uncaused, must be pure actuality (*Metaphysics* XII, 6, 1071b, 12–22), which implies its intellectual nature and immateriality. But this uncaused Mind is not a Creator, only an ultimate final cause of all things. It may be understood as an efficient cause only in the sense that all production and reproduction is for the sake of a final cause, just as building a house is for the sake of shelter. But it is not an efficient cause in the sense of bringing things into existence out of itself. On the contrary, this final cause or Unmoved Mover is depicted by Aristotle as rather unconcerned with things other than itself. For it is an intellect whose thought must be identical with its very substance. The object of this thinking needs to be proportionate to it in a way such that the thinking remains unalterable, at rest in the sense that the thinking is wholly its own end. Aristotle thus suggests that this intellect is thought thinking itself, and not thinking of lower things as such, for contemplating lower things, which are multiple and changing, would alter it (*Metaphysics* XII, 9, 1074b, 25–34).

Since in living things the final cause is linked to the formal cause, Aristotle approaches the question of the end or purpose of human life in the *Nicomachean Ethics* (Book I, chapter 7) by considering human nature. He applies his doctrine of the soul as the formal and final cause of living things to the question of the human good. The rational soul is the formal cause of the human being: human beings are like other living things in that their principle of actuality or formal cause is a soul. They are composites of soul and body. But human beings are what they are, and are distinct from other living things, because their soul or life principle is a rational one. The final cause or purpose of human beings is therefore actualization according to the rational soul, their form.

Aristotle argues that the good of a thing is performing its function well. The function of a thing, what a thing does, is shown by its definition, namely by what the thing is. In turn, what a thing is depends on its specific difference, the peculiar characteristic that distinguishes one kind of thing from other kinds. What is peculiar to human beings is the life of reason; human beings are rational animals. The human function or purpose is living this life of reason. Accordingly, the human good, the good performance of the human function, is living this life of reason *well*, namely with excellence or virtue. In the *Ethics*, Aristotle discusses the virtues or human excellences, including the virtue of friendship, pleasure, and happiness, as dimensions of this life. His basic insight concerning the nature of this kind of life relates to form as the principle of actuality and unity and to actualization according to form as the final cause. Living the life of reason well implies a unity ordered to reason. Aside from the nutritive dimension of the human soul, which is not specifically human and thus is outside the investigation into right rational living, the soul is characterized by a twofold rational dimension, namely what possesses reason and what can either obey or disobey reason (*Nicomachean Ethics* I, 13). Having distinct dimensions, the well-being of the soul lies in its harmony, while self-fragmentation is its vice or sickness. The intellectual virtues are perfections of the part of the soul that reasons. The moral virtues, all combining good desire and sound judgment, are the perfections of the part of the soul that can either obey or disobey reason.

The best activities are those most associated with living the life of reason well. For "that which is proper to each thing is by nature best and most pleasant for each thing" (*Nicomachean Ethics* X, 7:1178a5, in *The Basic Works of Aristotle* [New York: Modern Library, 2001], 1105). For human beings this is the life of reason, where it is performing the highest function it is capable of. This activity is theoretical contemplation of the truest and highest things (*Nicomachean Ethics* X, 7). Knowledge of these things is wisdom, the knowledge of first causes. Neither the various crafts, like architecture, nor the particular sciences, like biology, qualify as the highest rational activities, in that the former are subordinate to their products, while the latter only consider a part of reality. Wisdom, on the other hand, is called by Aristotle first philosophy because it considers the first causes by which all else is and is known. It is also called the science of being as being (*Metaphysics* IV, 1), which later came to be known as **metaphysics**, in that it considers the truths of all that is inasmuch as it is. Finally, it is called **theology** in two senses. First, it is called theology, because it ends in the consideration of divine things, and secondly because it is a science that seems more fitting to God than to humans, since humans are servile in so many ways, while this science is absolutely free. Being solely for the sake of knowledge, it aims at what is most real or knowable, eternal things, which are higher than mere mortals (*Metaphysics* I, 2, 983a, 6–11).

Happiness, strictly understood as the human activity most for its own sake, extends as far as contemplation does, for three reasons. First, contemplation gratifies what is best and most proper to us. Second, this activity is most self-sufficient and thus most for its own sake, since it is most immanent: nothing arises apart from the activity itself. It is pure knowing for the sake of knowing. Accordingly, third, this activity alone, for its self-sufficient and continuous purity, accommodates the greatest and best pleasure. Engaging in this activity is the highest and best actualization of the human form or rational soul.

In their efforts to reconcile reason with revelation, practically all medieval thinkers combined Aristotle and Plato, at least to the extent that nearly all held the Platonic doctrine of forms understood as God's creative art, as well as the validity of Aristotelian logic. The synthetic efforts of medieval thinkers built upon and benefited, especially, from previous Neoplatonic syntheses of Plato and Aristotle, such as those of **Plotinus** and **Proclus**. In addition, later syntheses of religion and Aristotelianism built upon and benefited from earlier ones; the Christian Thomas Aquinas was influenced by Moses Maimonides the Jew, who in turn followed the Muslim **Al-Farabi** in important respects. Yet, even though all medieval thinkers synthesized these intellectual trends together with revelation, in terms of their fundamental principles they still favored either the Platonic approach or the Aristotelian approach. Philosophical rigor demanded that they choose between a Platonic conception of knowledge as a comparison with a standard, with consistent theses, and an Aristotelian conception of knowledge as abstraction, with consistent theses. Thinkers who sought to combine these two approaches generally subordinated one to the other (and some still used the secondary approach profoundly). **Henry of Ghent**, for example, adopted the Aristotelian view of knowledge as abstraction. But for him this was only one stage in cognition;

the pure or sincere truth came only when the abstracted universal was compared with a transcendent exemplar. Contrariwise Thomas Aquinas subordinated Platonism to Aristotelianism, understanding **Augustine**'s (Platonic) view that the mind understands all things in the light of eternal exemplars through his interpretation of Aristotle's agent intellect. This intellect, which knows forms only through abstraction from sensible particulars, is individuated according to the number of bodies, and for Aquinas it is also a participation in God, who is the Uncreated Light containing all exemplars.

Aristotelians, however, still differed among themselves, often quite markedly. Avicenna (influenced by Neoplatonists, especially Al-Farabi) and his critic **Averroes** provided two very different and fundamental interpretations of Aristotle. **Averroism** designates one of the standard trends within Aristotelianism. Avicenna's interpretation became central in the different approach of **John Duns Scotus**, who developed an alternative Christian philosophy. **William of Ockham**'s new interpretation of Aristotle's logic and natural philosophy gave birth to the so-called *via moderna* (the modern way), a third classic form of Aristotelianism in the Christian tradition. In Judaism, the distinct philosophies of Maimonides and **Gersonides** have Aristotle as the central component. In theological discussions, Aristotelian principles were used extensively in the three traditions. For example, Christians used Aristotelian concepts in discussions on the Trinity and the status of theology, while in Muslim *kalam* and in Jewish theology, Aristotle informed discussions regarding the divine attributes. Refer to the introduction. *See also* ACCIDENT.

**ARISTOTLE.** *See* ARISTOTELIANISM; AUGUSTINIANISM.

**ARTS FACULTY.** When universities were established around the beginning of the 13th century, the Arts Faculty was essentially a preparatory faculty. It provided students with an education in the traditional **liberal arts** (grammar, dialectic or logic, rhetoric, arithmetic, geometry, astronomy, and music). The texts for these studies were the traditional works that were respected in these disciplines, for example, **Priscian** and **Donatus** in grammar, **Aristotle** in dialectic, etc. These studies prepared students for the more advanced fields of Scripture, medicine, and law. When Aristotle's philosophical works were translated into Latin, they began to exert pressure for more than the study of Aristotle's *Organon*, or the collection of his books on logic. The statutes at the University of Paris in 1255 mandated the exact number of lessons that had to be given on each book of Aristotle's philosophy. It was just a basic general knowledge that was gained at first, but soon teachers began to spend more time on individual works of Aristotle and became aware of the different interpretations that his various commentators presented concerning his teachings. Eventually, and with a great deal of conflict, the Arts Faculty became much more of an Aristotelian philosophy faculty. When the Arts Faculty was a preparatory faculty in the liberal arts, no one wanted to stay there to teach forever. The saying was "No one gets gray hair in the Arts Faculty." Matters changed when it developed more into an Aristotelian philosophy faculty. Some wanted to stay and face the philosophical challenges that were newly arising.

**ASHARI, AL-.** *See* ASHARITES.

**ASHARITES.** One of the principal schools of Muslim theology, this movement was founded by Abu al-Hassan al-Ashari (873–935). In his early years, in his *Theological Opinions of the Muslims*, Al-Ashari collected various Muslim theological views and followed the school of the **Mu'tazilites** that integrated them through the use of rational consistency. Around the age of 40, he dedicated himself to bringing theological opinions more in line with orthodox Muslim religious beliefs by uniting the teachings of the Koran and the sunna, the corpus of Islamic customs and practices founded on the words and deeds of Muhammad. His chief follower was **Al-Ghazali**, and his followers took his name, the Asharites. *See also* EXEGESIS; *KALAM.*

**AUFREDUS OR ANFREDUS GONTERI BRITO (fl. 1303–1325).** A **Franciscan** from Brittany, Aufredus was the author of *Quaestio de paupertate Christi* (*A Question on the Poverty of Christ*). However, he is mostly known as a defender of **John Duns Scotus**. Aufredus lived in the Franciscan community in Paris from 1303 to 1308. It was there that he heard the Parisian lectures of Scotus. When he later lectured on Peter Lombard's *Sentences* in Barcelona in 1322, he indicated that his commentary was a *compilatio* (a collection of texts from many authors). In 1325 he again lectured on the *Sentences* of Lombard, but this time in Paris. Again, his text includes numerous citations from contemporary authors. One of his sources in both commentaries is **Peter Aureoli**, who frequently opposed Scotus. At times the texts of Aureoli come directly from **Francis of Marchia**, not from Aureoli himself. However, both in representing and defending Scotus's positions, he gathers arguments that come from **Francis of Meyronnes**, **Gerard Odon**, **Peter Thomae**, **Robert Cowton**, and other **Franciscans**, as well as from Dominicans, such as **Hervaeus Natalis** and **James of Metz**, and **Augustinians**, such as Gerard of Siena. These texts are so abundant that he could be considered one of the most thorough historians of early Scotism.

**AUGUSTINE OF ANCONA (AUGUSTINUS TRIUMPHUS) (ca. 1275–1328).** Augustine is most generally known for his political writings that defend the supreme power of the pope. His *Summa de ecclesiastica potestate* (*Summa of Ecclesiastical Power*), following the lead of his fellow **Hermits of St. Augustine**, **Giles of Rome** and **James of Viterbo**, strongly defends the supremacy of papal power and the subordination of earthly power to the pope. He also defended Boniface VIII against the accusations of Philip the Fair, denied the right of the French king to judge the Knights Templar to be heretics, and subordinated the college of cardinals to the pope. Augustinus was a **lector** at Padua before the turn of the century and is known to have taught at Paris early in the second decade of the 14th century. He is mentioned by **Prosper of Reggio Aemilia** in the prologue of his *Commentary on the Sentences* as defending the position that a student in **theology** does not gain any habit of knowledge distinct from the **faith**. Prosper accuses Augustinus, a Hermit of St. Augustine, of thus betraying the teaching of his patron saint Augustine, who, in the beginning of Book XIV of *On the Trinity*, claims that a Christian teacher should seek the kind of knowledge that goes beyond faith by pursuing the knowledge that "begets, nourishes, strengthens, and defends that most wholesome faith that leads to true blessedness."

**AUGUSTINE, ST. (AUGUSTINE OF HIPPO) (354–430).** This native of Thagaste (in North Africa) became the most influential thinker among the **Fathers of the Church** in the West. His extensive writings, oriented by his efforts to synthesize **Platonic** philosophy with Christian revelation, contained for later thinkers the richest expression of Christian wisdom in its various dimensions. The son of a pagan father and a Christian mother (Monica), Augustine himself embodied the divergent traditions that he finally brought together as a coherent and seminal worldview. Even after **Aristotelianism** had gained a strong foothold in theology faculties at the **universities** of the 13th century, Augustine continued to be favored by many and incorporated by practically all.

A highly critical, passionate, and creative spirit, he describes his eventful path to God from early youth in his *Confessions*, a masterpiece in introspective analysis and expression. From early on, he displayed a keen drive for rational certainty, coupled with an equally keen critical instinct. The former impulse continually drove him to overcome skepticism by seeking the surest foundations for knowledge, while the latter motivated him to question and scrutinize thoroughly. As he reflected in later life, it was clear to Augustine that God had always been the object of his search, as God is the foundation of all truth, as well as the only object that satisfies the **soul** completely.

Cicero's *Hortensius*, which he read in 372–73 while he was a student of rhetoric at Carthage, elicited a profound thirst for wisdom that drove him to a variety of positions and bore its final fruit in his balanced harmony between reason and **faith**. At first, however, he found the Christian teachings encouraged by his mother, as he saw them in the Scriptures and in his church, unpalatable. In particular, he found unacceptable the apparent anthropomorphisms and inconsistencies, as well as what he saw as a demand for blind faith and for an unaccountable submission to authority. While at Carthage, he lived with a woman who bore him a son, Adeodatus, who, to Augustine's immense grief, died as a young man in 390. Also while at Carthage, he converted to Manichaeism, a sect that believed in two separate, eternal material principles of everything, good and evil, the former of which they identified with God. The Manicheans also pretended to follow Christ, but without faith and authority, claiming to reach God purely through reason. However, Augustine's demand for a rational account of things was ultimately unfulfilled by the Manicheans. Their leaders could not provide him with sufficiently convincing reasons for their tenets, and Augustine, especially through discourse with a friend, Nebridius, eventually came to see their worldview as inconsistent.

After Carthage, he moved to Milan as a professor of rhetoric, where he met Bishop Ambrose, who introduced him more deeply to the Catholic faith, which, though more attractive, still seemed inconsistent, like Manichaeism. At this point, convinced that unshakeable truth was unavailable, he embraced skepticism. The year 386, however, when he began to assimilate the teachings of the Platonists (particularly Plotinus), was a turning point. The Platonists helped him discern fundamental tenets, such as incorporeal reality, the dependence of evil upon the one good, and most importantly the agreement between philosophic truth and revealed truth. At the same time, however, he grew in his awareness of the insufficiency and possible errors of reason and philosophy taken on their own, and of their need for the strength of revelation and faith. Human beings need Christ, the Word made flesh, the Mediator between God and creatures. These results informed the spirit of his ongoing theological project: Platonic philosophy is sound in its basic orientation, though it needs to be revised and brought to its true fulfillment through the superior wisdom of divine revelation. While philosophy can be harmonized with revelation, belief is required for the understanding of the higher truths, the highest of which—God himself—is beyond our full grasp in this life and is made available only through His **grace**.

In 387, shortly before his mother's death, Augustine formally embraced Christ and was baptized. He devoted a few years to the monastic life as leader of a community at both Thagaste and Carthage. He often missed this contemplative life during the 35 years, beginning in 396, that he served as bishop of Hippo. As a Church official, he devoted much of his energy to the defense and clarification of the faith. He continued to debate against the Manicheans and was actively involved with other controversies, such as Donatism (a Church schism) and **Pelagianism**. Augustine died at Hippo on

28 August 430. His doctrines, especially those that were central in medieval thought, are discussed in more detail in the entry AUGUSTINIANISM. Refer to the introduction.

**AUGUSTINIANISM.** The thought of **St. Augustine** (354–430), the most influential of the **Fathers of the Church**, dominated Christian thought until the rise of **Aristotelianism** in Europe in the early 13th century (*see also* AVERROISM) and remained a major influence well beyond René Descartes, in whom we can discern important debts to Augustine. The transmission of Augustine's thought to the 13th century was facilitated by writers such as Paul Orosius, a compiler and friend of Augustine, Prosper of Aquitaine, Caesar of Arles (470–542), Fulgentius of Ruspe, Cassiodorus, St. Isidore of Seville, St. **Anselm of Canterbury**, **Hugh of Saint-Victor**, and **Peter Lombard**. Many 13th-century theologians observed the growing influence of the pagan Aristotle with alarm, and a new (medieval) Augustinianism that dealt with Aristotle in a variety of ways began to emerge. However, even opponents of the so-called Augustinians claimed that they were faithful to the true meaning of Augustine, whose name appeared in nearly all discussions. It could be argued that Augustine's defining impact in the history of medieval Christian philosophy and theology makes this history itself, in some senses, Augustinian.

Medieval Augustinianism, however, is a broad category referring to a rather eclectic group, whose relative integrity and grounding in Augustine have been a source of debate, to the extent that some historians have even rejected the term *medieval Augustinianism*. What is certain, at any rate, is that major figures like the **Franciscan St. Bonaventure** and the secular master **Henry of Ghent**, who both criticized and used Aristotelian philosophy thoroughly, still found in Augustine their main source of inspiration. Medieval Augustinianism is characterized by its opposition to Aristotelianism, which culminated in the ecclesiastical condemnation in 1277 of 219 propositions, the majority of which presupposed or advocated a philosophic wisdom independent from revelation. Important doctrines associated with many so-called Augustinians are the denial of a strict separation between rational and revealed truth, the primacy of the will over the intellect, the doctrine of knowledge as divine illumination, the **soul** as a complete substance individuated without reference to the body, the impossibility of creation from eternity, etc. Still the term *Augustinianism*, applied to medieval thinkers, cannot be used accurately in a strict way. Moreover, it should be used with some notion of the central features of Augustine's thought: **faith** and reason, God and creation, the soul and knowledge, and ethics and happiness.

For Augustine, true wisdom can only be an insight into revealed truth, whose highest manifestation is Christ. The right function of reason and philosophy, whose best exponents are **Plato** and his Neoplatonic followers, especially **Plotinus**, is to help in the search for God, to understand what is believed, as St. Anselm will later emphasize. Revelation and reason, faith and philosophy, are inseparable though distinguishable sources of true wisdom. Plato's philosophy without revelation is proof of the distinction between faith and reason, and of reason's essential desire for the divine, the eternal or immutable. Moreover, it is proof of reason's need of Christian revelation to fulfill its essential desire: the Platonists only knew something of the goal, but not the way, as the goal is divine and beyond the unaided reach of human beings. Since the goal of philosophy is happiness in wisdom, and true wisdom is in Christ, only the Christians who use reason to understand their faith, and who are wise through God's **grace**, are true philosophers. Reason assists faith, both complementing each other in the journey toward an ever deeper insight into God and his works. As **Thomas Aquinas** tells us, "whenever Augustine, who was imbued with the doctrines of the Platonists, found in their teaching anything consistent with the faith, he adopted it; and those things which he found contrary to faith he amended" (*Summa Theologiae* I, q. 84, a. 5, *Resp.*). True, Augustine's synthesis of reason and revelation is fundamentally theological, but for him this includes philosophy as such as a servant to the mistress.

The triune God of revelation is at the center of Augustine's thought. God is supreme "being" or, as the Scriptures put it, **HE WHO IS** (Exodus 3:14). This eternal and immutable Being is, following the Council of Nicaea (325), three persons in one substance: the Father who is supreme mind or intellect and will, the Son or Word who is the Father's self-understanding, and the Love between these two persons who is the Holy Spirit. Through the Word, God is supreme wisdom and truth; through the bonding Love with this absolute truth, God is supreme beatitude and Good. In the Word are also found the patterns for all that is and can be. Purely out of love, creation is a single, instantaneous, free act, and the world contained, at the instant of creation, the "seminal reasons" or germs of all that was, is, and will be in the world. Creation includes not only things that change, but spiritual substances or **angels**, which, though mutable in nature, are immutable in fact through God's grace. Plotinus had already placed Plato's ideas in what he calls Intellect, and Augustine, like practically all Christian theologians after him, identifies this principle of the ideas with God himself. This is enough to distinguish his entire system from Plotinus's, for whom the first principle is the One, followed by the Intellect (being and *nous*, or thought) and the World Soul respectively, each at a different ontological level. The Word is not only the model or exemplary cause of all that is not God, namely creatures, but the light of minds, as the Gospel of John (1:9) also tells us. For knowledge of creatures, which are images by definition, always implies some reference, however imperfect, to their divine models in the Word. Knowledge is possible only through some divine illumination.

According to Scripture, God created human beings in His image as compounds of soul and body. Though man is both soul and body, that he was created in the image of God, who is purely spiritual, implies the radical superiority of the soul over the body. Following the Platonists, Augustine sees the soul as somehow the user of the body. The soul is incorporeal, as it has no spatial dimension, which all bodies have. The soul knows itself, its existence and life as a thinking and knowing intelligence, immediately. It knows that it exists because in order to be mistaken about this it would have to exist to begin with. It knows because of its certitude of its existence, and that it lives because knowing is a kind of life that is a particular type of existence. The body, receiving life from without, passes away when separated from the soul; the soul, an intelligent life by essence, is immortal. As no inferior substance acts upon a superior one, the soul is the active, ordering principle in all bodily experience. Sensations do provide a good amount of certainty in regard to bodies, but they do not provide immutable truth, as the bodies that are sensed are changing. Only God provides this Truth, as God is the truth by which truths are true. The soul experiences the eternity, necessity, and immutability proper to truth itself through some judgments, such as "I exist" or "Seven and three equals ten." These properties of truth cannot come from the body, as mentioned, nor from an individual mind, since truth is common to many human minds, each of which is a mutable creature. Truth is always experienced as superior to the mind, which recognizes and submits to it and never creates it. The mind sees truths only in the light of what is itself immutable, necessary, and eternal. This can only be God, the Truth itself and source of truths. Augustine's account of knowledge is itself a proof of God's existence. The soul governs the body, and God governs the soul; to find God, one must turn from the exterior things to the interior things, and from these to the superior. This approach is characteristically Augustinian.

Moral truths display the same divine properties as speculative truths and come to the mind through God's illumination. All agree that wisdom is beatific knowledge, for instance, and many practical rules of wisdom are clear to all. Universal moral laws constitute the "natural law," and conscience is our awareness of it. The cardinal virtues of prudence, fortitude, temperance, and justice are manifestations of the eternal law, namely the rules of actual moral life. Vices are due to the will, which refuses to adhere to this "eternal law," to the will which favors pleasure in material things over pleasure in intelligible things. The human soul was not created to be imprisoned in its body, but after original sin this in effect happened through concupiscence and ignorance. The soul may submerge itself in the material world to the extent that it takes itself to be a body, its worst error. Though man fell through his own free will, free will is not sufficient to raise him again. Grace, in addition to free will, is necessary, as Augustine always stressed against Pelagius. Free will reaches its perfection and highest freedom when it adheres to God as the highest good, possessing what it fundamentally wants, to the extent that it is no longer able to do evil. This may be approached in this life, but only in the next one is ultimate liberation and beatitude possible. Man's ultimate happiness, therefore, entails both intellect and will: knowledge and love of the Trinity—the One Truth and Good. This view of man's end is the basis of Augustine's political thought, expressed in his *City of God* as a world history with God's love and justice at work to restore creation from its fallen state.

These positions of Augustine, in particular the one that is the basis of all the others—his approach to faith and reason—inspired the so-called medieval **Augustinians**, who opposed Aristotelianism primarily on the grounds that it separated, to too large an extent, the domains of reason and revelation.

**AUGUSTINIANS.** *See* ORDERS (RELIGIOUS).

**AVEMPACE (IBN BAJJAH) (ca. 1090–1139).** A native of Saragossa (in Spain), Ibn Bajjah or Avempace, as he was known in the Latin West, was the first major Muslim philosopher of the western caliphate. Competent in the various sciences, he wrote on logic and the different philosophic disciplines. Prior to his contributions in speculative philosophy that paved the way for **Moses Maimonides** and **Averroes**, Avempace made contributions in mathematics and **logic**. His untimely death, however, left the majority of his works (amounting to more than 30) in an incomplete state. A major theme of Avempace's **Aristotelianism**, as well as the chief goal of philosophy according to him, is union with the agent intellect, whereby the **soul** reaches its ultimate destiny, becoming part of the eternal separate intelligence governing the sublunary world. This conjunction is primarily the product of intellectual perfection or actualization (though it presupposes moral virtue) and is available only to the few who are capable of it. The final stage leading to this union goes beyond man's natural capacities, as it is consummated by an illumination of God toward His elect. Nevertheless, he notes that this illumination is reserved for the philosophers.

Even though Avempace recognizes with Aristotle that the human being is a political animal who is best actualized with other virtuous people, Avempace advises a solitary life in the pursuit of spiritual perfection, especially when one's social or political context is at odds with the fulfillment of this goal (as in the degenerate states described by **Plato**). He discusses this in his major work *The Conduct of the Solitary*, which was commented on in Hebrew by Moses of Narbonne. Thus, Avempace continues developing in his own way some of the key questions that had occupied his outstanding predecessors in the East, such as **Avicenna** and **Al-Farabi**. Avempace, especially in relation to questions concerning the intellect, was often quoted in medieval Christian philosophy (e.g., by **Albert the Great** and **Thomas Aquinas**). Though Christians generally rejected the understanding of the agent intellect as a separate intelligence, which was common among Muslim Aristotelians, Muslim philosophers still influenced their various approaches to this topic. Avempace was also influential in the Latin West in the natural sciences, particularly in astronomy and physics.

**AVERROES (IBN RUSHD) (ca. 1126–1198).** Along with **Avicenna** (Ibn Sina), Abu al-Walid Muhammad ibn Rushd represents the summit of Muslim **Aristotelianism**. Though his philosophy practically died with him in Islam, Averroism was influential in the medieval Jewish and Christian worlds. Born in Cordoba, Spain, Averroes lived in the empire of the Almohads, a Berber dynasty representing Muslim orthodoxy, that controlled much of the Iberian Peninsula. Under the rule of the Almohad caliph Abu Ya'qub Yusuf (fl. 1163–1184), he served in a number of high offices. An authority on Islamic law, like his father and grandfather, he became chief judge of Cordoba. His knowledge of natural science, especially of medicine, on which he wrote a treatise translated into Latin as *Colliget* (*Generalities* or *Principles*), earned him his appointment in 1182 as court physician. In 1168 or 1169, on account of his philosophical erudition, Averroes was commissioned by the caliph himself to write commentaries on all the available works of Aristotle, which bespeaks not only tolerance of but also the cultivation of philosophy by the Muslim regime. In 1195, however, the caliph's son and successor became an enemy of philosophy, and Averroes fell into disgrace. He was exiled to Lucena, near Cordoba, and his books were banned and ordered to be burned. However, by the time of his death at Marrakesh, Morocco, Averroes had regained royal favor.

Averroes's principal interest was philosophy, and for him this meant Aristotle's philosophy. His brilliant commentaries on Aristotle's works, coupled with his deep admiration for the wisdom of the Stagirite, made him known in the medieval philosophical tradition as the "Commentator." His approach to Aristotle illuminates other aspects of his thought, particularly his view of the relation between religion and philosophy. Two concerns pervade his scholarly efforts. First, he strives for a thorough explication of the original thought of Aristotle, which for him implies purifying Aristotle from extrinsic, particularly **Neoplatonic**, elements. In this effort, he is largely successful, in spite of some abridgments of Proclus and **Plotinus** that were at the time attributed to Aristotle, and which at points seem even to influence the Commentator. As a restorer of true Aristotelianism, his main opponent was an earlier commentator, Avicenna. His second concern was the defense of philosophy both as the highest activity available to humans and as wholly legitimate within Islam. In this latter effort, his main opponent is **Al-Ghazali**, who often criticizes philosophy both as a cognitive tool and as antithetical to Islam.

Of Averroes's commentaries on Aristotle's works, we have 38 in number. For most texts, he wrote both a short commentary, a summary or epitome, as well as a medium-length one, a more detailed, though selective, exposition with more paraphrasing than quotations. Aristotle's *Posterior Analytics*, *Physics*, *On the Heavens*, *On the Soul*, and *Metaphysics*, however, also received a long commentary, a thorough line-by-line exposition with full quotations. He also made a commentary on Plato's *Republic*, an important document for Averroes's political thought. In addition, he composed treatises that are not commentaries, among which *The Decisive Treatise Determining the Nature of the Connection between Religion and Philosophy* and his *Tahafut al-Tahafut* or *Incoherence of the Incoherence* are especially noteworthy. In the former work, Averroes defends philosophy's place in Islam. The latter is an attack on Al-Ghazali's *The Incoherence of the Philosophers*. His *Incoherence of the Incoherence* attempts to undermine what philosophy meant for Ghazali, namely Avicenna's Neoplatonism.

In his account of the universe, Averroes follows Aristotle. However, he is also innovative. In places where the Philosopher is unclear, and in regard to problems about which he is silent, Averroes often offers his own interpretation in accord with his systematic presentation of Aristotle. An example of this is his view of the most basic material principle of the universe, namely prime matter. For Averroes, prime matter is in potency to acquire the different forms displayed by physical substances, though only as already informed with the most basic, still amorphous, "corporeal form"; this form provides matter with tridimensional extension. Another example is his interpretation of Aristotle's agent intellect, the efficient cause of human thinking, whose nature and function are only vaguely described by Aristotle, usually metaphorically: as light actualizes vision, so does the agent intellect actualize knowledge. For Averroes, the agent intellect is the separate intelligence that governs the sublunary world, including the human form or intellect. It does so, not by being a giver of forms, as Avicenna's emanationism would have it, but as the actualizing principle of forms innate in matter. This intellect is the lowest among the separate intelligences, those governing the motion of the spheres, among which the first and ultimate cause of all is God. The agent intellect is also the highest one to which humans can aspire. Through their actualization in knowledge, human intellects may after death unite with this intellect. Unlike Avicenna, however, for Averroes this union never means personal immortality, but rather the absorption into one eternal intellect and knowledge—his theory of **monopsychism**. Thereby, Averroes stresses the Aristotelian principle that among things that change, in this case humans, only the species and not the individual is immortal. Finally, Averroes's philosophy describes God as relating to the world in a more direct way than Aristotle does. Adhering to Aristotle's conception of God as pure thought thinking itself and rejecting the Neoplatonic One from which all emanates, Averroes stresses that God's thought is not just a knowledge of self, as Aristotle seems to imply, but also of what is distinct from Him. Thus, God exerts providence in the universe, though its exact nature remains obscure to us, since God's knowledge is quite different from ours.

Averroes's analysis of reality begins with Aristotle's ontological priority of substance: what exists fundamentally and primarily is what does so on its own account, like my friend John, this dog, or that chair. Other aspects of reality, like quantities, qualities, relations, etc., namely **accidents**, have being only in relation to substances. As all substances are individual, the universal or essential features of things do not exist independently, as **Platonists** are inclined to think, but only in individual substances. Universality is therefore discovered by the understanding. Science knows not universals as such, but particular things in a universal way. Knowledge is the abstraction by the intellect of forms or essences from singular things. Knowledge corresponds to reality because substances are not just unique individuals but composites of form and matter. Essence is not really distinct from existence, as Avicenna contends, viewing essence as a prior principle of possibility to which existence is added. What exists are individual substances, nothing more. Form is the principle of actuality and universality, while matter is the principle of potentiality and individuality. For example, the form of a chair makes the chair actual as well as part of a class, while its wood had the potency to receive such a form, thus making the form individual, that is, the form of this chair. All substances in nature are both actual and potential, for they come to be and pass away. This movement, or becoming, proper to substances bespeaks their causes, ultimately God.

In rejecting Avicenna's distinction between essence and existence, Averroes also rejected Avicenna's view that metaphysics can reach God as the first giver of existence. To Averroes, this is a Neoplatonic and theological distortion of the true philosophy, namely Aristotle's genuine philosophy. To Averroes, philosophy's access to God is fundamentally based on natural philosophy or physics. It is the analysis of natural substances and processes that leads to the scientific knowledge of their causes, ultimately God. **Metaphysics**, on the other hand, primarily considers God as the First Cause.

Whatever is in motion is something in potency moved by something else in act. In terms of motion, things fall into one of three classes: things that are moved and do not move others, things that are moved and also move others, and things unmoved which nevertheless move others. Now the intermediate class of beings, though it may be vast, must be finite. There cannot be an infinite regress of movers, themselves moved, and still be movement, as nothing actualizes itself. Only through primary causes, themselves unmoved, can the series of moved movers be accounted for. The existence of the third class is evident. These unmoved movers are pure acts by definition, as they lack any potency for change in themselves. Accordingly, they are immaterial—specifically unique intelligences. As pure acts they move uniformly and perpetually. Since there is no motion without a moving body, motion and the world itself are eternal. There are as many unmoved movers as there are primary movements in the heavens, presumably 38. Each celestial body perpetually strives to approximate, through its motion which is actualization, the pure act on which it depends. The celestial body must therefore possess, not senses or imagination, as Avicenna held, but only intelligence, as it is thought—its immobile mover—that the celestial body strives for through its motion. That is why the separate intelligences also give the celestial bodies their form, namely their life. They are their efficient, formal, and final causes. Since the heavenly spheres form a hierarchy of motions from the moon to the firmament, their movers must be arranged similarly. There is a hierarchy of intelligences with One at the top. This First Intelligence by definition possesses the best knowledge among intelligences, upon which all order is based. Creation is viewed as the eternal process by which God is responsible for the order and nature of the universe.

In the Latin West, Averroes was usually attributed a "double truth theory," whereby philosophic truth may contradict, though not invalidate, religious truth, reason and revelation being separate domains. For the Muslim Ibn Rushd, however, religion and philosophy agree: "Now since this religion is true and summons to the study which leads to knowledge of the Truth, we the Muslim community know definitely that demonstrative study does not lead to [conclusions] conflicting with what Scripture has given us; for truth does not oppose truth but accords with it and bears witness to it" (*The Decisive Treatise Determining the Nature of the Connection between Religion and Philosophy*, Hyman and Walsh, 302). For Averroes, the **Koran** in fact requires the intellectual elite to pursue philosophy. These are the few who can distinguish between demonstrative and nondemonstrative arguments. The Koran expresses its truth at three levels corresponding to the three main intellectual classes of people, namely demonstratively, dialectically, and rhetorically. Demonstrations (valid reasonings from necessary premises), as Aristotle's *Posterior Analytics* shows, are the highest form of rational discourse, and only they produce perfect knowledge, the only form that guarantees unity of truth. However, the other two forms of discourse have an important social function: to help people live according to God's will. Philosophy knows revelation best, though philosophic wisdom ought not to be taught to those who are not fit for it, as this results in errors, fragmentation into sects, and heresies. The wisdom of revelation is supreme in that it addresses itself to all in appropriate ways and degrees.

Averroes's version of Aristotelianism greatly informed subsequent philosophy. His conclusions, particularly those concerning the immortality of the **soul**, the eternity of the world, and the relation between religion and philosophy, elicited strong and diverse reactions among those engaged in the project of reconciling reason and revelation. *See also* AVERROISM.

**AVERROISM.** Though it did not do so in Islam, the thought of the Muslim **Averroes** exerted great influence in Judaism and Christianity, to the extent that we can speak of Averroism in these two traditions. In late medieval and Renaissance Judaism, all aspects of Averroes's thought were widely and intensely studied; among philosophers, only **Moses Maimonides** attracted more attention. Averroes's entire work was translated from Arabic into Hebrew, most of it in the 13th and 14th centuries; his long commentary on *De anima* (*On the Soul*) was not translated until the late 15th century, from a prior Latin translation. These translations extended the study of philosophy among Jews outside the Islamic world and practically constituted the curriculum and vocabulary of Jewish philosophy in Europe, which remained close to its origins in Islam. The intense study of Averroes's commentaries resulted in a new genre of "supercommentaries," such as those of **Gersonides**, in which the Commentator even more than **Aristotle** himself became the primary source.

Jewish Averroism indicates a general approach to Aristotle rather than a rigid set of doctrines. Jewish Averroists are diverse and manifest different aspects of the thought of Averroes. Notable figures are Isaac Albalag and Shem Tov ben Falaquera in the 13th century; Joseph Caspi, Moses of Narbonne (Moshe Narboni), and Levi ben Gershom (Gersonides) in the 14th century; and Judah Messer Leon and Elijah del Medigo in the 15th century. Maimonides himself, Averroes's near contemporary and fellow Andalusian, recommended the study of Averroes's commentaries, and many Jews read Maimonides as a strict Aristotelian, after the manner of Averroes, in spite of the frequent **Neoplatonic** and **Avicennian** notions found in Maimonides's works. Central issues in Latin Averroism, such as the doctrines of **monopsychism** (the teaching that there is only one human intellect) and the double truth theory (reason and revelation may yield contradictory truths), were not as defining in Jewish Averroism. Translators largely avoided disputes over these issues, and few Jewish philosophers explicitly held these doctrines. Moshe Narboni, a strong exponent of monophychism, and Isaac Albalag, the only major thinker to adopt the double truth theory (probably due to Latin **Scholastic** influence), are more the exception. Jewish Averroism is for the most part an essentially scientific attitude, employing Averroes's Aristotle to understand the universe. Jewish critics of philosophy saw this attitude as an enemy of traditional beliefs and norms and blamed it for the suffering of the Jewish community in Spain that culminated in their expulsion in 1492. Jewish Averroists denied these accusations and always expressed their respect for and obedience to Jewish religion. Nevertheless, this picture of the Jewish Averroists became quite influential and contributed to the decline of philosophical activity in Judaism after the 15th century. On the whole, however, Averroes and Jewish Averroism sustained to a significant extent the life of Jewish philosophy well into the 16th century.

In the late 1260s, the philosophical movement labeled "Latin Averroism," as well as "Radical" or "Heterodox" **Aristotelianism**, appeared in the **Arts Faculty** of the University of Paris. In 1255, what had been a preparatory faculty focusing on the seven traditional **liberal arts** changed into an Aristotelian philosophy faculty. However, the faculty still served the purpose of preparing students for the higher studies of **theology**, medicine, and law. This began to change in the late 1260s, when some faculty members decided to stay as teachers in the Arts Faculty instead of moving on to the presumed higher disciplines. Their approach to philosophy as well as their doctrines became increasingly suspicious to theologians at Paris. For example, **St. Bonaventure** in his Lenten sermons of 1267 speaks of the improper use of philosophy in the Arts Faculty, and in his 1268 sermons he also indicates teachings antithetical to Christian truth, that is, the eternity of the world and monopsychism. In his fourth sermon *On the Gifts of the Holy Spirit* in 1268, Bonaventure criticizes those who remain in the Arts Faculty for dedicating themselves wholly to (Aristotelian) philosophy, in particular to Averroes, rather than to preparing students for theology. For Bonaventure and other Christian theologians, philosophy is and can only be an aid in the pursuit of the highest wisdom available to human beings, found only in the Scriptures.

The two main interpretations of Aristotle among masters of philosophy and theology in Christian Europe until 1260–1265 were Averroes and Avicenna. (**Thomas Aquinas**'s writings, from about 1261 on constituted the third main appropriation of Aristotle.) Many used Averroes as a standard text on Aristotle, who taught some useful things, as in **logic**, but whose picture of the world they did not necessarily accept. Even though Aristotle, Averroes, and Avicenna were cataloged as "philosophers," as outsiders by Christian theologians, Averroes in particular could not be ignored by theologians due to his explicit separation of philosophy and theology, about which he spoke many times when criticizing Avicenna's blending of Aristotle with religion. What for Averroes had been a harmonious separation between philosophy and religion, whereby both expressed the same truth, though philosophy knew this truth best, became on some key points a conflict in Latin Averroism as well as its distinguishing feature. For the Latin Averroists, following Averroes as the true exponent of Aristotle and thus of philosophy, some necessary philosophical conclusions indeed contradict Christian truths. To the Averroists, this per se does not invalidate Christian teachings, whose absolute certitude is accepted on the basis of **faith**, not reason. However, this was unacceptable to most theologians, for whom natural reason's ultimate end is to understand and clarify central truths of the faith, such as the Trinity, the temporal creation of the world, and personal immortality. To these theologians, truth is one, and what is true for reason cannot be false for faith.

Before 1270, there had already been opposition to Averroes himself, though not necessarily to Averroists. An example is **Albert the Great**'s treatise *On the Oneness of the Intellect against Averroes* (1256); Thomas Aquinas refutes Averroes's position on the intellect in his *Summa contra gentiles* (1258). However, the ecclesiastical condemnation in 1270 of Averroistic errors taught at the University of Paris is a sure sign of Latin Averroism. In his 1270 treatise *On the Unity of the Intellect*, Aquinas also speaks of a contemporary Christian author who approaches Christian teaching on the intellect from the outside, as it were, as something to be accepted unquestioningly as a law rather than as something to be elucidated by reason. **Siger of Brabant**, a prominent heterodox Aristotelian, taught that from a philosophical perspective the world was eternal and that the intellect is unique to mankind, without attempting to reconcile reason and revelation. His teaching on the intellect implied a denial of an individual afterlife, thus diminishing individual moral responsibility. Influenced by the events of 1270, including Aquinas's arguments, Siger became orthodox in his later writings. **Boethius of Dacia**, though not a heterodox Aristotelian, was nevertheless labeled a "radical" one for his sharp separation of philosophic and theological truth. To Boethius, the natural philosopher as such has the right to discuss the question of the eternity of the world. Within his own discipline, the natural philosopher cannot prove that the world began, as he can only approach nature as already in existence. The natural philosopher will deny creation as he grants only what is possible through natural causes. Creation, therefore, can only be accepted by a believer on the basis of faith. In this case, to Boethius, natural reason necessarily leads within its framework to a conclusion that contradicts Christian teaching. The condemnation (of 219 propositions) of March 1277 by the bishop of Paris further attests to the controversies of Latin Averroism. Though this condemnation was of a wider scope than the previous one in 1270, still many of the propositions were associated with figures such as Siger of Brabant and Boethius of Dacia and concerned the eternity of the world, monopsychism, the supremacy of the philosophic life, etc. Refer to the introduction, "The Beginning and Development of Medieval Arabian and Jewish Philosophy and Theology."

**AVICEBRON.** *See* GABIROL, IBN (AVICEBRON) (ca. 1021–ca. 1058).

**AVICENNA (980–1037).** The Muslim Ibn Sina or Avicenna, as he is known in the West, holds a very important place, not only in Islamic circles, but also in the history of philosophy. Among Islamic thinkers, only **Averroes** is as influential. Born near the city of Bukhara, in what is now Uzbekistan, and from an important family (his father was governor of the district), Avicenna was unusually gifted and for the most part self-taught. By the age of 10, he had studied Arabic literature, the **Koran**, and Islamic law. He then turned to the philosophical sciences, beginning with **logic** and mathematics and continuing with natural philosophy and **metaphysics**. Having mastered medicine, he began practicing it at 16 as court physician of the Samanid sultan of Bukhara, which gave him access to the sultan's great library. Although he had gained competence in the philosophic, literary, and religious disciplines of his day at a young age, he still found **Aristotle**'s *Metaphysics* obscure. He famously tells us that he read the work 40 times without gaining clarity. Only after reading the commentary by **Al-Farabi** did he grasp the necessary concepts that grew into his own seminal metaphysics. His adaptation of Aristotle made him one of the three most influential Aristotelians in the Middle Ages; the other two are Averroes and **Thomas Aquinas**. In 999, when the Samanid regime began to weaken, Avicenna left Bukhara. He held various posts as physician to different rulers; in the city of Hamadan, he was vizier in addition to physician, from 1015 to 1022. After an army mutiny that meant for him a four-month imprisonment, he moved to Isfahan and spent the rest of his life in the service of its ruler.

Avicenna developed and synthesized the Aristotelian and **Neoplatonic** traditions, seeking to reconcile philosophy with Islam. Though he was well versed in Islamic religion and law, Avicenna's most influential contributions were in the sciences, including logic, mathematics, natural philosophy, and, above all, metaphysics, which he understood as the study of being as being. Before Averroes became officially known in the philosophical tradition as the Commentator of Aristotle, Avicenna held that title. Avicenna wrote abundantly in various fields, from science to mysticism. More than a hundred of his works are known, most of them in Arabic and some in Persian. His most important medical work, *The Canon of Medicine* (*Al-Quanan fi al-Tibb*), remained the standard medical work in Europe until the 17th century. The essentials of his philosophy may be found in his chief philosophic work, *The Healing* (*Al-Shifa*), as well as in *The Deliverance* (*Al-Najat*), which is for the most part a summary of the former work. A summary of his account of reality follows.

Things exist either by nature or essence or by choice or will. Speculative philosophy deals with the former (the true) and practical philosophy with the latter (the good). All sciences study being, for all deal with aspects of reality. Metaphysics, the highest of the speculative sciences, differs from particular sciences such as biology in that its subject is not a part of being, but rather being as being. Avicenna's originality and influence as a metaphysician stems from his understanding and development of this starting point. Aristotle had distinguished between first and second substance (*ousia*), that is, between a concrete individual and the form determining its essence. Every thing we experience is a "this" (first substance) of a certain kind (second substance), such as this dog or this human being. To Aristotle, second substance or form is the principle of being, as things are actual by virtue of their form. For example, an object is actually a chair because the form of chair has been imposed on some material, and an animal is actually a dog because through generation it received the form of dog from its parents. Avicenna, in his interpretation of Aristotle, goes further. In order to account for actuality, we must distinguish not only between matter and form, but also between form (essence) and existence. For essence as such is still only possible. As Aristotle, Al-Farabi, and others had already pointed out, we can know what something is without knowing whether it is. Avicenna, more explicitly and systematically than his predecessors, applies this insight to his account of reality: if an essence actually exists, this is because it received existence from another.

This basic position enables Avicenna to develop a philosophical account of the creation spoken of in the Koran. Metaphysics goes beyond natural philosophy, which led Aristotle to conceive of God only as a final cause of the world. Natural philosophy takes the being of its subject matter (i.e., motion) for granted, as do other particular sciences concerning their subject matters. For example, biology does not seek to prove that there is life, but only deals with the nature of life. Thus, Aristotle's physical analysis cannot lead him to the cause of the being of motion, but only to the causes of the nature of motion, among which the Unmoved Mover is first. On the other hand, "the metaphysicians do not intend by the agent the principle of movement only, as do the natural philosophers, but also the principle of existence and that which bestows [existence], such as the creator of the world" (*The Healing*, Hyman and Walsh, 248). This position appeared to Avicenna's important critic, Averroes, as a (theological and Neoplatonic) distortion of Aristotle's genuine philosophy, which for Averroes was almost equivalent to rational truth. On the other hand, against the predominant understanding of God's freedom as spoken of in revelation, Avicenna's analysis also leads him to an understanding of this creation as a necessary event. This renders his philosophy inadequate in the eyes of **Al-Ghazali**, the great reformer of Islam, who nevertheless drew from philosophy to account for a universe governed freely by God. Others, Aristotelians (e.g., Thomas Aquinas and **John Duns Scotus**) and Platonists (e.g., **Henry of Ghent**), who draw amply from Avicenna, also try to go beyond the necessity embedded in Avicenna's account.

Avicenna begins his investigation into being as being by considering absolutely first notions, such as being, thing, and necessary. Presupposed by all thought, they cannot be demonstrated but only pointed out. A being is something that is; to think of anything is to think of some being. Thing is also presupposed by all thought, as any being is some thing or of a certain kind. Thing implies "whatness" or quiddity. The necessary is also presupposed by all thought. Nonbeing or no-thing is inconceivable and thus impossible. Thus, necessity accompanies the first two notions. A being is necessarily what it is, as long as it is that being. And necessity includes the notion of possibility; a being must be at least possible or not impossible. These notions are related to Avicenna's fundamental conception of essence and existence.

Essences exist either universally (in the mind), individually (in things), or in themselves (absolutely, neither universally nor singularly). Absolutely speaking, an essence includes necessarily neither singularity nor universality, for it can be both singular (as this humanity belonging to an individual) and universal (as the humanity common to many human beings). If essence would necessarily include either mode, it would exclude the other. Logic deals with essences in the first sense, natural philosophy (physics) considers them in the second sense, and metaphysics considers them in the third way. In itself, an essence is either possible or necessary (what is impossible cannot even be conceived). Essences in themselves possible, like humanity, can be defined without affirming their existence. Existence, unlike the definition (rational animal) and unlike a property (such as "able to laugh"), is not necessarily included in humanity. Thus, existence is an "**accident**" of essence; if it comes to it, it comes to it from without.

A necessary essence would be unique. Two (or more) necessary beings cannot be, for either they are the same essentially or not. If the same essentially, then their existences are different, and so they would be necessary not essentially but through another. If different essentially, then one of them would have something necessary essentially that the other does not have, and so the same thing would be both necessary and not necessary, which is impossible. Moreover, one of them would lack a part of necessary being, or essential necessity, making it therefore unnecessary. So there can be only one necessary being, which is uncaused and has no distinction between essence and existence. Its essence is necessary existence.

The necessary is by definition causeless, and the possible by definition needs a cause to exist. Therefore, an existing essence that is possible in itself is also necessary through another. While it exists it is still possible in itself, but while caused by another it cannot not exist. Thus, an existing thing that is possible in itself necessarily has a relation to a cause while it exists. The bare fact of existence necessarily implies a relation to a cause. Now an essence like humanity includes both matter and form; its definition, namely rational animal, cannot be understood without some reference to physical reality.

However, of itself the essence is only possible, and so the cause of existence is more than just the composition of matter and form. The natural agent cause causes, not existence, but a change or motion. The metaphysical agent cause causes the very existence of an essence, which as matter and form is merely possible. The origin of a change or motion is different from the origin of existence. Aristotle's efficient cause is the former, not the latter—it is not Avicenna's metaphysical efficient cause.

Essential causes are given simultaneously with their effects. These are causes that produce and preserve the existence of their effects. On the other hand, accidentally ordered causes are such that the cause may cease to be while the effect continues to exist, as when a tree generates another tree that outlives it. In any essential causal series of three, there must be an uncaused cause, a caused cause, and something caused that does not cause. (In a larger series, the intermediate class is greater.) This causing is called "creation," and so the First Cause is the Creator of the universe, not simply its final cause as Aristotle would have it. Creatures are beings whose essences owe actual existence to the First. The mere fact that possible beings exist means that there is a first, uncaused necessary being. For accidentally ordered causes may be infinite but not essentially ordered causes, as this would mean an actually infinite series, which is unthinkable. Any possible essence that actually exists leads to the first, necessary being.

The First is more than perfect since it is not only necessary through itself but also the cause of the rest. It is God that ultimately actualizes all possible things that exist actually. All is necessary and one in the First. The First knows and causes all by virtue of its necessity. This necessary being is a pure spirit or intellect, since anything material is subject to change. This First Intellect by definition possesses perfectly and immutably all possible knowledge. Moreover, what this intellect knows is also willed and thus created eternally. In the necessary being, willing must be identical with knowledge; otherwise, its necessity would be impaired. Accordingly, creation is a necessary and eternal process by which the First Cause gives and sustains all being. The First Cause, as necessary and perfect, creates not due to a lack, but as an overflow of being or goodness. Following the tradition of **Plato**'s *Timaeus* and **Plotinus**, creation is a giving whereby the First Cause brings all into existence from itself. On the other hand, also according to the Neoplatonic tradition, evil is understood simply as privation of being.

Avicenna explains creation according to intellectual emanation. The First Cause knows itself immutably and perfectly, which includes an understanding of itself as the principle of all things, as well as of the necessary order among all things. Since in the First, knowledge is willing, the knowledge by the First of its effects necessarily results in these effects, in a necessary order. The produced entity (not temporally but hierarchically) is an intelligence, the mover of the outermost heavenly sphere, the first of all motions. The first created intellect is like the First Cause in all respects, except that it is second and thus necessary through another. As a produced intellect, it knows its cause, God, as well as itself in a twofold way, namely as possible in itself and as necessary through its cause. These distinctions in the knowledge of the first created intelligence are the origin of all multiplicity. In knowing God, it generates a second created intelligence. In knowing itself as necessary through another, it generates the **soul** of the first heaven. Third, in knowing itself as possible in itself, it generates the body of the first heaven, matter being possibility. The second created intelligence then repeats, in regard to the first created intelligence, the process of the first created intelligence in regard to God. The third created intelligence proceeds similarly in regard to the second, and the fourth does the same in regard to the third, and so on, until the 10th intelligence, the agent intellect governing the sublunary world of generation and corruption, comes to be. This agent intellect is the giver of the forms governing all processes, as well as the efficient cause of human thinking. The contingency of generation and corruption is due to matter, not due to the agent intellect or the separate intelligences, which are necessary. Things come to be when their matters are fit to receive the forms eternally in the agent intellect, and they pass away when their matters are no longer fit for their forms.

The core of Avicenna's psychology is the identification of the substance of the human soul with the intellect. The substratum of ideas (the "material" or potential intellect) cannot be a body. If the intellect would be a body, then, like all bodies, it is either divisible or indivisible (a point). If divisible, then all ideas would be divided. Thus, they could not be understood, as they in fact are, as integrated unities. If indivisible, then all ideas would become extended, since it would still be a point in a quantified body, which would quantify it, since a point is the extremity of a line which is always extended in space. This would also prevent conceptual understanding. Universal, integrated concepts, abstracted from position and place, cannot occupy a physical place in the intellect and still remain what they, in fact, are understood to be. For conceptual forms received physically in a body become extended, divisible, and material. Another proof of the incorporeality of the soul is the fact that it can know itself immediately, without including the body in its definition: a man suspended in space without any sensations would still affirm his own existence, without any reference to the body.

The function of the soul with respect to the body is that of an Aristotelian form, but its intrinsic nature is that of the Platonic soul, that is, a substance. But sense is the starting point of certain kinds of knowledge. For it separates universals from singulars sensed with the body, which are then used in propositions and reasoning. The intellect can derive knowledge from experience, by seeing predicates regularly accompanying subjects. We can receive probable opinions through communal experience. But after it has derived knowledge it can operate on its own, like the man who needs a horse to get somewhere, but once there he may dispense with the horse.

The soul does not preexist the body, which means that it came to be in time. Human souls are essentially the same. If they would preexist the body, then they are either one or many. They cannot be the latter, since they cannot be many essentially. They can be many only through the subject recipient of the essence. They cannot be numerically one, for then it would be impossible to explain how one actual soul becomes many. Souls only come into actual existence together with their bodies (when the bodies are fit for them). Bodies are the principle of the multiplication and individuality of souls. After their separation from their bodies, souls remain individual as already individualized by their previous bodies. However, they were created already as individuals more disposed to this body than to that one. The body of each soul is both its domain and its instrument, having a natural affection to it that makes it renounce other bodies. On the other hand, the soul is incorruptible because, as an immaterial intellect, it is a substance distinct from the body. Body and soul are only joined accidentally. Thus, the destruction of one entails the destruction of their relation only, according to the Platonic tradition. The survival of the soul is then at least possible. Since the substance of the soul is simple, because it is incorporeal (indivisible), it cannot contain the cause of its own destruction. Moreover, the soul owes its being to a higher, necessary metaphysical agent and only owes the time of its realization to the body. That the body has its own peculiar causes of destruction shows its independence from the soul, as well as the immortality of the soul. The chief goal of the soul is to purify itself through wisdom so that it may join the agent intellect, the source of all intellectual light for the human intellect. Moral virtue is primarily aimed at this end, intellectual felicity.

Much of what is literal in the Koran should be taken metaphorically. This applies to creation in time, the resurrection of bodies, and divine providence, which Avicenna understands in terms of God's necessary knowledge. As dependent upon the necessary being in a necessary order, the world is as good as it can be. Evil is the privation of being or goodness. However, revelation teaches the same as philosophy, only expressed in terms accessible to all, as Al-Farabi had already pointed out.

Avicenna's tenets of essence/existence, the substantiality of the soul, and necessary being became central to subsequent philosophy. Troubling tenets for many inside and outside of his tradition were eternal creation, his view of providence, and the apparent lack of free will in God and humans. Averroes, Avicenna's greatest critic on philosophic grounds, defends him and other philosophers (such as Al-Farabi) against Ghazali's criticisms, principally by arguing for the appropriateness of philosophy in Islam and by establishing different methods of interpreting revelation. For the tremendous influence of his system, including the criticisms it elicited, Avicenna remained a central reference point in subsequent philosophy and theology. His thoughts, especially in later works, on the mystical journey of the soul to God were also important in **Sufism**. Refer to the introduction, "The Beginning and Development of Medieval Arabian and Jewish Philosophy and Theology."

**BAHYA IBN PAQUDA (fl. 11TH CENT.).** Primarily an ethical thinker, Bahya bar Joseph ibn Paquda did not focus on all aspects of **ethics**. His focus was on the so-called internal duties, the "duties of the heart," which are contrasted to the "duties of the body" that relate to ritual and outward religious practice. His chief work was written in Arabic under the title *Kitab al-Hidaja ila Faraid al-Kulub*. This was translated into Hebrew by Samuel ibn Tibbon around 1160 under the title *Hovot ha-levavot* or *Guide to the Duties of the Heart*. This work is a well-known classic of Jewish ethics and piety and has enjoyed popularity not only among philosophers. Bahya's work is meant for a large audience, for the intelligent reader. Fundamentally, his arguments are supported by reason and supplemented by Scripture. The influence of **Neoplatonism** in his thought is noteworthy. Not much is known about his life. A native of Spain, he lived and worked in Zaragoza.

**BEDE, THE VENERABLE (ca. 672–735).** A monk of Jarrow, this **Doctor of the Church** is best known as a historian and an exegete. He was, however, broadly educated and wrote also on grammar, poetry, and chronology. His most famous work is *Historia Ecclesiastica gentis Anglorum* (*The Ecclesiastical History of the Angle Nation*), a work that earned him the title "Father of English History." He also produced a *Vita Sancti Cuthberti* (*Life of Saint Cuthbert*) and a *History of the Abbots* [*of Jarrow*]. While he presented in his histories a basic sense of contemporary events, he interpreted them within a theological framework that brought out their more lasting religious significance. Bede the exegete wrote extensive commentaries on Scripture for his readers who were unfamiliar with the tradition of Patristic exegesis. His exegetical work had the merit of bringing them the various interpretations of the noted Latin Fathers of the Church, especially the explanations of Ambrose, Jerome, **Augustine**, and Gregory the Great. *See also* EXEGESIS.

**BENEDICTINES.** *See* ORDERS (RELIGIOUS).

**BERENGARIUS OF TOURS (ca. 1000–1088).** Berengarius studied at Chartres under Fulbert and then taught at the school of Saint-Martin in Tours. Although his **Eucharistic** teaching was condemned at the same time as the Eucharistic teaching of **Ratramnus**, namely at councils held in Rome and Vercelli in 1050, we know his position from **Lanfranc**'s report in his *De corpore et sanguine Domini* (*On the Body and Blood of the Lord*) and also in Berengarius's response to Lanfranc in his own *De sacra coena* (*On the Lord's Supper*). Berengarius was the first recognized Eucharistic heretic. His fundamental assumption was that the senses not only grasped the appearances of things but also their essence or substance. Thus, the substance of the bread and wine do not become, for him, the substance of the body and blood of Christ, since the appearances of bread and wine remain. He interpreted the teachings of the **Fathers of the Church** concerning the body and blood of Christ in the Eucharist to indicate not a real change of substances, but a change taking place in the believer who views the bread and wine as the body and blood of Christ. Berengarius's teaching led his contemporaries, like Lanfranc, to clarify and develop more precisely the Church's true teaching concerning the Eucharist. He himself finally accepted the Church's position when he accepted the formula stating that the substance of the bread and wine is converted (*substantialiter converti*) into the substance of the body and blood of the Lord.

**BERNARD OF AUVERGNE, O.P. (fl. 1294–ca. 1315).** Bernard is known to have been at St. Jacques, the **Dominican** house of studies in Paris, in 1294 and to have served as the prior there in 1304. Succeeding **Peter of Auvergne**, he was appointed bishop of Clermont in that year, although his appointment was canceled by Pope Clement V in 1307. Although Bernard's *Commentary on the Sentences* survives in part, it is his defenses of **Thomas Aquinas** against contemporaries that have gained the most attention. He has a famous collection of *reprobationes* (criticisms) against **Godfrey of Fontaines**, **Henry of Ghent**, and **James of Viterbo** and their attacks on Aquinas that won him the greatest attention. These defenses of Thomas, presented between 1298 and 1315 were widely studied on different points by **Peter Aureoli, Peter of Palude, James of Metz, Hervaeus Natalis, John Baconthorpe, Michael of Massa, John Capreolus** and **Pico della Mirandola.** *See also* ORDERS (RELIGIOUS).

**BERNARD OF CHARTRES (ca. 1060–ca. 1125).** Ivo, the bishop of Chartres, appointed him master of the cathedral school around 1110, and he became the teacher of some very famous students, **William of Conches** and **Gilbert of Poitiers**. They were the teachers of **John of Salisbury**, who lauded Bernard as an outstanding educator who held to the highest standards, in contrast to the Cornificians who championed a more pragmatic, less demanding curriculum. John passed on in his *Metalogicon* one of the more famous sayings of Bernard: that contemporary thinkers were "dwarfs seated on the shoulders of giants." In philosophy, Bernard's design was to attempt to reconcile **Plato** and **Aristotle**, but his bent was more in the direction of Plato.

**BERNARD OF CLAIRVAUX, ST. (1090–1153).** Born in Fontaines-les-Dijon (a village near Dijon) from a family of noble lineage, Bernard entered the monastic life in 1111 following the rule of the **Cistercians**, reputedly the strictest rule at the time. He so distinguished himself that after only three years he was chosen as leader for a new foundation at the valley of Clairvaux, near the Aube. His leadership, grounded in a model of strict observance, grew rapidly well beyond Clairvaux and became central in the development of ecclesiastical life at his time.

On the one hand, St. Bernard's **theology** is an example of so-called **monastic theology**, whose aim is to express truth in such a way as to dispose the **soul** to prayer and contemplation. Thus considered, what is characteristic of Bernard's work is its rich use of personal experience. On the other hand, St. Bernard is a founder of Western speculative **mysticism**. His theology is an original synthesis of Latin and Greek sources, primarily **Augustine** in the Latin tradition and Gregory of Nyssa and **Dionysius the Pseudo-Areopagite** in the Greek tradition. Bernard "unites the Greek theology, based on the relation of image to model, with the Latin theology based upon the relation of nature to **grace**" (Gilson, *HCPMA*, 164). This synthetic approach was a major influence in 12th- and 13th-century **theology** and beyond.

Love is at the core of his thought: God, who is Love, created man by love and redeemed him by love. Thus, the purpose of his intellectual program is, as he puts it, "to know Jesus, and him crucified." Reasoning and its secular learning should be for this end, not for its own sake. Otherwise we are led away from God through vain curiosity. This explains Bernard's opposition to what he saw as the excessive use of **dialectics** in theology, which easily leads to heresy, specifically in the cases of **Gilbert of Poitiers** and **Peter Abelard**. His attitude was not a complete anti-intellectualism. Bernard's writings show a high competence in **liberal arts**, especially a skill for making arguments and distinctions that foreshadows the Scholastic method of the **universities** that begin to emerge at the end of the 12th century.

The teaching of Christ, who is the truth, is humility: humility leads to truth. Humility results from man's knowledge of what he is. According to St. Bernard's Rule, there are 12 degrees of humility. After man has attained humility in its purest form, he is able to approach the truth through stages. Humility reveals our own misery as its first fruit. This misery, recognized also as our neighbor's, leads to the second fruit of humility—the love of our neighbor or charity. This compassion for human misery leads to our aspiration for justice, the virtue that purifies us for contemplation of divine things. The summit of human knowledge is only reached in the next life through grace, in the beatific vision, though it may be approached in this life. This is the perfect conformity and resemblance between our human will and the divine will, between the created and uncreated substance. This union is still contrasted to that of the persons of the Trinity, which is a unity of substance or unity itself. Since God, who is Charity, created man in His image, man reflects God primarily through the will. As God naturally loves Himself, man naturally loves God. God's love includes man, so man's self-love can still be in accord with divine love, provided that man loves himself as God loves him. To love as God loves is to be indistinguishable from God without being God. This is the highest goal for man. On the contrary, sin is to will for the sake of man himself, rather than for God. Sin is the disconformity between our human will and the divine will, which moves man away from God. Christian life aims at the recovery of this conformity with the divine will, which man lost as a result of original sin. *See also* ORDERS (RELIGIOUS).

**BERTHOLD OF MOOSBURG (ca. 1300–ca. 1361).** The first real evidence we have for this 14th-century **Dominican** is a report that he was a student at Oxford in 1316. The next information sets his arrival at Cologne shortly before 1330, just around the time of the condemnation of **Meister Eckhart**. Although he has a strong connection with the spiritual teachings of **Johannes Tauler**, his chief work is the *Expositio in elementationem theologicam Proclis (An Exposition of the Elements of Theology of Proclus)*, a keen commentary on the work of one of the most influential Neoplatonic philosophers that places Berthold philosophically in the Dominican school of **Albert the Great**, along with **Ulrich of Strasbourg** and **Dietrich of Freiberg**.

**BIBLE.** The collection of sacred texts for Jews and Christians, which are also held as sacred by Muslims, who interpret them in terms of the later revelation they believe was given to the Prophet Muhammad that is found in the **Koran**. The sacred character of these texts is based on the belief that, although they derived from the prophets or spokesmen of God, their one primary source, and thus the author of all sacred Scripture, is God. In the medieval Christian world, the Latin word *Biblia* was considered a feminine singular form that stressed the unity of the Old Testament and New Testament books. This unity was primarily based on the belief that the Bible had God as its primary author. The collection of the biblical texts also formed a unity, because its story is one story, that is, the story of God's chosen people in whom the promises made to Abraham in Genesis 17:7—that "I will confirm my covenant as a perpetual covenant between me and you. It will extend to your descendants after you throughout their generations. I will be your God and the God of your descendants after you"—are fulfilled.

The Bible was the chief book studied in the Faculty of Theology in medieval universities. Along with it, as assisting texts, were the **glosses** on the Bible; the *Historia Scholastica* of **Peter Comestor**, which organized the stories of the Bible into the one overall story of the history of salvation; and the *Sentences* of **Peter Lombard**, which dealt in a well-ordered way with the difficult doctrinal questions that arose from reading the Bible and provided a sustained effort to discover the wisdom of God that is revealed in the sacred text. *See also* ALLEGORY; EXEGESIS; FATHERS OF THE CHURCH; THEOLOGY.

**BOETHIUS (ca. 480–ca. 525).** Anicius Manlius Torquatus Severinus Boethius had a significant impact on medieval philosophy and **theology** because of the lengthy influence of his translations and commentaries on a number of Aristotle's logical works, his impressive *Consolatio philosophiae* (*The Consolation of Philosophy*), and his *Opuscula sacra* (*Theological Tractates*), which gathered commentaries over the centuries. His plan to translate into Latin all the works of **Plato** and **Aristotle**, and to show how they could be harmonized, never approached completion. He either translated or retranslated and commented on Porphyry's *Isagoge* (*Introduction to Aristotle's Logic*) and Aristotle's *Categories* and *On Interpretation*. He tells us also about translations of Aristotle's *Topics* and *Prior Analytics* (done at least in part). However, the edited translations of the *Prior* and *Posterior Analytics*, the *Topics*, and *Sophistical Refutations* that at times are attributed to him were the work of James of Venice. A number of other logical works dealing with various types of syllogisms are more rightly attributed to him, as are commentaries on **Cicero**'s *De inventione* and an original *De divisione*.

Through his own work, and that of his student, Cassiodorus, he encouraged education in the tradition of the Roman liberal arts. His commentaries on the *Categories*, especially his treatment of the categories of substance and relation, had lasting influence on medieval discussions in **logic**, **metaphysics**, and theology. Some, on the basis of the philosophical nature of his *Consolation of Philosophy*, have questioned his Christian faith; but his *Opuscula sacra* show him not only to be a religious Christian but also a deep-thinking technical theologian. The chapters on substance and relation also carried over into his *Opuscula sacra*, where he applied them to discussions of the Trinity and the Incarnation. In these works, especially in *De Trinitate* (*On the Trinity*) and *De persona et duabus naturis contra Eutychen et Pelagium* (*On the Person and Two Natures against Eutyches and Pelagius*), he gives precision to the meanings of *nature* when speaking of Christ as having both a divine and a human nature. In explaining how the two natures are united in the one person of Christ, he also presents a classical definition of *person* ("an individual substance of a rational nature") that will be discussed and debated throughout the medieval period and beyond. His *Consolation of Philosophy*, both in its prose and verse passages, provides philosophers and theologians with a treasury of themes, such as God's eternity, his foreknowledge of future contingent events, and divine omnipresence. Refer to the introduction, "The Beginnings of 'Philosophy' and 'Theology' in the Latin West."

**BOETHIUS OF DACIA (fl. 2ND HALF OF 13TH CENTURY).** The precise dates of the birth and death of this native of Denmark are unknown, though all of his works were written before 1277. He and **Siger of Brabant** are the best-known representatives of Latin **Averroism**, a movement characterized by its strict separation between philosophical and theological truth, whereby both may appear to contradict one another on some points. For example, to Boethius the natural philosopher as such must deny creation and affirm the eternity of the world, as he can investigate the universe only as already in existence and can grant only what is possible through natural causes. Reason contradicts Christian teaching on creation, which may still be held, though strictly on **faith**. Boethius's separation of faith and reason is also apparent in his ethics. There is a natural felicity proper to man in this life, namely the life of philosophic contemplation. This contemplation entails the investigation of God above all, but only insofar as God is available to natural reason. Christian teachings about man's end that extend beyond the natural order are proper to faith, not reason.

Boethius's general attitude seems to be not to deny matters of faith altogether (although the precise rational weight he gave them is not clear), but rather to concentrate on a truth and wisdom based on what is naturally available to human beings. Positions associated with Boethius and Siger were primary targets of the ecclesiastical **condemnation in 1277** launched at Paris by Bishop Étienne Tempier. This condemnation was motivated by what was seen as Latin Averroism's distortion of the right order between reason and faith. Tempier's action was affirming that reason's highest calling should be to seek understanding of Christian revelation.

**BONAVENTURE, ST. (1217–1274).** Born in Balneoregio, between Orvieto and Viterbo, in 1217, he was the seventh successor of St. Francis of Assisi as head of the **Franciscan** order. He received his early education at the Franciscan friary in his hometown. In 1234, he went to study in the preparatory school for theology, the **Arts Faculty** at the University of Paris. He entered the Franciscan order at Paris in 1243 and started his theological studies under **Alexander of Hales**, the most famous master of theology at Paris, who had entered the Franciscan order. Bonaventure also studied with two other renowned Franciscan masters, **John of La Rochelle** and **Odo Rigaud**. During his years as an advanced theology student at Paris, he lectured on the **Bible** (1248–1250) and also delivered his *Commentary on the Sentences* of **Peter Lombard** (1250–1252). Bonaventure continued to teach theology at Paris until his election as general minister in 1257, as is witnessed by his *Disputed Questions on the Mystery of the Trinity*, his *Disputed Questions on the Knowledge of Christ*, and *The Breviloquium*, all of them university works. His *Sermons on the Ten Commandments*, *On the Gifts of the Holy Spirit*, and *On the Six Days of Creation*, dating from the late 1260s and early 1270s, were given to University of Paris audiences.

Among Bonaventure's more widely read books is his *Tree of Life*, his meditations on Christ, who is the center of his theology. His *Legenda maior* (*Life of St. Francis*) is a work that was commissioned by a general chapter of the Franciscan order that portrays the poverty and humility of Francis, as the imitator of Christ, who inspired his followers in the order and throughout the Church. His most well-known treatise is the *Itinerarium Mentis in Deum* (*The Journey of the Mind into God*), a work of the spiritual journey to God inspired by Bonaventure's meditation on the miraculous stigmata experienced by Francis of Assisi. Bonaventure links in his imagination the wounds of his Seraphic father with the six stages of contemplation presented by **Richard of Saint-Victor** in *The Mystical Ark*. He takes us on a spiritual journey that he imagines is most in accord with Francis's union with God. The tone of the work is well expressed in its prologue, which also summarizes the attitude of Bonaventure throughout all his theological writings: "Wherefore, it is to groans of prayer through Christ crucified, in Whose blood we are cleansed from the filth of vices, that I first of all invite the reader. Otherwise he may come to think that mere reading will suffice without fervor, speculation without devotion, investigation without admiration, observation without exultation, industry without piety, knowledge without love, understanding without humility, study without divine **grace**."

Despite the affective accent in his theological books, his spiritual treatises, and his sermons, Bonaventure had a very strong theoretical ability and philosophical depth. His *Commentary on Lombard's Sentences* and *Disputed Questions* are rich witnesses to the seriousness with which he wrestles with philosophical problems concerning our knowledge of reality. In question 4 of *The Disputed Questions on the Knowledge of Christ*, Bonaventure outlines what must be established to provide a guarantee of a sure or certain knowledge of reality: there must be infallibility on the part of the knower and immutability on the part of the object known. Throughout questions 4 and 5, whether dealing with the nature and role of the eternal reasons, illumination, or ultimate analysis—understood in different ways by contemporary authors appealing to various interpretations of the **Augustinian** tradition—Bonaventure brings a certain reserve to any easy effort to guarantee infallibility on the part of the knower and immutability on the part of what is known by a claim that we know directly and immediately ideal standards. For even if our judgments require an infallible standard, this norm is not present in us as a conscious object or term of our knowledge. We do not see the eternal art, even though it is the means by which we judge. The divine art is present in our every judgment, whether at the sensory or intellectual level. It illuminates our judgments but is not their object.

A similar caution is present in regard to too quick a claim regarding our knowledge of God's existence. When one reads Bonaventure's *Commentary on the Sentences*, there might be a temptation to judge that he himself is guilty of claiming too much. He declares, "So great is the truth of divine being that you cannot judge it not to exist unless there is something wrong with your understanding, so that you do not know what is meant by 'God.' There cannot be on its part a lack of presence or evidence, considering God in Himself or the object of a proof for His existence" (*Commentarium in I Sententiarum* I, 154). Bonaventure, however, nuances his position in this way: "It is strange that the intellect does not consider that which it sees before all others and without which it can recognize nothing. It is like the eye that is so intent on various differences of color that it is not aware of the light through which it sees them. The intellect is thus distracted by all the various objects of knowledge so that it does not notice that being that is beyond all categories, even though it comes first to the mind and though all other things are perceptible only by means of it. If then, we fully resolve the facts of our experience, both internal and external, they lead us to the divine light." The existence of God cannot be doubted. Bonaventure thus explicitly ties the argument of Anselm to the Augustinian theory of illumination. As he puts it, "But for the intellect which fully understands the meaning of the word 'God'—thinking God to be that than which no greater can be conceived—not only is there no doubt that God exists, but the nonexistence of God cannot even be thought."

Why then does Bonaventure provide so many proofs in his *Disputed Questions on the Mystery of the Trinity*? It seems pointless to attempt to prove that about which no doubt is possible. Bonaventure replies that the truth "God exists" does not need proof because it lacks intrinsic evidence but because our faulty processes of reflection need correction. That is, we do not reflect on our internal or external experience in a way that brings us to an ultimate analysis of the truth of God. The arguments he presents, therefore, are exercises that lead the intellect to such an analysis rather than proofs that provide evidence and make the truth manifest for the first time. The light is always there. Our intellect, however, might need the stimulus of reasons to induce a full awareness of the content of our first ideas. It is this kind of analysis that is best carried on in *The Journey of the Mind into God*.

Bonaventure had the challenge of the arrival of Aristotle's properly philosophical works, such as *On the Soul*, *Physics*, *Metaphysics*, *On the Heavens*, and *Nicomachean Ethics*. Much of the challenge he was concerned with was particular interpretations of Aristotle's teachings, especially ones that were at odds with the truths of the Christian faith. Yet many of his more technical philosophical and theological concerns were focused on how to restate as well as possible the traditions of Augustine and Anselm in ways that better represented their closeness to the realities they attempted to make manifest. This is most noticeable in the effort he put into explaining certain truth or providing the arguments for the existence of God just considered. Refer to appendix 1.

**BONIFACE VIII, POPE (ca. 1235–1303).** Pope Boniface VIII, or Benedict Gaetani, was born in Anagni and died in Rome; his pontificate lasted from 24 December 1294 to 11 October 1303. In 1290, at the Council of Paris, he played a leading role as papal legate, defending the unlimited right of the priests of mendicant orders to hear confession, against the objections of secular masters of the University of Paris. Gaetani's deliberation in favor of the mendicants can be viewed as a turning point in the life of the Theology Faculty at the university. For almost a century before 1290, masters of theology at Paris had been increasingly influential in decisions by ecclesiastical authorities concerning truth and orthodoxy. Gaetani's deliberation marked the beginning of a trend to reduce this influence; theology masters were only to be consulted by ecclesiastical authorities, not treated as authorities. Boniface's papacy was characterized by intense political struggles with secular powers, such as King Philip the Fair of France. His principal objective, to establish a unified Christendom led by the pope, was in constant tension with the views of many kings and their supporters.

**BRADWARDINE, THOMAS (ca. 1290–1349).** Theologian, scientist, and archbishop of Canterbury, this native of England, often referred to as *Doctor Profundus* (the Profound Teacher), was probably born in Hartfield, Sussex. He studied at Oxford, where he was a fellow at Balliol College in 1321 and, by 1323, at Merton College. He wrote an influential treatise in logic, *De insolubilibus* (*On Insoluble Propositions*). He also wrote in 1328 *De proportione velocitatum in motibus* (*On the Proportion of Velocities in Moved Bodies*), an enormously influential breakthrough in the mathematical measurement of velocity and motion. By identifying motion with velocity, Bradwardine went beyond **Aristotle** in making it possible to mathematically measure motion. His basic formula was that velocity is a function of the whole ratio of the mover over the moved in geometric, not arithmetical, proportionality. His method was adopted and developed not only at Oxford but also at places like

Paris and Padua. At Oxford, a group of scholars at Merton followed and developed Bradwardine's approach to problems of kinetics. They became known as the **Oxford Calculators** since they applied mathematics to different types of change. Famous members were **William of Heytesbury**, John Dumbleton, and **Richard Swineshead**. Part of Bradwardine's approach to science, as expressed in *De proportione* and another treatise, *De continuo*, was that mathematics was both necessary and can provide the key to understanding nature. Thus, his general approach was a sign of the lessening of the gap between pure mathematics and natural philosophy, although it was not until the time of Galileo that mathematics and empirical science were more conclusively integrated into the study of motion.

Bradwardine was also important in the development of **theology** in the 14th century. His most important theological sources were **Augustine, Anselm**, and **Thomas Aquinas**. He also argues against important positions of **William of Ockham**, such as his conception of God's knowledge of future contingents. Bradwardine's chief theological work, *De causa Dei contra Pelagium et de virtute causarum* (*On God's Case against Pelagius and the Power of Causes*), completed in 1344, is a systematic proof of God's free efficient will over all secondary causes. In it he argued against contemporary **Pelagians** who, claiming that Pelagius was never refuted by reason and Scripture but only silenced by ecclesiastical authority, saw man's free will as exempted from God's prior causality in both nature and **grace**. Bradwardine was elected (4 June), appointed (19 June), and consecrated (19 July) in 1349 as archbishop of Canterbury after the death of John of Ufford. Shortly after, on 26 August 1349, he died of the plague at the residence of the bishop of Rochester in Lambeth.

**BRUNO THE CARTHUSIAN (ca. 1030–1101).** Born in Cologne, Bruno studied in Reims and became master of the cathedral school there and the director of education in the diocese from 1057 until 1075. He founded the Carthusian order in 1084 at La Grande Chartreuse. In 1090 he moved to Calabria, where he began another of his foundations, La Torre. He wrote his *Commentary on the Psalms* in Reims and his *Commentary on the Epistles of St. Paul* at Chartreuse. He also wrote a profession of faith affirming the mystery of the Trinity, in contrast to **Roscelin**'s tritheism, and the real presence of Christ in the Eucharist, joining the opposition of **Lanfranc** and others to **Berengarius**, whose dialectical thinking led him to deny the real presence of Christ under the species of bread and wine. *See also* ORDERS (RELIGIOUS).

**BURIDAN, JOHN (ca. 1295–1361).** Although little is known of his life, except that he was from the region of Arras, John Buridan was a student and master in the **Arts Faculty** at Paris, probably becoming master around 1320. He did not move on to any of the higher faculties of Theology, Medicine, or Law. He was, however, respected enough to be named rector of the university twice, in 1327 and 1340. He wrote commentaries on many of **Aristotle**'s works, especially his *Physics*, *Metaphysics*, *On the Soul*, and *Nicomachean Ethics*. Buridan's commentaries follow a question format that allowed him to present his own unified treatment of the subject matter he was considering. His primary **logic** work was his *Summulae de dialectica*, which was based on a restructured text of **Peter of Spain**'s *Tractatus*. Other logic works have also survived, such as his *Treatise on Supposition* and *Treatise on Consequences*.

Buridan's approach to logic and philosophy followed in the footsteps of **William of Ockham**'s **nominalism**. In treating the categories, he attempted to show that only three of the 10 categories pointed to distinct substances and inhering realities. Certain qualities, such as whiteness, inhere in substances. But being a father does not give a man an inhering quality of fatherhood. A father gains a son or daughter, but he does not gain an inhering characteristic. Other qualities also do not inhere in substances: when a piece of wire is said to be straight or curved, it does not have an inhering quality of straightness or curvedness. The wire is straight if its ends are as far apart from one another as possible. If the ends become closer to one another, then the wire is said to be curved. This nominalistic theory of the categories is applied by Buridan to the other areas of philosophy, as is evident especially in his *Questions on the Physics*.

**BURLEY, WALTER (ca. 1274–1344).** A secular priest, Walter was probably born in Burley, near Leeds. He began his studies in the **Arts Faculty** at Oxford before the end of the century and was a fellow of Merton College. In 1309, he went to Paris to study **theology**. There is no known copy of a *Commentary on the Sentences*, but through some surviving questions we have a record of his debates with **Thomas Wylton**, his teacher in theology. Burley is known especially for his works in the field of logic, although he also wrote commentaries on **Aristotle**'s *Physics*, *Ethics*, and *Politics*. He commented on some of Aristotle's logical works, for example, *Categories* and *Perihermenias*, as many as four times: he started with introductory lectures that were simply outlines of the work, then moved on to literal expositions, expositions with questions added, and finally to long detailed expositions of Aristotle's texts accompanied by questions.

Burleigh's chief opponent in his works on **logic** and physics was **William of Ockham**. It should be noted, however, that Ockham, particularly in his treatise on supposition in the *Summa logicae*, borrows very much from Burley. Yet, in their fundamental viewpoints, they are as opposed as a **realist** like Burley and a **nominalist** like Ockham can be. The conflict between the two men lasted for decades, particularly from the side of Burley, as is evident in the longer version of Burley's *De purltate artis logicae tractatus* (*Treatise on the Purity of the Art of Logic*).

# C

**CABALA.** This was originally a Jewish religious movement, rejecting Greek philosophy and its Muslim and Jewish versions, characterized by the understanding of creation and revelation as symbolic of the divine. It emerged first in southern Europe, specifically Provence (second half of the 12th century) and then Spain (early 13th century), focusing on Jewish theosophical texts believed to contain esoteric wisdom on the world and humankind's place in it. Although the original Jewish movement rejected philosophy, some Christian thinkers found insights in the Cabala that influenced their philosophic views. Thus, Christian Cabala emerged in the 15th century, through exponents such as **Marsilio Ficino** (1433–1499) and **Giovanni Pico della Mirandola** (1463–1494) in Florence, and continued through later centuries. In Cabala, the deity is viewed as both hidden and revealed. The hidden aspect is called *Ein-Sof* (Godhead), while the revealed aspect is described as 10 *Sefirot* (potencies or emanations). These *Sefirot* indicate either divine powers of the revealed aspect of the deity or instruments employed by the divine power in the creation and governance of the world. The *Sefirot* are represented in the form of a tree or human:

Crown (Keter)
Intelligence (Binah); Wisdom (Hokhmah)
Power (Gevurah) or Stern Judgment (Din); Love (Hesed)
Beauty (Tiferet) or Compassion (Rahmanin)
Majesty (Hod); Eternity (Nezah)
Foundation (Yesod)
Kingdom (Malkhut)

The earliest cabalistic work is the *Sefer Bahi* (*Book of Clarity*), written in Hebrew. It presents a theosophical view of the *Sefirot* with some ancient Gnostic influences. Though attributed to the ancient author Rabbi Nehunyah ben Ha-Kanah, the surviving document is from the second half of the 12th century. The first work in Cabala whose author is known is a commentary on *Sefer Yetzira* (*The Book of Creation*) by Rabbi Isaac Saggi Nehor (Isaac the Blind). This work, as well as that of Rabbi Isaac's followers, shows an important development: the tradition of *Sefer Bahi* had been combined with

Neoplatonic thought. Cabala grew considerably in the 13th century, and a number of different cabalistic schools, with different approaches and emphases, emerged. The *Zohar* or *Book of Splendor* is the most important work in Cabala, and the circle around it, including Rabbi Moses de Leon (the author of all sections of the *Zohar* except the *Raya Mehemna* and *Tikkunei ha-Zohar*), Rabbi Joseph Gikatilla, Rabbi Joseph of Hamadan, and the anonymous author of the last section of the *Zohar*, is the most noteworthy. In the *Zohar* there is powerful sexual imagery concerning the Godhead itself, as well as an emphasis on the influence of human beings on the divine, both in good and evil ways. Through devotion in prayer and through fulfillment of commandments, human beings, who are made in the image of God and originated from the Godhead, can be active participants in the unification of the divine forces and in the restoration of creation as a servant of God. The *Zohar* combines Jewish tradition with non-Jewish influences in a comprehensive cabalistic view.

In the second half of the 13th century, what is known as "prophetic" or "ecstatic" Cabala emerged in Spain, Greece, and Italy; its main purpose was the attainment of ecstatic experiences, and its main exponent was Rabbi Abraham ben Samuel Abulafia. There was also a Byzantine cabalistic movement that flourished in the middle of the 14th century and the Middle Ages through figures such as Isaac Luria, whose approach begot a movement called Lurianic Cabala, and Abraham Cohen Herrera (the most philosophical of the cabalistic writers), as well as in the Christian tradition. Cabala thus was incorporated along with other medieval and ancient sources into new theological and philosophical outlooks.

**CALIPHATE.** Derived from the term *caliph*, the successor of Muhammad (d. 632) as the leader of Islam, the caliphate is the government of the caliph. The capital of the eastern caliphate, dominated by the 'Abbasid dynasty that came to power in 750, started at Damascus and was then moved to Baghdad in 762 by the second 'Abbasid caliph, Al-Mansur. At this point, Islamic power stretched from the Atlantic Ocean to central Asia and the Indus Valley. A rival western caliphate was set up in the eighth century at Cordoba, Spain, by the Umayyads, who were overthrown in the east by the 'Abbasids. Cordoba was the capital of the western caliphate, which in 732 extended westward as far as central France. Cordoba became arguably the richest cultural center in medieval Islam and was the principal filter of classical learning to western Europe in the 12th century. Some of the greatest medieval thinkers, such as **Averroes** and **Maimonides**, lived at Cordoba. Despite political rivalries between eastern and western caliphates, there was considerable cultural exchange and unity between them. *See also* ISLAM.

**CANONS REGULAR OF ST. AUGUSTINE.** *See* ORDERS (RELIGIOUS).

**CAPREOLUS, JOHN (ca. 1380–1444).** Named "the Prince of Thomists" by Renaissance followers of **St. Thomas Aquinas**, this **Dominican** was born in Rouergue in the southern region of France. He began as a bachelor of theology at Paris in 1407 and became a master in 1411. His most famous work is his *Defensiones theologiae divi Thomae Aquinatis* (*Defenses of the Theology of the Well-Respected Thomas Aquinas*). Capreolus, following the general outline of **Peter Lombard**'s *Sentences*, organized 190 questions treated by Thomas Aquinas in his *Summa* and *Sentences* commentary into a solid defense of Thomas's teachings against the challenges of various 14th-century opponents. Those who disagreed with Thomas on these issues were mostly Franciscan authors: **William of Ware**, **John Duns Scotus**, **Peter Aureoli**, and **Adam Wodeham**. Added to this list are the Dominican **Durandus of Saint-Pourçain**, the secular priest **John of Ripa**, and the Carmelites **Gerard of Bologna** and **Guido Terrena**. Often the objections he considers do not come directly from each of these authors but from the reports of Peter Aureoli, whose *Scriptum* he used as a sourcebook.

**CARMELITES.** *See* ORDERS (RELIGIOUS).

**CARTHUSIANS.** *See* ORDERS (RELIGIOUS).

*CATEGORIES.* The logical works of **Aristotle** are set up to cover terms, combinations of terms that are put into affirmative or negative statements or propositions, and combinations of propositions that are organized in such a way that they effectively express an argument. The first of his treatises, that dealing with terms, is in a work called the *Categories* or the *Predicaments*. In this work, Aristotle indicates that terms point to the real world and speak about it in ways that might be divided into 10 classes. The main class is what he calls substances, that is, realities that can stand on their own: men, trees, stones, etc. These substances also have certain qualities, they exist in different sizes and quantities, and they are located at different places at different times, and maybe with one another. So Aristotle discovers that we can speak about realities as substances and their color, size, location, and so on in a manner that he classifies as the 10 categories: substance, quality, quantity, relation, place, time, etc. The medieval philosophers and theologians used this classification in discussing their various philosophical and theological issues and even debated whether or not each of the 10 categories expresses a different kind of reality or not.

**CICERO, MARCUS TULLIUS (106–43 B.C.).** This Roman writer and public figure played some role in the transmission of Greek thought, especially Stoicism and the Platonism of the Academy, to the medieval world. Though not an original thinker, in his works (principally orations, rhetorical pieces, philosophical dialogues, and letters) he expressed the main doctrines of the different Greek philosophical schools in beautiful Latin prose, of which he is considered the master. Later writers, who used and reacted to Greek thought in various ways and did not have access to Greek sources, often relied on Cicero and were influenced by his style. Cicero was also the first to give certain Latin terms (e.g., *essentia, qualitas, materia*—essence, quality, and matter, respectively) a philosophical meaning that continued in the tradition. It was Cicero's *Hortensius* that first implanted in **Augustine**, the most influential of the Latin **Fathers of the Church**, the love of philosophy. Moreover, Cicero, still the principal source on the development of skepticism in the Academy originated by **Plato**, provides the background to St. Augustine's *Contra Academicos*, his criticism of skepticism. Though medieval Latin thinkers did not have much access to Plato's own works, they did have some translations, among which there is a fragment of Plato's *Timaeus* translated by Cicero. They also learned basic views of Plato in works such as Cicero's *Tusculan Disputations*, which contains an account of Plato's influential view of the immortality of the **soul**. After the Middle Ages, when in the Renaissance the classics of antiquity became the chief source of intellectual life, Cicero received much attention, primarily as a master of Latin prose.

**CISTERCIANS.** *See* ORDERS (RELIGIOUS).

**CLAREMBALD OF ARRAS (ca. 1115–ca. 1187).** A teacher of the **liberal arts**, and later head of the school at Laon, this commentator on **Boethius**'s theological treatises was a student of Thierry of Chartres and Hugh of Saint-Victor at Paris in the late 1130s. His chief philosophical work links him to the school of Chartres. He wrote an introductory letter to Thierry of Chartres's *De sex dierum operibus* (*On the Works of the Six Days of Creation*) and a *Tractatulus* (*Short Treatise on "Genesis"*). In the introductory letter, Clarembald asks to be recognized for the effort he made in his *Tractatulus* to reconcile the many views of the philosophers with the Christian truth so that the word of Scripture might receive strength and protection even from its adversaries.

Clarembald's earlier commentaries on Boethius's *De Trinitate* (*On the Trinity*) and *De hebdomadibus* (*How Created Things Can Be Called Good Even Though They Are Not Substantially Good*) had already made many of the philosophic points he develops in the *Tractatulus*: his theory of the **cate-**

**gories** (*De Trin*. 4:1–46), the distinction between dialectical, demonstrative, and sophistical syllogisms (*De hebd*. 1:1–2), and his interpretation of Boethius's different levels of abstraction (*De Trin*. 2:17–19). On theological issues, he was a strong critic of **Peter Abelard** and **Gilbert of Poitiers**.

**CLEMENT OF ALEXANDRIA (ca. 150–ca. 215).** Although we know little of Clement's life, we are well aware that he praised the Jewish traditional respect for their elders, especially for their spiritual fathers. This respect for spiritual leaders is a theme that runs through his three main works. These works are the *Protreptikos* (*Exhortation to the Greeks*), the *Paidagogos* (*Tutor*), and the *Stromateis* (*Miscellanies*). In the first of these works, Clement urges non-Christians to realize that as searchers for truth they should look to Justin and other spiritual fathers whose honest search for truth led them eventually to abandon false forms of philosophic truth and to embrace the only true philosophy, Christianity. In the *Paidagogos*, Clement speaks to Christian believers about Christ as the true teacher who can lead us through his teachings in Scripture to a deeper understanding of the truths He proclaims. The *Miscellanies* speaks of the relationship of Christian faith to various forms of Greek philosophy and encourages believers to use their minds and the materials of philosophy to refute the false religious, moral, and spiritual principles that were used by Gnostics who would come to Christian communities and pretend to be Christians so they could lead believers to convert to their false way of living. In all three of these treatises he shows the importance of philosophy and the ways in which true Christian philosophers, like spiritual fathers, can help true believers to a deeper understanding of the faith and can show the erroneous character of the teachings that were used by heretics and other deceivers to undermine the true philosophy of the Christian faith. Refer to the introduction, "Medieval Justifications for the Use of Philosophy."

*COMMENTARY ON THE SENTENCES*. **Peter Lombard** collected a four-volume manual of theological questions that became very popular in the Middle Ages. It was called the *Sentences*, since it provided the sentences or logically ordered opinions of the Fathers of the Church regarding each issue discussed in the work. The secular master **Alexander of Hales** used the *Sentences* of Peter Lombard as a textbook to complement the **Bible**, especially when difficult doctrinal questions were being considered. **Richard Fishacre**, a Dominican, initiated Alexander's practice later at Oxford. Many university **masters** and students of theology wrote commentaries on Lombard's work. At times, these commentaries were works that simply assimilated the long tradition of teaching that came down from the Fathers; later they became very independent works that showed the originality and mastery of the theologians who wrote the commentaries.

**CONDEMNATIONS OF 1277.** One of the most dramatic events connected with philosophy and **theology** in the Middle Ages was the condemnation at Paris of 219 propositions by Bishop Étienne Tempier in 1277. As part of the background to this event, one must realize that in the early part of the century, there had been church decrees in 1210 and 1215 against the teaching of **Aristotle**'s natural philosophy and *Metaphysics* at Paris. The same policy was restated by Pope Gregory IX in 1231, at least until a committee headed by William of Auxerre could examine the works of Aristotle and "purge them of every suspicion of error." Since William died in the same year, the committee never undertook its task. No actions were taken over the next decade, and after Gregory IX's death in 1241, the decrees seem to have been ignored. In 1255, when new statutes of the university were promulgated, requirements for students in the **Arts Faculty** to have attended a specific number of lectures on each of the known works of Aristotle were mandated. Some of the difficulties that had been anticipated by the earlier decrees were indicated to be real in 1270, when Bishop Tempier condemned 13 errors related to Aristotle's teachings: the eternity of the world, his denial of divine providence or God's involvement with the world, the unicity of the intellectual **soul**, and his implied denial of freedom of the will.

The threat of excommunication for instructors who knowingly taught these errors seems to have had little effect on those who taught them in the Arts Faculty, since Bishop Tempier was asked by Pope John XXI (Peter of Spain) in 1277 to investigate the situation. Bishop Tempier set up a commission of 16 theologians, the most well known of whom was **Henry of Ghent**, to study the teachings of the Arts Faculty. The result, going beyond the papal mandate, was the gathering of 219 propositions from the writings of those in the Arts Faculty that seemed to teach errors. The original collection of items did not have any order to them, and they were judged by other theologians at Paris, for example, Godfrey of Fontaines, to be statements that were at times vague and that even seemingly contradicted one another. Along with this list of condemned propositions, movements were afoot to bring personal processes against **Thomas Aquinas** himself and also against his student, **Giles of Rome**. In fact, Giles was the subject of a personal investigation, and he was prevented from becoming a master of the *Sentences* at Paris. Only through a papal directive was he appointed master years later, in 1284.

The action under Bishop Tempier's authority seems to have had a twofold aim: to put an end to the establishment of an independent, self-determining, Aristotelian philosophical movement, and to slow down the development of a more Aristotelian-influenced Christian theology. In *Quodlibet XII*, q. 5, disputed in 1296 or 1297, Godfrey of Fontaines, often a critic of Aquinas's positions, asks whether Tempier's successor as bishop of Paris sins if he fails to correct certain articles (namely those associated with Thomas Aquinas) condemned by his predecessor. Godfrey argues that certain condemnations should be corrected, since many of the articles concern matters that are no danger to faith or morals and are open to different opinions. He states, "One article, for instance, condemns as error the position that God could not multiply many individuals in the same species without matter. Another following upon this, declares it erroneous that God could not make many **angels** in the same species, since they do not have matter. Yet to hold the condemned positions as opinions seems justified, since they are among the positions that have been held orally and in writing by many Catholic teachers." Godfrey continues on, stating a number of other condemned propositions that he associates with Aquinas. In his argument Godfrey concludes, "For, through the things found in his teaching the teachings of almost all the other doctors are corrected, and they are restored and made more tasty. So, if this teaching of brother Thomas is withdrawn from their midst, those who study will find little taste in the teachings of the others [whose taste he has restored]." Godfrey's argument did not have the desired effect. The condemned propositions associated with Thomas Aquinas were only rescinded after his canonization. Nor were the propositions themselves rescinded, but rather the propositions as taught by Brother Thomas were no longer censured. Refer to appendix 2.

**CORRECTORIA.** The medieval Latin term *correctorium* or *correctory* (plural: *correctoria*) generally refers to a 13th- or 14th-century critical revision of the **Bible** (Latin Vulgate), even though revisions of Latin biblical texts were also produced earlier (e.g., by **Alcuin** and Theodulf in the late eighth century, by Stephen Harding in 1109, and by Nicholas Maniacoria in the 12th century). In the 13th century, the University of Paris adopted a text based on Alcuin's revision, and various *correctoria* of it were produced, such as the correctory of Saint-Jacques (mid-13th century); the *Correctorium Sorbonnicum*; and those of **Hugh of Saint-Cher**, **William de la Mare**, and Gerard de Huy. Most *correctoria* were scholarly masterpieces, considering the Vulgate manuscript tradition, the ancient translations of the Greek Septuagint version (*Vetus Latina*), as well as Hebrew, Greek, and Aramaic originals. The term *correctorium* also was extended to cover works that critics produced to correct the teachings of certain authors. The Franciscan William de la Mare wrote a *Correctorium "Quare"* (*Correctory beginning with the word "Why"*) to challenge the doctrines of **Thomas Aquinas**. On their part, some of Aquinas's Dominican followers, such as **John of Paris**, responded with corrections of the correctors. John gave his work the title *Correctorium corruptorii "Circa"* (*Correctory of the Distorting Treatise that begins with the words "In regard to"*).

**COSTA BEN LUCA (864–953).** Also known as Constabulus or Constabulinus, this Christian philosopher born in Baalbek, Syria, was known in the East primarily as a translator of **Aristotle**'s works into Arabic. In the West he was known chiefly through a work attributed to him, *De differentia animae et spiritus* (*On the Difference between Soul and Spirit*). In this work, a compilation of **Plato**, Aristotle, Theophrastus, and Galen, the author maintains, following Galen, that the spirit is not incorporeal and higher than the **soul**, but rather a very subtle matter within the human body. Spirit is "the proximate cause of life"; soul is "the more remote or great cause." The work was translated into Latin from the Arabic before 1143 by John of Spain and was influential in medieval Latin thought. When the arts curriculum was reorganized at the **University** of Paris in 1255, it became a required text.

**CRESCAS, HASDAI (ca. 1340–ca. 1411).** Born in Barcelona, Crescas lived during a time when Jews suffered persecution in Spain. He lost his only son at an anti-Jewish riot in 1391, where thousands of Jews were murdered. Crescas dedicated himself to the reconstruction of Jewish life in Spain. He assumed important posts, such as advisor to the Aragonese monarchs and rabbi of Saragossa, and he was recognized by the throne as the judge of the Jews of Aragon. Through the influence of **Aristotle**, **Averroes** (his chief medieval commentator), and others such as **Moses Maimonides** and **Gersonides**, **Aristotelianism** elicited strong reactions in Jewish circles, including rejections against philosophy altogether as well as new philosophical alternatives within Judaism. Crescas criticized Aristotelianism and developed a philosophy of his own within a Jewish framework. In *The Book of the Refutation of the Principles of the Christians*, he also criticized central Christian tenets, such as the Trinity, transubstantiation, and original sin, as being irrational.

Maimonides was the first to attempt to establish a set of authoritative Jewish beliefs. Crescas followed him in this attempt, against those who saw the commandments of the Torah as the only binding core of Judaism. He presented a new version of these beliefs in his chief work, *Light of the Lord* or *Adonai* (completed in 1410), where he draws expertly from the biblical-rabbinic tradition, Jewish and Islamic philosophy, and even **Cabala** and late medieval Christian thought. This work includes a developed philosophy of nature. Crescas rejected important theses of Aristotle's physics, a domain upon which much of Aristotle's vision of reality is built, such as his concepts of time and space and his denial of actual infinity and the vacuum. Crescas proposed new influential understandings. He viewed time and space as infinite quantities, the latter as an infinite vacuum and the former as infinite duration. Both exist independently of physical objects: space is identified with three-dimensionality, and time is in the mind. Thus, the universe is conceived as containing an infinite number of worlds. This fits into the anti-Aristotelian movement in physics of the 14th century that will lead to Isaac Newton and other modern pioneers. His work has affinities to that of **Nicole Oresme** (1325–1382). Crescas's theory of space, however, seems wholly his own.

Crescas's critique of Aristotelian physics is a rejection of the basis of Aristotle's proofs for the existence of God, in particular Aristotle's premise that an infinite regress of causes is impossible. Crescas rather proves the existence of God on the basis of necessity and contingency, as **Avicenna** had done: contingent things ultimately depend on something that is necessary on its own account, namely God. Crescas's conception of the universe influences his view of human beings, including their freedom and purpose. As every event in the universe is necessitated by prior causes, ultimately by God, the human will is also determined. The will, a conjunction of appetitive and imaginative faculties, is free not in the sense that it is uncaused, but in the sense that it can choose between possibilities. As knowledge and belief are not voluntary in Crescas's sense of the term, God rewards and punishes more on account of human feelings than beliefs. Love and fear of God are the keys to happiness and immortality more than intellectual speculation or dogma. Crescas's ideas were influential in the development of modern science, as well as in the work of later philosophers, such as Giordano Bruno, **Giovanni Francesco Pico della Mirandola**, and Baruch Spinoza.

# D

**DAMASCENE, JOHN (JOHN OF DAMASCUS), ST. (fl. 8TH CENTU-RY).** Damascene is the last of the major Greek **Fathers of the Church** and an important influence in medieval Christian thought, particularly in the transmission of the wisdom of the Greek Fathers to the medieval Latin world. His chief work, *The Source of Knowledge*, has three parts: a philosophical introduction, a brief history of heresies, and a systematic arrangement of texts of his predecessors concerning the central truths of Christianity. The third part, translated ca. 1151 by Burgundio of Pisa, is frequently quoted as *De fide orthodoxa* (*On True Faith*). Some of the tenets presented by Damascene were extensively interpreted, developed, and debated. An example is his claim that knowledge of God's existence is naturally implanted in all human beings, although what God is remains unknowable to us. The nature and extent of this natural knowledge of God's existence and the relative unknowability of the divine essence were widely discussed and debated among famous Scholastics like **Thomas Aquinas, John Duns Scotus**, and **Henry of Ghent**. Furthermore, *On True Faith*, a systematic and technical work, was a model for some of the greatest works of Scholastic thought, including theological **summae** and **Peter Lombard**'s *Sentences* (as well as famous commentaries on this book). Damascene's writings on the Trinity were influential in the Eastern Orthodox and Western Latin Churches. For example, his argument that the Holy Spirit proceeds from the Father alone, followed by the Greek Orthodox Church, was addressed extensively by various Latin thinkers expressing their belief that the Holy Spirit proceeds from both the Father and the Son. Refer to the introduction, "The Beginnings of 'Philosophy' and 'Theology' in the Latin West."

**DANTE ALIGHIERI (1265–1321).** A native of Florence, Dante is considered by many as the greatest poet of medieval Europe and as one of the greatest in history. Active also in politics, his support of his city's independence from the Roman curia (led by Boniface VIII) led to an exile, beginning in 1302, from which he could not return. Dante, who wrote both prose and poetry, was influenced by classic sources and the philosophical and theologi-

111

cal tradition, including contemporary **Scholastics**. *De vulgari eloquentia* (*On Popular Speech*), *Convivio* (*The Banquet*, in Italian), and *De Monarchia* (*On Monarchy*) are important treatises. The first deals mainly with the origin of language, the second with knowledge as the source of happiness, and the third with politics (particularly the relation between church and empire). The second relies on Neoplatonic cosmology and **Aristotelian** anthropology within a Christian context. The third reflects the influence of Latin **Averroism**, with its stress on the separation between reason and **faith**.

These philosophical and theological themes are also developed in *La divina commedia* (*Divine Comedy*), his masterpiece and the first major work to appear in Italian, influencing the development of this language. This epic poem, drawing on philosophical and theological sources, is based on the Christian view of the human end: created in the image of God in virtue of possessing freedom, intelligence, and love, human beings are meant to use these possessions to return to God. In this work, Dante describes his own ethical journey through hell, purgatory, and paradise. His main inspiration is the poet Virgil, who guides him through hell and purgatory, and the woman he loved ("Beatrice"), his guide through most of heaven. The story, told in the first person, is rather innovative, among other things in its stress on the dignity of human beings and freedom.

**DAVID OF DINANT (fl. 2ND HALF OF 12TH CENTURY).** Along with **Amalric of Bène**, David of Dinant was posthumously condemned at the Council of Paris in 1210, at which his writings were ordered to be burned, as well as at the Fourth Lateran Council in 1215. This condemnation of 1210 also prohibited the study of **Aristotle**'s natural philosophy at the University of Paris. One of David's theses under attack was his identification of mind, matter, and God, which relied on his interpretations of Aristotle and **John Scotus Eriugena**. Years afterward, when the study of Aristotle at Paris continued to generate controversy, **Albert the Great**, arguing that Aristotle was not anti-Christian, attacked David for giving Aristotle, specifically in *On the Soul*, an unwarranted materialistic interpretation. Albert's student **Thomas Aquinas** also criticized David's materialism. Others, however, saw more affinity between David and Aristotle. As we have no access to David's own views except through the reports of others (chiefly his attackers), we cannot reconstruct them with complete certainty. David and Amalric were both condemned as pantheists: they did not distinguish sufficiently between God and creatures so as to preserve the clear transcendence of God according to Christian teaching. Influenced by John Scotus Eriugena's *On the Division of Nature*, David's *On the Divisions* also divides reality, though in its own way. David divides being into matter, mind, and the separate substances (including the highest, God). But these divisions, one of David's (so-called pantheistic) arguments goes, share in identity, since they fall within the notion of generic being. Thus, all these divisions of being are subordinate to a generic type of being.

**DECRETALS AND DECRETALISTS.** In general terms, a decretal (*epistola decretalis* or *littera decretalis*) is a document expressing a papal decision. The term, however, has more precise senses, meaning a decision concerning an issue of canonical discipline or, in its strictest sense, a *rescriptum* (rescript): a papal response to an appeal. Decretals could have a very limited application, depending on the context, and so not all decretals were treated as laws. Often, however, they imposed a norm to be applied to relevant cases. From the middle of the 11th century, decretals began to be increasingly issued as the papacy became centralized and thus gave more responses to various appeals within the Western Church. In the middle of the 12th century, Gratian composed a legal synthesis titled *Concordantia discordantium canonum* (*Concordance of Conflicting Canons*). It is better known as the *Decretum*. This work, considered as a *corpus iuris canonici* (a code containing the then effective ecclesiastical laws), became a model for later jurists who added to it. Decretals had been included in canonical collections, but after Gratian they grew as the chief element in collections. Under the influence of Gratian, the father of the science of canon law, decretals were approached with all the rigor of this science, commented on, and classified under different species and subspecies. The commentators on these post-Gratian collections are usually called decretalists. In time, some of these collections became officially recognized, such as that of Bernard of Pavia (composed ca. 1187–1191), an official text at the **University** of Bologna.

**DENYS THE CARTHUSIAN (DENYS OF RIJKEL/DENYS DE LEEU-WIS) (1402–1472).** Denys of Rijkel, born in Limburg, studied in the **Arts Faculty** at Cologne, where he became a master in 1424. He then joined the **Carthusians** in Roermund and became one of the most prolific authors of the Middle Ages, producing a corpus that fills 44 volumes in its modern edition. He was a correspondent with **Nicholas of Cusa**, to whom he dedicated a few of his works. He wrote commentaries on all the books of Scripture, on the complete corpus of **Dionysius the Pseudo-Areopagite**, and on **Boethius**'s *Consolation of Philosophy*, and he even produced in his cell, not at a university, a lengthy detailed *Commentary on the Sentences* of **Peter Lombard**. This 15th-century author shows his opposition to the teaching of both **realist** and **nominalist** theologies in the 14th century by ignoring them. He does at rare times criticize **John Duns Scotus** and **Durandus**, but he favors the theological teachings of **Hugh of Saint-Victor**, **William of Auxerre**, St.

**Bonaventure**, **St. Thomas**, and **Henry of Ghent**. His favorite author is Dionysius the Pseudo-Areopagite, and he stays close to those he considers his closest followers, especially **Albert the Great** and Henry of Ghent.

**DESCARTES, RENÉ (1596–1650).** Generally considered the father of modern philosophy, Descartes ushers in a new philosophical approach that breaks from the ancient and medieval tradition. His approach explicitly rejects (philosophical and theological) tradition as a viable source in the search for truth and seeks to ground all certitude in the activity of thinking, whose first truth is "I think, therefore I am." Descartes's work represents the end of the historical period of medieval philosophy and the beginning of properly modern currents of thought. Refer to the introduction, "Modern Criticisms of Medieval Philosophy and Theology."

**DEVILS.** *See* ANGELS.

***DEVOTIO MODERNA.*** The *devotio moderna* (modern devotion) was a reform movement of the late Middle Ages advocating an evangelical and apostolic way of life. Though it had its roots in the early Middle Ages with the women's religious movement, it grew significantly around 1375, partly as a reaction against abuses in the Church. The movement is associated with **Geert Groote** (1340–1384) of Deventer, a master at the University of Paris, who founded a community for religious women in 1374 after experiencing a religious conversion. After this, various similar brotherhoods and sisterhoods emerged, composed of men or women dedicated to a simple, austere life of religious work and spiritual devotion. In many respects, this movement aimed at the revival of declining monastic life. In 1387, the Brethren of the Common Life of Deventer founded a convent in Windesheim, while the Sisters of the Common Life of Deventer formed their own at Diepenveen around 1400. Several other such settings followed. Mystical thinkers, such as **Meister Eckhart,** were a source of inspiration for the movement. In the 16th century, with the Reformation and Counter-Reformation, the *devotio moderna* lost influence. *See also* ORDERS (RELIGIOUS).

**DIALECTICS.** Ancient authors, especially **Aristotle** and his ancient commentators and translators, greatly influenced the medieval understanding of dialectics or **logic**. Medieval thinkers studied and developed Aristotelian logic and applied it in new ways, most notably in theology. For example, Christian theologians used logical distinctions when seeking some clarity concerning the mystery of the Trinity, and medieval Jews and Muslims applied logic to issues concerning divine names and attributes. Aristotle considered logic as a necessary instrument for scientific inquiry, and his logical works are often referred to as an "instrument" or *Organon*. This collection is made up of *Categories*, an account of the 10 broadest classes or genera (i.e., substance, quantity, quality, relation, where, when, position, state, action, and passion); *On Interpretation*, dealing with propositions; *Prior Analytics*, dealing with argument validity; *Topics*, a treatise on dialectic understood as arguments based on generally accepted opinions; *Posterior Analytics*, dealing with demonstrative or scientific arguments; and *Sophistical Refutations*, dealing with argumentative fallacies. Only some of the highlights in the transmission of Aristotelian logic to the Middle Ages will be mentioned here.

Between the fifth and seventh centuries, translations of the *Organon* were made from Greek into Syriac by Nestorians (mainly) and Jacobites, and the first books of the *Organon* received a number of commentaries at that time. When the Muslims took over the Fertile Crescent in the seventh century, Arabic became the official language of the empire; at this point most translations were still from Greek to Syriac (a form of Aramaic that had become a literary language), though translations from Greek into Arabic began. Translations from Syriac into Arabic only took place up to the 10th century. Some of the greatest translators of this period were the two ninth-century Christian Nestorians Hunayn ibn Ishaq and his son Ishaq ibn Hunayn, whose work helped create a technical philosophical Arabic. Other outstanding figures were 'Abd Allah ibn al-Muqaffa (d. 757), who wrote epitomes on the *Isagoge* or *Introduction to Aristotle's Logic* by **Plotinus**'s student Porphyry (ca. 232–ca. 305) and the first books of the *Organon*, and the Syrian Ibn Bahriz, who wrote epitomes on the whole *Organon*. Works such as these contributed to the growth of dialectics in Islam. Medieval Jewish philosophy, which took place in Islamic and Christian regions, also yielded Hebrew translations and commentaries.

Latin translations and commentaries of the *Organon* formed in large part the basic sources of medieval dialectic or logic in Christian Europe. The *Categories* was translated by Marius Victorinus and paraphrased by Albinus in the fourth century. **Boethius** (ca. 480–ca. 525) provided a more exact translation of this work and included a commentary. In the beginning of the 10th century, a composite edition was made by an unknown author, relying greatly on Boethius's version. Porphyry's *Introduction to Aristotle's Logic* was translated by Boethius. Subsequently, a complement to the *Categories* titled *The Book of Six Principles* was prepared by either **Gilbert de la Porrée** or **Alan of Lille**. Boethius translated *On Interpretation*, a version superior to Marius Victorinus's earlier one (of which only fragments remain). Moreover, Boethius wrote two expositions of *On Interpretation*. The second commentary contains important analyses of the text by Greek commentators, especially Porphyry and Ammonius. *Topics*, *Prior Analytics*, and *Sophistical Refutations* were also known in the Latin West through Boethius's translations. Another translation of this last work from the 12th century, probably by **James of Venice**, also survives. *Posterior Analytics* was translated by James of Venice in the first half of the 12th century, and by **Gerard of Cremona** from an Arabic paraphrase of Abu Bishr.

In the medieval Latin West, *Categories*, *On Interpretation*, and Porphyry's *Introduction to the Organon* constituted what is called the "Old Logic" (*Logica Vetus*), while *Prior Analytics*, *Topics*, *Sophistical Refutations*, *Posterior Analytics*, and *The Book of Six Principles* formed the "New Logic" (*Logica Nova*). Comments on the Old Logic began to appear in the 10th century when Gerbert of Aurillac taught logic at Reims. While Gerbert did glosses on the *Topics*, most commentaries on the New Logic did not appear until the 12th century. In the 11th and 12th centuries, before the Latin West began in the 13th century to gain fuller access to Aristotle's other more purely philosophical works, such as *Physics*, *On the Soul*, and *Metaphysics*, intellectual disputes in the European schools were primarily anchored in questions of logic, such as the status of universal terms and the use of dialectic in theology. Authors such as **Peter Damian** and **Bernard of Clairvaux** were generally suspicious of dialectics in theological questions. **Anselm of Canterbury**, on the other hand, employed logic extensively in theology, thus influencing the general spirit of later theological works.

**DIETRICH OF FREIBERG (ca. 1250–ca. 1320).** This **Dominican** philosopher and theologian first studied in Germany and then at Paris (1272–1274). He was a master in theology at Paris in 1296–1297. Dietrich was part of a distinguished group of German Dominicans, including **Ulrich of Strasbourg**, **Meister Eckhart**, and their principal influence, **Albert the Great**, the celebrated teacher of **Thomas Aquinas** and one of the outstanding 13th-century synthesizers of Greek philosophy and Christian wisdom. In Dietrich, as in Eckhart, one finds a strong influence of Neoplatonism, particularly that of Proclus. While **Aristotle**'s influence on medieval science was largely responsible for developments in natural philosophy, **Plato** had great influence in the mathematical sciences, including geometry and optics, in which Dietrich was interested. Following the tradition of Roger Bacon, he contributed to natural science, developing an explanation of the rainbow. His most important philosophical contributions, however, concern the human intellect. His major work, *On the Intellect and the Intelligible*, combines doctrines of Proclus, **Avicenna**, **Augustine**, and other Neoplatonic thinkers and argues for a creation out of nothing, in conformity with biblical understanding. The One of Neoplatonic thought, the highest of the intelligences or spiritual beings, creates according to an intellectual emanation.

Dietrich's cosmogony also contains a psychology that stresses the spirituality, substantiality, individuality, and divine origin of the human intellect. Like most medieval theologians, Dietrich maintained that God knows and creates all things through ideas in His intellect. The human intellect, however, is related to God in a closer way than other material creatures. The intellect is an image of God. The intellect's thought is like God in that, like God's thought, its true and primary, though implicit, object is God himself. This very knowing of God is what constitutes the human intellect. In knowing itself, the intellect knows God and all things, since being like God means that the human intellect possesses (implicit) knowledge of everything. Though the intellect does abstract knowledge from sensible things, its fundamental knowledge is not abstractive but intuitive. Abstraction is really a reminder of God, the cause of all. Moreover, the intellect's likeness to God also implies that the intellect has some role in constituting the objects of experience, as he explains in *On the Origin of the Things which belong to the Aristotelian Categories*. The intellect is not a power flowing from the essence of the human **soul** but is the cause of the soul, something whose very being is knowing, and thus being that is like the being of God. Thus, Dietrich joins Neoplatonic philosophy with **Augustinian** divine illumination. His work *On the Beatific Vision*, a part of his treatise *On the Three Difficult Articles*, develops these themes further. Dietrich's Christian Platonism represents a reaction against **Aristotelianism** and **Thomism**, a reaction that can already be seen in earlier Christian thinkers such as **Henry of Ghent** and in Dietrich's fellow Dominican, Meister Eckhart.

**DIONYSIUS THE PSEUDO-AREOPAGITE (PSEUDO-DIONYSIUS) (fl. ca. 500).** This is the name given to the author of the famous collection of theological treatises (written sometime before 528, when the corpus came into historical view) often called the *Corpus Areopagiticum* or *Corpus Dionysiacum*, one of the main sources of medieval thought. During the Middle Ages these writings were generally ascribed to St. Paul's Athenian convert, Dionysius the Areopagite, and thus the reverence given to these writings was partly due to the mistaken view of their authorship, which stems from the author's use of a pseudonym. Without their rich content, however, these writings would not have had such seminal impact. They circulated widely. In the Eastern Church, **Maximus the Confessor** commented on them in the seventh century and St. **John Damascene** made ample use of them in the eighth century. In western Europe, **John Scotus Eriugena** in the ninth century translated them from Greek to Latin and commented on them. Others, such as **Hugh of Saint-Victor**, **Robert Grosseteste**, **Albert the Great**, and **Thomas Aquinas**, also commented on them. It gradually became evident to scholars that since the corpus was a synthesis of a developed **Neoplatonism** and Christianity, it had to be from a later period than that of the historic Dionysius the Areopagite. The question of the authorship of the writings also led to questions of orthodoxy, and opinions differed in this latter matter. The corpus consists of *De divinis nominibus* (*On Divine Names*), *De mystica* *theologia* (*On Mystical Theology*), *De coelesti hierarchia* (*On the Celestial Hierarchy*), *De ecclesiastica hierarchia* (*On the Ecclesiastical Hierarchy*), and 10 letters.

For the author, there is a positive and a negative way of approaching God, and these two are often combined. In *On Divine Names* he stresses the former, which consists in ascribing to God the perfections found in creatures that are compatible with God's spiritual nature—in this approach, goodness plays a prominent role. Even though such perfections can be attributed to God, they must be attributed to Him without the limitations that these spiritual or pure perfections have in creatures—in this sense, the approach is negative. These perfections should be understood (as far as possible, since God is ultimately incomprehensible to us) as existing in God in a most eminent way, that is, in an infinitely better way than the way they are found in creatures. The negative way, emphasized in *On Mystical Theology*, consists in excluding from God the limitation of perfections found in creatures. This distinction between positive and negative ways shows the influence of Proclus, the author who transmitted this approach to Christian philosophy and theology.

In Pseudo-Dionysius's view of the Trinity, the Neoplatonic influence is sharp. Though Pseudo-Dionysius maintains in God the distinction between the divine persons, he seems to stress the undifferentiated unity and total transcendence of the Neoplatonic First Principle to such an extent that some have seen in his account a failure to fully uphold the orthodox Christian position on the Trinity: three really distinct persons in one substance. With respect to creation, Dionysius the Pseudo-Areopagite combines Neoplatonic emanation with the Christian doctrine of creation. In creation (an intellectual emanation), God, who is pure goodness (as **Plato** had already noted in the *Timaeus*), gives of himself to the world, while still remaining in himself transcendent. Creation, however, is spoken of in terms likening it more to a natural, spontaneous act of goodness (in the way that Christians conceive of the necessary emanations of the Trinity) than a free, willing act, as Christian orthodoxy conceives of creation. In the Neoplatonic mode, the author stresses that God is the origin and end of all, reality circulating from and to the Good, a core idea of Neoplatonism that becomes the property of later Christian theologians.

Consonant with his conception of God as pure goodness and the origin of all is the author's approach to the question of evil: evil is a privation or the absence of a due goodness, not a positive reality in itself. This position is quite in line with the Neoplatonic tradition, including Augustine's teachings. In some of his accounts, such as the accounts of the Trinity and creation, there seem to be in Dionysius some tensions between Neoplatonism and Christianity. His writings, however, proved themselves fecund in later refinements in the ongoing syntheses of Greek philosophy and Christian revelation, as we see especially in many medieval Christian authors.

**DISPUTATION.** Refer to the introduction, "Methods of Study."

**DOCTORS OF THE CHURCH.** *See* FATHERS OF THE CHURCH.

**DOMINICANS.** *See* ORDERS (RELIGIOUS).

**DOMINICUS GUNDISSALINUS.** *See* GUNDISSALINUS (GUNDISAL-VI), DOMINICUS (ca. 1125–ca. 1190).

**DONATUS, AELIUS (fl. MID-4TH CENTURY).** This Roman teacher of grammar and rhetoric (one of his students was St. Jerome) was an important source for the teaching of the **liberal arts** in the Middle Ages. His *Ars maior* and *Ars minor* were part of the curricula at various schools and universities. His literary work also includes commentaries on Terence and Virgil.

**DUNS SCOTUS, JOHN, BL. (ca. 1266–1308).** A native of Duns in southern Scotland, Scotus did his early studies at the **Franciscan** convent of Northampton. He began his theological studies at Oxford around 1288 and completed them under William of Ware, regent master from 1291 to 1293. In the fall of 1302 he moved to Paris and began a new set of lectures on **Peter Lombard**'s *Sentences*, called the *Reportationes Parisienses* (*Parisian Reports*) under **Gonsalvus of Spain**. Like all foreigners who sided with **Boniface VIII**, he was exiled to England by Philip the Fair in 1303. He returned to Paris in 1304 to complete the *Reportationes*, and he was promoted to master of theology in 1305. He left Paris in 1307 to become a **lector** at the Franciscan convent in Cologne, where he died and was buried in 1308. Named the Subtle Doctor, Duns Scotus deserves the title for developing highly detailed and well nuanced positions in his efforts to settle the intense conflicts in Paris between **Thomas Aquinas**, **Henry of Ghent**, **Godfrey of Fontaines**, and their followers.

Duns Scotus's philosophical works generally date from the early part of his life, before 1288 when he began his theological studies. However, there are later revisions to some of these philosophical texts, as are evident especially in regard to Books VII–IX of the authentic nine books of his *Commentary on the Metaphysics*. His other commentaries are on Porphyry's *Isagoge* or *Introduction to Aristotle's Categories* and on the following texts of Aristotle: *Questions on the Categories*, two works on Aristotle's *Perihermeneias*, *Questions on the Sophistical Refutations*, and his *Quaestiones in De anima* (*Questions concerning On the Soul*), with later corrections by **Antonius Andreas**. His *Theoremata* is also an authentic work, though it was later corrected by **Maurice de Portu**.

Scotus's strongest contributions are in **theology**. His *Lectura in Sententias* (*Lecture on the Sentences*), begun around 1288, was followed by a more developed and deliberately arranged form of these lectures, called the *Ordinatio* or *Opus Oxoniense*, completed at Oxford before the end of the century. But he was quite likely revising this *Ordinatio* in 1300, and certainly during the school year 1301–1302. We know of a first collection of *Collationes* (or disputations or conferences) that must also be connected with Oxford. When Scotus moved to Paris in 1302, his *Reportationes Parisienses*, particularly on Book I, show a more mature response than the *Ordinatio* to the teachings of Henry of Ghent and Godfrey of Fontaines. The collection of **Quodlibet** questions, dating from Paris in the academic year 1306–1307, must likewise be taken as representing Scotus's most mature thought. His second *Collationes*, whose authenticity is verified by **William of Alnwick**, also derives from Paris. Finally, although the *De primo principio* (*On the First Principle*), which provides a full treatment of the transcendentals as well as formal proofs for the existence and infinity of God, is without doubt the work of Scotus, half of its text comes verbatim from the *Ordinatio*, and it thus has the character of a compilation. The works of Scotus, then, especially but not exclusively the theological works, are very complicated texts: he revised his original manuscripts over time, providing numerous additions and annotations, and his secretaries and students filled in many places that were incomplete.

In developing his description of theology, Scotus principally examined the positions of Henry of Ghent and Godfrey of Fontaines. Henry claimed for theologians a special light that provides enough evidence or understanding to warrant declaring theology a science of the realities of the Christian **faith**. While denying any special light and without reducing theology principally to a study of Scripture passages that justify the Church's beliefs, Scotus argued that believers can have some science or knowledge of the objects of Christian faith, since Christians develop arguments, especially **metaphysical** ones, that support Christian truths, and thus, while remaining believers, they go beyond the knowledge of the simple believer.

In his effort to guarantee some knowledge of the realities proclaimed in the Scriptures, Scotus went beyond Henry of Ghent's peculiar doctrine of **analogy** and defended man's ability to have a univocal concept predicable of God and creatures. It is a concept that prescinds from the proper modes of "infinite" and "finite" and that is presupposed by our analogous, proper concepts of God and creatures. It is by efforts such as these that Scotus attempts to solve the intellectual conflicts left by his predecessors. He makes these and other adjustments to respond to the tensions left especially by the teachings of Henry of Ghent and Godfrey of Fontaines. These authors forced him to adopt a number of subtle developments in his thought. A consideration of these complications will help, at least in part, to explain his ever-evolving positions in the *Lectura*, the *Ordinatio*, and the *Reportationes Parisienses* and the constant efforts at clarification that are given by his early disciples: **Anfredus Gonteri**, Antonius Andreas, **Francis of Marchia**, **Francis of Meyronnes**, **Henry of Harclay**, **Hugh of Newcastle**, **John of Bassolis**, **Peter of Aquila**, and William of Alnwick. *See also* ORDERS (RELIGIOUS).

**DURANDUS OF SAINT-POURÇAIN (ca. 1275–1334).** A Dominican friar, his academic career began around 1308 with the first redaction of his ***Commentary on the Sentences** of Peter Lombard*. This was at a time when the **Dominican** order was rallying around the teachings of **Thomas Aquinas** by requiring its members to avoid criticizing them and even to teach and defend them. Durandus was a disagreeing rebel who was criticized by the future general minister of the Dominican order, **Hervaeus Natalis**, who also led the movement that pushed for the canonization of St. Thomas. Durandus wrote two later commentaries on Lombard's *Sentences*, one in 1310–1312 that makes some compromises toward St. Thomas and another after 1316 wherein he returns to many of his earlier positions. Since only the third redaction has been published, editions of the first two redactions could clarify his changes of opinion in more detail. Durandus also has left three *Quodlibets*, dating from the years 1313–1317, and a *Treatise on Habits* written around the same time.

Durandus provides us with a summary of the various conceptions of the nature of **theology** in the prologue to the first redaction of his *Commentary on Book I of the Sentences*. According to him, *theology* at the time had three meanings. The first identifies it with sacred Scripture, whose teaching is accepted because it is divinely revealed. The second meaning is the human science whereby from the things revealed in the Scriptures more explicit further truths are deduced by using many biblical statements to deepen and extend the Christian understanding of God's revelation. Durandus tells us that this way of doing theology is the form that is most dominant in his era. The third meaning is given to the effort that theologians dedicate to defending and clarifying the faith by employing nonbiblical sources—an effort Durandus describes as "declarative and defensive theology." One of the chief issues that puts Durandus at odds with Thomas Aquinas in philosophy seems to be his theory of relations. Here he seems to be influenced by **Henry of Ghent** and **James of Metz**, and he appears to be anticipating the teaching of **William of Ockham**.

**EADMER OF CANTERBURY (ca. 1060–ca. 1130).** A Benedictine monk, born near Canterbury, who entered the monastery there that was under the direction of **Lanfranc**. He served as chaplain to **Anselm**. His *Vita sancti Anselmi* (*Life of Saint Anselm*) earned him the renown of being the first great English historian after **Bede**. Most notable among his theological works is his *Tractatus de conceptione sanctae Mariae* (*Treatise on the Conception of Blessed Mary*), the earliest theological treatise defending Mary's Immaculate Conception. *See also* ORDERS (RELIGIOUS).

**ECKHART, MEISTER (1260–1328).** Even though this German **Dominican**, from the school of **Albert the Great** and **Dietrich of Freiburg**, is primarily known as a mystic, since he was a mystical writer and a leader in the mystical way of life, he was also known as a theologian. He was master of theology at Paris in 1302–1303 and from 1311 to 1313. His works contain many influential and original philosophical ideas. A highly controversial figure who has been variously interpreted, he held theses that were condemned in 1329, shortly after his death. He was one of the first medieval theologians to write, aside from works in Latin (e.g., *Parisian Questions* and *Three-Part Work*), in the vernacular purposely for wide audiences (sermons and treatises in Middle High German), where some of his most important notions are to be found. In Eckhart, **Neoplatonic** ideas receive tremendous vigor. He takes the traditional idea that God is a being who thinks and interprets it in the (rather original) sense that God is because He thinks. Thus he challenges the whole tradition that conceives of God as the supreme being: he makes thinking somehow higher than being and the cause of being. However, in relation to creatures, God may be understood as containing all the perfections of creatures in a most eminent way, including the perfection by which he makes them exist. His conception of the human **soul** is also quite original. Like Dietrich of Freiburg, Eckhart stresses the divine character of the human intellect, but he goes even further. Whereas Dietrich sees the intellect as an image of God and as permanently turned toward God, for Eckhart the "basis" (*grunt*) or "spark" (*vunke*) of the soul does not belong to the soul, though it is in it. It is something uncreated and uncreatable; the true I is in fact God. Thus, Eckhart develops, with far-reaching consequences, the tradition of Albert the Great, according to which the highest part of the soul (the intellect) is made divine through its ability to be filled with knowledge derived from God.

Despite the many echoes of **Aristotelian** philosophy found in his writings, and despite the dominance of Aristotle and his commentators in the schools, Eckhart is someone who went back to the Neoplatonic tradition and contributed to the revitalization of that tradition, as seen in the work of later thinkers such as **Nicholas of Cusa**. These thinkers, when they used Aristotelian philosophy, generally subordinated it to their Neoplatonic principles. In their work, it was **Augustine** and **Dionysius the Pseudo-Areopagite** who most informed them.

**EDMUND OF ABINGDON (ca. 1174–1240).** Edmund studied grammar at Oxford and the **liberal arts** at Paris before 1190. He returned as a master of arts at Oxford (1195–1201). According to **Roger Bacon**, Edmund lectured there on the *Sophistical Refutations* of **Aristotle**. He went back to Paris to study **theology** and returned to Oxford probably around 1214. **Robert Bacon**, who became a master of theology before 1209, claims to have attended Edmund's lectures and to have been his assistant. In 1222, Edmund was appointed treasurer of Salisbury Cathedral, and in 1234 he became archbishop of Canterbury. He died on 15 November 1240 and was canonized shortly thereafter. His teaching is known first of all through his unedited *Moralities on the Psalms* and his *Speculum Ecclesiae* (*Mirror of the Church*), a collection of Scriptural glosses with a strongly moral bent, close to the style of **Stephen Langton** and **Peter the Chanter**. The moral character of his theology is revealed through his *Speculum religiosorum* (*Mirror of Religious*), a treatise showing religious how they may become holy through daily prayer and contemplation, a program whose goal is union of the **soul** with God that is strongly indebted to **Hugh of Saint-Victor** and **Richard of Saint-Victor**.

**ERIUGENA.** *See* JOHN SCOTUS ERIUGENA (ca. 810–ca. 877).

**ETHICS AND POLITICS.** This entry focuses on ethics and politics as present in medieval philosophy and **theology**. As subjects of study, ethics and politics are there interrelated, as they are also in Greek philosophy. Ethics considers the voluntary human actions leading to the best life and goals, and politics seeks an account of the state or community most fit toward these ends. This interrelation between ethics and politics is evident in the most influential Greek philosophical texts for these subjects in the Middle Ages, namely in **Plato**'s *Republic* and *Laws*, on the one hand, and in **Aristo-**

tle's *Nicomachean Ethics* and *Politics*, on the other. In Plato, the well-being (virtue) of the **soul** and the well-being of the state are both analogous and connected; in Aristotle, the *Politics* is introduced as a discussion complementary to the *Ethics*, since man, for Aristotle, is not a lone individual but "a social animal." Again, as in the Greek philosophy informing it, medieval ethics and politics are formulated as consistent with fundamental **metaphysical** and epistemological doctrines. In Plato and Aristotle, happiness consists primarily in knowledge, and so their (different) accounts of the human good depend on their (different) accounts of knowledge and reality. This grounding of ethics and politics in an overall conception of knowledge and reality is indeed pronounced in Jewish, Christian, and Islamic thought, where the God of revelation is the source and goal of human life. Thus, medieval thinkers, giving accounts of the path to God, amply discussed the nature, the habits, and the immortality of the soul. However, both Plato and Aristotle conceived of the highest good in terms of philosophic wisdom, and thus as available only to the few. On the other hand, medieval thinkers, even those for whom philosophy is the best way to God, incorporated more explicitly into their ethical and political frameworks God's accessibility to all men and his universal providence.

Aside from Greek philosophical texts, the other chief source in medieval ethics and politics is divine revelation, where the order created by God dictates the right rules and purpose of human conduct. As is the case with medieval philosophy and theology in general, medieval ethics and politics can be understood as a development growing out of two sources, reason and revelation, mutually informing each other: philosophy is developed in light of the basic doctrines of Scripture, and Scripture is interpreted in light of what is evident to reason. Thus, aside from various authors' doctrinal preferences, alternatives in regard to medieval ethics and politics among Judaism, Christianity, and Islam result largely either from differences of philosophical tradition or of religious tradition, or both. In terms of philosophic tradition, Aristotle's *Ethics*, available to Muslims and Jews by the ninth century, was not available in Latin in the Christian West until the 12th century (and better translations of it were made in the 13th). In the case of the *Politics*, its first translation into Latin was **William of Moerbeke**'s in the latter part of the 13th century, when it became the chief political text for Christian thinkers. Previously it was unavailable to medieval Muslims and Jews. Thus, various Islamic and Jewish Aristotelians still drew heavily from Plato in their political formulations. In the case of Plato's *Republic* and *Laws*, they were unavailable in Latin until the Renaissance, though medieval Christian thinkers had knowledge of basic Platonic ethical and political doctrines through the reports of ancient authors, such as **Cicero** and **Augustine**. In the Latin West,

Augustine's synthesis of **Platonism** and Christian wisdom as found primarily in his *City of God* dominated ethical and political doctrines. In the late 13th century, Aristotelianism emerged as the other chief influence.

In terms of religious tradition, Christian thinkers stressed the fallen state of human beings and their need of divine **grace** for salvation, to the extent that practically all, whether within the Aristotelian or Augustinian tradition, saw the moral and intellectual accomplishments based on human natural powers alone, which included philosophic wisdom, as insufficient. (Latin **Averroists** who formulated a version of happiness according to purely philosophic principles, such as **Siger of Brabant** and **Boethius of Dacia**, are the exceptions.) This insufficiency and the concomitant need of supernatural assistance are certainly stressed by a number of Jewish and Muslim authors in the context of their religious traditions; **Judah Halevi** and **Al-Ghazali**, both of whom elicited a significant following in Judaism and Islam respectively, are examples. However, among Jewish and Islamic philosophers, the fairly close identification between the human good attainable according to nature, as described by philosophers, and the human good as described by revelation was not uncommon. The highest beatitude of the next life is often described as the activity of the immortal part of the soul, the intellect, occasioned primarily by the pursuit of philosophy in this life. Among these same thinkers, one also finds the conception of religion as the popular expression of philosophy, resulting in the fairly close identification of the philosopher-king of Plato's *Republic* with the legislator-prophet. Some or all of these attitudes may be seen in **Al-Farabi**, **Avicenna**, and **Averroes** in the Islamic tradition, and in **Isaac Israeli**, **Gabirol**, **Gersonides**, and (some would argue) **Maimonides** in the Jewish tradition.

Another religious difference bearing upon ethics and politics between Judaism and Islam, on the one hand, and Christianity, on the other, has to do with the relation between religious and political authority. In Judaism and Islam, they are intimately fused together, religious law governing the political community. On the other hand, in medieval Christianity, debates concerning the powers of the Church and the state, and the emergence of religious and civil laws as distinct, were significant elements. In Islam and Judaism the main task of the legislative dimension of ethics and politics was interpreting and applying the religious law, and philosophy could have a role in this. In Christianity, philosophy could play a role in formulations of the distinction and relation between religious and civil powers. In the case of **Marsilius of Padua**, a representative of "political Averroism," philosophy was used to develop a theory of the state as separate from religion. Finally, in addition to the representatives of *falsafah* (philosophy) and *kalam* (theology) in Islam and of Jewish philosophy and theology, philosophical and theological ideas bearing upon ethics and politics may be found in representatives of **Sufism** and **Cabala**, Islamic and Jewish mysticism respectively.

**EUCHARIST.** Derived from the Greek *eucharistia*, meaning "thanksgiving," this term first appears in the first century. The Eucharist is the central sacrament of the Church, "the source and culmination of all Christian life" (Vatican Council II, *LG* 11). In addition to its first meaning as a liturgical activity, *Eucharist* refers to the body and blood of Christ received under the species or appearances of bread and wine. In the New Testament, Christ takes bread and wine, identifies them with his body and blood, and tells others to eat and drink them. From this context, the Eucharist is seen as a sacrifice: Jesus, giving his body and blood for men. The issue of the extent to which Jesus's presence in the bread and wine is real or symbolic became strongly debated in the West beginning in the ninth century, and the Church emphasized the physical presence of Christ in the Eucharist in very explicit terms. In the 12th century, theologians started using *transubstantiation* (employed by the Fourth Lateran Council in 1215), or the change of the substance, to refer to the type of change that occurs in the Eucharist. As **Thomas Aquinas** and other **Scholastics** put it, the **accidents** of the bread and wine remain, while the substance becomes the body and blood of Christ.

The Eucharist, along with the Trinity, is one of the Christian truths known as "a mystery." That God is triune, in some sense both one and three, and that in the exceptional case of the Eucharist there can be a change of substance without a change in accidents are beliefs to be taken on **faith**. Nevertheless, theologians still had to provide some account or justification for them. Even though as articles of faith these mysteries are not susceptible to demonstration, theologians focused on how arguments seeking to demonstrate the falsehood of these mysteries are inconclusive. Basically they argue that the realm of faith is neither reducible to nor contrary to reason. Theologians claiming to demonstrate the Eucharist or the Trinity, reducing the authority of revelation and faith to human reason, were generally considered heretical, as was the case with **Berengar of Tours**, who was criticized by **Anselm**'s teacher **Lanfranc of Bec**.

**EXEGESIS.** Medieval exegesis or textual interpretation focused primarily on the only text considered as offering salvation—revelation (the Torah for Jews, the New and Old Testaments for Christians, and the **Koran** for Muslims). This divinely revealed status of the Scriptures was enough to make the study of revelation the most important study. Authored by a transcendent God through human agency, these holy writings inherently demanded more than purely literal interpretation. The words of revelation, normally employed for interactions among human beings, may both reveal and conceal the divine message. In its effort to delve into revelation adequately, the medieval tradition produced a variety of exegetical approaches, some of which sought the assistance of secular disciplines, such as the traditional **liberal arts** and philosophy (or *falsafah* in Arabic). Exegesis was presupposed in the main areas of religious thought, namely law, **theology** (*kalam* in Arabic), **mysticism** (including Jewish **Cabala** and Islamic **Sufism**), and philosophy, to the extent that these areas sought agreement with revelation. Medieval philosophers and theologians of the three traditions faced and met in different ways the twofold exegetical challenge of revising the philosophical tradition in the light of revelation and interpreting Scriptural revelation with the help of philosophy. Thus, practically every thinker in this Dictionary engaged in his own way in exegesis. Only by studying them individually and on their own terms can one obtain the concrete details of their exegesis. Below we can make only general remarks concerning exegesis in the three traditions. The section on Latin exegesis is the most extensive, since we also deal with aspects of Jewish and Islamic exegesis in other general entries, namely **Jewish Philosophy and Theology**, Cabala, *falsafah*, *kalam*, and Sufism.

The Jewish **Torah** includes both the written law (the Pentateuch) and the oral law revealed to Moses, along with the written law and oral law passed on through rabbinic tradition. This oral law was codified in the **Talmud** and is considered by all Jews except **Karaites** to be part of the Torah and as necessary for proper understanding of the written law. Thus, the Torah itself includes a strong tradition of exegesis. Since the time of Ezra, in the fifth century B.C., Jews engaged in midrash, the rabbinic term for investigation into the meaning of Scripture. The fruits of this endeavor were collections of midrashim, or bible commentaries, in which four senses of Scripture were generally recognized: *peshat* (literal), *remez* (allegorical), *derash* (homiletical), and *sod* (hidden/mystical). Moreover, two leading schools of midrash were formed, that of Rabbi Akiva (ca. 45–135) and that of Rabbi Ishmael (fl. ca. 100–130). Both of these schools produced important works. A significant difference between them, however, is that the school of Rabbi Ishmael, holding that the Torah "speaks the language of men," tended to stress the literal sense of the Scriptures, i.e., *peshat*, more than the school of Rabbi Akiva.

In the Middle Ages, Jews in Islamic lands were influenced by Islamic culture. **Saadiah Gaon**, active in Babylon in the 10th century, translated the Bible into Arabic. His translation, along with the Hebrew original, became a standard among Jews of the Near East. Saadiah's exegesis was largely motivated by his debates against the Karaites, and he used both philology and philosophy to defend the legitimacy of the oral law. Saadiah became a model for exegetes in the next centuries. Medieval Spain also became an important center for Jewish exegesis. Along with the more philosophically informed exegesis of the **Neoplatonic** thinker Salomon **ibn Gabirol** in the 11th century, a strong philological trend may be seen among thinkers such as Johah Abu'l Walid Merwan ibn Janah (ca. 985–ca. 1040) and Moses ben Samuel ha-Kohen Gikatilla (d. ca. 1080). Abraham ibn Ezra (ca. 1092–1167), relying on rigorous grammar and a commonsense approach, produced a number of clear biblical commentaries containing a wealth of sources. He criticized especially what he saw as unfounded allegories (including midrashic interpretations), as well as the Karaites. David Kimhi (1105–1170), while respecting midrashic sources, still followed him in favoring the plain sense of the text. **Moses Maimonides**'s strong philosophical inclination (mainly **Aristotelian**) pushes him to use allegories to explain apparent inconsistencies in the Torah, as can be seen in his *Guide of the Perplexed*. This rational approach, and its concomitant allegorizing of the letter of Scripture, is even more marked in the Aristotelian **Gersonides**, active in France in the 14th century. This rational tendency to interpret the letter according to philosophical principles received criticisms. **Judah Halevi**, working before Maimonides, had already opposed philosophy in his defense of traditional Jewish wisdom. It should be noted that Jewish exegesis in Europe also influenced Christian approaches. The celebrated Rabbi **Solomon ben Isaac** (1040–1105) (also known as Rashi), the founder of a school, influenced important Christian exegetes, such as **Andrew of Saint-Victor** and **Nicholas of Lyra**, in their increasing appreciation of the literal sense of Scripture. Rashi is known for an approach to exegesis that is based on the proper establishment of context. Other important medieval Jewish exegetes are exponents of Cabala (the best-known cabalistic work is the *Zohar*, largely mystical midrashim), as well as pietistic thinkers known as Hasidé Ashkenaz. Finally, Karaites, rejecting the rabbinic tradition, focused their exegesis on the only revelation they accepted as authoritative: the whole written text of the Bible.

In the Christian tradition, the exegesis of the **Fathers of the Church** already interpreted biblical passages in various senses and at different levels. In general, Latin exegetes distinguished between the literal and the spiritual senses of Scripture, and within the spiritual sense they distinguished between the **allegorical**, the **anagogical**, and the moral senses. In the early medieval period, the spiritual sense was favored, often at the expense of the literal sense. However, the literal sense gradually gained importance, as may be seen, for instance, in the work of Andrew of Saint-Victor in the 12th century, and later on in the 13th century. To gain in precision, some scholars even sought to go beyond the Latin translation and equipped themselves with the requisite languages (Hebrew and Greek).

Earlier, in the sixth century, Gregory the Great, standing at the junction between the classical and the medieval periods and influenced by Patristic sources, such as Origen, Jerome, and **Augustine**, stressed the importance of maintaining a balance between the spiritual and literal senses. Taking metaphorically what should be understood literally or taking literally what should be understood metaphorically is error. The former, however, was much more likely in the early period, as exegesis was primarily grounded in the Patristic insight that the spiritual sense should be sought whenever possible. **Isidore of Seville** and **Bede** are some of the chief exegetes of the seventh and eighth centuries; the Carolingian Renaissance, with major figures such as **Alcuin** and **John Scotus Eriugena**, remained highly indebted to Patristic sources. At the end of this earlier medieval period, however, a greater awareness of the literal sense may be discerned in scholars such as **Rhabanus Maurus**, who studied Hebrew and revised the Vulgate, and Eriugena, who was competent in Greek. After the 10th century, a period of little exegetical production, the 11th century produced the first so-called **Scholastic** versions of exegesis, in contrast to the earlier exegesis of what is sometimes termed "Monastic theology." Whereas the exegesis from the 7th to the 11th century was primarily done by monks in the mode of recollection (knowing by heart any given passage, they were able to recall an array of associated notions and texts), after the 11th century the liberal arts (especially **logic** or **dialectics**), at schools and **universities**, increasingly began to provide a foundation for the practice of exegesis. The monastic style was still common, however, and some of its 12th-century adherents, such as **Bernard of Clairvaux** and **William of Saint-Thierry**, were suspicious of what they saw in some of their contemporaries' appropriation of logic into theology as an excessive rationalization of Scripture that could easily lead to heresy. Generally, however, biblical scholars regarded logic and the liberal arts as valuable tools, if used properly. It was on the extent and nature of its application that they differed.

With the increasing influence of dialectic came an increase in secondary and supplementary texts of various kinds. One of the first and greatest works in Scholastic exegesis was the *Glossa ordinaria* (a work gradually gathered from a number of glosses principally under the direction of **Anselm of Laon**), whereby Patristic texts were neatly placed as glosses alongside the Scriptural text. The exegetical work of **Peter Abelard** was important, as was the exegesis and theology of the school of Laon and the school of Saint-Victor, with such figures as **Hugh**, Andrew, and **Richard**. Paris, however, eventually became the most important center. After **Peter Lombard** wrote his *Sententiarum libri quattuor* (*Four Books of Sentences*) in 1155–1158, this work gradually became an undisputed companion to the Bible itself, dealing with the more difficult doctrinal questions facing the masters and scholars of Scripture. The *Sentences* retained this status well into the 16th century. In effect, then, when students in medieval universities in the 13th and later centuries wished to become masters of theology, they had the choice of writing commentaries on the Bible itself, on Lombard's *Sentences*, or on **Peter Comestor**'s *Historia Scholastica* (*Scholastic History*), a work that offered a unified vision of the history of God's people. The *Scholastic History* provided a historical order and unity to the Bible story, in contrast to Lombard's work, which followed a logical order of studying doctrinal questions.

Some of the most notable works of Scholastic theology, which were also among the greatest expressions of medieval philosophy, were commentaries on Lombard's *Sentences* (e.g., those of **Bonaventure**, **Aquinas**, and **John Duns Scotus**). This concern for logical order in theology pushed students of the Bible in a direction that would eventually lead to an orderly or scientific approach to theology. At its beginning, this logical tendency created an increased interest in well-defined themes or questions rather than following the flow of the Scriptural text itself. Later, it would lead to a linking together of these themes or questions according to a broader principle of order that formed a unified work, a **summa** or a treatise that aimed at being modeled on Aristotle's view of a science. Still, commentaries on the biblical texts themselves of both testaments were steadily produced throughout the Middle Ages.

With the influence of logic and philosophy came an emphasis on the literal sense in examining the Scripture texts. The literal sense was especially emphasized in *Commentaries on Lombard's Sentences* and summae, where logic and argument were applied in theology. Logical demands require a consistent signification for terms when they are used in arguments. The literal sense, however, as conceived by Thomas Aquinas and others, was understood broadly as the intended sense of the human authors, and it thus could include figurative language. Nicholas of Lyra, an influential follower of Aquinas who knew Hebrew and the rabbinic tradition, saw a twofold literal sense, the figurative and the obvious, as corresponding to the Old and New Testaments respectively. Nevertheless, the spiritual sense survived with its emphasis on allegory and symbolization and continued to be used by many as a means to furnish examples and allusions that conveyed moral and spiritual lessons. Even Nicholas of Lyra himself used it in his *Postilla Moralis* (1339), where he gives his view of the moral significance of the Bible. Important figures of 14th-century exegesis, which on the whole produced less in this area than did the 13th century, include **Robert Holcot**, **John Wycliffe**, and **John Gerson**.

In the early period of Islamic history, pressing tasks were the establishment of the so-called traditions (hadith) and the application of revelation to legal questions in the context of a growing empire. This challenge was met by various students of law. Then Islam, mainly through contacts with foreign traditions, faced the need to define itself as a unified and rationally defensible theological doctrine. This latter challenge was met by those who practiced *kalam* or theology, some of whom delved deeply into philosophy or *falsafah*. The Koran itself did not explicitly address a number of legal problems that arose as Islam matured and grew politically. In these cases, guidance was sought through the establishment of precedence in the living tradition of Muhammad, focusing on his customary practice (sunna). This approach and its abuses yielded at times a number of unreliable traditions. Scholars and exegetes then endeavored to establish reliable traditions through historical analysis. Al-Shafi'i (d. 820) propounded an approach that became widely recognized. The Prophet's sunna is the only authority for a tradition (hadith), and a tradition must consist of a chain of authoritative oral transmitters, as well as a text embodying the oral content. Traditions were then generally classified into sound, good, or weak. Written collections of traditions began to appear, first ordered according to the authority of the reports and later according to subject matter. Some of the most famous and authoritative collections are those of Malik ibn Anas (d. 795) and Ahmad ibn Hanbal (d. 855), both of which are arranged by subject, and those of Bukhari (d. 870) and Muslim (d. 875), arranged by authority.

The study of these collections, along with the Koran, is not only the principal subject in Islamic schools, law, and exegesis, but it is fundamental to Islam as a way of life grounded in a code of conduct. At first the principal criterion for the application of laws was generally textual or literal. Answers to specific questions should be grounded in the letter. This was not always easy, and so another approach emerged that also permitted itself the use of analogy and some independent judgment. These approaches are reflected in the four main schools of Islamic jurisprudence, which persist to this day. The schools founded by Abu Hanifah (d. 767) and Ash-Shafi'i (d. 820) are generally less literal than the schools founded by Malik ibn Anas (d. 795) and Ahmad ibn Hanbal (d. 855). This tension between the literal and the more liberal approach in legal interpretation was carried over into the field of theology.

Law purely on its own was not sufficient for the formulation of a rationally defensible and unified Islamic doctrine, and so theology emerged as a natural impulse to fulfill this need. However, to find doctrinal unity among seemingly incompatible passages, theologians were forced to go beyond the letter. This could be done in more than one way, however, and so different, conflicting theological approaches emerged, some relying on reason and philosophy more than others. In addition, there were those who opposed any kind of systematic theology, on the grounds that the role human reason played in it was bound to corrupt the truth embedded in Scripture and tradition, revealed by God's inscrutable will. To them, this truth should be sought purely through the analysis of language and history. Finally, there were those who used the philosophical tradition against philosophy and systematic theology, arguing for the sovereignty of law and tradition chiefly on the basis of the mysterious ways of God's supreme will. It was this latter group, the **Asharites**, that primarily established orthodoxy in theology, and its greatest spokesman was **Al-Ghazali** (Algazel), who is called the "proof" or "seal" of Islam. See also GLOSSA (INTERLINEAREA AND ORDINARIA).

# F

**FAITH.** Medieval treatises on faith most frequently centered attention on the words of the Letter to the Hebrews (11:1) attributed to the Apostle Paul: "Faith is the substance of things hoped for, the argument for things not seen." Although faith is also involved in the religious life of Jews and Muslims, these religions view themselves as religions of law; Christianity is seen by medieval writers primarily to be a religion of faith. Faith is the argument or ground for the realities of Christian belief, especially for the Triune God, the Incarnation of the Son of God, and the beatific vision of God as the fulfillment of human life. This centering on truth is not a purely medieval Christian construction. The **Fathers of the Church** often focused on this intellectual aspect of their religion. **St. Augustine** even presented the Hebrews text cited above as the definition of faith.

A further stimulus for the medieval focus on the truth aspect of faith came from the battle between **Peter Abelard** and **St. Bernard of Clairvaux** over Abelard's restatement of the traditional Pauline definition of faith. For Abelard, faith is "a judgment (*existimatio*) of things not seen." Bernard interpreted this alteration or substitution of "judgment" for "argument" or "conviction" to imply either that the Christian faith has the character of opinion or that each believer could choose the truths of the faith that he or she wishes to affirm. Abelard simply meant by judgment or *existimatio* that faith is not grounded on evidence that brings cognition. Faith, for him, does not provide experiential knowledge of the realities of the faith; it does not, however, exclude certitude. **Hugh of Saint-Victor** tried to resolve the dispute by attempting to present faith in contrast to opinion and evident knowledge: "Faith is the kind of certainty of the mind concerning things absent, established beyond opinion and short of knowledge."

In the early part of the 13th century, **William of Auxerre** in his *Summa aurea* (*Golden Summa*) tried to explain how a believer who accepted as certain the truths of the Christian faith could still look for arguments supporting it. He asks whether the Fathers of the Church and the masters of sacred Scripture did not appear to act perversely when they attempted to prove the articles of the faith by providing human arguments. After all, "faith is the argument for things not seen," not a conclusion justified by rationally grounded arguments. In his response, William offers three reasons why Christian teachers are justified in presenting rational arguments for the faith: first of all, natural reasons increase and strengthen the faith of believers, even though they are not the principal reason causing the faithful to assent to their truth. Second, arguments allow the learned to defend the faith against heretics. Third, arguments supporting Christian teaching lead the unlearned to accept the faith: they realize that learned believers have responses for the many objections that may come from nonbelievers. William concludes, "Nonetheless, when someone has true faith and also has reasons by which this faith can be manifested, he does not rest upon the First Truth because of these reasons, but rather he accepts these reasons because they agree with the First Truth (God) and bear witness to it." This would be the attitude of Christian theologians as they developed **theology** and used philosophy as the main instrument to help them do so.

**FALSAFAH, AL-.** The term *falsafah* in the Muslim intellectual tradition means literally "philosophy" (*falasifah*: philosophers). In contradistinction to **kalam** or **theology**, based on the revealed **Koran**, philosophy in Islam meant knowledge based on reason, inspired primarily by Greco-Roman philosophers. After **Al-Ghazali**'s attack on philosophy, the term could be used with a more polemical connotation, referring to a rationalism, associated with **Avicenna** primarily and with **Al-Farabi** secondarily, in conflict with *kalam* or theology. Philosophy in Islam grew as thinkers assimilated and developed classical philosophy, particularly Aristotle, Plato, and their followers, in various ways. Neither **Platonism** nor **Aristotelianism**, however, ever existed in their pure original form in medieval Islamic thought. Both were received as already combined to some extent (primarily through developments in Middle Platonism), and it was not uncommon for works to be misattributed. A famous example is the widely circulated *Theology of Aristotle*, a work of a **Neoplatonic** author (probably Porphyry) largely based on Plotinus. Both continued to be synthesized in various ways, and it was not rare for self-proclaimed Aristotelians, such as Al-Farabi, to favor important Platonic ideas. However, unlike the Arabic translations of Aristotle's works, it is uncertain whether any work of Plato was translated integrally into Arabic. Platonism was constructed in Islam primarily from summaries and versions of Plato, such as Galen's account of the *Timaeus*. Nevertheless there were translations from the *Republic*, the *Laws*, the *Timaeus*, the *Phaedo*, the *Crito*, and the *Sophist* (with Olympiadorus's sixth-century commentary); Hunayn ibn Ishaq (d. 873) and his school made the first translations of these works. Platonism was still a major influence; in **metaphysics** Neoplatonic emanationism largely dominated, and in **ethics and politics** Platonism's influence was even greater.

*Falsafah* also contributed to the formation of theology as a systematic discipline, which in turn preserved philosophy in Islam after the decline of philosophy as an independent pursuit. *Falsafah*, of non-Muslim origin, owed its growth in Islam to the translation of Greek philosophy into Arabic. Between the fifth and seventh centuries, the first Greek texts (primarily medical works and texts in **dialectics** or **logic**) began to be translated into Syriac (a form of Aramaic that had become a literary language) by Nestorians (mainly) and Jacobites. The Muslims took over the Fertile Crescent in the seventh century, and Arabic became the official language of the empire. At this point most translations were still from Greek to Syriac, though translations from Greek into Arabic followed, and, beginning in the 10th century, translations from Syriac into Arabic also were made. Translators, such as the two ninth-century Christian Nestorians Hunayn ibn Ishaq and his son Ishaq ibn Hunayn (d. 910), 'Abd Allah ibn al-Muqaffa (d. 757), and the ninth-century Syrian ibn Bahriz, contributed to the formation of a philosophical Arabic. **Al-Kindi** (d. ca. 870), active in Baghdad at the courts of Al-Ma'mun and Al-Mu'tasim, is considered the first Muslim philosopher. Collectively, his followers show interest in logic, metaphysics, natural science, ethics, and history, and in the relation between religion and philosophy. His students included the geographer Abu Zayd al Balkhi (d. 934), the historian and philosopher Ahmad ibn al-Tayyib al-Sarakhsi (d. 899), and the astronomer and historian Abu Ma'shar al-Balki (d. 866). The subsequent generation of Al-Kindi's so-called school was dominated by two students of Abu Zayd, the philosopher Abu al-Hasan al-'Amiri (d. 922) and the encyclopedist Ibn Farighun (fl. ca. 950).

*Falsafah* continued to thrive through the Peripatetic school at Baghdad. This school was an outgrowth of the philosophical school of Alexandria, begun around 900 when three Harran masters (al-Quwayri, Yuhanna ibn Haylan, and Abu Yahya al-Marwazi) began teaching philosophy professionally at Baghdad. It was different from Al-Kindi's in that its focus was purely philosophical, specifically Aristotelian. The great Al-Farabi was part of the first generation of students in this school, which produced a number of prestigious names, among them the Christian Yahha ibn 'Adi (d. 974), who influenced practically all major Baghdad intellectuals at the turn of the 11th century. This Baghdad school also resulted in a number of important philosopher-physicians; in fact, some of the greatest philosophers in medieval Islam (e.g., Avicenna, **Averroes**, and the Jewish thinker **Maimonides**) were also physicians. *Falsafah* reached new heights with Avicenna's Neoplatonized Aristotelianism in the eastern **caliphate** and with Averroes's more strict Aristotelianism at Cordoba, the capital of the western caliphate. The first major figure of Muslim philosophy in Spain is Ibn Bajjah (ca. 1070–1138), **Avempace** to the Latins. Philosophy practically died in Islam in the 12th century with Averroes (d. 1198), when Muslim orthodoxy began to regard philosophy with increasing suspicion. Averroes's influence was felt primarily among Jews and Christians, and only to a small extent in Islam, as evidenced by, for example, the work in social science and history of Ibn Khaldun (1332–1406) from Tunis. Islamic philosophy continued to develop mainly in terms of its influence on the former two traditions. However, elements also survived within Muslim scholastic theology, the *kalam.*

**FARABI, AL- (AL-FARABI) (ca. 870–ca. 950).** Abu Nasr Muhammad ibn Muhammad al-Farabi was probably of Turkish descent and was born in a district of the city of Farab (in Transoxania). He studied and taught at Baghdad, where he had contact with Christian philosophers and translators. From 942 until his death at Damascus, he remained mostly at Aleppo as a guest at the court of the Hamdanid ruler Sayf al-Dawalah. Farabi wrote on virtually all the philosophical disciplines, and a great number of works (over 100) have been attributed to him, though many (including commentaries on **Aristotle**) do not survive. There is evidence that for him **Plato** and Aristotle could and should be reconciled, an attitude that many thinkers of the three revealed religions adopted. Greatly revered in the Islamic intellectual tradition, he was called "the second teacher," Aristotle being the first. His influence was immense both in and outside of Islam. **Moses Maimonides**, the most influential medieval Jewish philosopher, apparently considered him to be the greatest of the Muslim philosophers. **Avicenna** claimed that, after much unsuccessful reading of Aristotle's *Metaphysics*, he finally came across a text of Al-Farabi (i.e., *On the Aims of Aristotle's Metaphysics*) that unlocked the chief goals of this work, a lesson that was to have a great impact in the history of philosophy.

In politics, Al-Farabi followed Plato primarily, especially the *Republic*; Aristotle's *Politics* was unavailable. In **dialectics** (**logic**), natural philosophy, and **ethics**, he relied chiefly on the Aristotelian tradition. His **metaphysics** and cosmology is a synthesis of Aristotelian and **Neoplatonic** elements, which also draws from Ptolemaic astronomy. Aristotle's prime mover is not only the final cause of all motion, according to Aristotle, but also, according to the Neoplatonists, the first cause from which all being emanates according to a hierarchy of intellects. This emanation descends all the way to the agent intellect that Aristotle speaks of in *De anima* III, 5, interpreted as the eternal principle governing the sublunary realm of generation and corruption. Human beatitude exists to the extent that the intellect approximates through acquisition of knowledge the pure intellectual actuality of the agent intellect.

The relative consistency and unity of Al-Farabi's work, as well as its ultimate intention, has been a source of debate among scholars. The problem has also been exacerbated by questions of authorship. Some scholars see him as harmonizing religion and philosophy, while others see him primarily as a philosopher for whom religion has a purely social function. He seems to be the originator of two greatly influential metaphysical positions: (1) the distinction between necessary and possible existence, which is used in proving the existence of God, who is necessary per se, and (2) the distinction between essence and existence, existence being something superadded to essence. These two metaphysical distinctions, whether adopted, rejected, or nuanced, are central subjects in fundamental debates and the source of important developments in subsequent metaphysics in Islam, Judaism, and Christianity. Avicenna, **Averroes**, Maimonides, and **Aquinas** developed some of their fundamental principles when approaching these questions. In his account of God, Farabi identifies the Neoplatonic One with Aristotle's thought thinking itself. God, who is wholly uncaused, contemplates Himself. From this contemplation, an intellect emanates that, like God, self-contemplates. Unlike God, however, this intellect depends on another, and so its contemplation is not only of self but also of its cause, namely God. From this first-emanated intellect, another proceeds that depends on it similarly. From this latter one another proceeds similarly, and so on until a 10th (the agent) intellect is produced. Each intellect governs its own celestial sphere (each sphere being identified with a celestial body) but exists separately from that sphere. The nine spheres are, in descending order, the first heaven, the sphere of the fixed stars, Saturn, Jupiter, Mars, the sun, Venus, Mercury, the moon, and the sublunary sphere of generation and corruption governed by the agent intellect. There is disagreement among scholars in regard to whether this emanation is for Al-Farabi voluntary or necessary and eternal; the evidence seems to favor the latter view.

His interpretation of Aristotle concerning the human intellect is also significant. Apparently following Aristotle's Greek commentator, Alexander of Aphrodisias, Farabi viewed the intellect as a power within the human body. The intellect acquires knowledge from sensible things through abstraction and thus becomes actualized according to its degree of acquisition of knowledge. In a way reminiscent of **Al-Kindi**'s distinctions, Farabi writes that "Aristotle set down the intellect which he mentioned in the *De anima* according to four senses, intellect in potentiality, intellect in actuality, acquired intellect and the agent intellect" (*The Letter Concerning the Intellect*, Hyman and Walsh, 215). These four senses correspond in ascending order to the levels in which intelligible forms are abstract in relation to matter. The agent intellect, the efficient cause of human thinking (as light causes vision), contains immutably the forms governing all sublunary processes. This conception of the intellect influences Al-Farabi's and other (e.g., Maimonides's) views on immortality, prophecy, and politics.

Individual immortality is fundamentally the incorporeal life of the intellect. It happens only to the few who attain the necessary actualization through knowledge. The **Koran**'s physical descriptions of the next life are metaphors for the masses. The prophet, both a philosopher and a political leader, possesses all the virtues, especially the intellectual virtues. As a legislator, the prophet takes on the role of Plato's philosopher-king, who governs well by judging in practical matters in light of his philosophical knowledge of the forms, especially the Good. Thus, the prophet, in addition to speculative knowledge, is able to convey this knowledge in the language of ordinary people, and in ways eliciting virtue. The highest knowledge (the prophet's) is chiefly philosophical or abstract, although it agrees with revelation. Revelation expresses the same truth as philosophy, though in metaphorical ways appropriate for orienting the masses, who are moved primarily through the imagination.

Ideally, political leaders should be philosophers who, like prophets, are able to convey their knowledge to the masses effectively and productively. The true philosopher is the one with this practical ability. Farabi calls the one who lacks this skill a false or vain philosopher. This political dimension of the relation between abstract knowledge and its popular manifestation depends on Farabi's conception of the relation between logic and grammar: the former contains universal truths expressed by the latter in conventional ways. This is then applied to the relation between religion and philosophy: "religion . . . is called popular, generally accepted, and external philosophy" (*The Attainment of Happiness*, Hyman and Walsh, 228). These positions, controversial in some religious circles, will be developed by major figures later on, such as Averroes and Maimonides. Farabi's view of religion and philosophy was interpreted by some as a belittling of religion or as a mere imitation of philosophy. Another side of the issue must also be considered: to Farabi, religion completes philosophy, putting it into practice.

Farabi integrates in seminal ways Aristotelianism and Neoplatonism within a Muslim framework. In the thought of practically all subsequent medieval thinkers, these three general components—Aristotelianism, Neoplatonism, and the principles of revealed religion—coexist in varying ways and proportions as the principal sources of intellectual life. Farabi's synthesis plays a major role in subsequent developments. Refer to the introduction, "The Beginning and Development of Medieval Arabian and Jewish Philosophy and Theology."

**FATHERS OF THE CHURCH.** They are the authors of the early Church who were generally known for their antiquity, orthodoxy, holiness, and Church approval, though some who held heretical or unorthodox positions enjoyed the title due to their great influence on the deeper understanding of the teachings of the Church. The Christian Fathers extend from the Apostolic Fathers, like Clement of Rome who died around 100, to the last of the Western Fathers, Isidore of Seville, who died around 636, and the last of the Eastern Fathers, John of Damascus, who died around 750. The more famous traditional Fathers of the Church were those who were also named Doctors, or chief teachers, of the Church. This was a group that for medieval writers included the Latin Fathers, Ambrose, **Augustine**, Jerome, and Gregory the Great, and the Greek Fathers, John Chrysostom, Basil, Gregory of Nyssa, Gregory of Nazianzus, and Athanasius. Augustine was the most influential Latin Father: he is quoted by the important medieval textbook writer **Peter Lombard** so often that many imagined Peter, as the **master** of the *Sentences*, to be a compiler of Augustinian quotations rather than an author in his own right. **Thomas Aquinas** indicated that Chrysostom was the most respected of the Greek Fathers when it came to his understanding of the Scriptures (*Lectures on the Gospel of St. John*, lect. II, n. 94).

The Fathers of the Church were not considered infallible. In a frank admission, St. Augustine in the introduction of his *Retractationes* indicated how much he feared God's words: "In a multitude of words you shall not avoid sin" (Proverbs 10:19). He feared the divine warning because he realized that many things could be collected from his "numerous disputations, which, if not false, yet may certainly seem or even be proved unnecessary" (*Retractationes* I, c. 1; PL 32:583–84). In his *Letter to Fortunatianus* (Ep. 148, n. 15; PL 33:628–29), Augustine went beyond the correction of his own works and extended the invitation of criticism to the works of others: "Still, we are not obliged to regard the arguments of any writers, however Catholic and estimable they may be, as we do the canonical Scriptures, so that we may not—with all due respect to the deference owed them as men—refute or reject anything we happen to find in their writings wherein their opinions differ from the established truth, or from what has been thought out by others or by us, with divine help. I wish other thinkers to hold the same attitude toward my writings as I hold toward theirs." Despite such solicitation for criticism by Augustine and others, the Fathers commanded great authority among medieval theologians as Christians who were attempting a more profound penetration of revelation. Such an effort demanded a loyal doctrinal communion with the Church, and although Tertullian and Origen might respectively have slipped into error by teaching the pure spiritual character of the Church and the preexistence of souls, they contributed strongly to the orthodox teachings of the Church by opposing errors and producing a deeper understanding of the faith. Refer to the introduction, "Faith and Reason."

**FICINO, MARSILIO (1433–1499).** Founder of the Platonic Academy in Florence, Ficino was in his early days influenced by **Aristotelian** Scholastic thinkers. When he later dedicated himself to **Plato** and the Platonic tradition, he began to view much of Aristotelian **Scholasticism** as antireligious and claimed that Christianity as the true religion needed a new marriage with a true and religious philosophy (Platonism). He dedicated himself to translating into Latin the works of Plato, Plotinus, and **Dionysius the Pseudo-Areopagite**. St. Augustine very much influenced the religious orientation of his reading of the Platonic tradition, and in Ficino's *Commentary on Plato's*

*Symposium*, the Christian charity of St. Paul and St. Augustine have informed and transformed Platonic love. His own major works are *Theologia Platonica* (*The Platonic Theology*) and *De Christiana religione* (*On Christian Religion*). His view of man as a bridge between the immortal and the mortal, with its portrait of man rising to God or descending to the earthly and mortal, had a strong impact on the philosophy of **Giovanni Pico della Mirandola**.

**FISHACRE, RICHARD (ca. 1206–1248).** This Oxford **Dominican** master, who lectured along with and succeeded **Robert Bacon**, was the first to be educated completely in England. He was also the first master to comment on the *Sentences* of **Peter Lombard** at Oxford, between 1241 and 1245. In following the move initiated by **Alexander of Hales**, Richard went against the desires of **Robert Grosseteste**, and this provided him with the occasion in his inaugural sermon to explain why he was doing so. He informs us that the traditional way of explaining Scripture was to offer a moral interpretation of the sacred text. Any attempts to deal with the more difficult doctrinal questions were shunted to afternoon discussions. Richard argued that by introducing the *Sentences* to the morning periods assigned for Scriptural classes, he was in effect uniting the two approaches to the study of the Scriptures. In other words, he considered that when you commented on the *Sentences*, you were finding another way, and a complementary way, of studying divine revelation. While commenting on the *Sentences* of Lombard, Richard often added sermons at the end of his lessons, which provided an affective dimension to his theoretical discussions. He was chided for this by the Franciscan **Richard Rufus**, who pointed out that a **master** had different offices he is obliged to carry out. Among these duties are the office of preaching and the office of treating difficult questions. The two functions, Rufus argued, should not be conflated: one should not preach in class. This well indicates the direction followed by other masters, for the *Commentary on the Sentences* by Fishacre seems to be the only surviving commentary that mixes together doctrinal discussions with sermons.

Throughout his *Sentences*, Fishacre refers to **Aristotle**, but he has not read him on the Philosopher's own terms. He cites him, but in general he reads him from an **Augustinian** perspective, unconsciously understanding his statements in a way that confirms the tradition that he has assimilated. His view of reality is basically Neoplatonic in its metaphysics. At times **Avicenna** seems to be his commentator. **Averroes**, with his paragraph-by-paragraph explanations of the Philosopher, has not yet entered Fishacre's world.

**FITZRALPH, RICHARD (ca. 1295–1360).** A native of Ireland, Richard came to Oxford before 1315 and became a master of arts there around 1322. His commentary on **Peter Lombard**'s *Sentences* dates from about 1327–1328. It is a work that already shows the manner in which such commentaries were written. It is a work that does not attempt to assimilate all the doctrinal matters treated by Peter Lombard but that centers more on the burning issues of his particular time. He is thus part of the trend in the method of commenting on the *Sentences* prevalent at Oxford in his era. His dialogue partners at Oxford were mainly **Adam Wodeham** and **Robert Holcot**, but he also had a strong influence on Parisian writers, perhaps through **Gregory of Rimini**, since he had some influence on **John of Mirecourt**, **Peter Ceffons**, and **John Wycliffe**. Richard is well known for his 1334 dispute at Avignon against the position of Pope John XXII concerning the beatific vision.

**FLAND, ROBERT.** *See* ROBERT FLAND (ROBERT OF FLANDERS) (fl. 1335–370).

**FONSECO, PETRUS (1528–1599).** A Portuguese Jesuit who taught at Coimbra, Pedro's *Summula* of **logic** was recommended in the Jesuit *Ratio studiorum* (*Curriculum of Studies*) in 1586 as a basic introduction to **Aristotelian** logic. In an era of contemporary attacks by Domingo de Soto and other **Dominicans** against treatises on Aristotelian logic that had been distorted by the intrusions of theological and metaphysical discussions, Fonseco's *Summula* was presented as a basic introductory-level work that was defended as being "broader, clearer and more adjusted to Aristotle" and as a treatise that "avoided sophistic manoeuvres that were useless and turned off beginners." His more advanced *Institutionum Logicarum libri octo* (*Eight Books of Logical Instruction*) was recommended in the *Ratio studiorum* of 1595, and with the spread of the Jesuit educational initiative it went through 53 editions between 1564 and 1625, making him one of the most influential logicians of his age.

**FRANCIS OF MARCHIA (ca. 1290–ca. 1345).** Also known as Franciscus de Esculo, this Franciscan lectured on the *Sentences* of **Peter Lombard** at Paris in 1319–1320. His longer commentary on the four books of Lombard's work, however, was produced slightly later and was completed before he moved to Avignon around 1324. There, he taught at the Franciscan *studium* when **William of Ockham** was undergoing investigation at the papal court. He opposed and criticized Pope John XXII's dealings with the general minister of the **Franciscans**, Michael of Cesena, and joined Michael and Ockham in flight from Avignon to seek refuge with Emperor Louis of Bavaria. It is reported that Francis later recanted his position before his death. Besides various redactions of his *Sentences* commentary, Francis has left a literal commentary on the *Physics* of **Aristotle**, commentaries on his *Metaphysics*, a set of *Quodlibet* questions, and his treatise directed against Pope John XXII. The content of his works is not well known, but we are aware that he plays a major role in the discussions of **Gregory of Rimini** in his commentary on the *Sentences* and criticizes a number of the positions of **Peter Aureoli** in his own commentary on that work. Studies on some portions of his *Physics* commentary show that he is an important source for the natural philosophy of **John Buridan** and **Nicholas Oresme**.

**FRANCIS OF MEYRONNES (ca. 1288–1328).** A native of Provence, Francis probably belonged to a noble family with connections to the House of Anjou. He lectured on the *Sentences* of **Peter Lombard** at Paris in 1320–1321 and was named a master of theology in 1323. His *Commentary on Lombard's Sentences* shows him to be a loyal follower of **John Duns Scotus**, at times defending him against the criticisms of **Peter Aureoli**. He does not always follow Scotus in a pure way, but at times qualifies his teachings with elements borrowed from **Henry of Ghent**. He is a strong defender of the Scotistic teachings on the univocity of being and the formal distinction. In a *disputatio* against the future pope Clement VI (Peter Roger), he vigorously defended the use of the formal distinction in discussions concerning the Trinity.

Francis's positions in the areas of politics and economics have been seriously studied. Although in opposition to Pope John XXII on the question of the absolute poverty of Christ, he still supported the pontiff on the issue of the sovereignty of the pope. In the field of economics, he viewed private property as the product of human positive law and as a complement to the natural laws stress on common use.

**FRANCISCANS.** *See* ORDERS (RELIGIOUS).

**FREDEGISUS (FRIDUGISUS) (ca. 765–834).** An Anglo-Saxon student of **Alcuin** at York, Fredegisus (one of the 17 variant spellings of his name) accompanied Alcuin to the court of Charlemagne. There, he taught Gisla, Charlemagne's sister, and his daughter, Rodtrude. He succeeded Alcuin as abbot of Saint-Martin in Tours in 804. In 819, he was chosen as chancellor by Louis the Pious, and he served in that position until 832. One year after he became chancellor, he was elected abbot of Saint-Bertin and Saint-Omer. He held this office until his death in 834. Fredegisus's famous work is *De substantia nihili et tenebrarum* (*On the Substance of Nothing and Darkness*), written in 800, a treatise that is his reflection on the story of creation. The "nothing" of which he speaks appears to be that from which God drew all creatures, a first matter that **St. Augustine** spoke of as *prope nihil* (almost nothing).

**FREEDOM.** The fact of freedom is generally accepted by medieval Jewish, Islamic, and Christian thinkers at two chief levels, namely at the levels of divine and human will. God is generally understood as a free agent with complete control over His creation, including the very fact of creation. Moreover, human beings are understood as free agents, who are responsible for their conduct, which is either rewarded or punished by God. However, regarding the nature of these two freedoms and their relations, as well as regarding the extent to which reason can demonstrate anything about them, a great variety of opinions exists. Concerning God's freedom in regard to creation, for example, there are two extremes with a number of intermediate positions. On one extreme, creation is understood as necessary, as the eternal and immutable sustaining of the universe by God. **Avicenna** (who draws much from **Al-Farabi**) and **Averroes** both use philosophy to support this in their own ways, the former in terms of **Neoplatonic** emanation, and the latter in terms of **Aristotle**'s view that God is the final cause of an eternal world. In this view, the perfection of God's will is understood in terms of His necessary and undivided essence: God's will is identical to His intellect, in the sense that what God knows about creation from eternity His will enacts also from eternity. In this general view, one of the chief challenges is accommodating the divine and human freedom spoken of in revelation. On the other extreme, God's will is seen as the inscrutable source of a contingent world. In this view, God's freedom in regard to creation is understood as incompatible with necessity, which would restrict the all-encompassing power of the God of revelation. One of the chief challenges to this general position is how to account for God's immutability as well as for human freedom in a way that does not limit divine power. Thus the Muslim **Asharites**, in their affirmation of God's unrestricted will, greatly restrict human will.

The majority of medieval thinkers would agree with the principle that, even though God has established an order in the universe, still the natural order is contingent. However, they uphold, emphasize, and apply this principle in diverse ways and to varying degrees. Thinkers such as **Al-Ghazali** and **John Duns Scotus** are among those who greatly stress contingency as essential to God's absolute freedom. In Christian thought, many of the **Augustinians**, such as **Bonaventure** and **Henry of Ghent**, also stress God's complete freedom, arguing, for example, on the basis of **faith** and reason the impossibility of creation from eternity. Some influential **Aristotelians**, such as **Moses Maimonides** and **Thomas Aquinas**, also adhere to the principle of God's absolute freedom in regard to creation but argue for key consequences, for example, that we know of the temporal creation of the world on the basis of faith alone and that it is not demonstrable by philosophical reason that the world is not eternal.

The polarity between those stressing divine necessity and those stressing God's unrestricted will becomes especially telling in the context of medieval Islamic **Scholastic** theology, the *kalam*. Islamic discussions concerning God's necessity/freedom and its relations to creation and human freedom accentuate necessity much more than is generally found in Jewish and Christian contexts.

Another important distinction concerns human freedom itself. In Islamic and **Jewish philosophy and theology**, human will is often (though not exclusively) understood as the practical intellect, as the intellect that decides between alternatives, as is the norm in Greek philosophy. (The Jewish philosopher **Hasdai Crescas**, for example, is exceptional in defining the will as the joining of appetite and imagination.) Naturally, different accounts of human freedom still exist among those who view the will as the practical intellect. In the Christian tradition, heavily influenced by **Augustine**, human will is generally understood as a faculty distinct (though inseparable) from the intellect. As Augustine puts it (*De Trinitate*, Book XV, chapter 27), the fact that one may know something and not love it, while one cannot love something without knowing it, shows both the coexistence and distinction between the intellect and the will. Thus, it is peculiar to the Christian tradition to give great emphasis to the question of which faculty is higher, the intellect or the will. In fact, the approach to this question is usually symptomatic of a medieval Christian thinker's deeper doctrinal affiliation: advocates of the primacy of the will are generally Augustinian while advocates of the intellect's primacy are generally Aristotelian. The specifically Christian aspect of this issue becomes especially evident in discussions of the **Trinity**, where the processions of the Son and the Holy Spirit are understood as flowing from rationally distinct, though substantially unified, sources in the divine nature, namely the divine intellect and will, respectively. These discussions profoundly influence Christian accounts of intellect and will in the human **soul**, which is seen as the image of the Trinity.

**FRIARS (DOMINICANS; FRANCISCANS).** *See* ORDERS (RELIGIOUS).

# G

**GABIROL, IBN (AVICEBRON) (ca. 1021–ca. 1058).** Primarily a philosopher, Salomon ibn Gabirol, or Avicebron as he became known in the Latin West, is one of the outstanding figures of Jewish Neoplatonism, a movement based chiefly on Plotinus and Proclus, though informed by **Aristotelian** ideas. In his understanding of matter, Gabirol also incorporated Stoic elements, possibly as transmitted by Galen. Pseudo-Empedocles and Isaac Israeli are also probable sources for his cosmology. Interestingly, he had a greater impact in the Latin West than in his own tradition. **Albert the Great**, **Bonaventure**, **Thomas Aquinas**, and **Duns Scotus**, to name but a few **Scholastics**, cited his work. A native of Muslim Spain when it was one of the richest cultural centers, he was born in Malaga and educated at Saragossa. He was also an accomplished poet who wrote primarily in Arabic. Only a few of his works are extant, of which two will be mentioned: *Meqor Hayim* (*The Fountain of Life*) and *Tikkum Middot Ha-Nefesh* (*The Improvement of Moral Qualities*). The latter, written in 1045 and available in the original Arabic, is his contribution to ethical literature. The focus here is practical **ethics**, with stress on the importance of the golden mean in moral virtue, as understood by Aristotle. He supports this doctrine with biblical passages and writings from the philosophers and poets. The end of human existence is described as the happiness of the **soul**, consisting primarily in knowledge and requiring a certain detachment from the passions of the body.

*The Fountain of Life*, surviving only in a 12th-century Latin translation (*Fons Vitae*) by Johannes Hispanus and **Dominicus Gundissalinus**, contains the fullest expression of Gabirol's **metaphysics** and cosmology. This work, comprised of five books, is unique in that, unlike other medieval Jewish works, it possesses virtually no references to Jewish sources. This may have contributed to its limited influence on Jewish philosophy; in fact, the work was never translated into Hebrew. It is written as a dialogue between a teacher and his student, a popular style in philosophical literature at the time. In this work we find God or the First Maker at the top of the metaphysical hierarchy, from which the divine will emanates, and from this divine will substances composed of matter and form proceed. These composites are further divided into spiritual beings available to the understanding and corporeal things perceptible to the senses. Gabirol's most original philosophical contribution is his view that all substances in the world, both spiritual and corporeal, are composed of matter and form. For him there are degrees of matter according to simplicity: general spiritual matter, general corporeal matter, general celestial matter, general natural matter, and particular natural matter. God is described in a typical Neoplatonic way, as wholly transcendent, infinite, eternal, and incomprehensible as to His essence (only His existence can be known). Scholars disagree as to the status of the divine will, whether it is identical to or separate from God; what seems clear is that by calling it divine will, Gabirol stresses a voluntary creation. Gabirol posits universal matter and universal form, both emanated from God and the divine will, as the highest principles in the created world. Other created things are determinations proceeding from these two principles. Lower matters and forms proceed from higher matters and forms; the higher matters and forms are always found in the lower, just as a genus is always found in a species. This implies that Gabirol, as seen by many of his interpreters, holds a multiplicity of substantial forms in a given substance—a debated position later on, particularly between **Augustinians** and Aristotelians in Scholasticism.

Gabirol views the human being as a microcosm of the world, the macrocosm. Intelligence, soul, and nature are metaphysical principles both of man and the world. The human soul, placed in the base world of nature, is meant to return to the spiritual realm. To this end it must purify itself, chiefly through knowledge of the highest things. His influential successor **Judah Halevi** criticizes what he saw in Gabirol as intellectualism, as well as an insufficient incorporation of traditional Jewish wisdom.

**GABRIEL BIEL (ca. 1414–1495).** Biel joined the **Arts Faculty** at Heidelberg in 1432 and became a master of arts there in 1438. His theological studies were begun a few years later at Erfurt and then continued at Cologne. These different venues gave him a strong background both in the *via antiqua* (the **realism** of authors like **Thomas Aquinas** or **John Duns Scotus**) and the *via moderna* (the **nominalism** of **William of Ockham** and his followers). It is necessary to add to this portrait of Biel's spiritual background his serious involvement throughout his life with the *devotio moderna* (the spiritual movement associated with the Brethren of the Common Life). When he was appointed to the **theology** faculty of the newly established University of Tübingen in 1484, he stood as a representative of the *via moderna*, and his *Collectorium circa quattuor libros **Sententiarum*** is highly dependent, even textually, on the *Sentences* of Ockham. His nominalistic positions, however, are at times complemented by the addition of texts from realistic authors, such as **Bonaventure**, Aquinas, Duns Scotus, **Gregory of Rimini**, and **Pierre d'Ailly**.

**GAETANO OF THIENE (1387–1465).** One of the most famous members of the **Arts Faculty** at Padua, succeeding the **Augustinian Hermit Paul of Venice** in 1422. He is renowned especially for his commentary on **William of Heytesbury**'s *Regulae* (*Rules for Solving Sophisms*). Heytesbury was one of the Merton Calculators, a group that specialized in the logical puzzles dealing with the continuum and with motion. Gaetano brought these discussions to Padua and also extended them beyond their character as logical conundrums. He also attempted to deepen the understanding of the issues of natural philosophy that were the subject matter of these logical problems.

**GERALD (GERARD) ODON (GUIRAL OT) (ca. 1290–1349).** A **Franciscan** from the south of France, Gerald was a bachelor of the *Sentences* before 1315. He taught again at Paris as regent master before 1326 and then at Toulouse. *Reportationes* (*Student Reports*) of his lectures on all four books of the *Sentences* and an *Ordinatio* of Book IV have survived. Following Michael of Cesena's conflict with Pope John XXII, Gerald replaced him as general minister of the Franciscans, elected at a general chapter presided over by the Franciscan cardinal Bertrand de la Tour. He served in this office from 1329 to 1342, when he was appointed patriarch of Antioch by Pope Clement VI. A number of his logic treatises (*On the Principles of Sciences*, *On Suppositions*, and *On Syllogisms*) have been edited, as has his *Commentary on the Ethics*. Like many Franciscans, he commented on particular works of both the Old and New Testaments. His choice, made at Toulouse before 1329, was to write commentaries on *The Book of Wisdom* and on Paul's Letters to the Corinthians and Galatians. Also during his years in Toulouse, he presented a *Lectio de signis diei judicii* (*A Lecture on the Signs of the Day of Judgment*). His latest treatise, written after 1342, was *De figuris Bibliorum* (*On the Figures of the Bible*), a portrait of some 30 biblical figures presented in relation to the Incarnation.

**GERARD (GERALD) OF ABBEVILLE (ca. 1220–1272).** A secular master in theology at Paris, he was also regent master in **theology** and archdeacon of Ponthieu in 1262. A disciple of **William of Saint-Amour**, he is well known because of his leadership in the movement to expel members of the mendicant **orders** from the **university**, as well as to take away their privileges. His attacks also concerned theological questions, such as his criticisms against the Franciscan ideal of poverty. His *Contra adversarium perfectionis Christianae* (*Against the Adversary of Christian Perfection*), written in 1256 but not circulated until 1269, received responses from **Bonaventure** of the **Franciscan** order and **Thomas Aquinas** of the **Dominican** order. Gerard persisted and wrote other works with this same general intention; he became the object of steady attacks from the mendicants, particularly the Franciscans. Writings against Gerard and his movement became known as the *Contra Geraldinos* (*Against Gerald and His Followers*).

**GERARD OF BOLOGNA (ca. 1245–1317).** Gerard was the **Carmelites'** first master of **theology** at Paris. He became the general prior of his order in 1297, a position he held until his death 20 years later. He fulfilled his theology office while general prior, leaving five *Quodlibets*, some *Quaestiones ordinariae*, and a *Summa theologiae*, which he never completed. His first three *Quodlibets* were disputed between 1309 and 1311; the other works thereafter. Gerard is cited by the **Augustinian Hermit Prosper of Reggio Aemilia** in the portrait he provides of the disputes over the nature of theology at Paris between 1311 and 1314. He is also cited by the Franciscan **Peter Aureoli** and more frequently by his fellow Parisian Carmelites: **Guy Terrena**, Siger of Beek, **John Baconthorpe**, and Michael Aiguani. The 15th-century Dominican **John Capreolus** cites him, basing his knowledge of Gerard, however, on the reports of Peter Aureoli. Gerard's *Quodlibets* show his doctrinal disagreement with the **Franciscan Duns Scotus** and the **Dominican Hervaeus Natalis**. The opening question of his *Summa theologiae* reveals his opposition to the position on the nature of theological study found in the first redaction of **Durandus of Saint-Pourçain**'s *Commentary on the Sentences*. *See also* ORDERS (RELIGIOUS).

**GERARD OF CREMONA (ca. 1114–1187).** Forty years after Toledo had been recaptured by the Christians (1085), Dom Raymundo, the archbishop of Toledo, initiated a movement to create in the city a center for scientific study and translation. Gerard, through the more than 70 translations from Arabic sources attributed to him, was one of the key contributors to this intellectual renaissance. Seemingly he was drawn to Toledo by his love of what he heard of **Ptolemy**'s *Almagest*, the most complete Greek encyclopedia of astronomy and mathematics. With the help of Jewish and Islamic teachers, he was able to finish his Latin translation of the *Almagest* in 1175. He then turned to the works attributed to **Aristotle**. He translated the 10th-century Arabic version of Book II of Aristotle's *Posterior Analytics*, along with the commentary on Book I of the same work by Themistius. He made an influential translation of the *Book of Causes*, which was attributed to Aristotle, though it is a commentary on certain theses taken from the *Theological Institutes* of the Neoplatonist Proclus. He also made translations from the Arabic of Alexander of Aphrodisias's commentaries on five of Aristotle's works and of **Al-Kindi**'s *Concerning Five Essences*, *On Sleep and Vision*, and *On Reason*. To Gerard also are attributed translations of **Al-Farabi**'s *On the Sciences* and the same author's *Commentary on Aristotle's Physics*. In providing just some of the many titles, we should also add to his list of translations Isaac Israeli's *Book of Definitions* and *On the Elements*. Through his many translations, the Latin West first came to know much of the natural philosophy of Aristotle and of the Greek and Arabian commentators on his corpus.

**GERSON, JEAN (1363–1429).** He studied the **liberal arts** and **theology** at the College of Navarre in Paris and became a master of theology in 1392. Almost immediately, he succeeded **Pierre d'Ailly** as chancellor of the university. After several years in this office, he threatened to resign because of heated debates among the theologians. A sample of his feelings in this regard makes his frustration evident:

> This is the philosophy which the Apostle and his disciple, Dionysius, call the wisdom, indeed, the revelation, of God. . . . I understand this revelation to be the "light of the Lord's countenance which is manifest upon us," precisely as the holy Bonaventure so beautifully and clearly concluded in his little work, which is beyond all praise, *The Journey of the Mind to God*. I do not know if the school of Paris will ever again have such a teacher. Hence I cannot bring myself to appreciate the way the **Franciscans**, having dismissed this great teacher, have turned to I know not what novelties and are prepared to fight tooth and nail for them.

In his *Mémoire sur la réforme de la faculté de théologie* (*Treatise on the Reform of the Faculty of Theology*), Gerson set out his plan to reform theological study, for example, by measures that called for less attention to the theoretical and truth-centered themes that dominated commentaries on Books I and II of the *Sentences* and greater attention to Books III and IV, which dealt with the Incarnation and Redemption of Christ and with the sacraments and last things that were more love focused and practice oriented. Gerson's *On Mystical Theology* and *On the Spiritual Life of the Soul* also set up a contrast between **Scholastic** theology, which he sees as anchored in nature and *Aristotle*'s natural philosophy, and the mystical tradition, which tastes and sees the sweetness of God's love. He was also in the center of Church life, writing *De unitate ecclesiae* (*On the Unity of the Church*) and many other treatises on the Church and on the authority of the pope and councils, and he led the French delegation at the Council of Constance (1414–1418). A large number of his works were written in Lyons during the post-counciliar period of his exile from Paris (1418–1429).

**GERSONIDES (GERSHOM, LEVI BEN) (1288–1344).** In the 13th century, Jewish philosophy began to be practiced in Hebrew in Christian, rather than Islamic, lands, where Arabic had been the chief language of educated Muslims and Jews. Rabbi Levi ben Gershom, or Gersonides, his Latinized name, is generally considered the most important medieval Jewish Aristotelian working in Christian Europe. He is also renowned for his highly rigorous brand of **Aristotelianism**, one drawing greatly from **Averroism**. The most influential medieval Jewish thinker was an earlier Aristotelian, namely **Moses Maimonides**, who recommended Averroes's commentaries on Aristotle. Even though he did not know Latin, Gersonides also shows some acquaintance with the Christian philosophy taking place at European universities at the time. Gersonides was born in Bagnols (in southern France), then a rich center for Jewish intellectual life, and he seems to have mostly remained there. He wrote commentaries on Averroes's own commentaries on Aristotle, commentaries on biblical texts, and significant contributions in astronomy and mathematics. His overall project was to reconcile religion and philosophy within a Jewish framework, as Maimonides had done. His chief work is *The Wars of the Lord*, written "to wage the Lord's war against the false opinions found among [his] predecessors," concerning topics such as immortality, creation, providence, and divine knowledge of particulars.

An independent and critical mind, he did not hesitate to disagree with authorities he respected. Thus, he sought to rectify what he saw as errors in Aristotle's account of the syllogism in the *Prior Analytics*. He also criticized Maimonides and others, maintaining that creation cannot be rationally demonstrated. Moreover, even though Gersonides, with **Averroes** (and **Aristotle**), sees immortality as the activity of the intellect, he defends individual immortality, while Averroes considers immortality as purely impersonal. In his own original arguments for individual immortality and providence, Gersonides relies on the general understanding, common among Jewish and Islamic Aristotelians, of Aristotle's agent intellect (in *De anima* III 5) as the intelligence (separate from God) that governs the sublunary world and as the efficient cause of human thinking. To Gersonides, prophecy is the result of intellectual actualization, whereby knowledge, ultimately emanated from God, is accessed by means of the agent intellect.

God, however, is unaware of particulars as such. Immortality, the utmost form of providence, is also the product of intellectual actualization; it is individual, since people obtain varying extents of knowledge. It is worth noting, however, that Gersonides does assign a role to moral virtue in the acquisition of knowledge. Gersonides appropriates an Aristotelian God, not immediately or personally related to human affairs, invariable as to His will, and with limited knowledge of the world. He then seeks to reconcile this in creative ways with the main themes of his biblical tradition, such as immortality and prophecy, as we have seen, as well as with free will, miracles, and creation, the longest and most complex issue in the *The Wars* as well as the most criticized. His solutions, technical, subtle, and ingenious, sharply impacted Jewish philosophy. Major Jewish thinkers such as **Hasdai Crescas**, Isaac Arama, and Isaac Abravanel rejected his views as heretical. Later on, however, Gersonides was to exert an important influence on Baruch Spinoza, who, in his effort to disassociate philosophy from religion, represents the beginning of the modern period in Jewish philosophy. It should be noted, however, that Gersonides himself considered the Torah to be a paramount source of his systematic thought (which both informs and is informed by philosophy), and not merely something to be superficially accommodated.

**GHAZALI, AL-, OR ALGAZEL (1059–1111).** Born in Tos (in Khorasan), Ghazali taught from 1091 to 1095 in Baghdad, where he experienced a personal crisis that led him to give up his wealth and position and adopt the life of a poor Sufi mystic for the next 10 years, traveling to a number of places. The growth of (Neoplatonic and **Aristotelian**) philosophy in **Islam**, particularly as found in **Al-Farabi** and **Avicenna**, elicited strong reactions against philosophy by those who saw many central Greek ideas as incompatible with revelation. Ghazali is best known for launching the grandest attack against philosophy at the time, though his work is not only deconstructive. He was a major influence in other intellectual trends, such as skepticism, **Sufism** (Islamic mysticism), and *kalam* (dialectical theology). His **theology**, a refinement and development of **Asharite** *kalam*, became almost equivalent with orthodoxy. His criticism of philosophy and his defense of theology included in-depth knowledge of the philosophical tradition and an adept use of logical principles, which earned him an important position in the history of philosophy. **Averroes**, the greatest figure in Muslim Aristotelianism, developed many of his positions in response to Ghazali; his important work *The Incoherence of the Incoherence* is directed against Ghazali's *The Incoherence of Philosophy*. Ghazali's tremendous influence in his tradition can be gauged by a common appellation given to him: the "seal" or "proof" of Islam.

Ghazali's principal target was Avicenna. In fact, a large part of Averroes's criticisms of Ghazali sought to show that because Avicenna's Platonized Aristotelianism was inadequate on certain key points, Ghazali's criticisms of philosophy were also inadequate to the extent that they identified philosophy with Avicenna. They did not at all, argued Averroes, touch the pure Aristotelianism that he himself defended. In his *Incoherence*, Ghazali criticized various philosophical propositions, which he sought to refute both on rational grounds and by showing that they were ultimately incompatible with Islam. Some of them are especially noteworthy. One concerns the identification of the Neoplatonic One with Allah. This move implies that emanation is identical with creation, a position that entails the view that the world is eternal. Another was the Aristotelian position that God lacks knowledge of the world, which threatens divine omnipotence and individual providence. Ghazali also attacked the Aristotelian denial of bodily resurrection, which goes against the **Koran**'s explicit statements and the ethical elements associated with them. Ghazali also focused on the issue of causality, denying all necessary connections between causes and effects. God's omnipotence implies that no secondary cause is necessary in its own right and that God, if he wills, can do anything without the assistance of anything else. This latter position, common in *kalam*, associates Ghazali with the development of skepticism. However, though Ghazali was for some time a radical skeptic, he later moderated his position, considering unnecessary the complete rejection of philosophy. It was as a mystic that Ghazali spent the last portion of his life.

**GILBERT OF POITIERS (GILBERT DE LA PORRÉE) (ca. 1085–1154).** A teacher at Paris and probably at the **school** at Chartres, Gilbert made contributions in both philosophy and **theology**. At the time of his death, he was bishop of Poitiers. The *Book on the Six Principles*, generally attributed to him in medieval times (though it could have been written by **Alan of Lille**), was an influential metaphysical account of **Aristotle**'s *Categories*, one of Aristotle's treatises in **dialectics**. In a **Platonic** vein, Gilbert interprets Aristotle's categories as being not just logical classes but real forms: **substance** (the only category existing by itself) and the three categories existing in substance, namely quantity, quality, and relation, are called inhering forms in that all exist as or in substance regardless of the substance's relations to other things. The other six principles (where, when, position, state, action, and passion) are described as assisting forms (*formae assistentes*), extrinsic elements connecting substances to other things. Gilbert classified relation as an inherent form because it is part of the nature of a substance to relate to other things, to be one of the two terms of a relation. However, Gilbert still calls relation a form, which implies, at least according to several of Gilbert's medieval interpreters, that relation has a proper reality similar to inhering forms. This question of the extent and type of reality to be accorded to relation generated intense debates and provided the context for important developments in medieval thought, especially in the context of discussions of the **Trinity**, where relation (in the tradition initiated by **Augustine** and **Boethius**) accounted for the real distinctions among the divine persons, while substance accounted for their unity. Thinkers such as **Bonaventure** and **Henry of Ghent** formulated some of their central positions and criticisms in the context of such discussions, where Gilbert often appears, especially, as a proponent of relations as real things.

Gilbert's own **metaphysics** was developed further and gained historical significance when he applied it to theology, especially in his commentary on Boethius's *On the Trinity*. Some of his theological positions, specifically his use of the categories in regard to the Trinity, were attacked by **St. Bernard of Clairvaux** as heretical in that they impaired the divine unity. They were condemned at the Council of Rheims in 1148. He later retracted his censured positions. Later thinkers continued to apply the categories to the Trinity, in highly nuanced ways developed in light of the criticisms against Gilbert's teachings. Gilbert's Platonism was quite influential, generating a good number of followers called the Porretani. Among them figure Alan of Lille, Raoul Ardent, and John Beleth. It also informed philosophical and theological developments of later centuries.

**GILES OF LESSINES (ca. 1235–ca. 1304).** This Belgian **Dominican** is very much linked by his writings to **Albert the Great** and **Thomas Aquinas**. There are elements in his writings that tie him to Albert and suggest that he studied with him in Cologne. His work *On the Essence, Motion, and Meaning of Comets*, written in 1264, shows his interest in the natural sciences that was characteristic of Albert. The same holds for his *Treatise on Sunsets*. Furthermore, he wrote a letter to Albert the Great seeking his judgment on the propositions condemned at Paris in 1270, which indicates a close connection to him. On the other hand, Giles's concern with these Parisian propositions would link him to Paris, and his treatise *De unitate formae* (*On the Unity of Form*), a detailed defense of the doctrine of the unicity of substantial forms, shows a close loyalty to St. Thomas. Also, his closeness to Thomas is further indicated by his treatise *De usuris* (*On usury*) that was at first attributed to Aquinas. Despite his association with Albert, then, he was considered by many Dominicans to be a member of the early Parisian Thomist school.

**GILES OF ROME (AEGIDIUS ROMANUS) (ca. 1245–1316).** A student of **Thomas Aquinas**, Giles was the first member of the **Hermits of St. Augustine** to become a master of theology. Within the turmoil surrounding the **condemnations of 1277** at Paris, Giles was subjected to an individual inquiry concerning his teaching of certain of the condemned propositions. His license to teach was rescinded and was only restored by Pope Honorius IV in 1285. He served as a regent master from that time until 1291. In 1292, he was elected general prior of his order. In 1295, he was appointed archbishop of Bourges. Throughout his life, Giles was involved in a number of ecclesiastical and political debates. Even while suspended from teaching from 1277 to 1285, he wrote *De regimine principum* (*On the Regime of Princes*) at the request of Philip the Fair. In 1297, he wrote *De renuntiatione papae* (*On the Abdication of the Pope*), defending the legitimacy of the election of **Boniface VIII**. He supported the pope in his dispute with Philip the Fair, again defending Boniface through his *De ecclesiastica potestate* (*On Ecclesiastical Power*). His last political writing was *Contra exemptos* (*On the Knights Templar*), written during the Council of Vienne (1311–1312). He died at the papal court in Avignon in 1316.

Giles was close to Aquinas on many of his philosophical positions. There was, however, a drive in Giles to make his positions his own. On certain issues, then, even while agreeing with his teacher, he established them in his own manner. In regard to the real distinction between essence and existence,

Giles held that they were distinct as *res* and *res*, that is, as thing and thing. Since essence and existence were not two substances, Giles in effect was defending a position that came close to **Avicenna**'s teaching that existence is an accident of a substance or essence, not exactly the view of Aquinas. Also, in regard to Aquinas's defense of the unicity of form in substances, Giles accepts this teaching absolutely in his *De gradibus formarum* (*On the Grades of Forms*) in 1278. However, his writings after this date show more reservations regarding the universal application of this theory: he holds back in applying it to human beings.

In **theology**, Giles is best known for defending the thesis that theology is an affective science. It is a thesis that was defended by **Albert the Great** in his *Commentary on the Sentences* and in his *Summa theologiae*: theology is properly affective, since it does not deal with truth as divorced from the good, and therefore it perfects the intellect and the affective faculty. This position is continued by Giles, who for 25 years defends the thesis, mainly against **Godfrey of Fontaines**, that the love of God is the goal of studying theology. *See also* ORDERS (RELIGIOUS).

**GLOSSA (*INTERLINEAREA* AND *ORDINARIA*).** The term *glossa ordinaria* refers to compilations of notes (glosses) on a text, usually in the field of law or **theology**. These notes may be either on the margin or between the lines of the text. In the latter case, the notes are also called *glossa interlinearea* (interlinear gloss). Some of the glosses were quite authoritative and formed part of the curricula. The earliest gloss was on the **Bible**, probably in the 12th century, while the first one in canon law was composed by Joannes Teutonicus (soon after the Fourth Lateran **Council**, 1215–1216) as a marginal commentary on **Gratian**'s *Decretum*. The greatest medieval biblical gloss is the *Glossa ordinaria*, a compilation from various glossators directed especially by **Anselm of Laon** (d. 1117), while in canon law those of Tancred of Bologna (ca. 1220), Bernard of Parma (revised 1234–1263), and Joannes Andreae (ca. 1301) are noteworthy. *See also* EXEGESIS.

**GODFREY OF FONTAINES (ca. 1250–ca. 1306).** A secular master of theology, Godfrey was born in Liege and studied in the **Arts Faculty** at Paris during the time of **Thomas Aquinas**'s second stay there (1269–1272), possibly with **Siger of Brabant**. Probably he also studied **theology** with **Henry of Ghent**. He became a master of theology by 1285, since his chief surviving works are his 15 *Quodlibets* and the first of these dates from that year. He has also left a number of *Disputed Questions*. Godfrey was an independent and critical thinker, though quite sympathetic to Thomas Aquinas, whom he praises very strongly in a question of *Quodlibet XV*. In this question where he is asked if the **condemnations of 1277** should be rescinded, he responds by telling how these condemnations have hurt the study of theology, particularly by making Thomas's teachings suspect in general and robbing the faculty of one who brings salt to the food of theology.

Godfrey engaged Thomas on most of the significant philosophical issues of the time. He is strongly **Aristotelian** in his theory of knowledge, emphasizing the passivity or receptivity of sense and intellect to guarantee the objectivity of knowledge. In his evaluation of theology, he places a strong accent on evidence as the requirement for science to be science in the proper sense of term. In *Quodlibet IV* he criticizes Aquinas for making too strong a claim for theology by saying that it is a science, albeit a subaltern science. According to Godfrey, theology can only be a science in a less proper sense of the term, and in *Quodlibet XIV* he explains why philosophy, which is based on evidence, can assist theology in coming to a better knowledge of the divine realities revealed in Scripture. His theology has a strongly metaphysical thrust, since he thinks this is the superior evident science and the one that provides the most solid base for a study that aims at being more scientific.

**GONSALVUS HISPANUS (GONSALVO OF SPAIN) (ca. 1255–1313).** After completing his studies in the **liberal arts** in Spain, he became a bachelor of the *Sentences* in 1288 and regent master in 1302–1303. He was elected provincial of the province of Castile in 1303 and the 15th general minister of the **Franciscans** in 1304, a position he held until 1313. His most challenging task was keeping in line the various Franciscan groups that were split over the nature of poverty. He wrote a treatise on the Franciscan rule, compiled a catalog of the general ministers of the order and their cardinal protectors, and wrote many letters dealing with the poverty issue. His *Commentary on the Sentences* has not survived, but his *Conclusiones metaphysicae* were once attributed to **John Duns Scotus**, who was in Paris when he was regent master. Both of them fled, as did all foreign Franciscans, when they refused to sign the letter of Philip the Fair against **Boniface VIII**. His *Disputed Questions* and *Quodlibets* show intense debates with the **Dominicans John of Paris**, **Peter of Palude**, and **Meister Eckhart**, as well as **Godfrey of Fontaines**.

**GOTTSCHALK OF ORBAIS (ca. 803–ca. 867/9).** A **Benedictine** theologian and poet of Saxon origin, Gottshalk is best known for his doctrine of predestination, which was seen with alarm by the Church in Germany and France. Having reluctantly entered the monastic life, he studied **Augustine** and Fulgentius of Ruspe intensely. He developed a position upholding double predestination in a strict form, claiming to have found support in the writings of Augustine, and avoided all mention of human **freedom**. For him predestination is based on God's unchanging nature. He did not say that certain individuals are predestined to evil but that the unrighteous are predestined to be punished, while the righteous are predestined for rewards. "For just as the unchangeable God, prior to the creation of the world, by His free **grace** unchangeably predestined all of His elect to eternal life, so has this unchangeable God in the same way unchangeably predestined all of the rejected, who shall be condemned to eternal death for their evil deeds on the judgment day according to His justice and as they deserve" (*Migne*, PL 121, 368A). Before the Synod of Mainz, he was opposed by the leading theologian and archbishop of Mainz, Rhabanus Maurus (also known for his work in **liberal arts**), and condemned as heretical in 848. In 849, Bishop **Hincmar of Reims**, Gottschalk's metropolitan, placed him under house arrest at the monastery, and again he was condemned. He was even flogged, near to the point of death, and his status of priest was taken away. Despite ensuing debates among theologians on the issue of double predestination, Hincmar's view won, and Gottshalk's doctrine was officially condemned at the Synod of Quiercy-sur-Oise in 853. Gottshalk lived as a prisoner for the next 20 years and never retracted his position. The influence of the interpretation of Augustine that stressed freedom of the will with the cooperation of grace dominated. *See also* ORDERS (RELIGIOUS).

**GRACE.** Grace is a gift. It is something given freely and is something unmerited or unearned. For medieval Christian authors, grace can often mean a particular momentary free gift, which they might technically call actual grace. Some graces, however, last longer. They might be presented, as **Peter Lombard** is often said to have taught, as the lasting presence of the Holy Spirit in us. Later theologians considered more lasting graces as habits of the **soul**. They are not habits developed after the manner of the virtues of courage or temperance that we may develop through repeated courageous or temperate acts that make it easier to do the same kind of acts later on. Habitual grace or charity is a gift from God. It is unearned by us. Some theologians teach that it is given in baptism, that by this grace we are made children of God, pleasing to God. They affirm that when we do morally good acts while we are in this state of grace, these acts become meritorious acts; that is, they are acts that are pleasing to God in a way that they can merit eternal life with Him. Throughout the Middle Ages there are continual debates about grace, especially concerning sanctifying or habitual grace or charity.

**GRATIAN (fl. 12TH CENTURY).** Little is known about the life of Joannes Gratianus, a native of Italy who died before 1179. A monk and a teacher (at the monastery of Sts. Felix and Nabor in Bologna), he is regarded as the father of canon law as a **university** discipline, just as his contemporaries, **Peter Lombard** and **Peter Comestor**, are considered as the fathers of university **theology** and university biblical history respectively. His major work, *Concordantia discordantium canonum* (*Concordance of Conflicting Canons*), also known as the *Decretum*, is a legal synthesis that was recognized as the *corpus iuris canonici*, that is, the code embodying the effective ecclesiastical laws. Later jurists who added to this code were greatly influenced by Gratian's methods. *See also* DECRETALS AND DECRETALISTS.

**GREGORY OF RIMINI (ca. 1300–1358).** This **Hermit of St. Augustine** was born in Rimini and began his theological studies in Paris in 1323. He attained the rank of **lector** there in 1329 and then taught at various Augustinian houses of study (Bologna, Padua, and Perugia) before returning to Paris in 1341 or 1342 to prepare for the lectures on the *Sentences* of **Peter Lombard** that he gave as a baccalareus in 1342–1343 or 1343–1344. Gregory returned to his native Rimini as regent of the Augustinian house of studies in 1351 and taught there until 1357. He replaced **Thomas of Strasbourg** as general prior of the Augustinians in 1357 but died a year later.

Gregory's chief work was his *Lectura super Primum et Secundum Sententiarum* (*Lectures on Books I and II of Lombard's Sentences*). It must have been during his years of teaching in Italy or while he prepared his lectures on the *Sentences* that he became familiar with the works of many contemporary English authors. He helped introduce to Paris **William of Ockham**, **Walter Chatton**, **Adam Wodeham**, **Richard Fitzralph**, and, to a lesser degree, **Thomas Bradwardine**, **Richard Kilvington**, **William Heytesbury**, **Thomas Buckingham**, and **Robert of Halifax**. His philosophical works, *Tractatus de intensione et remissione formarum corporalium* (*Treatise on the Intention and Remission of Corporeal Forms*) and *De quattuor virtutibus cardinalium* (*On the Four Cardinal Virtues*), are complemented by a number of Scriptural commentaries and theological treatises.

To evaluate the label of **nominalism** is a complex affair, especially in the 14th century, when it swelled from a denial of real entities corresponding to our universal concepts to include a dozen other points. The more recent editors of his *Lectura* label him "a nominalistic alternative to William of Ockham." This association with Ockham is justified at least by the way he accepts the claims of Ockham's natural philosophy. However, he distances himself from Ockham at times, especially when he accuses the Venerable Inceptor of having a Pelagian view of man. Gregory accepts with little alteration many claims of Ockham's natural philosophy. Gregory, like Ockham, employs a razor to establish that motion, time, and sudden change are not distinct and definable entities in themselves. "Sudden change," for example, does not signify some thing over and above the permanent things involved in the change—that is, over and above the subject that is changed and the form gained which the subject did not have previously or the form lost which it previously had. Gregory stresses the contingency of the natural world. Since

God is the only necessary being, all creatures and thus the whole created universe are contingent. The laws of nature have been freely chosen by God and have no absolute necessity of their own.

**GREGORY PALAMAS (1296–1359).** Born in Constantinople, Gregory entered the monastery of Mt. Athos and was ordained there in 1326. In 1337, he began to correspond with the philosopher Barlaam the Calabrian. Barlaam defended the absolute transcendence of God. Gregory admitted God's transcendence in regard to his essence, but following the mystical tradition he also stressed God's divine energies that lead to communion with His creatures: through the Incarnation, liturgies, and mystical experiences. His most famous theological work was *For the Defense of the Holy Hesychasts* (*Contemplatives*). A number of Greek councils upheld his teaching (1341, 1347, and 1351). He was consecrated archbishop of Thessaloniki in 1347 and was canonized a saint in 1368.

**GROOTE, GEERT (GERARD) (1340–1384).** Born in Deventer, Groote attended the **Arts Faculty** at Paris and became a master of arts at age 18. He moved on to study canon law. When he returned to Holland, he at first led a worldly life, but at the age of 34 he entered the Carthusian monastery at Monnikhuizen. He translated into Latin Ruysbroeck's *Adornment of the Spiritual Wedding*. He was ordained a deacon in 1379 and became a renowned preacher throughout the Netherlands, urging the laity to deepen their spiritual lives and live in poverty. He established the ***devotio moderna*** or Brethren of the Common Life as a reformed way of living for those who would follow him. He died of the plague in 1384, urging his followers to unite with the **Canons Regular of St. Augustine**, since their rule corresponded best to the rule he himself formulated in his *Conclusa et praeposita, non vota* (*A Beneficial Dedicated Way of Life, without Vows*).

**GROSSETESTE, ROBERT (ca. 1168–1253).** Born of a poor Norman-English family in Stradbroke in the diocese of Norwich, Grosseteste wrote a religious poem *Le Chasteau d'Amour* (*The Castle of Love*) and some prayers in Norman French, suggesting that this might be his first tongue. He also spoke a dialect of English and mastered Latin and Greek, reading extensively from the **Fathers of the Church** in both languages. Although some historians place his educational development late (1225–1235), it seems more likely that it must be spread out over a broader and earlier period. He must have become a master of arts before the end of the 12th century and was probably teaching **theology** at Oxford from at least 1214 on. He continued his theological teaching with the newly arrived **Franciscan** friars from 1229 to 1235, when he was elected bishop of Lincoln (with jurisdiction over Oxford), an office he held until his death in 1253.

Grosseteste gives evidence of his knowledge of Greek by 1230, and he became well known as a translator of **Aristotle**'s *Nicomachean Ethics* and parts of *On the Heavens*, the *Letters* of St. Ignatius, and the *Testaments of the Twelve Patriarchs*. He also translated, among other texts, the works of **Dionysius the Areopagite**, **John Damascene**, and Greek commentators on Aristotle's *Ethics*. His speculative abilities led him beyond the role of translator. The first step in this new direction might be his commentaries on Aristotle's *Posterior Analytics* and a number of other logical treatises. He began but never completed a commentary on Aristotle's *Physics*. Among his independent works, the most impressive is his *Hexaëmeron* (commentary on Genesis 1–2). (It also is a strong indicator of his general approach to theology: studying the Bible—he was opposed to the introduction of the ***Commentary on the Sentences*** as an alternative way of studying theology initiated at Oxford by **Richard Fishacre**.)

Grosseteste's *De libero arbitrio* (*Concerning Freedom of Decision*), another of his long works, investigates the many issues involved in human **freedom** and responsibility and God's knowledge, examining the modes of contingency and necessity and God's eternal perspective on temporal events. Most of his other theoretical works are short. For example, *De luce* (*On light*) presents in brief form his basic cosmology; and his truncated *De finitate motus et temporis* (*On the Finiteness of Motion and Time*) offers his refutation of Aristotle's thesis concerning the eternity of the world. His biblical **exegesis** is extensive. Beyond the *Hexaëmeron*, he also wrote extensive commentaries on Psalms (1–100) and on Paul's Letter to the Galatians. There are also **glosses** on the other letters of Paul, as well as treatises dealing with biblical matters, for example, *De cessatione legalium* (*On the Cessation of the Ritual Torah*). Grosseteste argues that the Mosaic Law pointed to its own fulfillment in Christ. *De decem mandatis* (*On the Ten Commandments*) was also intended as a commentary on Exodus 20:1–17, explaining it always from the perspective of Paul's Letter to the Galatians. Grosseteste's writings are strikingly diverse, even without taking into consideration his sermons and letters.

**GUIDO (GUY) TERRENA (ca. 1265–1342).** Guy, born in Perpignan, succeeded **Gerard of Bologna** as the general prior of the **Carmelites** in 1318, an office he held until he was named bishop of Majorca in 1321. In 1332, he became bishop of Elna and held that position until his death in 1342. Like Gerard of Bologna, some of his theological work was undertaken after he became general prior. The first five of the eight *Quodlibets* attributed to him likely date from 1313–1316, but *Quodlibets VI–VIII* probably should be placed after 1318. Guy's *Commentary on the "Decretum"* and his *Concordia Evangeliorum* (*Harmony of the Gospels*) cite *Quodlibet VI* and must be located after 1320. His *Quaestiones in libros Ethicorum* (*Questions on the Nicomachean Ethics*) quotes *Quodlibet I*, so it is one of his earliest surviving works.

Guido was a student of **Godfrey of Fontaines** and became a master of theology in 1312. His ***Commentary on the Sentences of Peter Lombard*** has survived only in fragments, so our knowledge of his teachings in philosophy (he wrote commentaries on Aristotle's *On the Soul*, *Physics*, and *Metaphysics*) is more complete than on his positions in **theology**. Like Godfrey, he criticizes the illumination theory of knowledge of **Henry of Ghent** and stresses the primacy of the intellect over the will, defending the receptive and objective character of human knowledge. He is also known as the first **Scholastic** defender of the pope's doctrinal infallibility.

**GUNDISSALINUS (GUNDISALVI), DOMINICUS (ca. 1125–ca. 1190).** Mainly known as a translator of Arabic texts, he also wrote a number of philosophical treatises. We know that he worked under the sponsorship of John the archbishop of Toledo from 1151 to 1166. For some of his translation work, he joined up with Avenduth (Ibn Daud), who would translate the works from the Arabic into Castilian, and then Gundissalinus would transform the Castilian into Latin. The works he translated were **Avicenna**'s *On the Soul* and *Metaphysics*, **Al-Ghazali**'s *Summa of Theoretical Philosophy* (logic, physics, and metaphysics), and **Avicebron**'s *Fountain of Life*. He probably also translated part of Avicenna's *Logic* and *Physics*, as well as the treatise *On the Heavens* that was attributed to him. His own *De divisione philosophiae* (*On the Division of the Sciences*) also contains translated passages from other Arabic works. His *On the Soul* and *On the Immortality of the Soul* show his effort to adapt the teachings of Avicenna and Avicebron to the teachings of the Christian West. His chief Latin sources are **Boethius** (his *On Unity and the One* was once attributed to Boethius) and **Augustine**, so in effect he was attempting to reconcile Augustine and Avicenna in his psychological works.

# H

**HALEVI, JUDAH (ca. 1075–1141).** A native of Tudela in northeastern Spain, the Jewish thinker, poet, and physician Judah ben Samuel Halevi also spent time in southern Spain, which at the time was under Muslim control. At a time when Jewish life in Spain was in great part dictated by political struggles between Christianity and **Islam**, Halevi's work was motivated by his emphasis on traditional Jewish wisdom as the one stable core for Jews and a true guide to God. His poetry, whose central themes concern Jewish culture, wisdom, and the Holy Land, is still regarded as among the most beautiful and meaningful in Hebrew literature. His famous *Kuzari* or *Book of Refutation and Proof, in Defense of the Despised Faith*, is the text where Halevi develops a comprehensive and more systematic account of his views. Written in the form of a dialogue between the king of the Khazars and representatives of Islam, Christianity, and philosophy, it argues for the superiority of traditional Jewish wisdom. For, God has chosen a people, the people of Israel, and God cares that His people follow the set of rites and laws He prescribed in the **Torah**. This also shows the insufficiency of philosophy and of the religious rationalism that, like that of **Gabirol** and others, conceives of the attainment of God as fundamentally intellectual. True, human beings through their own efforts and discursive reasoning may gain some wisdom and thus come closer to God, but the path to God is ultimately beyond any human wisdom, and it is the path provided by the revealed Torah.

**HASDAI, CRESCAS.** *See* CRESCAS, HASDAI (ca. 1340–ca. 1411).

**HENRY OF GHENT (ca. 1217–1293).** The Solemn Doctor (*Doctor Solemnis*) was born at Ghent or Tournai in what is now Belgium, though the date is not known. Regent master in theology at the University of Paris from 1276 until his death, he was a seminal thinker and is probably the most influential theologian in Europe between **Thomas Aquinas** and **John Duns Scotus**. His influence was felt both inside and outside the **universities** and in a variety of traditions, doctrines, and movements, such as **Scotism**, **nominalism**, and **mysticism**, to name but a few. Henry developed his theological system sharing a concern of special relevance among Christian theologians of the latter half of the 13th century: to address in a manner congenial to reason and revelation non-Christian philosophy, particularly that of **Aristotle** and his commentators, which had just recently been received in its totality in the Latin West. The synthesis of Thomas Aquinas was far from universally accepted as the final answer to the question of the right relation between revealed and philosophic truth. The question still generated much controversy, as evidenced by Bishop **Étienne Tempier**'s famous **condemnation** at Paris, 7 March 1277, of 219 philosophical and theological propositions.

Henry, one of the theologians assisting Tempier, developed his own synthesis of reason and revelation. His major work *Summa quaestionum ordinariarum* (*A Summa of Ordinary Questions*) is such a synthesis, one analogous in comprehensiveness, though shorter in extension, to the *Summa theologiae* of Thomas Aquinas. (Many of the themes of Henry's *Summa* are also developed in his 15 *Quodlibets*.) Henry's thought is inspired primarily by **Augustine** and **Bonaventure** and is in part a response to **Aristotelianism**, particularly that of Thomas Aquinas. Partly due to the great controversy generated by Aristotle's philosophy during his career at Paris, Henry, unlike most of his **Neoplatonic** predecessors, appropriates Aristotle and his commentators critically and uses them extensively and profoundly. His use of **Avicenna**, particularly in **metaphysics**, is especially noteworthy. In providing a Neoplatonic alternative to Thomism that addresses and criticizes Aristotle thoroughly, he not only stimulates Neoplatonic thought, such as is found in Christian mysticism, but also influences thought more grounded in the Aristotelian tradition, such as is found in Scotism.

Aristotelianism, by stressing that we know philosophically the first cause *only* through its effects, fails to account fully for the symbolic or higher-pointing character of created reality. Rather, God is the ultimate source of all light and all seeing, and so any knowledge we have of God through reason and revelation, especially of His triune nature, is the foundation of our knowledge of everything else. Accordingly Henry devotes a large part of his work to questions concerning the **Trinity**.

Aristotelians are correct to the extent that purely natural, sense knowledge does accurately capture common features of physical things and is grounded in self-evident, first principles. However, this purely natural knowledge does not reach what Henry calls the sincere and fixed truth of a thing. This truth is obtained when the universals abstracted from things are seen in the light of the ideas in God, by which God knows and creates things. In this life, this knowledge can only be partial, as a perfect comparison of the created to the eternal exemplar would require the open (beatific) vision of the exemplars in the divine essence, which vision can only be had in the next life. Accordingly, in this life, this knowledge is not a direct knowledge of God nor knowledge of the ideas as known by God, but only a knowledge of the essence of a created thing in the light of the idea. True knowledge can only be had through divine illumination that perfects abstraction; thus Henry subordinates Aristotelianism to **Augustinianism** in his Christian vision of reality. Any essence as truly known and loved is constituted in the **soul** only in the light of the supreme Truth and Good. An essence is therefore present to the soul as an intentional participation of essential being as such, the subject of metaphysics as a distinct discipline. However, it is the theologian, who investigates the Trinity, who sees the ultimate truth of metaphysics, for the metaphysician considers being absolutely, while the theologian considers it in relation to its ground in the Trinity. For God eternally gives essential being to all possible creatures when, in knowing himself through the Word, He knows himself as imitable in different ways. Actual existence is in turn given to the creature through a free action of divine will, which will can be a totally free choice in regard to creatures because prior to its creative action it is perfected in the divine nature in the person of the Holy Spirit.

Since God knows from eternity what is or is not to be actualized or created by His will, and in God intellect and will are only rationally distinct, Henry adopts what he calls an intentional distinction between essence and existence in the created composite, rejecting the real distinction of one of his chief opponents, **Giles of Rome**. As Avicenna pointed out, an essence like horseness may be considered absolutely, as neither one nor many, or as instantiated existentially in many individuals and thus predicable as a universal of many. However, since in fact all there is are existing horses, horseness and its existence as this horse are only intentionally, not really, real.

Henry uses this intentional distinction in other important ways, such as in his explanation of the reality of relations. To Henry, accounting for relations is central, since at the heart of all things lie their relations to the Creator. A relation and its foundation are only intentionally distinct, since a thing may be considered absolutely without its relations, which are nevertheless real aspects of the foundation insofar as it relates to other things. For example, a white thing may be considered absolutely without its relation of similarity to other white things. Moreover, whiteness and similarity are not really distinct. If all but one white thing disappears, the remaining white thing is just as white as it was when other similar white things existed. The relation adds nothing to the reality of the foundation. Yet relation is real as the relatedness of the foundation itself, presupposing only as a necessary condition the term to which the foundation relates. Thus, all creatures may be considered absolutely as **substances**, as in the science of metaphysics. Ultimately, however, a substance's relation to the divine intellect and will constitutes and preserves it. Theology, considering the aspect that grounds metaphysics or first philosophy, is the highest science.

A more perfect image of the divine spirit than physical entities, the soul can find in itself a more explicit analogical knowledge of God. Though he rejects the doctrine of innate ideas, Henry holds that the concept of being, understood as an absolutely prior criterion for judgment, is virtually innate to the soul. This concept depends on a different concept that grounds it, that of God, since the soul's judgments about finite, contingent being presupposes some implicit notion of unlimited, necessary being. (Duns Scotus develops his central and influential doctrine of the univocity of the concept of being in response to this view.) And this notion of divine being may be made more explicit in this life, according to the degree of divine illumination available to the wayfarer through God's will.

Therefore, if any insight into the Trinity is available to us at all, it is to be found above all by examining our knowing and loving operations, as Augustine and Bonaventure rightly saw. Thus, it is not surprising that Henry's psychology is quite extensive, intricate, and rich, having fundamental theological and metaphysical implications. The ultimate basis for his conception of the Trinity in itself and as a source of creatures is a psychology of divine intellect and will, inspired first and foremost by Augustine, though informed by the philosophical tradition. In turn, Henry's understanding of the Trinity in terms of Aristotelian **categories** applicable to God and creatures depends on his understanding of the Trinity according to itself and as a cause of creatures in terms of intellect and will. Interestingly, this means for Henry's view of reality a revised and original understanding of the Aristotelian categories that is applied pervasively and profoundly in his system. Refer to the introduction, "Developments in the Theology Faculty from the 13th Century Onward."

**HENRY OF HARCLAY (ca. 1270–1317).** A native of England, Henry was master of both the **liberal arts** (by 1296) and **theology** (by 1312) at Oxford, where he served as chancellor (1312–1317). He later became bishop of Lincoln. As an administrator, he is known for siding with the **university** in various intense debates against **Dominicans** concerning privileges they demanded. This anti-Dominican stance was also reflected in his opposition to central theses of **Thomas Aquinas**. His theological works include a commentary on **Peter Lombard**'s *Sentences* and his *Quaestiones ordinariae*. Doctrinally his main influence, as well as a target of his criticisms, was **John Duns Scotus**, whose **realism** he rejects on certain key points (individuation, the status of universal natures, and essence/existence). In trying to restore **Aristotle**'s original positions on these issues, Henry adheres to the principle that all extra-mental reality is singular. **William of Ockham** goes even further than Henry (still criticizing him as a realist) in this trend away from realism, adopting a position generally labeled as **nominalism**.

**HENRY OF ZOMEREN (ca. 1416–ca. 1480).** Born in a small town in Brabant, Henry began his studies at the University of Louvain in 1434 and became a master of arts in 1441. He began teaching immediately. It was only later that he received his **theology** degrees: as a bachelor in 1451, master in 1456, and doctor in 1462. He became an ordinary professor in the Faculty of Theology in 1460. Henry is very well known for his participation in the debate at Louvain over God's knowledge of future contingents with Peter of Rivo of the **Arts Faculty**, lasting from 1465 to 1456. Peter's position was found to be made up of "opinions ill-sounding, scandalous and offensive to Christian ears" by a papal court in 1473. When he later tried to justify his position, Peter was further forced to retract in September 1476. In Cardinal Bessarion's *De arcanis Dei*, a discussion of the same issue in Rome is again presented in 1471. It not only lacks the bitterness of the Louvain debate but also offers a gentler way of representing the opinions of Henry and Peter, and it does so with much greater breadth of intellectual perspective.

**HENRY TOTTING OF OYTA (ca. 1330–1397).** Henry Totting taught at Paris, Prague, and finally at the Faculty of **Theology** in Vienna. His chief works are a ***Commentary on the Sentences***, questions on the *Isagoge*, three *Treatises on the Soul and Its Powers*, and the *Tractatus moralis de contractibus reddituum annuorum* (a work on economics). He is associated with the **nominalists**, also called terminists, meaning, generally speaking, the followers of **William of Ockham** and opponents of the so-called **realists**, a broad designation that referred to Scotists (followers of **John Duns Scotus**) and Thomists (followers of **Thomas Aquinas**).

**HERESIES.** In a technical sense, heresy is the stubborn denial or doubt, by a baptized person, of a truth that must be believed. The truths that must be believed are the truths contained in the Scriptures and that have been proposed by the Church to be divinely revealed. **Faith**, then, is the response of the believer to God who has revealed the truths to the Church. Heresy must involve a stubborn denial, so it may be distinguished from a denial that is based on inculpable error. In this more precise sense of heresy, Catholics would say that those belonging to other Christian faiths are not heretics, since it is presumed that any erroneous teachings they proclaim are affirmed in good faith.

In the course of history, many heresies have forced the Church to clarify the teachings of the Christian faith. In the fourth century, the **Arians** accentuated the position that the chief characteristic of God is that he is "unbegotten." This entailed the consequence that the Son is not God, since he is begotten. The Council of Nicaea (325) countered this heretical teaching, as is evident in the Nicene Creed, where the Son is declared to be "begotten, not made, one in Being with the Father." This determination will be repeated in the next ecumenical council, that of Constantinople in 381. In the next century, the Nestorians posited two persons in Christ, denying the hypostatic union of the two natures, divine and human, in the one divine person. This heresy was corrected by the Council of Ephesus in 431. The Pelagians, in reaction to Manichean fatalism, emphasized the human capacity to do good. For them, no supernatural grace was needed for one to choose the good. **St. Augustine**, in his treatise, *On Nature and Grace*, argued against this error that effectively denied original sin and overplayed man's natural moral strengths.

Heresy is often understood in a less technical sense for what is considered as theologically false teaching. At the beginning of the medieval period, there was the *Filioque* controversy, i.e., the dispute over whether the Holy Spirit comes forth from the Father alone or from the Father and the Son—*see* PHOTIUS (ca. 810–ca. 893)—the predestination debate (*see* GOTTS-CHALK OF ORBAIS (ca. 803–ca. 867/9)—and the various Eucharistic conflicts—*see* BERENGARIUS OF TOURS (ca. 1000–1088), PASCHASIUS RADBERTUS (ca. 785–ca. 860), and RATRAMNUS OF CORBIE (fl. 844–868). **John Scotus Eriugena**, seemingly due to a misunderstanding of his *De divisione naturae*, was accused of pantheism, though it was far less a case of misunderstanding with **Amalric of Bène** and the Amalricians.

**HERMITS OF ST. AUGUSTINE.** *See* ORDERS (RELIGIOUS).

**HERVAEUS NATALIS (HARVEY NEDELLEC) (ca. 1250–1323).** Born in Brittany, he joined the **Dominican** order around 1276. He lectured on the *Sentences* of **Peter Lombard** in either 1301–1302 or the following academic year. Like all Frenchmen, he sided with Philip the Fair in the dispute with **Boniface VIII.** He became regent master of the Dominicans in 1307 and held that chair until he was elected provincial in 1309. He became general minister in 1318. During his tenure, he strongly pressed for the canonization of **Thomas Aquinas.** He wrote a *Defensio doctrinae fratris Thomas* (*Defense of the Teaching of Brother Thomas*), though he differed from him on a number of **metaphysical** issues, such as the real distinction between essence and existence and the principle of individuation. His theological works include his *Questions on the Sentences*, *Disputed Questions*, and four authentic *Quodlibets.* Among his philosophical writings are his commentaries on **Aristotle**'s *Categories* and *Perihermenias* and his treatises *On the Knowledge of the First Principle* and *On Second Intentions.* He is known as a fierce critic of **Henry of Ghent, James of Metz, Peter Aureoli,** and especially **Duran-**

dus of Saint-Pourçain. A commission he headed that was assigned to investigate Durandus's writings found 91 objectionable propositions. *See also* ORDERS (RELIGIOUS).

**HEYTESBURY, WILLIAM (ca. 1313–ca. 1373).** We know that Heytesbury was a fellow of Merton College, Oxford. He is, along with Richard Swineshead and others, part of the group of pioneering Oxford scientists called the **Oxford Calculators**, since they, following the example of **Thomas Bradwardine**, applied and developed mathematical methods in the study of nature, particularly kinetics. His work in **logic** and language is also noteworthy; his *Sophismata* is a collection of treatises on these subjects.

**HILDEGARD OF BINGEN (1098–1179).** Hildegard received the **Benedictine** habit at the age of 15 in the cloister of Disinbodenburg. She was elected abbess 23 years later, and after another 10 years, with 18 other religious, she moved the monastery to Rupersberg, just outside of Bingen. She founded another convent in Eibingen around 1162, and many of her writings were preserved in manuscript form at that convent. She had visions even in early life, but they increased as the years went on, and they were examined and authenticated by the archbishop of Mainz. Her theological writings were based on these visions, and her principal work, *Scivias*, is an account of her visions dealing with the relations between God and man in creation, redemption, and the Church. Hildegard's theology is marked by concreteness, using the image of life, expressed as "greenness," connoting abundance, fecundity, and vitality, to portray God. Men and women are images of God in their bodies, souls, and minds, though through sin they have become blind to God's living presence in themselves and the world around them. Pope Eugene III appointed a commission to examine her writings, and they were approved as orthodox. She also wrote works on medicine, hymns (both words and music), 50 homilies, a morality play, and innumerable letters to popes, kings, and men and women at all levels of society.

**HILDUIN (ca. 775–ca. 859).** Hilduin was a student of Alcuin and the teacher of Hincmar of Reims and Walafrid of Strabo. In 815, he was made abbot of Saint-Denis. He translated into Latin the writings of Dionysius the Pseudo-Areopagite, and, commissioned by Emperor Louis I, he also wrote a life of St. Denis that contributed in part to his identification with Dionysius, the convert and disciple of St. Paul associated with the Areopagus. The translations he made of the works of Dionysius were found to be faulty, and another more respected translation was made by John Scotus Eriugena.

**HINCMAR OF REIMS (ca. 806–882).** A student of **Hilduin** at Saint-Denis, Hincmar was already a priest when he was elected archbishop of Reims in 845. His tenure there was marked by many political challenges to his appointment. When **Gottschalk of Orbais** was condemned at the Council of Mainz in 848 for erroneous teachings concerning predestination, Hincmar wrote a refutation of Gottschalk's position titled *Ad reclusos et simplices* (*To Hermits and the Unschooled*). When this treatise was attacked by Prudentius of Troyes and Lupus of Ferrières, Hincmar wrote a second work on predestination in 856–857, and a third one in 859–860. Although this predestination crisis has been the center of the attention regarding Hincmar, it should be noted that he produced works in a large number of areas. In history, he is remembered for his *Vita sancti Remigii* (*Life of St. Remigius*); in politics, for his *De institutione regia* (*On Ruling Power*); in canon law, for his *Opusculum quinquaginta capitulorum* (*Little Book of Fifty Chapters*); and in philosophy, for his *De diversa animae ratione* (*On the Diverse Nature of the Soul*), as well as for an important collection of letters.

**HOLCOT, ROBERT (ca. 1290–1349).** The Cambridge **Dominican** Robert Holcot is known chiefly as a follower of **William of Ockham**, although he disagreed with Ockham on important epistemological and psychological issues. He also owed much to others, such as **Richard of Campsall**, **John of Rodington**, and **Richard Fitzralph**. He wrote a commentary on **Peter Lombard**'s *Sentences*, *Quodlibets*, *Sex articuli* (Six Articles), and several influential biblical commentaries. To Holcot, logical principles do not apply in theological questions as they do in philosophical questions: this is especially true in the case of the mystery of the **Trinity**. Holcot advocates in the case of such theological investigations a "logic of faith," which is rational in its own way, though distinct from classical Aristotelian logic (**dialectics**). Holcot is also known for his sharp stress on the absolute power of God's will and causality and on the inability of the mind to derive concepts from anything other than sensible things. These positions weaken natural **theology** at its basis, since the mind cannot rise from the natural order, which is totally contingent upon God's inscrutable will to begin with, to the discovery of spiritual realities, least of all God. In turn, and as (part of) a theological reaction against the **Averroist** movement, these positions greatly widen the scope of Christian revelation and **faith**.

**HONORIUS OF AUTUN (ca. 1085–ca. 1156).** A monk of Regensburg, he took the name Augustodunensis ("the hill of Augustus") from the supposed victory site of Charlemagne in a battle that took place near Regensburg. His chief renown is derived from his *Elucidarium* (*Clarification*), which is found in so many manuscript copies, early printings, and translations that he must be respected as a capable theologian in his own right and not reduced to a compiler of **Anselm**'s texts. Honorius joins Anselm as a new kind of theologian and is known as an inveterate defender of Christ's real presence in the **Eucharist**. He argued that a priest in union with the Church who confected a sacrament while in the state of serious sin still acts validly through Christ's power. At the same time, Honorius championed high moral standards for priests. In his *Inevitabile*, found in at least two redactions, he shows his independence from Anselm's *Cur Deus Homo* (*Why the God-Man*) by arguing that it is not the fall but rather man's predestination to deification that is the cause of the Incarnation. In his *Clavis Physicae* (*Key to Nature*), Honorius indicates his familiarity with **John Scotus Eriugena**'s thought and shows his effort to blend it with that of Anselm at times, for example, in regard to the predication of *esse* of God. Here, he goes beyond summarizing and provides evidence of real philosophical creativity.

**HUGH OF NEWCASTLE OR CASTRO NOVO (ca. 1280–ca. 1322).** This theologian of the **Franciscan** order was a native of either Newcastle in Durham or Neufchâteau in Lorraine. Also called *Doctor scholasticus*, he died at Paris, where he was a **university** master in **theology**, commenting on **Peter Lombard**'s *Sentences* between 1307 and 1317, and a doctor of (both) laws. His philosophy and theology, a systematic and comprehensive account, is largely a development of that of his Franciscan teacher, **John Duns Scotus** (though he also draws from other important current figures at the University of Paris), and he takes issue with the Dominican **Thomas Aquinas** on various points. Hugh is also known for his influential defense of the Immaculate Conception, which also reveals the influence of other major Franciscan thinkers like **Bonaventure** and Duns Scotus. Aside from his *Commentary on the Sentences*, other works of Hugh are his *De victoria Christi contra antichristum* (*On the Victory of Christ over the Anti-Christ*) and some *Quaestiones Quodlibetales*.

**HUGH OF SAINT-CHER (ca. 1200–1263).** Already a doctor in canon law and a bachelor in **theology** at Paris, Hugh joined the **Dominican** order at the convent of Saint-Jacques in 1225 and continued his theological studies under the first Dominican master of theology at Paris, **Roland of Cremona**. Hugh was elected provincial of France almost immediately after joining the Dominicans. He served in this office from 1227 to 1230. He became a **lector** on Peter Lombard's *Sentences* probably in 1231–1232 and served as master of theology at Paris until 1233. He was named head of Saint-Jacques from 1233 to 1236 before being reelected provincial of France for a second term, serving from 1236 to 1244. In 1244, he became a cardinal, with Saint Sabina as his titular church. He died in 1263 and was buried in Lyons in 1264. Hugh demonstrated his biblical expertise by making a *Correctory* or *Correctorium Bibliae*, suggesting alterations to the Vulgate text. Around 1235, he also made a *Concordantiae dictae de S. Jacobo* (*A Biblical Concordance Entitled "The Saint-Jacques Concordance"*). The statutes of the Dominican order specified three alternatives for showing a mastery in **theology**: writing commentaries on the **Bible**, **Peter Comestor**'s *Scholastic History*, or *The Sentences of Peter Lombard*. Hugh wrote commentaries on all three of these alternatives.

**HUGH OF SAINT-VICTOR (ca. 1097–1141).** A distinguished and influential Christian theologian born in Saxony, Hugh (called by some of his contemporaries "a second **Augustine**") studied and taught at the abbey of Saint-Victor, founded in 1110 by **William of Champeaux**. Hugh had a number of illustrious students, such as **Andrew of Saint-Victor**, who developed Hugh's **exegesis**, and **Richard of Saint-Victor**, who developed Hugh's speculative **mysticism**. A widely educated and inquisitive intellect, he sought knowledge for the sake of the mystical contemplation of God, obtained primarily through prayer and meditation on God's revelation (as St. Gregory had taught him), though with the assistance of the secular disciplines. Following Augustine, Hugh stressed that an essential part of contemplation is love, as God is love according to revelation. Learning not to this end is to be rejected as vain curiosity, as Augustine had noted, and as other mystical thinkers of his time, such as **Bernard of Clairvaux** and **William of St. Thierry**, had indicated as well. His *Didascalion*, where he discusses the order of learning and the art of biblical interpretation, seeks to restore the spirit of Augustine's *De doctrina Christiana* and is an important testament to the **liberal arts** at the time. To Hugh, the monastic life should integrate all activities perfecting the **soul**, namely (in ascending order) study, meditation, prayer, action, and mystical contemplation, their crowning fruit and a foreshadowing in this life of the next life's eternal beatitude. He wrote a comprehensive theological work that may be considered as the first summa of **theology**, *De sacramentis christianae fidei* (*On the Sacraments of the Christian Faith*), where he at points uses philosophy to defend **faith**, after the manner of Augustine. Thus, he is an important forerunner of the theology practiced at the **universities** that began to emerge at the end of the 12th century. Hugh's important place in subsequent theology may be gathered from the high praise given to him by **Bonaventure** in his *De reductione artium ad theologiam*. Another of Hugh's works is the *Art of Reading*, which deals with teaching and learning. In general, his writings are characterized by their unity and consistency, each part contributing to the whole. Refer to the introduction, "The Beginnings of 'Philosophy' and 'Theology' in the Latin West."

**HUS, JAN (1370–1415).** Born in Husinetz in lower Bohemia (now Husinec in the Czech Republic), Jan moved to Prague in about 1390 where he entered the Charles University. He received his bachelor's degree in arts in 1393 and his master's degree in 1396 before becoming ordained as a priest in 1400. In 1402 he became rector of the university, a role he held at different times in the following years. Theologically he was strongly influenced by **John Wycliffe**'s writings, and he even translated his *Trialogus*, a work parallel in general to Lombard's *Sentences*, but a text aimed at educated members of society and as an aid for preachers. In his own preaching he picked up strongly on Wycliffe's theme of *De dominio divino* (*On Divine Dominion*), namely, that only a man in the state of righteousness can properly exercise authority. Authority, then, is not found in an office, and the clergy and the pope cannot hold a claim to jurisdiction solely by occupying their position. Hus preached this reform message of Wycliffe's often. In 1406, furthermore, when two Bohemian students returned from England carrying a document that praised Wycliffe with the seal of Oxford University on it, Hus read it with enthusiasm from the pulpit.

Two years later, when Pope Gregory XII warned Prague about the spread of the Wycliffite heresy and ordered a correction of the situation, the June synod ordered that all the writings of Wycliffe be handed over to the archdiocesan chancery for correction. Hus was obedient and showed willingness to reject any errors that Wycliffe's writings might contain. However, along with many other issues, he continued to defend Wycliffe, especially against John Stokes from Cambridge, who came to Prague and argued that in England Wycliffe was considered a heretic. Hus also continued his writings (*De ecclesia* [*On the Church*] and *De sex erroribus* [*On Six Errors*]), which continued to push ecclesiastic reform. Shortly after the Council of Constance, in 1415, **John Gerson** extracted from these works propositions he considered heretical, and Hus was called to give an account of his teachings. He was tried, found guilty, and burned at the stake in Constance in 1416.

# I

**IBN ARABI (1165–1240).** Considered a profound and original thinker, as well as an outstanding scholar in a wide spectrum of Islamic sciences, Abu Abdallah Muhammad ibn Ali ibn al-Arabi al-Ta'i al-Hatimi was born in Murcia, Spain. Well trained in *falsafah* (philosophy) and *kalam* (dialectical theology), he also recognized the limits of rational perception, as he is reported to have expressed personally to **Averroes**, chief among Muslim **Aristotelians**. Ibn Arabi's work, though multifaceted, has a strong emphasis on intuitive vision and the mystical path, for which reason many have seen him fundamentally as a Sufi. Yet his **Sufism** includes a full-fledged and complicated metaphysics and epistemology. His many works (hundreds) aim at synthesis, integrating from various disciplines. Among these, *The Ringstones of Wisdom* (*Fusus al-hikam*) became especially important for interpreting his thought. His writings generated numerous commentaries, and in later Sufism Ibn Arabi is frequently called the "Greatest Master." Sadr al-Din Qunawi (1210–1274), his stepson, is also his most influential student. Ibn Arabi's work has not been without critics, however, and several have questioned his orthodoxy. A good part of his literary corpus remains to be edited and published, and scholars are still assessing the full significance of his thought. Ibn Arabi died in Damascus in 1240, where he had settled in 1223 after traveling for many years outside of Spain.

**IBN BAJJAH.** *See* AVEMPACE (IBN BAJJAH) (ca. 1090–1139).

**IBN GABIROL.** *See* GABIROL, IBN (AVICEBRON) (ca. 1021–ca. 1058).

**IBN KAMMUNA (d. 1284).** Details on the life of Sa'd ibn Mansur ibn Kammuna, a Jewish thinker from Baghdad who also lived for some time in Aleppo, are scanty. He wrote in Arabic extensively on a variety of philosophical and religious topics. His *Examination of the Three Faiths* (*Tanqih*) is his best-known work, where he argues that Judaism, Christianity, and Islam share a conception of prophecy that is also in agreement with philosophical truth, and he also discusses claims peculiar to each of the three faiths. His assessment of the Jewish position (which he favors) is based mainly on **Maimonides** and **Judah Halevi**. His presentation of the Christian and Muslim positions did receive criticisms. Still, his work is praised as an honest and exceptional attempt at interfaith discourse. Perhaps the chief topic in his thought is the nature of the soul and its immortality, where the influence of **Avicenna** is, though fundamental, by no means determinative. For instance, he disagrees with Avicenna's view that the soul is generated together with the body; for Ibn Kammuna, the soul preexists bodily existence. In this respect, he is closer to Plato. Ibn Kammuna's commentary on *Al-Talwihat* (*Intimations*) by Shihab al-Din al-Suhrawardi (1154–1191), the founder of Illuminationist philosophy in the Islamic East (an outgrowth of **Platonism**), was essential in the historical transmission of this school of thought. Scholars are still editing many of Ibn Kammuna's writings and coming to terms with the significance of his ideas.

**IBN KHALDUN (1332–1406).** The Muslim philosopher and scholar Abd al-Rahman ibn Muhammad ibn Khaldun al-Hadrami was born in modern-day Tunisia. The details of his eventful life are fairly well documented in his *Autobiography*. Ibn Khaldun is a pioneer historian, philosopher of history, and social scientist. Some think that Ibn Khaldun, not Adam Smith, is the true father of economics. His best-known work, *Muqaddimah* (*Prolegomena* or *Introduction*), earned high praise among modern scholars, and many consider him one of the greatest philosophers of the Islamic world. This work has come to be known as Ibn Khaldun's "history of the world" or "universal history."

**IBN RUSHD.** *See* AVERROES (IBN RUSHD) (ca. 1126–1198).

**IBN SINA.** *See* AVICENNA (980–1037).

**INQUISITION.** Originally, "inquisition" was one of the three basic procedures of Roman law: accusation, denunciation, and inquisition. Anyone could accuse others, but it had to be done formally and the accuser had to pay the court charges. If the accusation was not sustained, he also had to pay a penalty. Denunciation was aimed not at punishment but at rehabilitation by making persons aware of their misconduct, mainly through admonition, with the hope that they would change. Inquisition grew out of denunciation when the offenses became notorious and created scandal. Pope Innocent III (1198–1216) used "inquisition" as a procedure to deal with notorious clerical abuses and scandalous episcopal negligence. In dealing with "heretical" (*see* HERESIES for strict and broad meanings) individuals and groups, the usual procedure was to pursue "denunciation" through instruction and preaching.

Often this pastoral approach worked, but when it did not, in cases that were notorious and scandalous, then "inquisition" became the procedure followed, as suggested by the decree *Ad abolendam* (*In Order to Abolish*) published by one of Innocent's predecessors, Pope Lucius III (1181–1185). Lucius's decree was aimed at the Cathars, and to a lesser degree some Waldensians, since many of the latter, as is evident in the case of their theological leader, Durand Huesca (Osca), were moved to orthodoxy by "denunciation." There were cases where "inquisition" may have been abused, for example, in the case of **Margaret Porete**.

**ISAAC ISRAELI (ca. 855–955).** A native of Egypt who later worked in Qayrawan, Isaac Israeli is reputedly the first major philosopher among Jews of the Middle Ages. Since Israeli's focus was primarily philosophical, however, **Saadiah Gaon** (882–942) is usually credited as the first medieval thinker who created a comprehensive Jewish philosophy, a philosophy guided by Scripture. Also a (court) physician, Israeli wrote both medical and philosophical works. While his contributions exerted some influence in later philosophy, especially his *Book of Definitions* and his *Book of Elements* (which were translated from the Arabic into both Hebrew and Latin), the full significance and nature of his work did not come to light until the 20th century. His thought is predominantly **Neoplatonic** and indebted to various sources, including versions and abridgments of **Plotinus** and Proclus (both of whom were often confused with **Aristotle**), as well as the work of the first of the Muslim philosophers, **Al-Kindi**. Israeli synthesizes Neoplatonic and **Aristotelian** themes, most notably emanation with hylomorphism, an approach followed by various Neoplatonists. Israeli's work also contributes to the reconciliation between philosophy and religion, transforming the Neoplatonic One through descriptions proper to the God of revelation, such as prophecy as the highest form of illumination. Israeli also, like many Muslim philosophers, such as **Al-Farabi**, recognizes the important political role of the prophet, who after the manner of a Platonic philosopher-king, needs to be able to express and implement philosophical truths in a political context. Religion in this context takes on the role of a popular expression of philosophy.

Isaac Israeli is one of the outstanding Jewish Neoplatonists. One central feature of his thought is the attempt to understand the biblical account of creation in terms of emanation as voluntary and as creation out of nothing. Other thinkers, such as rabbis and poets, also stressed Neoplatonic ideas in ethical and mystical terms, especially the soul's orientation to the higher, purer levels of being, ultimately to God. The Andalusian **Bahya ibn Paquda** (ca. 1050–1080), whose *Guide to the Duties of the Heart* remains a widely read work in Judaism, as well as the Spanish natives and poets Moses ibn Ezra (1055–ca. 1135) and Abraham ibn Ezra (ca. 1092–1167) are examples.

Another major figure of Jewish philosophy in Islamic lands is the influential Neoplatonist Salomon ibn **Gabirol** (or Avicebron, as he was known in the West), who is also an important figure in Hebrew poetry.

**ISAAC OF STELLA (ca. 1100–ca. 1169).** This philosopher and theologian from England joined the **Cistercian** order during the reforms of **Bernard of Clairvaux**. As was the case with Bernard and other **monastic** theologians, Isaac was greatly influenced by **St. Augustine** and **Neoplatonism**. In particular, he develops Augustine's **Platonic** theory of illumination, namely that the mind assesses all things in the light of eternal ideas in God, and stresses God's intimate presence to the mind. Drawing from **Boethius**, Isaac distinguishes himself as a solid **metaphysician** and **dialectician** who brings systematization to his **mysticism**. His *Letter on the Soul* (1162), addressed to **Alcher of Clairvaux**, is his main work. In it, Isaac meticulously distinguishes the faculties of the **soul** and discusses the three chief realities, the body, the soul, and God. Like other Cistercians, Isaac also wrote a series of sermons on the *Canticle of Canticles*. Isaac died in Étoile, Aquitaine.

**ISIDORE OF SEVILLE, ST. (ca. 560–636).** "The last of the **Latin Fathers of the Church**," Isidore was educated by his older brother, Leander, archbishop of Seville, whom he succeeded around 600. He was very active in Church councils, and his summations of the Christian faith were so adept that they were included in the canons of the Second (619) and Fourth (633) Councils of Toledo. He died in 636, and after his canonization in 1589, he was declared a **Doctor of the Church** (1722). He worked hard to establish a strong centralized church and monarchy in the Visigothic kingdom. He attempted to guide the Church through his *De ecclesiasticis officiis* (*On Ecclesiastical Offices*) and especially through canon 75 of the Fourth Council of Toledo, which stresses the obligations of the king to rule well and of the subjects to obey the king as "the Lord's anointed one." Isidore's most influential work, surviving in over 1,000 manuscripts, is his voluminous *Etymologiae* (*Etymologies*), the most important encyclopedia of thousands of sacred and secular topics. This 20-book achievement is complemented especially by Book II of his *Differentiae* (*Differences*), which focuses on the meanings of theological terms in particular.

**ISLAM.** The word *Islam* means literally "surrender" or "submission." Those who follow the religion of Islam, Muslims, are those who submit to the will of the one God, Allah. Allah's will was communicated between 610 and 632 to his prophet, Muhammad (ca. 570–632), a native of Mecca who transmitted this divine message in the **Koran**, the sacred text of Muslims. Accordingly, the profession of faith shared by all Muslims across the different sects and

parties of Islam is "There is no god but Allah, and Muhammad is His prophet." Islam as a way of life is grounded in law, in the Koran's code of conduct,
as well as in the traditions (hadith) following Muhammad's customary practice (sunna). These traditions were established by **exegetes** as official legal
collections supplementing the Koran's jurisdiction. The collections of Bukhari (d. 870) and Muslim (d. 875) are among the most respected. The five
"pillars" of Islam, grounded in the Koran and developed through the traditions, are the profession of faith, ritual prayer, almsgiving, fasting, and pil-
grimage, each with its own regulations. Some, however, consider holy war as
the fifth pillar and see the profession of faith as a basis for the five pillars.
Islam spread quickly through the preaching and enterprises of Muhammad,
who by the time of his death had achieved, for the first time in history, the
unity of the tribes of the Arabian Peninsula under one authority. At the height
of its political dominion during the Middle Ages, Islam consisted of the
eastern and the western **caliphates**. The eastern caliphate, which extended
eastward as far as central Asia and the Indus Valley, first had Damascus as its
capital, and then Baghdad. Cordoba was the capital of the western caliphate,
which in 732 extended westward as far as central France.

The two principal subgroups of the Muslim religion are the Shi'ites and
the Sunnis. They differ mainly in regard to their distinct views of the tradition of the legitimate heirs to the Prophet Muhammad. About 80 percent of
all present Muslims, however, are Sunnis, and in the Middle Ages, Shi'ites
were an even smaller minority. Shi'ites recognize only the members of Ali's
family as heirs to the Prophet and as having rights to the caliphate, and they
consider the first three caliphs after Muhammad as illegitimate. Within
Shi'ism, however, there are differences, chiefly in terms of the leaders recognized as legitimate, resulting in three main sects, the Zaydis, the Ismalis, and
the Imamis (or Twelvers). Moreover, Ismalis and Imamis believe in a secret
knowledge given by Muhammad to Ali's descendants. Accordingly, the
Shi'ite leader (imam) of these sects has a prophetic role beyond that of the
Sunni caliph. Unlike Shi'ites, Sunnis recognize the first four caliphs as legitimate, as well as the Umayyad and 'Abbasid caliphates. They are known as
orthodox, "the people of custom (sunna)," and are divided according to four
schools of law: Hanbali, Shafi'i, Maliki, and Hanafi. *See also KALAM.*

# J

**JAMES OF ASCOLI (ca. 1270–ca. 1315).** A **Franciscan** theologian who studied at Paris, he has left a sizeable collection of writings that still need to be edited: his *Commentary on the Sentences*; his *Quodlibets* and *Disputed Questions*, the products of a master in theology; and a set of *Quaestiones diversae*. He must have already been a master of theology before 1309, since he was among the masters who were consulted in the process of dealing with **Margaret Porete**. Along with his fellow Franciscan, **Richard of Conington**, he was one of the theological consultants at the Council of Vienne in 1311. His *Quodlibets* have been dated to 1311 or 1312, although they might be a year or two earlier. In the first question of *Quodlibet I*, he defends the formal distinction of John Duns Scotus, gaining his knowledge of it from Scotus's *Reportatio Parisiensis* (Paris commentary on Lombard's *Sentences*). Later authors, such as **William of Alnwick**, would criticize his portrayal of this famous Scotistic distinction. In his *Quodlibets*, James also debates against **Robert Cowton** on the issue of God's knowledge of future contingencies.

**JAMES OF METZ (fl. 1300–1310).** Very little is known about the life of this **Dominican** theologian, who twice commented on **Peter Lombard**'s *Sentences*, probably at the University of Paris (ca. 1300–1301 and 1301–1302). Some, however, place the second commentary, which often repeats the *reportatio* (student report) of his earlier lectures, in the years 1308–1309. In general, he followed the principle of his fellow Dominican **Thomas Aquinas**, which became one of the dominating attitudes of Dominicans at this time: follow the Philosopher—that is, **Aristotle**—when his text does not contradict the Catholic faith. James, however, did not always himself follow Aquinas. He criticized his account of individuation by matter, positing form as the cause of individuality, as did **Peter of Auvergne**. Regarding the process of knowledge, especially in regard to the knowledge of God and immaterial substances, James also departs from Aquinas, seeking to synthesize **Aristotelian** and **Augustinian** views of knowledge. James's criticisms of Aquinas elicited the attacks of **Hervaeus Natalis**, who wrote a *Correctorium fratris Jacobi Metensis* (*A Correction of Brother James of Metz*).

**JAMES OF VENICE (fl. 1136–1148).** A native of Venice, James was the most important translator of Aristotle in the 12th century. The facts known about his life are few. He was present in 1136 at the theological debate in Constantinople between Anselm of Havelberg and the archbishop of Nicomedia, and he served as an advisor to the archbishop of Ravenna in 1128. A number of 12th- and 13th-century authors mention his translations of Aristotle's *Posterior Analytics*, and through identity of style, James must be acknowledged as the translator of the *Physics, On the Soul, Metaphysics, On Memory, On Longitude, On Youth, On Respiration, On Death, On Intelligence, Sophistical Refutations*, and most of the *Parva Naturalia*, that is, many important works on natural philosophy. The only other 12th-century translator of Aristotle was a certain Ioannes, who also did a translation of the *Posterior Analytics* that is mentioned by John of Salisbury. As a translator of Aristotle, James was followed in the late 1250s by Henricus Aristippus, who translated Book IV of the *Meteorologica* (*Meteorology*).

**JAMES OF VITERBO, BL. (ca. 1255–1308).** A native of Viterbo, James joined the **Hermits of St. Augustine** there around 1270 and received his preparatory education at the convent in his hometown. He studied philosophy and **theology** at Paris from 1275 to 1282. He succeeded **Giles of Rome** as **Augustinian** regent master in theology in 1293 and held that position until 1300. In that year, he was appointed director of the *studium generale* (international house of studies) for the Augustinians in Naples. In the late 1290s, he commented on the Gospels of Matthew and Luke and on the Pauline Epistles, but these works are lost. Among his surviving texts are a large number of *Quaestiones disputatae* (*Disputed Questions*): *De praedicamentis in divinis* (*On the Categories as Applied to God*), *De Verbo* (*Concerning the Divine Word*), *De Spiritu Sancto* (*On the Holy Spirit*), and *De angelorum compositione* (*On the Composition of Angels*).

James, like Giles of Rome and **Thomas Aquinas**, admits a real distinction between essence and existence, but he explains it in a different way than either of these authors, seemingly influenced by **Godfrey of Fontaines**. He shows his Augustinian background very boldly in his portrait of matter, portraying it as not purely passive but as possessing seminal reason, which he interprets as inchoate active forms. In political thought, James is credited with writing, in 1302, the earliest treatise on the Church, *De regimine Chris-*

*tiano* (*On the Christian Regime*). He was appointed bishop of Benevento in 1302 and archbishop of Naples one year later. He died in Naples in 1308 and was beatified in 1914.

**JAN HUS.** *See* HUS, JAN (1370–1415).

**JEAN GERSON.** *See* GERSON, JEAN (1363–1429).

**JEWISH PHILOSOPHY AND THEOLOGY.** Basic principles of medieval philosophy and **theology** can already be found in works of the early Jewish thinker **Philo of Alexandria** (30 B.C.–40 A.D.), even though medieval thinkers had little (or no) direct access to the texts of Philo and knew only generally (if at all) of his principles. Philo continues the tradition of Greco-Roman philosophy but also breaks from it, ushering in the religious philosophy that is characteristic of the medieval period, whereby revelation is interpreted in light of philosophy and philosophy is revised in terms of revelation. For Philo, there is one infallible source of truth, divine revelation. However, God is also the source of truth in the sense that He furnished human beings with reason, which on its own may acquire some (though not a complete or infallible) knowledge of God. Since truth is one, any conflict between reason and revelation cannot be real but only apparent, due either to a misunderstanding of Scripture or to a flaw in human reason. But if the language of Scripture could be properly understood and if reason were not misguided, both reason and revelation would always agree. Thus, the proper approach is to interpret revelation in terms of what is most evidently true to reason, and reason must be guided in terms of what are most evidently the true teachings of Scripture. Aside from differences among Judaism, Christianity, and Islam, medieval thinkers of the three traditions shared principles found in Philo, such as the existence of God, the unity of God, the creation of the world, divine providence, and the divine origin of the rules of human conduct. Medieval thinkers of the three traditions continued in the spirit of Philo, seeking to reconcile reason with revelation in their own ways.

Medieval Jewish philosophy and theology took place in Muslim regions, roughly from the 9th to the beginning of the 13th century, and in Christian Europe from the 12th century on. Unlike medieval Islamic and Christian thought, where philosophy and theology were often clearly demarcated as separate fields, in Judaism they were generally more blended: philosophical ideas were used primarily to provide systematic articulation of Jewish tradition. The adoption by **Karaite** Jews (who accepted only the Bible as authority, not rabbinic tradition) of a separate theology after the manner of *kalam* is an exception. This effort expressed itself in various areas, such as **mysticism**, theology, **logic**, and the other philosophic disciplines, and polemics; the contributors were also multifaceted, including rabbis, poets, doctors, statesmen, mystics, etc. However, rabbinic literature, focused on biblical and legal interpretation, continued as a distinctive enterprise, and many rabbis and Jews saw philosophy and theology (as the systematization of Judaism) as something foreign. Jewish thinkers in Muslim regions drew from *kalam* (the **Mu'tazilite** school especially), **Neoplatonism**, and **Aristotelianism**, basically the same intellectual trends as those informing medieval Islamic thought. The translation of Hellenistic works into Arabic facilitated for Jews, as it did for Muslims, their assimilation of philosophy. This foreign science came to be seen by some not as antithetical to Judaism, but as an important supplement to Judaism, especially for the educated.

The work of Dawud ibn Marwan al-Muqammis, of the ninth century, and of the Karaites Jacob al-Kirkisani and Japheth ben Ali, both of the 10th century, reflects the important influence of *kalam* in medieval rabbinic thought. **Saadiah Gaon**, a native of Egypt who later worked in Babylon, made important contributions in a variety of fields, including biblical scholarship, law, poetry, and philosophy. His *Commentary on the Book of Creation* and his *Book of Doctrines and Beliefs* are influential, systematic expositions in Jewish theology, originally using elements from *kalam* and philosophy (e.g., a version of Aristotelian physics against Mu'tazilite atomism) and defending the truth of rabbinical Judaism against the views of the Karaite Jews and against other religions. Refer to the introduction.

**JOACHIM OF FIORE (1130–ca. 1202).** Joachim entered the **Cistercian** monastery of Sambucina in Sicily without taking the habit, but church criticism of him as a lay preacher led him to take the Cistercian habit in Corazzo. Ordained in 1168, he was elected abbot but chose to found a stricter branch of the order. In 1202, he submitted his theological writings to the Holy See but died before they were judged. His most significant teachings concerned the **Trinity** and his Trinitarian view of history. He opposed the teachings of **Peter Lombard** on the Trinity and argued that the unity of the Father, Son, and Holy Spirit was not "true and proper" but "collective." In effect, he was judged, after his death, to be a tritheist at the Fourth Lateran Council of 1215. Joachim's views of the Trinity were likewise applied to history. He spoke of the times of the Old Testament, marked by fear and servile obedience, as the age of the Father. The New Testament period, characterized by faith and filial obedience, was the age of the Son. Around 1260, Joachim expected the arrival of the age of the Holy Spirit where universal love and the beatitudes would reign. This expected arrival of the age of the Spirit was preached and predicted by the Spiritual **Franciscans**, who were also called Joachimites, though they went far beyond what Joachim himself had ever preached. They, and he by implication, were condemned by Pope Alexander IV in 1256.

**JOHN XXI, POPE.** *See* PETER OF SPAIN (ca. 1205–1277).

**JOHN BACONTHORPE (1290–ca. 1348).** The *Doctor Resolutus* (Unhampered Teacher) is the best known of the early **Carmelite** authors, perhaps because both his *Commentary on the Sentences* and his three *Quodlibets* were printed at Venice in 1526 and again at Cremona in 1618. In the 17th century, he was generally considered to be the official doctor of the Carmelites. Baconthorpe, like the Parisian Carmelites **Gerard of Bologna** and **Guido Terrena**, was also involved in administrative work for his order. He was the prior provincial in England from 1326 until 1333. Quite likely he became a master of theology in 1323, so he lectured on the *Sentences* of **Peter Lombard** before this time, maybe as early as 1320–1321. His first two *Quodlibets* were probably disputed between 1323 and 1325, but since the published version is well crafted, he may have written them slightly later. Independent manuscript copies of *Quodlibet III* indicate that it was disputed in Paris, not in England, and done in 1330 while he was still prior provincial in England. Like the other Carmelites of his era, he seems to be free of allegiances to the **Thomists**, **Scotists**, or **Ockhamists**, preferring to follow an independent or unhampered path. *See also* ORDERS (RELIGIOUS).

**JOHN BASSOLIS (OF BASSOL) (ca. 1275–1333).** John was a French Franciscan who studied under **John Duns Scotus** at Paris in the first decade of the 14th century. He was one of Scotus's favorite students and one of his most loyal followers. A story is told that Scotus came to teach one day and the only student in the classroom was Bassolis. Scotus said, "Bassolis is present; the auditorium is full." John lectured on *Book IV of the Sentences* at Reims in 1313, but his complete *Commentary on Books I–IV of the Sentences*, printed in Paris in 1516–1517, probably dates from his later lectures at Rouen and Malines, or is at least an updated version of lectures given earlier in Reims.

**JOHN BLUND (ca. 1170–1248).** John was the first master of arts at Oxford whose writings survive. His *Treatise on the Soul*, written before 1204, quite likely had its origins at Oxford, although he is also asserted to have taught the **liberal arts** at Paris. He certainly studied **theology** at Paris, probably during the disturbing period (1208–1214) of political conflict when masters and students left Oxford for Paris, Cambridge, or Reading. In 1227, he was in the service of King Henry III. He was elected archbishop of Canterbury in 1232, but in a dispute his election was contested and he was replaced by **Edmund of Abingdon**. Blund was chancellor of York in 1234 and remained in that office until his death in 1248.

In his *Treatise on the Soul*, John follows **Avicenna**'s *De anima* (*On the Soul*) to help him clarify the puzzling positions held by Aristotle. Blund distinguishes between the way the natural philosopher treats the **soul** insofar as it is united to the body and the manner it is dealt with by the **metaphysician** as a **substance** in itself. The theologian is concerned with the soul not in itself but with the conditions of its salvation or punishment. Blund thus shows in this treatise a strong dedication to the philosophical study of the soul. He, following Avicenna, presents the soul as the perfection of the body. He departs, however, from Avicenna in adding a chapter on free will, which he borrows largely from **Anselm of Canterbury**.

**JOHN BURIDAN.** *See* BURIDAN, JOHN (ca. 1295–1361).

**JOHN CAPREOLUS.** *See* CAPREOLUS, JOHN (ca. 1380–1444).

**JOHN DUNS SCOTUS.** *See* DUNS SCOTUS, JOHN, BL. (ca. 1266–1308).

**JOHN LUTTERELL (ca. 1280–1335).** John received his degree as a doctor of theology at Oxford sometime around 1315 and was elected chancellor of the **university** in 1317. He was involved in a dispute between the university and the **Dominicans** during his first year as chancellor and was the leading figure in a battle with the masters and scholars at the university in 1322 that almost ended in schism. He was deposed as chancellor in September, 1322 and went to Avignon for two years. Pope John XXII justified his long stay, since he was involved in proceedings against certain teachings, which recent scholars are sure were the teachings of **William of Ockham**. The grounds for this conclusion is that Lutterell was examining the *Commentary on the Sentences* of Ockham and found 56 propositions there that were against true and sound doctrine. The list can be found in his *Libellus contra doctrinam Guillelmi Ockham* (*A Pamphlet against the Teaching of William of Ockham*) written during 1323–1324. He also was one of the masters of theology who condemned 51 articles of Ockham that were censured at Avignon in 1326. Some scholars suspect that Lutterell was also trying to take revenge on Ockham as one of the leaders of the group that had him deposed as chancellor. He was again in Avignon from 1327 until 1333, and there he wrote his *Epistola de visione beatifica* defending Pope John XXII's theology of the beatific vision. During these years, he was frequently sent on papal missions.

**JOHN OF DAMASCUS.** *See* DAMASCENE, JOHN (JOHN OF DAMASCUS), ST. (fl. 8TH CENTURY).

**JOHN OF JANDUN (ca. 1275–1328).** The most **Averroistic** member of the **Arts Faculty** at Paris in the early 14th century. He wrote commentaries on Aristotle's *Physics*, *Metaphysics*, *On the Soul*, and *On the Heavens*. In them, he defended all the Averroistic interpretations of Aristotle's teachings that presented problems for the Christian faith: the unicity of the intellect, the denial of personal immortality and personal moral responsibility, and the eternity of the world. He held that philosophical argumentation supported these positions, even though the Scriptures, the **Fathers of the Church**, and faith defended the opposite. In his *Treatise on the Praises of Paris*, Buridan chides theologians for their weak, or even sophistical, arguments supporting the faith. He was also associated with **Marsilius of Padua** to some extent in the production of the antipapal *Defensor pacis* (*Defender of the Peace*). He was officially mentioned in the formal condemnation in 1327 of many of the propositions contained in the work. When the authorship of the *Defender of the Peace* was revealed earlier, in 1324, he fled Paris along with Marsilius and also sought with him the protection of Emperor Louis of Bavaria.

**JOHN OF LA ROCHELLE (OF RUPELLA) (ca. 1190–1245).** Quite likely, John was already a master of theology when he entered the **Franciscan** order sometime before 1238. In entering the Franciscans, he became closely associated with **Alexander of Hales**. Their works from this point on are very much intertwined. The *Summa fratris Alexandri* (*The Summa of Brother Alexander*) has to give the title of authorship to John of La Rochelle for Book I (on God) and Book III (on the Incarnation, the suffering and death of Christ, law, **grace**, and **faith**). On the other hand, one of John's most famous treatises, called "the first scholastic textbook on psychology," his *Summa de anima* (*Summa on the Soul*), owes a great deal of its material to Alexander's *Gloss on the* **Sentences** *of* **Peter Lombard**. Their *Quaestiones disputatae* (*Disputed Questions*) are so interrelated that it is hard to distinguish which material comes from which author. John's fame as a preacher, however, stands out, especially his *Eleven Marian Sermons*. He and Alexander, so close in life, were also joined in death, both dying in the same year, 1245.

**JOHN OF LICHTENBERG OR PICARDY (ca. 1275–ca. 1315).** A **lector** at Cologne, this **Dominican** later delivered his ***Commentary on Peter Lombard's Sentences*** at Paris between 1305 and 1308. He became provincial of the Teutonic province of the Dominicans from 1308 to 1310 and thereafter became regent master in **theology** at Paris beginning in 1310. Only part of Book IV of his *Commentary on the Sentences* survives, along with 36 *Disputed Questions*.

**JOHN OF MIRECOURT (ca. 1310–ca. 1357).** John was a **Cistercian** who taught at the house of studies of his order in Paris. He commented on **Peter Lombard**'s *Sentences* twice, between 1334 and 1336 and between 1344 and 1345. Described later by **Peter of Candia** as one of the *filii Ockhami* (Sons of **William of Ockham**), a number of his Ockhamist teachings were challenged by the **Benedictine** John Norman. In 1346, 63 of his propositions were labeled suspicious. John wrote a *Declaratio* or *Explanation* of his positions, but more than half of them were condemned by the chancellor of the university in 1347. Mirecourt wrote a second *Declaratio*, but this second apology was also unsuccessful.

**JOHN OF NAPLES (ca. 1280–ca. 1350).** The first knowledge of this **Dominican** is that he was a student at the convent of St. Dominic in Bologna during the school years 1298–1300 and taught at the Dominican *studium* in his native Naples from 1300 on. We know that he did his theological studies at Paris and that he served as regent master there from 1315 to 1317, before returning as master at Bologna. He was part of the commission, along with **Peter of la Palude**, that examined the writings of **Durandus of Saint-Pourçain**. He was one of the witnesses in Naples for the canonization process of **Thomas Aquinas**, and he was likewise one of the promotors of Aquinas's cause in Avignon in 1322–1323. His fidelity to Thomas in his teachings is witnessed by many of his 42 *Disputed Questions* and the questions of his 13 *Quodlibets*.

**JOHN OF PARIS OR JEAN QUIDORT (ca. 1265–1306).** John read the *Sentences* at Paris sometime between 1292 and 1296, and he became master of theology there in 1304. His teaching on the body of Christ in the Eucharist, however, brought a prohibition against his position, and he died while awaiting a definite decision regarding this issue. Scientific treatises on meteors, on the rainbow, and on forms are attributed to him, but his *Sentences* commentary, responding at times on behalf of **Thomas Aquinas** to the criticisms of **Henry of Ghent**, comes down to us only in a *Reportatio* (a student report).

**JOHN OF READING (ca. 1285–1346).** John, a **Franciscan** theologian and philosopher, was one of **John Duns Scotus**'s most loyal and dedicated defenders. He is well known for his strong defense of Scotus's positions, particularly against the criticisms that **William of Ockham** brought to them. Surprisingly, however, in q. 3 of the prologue to Ockham's *Commentary on Book I of the Sentences*, John of Reading appears as one of Ockham's sources. The Venerable Inceptor (Ockham) quotes him verbatim, picking pieces here and there from q. 2 of John of Reading's prologue to his *Com-*

*mentary on Lombard's Sentences.* In short, it seems necessary to postulate that John made two commentaries on Lombard's *Sentences*—one before, and a source for, Ockham's *Sentences* commentary and another criticizing the same work of Ockham. Yet, despite such a postulate, it seems that both commentaries would have large portions verbally in common, since the text that survives and serves as Ockham's source is the same as the later, and sole surviving, text that comes down to us as a Scotistic response to Ockham. Eccleston lists him as the 45th regent master of the Franciscans at Oxford.

**JOHN OF RIPA (fl. 1357–1368).** This **Franciscan** author, who taught in Paris between 1357 and 1368, was known as the *Doctor Difficilis* (Difficult Doctor) and *Doctor Supersubtilis* (Extra-subtle Doctor). The latter title connotes his relationship with the Subtle Doctor, **John Duns Scotus**: he is considered a disciple, even though he criticized him quite often. He earned the former title, the Difficult Doctor, through the way he organized his discussions in his *Lectura super primum Sententiarum* (*Lectures on Book I of the Sentences*), which do not follow the normal structure of **Peter Lombard**. He has also left a set of *Conclusiones* regarding Book I of the *Sentences*, some partial comments on the other books of the *Sentences*, and a set of *Determinationes*, which are also difficult reading. John himself never had any of his positions censured, but his Franciscan student, Louis of Padua, had 14 of his articles condemned in 1362. John commanded the respect of **Paul of Venice**, who judged his *Book I of the Sentences* to be such a worthwhile text that he made an abbreviation of it.

**JOHN OF RODINGTON (ca. 1290–ca. 1348).** Portrayed as a follower of **John Duns Scotus**, this English **Franciscan** rather shows more of an Augustinian orientation in some of the questions of his *Commentary on the Sentences*. He holds to the illumination theory of knowledge that is more proper to **Henry of Ghent** and his Franciscan follower **Richard of Conington** than to the path of Scotus. His *Quodlibet*, referred to as a *Treatise on Conscience*, really covers in an integral way all aspects of morality, and it does so with frequent references to **Augustine, Anselm**, and **Richard of Saint-Victor**. If he seems more distant from Scotus than expected, then he also appears not only distant, but opposed, to **William of Ockham**. John, the 56th Franciscan **lector** at Oxford, was regent master there from 1325 to 1328. He was elected 19th provincial of the English Franciscans sometime after 1340 and is reported to have died of the Black Death in 1348.

**JOHN OF ST. THOMAS (JOHN POINSOT) (1589–1644).** John received his bachelor in arts degree from the Jesuit university of Coimbra in 1605, became a member of the Trinitarian order, and began his theological studies there. After a year he transferred to the University of Louvain and studied under a Spanish Dominican, Thomas de Torres. He entered the **Dominican** order when he finished his studies as a *baccalareus biblicus*. After teaching the **liberal arts** at Madrid, he began his theology teaching at the University of Alcalá in 1620 and remained there until his death in 1644. His chief works are his *Cursus Philosophicus*, which covers **logic** and natural philosophy (cosmology and rational psychology) in a Thomistic way. His *Cursus Theologicus* follows the order of theological questions in **Thomas Aquinas**'s *Summa theologiae* but is written in relation to the post-Reformation world. In general terms, he remains in accord with the representations of the philosophy and **theology** of St. Thomas that is also found in **Capreolus** and Cajetan.

**JOHN OF SALISBURY (ca. 1115–1180).** As a student of **Peter Abelard** and **Robert of Melun**, John, an Englishman, started his studies in Paris in 1136. A year later, he began to study grammar in Chartres with **William of Conches**. Other notables with whom he studied during the next 10 years were **Gilbert of Poitiers** and **Thierry of Chartres**. In 1147, he returned to England, working for Theobald, the archbishop of Canterbury, for the next 20 years as consultant and secretary. After many church missions, John was elected bishop of Chartres in 1176. He attended the Third Lateran Council three years later and died in Chartres, where he is buried, in 1180.

John's principal works are his *Metalogicon* and *Polycraticus*. The first is a strong defense of the **liberal arts** as taught by the teachers he admired most and an attack on the more pragmatic approach of Cornificius and the Cornificians who wanted to water down the curriculum of the trivium and quadrivium to move students on to their practical careers more quickly. In this work he praises the teachers he admires, especially **Bernard of Chartres**, who taught his teachers. The *Polycraticus* is a treatise on the art of government, attempting to unify ancient political philosophy with the Patristic and medieval teachings around the governance of society. He argues for a view of government that would allow the state to govern without too much interference from church authorities. John also wrote a *Historia pontificalis* (*A Papal History*), providing a detailed portrait of life at the papal court during the years from 1148 to 1151. He also left two biographies: *The Life of Saint Anselm* and *The Life of Thomas Becket*.

**JOHN OF STERNGASSEN (ca. 1275–ca. 1327).** A **Dominican** theologian who taught at Strasbourg and Cologne (1310–1327), he avoided the **Neoplatonic** direction of many Dominicans in the Rhineland and stayed so close to **Thomas Aquinas** in his teaching that he has often been represented as an immediate disciple of St. Thomas. The proof of his loyalty to Thomas can be found in his *Commentary on the Sentences*, which is markedly **Aristotelian** in the tradition of Aquinas.

**JOHN PECKHAM.** *See* PECKHAM, JOHN (ca. 1230–1292).

**JOHN PHILOPONUS OR JOHN THE GRAMMARIAN.** *See* PHILOP-ONUS, JOHN, OR JOHN THE GRAMMARIAN (fl. 6TH CENTURY).

**JOHN RUYSBROECK.** *See* RUYSBROECK, JAN VAN, BL. (1293–1381).

**JOHN SCOTUS ERIUGENA (ca. 810–ca. 877).** A native of Ireland, John arrived around 845 at the palace school of Charles the Bald, where he taught grammar and **logic**. From this teaching period dates his *Annotationes in Martianum Capellam* (Notes on *The Marriage of Philology and Mercury* of Martianus Capella). In the 850s, he became involved in a controversy with Prudentius of Troyes and Florus of Lyons over predestination. In his *De praedestinatone* (*Concerning Predestination*), he defended the thesis that there is but one predestination, a predestination to good, and that no one is forced by God's foreknowledge to do evil. A whole new phase of his life began around 860, when he was commissioned by Charles the Bald to correct **Hilduin**'s Latin translations of **Dionysius the Pseudo-Areopagite**'s works. He produced new translations of *On the Divine Names*, *Mystical Theology*, *On the Celestial Hierarchy*, and *On the Ecclesiastical Hierarchy*. He then translated the *Ambigua* or commentaries of **Maximus the Confessor** on Dionysius's works. His Latin translations continued with the production of Gregory of Nyssa's *Sermo de imagine* (*A Sermon concerning Images*) and Epiphanius's *De fide* (*On Faith*).

Eriugena began his own creative work in the 860s. This included commentaries on the *Gospel of John* and on Dionysius, and between 862 and 866 he produced his most important work, *Periphyseon* or *On the Division of Nature*. This was a work that had some serious difficulties when it was used and interpreted by Amalric of Bène and David of Dinant to explain Aristotle's philosophy. In fact, it was condemned at the Council of Sens in 1210, and Honorius III ordered all copies to be burned. In his work, Eriugena divided nature into four types: *natura creans et non creata* (nature that creates and is not created), *natura creata et creans* (nature that is created and also creates), *natura creata et non creans* (nature that is created and does not create), and *natura non creata et non creans* (nature that is not created and does not create). His explanations of these four types is at times in language that is pantheistic. He speaks of "God being made in His Creatures." Also, since

God is in creatures, he speaks of God as being the essence of creatures. Yet, read carefully, he insists that God is transcendent. Eriugena is certainly not a pantheist. Refer to the introduction, "The Beginnings of 'Philosophy' and 'Theology' in the Latin West."

**JOHN THE CANON OR JOHN MARBES (fl. 1300–1343).** John the Canon has been portrayed as a Catalan canon of Tortosa who taught philosophy and theology at Toulouse in the 15th century. His sole surviving work is his *Questions on the Eight Books of Physics*. However, he is such a close and faithful follower of **John Duns Scotus** and the early **Scotists** that it seems more accurate to place him back in the first half of the 14th century. The opponents he faces in his *Physics* commentary notably are **Thomas Wylton** and **Gerard Odon**, authors from the second and third decades of the 14th century. These are not the authors we would expect to be cited on the issues of physics in the 15th century, but rather others, like John Buridan, whose *Physics* manuscripts were numerous at that time. John the Canon holds strong to many traditional Scotistic doctrines: the univocity of the concept of being, the formal distinction, and *haeceitas* (thisness) as the formal principle of individuation. His *Physics* commentary was first published at Padua in 1475 and then five more times in Venice between 1481 and 1520.

**JOHN WYCLIFFE.** *See* WYCLIFFE, JOHN (ca. 1335–1384).

**JUDAH HALEVI.** *See* HALEVI, JUDAH (ca. 1075–1141).

**JULIAN OF NORWICH (1342–ca. 1423).** This English anchoress and mystic, author of *Showings* or *Revelations of Divine Love*, is well known for her saying "All shall be well." It is only in reading her work that one discovers that her words do not convey an optimism based on blindness to life's difficult trials but an awareness that man's whole being is centered in the loving hands of God. Her *Revelations* is based on 16 showings or visions she received in 1373 when she was suffering from a serious illness and near to death. The book was written in two forms: a short version made almost immediately after her experiences and a longer version, based on her meditations concerning these events, that was written about 20 years later. Her prayers to God had been that she might obtain the same experience of Christ's suffering as that had by his mother and his friends beneath the Cross, that she might be purified by these sufferings, and that she might receive three "wounds": true contrition for her sins, a desire to suffer with Christ, and a thirst for God. Margery of Kemp after visiting Julian praised her "theology of tears" and her ability to counsel others in their sufferings.

# K

*KALAM.* In Arabic, *kalam* means literally "speech" or "word" and may be used in a wide range of senses. In translations of Greek philosophical works, it often stands for *logos* in its various meanings (e.g., word, speech, reason, argument, account). *Kalam* later acquired the more specialized meaning of theology as the systematic study of revelation, which for Muslims is the **Koran**, revealed by God to the prophet and founder of Islam, Muhammad (d. 632). *Kalam* will be dealt with in this latter sense, which includes approaches to **exegesis**.

The systematic or theological approach to Scripture inevitably arose through the need to establish official Islamic doctrine by unifying seemingly incompatible Koranic passages and through the need of **Islam** to define itself in the face of other traditions, namely Judaism, Christianity, and Greco-Roman culture. However, as readers sought to derive meaning from the Koran's sacred wisdom, different theological approaches and formulations emerged. The question of free will versus predestination was one of the first to generate controversy, as evidenced by writings beginning at the end of the seventh century. Though philosophy or *falsafah*, grounded in natural reason, is a separate discipline, it was not uncommon for philosophy to be used, in varying ways and degrees, in Muslim theology. After the decline of philosophy as an independent pursuit in Islam at the end of the 12th century with the death of **Averroes**, it was primarily in *kalam* that Islamic philosophy lived on. The **Mu'tazilite** movement arose in the eighth century at Basra with Wasil ibn 'Ata' (d. 748/9). At Baghdad, it developed the first systematic theological school with the organizing assistance of philosophy. What the Mu'tazilites took to be certain fundamental tenets, especially divine unity and justice, they used as principles of deduction, interpretation, and, as in debates against the Christian dogma of the **Trinity**, polemics. For example, different qualities such as justice and knowledge, attributed to God by Koranic passages, had to be understood as somehow not impairing divine unity. Taking God's justice (with its rewards and punishments) as a premise, room needed to be made for human freedom and responsibility, though always in harmony with the Koran's descriptions of God's complete control over all

191

creation. In epistemology, **metaphysics**, and physics (they had their own theory of atoms), Mu'tazilites were evidently indebted to Greek philosophy. They viewed reason as an autonomous source of truth that could be used even to correct tradition; in fact, reason could even by itself lead one to believe in Allah.

The other major movement in *kalam*, the **Asharites**, was initiated by the former Mu'tazilite Al-Ashari (d. 935), the "Hammer of the Mu'tazilites," after abandoning what he saw as their unorthodox views. This movement gained wide influence, to the point of becoming identifiable with orthodoxy. The great **Al-Ghazali** (d. 1111), also known as the "proof" or "seal" of Islam, refined Asharite insights. The Asharites, like the Mu'tazilites, also employed philosophy when handling philosophical-type questions, but they differed from them both in terms of the extent and kind of philosophical usage: they placed greater emphasis on tradition (*hadith*) and less on reason as a source of truth. Also, their fundamental principles differed. Adhering to the principle of God's all-powerful and unrestricted will, they seem to have embraced a kind of occasionalism, which placed significant restrictions on reason's capacity to interpret facts accurately. The Asharites nonetheless sought to preserve human responsibility while still clinging to God's omnipotence: God creates the act of willing as well as the external action. God also creates in a third instant another component that enables the act to be attributed to the agent. This became known as their theory of "acquisition," a development of earlier formulations of the Mu'tazilites, since it was probably already implicit in some Mu'tazilite circles. Al-Maturidi (d. 944) and his followers the Maturidites, who along with the Asharites became the major forces in Islamic theology in Sunnite regions, further elaborated on this theory of acquisition to harmonize predestination with human responsibility. Put simply, to them the solution is that God creates the acts man chooses or acquires.

Aside from alternatives and debates within theology, theology as a systematic approach to revelation met with opposition on the grounds that it was bound to corrupt revelation through human standards. Such was the attitude of the Baghdad jurist Ibn Hanbal (780–855), who also emphasized that neither Muhammad nor his followers, the models of tradition, had engaged in this approach. Hanbal's position and exegesis, however, itself became the source of a theological stance, followed by influential theologians such as Ibn Taymiya (1263–1328) from Damascus, known among other things for his attack against the validity of traditional **logic**. Even before the Asharites, another important trend in the Islamic study of revelation began as a traditionalist reaction against the Mu'tazilites. The traditionalist approach, initially advocated by Sunnite theologians in the ninth century, was based on a textual approach to revelation that took its guidance from traditional sources; human reason was not to be followed as an independent source of truth. The traditionalists still emphasized certain principles within the letter of the Koran, however, such as the omnipotence of God, which some used as a basis to deny the fixed order of nature and to propound instead a theory of atoms more consonant with God as sole and absolute cause. Against the Mu'tazilites, God's omnipotence means (say the traditionalists) that good and evil (and justice and injustice) are based on God's inscrutable will and not absolute standards to which he submits. Justice is ultimately beyond human grasp; in practice, it is simply following God's will and its laws. After the legal thinker Al-Shafi' (d. 820), this principle grounded Islamic law in most **schools**. Though closer to the traditionalists, the Asharites may be seen as moderating between the rational approach of the Mu'tazilites and a purely traditional approach.

**KARAITES.** The Karaite movement began in the eighth century as a sect of Judaism that wished to set aside the oral tradition of the rabbis and the **Talmud** and to preserve the **Torah** as the only source of religious teaching and practice. They assumed that the Bible presented clear directions for Jewish life, and it simply needed to be read. The word *Karaism* comes from *qara* (to read). The Karaites encouraged personal interpretation of the Scriptures and stressed rigorous asceticism: fasting, strict dietary laws, and ritual purity and dress. *See also* EXEGESIS; *KALAM*; SCHOOLS.

**KILWARDBY, ROBERT.** *See* ROBERT KILWARDBY (ca. 1215–1279).

**KINDI, AL- (ALKINDI) (d. ca. 870).** Abu Yusuf Ya'qub ibn Ishaq al-Kindi, generally considered the father of Islamic philosophy or *falsafah*, wrote on practically every discipline of his day (including the natural sciences, medicine, **logic**, politics, and mathematics). However, only about one-tenth of his production survives, which makes it difficult to determine the details of his views on certain issues, such as human freedom. He is also a philosopher, in the proper sense of developing a comprehensive view of reality and of man's place in it. He worked in Baghdad at the courts of the Abbasid **caliphs** Al-Ma'mun and Al-Mu'tasim, who favored the cultivation and translation of the foreign Greek learning, then new to Islam. Al-Kindi is also the originator of a school that developed his interests through contributions in a wide range of scientific fields. His philosophical system, expressed most completely in his *Book of First Philosophy*, incorporates Aristotelian elements, as passed down in the tradition of Porphyry and the Alexandrine commentators, within an overall scheme that places the transcendent **Neoplatonic** One at the top and origin of reality. Al-Kindi appropriates this tradition in his own way. He argues, following **Islam** and **John Philoponus**, against those claiming the eternity of the world (e.g., Proclus and **Aristotle**), that the world both began and will end. His argumentation is detailed and rigorous, amply drawing from the mathematical sciences. This text is a pioneer work of Muslim philosophy not only in terms of its content and its (synthesizing) attitude toward **Platonism** and **Aristotelianism**, but also in terms of its approach to philosophy and religion.

Philosophy agrees with Islam, argues Al-Kindi, as truths of reason and revelation are one. Philosophy should therefore be developed and harmonized with Islam, fostering a more perfect knowledge of the things spoken of in revelation. His position as to the harmony between religion and philosophy is also expressed in his *Letter on the Number of Aristotle's Bodies*.

His cosmological views are also presented in his *Letter on the Prostration of the Farthest Body* and the *Letter on the True, First and Perfect Agent Cause and the Imperfect Agent Cause [which is called agent] by Extension*. Al-Kindi is also well known for his account of the **soul**, a synthesis of **Plato** and Aristotle, explaining the purification of the soul in its journey toward the vision of God. In his influential *Letter on the Intellect* (one of his only works translated into Latin), he distinguishes four senses of reason or intellect, which he claims to derive from Plato and Aristotle: "The first is reason which is always in act; the second is the reason which is in potentiality and is in the soul; the third is reason which has passed from the state of potentiality in the soul to the state of actuality; and the fourth is the reason which we call the manifest" (Fakhry, 87). His successor, **Al-Farabi**, born around the time of Al-Kindi's death and one of the most influential medieval thinkers, later used similar distinctions to develop central tenets in his Neoplatonic account of reality according to a hierarchy of intellects and intelligibles expounded in his own *Letter Concerning the Intellect*. Refer to the introduction, "The Beginning and Development of Medieval Arabian and Jewish Philosophy and Theology."

**KORAN.** (Arabic: Al-Qur'an, "reading" or "recitation"). The Koran is the holy book of the Muslim religion, teaching of the one god, Allah; His creation; and right human conduct. It is considered God's own revelation, communicated over a period of approximately 20 years to the one Prophet and founder of **Islam**, Muhammad (ca. 570–632), who was only a medium contributing nothing in form or content to the divine message. Not all of the Koran was written during Muhammad's lifetime; some was preserved orally and written down after his death. The canonical text of the Koran was not fixed until the reign of the third **caliph**, Uthman (644–656). Moreover, apocryphal materials from the traditions (hadith) that circulated orally were added for over two centuries to what must have been the original corpus. By the ninth century, **exegetes** endeavored to establish compilations of the canonical traditions. The compilation of Al-Bukhari (d. 870) is most famous and authoritative. For Muslims, the Koran is the final divine revelation that confirms, restores, and is the heavenly source of all previous ones, including the Christian Gospels and the Jewish **Torah**. Written in rhymed prose, it is celebrated as the summit in Arabic expression. It is divided into 114 suras or chapters, each of which is divided into verses. The work of medieval Muslim theologians and philosophers can be seen largely as an attempt to harmonize human reason and the Koran in various ways. The Koran's central teachings, such as its marked stress on Allah's absolute unity, omnipotence, and omniscience, are the fundamental principles in Muslim accounts of the world and humanity.

# L

**LAMBERT OF AUXERRE (OF LAGNY) (fl. 1250–1265).** Most of our information about this French **Dominican** comes from a Paduan manuscript containing his *Summula logicae* (*A Short Summa of Logic*). From it we learn that the author of this logical work was named Lambert, that he taught the future king of Navarre, and that he was a Dominican who was buried at the convent of Saint-Jacques in Paris. He was one of the four major logicians of his day, along with Peter of Spain, Roger Bacon, and William of Sherwood, and produced his main work, which seems to be an independent effort, probably at Navarre while teaching Duke Thibaud V between 1250 and 1255. Lambert also wrote some separate logical treatises on supposition and appellation. Since he has a separate treatise on appellation, he still presents a theory of terms which holds that terms on their own naturally stand for certain objects. When supposition began to be considered the property of a term in a proposition, natural supposition was set aside and supposition treatises also assimilated into their domain the formerly separated treatise on appellation. In his theory of appellation, Lambert seems less independent, however, endorsing many of the teachings of the earlier 13th-century logician John la Page.

**LANDULF (LANDULPHUS) CARACCIOLA (ca. 1287–1351).** A native of Naples, he quite likely studied the **liberal arts** there before going to do his theological studies at Paris. He followed **Peter Aureoli** as the **Franciscan** *baccalareus Sententiarum* (**lector** on the *Sentences*) in 1318–1319. He himself was followed by **Francis of Marchia** and **Francis of Meyronnes**. All three are mentioned by **Peter of Candia** in 1378 as the most notable followers of **John Duns Scotus** in the early 14th century. Landolf became a master of theology and wrote *Commentaria moralia in quattuor Evangelia* (*Moral Commentaries on the Four Gospels*) and *Postilla super Evangelia dominicalia* (*Postills on the Sunday Gospels*). Landolf is reported to have written also on *Zacharias* and the Epistle to the Hebrews. However, these commentaries have been lost. He is viewed, as Peter of Candia indicated, as a very loyal Scotist. This is true of him especially in his defenses of Scotus against Peter

Aureoli's criticisms on many points. Nonetheless, Landolf also at times disagreed with Scotus, though later authors who note it indicate that they are shocked when he does so. After serving as provincial of the Naples province of the Franciscans, he was made bishop of Castellammare on 21 August 1327 and archbishop of Amalfi on 20 September 1331. He died in Amalfi in 1351.

**LANFRANC OF BEC (ca. 1010–1089).** Aside from his role as teacher of **St. Anselm** of Canterbury, Lanfranc is known for his debates against theologians, such as **Berengarius of Tours** (ca. 1000–1088), who in their enthusiasm for the growing science of **dialectics** sought to reduce the mysteries of the Christian faith to human reason and thus reached inappropriate or even **heretical** conclusions. The very nature of logic's role in theology was a central question of debate at the time. Unlike **St. Peter Damian** (1007–1072), who saw philosophy and classical learning chiefly as corrupting influences not to be mixed with the wisdom of Scripture, Lanfranc recognized that logic may prove useful in **theology** when employed as a tool and not as an absolute domain. This attitude is reflected in his pupil Anselm, who systematically approached some of the central questions in Christian theology without thereby reducing Christian mysteries to mere logic, as is evident in Anselm's (**Augustinian**) position that one ought to believe in order that one may understand.

**LANGTON, STEPHEN (ca. 1155–1228).** Stephen was an English theologian who studied at Paris, first in the **Arts Faculty** and then in the Theology Faculty. He became regent master in theology at Paris in 1180 and taught there for 20 years. His commentaries on the whole of the Bible are among his most important writings. He also commented twice on Comestor's *Historia Scholastica*. Although his division of the books of the Bible into chapters is not the first such division, it is nonetheless the one followed today. Besides these contributions related more directly to the order of the biblical text, there are also his treatises that pursue a logical order of treatment, such as the order found in his early *Summa theologiae* and his *Quaestiones disputatae* of 1203–1206. The latter questions have left their presence in the works of **Alexander Nequam, William of Auxerre, Hugh of Saint-Cher**, and **Roland of Cremona**.

Beyond this academic life, Stephen lived an extremely active and influential ecclesiastical regimen. While teaching at Paris, he became a very close friend of the future Pope Innocent III. Innocent made him a cardinal in 1306. The pope also did not accept either of the competing candidates for archbishop of Canterbury. At his suggestion, the monks elected Stephen archbishop. After many disputes, Langton finally arrived in England in 1213. In London, he preached a sermon and held meetings with the barons who had been disputing with the king. It was an effort that eventually led to the signing of the Magna Carta in 1215. His friend Innocent III, however, was not happy with the settlement between the king and the barons, so he suspended Langton. Nonetheless, after Innocent's death, Pope Honorius III restored Langton to the See of Canterbury, where for the last 10 years of his life he was a very strong leader of the Church in England.

**LAW.** An important difference in the medieval intellectual world between Judaism and Islam, on the one hand, and Christianity, on the other, concerns the law, especially its political dimension. In the former two traditions, revealed law (the **Torah** for Jews and the **Koran** for Muslims) governs all aspects of life. In medieval Christianity, however, civil law was distinct from canon law, and debates concerning the right relation between evolving powers of the empire and the papacy were not uncommon. **Marsilius of Padua** even developed a theory of the state on purely philosophical principles. In Islam and Judaism, on the other hand, the chief legislative task was interpreting and applying the religious law, and for this purpose scholars and **exegetes** sometimes availed themselves of secular learning, even philosophy.

This difference manifested itself in the study of law. The various Talmudic academies, as well as the various **schools** of Islamic law, focused on the interpretation of the law of Scripture. On the other hand, at European **universities**, canon law was a separate study from civil law. Around 1140, **Gratian**, a monk from Bologna, published his *Decretum*, an ordered synthesis of ecclesiastical law that soon dominated legal instruction at the nascent universities. Gratian's work was organized according to topics and followed a logical order influenced by the dialectical methods of **Scholastic** theologians such as **Peter Abelard** and **Peter Lombard**. Though Gratian's work was eventually supplemented by the works of later jurists who were influenced by his methods, the *Decretum* became the first basis for canon law as a university discipline at important centers like Bologna and Paris, much like Peter Lombard's *Sentences* served that role for university theology. University civil law, on the other hand, was based on Roman law. Naturally, graduates of civil law worked in the various areas of secular administration, while graduates of canon law worked with the Church. Bologna, Padua, and Naples were important 12th- and 13th-century centers of civil law. In 13th-century France, Paris had only a school of canon law. It was complemented by a faculty of civil law at the University of Orléans. In the 13th century, Oxford had programs in both laws. The 14th and 15th centuries witnessed a significant growth in the study of civil law. *See also* DECRETALS AND DECRETALISTS; ETHICS AND POLITICS; EXEGESIS.

**LECTIO (LESSON).** Refer to the introduction, "Methods of Study."

**LECTOR (READER).** Refer to the introduction, "Methods of Study."

**LEVI BEN GERSHOM.** *See* GERSONIDES (GERSHOM, LEVI BEN) (1288–1344).

*LIBER DE CAUSIS.* A brief work of **Neoplatonic metaphysics** that was translated by **Gerard of Cremona**. The *Liber de causis* (*The Book of Causes*) was also mistakenly titled *Liber Aristotelis de expositione bonitatis purae* (*The Book of Aristotle on the Exposition of the Pure Good*). The attribution to **Aristotle** was first challenged by **Thomas Aquinas** when he read **William of Moerbeke**'s Latin translation of Proclus's *Elements of Theology* and realized that the ultimate source of the *Liber de causis* was Proclus. The mistaken attribution had led some medieval authors before the time of Aquinas to attempt a reconciliation of this work with **Aristotle**'s authentic works. In effect, they were actually trying to reconcile its Neoplatonic teaching with authentic Aristotelian metaphysics.

**LIBERAL ARTS.** The liberal arts or skills, a term of late Roman origin, are traditionally seven, the four arts of numbers designated collectively as the quadrivium (arithmetic, geometry, music, and astronomy) and the three arts of letters designated collectively as the trivium (**logic** or **dialectics**, grammar, and rhetoric). Classical Greek education, originally based on "music" and "gymnastics," included under the former rubric literature and later (fifth century) also rhetoric (for public speaking) and dialectic (for debate). This expansion constituting the trivium, as well as the addition of the quadrivium (based largely on Pythagorean achievements) around the same period, was largely influenced by the Sophists, who used these arts primarily for the sake of success in public life.

The Sophists' attitude toward learning was criticized by the philosophers **Plato** and **Aristotle**, who conceived the function of the liberal arts differently. To them, their chief end was not action or production (though they still had this role in certain areas) but knowledge of truth. In the *Republic*, Plato outlines a course of studies covering the liberal arts, though culminating in something distinct as their end—the vision of truth. Though Aristotle's different philosophy emphasizes mathematics less than Plato's and gives logic a more fundamental role, Aristotle also conceives of the ultimate end of all intellectual endeavor as contemplative. The liberal arts played less of a role for other Greek philosophers, such as the Epicureans and the Skeptics, who questioned the human possibility of gaining objective knowledge. With the Stoics, these arts (especially logic and grammar) played a greater role, and it is in the writings of the Latin author Martianus Capella (fifth century A.D.), partly drawing from Varro (first century A.D.), that the seven arts are first designated as liberal or free. According to Seneca and the Stoic ideal of freedom, they are important for the education of free citizens, as well as conducive to the only true freedom, the freedom found through wisdom.

This Greek educational heritage was assimilated and transformed in the West in the Jewish, Islamic, and Christian traditions, where the liberal arts became preparatory not only to philosophy (as classically conceived) but also to **theology** (to the extent that philosophy became instrumental in theology). In these three traditions, Aristotle's logical works, collectively known as the *Organon*, almost monopolized the curriculum of the liberal arts, since they provided the methodology for all the different disciplines, and especially for philosophy proper and for theology. In the Middle Ages, even self-proclaimed Platonists used Aristotelian logic as a neutral tool. Medieval Islam, where most **Jewish philosophy and theology** took place until the 12th century (and subsequently in Christian Europe), employed the liberal arts in the traditions of *falsafah* or philosophy, which included the sciences, and *kalam* or theology.

In the Western Christian tradition, before the central works of Aristotelian philosophy were finally received in their totality in the 13th century, texts in liberal arts provided most of the available classical learning except for the writings of the **Fathers of the Church** and the philosophy of Cicero and Seneca. In the Carolingian Renaissance, which produced **John Scotus Eriugena** (ca. 810–ca. 877) as the first major thinker since the sixth century, **Alcuin** (ca. 735–804) and his student Rhabanus Maurus (the author of the influential *De clericorum institutione*) cultivated the liberal arts at their **schools**, though their textbooks were largely based on late antique Latin authors, such as **Boethius** (ca. 480–524), Donatus (fourth century), Priscian (sixth century), and Martianus Capella. By the 12th century, Boethius (who translated into Latin some of Aristotle's logical works and wrote commentaries on them) and Martianus Capella furnished a substantial portion of logic and the quadrivium. The writings of Donatus and Priscian dominated grammar, while those of Cicero and Martianus Capella were the standards in rhetoric.

In the 13th century, when the more properly philosophical works of Aristotle arrived in the Christian West, along with important Arabic and Jewish commentaries, the preparatory status of the liberal arts as instruments for philosophy became even more important. However, all along, since the time of **St. Augustine** and the Fathers of the Church, they had assisted theology, whether in Platonic or Aristotelian frameworks, to the extent that theology used Greek and Roman learning as a key instrument. In medieval universities, focused on the systematic handling of philosophical and theological questions, logic tended to dominate the methodology that was used. Later, the Renaissance's emphasis on classical literature brought with it a new emphasis on rhetoric and grammar, while the scientific movements of the 16th and 17th centuries stressed the mathematical arts. *See also* ARTS FACULTY.

**LOGIC.** *See* DIALECTICS.

**LOLLARDS.** The Lollards were the groups of 15th- and 16th-century English Christian believers who in a general way inherited the legacy of **John Wycliffe**. To different degrees they locate theological authority not in Church institutions but in Scripture rightly understood; they avoid mixing spiritual and secular areas; they challenge Church regulations that are not Scripturally based; they establish true believers and false believers through divine predestination; they deny transubstantiation; they favor religious resources in English over Latin; they try to work with other Lollards; and they appreciate being excluded from the institutional church.

In the early 15th century, two students from Bohemia copied some works of Wycliffe (*De dominio divino* [*On Divine Governance*], *De ecclesia* [*On the Church*], and *De veritate sacrae scripturae* [*On the Truth of Sacred Scripture*]) and also brought back a letter allegedly authorized by the chancellor of Oxford praising Wycliffe as a scholar and teacher of Scripture and asserting that he had never been condemned for heresy. **Jan Hus** and Jerome of Prague used this letter to establish Wycliffe's theological integrity and also the legitimacy of their own theological positions. They thus extended the world of the Lollards into Bohemia.

**LOMBARD.** *See* PETER LOMBARD (ca. 1095–1160).

**LULL, RAYMOND (ca. 1233–1316).** After experiencing a religious conversion at the age of 30, this native of Majorca in Spain, also called the Enlightened Doctor (*Doctor Illuminatus*), renounced his married life and worldly privileges and joined the **Franciscan** order. The conversion of infidels absorbed much of his work. A student of Arabic, he sought to convert Muslims, making two missionary trips to Tunis in 1293 and 1314–1315 and one to Algeria in 1307. During these travels he was arrested, imprisoned, and even flogged. He is known for attacking the Latin **Averroists** at the University of Paris, particularly for the separation they established between philosophy and theology.

Lull was a prolific writer. More than 200 works are attributed to him, and most of them survive. His most influential one is his *Ars generalis ultima* (*The Ultimate General Art*), where he proposes a method and certain self-evident principles, common to all science, through which all may be led to the truths of Christianity. His thought was expressed chiefly in an apologetic style aimed at conversion. In this respect, its spirit may already be seen, though perhaps in a less intense and pervasive form, in **Roger Bacon**'s *Opus maius* (*Major Work*), **Alan of Lille**'s *Ars catholicae fidei* (*Art of the Catholic Faith*), and even **Thomas Aquinas**'s *Summa contra gentiles* (*Summa against the Gentiles*). Doctrinally, Lull seeks principally to restore the Christian wisdom of Augustine as formulated by the Franciscan **St. Bonaventure**, wherein philosophy is both subordinated to and illuminated by theology and wherein all creation is seen as a symbol of God. Interestingly, Lull's exact contemporary and fellow Franciscan, Duns Scotus, questioned and ultimately rejected some of Bonaventure's central theses, such as his view of knowledge as involving divine illumination.

**MAGISTER.** A title given to a special advanced **lector** or reader. The beginning teachers of standard medieval texts in the liberal arts, law, medicine, and theology would read the established texts and provide glosses in the margins or between the lines. More advanced readers, for example, in **theology**, would add the comments of various **Fathers of the Church** to bring further understandings to the sacred texts of Scripture. When the reader had advanced to the point that he could properly organize the Patristic citations and resolve seeming conflicts between the comments of the different Fathers, he was considered someone who had mastered the text tradition in regard to that work. Such teachers would be called masters. **Peter Lombard** was considered a person who had achieved this status in regard to the various Patristic authorities related to the Scriptures. He was called *magister* or master, and this title was awarded to him uniquely by referring to him as "the Master" or "the Magister," in much the same way as St. Paul was uniquely and antonymously called "the Apostle."

**MAGISTER MARTINUS (fl. 1200).** Little is known of Magister Martinus. Even his name is known only because of the title of his theological text: *Compilatio quaestionum theologiae secundum Magistrum Martinum.* When we search this compilation of texts, we discover that his sources are **Gilbert of Poitiers**, **Simon of Tournai**, **Alan of Lille**, **Magister Udo**, and Odo of Ourscamp, but not **Praepositinus** or **Stephen Langton**. Given this internal evidence, scholars date the work to have been written at about 1200. Since Martin refers at one place to the Seine, it seems that he must be a master of theology in Paris. The compilation of texts from other authors suggests furthermore that he is a mature master, who borrows freely from his well-known sources.

Martin's methodology seems to follow in the footsteps of Gilbert Porreta. His way of organizing his discussions fits with the method of the Porretan school. However, in dealing with particular subject matters, such as the Incarnation, his texts show that he does not automatically take a straight Porretan road. His use of many of the precise definitions of such key words as substance, *nature*, *person*, and *essence*, definitions he derives from the *Theologiae Regulae* (*Rules of Theology*) of Alan of Lille and the *Disputationes* (*Disputations*) of Simon of Tournai rather than from the texts of Peter of Poitiers, is key to his Christology on points where he differs from Porreta. However, Alan of Lille and Simon of Tournai lack the clarity of argument of Porreta. Martinus then advances the theology of Christology by combining the method and precision of definitions—a combination that was less strong in the earlier members of the Porretan school.

**MAGISTER UDO (fl. 1160–1200).** He is one of the earliest commentators on the *Sentences* of **Peter Lombard**. His *Commentarium* is assumed to have been written between 1160 and 1165, and it is judged to be one of the sources for **Peter of Poitier**'s *Commentarium*. One of the chief characteristics of Magister Udo's *Commentary on the Sentences* is that he debates with Peter Lombard. He does so by going to Scripture and **Fathers of the Church** for traditional teachings related to Lombard's presentation that might challenge his readers to deepen their understanding of Lombard's teaching on nature and grace. These traditional teachings serve as *pro* and *contra* arguments to challenge students to evaluate Lombard's presentation. Magister Udo, in effect, invites his students to deepen or correct their views of human nature and of grace. Man, Udo argues, can move toward God by his good acts, but *without grace* he cannot by the good acts of his free will be elevated to life with God.

**MAIMONIDES, MOSES (1138–1204).** Moshe ben Maimon, known as Maimonides in the Latin West, is easily the most influential Jewish philosopher of the Middle Ages, and perhaps even of all time. He furnished a great deal of the background from which major Jewish thinkers such as **Gersonides** and **Hasdai Crescas** launched their intellectual projects. In non-Jewish circles, Maimonides was also influential. For example, his synthesis of **Aristotelianism** and revelation served as an important example to thinkers seeking to reconcile these two domains, such as the Christian **Thomas Aquinas**. Maimonides is also one of the greatest scholars and **exegetes** of Jewish law who ever lived.

Moses was born in Cordoba, Spain, a cultural Mecca in medieval Islam, where the sciences, art, and religion enjoyed a fruitful relationship. In Spain, major Jewish and Islamic thinkers flourished, such as his predecessors **Ibn Gabirol** and **Avempace** and his contemporary **Averroes**, whose commentaries on Aristotle's treatises Maimonides recommended (though the extent to which he knew Averroes's works remains a question). This cultural background, combined with his family's tradition of learning (his father was as an astronomer, mathematician, and rabbinic judge), provided a stimulus for

Maimonides's later achievements in philosophy, medicine, and legal scholarship. Maimonides and his family were compelled to leave Cordoba when the Almohads took over the city in 1148, replacing the more tolerant Umayyads and forcing all non-Muslims either to convert or leave the country without their belongings. The family finally settled permanently in Egypt in 1165, where Maimonides's rabbinic and legal learning made him head of the Egyptian Jews and his medical expertise earned him the position of court physician to the vizier of Saladin. His *Guide of the Perplexed* (*Moreh Nebukim*) (1190) is his most influential work in philosophy and theology. His work in legal scholarship includes his *Mishneh Torah* (1180), an unprecedented attempt to codify the totality of Jewish law, and his commentary on the Mishnah, the *Book of Illumination* (1168). Maimonides also wrote on medicine and **logic**.

The *Guide* is a complex work, lending itself to a variety of interpretations. Moreover, the *Guide* is not a straightforward exposition but was personally developed for a former student, Joseph ben Judah. In addition, Maimonides himself tells the reader he will deliberately state seemingly contradictory things at some points. This suggests Maimonides's view that certain truths should not be divulged without caution to the masses, but only to those with the requisite training. For the proper guidance of children and the masses, revelation without philosophy suffices. Maimonides's conception of the universal appropriateness of revelation in contradistinction to philosophy was influential in later syntheses of religion and philosophy. At the beginning of his *Summa theologiae*, Thomas Aquinas employs a number of Maimonides's observations when he deals with the relation of philosophy to revelation. Nevertheless, all of Maimonides's works, those for the general public and for philosophy students alike, contain philosophy. Maimonides clearly esteemed philosophy as the domain yielding rational certainty, and he attacked the atomism and occasionalism of *mutakallimun* (sects of **kalam**), whereby all things lack inherent properties, since they exist in absolute and constant dependence on the divine will, as antiscientific.

The *Guide* seems intended neither for the simple believer nor for the pure philosopher, but rather for students with some expertise in philosophy and the sciences who were perplexed in their efforts to harmonize secular knowledge with the letter of Jewish revelation, where, for example, anthropomorphic allusions to God are quite common. This perplexity, according to Jewish legal norms, can affect someone's life in serious ways, and so the *Guide*, with all its theoretical content, also has the important practical dimension of addressing the person who experiences this confusion. The very order of the *Guide* reveals the good life as the goal of all learning; this life, unlike that of pure philosophers, includes revealed wisdom. Thus, the final part is devoted to ethical, moral, and political challenges.

Even though the wisdom necessary for dealing with reason on its own is quite limited with respect to the divine, Moses adheres to the unity and consistency of truth. A conflict between reason and revelation can only be apparent either through a misinterpretation of Scripture or through a failing of reason. Scripture has both a literal and a spiritual meaning, and its anthropomorphisms should not be understood literally, as the one God is incorporeal. However, God being wholly transcendent and unlike anything in experience, language can describe Him mostly in negative ways. This should be kept clearly in mind, lest we fall into the dangerous habit of thinking and speaking about God in terms proper only to creatures. Idolatry, the chief source or error and sin according to the Law, should be avoided above all.

Maimonides is perhaps best known for his so-called negative theology, which he developed at a time when the status of divine attributes was an intensely debated issue among students and sects of dialectical theology, the *kalam*. Maimonides's theology is largely grounded in his Aristotelian conception of the extent and nature of man's natural knowledge. Put simply, our concepts, as abstracted from sensible composites, are adequate for the understanding of our experience, not for understanding God Himself, who is one and simple. Accordingly, it should "become clear to you that every attribute that we predicate of Him is an attribute of action or, if the attribute is intended for the apprehension of His essence and not of His action, it signifies the negation of the privation of the attribute in question" (*Guide*, Hyman and Walsh, 383). We may attribute to God diverse actions when these actions are understood only as His effects and not in any way as belonging to His one simple essence. For example, we can say that fire burns, melts, and heats without impairing in our conception the unity of the nature of fire. Similarly, we may say that God creates and guides, if we refer these actions to His effects on creatures and not to God's essence. Other divine attributes that do not refer to actions are appropriate only when they negate a limitation found in creatures and thus do not posit anything in God distinct from his essence. For example, when we say that God is infinite, we are saying that He is not like finite creatures. To Maimonides, however, it is still possible for one to grow in the knowledge of God, to the extent that one knows demonstratively the attributes that apply negatively to God.

Like Aristotle, we may arrive at the knowledge of God's existence by reasoning from effects in the natural world to their ultimate cause, the Unmoved Mover. All of the arguments Maimonides intends as demonstrations for the existence of God seem to be based on natural philosophy or physics. In this respect, he seems closer to the Aristotelianism of his contemporary Averroes than to that of his predecessor and other source, **Avicenna**, who stressed the superiority of **metaphysics** (as he understood it) as the best rational way to God. (On the other hand, like Avicenna, Maimonides at points speaks of God's emanation and governance in a **Neoplatonic** fashion.)

Nonetheless, Maimonides underscores the fact that Aristotelian natural philosophy has serious limitations in its attempt to access anything about God except His existence. Aware of the difficulties in explaining, using Aristotle's principles, astronomical phenomena described by Ptolemy's *Almagest*, Maimonides states that Aristotle's natural philosophy is absolutely demonstrative only at the sublunary level (*Guide*, Hyman and Walsh, 398). Among others, Thomas Aquinas and **Duns Scotus**, also using Aristotelian frameworks (greatly informed by Avicenna), will try to go beyond Maimonides's negative theology and establish a firmer basis for terms applicable to God. Naturally, they will endeavor to do so through their own accounts of the knowledge of God available naturally to human beings. As alternatives to Maimonides's theory of negative attribution, Aquinas will propose a theory of analogy and Duns Scotus a theory of univocity.

Aside from the Scriptural anthropomorphisms in apparent conflict with the philosophical understanding of God as immovable and, therefore, incorporeal, another apparent conflict between reason and Scripture concerns the status of the world. Aristotle holds that it is eternal, Plato that it is created from preexistent eternal matter, while Scripture tells us that it is created out of nothing. To Maimonides, of the accounts by Plato and Aristotle, only the latter portrait, which does not leave room for divine omnipotence, is inconsistent with revelation. Maimonides argues that creation in the Scriptures is reconcilable with reason, as the philosophical arguments of Plato, Aristotle, and others on this issue are not conclusive. Neither side of the issue can be determined by reason. Accordingly, believing in creation out of nothing is strictly a matter of faith, for neither is it demonstrable by reason nor does it contradict reason. Trying to demonstrate creation out of nothing in fact weakens belief in it, as the arguments for it cannot be demonstrable. Establishing this was of paramount importance to Maimonides, for whom the validity of the Law, the heart of Judaism, depended on the belief in Scriptural creation (*Guide*, Hyman and Walsh, 401). Thinkers such as Aquinas will be influenced by and generally follow this attitude concerning this problem, as well as in regard to other articles of faith.

Maimonides accepts revelation as a historical fact, which implies that God is wholly free and omnipotent and is thus able to create the world out of nothing in time. This omnipotence includes a divine providence reaching particulars, though still preserving human freedom and divine justice in terms of rewards and punishments. Though Maimonides maintains with Aristotle that the highest reward or happiness consists primarily in intellectual virtue, culminating in knowledge of divine things, his view of providence and prophecy makes his ethics distinct. Maimonides's view of providence counters, on the one hand, the Aristotelian conception of divine knowledge as only universal and unconcerned with concrete human affairs and, on the other, determinist conceptions of divine providence, such as that of the Muslim **Asharites** (a school of *kalam*). This is related to his well-known account of prophecy, which is influenced primarily by **Al-Farabi** (also one of his chief sources in other areas, particularly logic and politics), who interpreted Plato's *Republic* in light of Muslim religion. The prophet, the summit of moral and intellectual virtue (requiring both natural and divinely infused excellence), is a statesman similar to Plato's philosopher-king. In this important respect, intellectual virtue has a crucial political function that is largely absent in Aristotle. Maimonides's ethics, aside from philosophy, law, and politics, also stresses pious devotion.

Maimonides is also known for being the first to propose a set of 13 authoritative Jewish beliefs that should be added to the commandments of the Torah as part of the binding core of Judaism. Thinkers such as Hasdai Crescas were deeply influenced by this approach. These 13 truths are as follows: only God is to be worshipped, prophecy exists, the divine origin of the **Torah**, the eternity of the Torah, the superiority of Moses's prophecy over other prophets, the resurrection of the dead, reward and punishment, days of the Messiah, God's existence, His unity, eternity, incorporeality, and His knowledge of human affairs. On Maimonides's grave (in Tiberias, near the Sea of Galilee), it is inscribed, "From Moses [the prophet] to Moses [Maimonides] there had arisen no one like him." Refer to the introduction, "The Beginning and Development of Medieval Arabian and Jewish Philosophy and Theology."

**MANICHAEANISM.** This ancient form of dualism, claiming that there are two competing gods of divine principles, the Principle of Light and the Principle of Darkness, still carried a presence into the time of **St. Augustine**. In his *Confessions*, Augustine indicates that he was attracted to this form of dualism, even though he had questions concerning it. However, he argues against it when, despite attractive aspects, he realizes that it removes personal responsibility by allowing men to blame the principle of evil as the source of their own sinful conduct. Medieval forms of dualism can be found among the Cathars and Albigensians, and also among lesser-known groups, such as the Bogomils and Paulicians.

**MARSH, ADAM.** *See* ADAM MARSH (ca. 1210–1259).

**MARSILIUS OF INGHEN (ca. 1340–1396).** A native of Nijmegen, he studied under **John Buridan** at the University of Paris, where he became master of arts in 1362. Marsilius went to Heidelberg University and became its first rector beginning in 1386. He wrote on **Aristotle** (his chief philosophic influence), both natural philosophy (*Abbreviationes libri Physicorum* and *De Generatione*) and logic or **dialectic** (*Quaestiones super libros Priorum*

*Analyticorum* and *Parva Logicalia*). He also composed a commentary on the *Sentences* of **Peter Lombard** (*Quaestiones super quattuor libros Sententiarum*). Marsilius, influenced by his teacher Buridan, falls in the **nominalist** or terminist tradition initiated by **William of Ockham**, the so-called *via moderna* (modern way) of interpreting Aristotle. According to them, universals refer to concepts and names and not to extra-mental universal realities, as the so-called **realists** (such as **Walter Burley**) are inclined to think about universals. There were various and different versions of this modern way. Like his teacher Buridan, Marsilius was no skeptic and held that reason can prove metaphysically the existence of God as well as some of His essential attributes, such as His uniqueness. In this, they were in agreement with **John Duns Scotus**. As Ockham and Buridan had maintained, however, and against the position of Duns Scotus, natural reason cannot prove the absolute infinity and omnipotence of God's power, which enables Him to create all things freely and immediately out of nothing. **Faith** alone can hold this. Marsilius had great influence and was seen in the 15th and 16th centuries, along with Ockham and **Gregory of Rimini**, as an outstanding nominalist. Several of his texts circulated as textbooks, and his theological and philosophical positions impacted early modern thinkers.

**MARSILIUS OF PADUA (ca. 1280–1343).** A native of Padua, Marsilius studied at Paris in the **Arts Faculty**, then in **law** and medicine. He became rector of the **university** in 1313. His major work was the *Defensor Pacis* (*Defender of the Peace*), completed in Paris in 1324. The first two books of this work show his awareness of the battles in Paris between **Boniface VIII** and Philip the Fair at the turn of the century and the later conflicts between the Spiritual **Franciscans** and Pope John XXII. His work, however, is not simply a practical reflection on these problems that caused so much disturbance. It is a book that is theoretically argued. In Book I, he urges along **Aristotelian** lines that the state exists for men to live and to live well. Marsilius contends that this goal can best occur when the citizens make laws to promote the common welfare. This entails a united body politic. Book II portrays the papacy as having an excessive desire for ruling and that this drive undermines the necessary unity for a state to attain its unified and peaceful purpose. Going even further, he reversed the claim of the pope that unity could only be achieved by having the temporal power under him. Marsilius held that the very opposite would better achieve the desired unity: the state, through its temporal ruler, should control church appointments. Book III presents a list of concluding propositions regarding the Church: all temporal goods of the Church belong to the ruler, Christ did not establish any positions of leadership in the Church, the ruler's duty is to correct and depose the pope, all priests have equal authority, and any coercive power of the Church and its officials comes from the ruler.

Pope John XXII condemned Marsilius's views, and Marsilius fled Paris and took refuge with Emperor Louis of Bavaria, who was also in a dispute with Pope John XXII. In 1342, Marsilius wrote another treatise, the *Defensor minor*, a short version of the teachings of his more famous work where he reaffirmed the conclusions of that work.

**MARSTON.** *See* ROGER MARSTON (ca. 1235–ca. 1303).

**MARTIANUS CAPELLA.** *See* LIBERAL ARTS.

**MARTIN OF DACIA (ca. 1225–1304).** Martin was a Danish master of arts and **theology** at Paris from about 1250 until he was appointed chancellor to the King of Denmark in 1287, a role he held until his death. His known university work at Paris is in the field of grammar. His *Modi Significandi* (*Modes of Signifying*) is his attempt to develop grammar into a theoretical science in the way that contemporaries (**Peter of Spain**, **William of Sherwood**, **Roger Bacon**, and **Lambert of Auxerre**) were attempting to develop the varying treatises in **logic** into more organized forms. His work in grammar was continued by **Thomas of Erfurt**, **Boethius of Dacia**, **Radulphus Brito**, and **Siger of Courtrai**.

**MASTER.** *See MAGISTER*; PETER LOMBARD (ca. 1095–1160); SENTENCES (*SENTENTIAE*).

**MATTHEW OF AQUASPARTA (ca. 1238–1302).** Matthew, who often provided a response from the school of **Bonaventure** to the philosophy and **theology** of **Thomas Aquinas**, qualified as a *baccalareus biblicus* (**lector** in the Bible) at Paris in 1268 and *baccalareus Sententiarum* (lector on **Peter Lombard**'s *Sentences*) in 1273. He lectured at Bologna from 1273 to 1277 and then became regent master at Paris from 1277 to 1279 before being named lector at the Roman Curia from 1279 to 1287. He was elected general minister of the Franciscans at Montpellier in 1287 and fulfilled this charge until 1289, although named a cardinal in 1288. He served the Holy See under Pope Boniface VIII until his death in 1302.

Matthew walked in the footsteps of Bonaventure, following the lead of his first followers, **Walter of Bruges**, **John Peckham**, and **William de la Mare**. For them, the knowledge of God's existence is the first truth implanted in the human mind. God's existence cannot be proved a priori (from something prior to it), since it is the first truth. It is a truth that is immediately known, not in the sense that there is actual knowledge of God implanted in the mind at birth but rather because any judgment we make already presupposes that the mind has contact with the Truth that is the measure of all truth. Matthew, however, holds that it is also necessary to approach the question of God's existence from empirical grounds. Such an approach allows us to make more explicit the knowledge of God that is implied in any of our original judgments. He argues, first of all, from the imperfection and mutability of finite beings to the need for their perfect and immutable foundation, and then (from the orderly way in which the world runs and the goals things naturally pursue) to a first efficient and final cause.

In treating of creation, Matthew enters into the debate raging in the 1270s at the University of Paris between the **Averroists**, who contended that the eternity of the world could be rationally demonstrated, and the theologians who denied the validity of their proofs. Aquinas, admitting the temporal character of creation as an article of faith, contended that reason could demonstrate neither the temporal nor the eternal nature of creation. Matthew attacked Aquinas's efforts to show that specific arguments against the eternity of the world are not demonstrations. For Matthew, an eternal world would imply the existence of an infinite number of souls or revolutions of the sun. These arguments against an eternal creation are, for him, necessary reasons, and the attempts of Aquinas to rebut them are sophistical. Matthew, nonetheless, is very much influenced by Aristotle's philosophy as elaborated by Aquinas. Even when he rejects Aquinas's positions, Matthew's arguments are not simply repetitions of those of Bonaventure and his early followers. They are serious attempts to overcome Aquinas's theses by employing **Aristotelian** arguments.

**MAURICE O'FIHELY (MAURITIUS DE PORTU) (ca. 1455–1513).** This famous editor of the works of **John Duns Scotus** was born in Cork, Ireland, and joined the Conventual **Franciscans** in about 1475. He did his studies at Oxford and was named the regent of studies at the Franciscan school in Milan in 1488. He became regent master of **theology** at Padua in 1491 and taught Scotistic theology there at least until 1505. In 1506, he became archbishop of Tuam and attended the Fifth Lateran Council in 1512. He died a year later in Galway. Maurice edited many works of Scotus that were published between 1497 and 1517, and during the same time he provided many expositions on the Subtle Doctor's **logical** and **metaphysical** treatises. His study of Scotus's doctrines led him to examine and edit works of the Scotists **Antonius Andreas** and **Francis of Meyronnes**. His own works include an *Enchiridion fidei* (*A Handbook of Faith*), which also has the title *De rerum contingentia et divina predestinatione* (*On the Contingency of Created Things and Divine Predestination*). His commentary on the *Sentences* under the title *Compendium veritatum* (*A Compendium of the Truths of Faith*), based on his lectures at Padua, was published in hexameters at Venice in 1505.

**MAURICE OF SULLY (ca. 1120–1196).** Successor to **Peter Lombard** as bishop of Paris in 1160, Maurice was a student of Peter **Abelard** and a teacher of Scripture during the years leading up to the foundation of the University of Paris. He replaced the Carolingian church of Notre Dame, breaking ground for the renowned Gothic cathedral in 1163. Maurice has left an admired collection of sermons, *Sermons on the Gospel*, written originally in the vernacular and later translated into Latin. He retired to the monastery of the **Canons Regular of St. Augustine** at Saint-Victor, where he died in 1196.

**MAXIMUS THE CONFESSOR, ST. (ca. 580–662).** This great Byzantine theologian and **mystic** was born in Constantinople and belonged to an influential family with relations to the royal court. After a short career in public affairs as secretary to Emperor Heraklios I (610–641), he entered the religious life, first at a monastery in the vicinity of the capital. With the invasions of Constantinople beginning in 626, he traveled to various places (Crete, Cyprus, North Africa), including Rome, where he played a prominent role at the council (649) that condemned Monothelitism (the doctrine that Christ had only one will). A cornerstone of the **theology** of Maximus was his belief in the two distinct natures of Christ, the divine and the human, and he actively opposed as heretical the doctrines that compromised this duality. However, before these positions of Maximus became orthodox teaching in the Byzantine world (in 680 at the Sixth Ecumenical Council of Constantinople), Emperor Constans II (641–668) violently sought to impose Monothelitism and saw Maximus and his chief supporter, Pope Martin I (649–655), as traitors. He arrested them in 653 and charged them at Constantinople. The pope was exiled to Crimea until he died, and Maximus to Byzia (in Thrace). Later in 662, still refusing to accept Monothelitism, Maximus had his tongue ripped out and his right arm amputated by the emperor's supporters.

The philosophy and theology of Maximus draws from **Aristotelianism** and from Christian **Neoplatonism** (notably the thought of **Dionysius the Pseudo-Areopagite**) and the Greek **Fathers of the Church**. In his scheme, the dual nature of Christ was central since creatures act and will according to their inherent natures (according to Aristotle), natures that seek their origin or union with God (according to the Neoplatonists). However, creatures are fallen; their wills are disordered, and so the Incarnation of Christ is necessary to restore the creatures' order to the Creator. It is the dual nature of Christ that mediates between creatures and Creator by enabling the creature to fulfill its own original nature as planned by God. In other words, Christ's dual nature preserves the distinction between creature and Creator while enabling the former to fulfill its end in relation to the latter. Maximus's extensive writings (around 90 pieces found in PG 90–91 [1860]) include Scriptural commentaries, letters, polemical works, and Eucharistic reflections.

**MEDICINE.** The development of medicine in the medieval period largely depended on the infusion of Hellenistic medical texts. Contributions were made, however, and in the Middle Ages some of the important features of modern medicine began to emerge. Designated, along with theology and law, as one of the three faculties of higher studies (arts was preparatory) at the nascent **universities** in Europe, medieval medicine became a science that related theoretical and practical aspects, as well as a controlled profession. The university setting provided for a systematic control of medical competences that had not been present in the ancient or Arabic worlds, even though healing also continued (and in fact continues) to be exercised by various kinds of practitioners. In the sixth century, Cassiodorus, cultivating medicine at his monastery at Vivarium, cited some of the Hellenistic medical works available in Latin, including writings from Hippocrates, Galen, Dioscorides, and Caelius Aurelianus. These and other works, for example, the *Oribasius* and *Soranus* (translated by Caelius Aurelianus), including some of unknown authorship, constituted the medical heritage at Carolingian monasteries. This was where most medical knowledge was housed and implemented, as evidenced by the insistence of **Alcuin**'s influential student **Rhabanus Maurus** (ninth century) on the importance of medical knowledge for monks. Most of this body of medical knowledge was practical rather than theoretical; it focused on the description of illnesses and cures and provided little theoretical explanation.

At the cathedral schools of the 10th and 11th centuries, medicine began to be pursued in addition to the liberal arts by secular clergy, although this pursuit remained more practical than theoretical. Nonetheless, medical theory also began to flourish at the end of the 11th century, principally at Salerno and at the neighboring Benedictine abbey at Monte Cassino. In the 12th century, Constantine the African at Salerno translated various medical texts from Arabic into Latin, including additional texts from Galen and Hippocrates, as well as from Jewish and Muslim authors such as Isaac Israeli and Haly Abbas. Constantine, apparently stressing the connection between medicine and philosophy, translated theoretical texts that were new to the West. In addition, 12th-century translations of Greek and Arabic texts by scholars such as Burgundio of Pisa and **Gerard of Cremona** (and his disciples) at Toledo helped raise medicine to a theoretical science that governed its practical applications. It is worth noting that some of the major medieval philosophers in the Islamic and Jewish traditions (including **Avicenna**, **Averroes**, and **Maimonides**) were also physicians who saw the subject matter of medicine as part of their philosophical view of the universe. The influence of

**Aristotelianism** deepened medicine's connections with theory and philosophy. Avicenna's *Canon* (translated by Gerard of Cremona), which remained a standard text in Europe until the 17th century, was a paradigm of medicine as a systematic discipline open to logical methodology and closely connected to philosophy.

Through its 12th-century growth, principally at Salerno, medicine became in the 13th century one of three faculties of higher studies at universities. As was the case with other university studies, lectures on authorities were given, and a logical or dialectical method was applied to specific questions. In addition, the practical dimension of medicine was increasingly emphasized. Students at most faculties were also required to follow a practical course with a master. At Paris, this requirement began in 1335. Dissection for pedagogy began clandestinely in the late 13th century at Bologna, and then officially from the 14th century onward. Thus, in the Middle Ages, the theoretical and practical dimensions of medicine, of reason and experience, were increasingly defined. Montpellier, Paris, and Bologna became the chief granters of medical degrees in the 13th century; in the 14th and 15th centuries, medical faculties emerged across Europe, Padua being one of the most important.

**MEISTER ECKHART.** *See* ECKHART, MEISTER (1260–1328).

**METAPHYSICS.** One of the main works of Aristotle was his *First Philosophy*, or what his commentators called his *Metaphysics*. The word originally meant literally "After the *Physics*," but it came to designate what Aristotle considered the universal science. It was a science that did not consider certain particular areas of reality but was the science of all things, "being *qua* being." It pursued the most fundamental questions. In the Arabic world, **Avicenna** and **Averroes** wrote different and competing interpretations of Aristotle's *First Philosophy* in their works titled *Metaphysics* and *Commentary on the Metaphysics*, respectively. These two commentaries played an important role in the treatment of metaphysical questions in the universities of the Latin West. Also, metaphysics played an important role in theology, since theologians wanted to employ the most basic and most solid science in their work and not depend on or employ varying views of physical nature or the soul in establishing their discipline.

**METZ, JAMES OF.** *See* JAMES OF METZ (fl. 1300–1310).

**MICHAEL OF MASSA (ca. 1300–1337).** Michael, whose *Commentary on Books I and II of the Sentences of Peter Lombard* was written in 1335, moved away from the intellectual heritage of the early school of his religious order. The early **Hermits of St. Augustine**, following the lead of **Giles of**

**Rome**, had strong **Dominican** intellectual ties. Michael, and later Augustinians, like **Gregory of Rimini**, for instance, were more notably influenced by the philosophy and **theology** of **Franciscan** authors, especially English theologians. Since Michael is one of the first to mention the presence of Ockham's thought in Paris, he might well be one of the roots of Gregory of Rimini's orientation toward the Oxford theologians.

**MICHAEL SCOT (ca. 1170–ca. 1235).** Michael, born either in Scotland or Ireland, was a translator of texts of natural science and philosophy from the Arabic into Latin. He was an advisor at the Fourth Lateran Council in 1215, after spending his career translating works of **Aristotle** and **Averroes** into Latin. Around 1217, he stopped his translating efforts, which took place in Toledo. From 1220 on, he lived in Bologna, then went into the service of the archbishop of Cashel in 1225. He joined the service of King Frederick II and died in his palace around 1235. His translating work was very helpful in preparing the arrival and assimilation of the works of Aristotle and especially Averroes into the Latin West.

**MIDDLETON, RICHARD.** *See* RICHARD OF MIDDLETON (ca. 1249–1302).

**MIDRASH.** *See* EXEGESIS.

**MISHNAH.** The oldest part of the Talmud, this collection of the oral teachings of the rabbis concerning the **Torah** was gathered by Rabbi Judah Ha-Nasi in the third century A.D. The title derives from the Hebrew word for "repetition," the way of providing instruction in the oral law. *See also* EXEGESIS.

**MONASTIC THEOLOGY.** As referring to a class of Christian theology, the now commonly used term *monastic theology* was first used in the 20th century to designate thinkers, such as **Peter the Venerable**, **Rupert of Deutz**, **Bernard of Clairvaux**, **William of St. Thierry**, and **Isaac of Stella**, who in the cloister followed in practice, study, and prayer the **Augustinian** program of reflecting on the **faith**. Monastic theology is a development of Patristic theology that sought to achieve the fruits of the contemplation of God in a life of devotion and love. In this sense, monastic theology is ultimately geared to practice, to the living of Christian wisdom, and ultimately to the mystical experience of God. Accordingly, monastic theology is sometimes contrasted to the approach of some theologians at **schools** and **universities** (some exponents of so-called **Scholastic theology**), whose chief concern was logical analysis, scientific organization, and intellectual understanding. Thus, Bernard of Clairvaux, the great **Cistercian** reformer, attacked what he saw as the excessive and dangerous use of **dialectics** in theology (especially in **Gilbert of Poitiers** and **Peter Abelard**), insofar as for Bernard it distracted believers from their chief goal, namely spiritual growth in the search of God. Before Bernard, **Peter Damian**, another leader of monasticism, had already denounced the dangers of dialectics.

The monastic and Scholastic attitudes are by no means mutually exclusive, however. Some of the monks, such as Bernard, had tremendous rigor in their theological writings, while some of the outstanding Scholastics, such as **Bonaventure**, saw speculation fundamentally as a means for holy living and **mystical** experience. Their core concern for spiritual growth motivated monastic theologians to reflect deeply about issues central to philosophy and theology, such as human nature and psychology, as well as **metaphysics** and **grace**. One of the most influential monastic works on the **soul** was the large compilation by **Alcher of Clairvaux** titled *De spiritu et anima* (*On the Spirit and the Soul*), reputedly a response to Isaac of Stella's *Letter on the Soul*. Both authors provided thinkers of the 13th century with various traditional sources on the subject.

**MONOPSYCHISM.** This is the doctrine that there exists only one human intellect and that consequently human immortality is universal (impersonal). In the Middle Ages, **Averroes** was the champion of this doctrine (formulated in his *Long Commentary on Aristotle's "De anima"*), which he developed through his interpretation of **Aristotle** and Aristotle's Greek commentators, notably Alexander of Aphrodisias and Themistius. Averroes also drew from previous figures in Islamic philosophy (*falsafah*) who explained human knowledge and immortality through the agent intellect, understood as the separate intelligence governing our sublunary realm of generation and corruption and functioning as the efficient cause of human thinking. For Averroes, however, unlike **Avicenna** and **Al-Farabi**, immortality becomes explicitly impersonal: the absorption into one eternal intellect. Averroes also explains human knowledge in this life in terms of an intellect unique to mankind, the so-called material intellect, which is illuminated by the agent intellect. His doctrines were attacked on both philosophic and theological grounds.

Even though Averroes holds that philosophy and revelation agree, many thinkers both within and outside of Islam saw his views as contrary to revelation. One of the criticisms launched against his doctrine was that it was inconsistent with individual responsibility and its concomitant rewards and punishments. Christian thinkers such as **Bonaventure** and **Thomas Aquinas** expressed this while debating against contemporary representatives of Latin **Averroism** and providing their own alternative epistemologies. The vast majority of Christian theologians rejected not only monopsychism but also the doctrine of a separate agent intellect (common in Islamic and Jewish thought) and understood this intellect as a faculty of the individual human soul. Averroes's doctrine on the intellect was one of the chief objects of the **condemnation of 1277** at Paris. Even though Averroes was very influential in both Jewish and Christian circles (i.e., Latin Averroism), there were even Averroists, such as the Jewish philosopher **Gersonides**, who criticized him and tried to incorporate individual immortality into his philosophy.

**MUSIC.** *See* LIBERAL ARTS.

**MU'TAZALITES OR MUTAZALITES.** Literally, Mu'tazalites are "those who stand apart" or "those who do not take sides." As a theological school, the Mu'tazalites are traceable to a student of Al-Hasan al-Basri (fl. ca. 725) who withdrew from his circle due to a dispute over the interpretation of the nature of the **Koran**. The eighth-century Mu'tazalites who followed the rebel's lead were the first Muslims to use Hellenistic philosophy to present their main religious tenets. First, they established the Oneness of God. Second, they concluded that the Koran could not be judged to be the word of God, which the orthodox believed, as God had no separable parts like the Koran. So it had to be created and was not coeternal with God. Thus, it always had to be interpreted, and philosophical methods and categories provided the means to do this. The movement essentially abandoned or set itself apart from orthodox teachings. **Al-Ashari** and the **Asharites** broke away from the Mu'tazalites and refuted their teachings with the same Hellenistic rational methods, but they did so in a way that defended orthodox teachings. The Shi'ites accept the premises of the Mu'tazalites; the Sunni Muslims do not. *See also* ISLAM.

**MYSTICISM, CHRISTIAN.** Since medieval Jewish mysticism is discussed in the entry **Cabala** and medieval Islamic mysticism in the entry **Sufism**, this entry is a brief statement on medieval Christian mysticism, insofar as it receives theological expression in certain authors. The term *mysticism*, from the Greek word meaning "to initiate," connotes mystery and is now used chiefly in relation to the mystery of the divine. As a human endeavor, mysticism in its various forms aims at the experience of union with God. Mystical **theology** seeks to express how this takes place. In so doing, medieval Christian mystical theologians, as their Jewish and Islamic counterparts, generally drew from the **Platonic** and **Neoplatonic** traditions, which provide a general framework wherein all comes from and seeks to return to God, including the human soul. **Augustine**'s and **Dionysius the Pseudo-Areopagite**'s syntheses of Platonism and Christian wisdom were some of the most influential sources for medieval Christian mystics. Augustine's doctrine of divine illumination, whereby God is intimately present to the human soul as the light by which the soul sees and loves all things, was especially seminal for Christian mysticism.

To mention only a few, **Bonaventure**, **Richard** and **Hugh of Saint-Victor**, **Henry of Ghent**, **Denys the Carthusian**, **Meister Eckhart**, and, generally, the great representatives of **monastic theology**, such as **Bernard of Clairvaux**, are important medieval mystical thinkers. In a broad sense, all thinkers for whom the ultimate end of human endeavor is the beatific vision of God in the next life may be considered mystical in orientation, and this would include practically all medieval Christian thinkers. However, mystical thinkers, in a narrower and more proper sense, are those who grant, aside from special divine gifts, some intuitive grasp (however imperfect) of God in this life. This would exclude the more fundamentally **Aristotelian** thinkers, for whom God may be discerned naturally in this life only through His effects. In its efforts to access God, the mystical impulse also yielded a number of unorthodox positions, generally either by confusing God and creatures—pantheism—or by deifying humanity. **Amalric of Bène** and **David of Dinant** were accused of the former, while the highly controversial and variously interpreted Meister Eckhart was condemned during his lifetime as associated with the latter.

# N

**NATURAL LAW.** Proponents of natural law understand it as a moral law proper to rational agents, from which at least some universal moral principles and rules may be derived without direct reference to the revealed Scriptures. However, the natural law in the Middle Ages was seen as agreeing with the Scriptures and in fact as alluded to by the Scriptures, as, for instance, in the words of St. Paul regarding the Gentiles: "the demands of the law are written in their hearts" (Romans 2:14–16). Pagan sources grounding morals in human nature, such as **Stoicism**, Roman law, and **Aristotelianism**, provided a great deal of the philosophic framework for the formulation of natural law theories in the Middle Ages. For example, Aristotle's teleology provided the background of **Thomas Aquinas**'s theory of natural law (probably the most influential one of the Middle Ages), whereby rational agents through the natural law are ordered to their proper ends and thus participate in God's eternal law or providence. Refer to the introduction, "Modern Criticisms of Medieval Philosophy and Theology."

**NATURE.** This term can have different meanings, even among individual authors. Like most terms in medieval philosophical and theological vocabulary, *nature* is related to the term corresponding to it in Greek philosophy, namely *phusis*. *Nature* primarily refers to that which defines a thing, its essence or form. **Aristotle**, in his *Physics* (or *Treatise on Nature*), speaks of nature (Book II, chapter 1) primarily as the specific form of a thing—the immanent principle by which a thing grows and acts according to its species. **Plato**, who has a different view of reality, at times speaks of nature as the essential character of a class of things, as when he speaks of the nature of justice (e.g., *Republic* II, 359b4). However, in Greek thought, as in medieval and modern usage, *nature* can also refer to the character of an individual. Thus Plato (e.g., *Republic* II, 370a9) speaks of different human beings as having different natures in the sense of vocations or dispositions. Aside from nature as specific essence and nature as individual disposition, *nature* can also refer to the natural world as a whole. Thus Aristotle's *Physics* considers the whole class of natural things (as opposed to artificial things).

In medieval philosophical and theological discussions, *nature* is used for the most part in one of these three senses. This is true even in discussions that consider subjects not entertained in Greek philosophy. In regard to the **Trinity**, for example, *nature* refers to the essence shared by the Father, the Son, and the Holy Spirit. *Nature* may also be used to describe the human and divine aspects of Christ. Or *nature* may refer to the whole of the natural world insofar as it is a manifestation of the God of revelation. There are disagreements, of course, as to the realities indicated by the different senses of the term *nature*, notably regarding nature as species. A much-debated question in **Scholastic** philosophy is the following: Is there a common nature aside from individuals and inhering in them? This is one way of stating the famous medieval problem of **universals**. Important thinkers like **William of Ockham** and **John Duns Scotus** provide different answers.

**NEOPLATONISM IN THE MIDDLE AGES.** *See* PLATO (IN THE MEDIEVAL WORLD).

**NESTORIANISM.** The heretical teaching of Nestorius, the patriarch of Constantinople (428–431), claimed that there were two distinct subsistent natures, one fully divine and one fully human, joined by indwelling without confusion in the one person of Jesus Christ. Thus, Nestorius ended up denying a real unity to the person of Christ by holding that there could be no communication of attributes in one person. You could not say the Word suffered and died or that Mary was the Mother of God. The theology of Nestorius was condemned at the third general or ecumenical council held at Ephesus in 431.

**NICHOLAS OF AUTRECOURT (ca. 1300–ca. 1350).** After completing his arts degree at Paris, Nicholas became a bachelor of theology. He raised suspicion of erroneous teaching in 1340, and Pope Clement VI condemned him in 1346 and had his books burned. The result is that his surviving writings are nine letters to Bernard of Arezzo, a letter to Giles of Medonta, a question concerning beatific vision, and a prized treatise: *Ad videndum an sermones Peripateticorum fuerint demonstrativi* (*An Investigation into Whether or Not the Arguments of the Peripatetics Were Demonstrative*). His effort in this work was aimed at showing the plausibility of a teaching opposed to that of Aristotle or else to prove that an Aristotelian argument was insufficient. The judges at his trial accused him of many subterfuges, and readers of his surviving literature often suspect him of skepticism or a philosophy that aims at nothing more than probabilities.

**NICHOLAS OF CUSA (1401–1464).** A student of law at Padua and theology at Cologne, Nicholas was part of the Council of Basel in 1437 and an official of the Church in a number of capacities, including archdeacon of Liège. His chief ideas may be found in his work *De docta igorantia* (*On Learned Ignorance*) and in his *Apologia doctae ignorantiae* (*Apology for Learned Ignorance*). At a time when the debate among nominalists and realists, whose reference point was Aristotle, was the dominating philosophical discussion, Nicholas of Cusa found his primary source of inspiration in the Neoplatonic tradition initiated by **Plotinus**, whose last outstanding exponent had been **Meister Eckhart**. For Nicholas, Aristotle's wisdom was not summed up by his doctrines but by his remark that the intellect is to ultimate truth as the eyes of bats are to the light of day. Aristotle is the undisputed master of reason, a faculty grounded in the principle of noncontradiction, whose power lies in analysis and in making distinctions. Remaining in the context of oppositions, reason is unfit for genuine theology, which seeks a God that is purely one, transcending all created categories, perfections, and distinctions. In order to approach this source of all reality, one must go beyond discursive reasoning and reach the level of insight of pure intellect, which sees the underlying unity in all things. Thus, **Aristotelianism** remains deficient, and true wisdom is to be sought in mystical sources of Neoplatonism, such as **Augustine**, **Dionysius the Pseudo-Areopagite**, **Avicenna**, and **Henry of Ghent**. Meister Eckhart and Nicholas are some of the important voices raised against the dominant presence of Aristotle in the universities and in their approach to theology. In favoring Platonism, they will be followed by a number of philosophers in the Renaissance.

**NICHOLAS OF LYRA (ca. 1270–1349).** A **Franciscan** theologian known primarily as a biblical **exegete**, he studied theology at Paris and became regent master there from 1309 to 1311. After serving as the Franciscan provincial of Paris (1319–1324) and Burgundy (1324–1330), he began his long teaching career at Paris (1333–1339). Although he wrote a *Commentary on the Sentences* and delivered innumerable sermons, he is rightfully renowned for his work as an interpreter of the Bible. His *Postillae perpetuae super totam Bibliam* (*Long Postillae on the Whole Bible*) was copied by hand more than a hundred times and went through many printed editions. His *Postilla moralis* (*Moral Postilla*), written in 1339, presented the spiritual meanings of the biblical texts in a way that could be used for preaching and moral instruction. His work is a strong testament to his knowledge of the Hebrew Bible, the **Midrash** and **Talmud**, as well as the exegetical works of **Rashi** and **Maimonides**.

**NICHOLAS OF OCKHAM (ca. 1242–ca. 1320).** This **Franciscan** theologian and philosopher is closely linked to **Roger Marston, John Peckham, William de la Mare,** and **Richard of Mediavilla,** all of whom followed the intellectual tradition of **Alexander of Hales** and **St. Bonaventure.** Nicholas was born in Ockham, a town in Surrey, probably around 1242. After joining the Franciscan order, he was sent to Paris (1270–1274) for his first theological studies, most likely attending the lectures of Roger Marston. Quite likely he was a bachelor of the Bible at Oxford from 1278 to 1279 and a bachelor of the *Sentences* from 1280 to 1282. Finally, he served, according to Eccleston, as the 18th regent master of the Franciscan house of studies at Oxford, probably from 1286 to 1288. We know nothing of his later life.

Recent scholarly research has turned up 10 complete and incomplete manuscript copies of Nicholas's *Commentary on the Sentences.* Fifteen *Quaestiones disputatae* (*Disputed Questions*) belonging to Nicholas have also be found. Among these disputed questions is a question on the plurality of forms. This dispute is the response of Nicholas to **Thomas of Sutton**'s *Treatise against the Plurality of Forms.* Some of the other disputed questions fall into organic wholes, such as the questions dealing with the fall of man or the four questions that are united in the recent edition titled *Quaestiones disputatae "De dilectione Dei"* (*Disputed Questions on the Love of God*). The latter questions show his subtle knowledge of Aristotle's treatment of friendship in the *Nicomachean Ethics* and his effort to show how a Christian theology of friendship can build on it.

**NICOLE ORESME.** *See* ORESME, NICOLE (ca. 1320–1382).

**NOMINALISM.** In its original form, this term was used to describe the position of certain 12th-century logicians who held that there was no universal reality corresponding to common terms, such as *man* or *animal. Man* was simply a common name that was given to a number of individuals we put into a certain class. There was nothing in these individuals that was shared by others, except the name. As the debate raged between **William of Champeaux, Peter Abelard, Gilbert of Poitiers,** and **Roscelin of Compiegne,** more nuanced positions regarding the real foundation for universal common nouns or concepts developed. Later, in the 14th century, the debate concerning universals raged again, this time involving **William of Ockham, Walter Burley,** and many others. Much more precise theories developed that might classify some as nominalists, conceptualists, moderate **realists,** and exaggerated realists: each providing its own explanation for holding that there are only common written or spoken words, or common concepts, or that there are really common realities that justify our universal categories. *Nominalism* took on a much broader meaning in the 14th and 15th centuries when it was extended as a title to describe certain theological positions, such as explanations of God's absolute and ordained power and what things were absolute and unconditioned realities and what were chosen and conditioned things. Most often, nominalism is associated with Ockhamism or the tradition flowing from William of Ockham.

**NONCONTRADICTION, PRINCIPLE OF.** This principle essentially states that the same thing cannot both be and not be at the same time and under the same respect. For example, it is impossible that this animal next to me at this moment is both a horse and not a horse, if by "a horse" we mean one thing, not two or more, and by "this animal" we mean one thing, not two or more. This is the basic principle of all reasoning and knowledge. As part of the subject of a discipline, however, it is considered explicitly in **dialectics** or **logic**, where it serves as a fundamental axiom. The principle is already formulated by Plato (e.g., *Republic* IV, 437a) and later by Aristotle (e.g., *Metaphysics*, 1005b10–20), whose collection of logical treatises, also known as the *Organon* or instrument of philosophy, constitutes the first systematization of dialectic or logic. Aristotle speaks of this principle as the most certain and the most basic; in fact he says that it is impossible to be mistaken about it if rightly understood. Medieval thinkers, irrespective of theological and philosophical differences, adopted and employed this principle and used Aristotelian logic as a neutral tool.

**NOTTINGHAM.** *See* WILLIAM OF NOTTINGHAM (ca. 1280–1336).

# O

**OCKHAM, WILLIAM OF.** *See* WILLIAM OF OCKHAM (ca. 1285–1347).

**OCKHAM'S RAZOR.** Basically, Ockham's razor is the name given to the popular version of the principle of parsimony enunciated in Book I, chapter 4, of Aristotle's *Physics* (188a 17–18): "Pluralitas non est pondenda sine necessitate" (Plurality should not be posited without necessity). **William of Ockham** himself used this principle frequently in his explanations of Aristotle's *Physics* and in many other contexts. For instance, in regard to the 10 Aristotelian categories, Ockham claimed that the 10 categories did not mean that there were for Aristotle 10 different kinds of realities. Certainly, there are qualities that are realities inhering in substances. A white wall has whiteness in it. However, a curved yardstick does not have curvedness in it. If you simply bend the yardstick so that the ends are closer to each other, then the yardstick is said to be curved. "Curvedness," then, is not an inhering quality like whiteness. Nor do children who are twins have "twinness" inhering in each of them. When you have two children born of the same mother shortly after one another, then you call them twins. "Twinness" is not an inhering quality. Ockham was attacked by **Walter Chatton**, for example, for using the principle of parsimony without warrant. He formulated an "anti-razor": if you cannot explain something without appealing to three realities, then appeal to three; if you cannot explain something without appealing to four realities, then appeal to four. In reaction, Ockham reformulated his razor to parallel Chatton's formula: "If you can explain something by appealing to three realities, then do not appeal to four; and if you can explain something by appealing to two realities, then do not appeal to three," etc.

**OCKHAMISM.** This is a general title used to describe the methods and teachings of **William of Ockham** and his many followers during the time from 1325 to the beginning of the 16th century. Among those generally named as his followers are **Adam Wodeham, Robert Holcot, Nicholas of Autrecourt, John of Mirecourt, Gregory of Rimini, John Buridan, Al-**

bert of Saxony, Pierre d'Ailly, and Gabriel Biel. Their positions on certain points may differ significantly, but they are usually interpreted as having related views on the relation between faith and reason, the divine order of reality, the nature of grace, man's fallen character, and the process of justification, as well as on philosophical matters, such as the question of **universals**.

**ODO RIGAUD (RIGALDUS) (ca. 1220–1275).** One of the early Franciscan masters at Paris. He was a student of **Alexander of Hales**, along with his confrere **John of La Rochelle**, and was one of the authors (also Alexander of Hales, John of La Rochelle, and Robert de la Bassée) of the *Expositio Regulae Quattuor Magistorum* (*Exposition of the Rule of St. Francis by Four Masters*). He lectured on *Books I–III of the **Sentences** of **Peter Lombard*** between 1241 and 1245 and succeeded John of La Rochelle as regent master in theology upon the latter's death in 1245. He later became archbishop of Rouen (1248) and took an active part at the Council of Lyons in 1274. *See also* ORDERS (RELIGIOUS).

**OPTICS.** In the Middle Ages, optics was primarily a theoretical discipline, even though practical applications were developed, such as the making of lenses to correct vision around 1280. This understanding largely depended on Aristotle's view that optics, like astronomy, is a mathematical science that nevertheless applies to the sensible. In the Islamic world, the translation movement of Greek scientific works in the eighth and ninth centuries provided a variety of materials on scientific subjects, including optics (*see FAL-SAFAH, AL-*), and stimulated work on different topics concerning light and vision, including its anatomical, mathematical, and philosophical dimensions. Works by Euclid and **Ptolemy**, providing a mathematical explanation for visual phenomena, were influential. Also important were Galen's description of eye anatomy and his visual ray account of vision, whereby the visual spirit coming from the eye transformed the air into an instrument of vision. **Aristotelian** philosophers, such as **Avicenna** and **Averroes**, approached vision within a general account of sensation, which was part of natural philosophy (as in Aristotle's *De anima*), and understood vision and the other sensations as types of abstraction (and intellectual abstraction as analogous to sensation): vision is the reception in the eye of the object's visible species or likeness; hearing is the reception in the ear of the object's audible species or likeness, etc. Avicenna, in his influential *Book of Healing*, develops Aristotle's theories, criticizes him on certain points, and furnishes original arguments. Some thinkers influenced by Aristotle, though of a more Platonic inspiration, such as the **Augustinian Bonaventure**, will appropriate this understanding of vision, although they generally ascribe a more active role to the soul in vision (and in the formation of concepts) than do Aristotelians.

Islamic physicians, such as Hunayn ibn Ishaq (809–873), the renowned translator, generally followed Galen's account of vision. **Al-Kindi**'s *De aspectibus*, one of the greatest medieval Islamic works in optics, draws from and develops Greek optics, especially the theories of Euclid and Ptolemy. Aside from other important treatises, the monumental and influential *Book on Optics* by Ibn al-Haytham (965–ca. 1040) (translated into Latin in the 12th century and commented on in the 14th century by Kamal al-Din al-Farisi) also develops Greek optics (notably Ptolemy's *Optics*) and is innovative in the way it combines experimentation and observation with mathematics. Aside from classic sources, the work of Al-Kindi, Avicenna, and especially Ibn al-Haytham (known in Latin as **Alhacen**) was central in the development of optics in **Islam**, and important writings of all three were translated into Latin, influencing the development of optics in Europe.

In the Christian West, Plato's theories of optics (in Chalcidius's translation of the *Timaeus*), adopted by Augustine, were authoritative until the 11th century, when Aristotelianism began to flourish. For Plato, the visual fire coming out through the eye joins daylight, whereby a medium is created through which the soul accesses visible forms. Constantine the African's translations in the 12th century (e.g., of Johannitius's *Liber de oculis*) and the encyclopedia of Bartholomew of England were important contributions to the physiology and anatomy of the eye. Latin translations in the 12th and 13th centuries of Euclid, Ptolemy, Aristotle (and his commentators), and others such as Ibn al-Haytham were also fundamental. The Platonic view, though informed by new sources, still had proponents, however, as evidenced by the work of **Robert Grosseteste**. **Albert the Great** promoted Aristotle's conception of vision, while **John Peckham**, **Roger Bacon**, Blasius of Parma, Henry of Langestein, and Witelo were among the scientists who depended on theorems and principles of Ibn al-Haytham (and Ptolemy). Through the work of this latter group especially, optics began to be approached geometrically, and in the 13th century it reached the status of a mathematical science, the *scientia perspectivae* (the science of perspective), and was studied under different headings at **universities**. As such, investigation into optics bore fruit during the rest of the Middle Ages and into the Renaissance. In 1304, for example, the **Dominican** Theodoric of Freiberg first successfully provided an explanation of the rainbow's formation of colors, an explanation absent in Aristotle's *Meteorologica*. Optical topics were also dealt with in theological contexts, where, for example, metaphors of light informed treatments of cognition and the role of light in creation was considered.

In medieval discussions concerning the status of a science, usually generated by Aristotle's *Posterior Analytics*, optics is a favorite example of a subalternate science. A subalternate science is one whose principles are established as conclusions by another science. Thus, for **Thomas Aquinas**, optics is subalternate to geometry because the principles of optics are borrowed from conclusions in geometry. The issue of subalternation in science becomes central in debates concerning the scientific status of theology. Aquinas uses his understanding of subalternation and the example of optics to conclude that theology is a subalternate science. Just as optics accepts its principles on the authority of geometry, theology accepts its (revealed) principles on the authority of God and the blessed. Just as the optician as optician cannot give an account of the principles of optics (only the geometer can), the theologian cannot give an account of the principles of theology, which belong only to the higher science of God and the blessed. This approach to theology depends on Aquinas's Aristotelian principles: since the human intellect is the form of its body, its knowledge is abstractive and proceeds from effects to causes; the most the intellect can know about the first cause is its existence, and so it must accept other truths about God's nature and will on the basis of divine revelation and faith. Thinkers of a more **Augustinian** inspiration, holding that God himself is the source of all intellectual seeing, will challenge Aquinas's view of subalternation. Thus **Henry of Ghent** argues that theology does not fit the model of subalternation in Aristotle's *Posterior Analytics*; it is not analogous to optics. For theology is a science proceeding simply from first principles; that these principles are known more or less obscurely by a given theologian does not make theology subalternate.

**ORDERS (RELIGIOUS).** Religious orders in the Middle Ages were groups that followed a rule, i.e., a set of principles governing their religious life. St. Augustine of Hippo (354–430) wrote a rule that became the model for the Order of Hermits of St. **Augustine**, formed in 1244 by Pope Innocent IV. Members of this Augustinian order played an active role in university and ecclesiastical life. **Giles of Rome** and **Gregory of Rimini** were among their outstanding theologians at the University of Paris. Martin Luther was also an Augustinian. St. Benedict of Nursia (ca. 480–ca. 547) founded according to his rule a monastery at Monte Cassino that became the root of the medieval monastic system. Destroyed by Lombards around 577, the monastery was reestablished in the eighth century. Through Charlemagne's influence, the Rule of St. Benedict was predominant at Carolingian monasteries. In 21 March 1098, Robert, abbot of the Benedictine Abbey at Molesme, went with some of his companions to Citeaux to follow the Rule of St. Benedict in its original purity and fullness. Although Robert was recalled to Molesme by papal ordinance, Citeaux was the origin of a rich reform of the Order of St. Benedict, the Cistercians. Bernard of Fontaines, who became **St. Bernard of**

Clairvaux, the great mystical theologian, was admitted to Citeaux in 1112 by its leader, **Stephen Harding**. Bernard founded Clairvaux, a focal point of further reform, and organized the institution of numerous other foundations. The Carthusian order, known for their austere and nearly eremetical life, was founded by St. Bruno (ca. 1030–1101) in France. Carthusians follow their own rule, the *Consuetudines* or *Statutes*. **Denys the Carthusian** is one of their most influential thinkers. The Carmelites, a mendicant order whose exact origin has been a source of debate, produced a number of prominent university theologians, **Gerard of Bologna**, **Guido Terrena**, and **John of Baconthorpe**. As the canon regular Erasmus of Rotterdam put it, canons regular, essentially religious clerics, are "something in between" monks and secular priests. In the 12th century, a new order of canons regular, notably at the Abbey of Saint-Victor in Paris, played an important role in philosophy and theology: **Hugh**, **Adam**, **Andrew**, **Richard**, and **Thomas Gallus**, all members of the Canons Regular of St. Augustine at Saint-Victor, made important contributions. Their "in-between" or combined status served as a bridge between monastic theology and the Scholastic theology practiced at the nascent universities of the late 12th century.

In the university setting, Dominican and Franciscan friars (both mendicant orders) made some of the greatest contributions to philosophy and theology. The Dominicans, founded around 1210 by St. Domingo de Guzmán (ca. 1170–1221), produced major figures such as **Albert the Great**, **Thomas Aquinas**, **Dietrich of Freiberg**, and **Meister Eckhart**. Among the Franciscans, founded in 1210/1212 by St. Francis of Assisi (1182–1226), **Alexander of Hales**, **Bonaventure**, **John Duns Scotus**, **Matthew of Aquasparta**, **Peter John Olivi**, and **William of Ockham** were very influential. At the University of Paris, Dominicans were established as part of the teaching staff in 1217, and the Franciscans in 1220. The distinction between secular masters (such as **Henry of Ghent** and **Godfrey of Fontaines**) and masters from the mendicant orders had political ramifications in the universities, including struggles between seculars and mendicants concerning rights and privileges. Figures like **William of St. Amour** and his follower **Gerard of Abbeville** opposed the very idea of the mendicant orders and intensely sought to undermine the mendicants at the University of Paris. In turn, leaders like Bonaventure and Aquinas wrote their own responses to these challenges. The mendicants ultimately won, with the favor of Pope Alexander IV (the successor of Innocent IV in 1254), becoming undisputed doctors at the university. *See also STUDIUM GENERALE.*

**ORESME, NICOLE (ca. 1320–1382).** A native of Normandy, Oresme studied theology at the University of Paris and became a master in 1362. A highly accomplished scholar who held influential posts (he became bishop of Lisieux in 1377), he wrote in Latin and French and contributed in various fields, including physics, astronomy, politics, and ethics (he also translated **Aristotle**'s *Politics*, *Ethics*, *Economics*, and *On the Heavens* into French). In addition, he composed pioneering treatises in political economy. However, he is best known as one of the most accomplished medieval contributors to the mathematical and natural sciences, influencing later advances of **René Descartes**, Galileo Galilei, and Nicolaus Copernicus. He wrote questions (*Quaestiones*) on Aristotle's *Physica, De caelo, De generatione et corruptione, Meteorologica, De sensu*, and *De anima*, as well as other treatises on natural philosophy, such as the *Treatise on the Sphere* and *On the Deformity of Qualities*. The law of falling bodies, the employment of coordinates in the analysis of the movement of bodies, and the diurnal movement of the earth are scientific advances toward which Oresme's work played some part.

**ORIGINAL SIN.** In the biblical tradition (in connection with Genesis 1–3), *original sin* can have two related meanings. First, the term can refer to the original transgression of mankind's first parents, Adam and Eve. They were expelled from the Garden of Eden for disobeying God's prohibition for them in that place: they were not to eat the fruit of the tree of the knowledge of good and evil. In general, Christianity views the consequences of the first sin differently than do Judaism and **Islam**. To Christians, the whole of mankind inherited the guilt of the first sin and needs redemption. For Christians, it is not only the sin of Adam, but through him all men have sin. The focus of Judaism and Islam is more on the sin of Adam as affecting the circumstances of our life so that we now live in a world where Adam's sin shows us the wrong path that we might also follow.

For the Christian understanding of original sin, St. Paul's writings are fundamental, especially Romans 5:12, which states that sin and thereby death extends to all mankind on account of the first sin. Medieval Christian teaching on this issue was defined by **Augustine**'s interpretation of St. Paul and by his arguments against the **Pelagians**. For Augustine, all mankind suffers because of the real inherited guilt contracted at birth, and this suffering extends well beyond mortality. Moreover, original sin does not mean that human beings are sinful like Adam, on account of their free will. Rather, and more importantly, all who sprang from Adam are corrupted because of Adam's sin, and this applies even to children, who do not sin by their will (hence the Catholic understanding of baptism as remission of sin). Adam's sin corrupted man's soul and thereby man's ability to reach his end—eternal happiness in union with God. God's redeeming grace is necessary.

In the later Middle Ages, Augustine's view of original sin also became fundamental in the Protestant theologies of Martin Luther and John Calvin. For them, original sin is understood as an essential corruption of man's nature. After the fall, men's relations with nature, with each other, and with

God became corrupted so that sin became part and parcel of human life, and man's attainment of beatitude was nullified. Human beings could regain blessedness only through the help of Christ's grace, not by their own efforts.

As already implied, perspectives on original sin have important theological implications. In Christianity, this doctrine is intimately related to Christology, since Christ is seen as the necessary redeemer of mankind. **Anselm**'s *Cur Deus Homo* (*Why God Became Man*), for example, is both a conception of original sin and of the Incarnation. In philosophy, original sin is also an important topic, as it relates to anthropological and ethical questions. Augustine, for example, provides some of his most profound insights on the soul while exploring man's fallen nature and need for grace. On the other hand, the absence in Judaism and Islam of the doctrines of original sin and the Incarnation implies different frameworks for the conception of human nature and its relation to God, wherein human beings are seen as able to approach God with less difficulty through their own efforts.

**OTTO OF FREISING (ca. 1112–1158).** Although Otto studied in Paris and perhaps under **Peter Abelard** or **Hugh of Saint-Victor**, his interest was not in philosophy or theology, but rather history. He joined the **Cistercians**, was elected abbot in 1137, and was made bishop of Freising at an early age. His chief work was his *Historia de duabus civitatibus* (*History of the Two Cities*), a work obviously modeled on **Augustine**'s *City of God*. Like Augustine, Otto portrayed the City of God as the communion of saints both living and dead. However, in portraying the city on earth, he does not represent it as evil but rather as the place where the two cities were both present and intermingled. A sequel to this historical text was his *Gesta Friderici imperatoris* (*Deeds of Frederick Barbarossa*), written in 1146.

**OXFORD CALCULATORS.** This term refers to a group of pioneering 14th-century Oxford scientists that, following the example of **Thomas Bradwardine**, applied and developed mathematical methods in the study of nature, particularly kinetics. This group includes thinkers such as **William Heytesbury**, **John Dumbleton**, and **Richard Swineshead**.

**PALAMAS, GREGORY.** *See* GREGORY PALAMAS (1296–1359).

**PARIS, UNIVERSITY OF.** *See* UNIVERSITIES.

**PASCHASIUS RADBERTUS (ca. 785–ca. 860).** Paschasius joined the Benedictines at the Abbey of Corbie and soon was elected abbot. He served in this role from 843 to 853, resigning because of resistance to his desired reforms. Paschasius wrote the first treatise on the Eucharist: *De corpore et sanguine Domini* (*Concerning the Lord's Body and Blood*), wherein he argued that "the substance of the Bread and Wine is changed into the Body and Blood of Christ" and that the Eucharist "is the very flesh that suffered on the Cross." He was attacked by **Ratramnus of Corbie** and **Rhabanus Maurus**, who viewed the Eucharist as a symbol of Christ's body and blood, but Paschasius defended his position until the very end of his life.

**PATRISTIC AUTHORS.** *See* FATHERS OF THE CHURCH.

**PAUL OF VENICE (1369–1429).** Born in Udine, the ancient capital city of Friuli, Paul joined the **Hermits of St. Augustine** at a young age and was educated at the *studium generale* (international house of studies) of the order in Padua, and then at Oxford. He had a long career in teaching, particularly at the University of Padua. He served as provincial for a short time in his religious order and also as an ambassador of the Venetian Republic to Poland and Hungary. He is known for his many works in **logic** and philosophy, but he is also acknowledged as the author of an *Abbreviatio lecturae super I Sententiarum Ioannis de Ripa* (*An Abbreviation of the Lectures of John of Ripa on Book I of the Sentences*). His earliest work was his *Logica Parva* (*An Abbreviated Logic*), written in 1401 and found in 82 manuscripts and printed in 25 editions. The *Logica Magna* (*A Long Treatise on Logic*), a much more impressive work assigned to his teaching at Oxford, has had its authenticity challenged in recent years.

**PECKHAM, JOHN (ca. 1230–1292).** The successor of **Robert Kilwardby** as archbishop of Canterbury from 1279 until his death, this English **Franciscan** is best known for his reactions against **Aristotelianism** at Oxford, especially that of the followers of **Thomas Aquinas**, and his defense of the tradition of **Augustine** and **Anselm**. He served as regent master in theology at both Paris and Oxford. His doctrinal orientation is perhaps best summarized in a letter he wrote to the Bishop of Lincoln (1 June 1285): "I do not in any way disapprove of philosophical studies, insofar as they serve theological mysteries, but I do disapprove of irreverent innovations in language, introduced within the last 20 years into the depths of **theology** . . . to the detriment of the **Fathers of the Church** whose positions are disdained and openly held in contempt. Which doctrine is more solid and more sound, the doctrine of the sons of Saint Francis, that is, of Brother **Alexander of Hales** of sainted memory, of Brother **Bonaventure** and others like him, who rely on the Fathers and the philosophers in treatises secure against any reproach, or else that very recent and almost entirely contrary doctrine, which fills the entire world with wordy quarrels, weakening and destroying with all its strength what Augustine teaches concerning the eternal rules and the unchangeable light, the faculties of the **soul**, the seminal reasons included in matter and innumerable questions of the same kind. Let the Ancients be the judges, since in them is wisdom. Let the God of heaven be the judge, and may he remedy it" (*Registrum epistolarum fr. Johannis Peckham*, III, 871, 901–2; translation from Gilson, *HCPMA*, 359).

This utterance comes a few years after the famous **condemnation** of 219 philosophical and theological propositions (most of them Aristotelian) launched by Bishop **Étienne Tempier** at Paris on 7 March of 1277. It shows the controversy regarding the introduction of Aristotelianism into an intellectual tradition dominated largely by the Church Fathers (especially Augustine) in the years following the death of Thomas Aquinas in 1274. It also shows that, at least in the mind of Peckham, the fundamental doctrinal alternative at the time was either Augustinianism (represented primarily by Franciscans and others, such as Henry of Ghent) or Aristotelianism (represented primarily by Dominicans). As suggested by Peckham above, the problem of the soul and its knowledge was quite important to him, including its **metaphysical** foundations. His *Quaestiones tractantes de anima* (*Questions Treating the Soul*), *Tractatus de anima* (*Treatise on the Soul*), and *Summa de esse et essentia* (*The Summa concerning Existence and Essence*) are some of his contributions in this general area. His *Perspectiva communis* (*General Optics*), *Theorica planetarum* (*A Theoretical Study of the Planets*), *Mathematicae rudimenta* (*The Basics of Mathematics*), and *Tractatus spherae* (*Treatise on the Nature of a Sphere*) provide evidence for his engagement in scientific studies, in which he followed the tradition of thinkers like **Roger Bacon** and **Robert Grosseteste**.

**PELAGIANISM.** This **heresy** in its original form stressed the complete freedom of the human will in regard to its choice of good or evil. The **sin** or sins of others, including Adam, cannot interfere with this freedom; nor can God's grace. The implications of this teaching are that there is a denial of **original sin**, and thus the human race did not inherit sin that required redemption. Also, children do not require baptism, and people were sinless in their way of living before the arrival of Christ. Neither do prayers for sinners bear any fruit, since only free will makes acts good. In the Middle Ages, the name Pelagian or Semi-Pelagian was attached to many who stressed freedom or the ability of men to perform morally good acts without grace. One of the more famous attacks on what he considered medieval Pelagianism and Semi-Pelagianism can be found in **Thomas Bradwardine**'s *De Causa Dei contra Pelagium* (*On God's Case against Pelagius*).

**PERALDUS (PEYRAUD), WILLIAM (ca. 1199–ca. 1271).** William studied at Paris and is thought to have joined the Dominicans at Saint-Jacques as a mature man due to the inspiring sermons of Jordan of Saxony. He thus would have been at Paris with his fellow Dominicans Humbert of Romans and **Hugh of Saint-Cher**. He was sent to the Dominican convent in Lyons before the Lent of 1249 and there held the office of prior from 1264 to 1266. His *Sermones* and his most famous Scriptural and Patristic sourcebook, *Summa de vitiis et virtutibus* (*Summa of Vices and Virtues*), were written before 1249. The latter was printed often from the 15th to the 17th century. Other works, such as his *De regimine principum* (*On the Rule of Princes*) and *Speculum religiosorum* (*Mirror of Religious*) or *De eruditione religiosorum* (*On the Training of Religious Men*) have often escaped attention because they have been attributed to other authors. His chief influence, however, has been through his *Summa*, which dealt with the vices and virtues, not in the technical Scholastic manner but in a way that could nourish pastors who preached and religious souls who searched for spiritual nourishment.

**PETER AUREOLI (AURIOL) (ca. 1289–1322).** Born in Cahors, in Aquitaine, Peter entered the **Franciscan** order at an early age. By 1312, he was a **lector** at Bologna. There he wrote *A Treatise on Poverty and Poor Use* and a work on natural philosophy titled *Tractatus de principiis* (*A Treatise on Natural Causes*). Two years later, he taught at Toulouse, where he produced his *Tractatus de conceptione beatae Mariae Virginis* (*Treatise on the Conception of the Blessed Virgin Mary*). He was chosen, at the general chapter at Naples in 1316, to go to Paris to lecture on all four books of the ***Sentences***. He must have completed most of his *Scriptum in I Sententiarum* (*Written Commentary on Book I of the Sentences*) during the years at Toulouse, since a finished illuminated copy of it dedicated to Pope John XXII was completed in May 1317, and we have *Reportationes* on all four books of the *Sentences* produced at Paris in 1316–1318. Peter was made a master of theology in 1318 at the written request of Pope John XXII and stayed in Paris as *magister*, producing by 1320 his *Quodlibet*. In 1321, he was appointed archbishop of Aix-en-Provence, but he held this office only for a short time, since he died in 1322. His *Scriptum* and *Reportationes* are good illustrations of the changes taking place in regard to commentaries on **Peter Lombard**'s *Sentences*. Writing commentaries on Peter Lombard's *Sentences* is, for Aureoli, no longer an exercise in assimilating the traditional learning, but more of a major vehicle expressing one's own developed theology.

**PETER CANTOR.** *See* PETER THE CHANTER (PETER CANTOR) (ca. 1130–1197).

**PETER CEFFONS (ca. 1320–ca. 1380).** Peter was a French **Cistercian** who, like **John of Mirecourt**, quite likely studied at the College of St. Bernard and the University of Paris. In general, Cistercians tended to limit study to Scripture and the commentaries of the **Fathers of the Church** on Scripture, so the names of French Cistercian **Scholastics** are limited. Peter, who lectured on the *Sentences* of **Peter Lombard** at Paris in 1348–1349, four years after his confrere, John of Mirecourt, shows the influence of English philosophy and theology at Paris. This influence was present in the writings of **Gregory of Rimini**, a **Hermit of St. Augustine**, and in Peter Ceffons's Cistercian predecessor John of Mirecourt, but when it came under attack by the more traditional Parisian theologians, Ceffons defended the new English approaches with stunning ridicule of its opponents. He, however, is not ignorant of the earlier Parisian tradition, which he readily cites. His association with the English theology that was in his era under attack at Paris did no harm to him within his order. He was in his later life elected abbot of Clairvaux.

**PETER COMESTOR (ca. 1100–ca. 1180).** As chancellor of the cathedral school in Paris (1164–1168), he taught theology there before becoming a canon regular at the Augustinian monastery of Saint-Victor. Although he wrote a large collection of sermons, a treatise *De sacramentis* (*On the Sacraments*), Peter became most renowned for his *Historia Scholastica* (*Scholastic History*). It is the story of salvation history that attempts to unify the books of the Bible into a narrative with historical unity. Influenced by the Scriptural commentaries of **Peter Lombard**, Comestor's *Historia Scholastica* joined the curriculum of theology, along with Lombard's *Sentences*, as one of the three alternative ways of studying the Scriptures: reading them directly; studying the unified account of God's creative and redemptive involvement with men (*Historia Scholastica*); or dealing with the more difficult doctrinal questions raised by the Scriptures (Lombard's *Sentences*). *See also* PETER OF POITIERS (ca. 1130–1205).

**PETER DAMIAN, ST. (1007–1072).** St. Peter Damian was cautious about the influence of secular disciplines (especially **dialectics**) on Christian learning. "If skill in the humane art is sometimes used in dealing with Scripture, it should not arrogantly grasp for itself the right of master, but rather play a certain subordinate role as a servant, like a handmaid to a mistress, lest it should fall into error if it take the lead." A teacher at Ravenna (his town of origin) who studied **liberal arts** at Faenza and Parma, Peter became one of the leading advocates and organizers of monastic life in Italy. Though learned and eloquent, his version of the ideal monastic life emphasized contemplation and asceticism more (and education and art less) than other monastic models in Europe. In his letter to Desiderius, the abbot of Monte Cassino, titled *De omnipotentia divina* (*On Divine Omnipotence*), he cautions against the arguments of logicians or rhetoricians becoming the measure of divine things. The only legitimate role of reason and philosophy is to aid in the study of Scripture. Among those who held this view, Peter is quite at the extreme of the spectrum. He is famous for saying that the first teacher of grammar was the devil: he taught Adam to decline *deus* (God) in the plural. For Peter, reason should be cultivated only for the sake of living in a holy way (the monastic life being the best example). Philosophical pursuits can easily lead the **soul** astray through vain curiosity (as **Augustine** and other **Fathers of the Church** had already noted) or may easily result in heresy. This misuse of dialectics in theology was evident to Peter in **Berengar of Tours** (also opposed by **Anselm**'s teacher **Lanfranc of Bec**), whose analysis of the **Eucharist** denied transubstantiation. Some of Peter's influential successors, such as Anselm, will criticize Peter and assign a greater role to reason, without reducing the truth of the Christian faith to human categories.

**PETER HELIAS (ca. 1100–ca. 1166).** A student of Thierry of Chartres, Peter became a very famous teacher of grammar and rhetoric. His *Commentary on Cicero's "De inventione"* followed **Boethius**'s lead and traveled the path of other glosses on works of this respected author. Peter's *Summa super Priscianum* (*A Summa on Priscian's Institutions*), however, is a structured textbook that attempts to provide within the framework of **Priscian**'s text the basic structure that would present the causes or principles to explain the different kinds of linguistic materials.

**PETER LOMBARD (ca. 1095–1160).** This theologian, and later bishop of Paris, was born near Novara in Lombardy between 1095 and 1100 and died in Paris on 21 August 1160. **Bernard of Clairvaux** sponsored his studies at Reims and recommended him to Gilduin, the prior of Saint-Victor in Paris, where he likely studied under **Hugh of Saint-Victor** around 1136. He taught at the cathedral school of Notre Dame from at least 1145 on and became a canon there in the same year. Ordained a subdeacon in 1147, he attended the Council of Reims in 1148. Advanced to deacon and archdeacon, he was consecrated bishop of Paris on 28 July 1159.

Peter's *Commentary on the Psalter*, written around 1136, aimed at making the reading of the Divine Office more spiritually fruitful. His *Collectanea* or *Commentary on the Epistles of Paul*, famous under the title *Magna Glossatura*, written between 1139 and 1341 and later revised, undertook more complex doctrinal discussions. Both commentaries served as sources for his ***Book of the Sentences***.

The *Sentences*, the fruit of Peter's doctrinal teaching during his Paris years, reached its final form between 1155 and 1157. Thirty of Peter's sermons survive, for the most part published among the works of Hildebert of Lavardin. The *Sentences* was the most successful collection of theological questions of the 12th century. Other collections, the anonymous *Summa sententiarum* and Hugh of Saint-Victor's *De sacramentis*, assembled texts of Sts. Ambrose, **Augustine**, and Hilary throughout; in specific areas, they included Julian of Toledo's treatment of the last things, and for the sacraments they used the guiding practical texts of **Gratian** and Ivo of Chartres. If Peter Lombard's *Sententiae* won out in influence, it was due to his balanced choice of questions and his avoidance of minor controversies. Its content was based on the teaching given in Augustine's *De doctrina Christiana* about the things that are real and the things that are signs leading us back to what is most real. In four books, Peter treated the triune God and his attributes, the creation and the fall, Christ, the remedy for the fall, and the sacraments and last things. The *Sententiae* was not a perfect work, and later theologians who revered it also listed its weaknesses. Overall, it was a solid, balanced work that commanded respect up to the time of Philip Melancthon and beyond. **Alexander of Hales** made it his doctrinal textbook in Paris around 1222, to complement the moral interpretation of Scripture that was then dominant. **Richard Fishacre**, at Oxford ca. 1245, followed Alexander's lead.

Thereafter, commentaries on Lombard's *Sentences* became the chief way, along with commentaries on the Bible and Peter **Comestor**'s *Historia Scholastica*, to attain the grade of master of theology. At first, the commentaries on the *Sentences* were instruments for learning the subject matter of the total collection of traditional questions; later, they became works that demonstrated mature theological expertise in treating such questions. At first, the commentaries covered all the areas examined by Peter Lombard; later, they often became collections of the most burning questions that concerned theologians at the time. Under its various usages, the *Sentences* of Peter Lombard remained the single most important theological text of the Middle Ages.

**PETER OF AQUILA (ca. 1280–1361).** Peter was a Franciscan who taught at Paris around 1330 and was so attached to the thought of **John Duns Scotus** that he earned the title *Scotellus* (Little Scotus). In 1334, he became provincial of Tuscany. Ten years later, he was chosen to be chaplain to Queen Johanna of Sicily. In 1347, Peter was appointed bishop of Sant'Angelo dei Lombardi in Calabria, and a year later he became bishop of Trivento. His *Quaestiones in IV libros Sententiarum* was published in 1480 and reprinted in 1967. This work is to a great extent a reworking of the *Ordinatio* of Duns Scotus. He has also left in manuscript form a *Compendium of the Books of the Sentences*, an *Exposition of the Books of Aristotle's Ethics*, and a *Treatise on the Sacraments*.

**PETER OF AUVERGNE (ca. 1230–1304).** A distinguished secular master in both the Arts and Theology Faculties at the University of Paris, Peter was appointed rector of the university on 7 March 1275. He is probably the same Peter of Auvergne appointed bishop of Clermont on 21 January 1302 by **Pope Boniface VIII**. In the **Arts Faculty**, he focused on **Aristotelian** and **Averroist** philosophy (his principal philosophical inclination), as was the norm at that faculty, and is credited with several commentaries on Aristotle. A commentary on **Peter Lombard**'s *Sentences* and *Quodlibets* is also attributed to him. The authenticity of some works associated with his name remains a question, and a number of them still need to be carefully edited to determine what parts of these works belong to him and what parts to others.

Reputedly a most faithful disciple of **Thomas Aquinas**, Peter was influenced by him. However, there is no evidence that he studied directly under Thomas, and his doctrines differ from Thomas's on some points. For example, his rejection of a real distinction between essence and existence is more in line with **Averroes**'s interpretation of Aristotle. After Aquinas's death in 1274, Peter's work was used to complete some of Aquinas's unfinished writings, especially his *Commentary on the Politics of Aristotle*. In theology, his main influences are **Henry of Ghent** and **Godfrey of Fontaines**, the positions of whom he occasionally followed against Aquinas's positions. Under the influence of the latter, for example, he changed his originally Thomistic opinion on individuation. Peter is also known as a speculative grammarian (or modist), holding a close correlation between thought, language, and reality.

**PETER OF BLOIS (ca. 1130–ca. 1211).** Between 1140 and 1155, Peter studied rhetoric and **theology** at Tours, Bologna, and Paris. Among Peter's works is an unedited *Libellus de arte dictandi rhetorice* (*A Brief Treatise on the Art of Rhetoric*). He, however, is better known for his letters, his apologetic treatises, and his *Compendium on Job*. In the latter work, written probably in 1183, he strongly criticizes the conduct of the king, the princes, and the prelates as he holds up Job as the model of human conduct. He wrote an *Instructio fidei catholicae* (*Instruction for the Catholic Faith*) in the name of Pope Alexander III for a sultan who was considering conversion to the Catholic faith, explaining the main Christian teachings, especially concerning the Incarnation and Redemption. He also wrote a treatise titled *Contra perfidiam Judaeorum* (*Against the False Belief of the Jews*), employing Scriptural citations and rational arguments to establish his case. The work most closely approaching a **Scholastic** character is his *De testimoniis fidei* (*On the Witnesses of the Faith*), whose last chapter attacks the *habitus* theory of the Incarnation that was proposed by **Peter Lombard**. His treatise *On Christian Friendship and the Love of God and Neighbor*, for a long time attributed to Cassiodorus, is very dependent on Aelred of Rievaulx's *De amicitia spirituali* (*On Spiritual Friendship*) and *Speculum caritatis* (*Mirror of Love*). Despite his many writings, Peter's life was essentially an active one, serving at various royal and episcopal courts.

**PETER OF CANDIA (ca. 1340–1410).** Born in Crete and left an orphan at an early age, Peter was given his basic education by a Franciscan who recommended him for studies at Padua when he joined the Franciscans in 1357. He studied at Padua and at the Franciscan *studium* in Norwich. He became a bachelor of theology at Oxford and then a master of theology at Paris, constructing his commentary on the *Sentences* of **Peter Lombard** in 1278–1280. Some logical treatises, e.g., *De suppositionibus* (*On the Kinds of Supposition*) and *De consequentiis* (*On Consequences*) are attributed to him, as is a *Tractatus de immaculata Deiparae conceptione* (*A Treatise on the Immaculate Conception of the Mother of God*). By the middle of the 1280s, he was at the court of Gian Galeazzo Visconti, and with the support of his patronage he held the chair of theology at Pavia, where he helped restore the **university**. Peter was made a counselor to the Duke of Milan in 1378 and was appointed bishop of Piacenza, then Vincenza, and finally Novara before becoming archbishop of Milan in 1402. In the Great Schism (1378–1417), he stood with Rome. He was made a cardinal by Pope Innocent VII in 1405. When Innocent's successor, Gregory XII, and the antipope Benedict XIII were declared heretics at the Council of Pisa (1409), he became pope, assuming the name of Alexander V. He died a year later before accomplishing any of the Church reforms that he promised at the Council of Pisa.

**PETER OF JOHN OLIVI (1248–1298).** Trained by a Joachimite **Franciscan** Raimondo Barravi in his youthful start as a Franciscan, Peter very much favored a life dedicated to poverty and asceticism. When he moved on to **theological** studies at Paris, Peter studied under **Matthew of Aquasparta**, **John Peckham**, and **William de la Mare**, all students of **St. Bonaventure**. In 1268, he first heard St. Bonaventure himself deliver his Parisian Lenten sermons *On the Gifts of the Holy Spirit*, and in 1273 he was again present for the Lenten sermons *On the Hexaëmeron* or *Six Days of Creation*. Although he rejected certain elements of Bonaventure's theology, such as the *rationes seminales* (seminal reasons) and the theory of Illumination, he generally stayed in the **Augustinian** tradition of Bonaventure, especially in his view of the spiritual nature of the soul and its active role in intellectual cognition. He viewed **Aristotle**, **Averroes**, and **Avicenna** as *"dei huius saeculi"* (gods of this world) who were awarded too easy an acceptance and too much reverence. For him, philosophy was meant to be a servant of theology.

Peter produced very few works in the **liberal arts** beyond his *Quaestiones logicales* (**Logic Questions**). He wrote a **Commentary on the Sentences**, of which Book II has been edited. But he never wanted to become a doctor of theology, since such an honor he believed was not to be sought by a friar dedicated to humility. He wrote serious works on living the Gospel life (*Questions concerning Evangelical Perfection*) and a commentary on the Franciscan rule (*Exposition of the Rule of the Friars Minor*). These works in particular had great influence on the reformed Franciscan movement that grew up under Bernardine of Siena. Peter's spiritual treatises brought him a great deal of grief in his own day as a Franciscan, often suffering suspicion or enduring outright attack. When he seemed most under siege, however, he was rescued by his teacher, Matthew of Aquasparta, the general minister of the order, who appointed him **lector** first in Florence and then in Montpellier. He moved on to Narbonne around 1295 and continued to live a strong spiritual life until his death in 1293.

**PETER OF LA PALU (PALUDE) (ca. 1280–1342).** This **Dominican lector** on the *Sentences* of **Peter Lombard** at Paris in 1310–1312 became regent master there from 1314 to 1317. Like many Dominicans, he produced *Postillae in Bibliam*, that is, brief commentaries on all the sacred writings. His *Commentary on the Sentences* that survives provides a text that has been reworked, stretching from Book I in 1310–1311 to Book IV in 1315. His chief opponent in this work seems to have been **Durandus of Saint-Pourçain**, and he was a member of the Dominican committees that passed judgment on Durandus's commentaries in 1314 and again in 1316–1317. As a master, Peter fulfilled the requirement of disputing **Quodlibet Questions**. In 1318–1319, he was involved in the process against John of Polliaco at Avignon, and two of his works, *Judgment against John of Polliaco concerning*

*Thirteen Articles* and *Conclusion against the Response Given by John of Polliaco*, date from this period. In 1313, he wrote a treatise *De potestate papae* (*On the Power of the Pope*). Also in the field of church life, he wrote a criticism of the **Franciscan Michael of Cesena**'s views on poverty, titled *On the Poverty of Christ and the Apostles*.

**PETER OF POITIERS (ca. 1130–1205).** Probably a student of **Peter Lombard**, Peter studied and then, beginning in 1167, taught **theology** at Paris. From 1193 to 1205 he was chancellor of the University of Paris, which was (during this very period and partly due to Peter's efforts) emerging as a **university** from the cathedral school. Due to the fundamental importance of the university as an institution in Western intellectual development, Peter's role in this transformation has earned him a place in history. In his own teaching and writing, Peter is one of the fathers of the so-called **Scholastic** method of medieval universities, whereby logic or **dialectics** is applied to the study of theology and questions are dealt with in a logically ordered manner. The translation of classical texts in **liberal arts**, particularly **Aristotelian** logic, provided medieval theologians with important methodological tools, and Peter, following the tradition of **Peter Abelard**, used them enthusiastically.

Peter of Poitier's main work is his *Sententiarum Libri Quinque* (*Five Books on the Sentences*), a systematic series of questions arising from the study of Scripture that partly follows in format and content **Peter Lombard**'s *Sentences*. Only about one half of Peter's questions are found in Lombard. Moreover, Peter's division into five books is in contrast with Lombard's fourfold division. Finally, Peter gave much more emphasis to moral questions than Lombard did. In addition to contributions in **exegesis**, Peter also wrote a *Compendium historiae in genealogia Christi* (*A Compendium of Biblical History Viewed from the Descent of Christ from Adam*). It is probable that the last part (*Historia Actuum Apostolorum*) of **Peter Comestor**'s *Historia Scholastica* (the second most influential theology textbook in medieval universities after Lombard's *Sentences*) was written by Peter of Poitiers.

**PETER OF RIVO (ca. 1420–1500).** Peter van den Becken studied at Louvain beginning in 1437. He became master of arts five years later and then studied theology, lecturing on **Peter Lombard**'s *Sentences* in 1448–1449. Knowledge concerning Peter of Rivo is almost limited to his defense of **Peter Aureoli**'s special explanation of future contingent propositions, which are, for both authors, neutral prior to their occurrence or nonoccurrence. He became embroiled in a battle with another Louvain theologian, Henry of

Zomeren, over this issue. Henry of Zomeren appealed to his friend Cardinal Bessarion, and through the influence of Bessarion's circle, Peter of Rivo's teaching was eventually condemned in 1474.

**PETER OF SPAIN (ca. 1205–1277).** Born in Lisbon, Portugal, this future pope studied in the **Arts Faculty** of the University of Paris from 1320 to 1329, before entering the Faculty of **Medicine**, probably at Montpellier. We know for certain that he taught medicine at Siena from 1245 to 1250. He was renowned traditionally as the author of the *Thesaurus pauperum* (*Treasury of the Poor*), a medical text that gained him great respect, though some scholars today challenge its authenticity. His more famous work, from his earlier stay in Toulouse in the 1230s, was a basic **logic** book, his *Tractatus* (*Treatise*), which later became known as the *Summulae logicales* (*Brief Logical Summa*), one of the competing textbooks of the late 13th century in logic. Peter returned to his native Portugal around 1250 and remained there except for certain short visits to the papal court in Anagni. In 1263, he was appointed as master at the Cathedral **School** of Lisbon, and the records go silent on him until his election as archbishop of Braga in 1273, a position he filled until 1275. He was elected successor to Pope Gregory X on 15 September 1276. He became involved with the **University** of Paris within months, instructing the archbishop of Paris, Étienne Tempier, to look into the errors being taught in the Arts Faculty. This would lead into the **condemnation of 1277**. He died less than two months after the event.

**PETER OF TARANTAISE (ca. 1230–1276).** After producing his *Postillae* on the books of the Bible, Peter lectured on **Peter Lombard**'s *Sentences* at Paris as a bachelor in 1257–1258 and became a regent master there in 1258–1260. He served as regent master for a second time in 1267–1269 between his terms as provincial of the French Dominicans (1264–1267, 1269–1272). He involved himself in the debates raging at the **university** at the time and has left us a taste of them in his *Quaestiones quattuor de materia caeli et de aeternitate mundi* (*Four Questions concerning the Matter of the Heavens and the Eternity of the World*). His *Commentary on Lombard's Sentences* and his **Quodlibet** are from his university years, and quite likely from the period of his second regency. Later, in 1272, he became archbishop of Lyons, then cardinal a year later, and was elected pope in 1276. He took the name Innocent V, but his pontificate was short lived, as he died the same year.

**PETER RIGA (ca. 1140–1209).** A native of Rheims (canon of Notre Dame of Rheims and later canon regular of Saint-Denis in Paris), this religious poet of Latin verse studied at Paris in the 1260s and is best known for his *Aurora* (end of 12th century), a verse presentation of the chief books of the **Bible** containing moral interpretations and allegories, as well as allusions to standard theological authorities (e.g., **Peter Comestor**'s *Historia Scholastica*). The *Aurora*'s popularity among educators, poets, and religious resulted in three editions and is evidenced by ample quotation by medieval authors, such as Chaucer. Peter wrote other poetic works, such as the earlier *Floridus aspectus* (containing some material incorporated into his *Aurora*), a collection he dedicated to Samson, archbishop of Rheims.

**PETER THE CHANTER (PETER CANTOR) (ca. 1130–1197).** Peter was educated at the cathedral **school** of Reims and became a professor there and a canon and chanter at the cathedral. Around 1170 he became a professor at Paris and a canon of Notre Dame. About 1180 he became chanter, a role he played until he was elected dean of the cathedral of Reims in 1196. Traveling toward Reims, he visited the Cistercians at Long Pont Abbey where he fell ill and died in 1197.

Peter had some very eminent students, such as **Stephen Langton** (archbishop of Canterbury) and **Robert of Courçon** (papal delegate for France from 1212 to 1219). Peter wrote, with the help of students, commentaries on the Bible. His disputations on special problems arising from lectures constituted his questions, which were collected as his *Summa de sacramentis*. The published *Summa* of Robert of Courçon is the final reworking of this collection. Though a celebrated preacher, almost nothing from his sermons survived, but he did compose a widely copied treatise, the *Verbum Abbreviatum* (1191–1192), that likened the study of theology to a building, where he portrays "reading" as the foundation, "disputation" as the walls, and "preaching" as the ceiling. Near the beginning of this work, he criticized those who portray Christianity as a religion of the Book. The *Verbum Abbreviatum* argues that the single Word, who is Christ the Son of God, is the key to understanding all the words of the Scriptures.

**Thomas Aquinas**, in his inaugural sermon at the beginning of his career as a master of sacred Scripture, introduced as important three functions found in the *Verbum Abbreviatum*. These functions are the duties of a master, and they are grounded in Titus 1:9: "So that he may be capable of exhorting people" (this refers to "preaching") "in sound teaching" (this refers to "reading") "and of defeating those who contradict" (this refers to "disputing"). One of Thomas's contemporaries, the **Franciscan Richard Rufus**, in the introduction to his Oxford *Commentary on the Sentences*, without mentioning Peter Cantor, refers to the same three functions of a master: to read, to dispute, and to preach. "Reading" is teaching aloud and bringing clear understanding; "disputation" is untying knots, explaining difficult points, and, to the degree that it is possible, "bringing light to obscure places." Only after learning how to read and dispute is one capable of preaching well, that is, teaching the faithful how to live a Christian life. Rufus, however, joins to the list of Peter Cantor's duties a fourth function: he completes the list by adding *iubilatio* (praising God by chanting the Office and celebrating Mass).

**PETER THE VENERABLE (ca. 1092–1156).** The ninth abbot of Cluny, he entered the monastery as a young man and made his profession in 1109. He was soon prior of the cloister at Vézelay, then prior of the convent at Domène, and he was made abbot of Cluny in 1122. He ruled over almost 400 monks at Cluny and over numerous dependent houses. He was a man of peace and reasonableness who brought reconciliation to **Peter Abelard** after his troubles at the Council of Sens (1140). He appealed for a dialogue with the Muslims at the time of the Crusades instead of a policy of conquest.

**PETER THOMAE (ca. 1280–ca. 1340).** Little is known of his life except that he was a **Franciscan** who taught at the *studium generale* (international house of studies) of the order in Barcelona. He is mainly remembered as a loyal follower of **John Duns Scotus**, and that he wrote a *Commentary on Book I of the Sentences* and a long set of 15 questions entitled *De ente* (*On Being*). The latter work shows him to be an adept expositor of Scotus's teaching concerning the univocity of being, defending him against the criticism of a fellow Franciscan, **Richard of Conington**, who attacked Scotus in defense of **Henry of Ghent**'s theory of the analogy of being. In theology, he is known for his *Liber de originali Virginis innocentia* (*A Book on the Original Innocence of the Blessed Virgin*), a long Scriptural defense of the Immaculate Conception that also depends on Scotus and on **Peter Aureoli**.

**PETRUS DE ALLIACO.** *See* PIERRE D'AILLY OR PETRUS DE ALLIACO (1350–1420).

**PETRUS DE TRABIBUS (fl. 1290–1295).** Petrus was a faithful disciple of **Peter of John Olivi**, the idol of the Spiritual Franciscans. At one time Petrus de Trabibus was thought to be a pseudonym of the persecuted Peter John Olivi. They are distinct, although in fact their positions are quite identical.

Petrus commented on the *Sentences* of **Peter Lombard** between 1290 and 1295. The question whether God could have created more things or otherwise than He actually did was commonly answered by distinguishing between God's absolute and ordained power. What Petrus says about the distinction had been stated before, even back in the time of **Peter Abelard** (d. 1142), but Petrus expresses it with his customary lucidity. He understood the distinction correctly: "Absolute power" is power in itself or power considered purely and absolutely, not unrestrained or despotic power. Neither is "ordained power" the same as orderly power as opposed to disorderly power;

nor is it ordinary power as opposed to extraordinary power, but it is the one and the same power considered in relation to what God has foreseen and decreed he would realize from all eternity. We speak of ordained power with regard to things God de facto wills and does, and we speak of absolute power with regard to things God could will and do but never intended to do. In other words, the distinction is not in God but in our mind and in our way of speaking: there is only one, infinite power in God, which is identical with His essence and his wisdom, and this power is coextensive with the whole realm of possibilities; but since God does not act of necessity but has freedom of choice, of these possibilities he realizes only those which He in His wisdom chooses to realize. This is the original meaning of the *potentia absoluta–potentia ordinata* dichotomy.

**PHILIP THE CHANCELLOR (ca. 1170–ca. 1237).** Not to be confused with Philip of Grève, this native of Paris undertook theological studies at the University of Paris. The son of Archdeacon Philippe of Paris, he is first mentioned as archdeacon of Noyon in 1211 and as chancellor of Notre Dame in 1218. Having limited jurisdiction as chancellor over students and masters at the university, he is known to have engaged in conflicts with the university (e.g., for excommunicating masters and students), which was then increasingly emerging as an autonomous entity. Philip's chancellorship coincided with the establishment of the first **Dominican** and **Franciscan** chairs of theology. He experienced conflicts with the former order and remained friendly with the latter (he is buried in the Franciscan church). Aside from his theological *Quaestiones* and sermons, his chief work is his *Summa de bono* (*A Summa on the Good*), written between 1230 and 1236, one of the first major 13th-century **Augustinian** accounts of reality influenced by **Aristotelian** philosophy. This rather original work relies on and shows affinity with the Franciscan **Alexander of Hales** and is an important source for **Albert the Great** (**Thomas Aquinas**'s teacher) and for early Franciscan authors. Philip is also known as an outstanding poet and preacher; he composed poems in Old French and Latin and more than 700 sermons.

**PHILO OF ALEXANDRIA OR PHILO IUDAEUS (ca. 40 B.C.E.–20 C.E.).** Little is known about the life of Philo Judaeus, Jewish thinker and prominent citizen of Alexandria. A product of both Hellenic and Jewish culture, he is credited as being a pioneer in the development of a new approach in the history of thought, which later became central in medieval philosophy and theology. Philo's goal was to marry Greek philosophical thought and the Hebrew Scriptures. Although Philo's work was not well known in the Middle Ages, it did exert influence among some **Fathers of the**

**Church**, such as **Clement of Alexandria**. Aiming at the synthesis of religion and philosophy, Philo anticipates in broad outline the spirit behind medieval Jewish, Christian, and Islamic thought.

**PHILOPONUS, JOHN, OR JOHN THE GRAMMARIAN (fl. 6TH CENTURY).** A disciple of Ammonius, one of the Greek commentators on **Aristotle**, Philoponus wrote some grammatical treatises, which explains his title. However, for the history of philosophy and **theology**, he is most important for his commentaries on Aristotle's *Categories*, *Prior* and *Posterior Analytics*, *Metaphysics*, *Meteors*, *Generation of Animals*, *Generation and Corruption*, certain books of the *Physics*, and Book III of *On the Soul*. Although a Christian, he is not always Christian in his philosophical and theological expressions. For instance, in Christ he admits only one nature, though a composite one. His explanations of nature, substance, essence, hypostasis, and individual lead him to confused views in regard to both the Incarnation and the **Trinity**. The place where he contributes most in medieval discussions concerns the nature of the agent intellect. For Philoponus, the agent intellect is within the soul, and so his *Commentary on Book III of the De anima* is cited frequently in medieval texts opposing the teaching of **Averroes**.

**PHOTIUS (ca. 810–ca. 893).** The affluent family of this philosopher, **theologian**, and public figure was prominent both politically and intellectually; it was related to Empress Theodora and included the patriarch Tarasios (d. 806). The family was condemned and exiled in 833 on account of its opposition to iconoclasm, though Photius and his brothers remained in Constantinople, still able to gain the benefit of an excellent education. Although his parents died in exile, the fortune of the family changed with Theodora's (and the iconophiles') rise to power in 842, when Photius became professor of philosophy at Constantinople. Considered by many as the chief Byzantine thinker of his time, Photius served twice (in the years 858–867 and 878–886) as patriarch of Constantinople, even though he was a layman. His patriarchates were controversial. The first resulted in the so-called Photian Schism with Rome and the supporters of the patriarch he replaced, Ignatios. In 867, Emperor Basil I restored Ignatios and exiled Photius, but after the death of the former he made Photius patriarch again. However, Basil's successor, Leo VI (d. 912), made his own brother (Stephen) patriarch and exiled Photius a second time in 886.

Notable aspects of Photius's writings (PG 101–4) include his position (expounded in his *Mystagogia*) against the *Filioque*, namely his **Trinitarian** position that the Holy Spirit proceeds only from the Father, not from both the Father and the Son as taught by the Latin Church. His *Bibliotheca* is a vast work that indicates his various textual sources (ranging from classical Greece up to his own time—a valuable reference for important works of the times, including ones that are now lost). His work includes philology, namely the *Lexicon* and the *Etymologicum*, as well as *Homilies*, *Letters*, and the *Amphilochia* (where he gives his position on a number of theological issues). Photius was at the center of Byzantine learning during his time and was very influential, notably in the defense of the theological positions of the Eastern Church against the Latin Church. He also played an important role in the revival of classical education, especially as part of the curriculum for the clergy. He was canonized by the Eastern Church, probably at the end of the 10th century.

*PHYSICS.* Refer to the introduction.

**PICO DELLA MIRANDOLA, GIOVANNI (1463–1494).** After studying canon law at Bologna at the early age of 14, Giovanni made his first contact with **Marsilio Ficino** in Florence. He went on to study **Aristotelian** philosophy at Padua for two years but returned to Florence in 1482 to read Ficino's *Platonic Philosophy*. Four years later, he arranged a disputation in Rome on 900 theses; but he was accused of defending heretical positions, so the disputation was canceled by Pope Innocent VIII. He fled to France but was arrested for a short time. Protected by the Medici family, he returned to Florence and composed his *Heptaplus* (*Commentary on the Story of Creation*). In 1492, Pico della Mirandola wrote a work, *De ente et uno* (*On Being and Unity*), that attempted to harmonize the philosophies of Aristotle and Plato. This syncretistic tendency marks most of the works of a young man who died at the age of 31. His most famous work was his *Oratio* (*Oration on the Dignity of Man*), where he picks up the theme of Ficino on man's calling to ascend to the level of the angels through a life of contemplation.

**PIERRE D'AILLY OR PETRUS DE ALLIACO (1350–1420).** A theologian, philosopher, and man of public affairs, Petrus began his studies in 1363 or 1364 at the University of Paris, where he had a distinguished career from his student years all the way up to his election as chancellor of the **university**. He became doctor of **theology** in 1381; he was also cardinal of Cambrai. A prominent figure in the political and ecclesiastical affairs of his day, he left a large number of writings on theological, ecclesiastical, philosophical, and scientific topics, as well as letters, poems, and sermons. Among them are his commentary on **Peter Lombard**'s *Sentences*, a treatise on the soul (*Tractatus de anima*), and *Imago mundi* (*Image of the World*), a geographical work that depends heavily on other sources and that acquired fame because it was supposedly studied by Christopher Columbus prior to his voyage to America. His chief philosophic influence is **William of Ockham**, whom he follows on central issues, though not uncritically. The majority of his writings concern the theme that most occupied Petrus's life, the ecclesiastical events of his day. His *Tractatus de materia concilii generalis* (*Treatise on the Subject Matter of a General Council*) and his *Tractatus de reformatione ecclesiae* (*Treatise on the Reformation of the Church*) relate to his efforts to end the Great Schism initiated by the disputed papal election of 1378 and to his role in reforms in ecclesiastical policy.

**PLATO (IN THE MEDIEVAL WORLD).** Unlike the works of Aristotle, most of which were translated and amply commented upon, medieval thinkers knew little of the actual writings of Aristotle's Athenian teacher Plato (ca. 427–347 B.C.). However, Platonism, the philosophy of Plato as interpreted and adapted through the centuries, was one of the two chief currents in the medieval period, influencing practically all areas in Jewish, Christian, and Islamic thought. The other chief current was **Aristotelianism**. Greek Neoplatonists, such as Plotinus and Proclus, who developed the philosophy of Plato against the background of other Greek thinkers (e.g., Aristotle and the Stoics), contributed to the great influence of Platonic thought in the Middle Ages. In the Latin West, for example, **Augustine** drew from and revised Neoplatonic doctrines in order to formulate his seminal synthesis of Platonic and Christian thought. The Neoplatonic view that all things emanate from and return to one divine principle was seminal. Ironically, due to misattribution, important Neoplatonic ideas exerted influence in the name of Aristotle. A famous example is the widely circulated *Theology of Aristotle*, a Neoplatonic work (probably Porphyry's) largely based on Plotinus. As is the case with medieval Aristotelians, medieval thinkers influenced by Plato had to reinterpret or correct what they saw as lacking in a philosophy without reference to revelation. Certain doctrines relying on Plato were controversial. Examples are the doctrine that the world is created necessarily (an interpretation of the *Timaeus*), that the soul is indestructible by nature (found, e.g., in *Republic* X, 608d–612a), and that the so-called forms are necessary of themselves. These doctrines seemed to some to challenge the view, based on revelation, that God is totally free and omnipotent. Still, some of the outstanding medieval thinkers saw in Platonism more than in other philosophies the truer and more compelling rational principles, reconcilable after some adjustments with the infallible truth of revelation. In particular, Plato's arguments that the sensible world is a copy of intelligible reality informed medieval philosophical accounts of the Creator and His creatures.

It is uncertain whether any work of Plato was translated integrally into Arabic. Platonism was constructed in Islamic philosophy (and in the Jewish philosophy in Islamic lands) primarily from summaries and versions of Plato, such as Galen's account of the *Timaeus*. Nevertheless, there were translations of the *Republic*, the *Laws*, the *Timaeus*, the *Phaedo*, the *Crito*, and the *Sophist* (with Olympiadorus's sixth-century commentary). Hunayn ibn Ishaq (d. 873) and his school made the first translations of these works. In the West, similarly, the actual Platonic corpus was only fragmentarily known. Medieval Christian thinkers had only a portion of the *Timaeus*, translated into Latin in the fourth century by Chalcidius. The *Parmenides* was transmitted only partially as sections in Proclus's commentary, translated into Latin in the 13th century by **William of Moerbeke**. Finally, Henricus Aristippus in the 12th century rendered the *Meno* and the *Phaedo* into Latin. Platonic principles and concepts, however, were quite known, principally through the writings of authorities, such as **Cicero**, Augustine, **Boethius**, and **Dionysius the Pseudo-Areopagite**. The many translations of Aristotle in the 12th and 13th centuries also provided his influential, though sometimes questionable, reports on Platonic doctrines. It was not until the Renaissance, principally through the work of **Marsilio Ficino** (1433–499), that the actual Platonic corpus came to light in the West.

What Plato actually held concerning his various inquiries is still a subject of debate, primarily because of the tentative nature of many of his remarks and the varying contexts of those remarks. However, there are recurring attitudes and themes in Plato's writings. What follows is a brief summary of basic ideas found in Plato, particularly those concerning topics of major interest to medieval thinkers.

Through reflection on the soul's judgments, Plato discovered what he calls forms, as well as the immortality of the soul. This is evident, for example, in the *Phaedo* (74a–77d). In this text, Plato notes that when we judge two things as equal we are also aware that they are not equal absolutely, that their equality is still deficient with respect to equality itself. Similarly when we judge a thing to be more beautiful than another, we recognize that its beauty is still deficient, that it is not beauty itself. Equality and beauty (and the other forms by which the mind judges) do not and cannot appear to us through sense experience. Only equal and beautiful things appear. Appearing, either in perception or in the imagination, would make them into one more equal thing or beautiful thing. In such a context, they themselves could be compared to other things in terms of equality and beauty. The mark of equality itself and beauty itself, therefore, is that they are available to the understanding soul only. Equal and beautiful things are available to the senses as well as the understanding, to the extent that they are judged in reference to some standard. True, when we make these comparative judgments we do not do so with a perfectly clear grasp of the standard by which we judge, in this case beauty and equality. The nature of pure beauty still escapes us, even though we assess things of our experience as beautiful. However, to recognize this deficiency in the things judged we must possess at least a latent connection to the standards by which we judge. As Plato puts it, equal and beautiful things remind us of the Equal itself and the Beautiful itself.

As available to the understanding alone, each of the forms is manifestly one and unchanging. Pure equality, the standard in reference to which equal things are deficient, is understood as one unchanging essence. For if it were somehow many or different from itself, it could then be judged as an equal thing, and that by which it would be so judged would then be Equality itself. The soul that judges through these forms therefore possesses at least some partial knowledge of what is unchanging. Knowledge, properly speaking, can be only of unchanging things, as only they can yield unwavering truth. Of changing things we can have only opinion, as he notes in *Republic* V (476a–480a). This access to unchanging realities transcending the sensible world is evidence, for Plato, of the preexistence of the soul, as some type of reality, before birth. For this access is not derived, but only recollected, from experience. The soul preexists its temporal, earthly existence since the knowledge of the soul depends on its connection to eternal forms.

From the point of view of the order of premises in Plato's arguments, the theory of recollection is the basis of the theory of forms. The theory of forms, in turn, yields two fundamental consequences. From a metaphysical standpoint, the forms are models imitated or participated in by sensible things. The relation between sensible and intelligible reality is one between a copy and the original by which the copy has reality. Moreover, even though the forms are each one of a kind, they are still many essences. As sharing in unity, being, and truth, the forms owe their reality to their one source and ultimate principle—the Good. The forms bespeak the Good, just as sensible things bespeak the forms. That by which the forms possess specific unity or formal being cannot be itself a specific unity or formal being as the forms are, just as that by which equal things are equal cannot be itself an equal thing. The Good transcends the forms as their principle as equality transcends equal things as their principle. The Good is thus said to be beyond being. Even though it is sometimes referred to as a form, it cannot be a form among the other forms, but only a Form of forms which, by definition, is beyond being understood as formal specificity (see *Republic* VI, 507a–509c).

From a psychological and epistemological standpoint, the theory of forms is the basis of the Platonic doctrines of knowledge and of the nature of the soul. The relation between experience and judgment is one between assessed objects and the unchanging standards by which they are assessed, objects reminding the soul of the standards through their deficiency with respect to these standards. Only these unchanging standards, however, are the true objects of knowledge, so the soul to know verily must turn its gaze from assessed appearances to the unchanging sources of assessment, with which it always had contact, even and especially prior to birth. The highest knowledge, true wisdom, would be the contemplation of the Good, the ultimate principle of all reality and, thereby, the truest object of knowledge.

Since the soul's preexistence means that it is some complete entity prior to birth, the soul cannot be individuated by the body. After birth the soul remains essentially what it was prior to birth, a distinct, intellectual nature. However, while in a body the soul is constantly and intimately tied to sense experience. The soul brings unity and life to all bodily dimensions: the one soul thinks, has emotions, and has desires; the one soul both thinks and perceives. Through the common sense, the soul organizes the data that comes through the five senses, and upon this organized data it judges and thinks about experience (see *Theaetetus*, 184d–186d). In spite of these important functions with respect to the body, however, the soul itself—the preexistent and true soul—is still essentially intellectual, a knower, a lover of true reality, which is invisible and unchanging. Nevertheless its relation to the body puts the soul in a challenging situation. If the soul is to acquire knowledge while in the body, it must use sense experience, a copy of true reality, correctly, namely as a reminder that lifts it toward the contemplation of true reality and toward a more explicit awareness of its own intellectual nature. (Perhaps Plato's best illustration of this is his famous allegory of the cave in *Republic* VII, 514a–519c.)

The intellectual nature of the soul implies its core yearning to be with what is akin to it. The soul is essentially a lover of true reality, and it seeks to be one with it according to its intellectual nature, namely through knowledge. The soul, as Plato describes it, is a lover. Primarily, the soul is a lover of wisdom, since true reality is the only food that will satisfy its intellectual nature. However, the incarnate soul may become disordered or vicious. For the human soul has three functions or parts, the rational part by which it learns, the part by which it experiences emotions such as fear and anger, and the part by which it experiences physical appetites. The virtuous soul is the soul in harmony, and such harmony only happens when reason rules and the other parts are happy to obey reason. When reason does not rule, a soul may live for the sake of fulfilling its physical desires, calculating and fighting to this end. Plato calls such a soul a lover of profit, the means to get physical satisfaction. Or it may live for the sake of fulfilling its desire for recognition and power, calculating and governing its appetites to this end. Such a soul is purely a lover of honor. The relative virtue (justice) or vice (injustice) of all souls lies in the relative harmony or tension among these three parts, as he explains in *Republic* IV (435e–445e).

The soul's core yearning for true reality is always actively manifested, since bodily experience prevents it from a complete communion with what is by nature akin to it. All modes of living are ultimately expressions of this core yearning of the soul to fulfill its nature. These modes of living are satisfying to the extent that they approach wisdom, knowledge of true reality. To approach wisdom, the soul must learn to see and treat sense experience for what it is—a symbol of true reality. Here lies the greatest challenge of the soul and the greatest source of error and thus of wretchedness: idolatry. The soul may mistake the symbol for the symbolized. Aspects of experience may appear supremely attractive precisely because they appear so real, particularly those that result in intense pleasures and emotions. For Plato, the soul by nature loves true reality, though it may be mistaken as to what true reality is through vice and ignorance. Thus the soul may misguidedly pursue money or power as ends in themselves. By nature, however, the soul loves knowledge because knowledge is communion with true reality, to which the soul is akin—the forms and the Good. The fact that sensible things share in reality makes it easy to mistake them for true reality. However, they are not real in virtue of themselves; they are real only as reflections of the forms and the Good. The more the soul treats material things and recognition from others as ends in themselves, the more it descends toward the many and changing and the more it becomes fragmented through its infinite desires, as its desires are multiplied in this descent toward the manifold. Thus, the yearning of the soul for true reality is less and less able to be fulfilled. The soul becomes like a vessel full of holes. The more it seeks the wrong nourishment, the less fulfilled it is, and the more closely it bonds with the body, the farther it is from what is truly akin to it and can relieve it. On the other hand, the more the soul collects itself in the pursuit of knowledge for its own sake, in the contemplation of the truth, the more it abides with what is akin to it and can fulfill it, as Plato explains in *Republic* IX.

The yearning at the heart of the soul, however, its love of wisdom, is ultimately a yearning for what is higher than itself. It is a yearning for its source and means of existence, for the fountain of light that is its absolute prior and that always governs and sustains its intellectual vision, however myopic or acute it might be. Even though the soul belongs essentially to the intelligible realm, neither is the soul the highest reality nor is its true fulfillment other than the source of all reality and intelligibility. The yearning of the soul for truth and knowledge means that the soul is only fulfilled through union with the source of all truth and intellectual life, the Good. Philosophy, or love of wisdom according to Plato, is therefore the soul's core yearning to be one with its ultimate source, the source of its intellectual light, vision, and nature, whether it is explicitly aware of this or not.

Plato sees this world of ours as a copy of true reality. The world possesses reality to the extent that it reflects its original, intelligible source. This means that the sensible world has a borrowed reality, that it owes its existence. In other words, this means that the world is created and that the ultimate principle of reality is a Creator. (The nature of this creation is interpreted in various ways by Plato's successors.) But why does the Creator, being wholly perfect, eternal, and self-sufficient, create? He does not need to create, as need would imply a lack and dependence, which the First Principle by definition cannot have. The Creator, the Good, created out of his own essential goodness, for the Good by nature gives of itself. Creation is the diffusion and sharing of this primal goodness (*Timaeus*, 29e–30b). In other words, the Creator can be said to create out of love. There are important reasons, therefore, why Plato calls the First Principle the Good, not the True or the Real, which the Good also is. The First Principle is the principle and origin of lesser things in virtue of His goodness and nothing else. The borrowed and symbolic character of the world bespeaks a giving principle or source. Thus, the Good, as the source of being, is also the source of love at the heart of all being, since each being desires its origin. For the origin is pure goodness, the ultimate object of all desire.

In terms of the human soul, the ultimate expression of this desire is called love of wisdom or philosophy. Philosophy in Plato is the highest expression of the core yearning of the soul for its source, its ultimate happiness. This is its desire to liberate itself from the lower levels of reality and thereby abide ever more intimately in the intelligible realm.

**PLOTINUS (204/5–270).** Born in Lycopolis, Egypt, Plotinus is generally considered the founder of **Neoplatonism**, as well as its most influential representative. He was the chief source and mediator of **Platonic** thought in late antiquity and the Middle Ages. Like other Neoplatonists, Plotinus saw himself fundamentally as a student of Plato. However, he interpreted and developed Platonic philosophy and combined it with other currents, notably Aristotelian and Stoic thought. His chief work, the *Enneads*, edited by **Porphyry**, had continuing influence in the development of Platonism in Judaism, Christianity, and Islam. For instance, it is well known that **St. Augustine**'s encounter with Platonic thought as presented by Plotinus was decisive and that Plotinus's ideas play a major role in **Avicenna** and **Gabirol**, both seminal thinkers from the Islamic and Jewish traditions, respectively. Plotinus spent the latter part of his life in Rome. Refer to the introduction.

**POLITICS.** *See* ETHICS AND POLITICS.

**PORETE, MARGARET (fl. 1300–1316).** In the region of northern France, Belgium, Holland, and the Rhineland, movements grew up in the latter part of the 13th century that aimed at fostering a richer spiritual experience. Many attached to these movements adopted a form of severe personal and communal asceticism that aimed at mystical union with God, a rediscovery of the spirit of the Garden of Eden, and an anticipation of the heavenly paradise. This mysticism risked stressing interior freedom at the expense of orthodoxy and all laws. It is within this framework that Margaret Porete wrote *The Mirror of Simple Souls*. Between 1296 and 1306, the famous Parisian theologian **Godfrey of Fontaines** approved the book, even though he advised Margaret to practice prudence in following her way of life. Before 1306, however, Guy de Colmieu, the bishop of Cambrai, burned the book and forbade its diffusion. The **inquisitor** with jurisdiction over Cambrai interrogated Margaret Porete and condemned her. She was arrested in 1309, handed over to the secular arm, and burned at the stake. The Council of Vienne, which later (1311–1312) examined the challenges coming from the Beghards and other "free spirit" movements, also examined Margaret's work and added eight articles taken from the *Mirror* to the propositions condemned by Pope Clement V.

**PORPHYRY (ca. 234–305).** A **Neoplatonic** philosopher born in Tyre (Phoenicia), Porphyry was a student of **Plotinus** as well as a prolific writer (but not all his writings survived). His edition of the *Enneads* preserved this important work for future generations. His work on Aristotelian logic, translated into various languages (such as Boethius's Latin translation), became basic texts in medieval curricula. Deeply influenced by Plotinus, his work defends the philosophy of Plato while also combining it with Aristotelian elements, notably logic. *See also* DIALECTICS.

**PORRÉE, GILBERT DE LA (PORRETANUS).** *See* GILBERT OF POITIERS (GILBERT DE LA PORRÉE) (ca. 1085–1154).

**PRAEPOSITINUS (PRÉVOSTIN) OF CREMONA (ca. 1130–ca. 1210).** A student of **Maurice of Sully** and **Peter Comestor**, this native of northern Italy taught at Paris before 1194. His *Summa theologica* or *Theological Summa*, in four books, was based on his Paris lectures between 1190 and 1194, although manuscripts of the work indicate some later revisions. From 1194 to 1203, he was master of the cathedral school of Mainz and then became chancellor of the University of Paris in 1206, an office he held until 1209. He died quite likely in or just after 1210, on 25 or 26 February. Records indicate that besides his academic work, he was used as a judge in certain matters by Pope Innocent III and also had lived among and had extensive knowledge of the Cathari in northern Italy. His *Summa theologica* follows very closely the structure of **Peter Lombard**'s *Sentences*, though it is not officially a commentary on that work. Praepositinus also wrote a *Summa on the Psalter*, whose references to liturgical revisions going on in Paris would date it to around 1196; his *De officiis* (*On Liturgical Offices*) is written around the same time and quite likely before 1198. A number of other works once attributed to him (*Summa on Penances to Be Imposed, Summa against Heretics, Treatise on Original Sin*, and two groups of *Quaestiones*) are now considered inauthentic.

**PREACHING.** *See MAGISTER*; PETER THE CHANTER (PETER CANTOR) (ca. 1130–1197); THEOLOGY; UNIVERSITIES.

**PRISCIAN (fl. ca. 500).** This famous Latin grammarian taught at Constantinople. His work in Latin and grammar, particularly his *Institutiones grammaticae* (*Grammatical Foundations*), was one of the chief components in the **liberal arts** curricula at medieval **schools** and **universities**. His other grammatical works include *De nomine, pronomine, et verbo* (*Concerning the Noun, Pronoun, and Verb*) and *Praeexercitamina* (introductory Greek rhetorical exercises adapted for Latin students). His work was also a factor in the development of the study of linguistic logic or speculative grammar in the Middle Ages.

**PROCLUS (ca. 410–485).** A pagan Greek Neoplatonist, Proclus headed the Platonic Academy at Athens. He was very hostile to the Catholic Church and yet had great influence on early Christian authors, like **Boethius**, and on a large number of medieval and Renaissance philosophers and theologians. His anti-Christian writing is illustrated by his *Eighteen Arguments in Favor of the Eternity of the World against the Christians* and *Ten Doubts concerning Providence*. The work that had the most influence on medieval and Renaissance authors was his *Elements of Theology*, later on its own and earlier as the main component in a very influential treatise called the *Liber de causis* (*The Book of Causes*). This same work was also given the title *Liber Aristotelis de expositione bonitatis purae* (*The Book of Aristotle on the Exposition of the Pure Good*) and thus was wrongly thought to be a work of Aristotle, not Proclus. *See also* BERTHOLD OF MOOSBURG (ca. 1300–ca. 1361).

**PROSPER OF AQUITAINE, ST. (ca. 390–ca. 460).** Learned in the classics and **theology**, this native of southern Gaul is best known for his defense of **Augustinian** positions. **Augustine**'s work *On Reproof and Grace* was unfavorably received in Gaul, to the point of being considered a heresy of predestination. In 427, Proper and his friend Hilary of Aquitaine communicated with Augustine. Prosper then wrote *Epistola ad Rufinum de gratia et libero arbitrio* (*Letter to Rufinus concerning Grace and Free Will*) and *De ingratis* (*Concerning Those without Grace*) in defense of Augustine, and he even went with Hilary to Rome in 431 to seek approval from Pope Celestine I. He also composed, among other writings in the same vein, *De gratia et libero arbitio contra collatorem* (*Concerning Grace and Free Will against* *the Author of Conferences*) attacking one of the "Conferences" of John Cassian, in which Prosper inaccurately accused as Pelagian members of the southern Gallic church. However, the anti-Augustinians, also mistakenly called Semi-Pelagians, prevailed in Gaul until the Council of Orange in 529. Prosper then moved to the chancery of Pope Leo I, authoring apparently some of the pope's best tracts. In his efforts to defend Augustine, Prosper also introduced modifications of his own, as is evident in *De vocatione omnium gentium* (*Concerning the Calling of All Peoples*). Under the name Prosper of Tiro, some other important works have been attributed to him, probably accurately, such as *Epitoma Chronicon* (*A Digest of History*), a summary of world history from Adam to 455. His writings provide useful evidence of the development of church doctrine, especially in relation to Pelagianism. He probably died in Rome. *See also* HERESIES.

**PROSPER OF REGGIO EMILIA (ca. 1270–ca. 1332).** A Hermit of St. **Augustine**, Prosper has the same name as the patron saint of his city. He was teaching theology at the Augustinian convent of Bologna when he died. This is known, since early in 1333, Pope John XXII appealed for the conferment on Denis of Modena of the title "master of theology" so that he could replace the deceased Prosper. There are three other facts that are well established concerning this Hermit of St. Augustine. He was named general vicar of his order in 1311, serving in this role just before he went to study theology at Paris. His *Commentary on Lombard's Sentences*, which could date anytime between 1313 and 1318, is very incomplete. Yet it provides a unique picture of the debates over the nature of theology in the clarity with which it summarizes all the main issues being discussed at that time and also in the fullness of the information it provides about individual theologians and their doctrinal positions. His account adds to a list of famous personages the names of many others who are less known and for whom he provides their names and teachings. After completing his studies in Paris, Prosper returned to the convent of his order in Bologna, where he taught until his death.

**PSELLOS, MICHAEL (1018–ca. 1078).** Born in Constantinople, this Byzantine statesman and scholar was probably the first great popularizer of Greek learning in the Byzantine world, stimulating much interest in that tradition. His writings on various subjects (e.g., **theology**, **metaphysics**, astronomy, mathematics, music, **ethics**, alchemy, **medicine**, and **law**) are largely summaries or compilations of earlier sources, making them accessible to larger audiences. His scholarship is historically significant as it refers to otherwise unknown sources. Psellos was also considered in the later Byzantine period, along with Demosthenes and Gregory of Nazianus, as a great rhetorician cultivating the Attic style. His main work, *Chronographia*, which did not receive full attention until the 19th century, provides a history of the Byzantine imperial court from 976 to 1077. Aside from a good deal of works attributed to him (uncertainly), he composed funeral orations for contemporaries and many rhetorical letters providing his views on events in the Byzantine Empire in the 11th century. His work benefited from the sponsorship of imperial patrons, and he was also active in politics. Under Michael IV and the next emperors, he held various important offices. In the last year of the reign of Constantine IX Monamachos (1042–1055), Psellos lost royal favor, changed his name from Constantine to Michael, and moved to Mt. Olympus. Later, Empress Theodora called him back, and he played a role in the deposition of Michael VI Stratiotikos and the accession of Isaac I Komnenos. He regained his full political influence when his former pupil Michael VII Doukas (1071–1078) reached power.

**PSEUDO-DIONYSIUS.** *See* DIONYSIUS THE PSEUDO-AREOPAGITE (PSEUDO-DIONYSIUS) (fl. ca. 500).

**PTOLEMAIC ASTRONOMY.** When accessible, the chief work of the Greek thinker **Ptolemy**, the *Almagest* (composed around 150 A.D.), dominated astronomy in the Middle Ages until Nicolaus Copernicus's 1543 *De revolutionibus orbium coelestium* (*On the Revolutions of the Celestial Bodies*). In the interim, astronomy focused mainly on the practical aspect of Ptolemaic theory (e.g., production of instruments, tables, and almanacs), although Islamic scientists did fill some theoretical gaps. Translated from Greek to Arabic in the eighth and ninth centuries, from Greek to Latin in 1160, and from Arabic to Latin in 1175, the *Almagest* provides a geocentric model of the universe that "saves the phenomena," accounting for the motions of the heavenly bodies mathematically. However, Ptolemy anticipates Copernicus when he mentions that the appearances perhaps may also be accounted for through a theory assuming the movement of the earth, although he does not follow this line of inquiry due to the seeming unlikelihood (according to regular experience) of this assumption. **Plato**'s *Timaeus*; Aristotle's work in natural philosophy, especially *De caelo*; and of course Holy Scripture were the other chief sources in medieval conceptions of the heavens.

**PTOLEMY (ca. 100–ca. 170).** An Egyptian of Greek descent active at Alexandria, this astronomer, mathematician, and geographer represents the summit of Greek science in these areas. *See also* PTOLEMAIC ASTRONOMY.

**PTOLEMY OF LUCCA (ca. 1236–1327).** He was born in Tuscany, on the other side of the mountain from Pisa, around 1236. He joined the **Dominicans** as a young man and studied at the University of Paris from 1261 to 1268, at times under **Thomas Aquinas**. He traveled with Aquinas to Italy, was with him when he died in 1274, and provides in his writings much of the information we have concerning Aquinas. Between 1280 and 1300, he was often named the prior or religious superior at various Tuscan Dominican houses, most notably that of Santa Maria Novella in Florence. Among his writings are a *Commentary on the Hexaëmeron* or *Six Days of Creation*, a history of the Church (*The Ecclesiastical Histories*), and some Tuscan annals. His works that have gained the most attention are his political writings: the extent of his contribution to the *De regimine principum* (*On the Government of Rulers*) that is attributed to Thomas Aquinas and his *Determinatio compendiosa de iuribus imperii* (*Brief Determination of the Jurisdiction of the Roman Empire*). Ptolemy spent much of his time from 1300 onward at the papal court in Avignon until he was appointed bishop of Torcello, outside Venice, in 1318. He died there in 1327.

# Q

**QUADRIVIUM.** *See* LIBERAL ARTS.

**QUAESTIO OR QUESTION.** Refer to the introduction, "Methods of Study."

*QUODLIBET.* Different exercises were employed in the universities to challenge masters and lectors and to test their skills. Masters were required to debate with other members of the university in the exercise of *Quaestiones disputatae* (*Disputed Questions*). The topic for the disputation could be a single theme, as we see, for example, in Thomas Aquinas's *Disputed Questions on Truth* or *Disputed Questions on God's Power*. Here the exercise was testing the breadth and depth of a master on a specific subject. Another exercise was the *Quaestiones disputatae de quolibet* (*Disputed Questions about Whatever Pleases You*). This exercise was aimed at testing the dexterity of the master, who was expected to carry out such disputations twice a year (during Advent, just before Christmas, and during Lent, just before Easter), answering questions set by others. The master did not choose the questions. The listeners did, and they could pick whatever they pleased. In the case of authors like Henry of Ghent and Godfrey of Fontaines, such questions are extensive and provide us with most of what we know of their teachings. Certainly this is the case with Godfrey. The final version of a *Quodlibet* was usually put together after the event by the master, who also incorporated objections from his challengers and his responses to them. Surviving *Quodlibets* might differ in quality, since some are based on the notes of a student attending, whereas others are student versions that have been corrected by the master. Finally, there might be some surviving *Quodlibets* that are the finished products of the masters themselves.

**RADULPHUS (RAOUL) ARDENS (ca. 1120–ca. 1200).** Radulphus was born in Beaulieu in the west-central Poitou region of France. He probably studied at Poitiers under **Gilbert**, and he was certainly influenced by the Porretani, such as by the *Institutiones in sacram paginam* of **Simon of Tournai** and by numerous texts of **Magister Martinus** and **Praepositinus**. Radulphus is known for a number of his epistles, but his most famous work (written between 1193 and 1200) is his *Speculum Universale*, which is also known under the title *Summa de vitiis et virtutibus*.

Radulphus joins many 12th-century theologians who disagree with Peter Lombard's treatment of grace. Lombard, in distinction 17 of Book I of his *Sentences*, holds that grace is the presence of the Holy Spirit in the human soul; for Radulphus and other critics of Peter Lombard, grace is a gift of the Holy Spirit, but its reality is that of a created quality that is given by the Holy Spirit and that elevates the soul. Radulphus, in his discussion of virtue in the *Speculum Universale*, also provides a distinction between political or philosophical virtues and Christian virtues. For him, virtue in the strict sense must have God as its end. Those who act in morally good ways can please God by their acts of courage or morally good acts of other kinds, but such morally good ways of acting are not meritorious of eternal life.

**RADULPHUS (RAOUL) BRITO (ca. 1270–ca. 1320).** He was a master of arts in Paris by 1296 and master of theology there in 1311. Most of our knowledge of his work is in the field of **logic** and grammar, where he wrote commentaries in question format. He also wrote *Quaestions on Aristotle's "Physics," "On the Soul,"* and *"On Meteors."* His *Commentary on Books I–III of **Peter Lombard's** Sentences*, *Disputed Questions*, and ***Quodlibet Questions*** survive in unedited manuscripts.

**RALPH STRODE (ca. 1335–1387).** A fellow of Merton College, Oxford, Ralph wrote two books on basic **logic**—*On the Logical Art* and *On Logical Principles*—and a number of treatises on particular areas of logical concern:

*On the Kinds of Suppositions*, *On Consequences*, and *On Insoluble Proposi-tions*. A friend of **John Wycliffe** and Geoffrey Chaucer, he studied and practiced **law** in the latter part of his life.

**RASHI.** *See* SOLOMON BEN ISAAC (RASHI) (ca. 1040–1105).

**RATRAMNUS OF CORBIE (fl. 844–868).** A priest, theologian, and teach-er at the **Benedictine** abbey of Corbie (Somme, France), Ratramnus wrote, among other works, two influential **theological** pieces (both around 850) at the request of King Charles the Bald: *De praedestinatione* (*Concerning Pre-destination*) and *De corpore et sanguine Domini* (*On the Body and Blood of the Lord*). In the former he discussed God's governance and defended, against Archbishop Hincmar of Reims, **Augustine**'s predestination of the elect and damned. In the latter, against an overly realistic conception of the presence of Christ in the **Eucharist** on the part of his teacher, **Paschasius Radbertus**, he interprets the Eucharist rather symbolically. The *De corpore* elicited mixed reactions in history, although now it is largely viewed among Catholics as orthodox. Wrongly attributed to **John Scotus Eriugena**, it was condemned at the Councils of Rome and Vercelli in 1050. It was favored in Protestant circles, which contributed to its inclusion in the first Catholic Index of Prohibited Books in 1559, remaining there until the edition of the Index in 1900. Ratramnus's *Contra Graecorum opposita* (*Against the Op-posing Teachings of the Greeks*) defends traditions of the Latin Church, notably the *Filioque—see* TRINITY (TRINITARIAN DOCTRINE)— against Byzantine criticisms. His *De nativitate Christi* (*On the Birth of Christ*) argues, against his teacher Paschasius, that Mary's parturition of Jesus was a natural physical event rather than a miraculous one.

**RAYMUNDUS BEQUINI (ca. 1280–1328).** He was a member of the Aqui-taine province of the **Dominicans** and pursued his studies in various con-vents of the order in that region, e.g., in Montpellier (1302), Toulouse (1305), and Cahors (1311). He was prior of Toulouse (1313–1315) and later became very familiar with the *Scriptum in Primum Sententiarum* (1316–1318), which the Franciscan **Peter Aureoli** produced there. To a great extent his attention to Aureoli's works indicates the seriousness of Aureoli's challenge to Thomas Aquinas. This is evident from Raymundus's 14-ques-tion *Correctorium* of the beginning of Aureoli's *Scriptum* where he criticizes Aureoli's views of theology, rational psychology, and metaphysics from a general Thomistic perspective. However, in his two *Quodlibets*, Bequini con-fronts from his own viewpoint Aureoli's *Quodlibet* teachings concerning the causes of the beatific vision.

**REALISM.** In its medieval context, this is a discussion in contrast to the positions of **nominalism** and conceptualism. The word *nomina* in Latin has a twofold reference. It can refer to written or spoken words that we use externally, and this use would be the most normal one. On the other hand, *nomina* might refer to interior words or concepts. Conceptualism might, then, at times be called "nominalism" in this second sense of its meaning. The same holds for realism. *Realism* might refer to those who claim that our universal concepts and external words have a universal reality in things that correspond to them. It might, less boldly, claim that there is a real foundation for universals in things prior to any operation on the part of the knower but that the foundation itself is not a universal reality. Things, in this latter case, are not universal but individual realities belonging to the same genera and species that do have an essential likeness. The first of these forms of realism is called exaggerated realism; the second is often called moderate realism.

**REMIGIUS OF AUXERRE (ca. 841–908).** Remegius became a Benedictine monk at the monastery of Saint-Germain in Auxerre, where he taught before moving on to Reims and then to Paris. At Paris, he taught Odo of Cluny. He continued the tradition of the Carolingian Renaissance, writing commentaries and glosses on many of the classical Latin authors (Cato, Virgil, Terence, Juvenal, Sedulius, and Prudentius). He also wrote commentaries on the grammarians Donatus, Priscian, and Martianus Capella. In theology, Remigius commented on **Boethius**'s *Consolation of Philosophy* and also wrote the earliest commentary on Boethius's *Opuscula sacra* (*Theological Tractates*) with some influence from **John Scotus Eriugena**. He also left Scripture commentaries on Genesis and the Psalms and *Homilies on Matthew's Gospel*.

**RHABANUS MAURUS.** *See* LIBERAL ARTS.

**RHETORIC.** *See* LIBERAL ARTS.

**RICHARD BRINKLEY (ca. 1325–1373).** An Oxford **Franciscan** known only through his **logical** and theological works. He wrote a *Summa logicae* (*Sum of Logic*), which, unlike **William of Ockham**'s famous work with the same title, was a simple text meant for beginners, and it was also written from a **realist** rather than a **nominalist** perspective. It thus was like an earlier introductory logic text produced by **Gerard Odon** at Paris. Brinkley has also left a **theological** inheritance through his *Commentary on the Sentences* and his collections of *Quaestiones magnae* (*Long Questions*) and *Quaestiones breves* (*Short Questions*), which, though produced at Oxford, were known in Paris in the 1360s.

**RICHARD FITZRALPH.** *See* FITZRALPH, RICHARD (ca. 1295–1360).

**RICHARD KILVINGTON (ca. 1302–1361).** A fellow of Oriel College, Oxford, in 1333, Richard was already master of arts. He became a **lector** on **Peter Lombard**'s *Sentences* in 1335 and a regent master in **theology** in 1338. Although he wrote commentaries on **Aristotle**'s *Physics* and *Ethics*, he is known especially for his detailed work on *Sophismata*. His exacting approach to study is also characteristic of his *Commentary on the Sentences*: it is made up of a few long, almost endless questions. After arguing a position, he raises objections, answers them, and then raises further objections to his own responses, which he then also answers.

**RICHARD KNAPWELL (ca. 1250–ca. 1288).** Not very much is known of the life of Richard Knapwell. The first information about him concerns his *Notes on the Sentences of Peter Lombard*, given at Oxford between 1272 and 1277. These *Notes* provide us with the dates. Since he quotes the *Secunda Secundae* of **Thomas Aquinas**'s *Summa theologiae*, we know this work was written after 1272. Silence about the **condemnation of 1277**, a subject that would have gotten his attention, sets the *terminus ante quem*. Richard incepted as a regent master at Oxford in 1284–1285, and soon thereafter he disputed his *Question on the Unity of Form*. He completed the commentaries on the *Perihermeneias* and *De generatione* of Aquinas. His treatise on the unity of form led to his excommunication and the end of his career. He died in Bologna around 1288.

**RICHARD OF CAMPSALL (ca. 1280–ca. 1350).** A fellow of Merton College, and later of Balliol College, Richard became regent master of arts before 1308. He served as regent master of **theology** from 1322 to 1324 and was vice chancellor of the university in 1325–1326. From references by **Walter Chatton**, **Adam Wodeham**, **Robert Holcot**, and **Peter of la Palu**, we know that he produced a *Commentary on the Sentences*, probably around the same time as **William of Ockham**. His *Questions on the Prior Analytics* accentuates the importance of **logic** for studying philosophy and theology. Yet, for him **Aristotle**'s logic has problems, for, like Robert Holcot a little later, he finds difficulties involved in applying Aristotle's logic to the **Trinity**.

**RICHARD OF CONINGTON (ca. 1275–1330).** Richard became a master of theology at Oxford around 1305–1307 and then a **lector** at the **Franciscan** convent in Cambridge from 1308 to 1310. He was subsequently elected provincial of the English province of the Franciscans, an office he served in from 1310 to 1316. He was a theological consultant at the Council of Vienne

(1311–1312), where he was involved in a great debate with the Spiritual Franciscans over poverty. This debate resulted in a treatise on poverty, titled *Beatus qui intelligit* (*Blessed Is He Who Understands*), that was mocked by Ubertino de Casale. Regretably, his **Commentary on the Sentences** has not survived, but his *Quaestiones disputatae* and two **Quodlibets** reveal an author who, on certain questions, favors the positions of **Henry of Ghent** over those of his fellow Franciscan, **John Duns Scotus**. In a manuscript of Scotus, there is even an indication that when the Subtle Doctor seems to be responding to Henry of Ghent, in reality he is responding to Henry's defender, Richard of Conington.

**RICHARD OF LAVENHAM (LAVINGHAM) (ca. 1335–1381).** An English **Carmelite** who was confessor to Richard II, Richard taught at Oxford. He was a prolific writer, producing over 60 works. He is best known for his logical works: *On Insoluble Propositions*, *On Modal Propositions*, *On Hypothetical Propositions*, *On Obligations*, and many other tracts in **logic**. He also wrote on natural philosophy and on **ethics**. His **theological** works were on Scripture and **Peter Lombard**'s *Sentences*, along with a number of anti-Wycliffite treatises.

**RICHARD OF MIDDLETON (ca. 1249–1302).** A **Franciscan** theologian and philosopher, Richard was born either in England or France around 1249. It is certain that he studied at Paris during the years 1276–1278, probably under **William de la Mare** and **Matthew of Aquasparta**. His *Commentary on Peter Lombard's Sentences* was probably begun in 1281 and completed in 1284. He then became the regent master of the Franciscans, an office he performed until 1287. His *Sentences* commentary provides a sober assessment of many of the positions of **Thomas Aquinas**. The tone of his 80 **Quodlibet** questions, however, shows a more critical attitude toward Aquinas. In his theory of knowledge he follows close to Aquinas, rejecting the illumination theory of **Augustine**, **Bonaventure**, and **Henry of Ghent**. Yet Richard stresses the superiority of the will over the intellect. The intellect plays a role in **theology**, since the study of the Scriptures attempts to clarify human knowledge of both Creator and creatures. Principally, however, theology aims to stimulate man's affections. Middleton believes that Scripture prescribes laws, attracts men through promises, and shows them models of behavior that they should follow or avoid. The study of Scripture, for Richard, perfects the soul, moving it toward the good through fear and love.

**RICHARD OF SAINT-VICTOR (ca. 1120–1173).** Although probably a native of Scotland, Richard joined the **Canons Regular of St. Augustine** at Saint-Victor outside of Paris in the 1140s or early 1150s. He became subprior of the abbey in 1159 and prior in 1162. In his various works, he followed the basic vision of **Hugh of Saint-Victor**: intellectual pursuits are to be based on all the senses of Scripture. The literal sense focuses on natural truths related to creation and on the history of salvation. The spiritual sense includes the allegorical meanings of Scripture, which indicate how creation and the events of history are fulfilled in Christ. Further, the spiritual sense also includes both the tropological meanings that teach the moral path of Christian living and the **anagogical** meanings that lead to the contemplation that anticipates the light and life of eternal glory.

For Richard, this is a unified program. Although those who classify his works might distribute them to areas called **exegetical**, doctrinal, and contemplative, they all form a unity in the actual intellectual, moral, and spiritual striving of Richard. For sure, his debt to Hugh of Saint-Victor for this achievement is great. Richard's *Liber exceptionum* depends on Hugh's *Didascalicon* and *Chronicon*. His knowledge of **Dionysius the Pseudo-Areopagite** is often mediated through Hugh's writings, as is much of his knowledge of **Boethius** and **John Scotus Eriugena**. His allegorical interpretations in *The Twelve Patriarchs* (*Benjamin minor*) and *The Mystical Ark* (*Benjamin maior*) manifest the mystic's path to contemplative union with God, following Hugh's practices. Yet, in all this, Richard is a giant standing on the shoulders of a giant. Especially does he achieve this stature in his *De Trinitate* (*On the Trinity*). For the special stamp he has put on this spiritual inheritance, he was highly admired by **Alexander of Hales**, **Albert the Great**, **St. Bonaventure**, and **Henry of Ghent**.

Richard's six steps to contemplation, developed through his expansion of the Proclean framework of Boethius, focused on the objects of the natural world (*naturalia*), of the interior world of man (*intelligibilia*), and of the transcendent divine world (*intellectibilia*). His inventive extension of this model that incorporated the searcher's alternative approaches to the examination of these three types of objects later provided the path for the spiritual climb of many Augustinian canons at Saint-Victor as well as for the structure of St. Bonaventure's *Journey of the Mind to God* and Bernardine of Laredo's *Ascent of Mount Sion*. Refer to the introduction, "The Beginnings of 'Philosophy' and 'Theology' in the Latin West."

**RICHARD RUFUS (ca. 1210–ca. 1260).** After becoming a master of arts, Richard joined the **Franciscan** order in 1238. He commented the *Sentences* of **Peter Lombard** twice: once in Oxford covering Books I–III (around 1251–1253) and later in Paris, where he copied, condensed, and at times altered the *Sentences* of St. Bonaventure. In 1256, he returned to Oxford to serve as the regent master in theology at the *studium generale* (international house of studies) of the Franciscans. Quite likely a *Commentary on the Metaphysics of Aristotle* that is attributed to him is authentic; but a *Commentary on the Physics of Aristotle* doubtlessly is not his.

**RICHARD SWINESHEAD (fl. ca. 1344–1354).** Author of a *Liber Calculationum* (*The Book of Calculations*), which made him known among contemporaries as "the Calculator," Richard is one of the important members, indeed the original member, of the so-called **Oxford Calculators**, a group of 14th-century scientists that, continuing the work of **Thomas Bradwardine**, was characterized by their (then pioneering) use of mathematics in the study of motion. Richard must be considered the leading member of the **Oxford Calculators**, since he is the author of the main text of the movement. Richard was viewed by Gottfried Wilhelm Leibniz as the first medieval author who introduced mathematics into the study of natural philosophy.

**ROBERT BACON (ca. 1190–1248).** Robert was a student of John of Abbeville at Paris around 1210. He was also a fellow student and friend of **Robert Grosseteste** at Oxford, where he describes himself as a scholar who attended the lectures of **Edmund of Abingdon** and served as his assistant. By 1219, he was already a regent master of **theology** at Oxford, where he taught the young **Dominicans**, a religious order that arrived in England in 1221. When he himself joined the order, the Dominicans had their first chair at Oxford. The first Dominican student to incept and to become a master in theology was his student **Richard Fishacre**, who shared teaching duties with him until Robert retired in 1244. He died in 1248 and is buried at the Dominican Church in Oxford. Very little can be known of his teaching, since, besides a sermon, the only work that has come down to us is his unedited *Glossa in Psalterium* (*Gloss on the Psalter*).

**ROBERT COWTON (ca. 1274–ca. 1315).** Robert, a Franciscan theologian, was ordained in 1300 and was perhaps one of the first English Franciscans not sent to Paris to study theology and become a master there. If this is so, then, he broke a tradition that began around 1260 with **John Peckham** and continued with **William de la Mare**. Robert wrote his *Commentary on the Sentences* in 1309–1311, enjoying a great deal of influence from **William of Nottingham**, with whom, however, he at times disagrees. He followed Nottingham and **Richard of Conington**, also Franciscans, in opposing Scotus on many points. They all to a marked degree interpreted **Henry of Ghent** differently than did Scotus. His *Sentences* were abbreviated by Richard Snettisham, and these abbreviations were popular, since 10 copies of them have survived.

**ROBERT FLAND (ROBERT OF FLANDERS) (fl. 1335–370).** Robert is presently known only as a mid-14th-century logician. All the information concerning him is provided by the manuscript in Bruges that contains his three surviving logical works: *Consequentiae* (*Consequences*), *Obligationes* (*Obligations*), and *Insolubilia* (*Insolubles*). The manuscript speaks of these works as treatises of Roberti Fland or simply Fland. *Fland* in each case is followed by a period, suggesting that *Fland* is an abbreviation—perhaps for *Flandriae*, that is, Robert of Flanders. The sources he uses in these works indicate that they were written between 1335 and 1370 at Oxford. His *Consequences* shows a dependence on **William of Ockham**. His *Obligations* represents two different traditions concerning obligations: the traditional theory followed by **William of Sherwood, Walter Burley, Ralph Strode, Albert of Saxony, Peter d'Ailly**, and Paul of Pergula, and the new response defended by **Roger Swineshead** and **Richard of Lavenham**. His *Insolubles* continues his contribution to the history of **logic**, since in it he again represents two camps: the first tradition defended by **Thomas Bradwardine** and the second approach favored by **Richard Swineshead**.

**ROBERT HOLCOT.** *See* HOLCOT, ROBERT (ca. 1290–1349).

**ROBERT KILWARDBY (ca. 1215–1279).** Robert was born in Leicestershire. He studied in the Arts Faculty at Paris ca. 1231 and became a master of arts there from 1237 to 1245, focusing mainly on **logic** and grammar. In 1245, he entered the **Dominican** order in England and studied theology at Oxford, where he became a *baccalareus* in about 1250 and a regent master around 1254. As the occupant of the Oxford Dominican chair in theology, he succeeded **Richard Fishacre**. He was elected provincial of the English province of the Order of Preachers and served in that position from 1261 to 1272. He was named archbishop of Canterbury in 1272 and was consecrated archbishop in 1273. Among his most noteworthy actions in this position was the list of 30 errors that he condemned on 18 March 1277. This action followed Bishop **Étienne Tempier**'s **condemnation** (7 March) at Paris of 219 propositions. Some of the more philosophically and theologically significant propositions Kilwardby condemned were opposed to his own **Augustinian** tenets (seen as traditional Christian wisdom), such as the doctrine of seminal reasons, the plurality of forms in man, and divine illumination. He attended the Council of Lyons in 1274 and was appointed cardinal of Porto and Santa Rufina in 1278. He died at Viterbo on 10 September 1279 and was buried at the now-destroyed church of S. Maria ad Gradus. Kilwardby wrote commentaries on **Aristotle**'s logic or **dialectics**, his natural philosophy (including *On* *the Soul*), and his *Metaphysics*; on the **Sentences** of **Peter Lombard**; and various original treatises (including *On the Origin of the Sciences*, *On the Unity of Forms*, and *On Theology*).

**ROBERT OF COURÇON (ca. 1150–1219).** Robert studied theology around 1175 at Paris under **Peter Cantor**. He taught theology at Paris from 1202 to 1208, producing a **summa** that very much focuses on practical questions related to the **Sacraments** and canon **law**. He was a canon at Notre Dame in Paris and was made a cardinal by Pope Innocent III in 1202. He was also appointed legate for France. In 1215, he drew up the statutes for the university and repeated the prohibition against the reading of the *Metaphysics* and *Physics* of **Aristotle**. He also took part in the Fourth Lateran Council.

**ROBERT OF MELUN (1100–1167).** A native of England, Robert studied at Oxford and then at Paris, where he was a student (as well as a critic) of **Peter Abelard** and also a student of **Hugh of Saint-Victor**. In 1137, he became a master of arts at Mont Saint-Geneviève in Paris, where one of his well-known students was **John of Salisbury**. He was director of a school in Melun and quite possibly later a teacher at Saint-Victor. He opposed the **Trinitarian** teaching of **Gilbert of Poitiers** as well as some points in the Christology of **Peter Lombard**. Robert returned to England in 1160 and became bishop of Hereford in 1163. In the conflict concerning Thomas à Becket, he sided with the king. The prologue to his *Quaestiones de divina pagina* (*Questions concerning the Divine Page*), using texts from **St. Augustine**, presents a very strong portrait of the nature of a *quaestio* that will beget understanding rather than a routine answer. His *Sententiae* is a **summa** that follows the model of Hugh of Saint-Victor's *Sacraments of the Christian Faith*. Refer to the introduction, "Methods of Study."

**ROBERT OF ORFORD (fl. 1284–1299).** Robert's life is known only from his writings. Elements of his academic career suggest that he was born around 1260. Estimates point to an academic career that began around 1284. Quite likely he incepted between 1285 and 1290, and his *Commentary on the Sentences* dates from this period. He joined other **Dominicans** in their responses to **William de la Mare**'s *Correctorium fratris Thomae* (*Correctory of Brother Thomas*) before 1284. Robert's defense of **Thomas Aquinas** is found in his *Correctorium "Sciendum"* (*Correctory beginning with "Sciendum"*). His defense of Thomism took on wider dimensions, since he attempted to respond to the criticisms of Thomas found in **Henry of Ghent**'s *Summa* and *Quodlibets* with his *Impugnatio Henrici de Gandavo* (*Disagreement with Henry of Ghent*), produced between 1288 and 1291 at Paris. Correspondingly, between 1289 and 1293, he met the criticisms that **Giles of**

Rome brought against Aquinas in his *Commentary on the Sentences* and *Quodlibets* with his *Reprobationes dictorum a fratre Aegidio in Sententiarum libris* (*Responses to the Declarations Made by Brother Giles in His Book on the Sentences*). Robert's responses to critics of Thomas Aquinas vary in tone, since the opposition of authors such as Giles of Rome and **James of Viterbo** to Thomas was much milder than the criticism of Henry of Ghent. It is probable that he died before 1300.

**ROBERT OF WALSINGHAM (ca. 1270–ca. 1314).** Robert was a **Carmelite** theologian and regent master at Oxford. We know that he became master of **theology** before February 1312 and that he chose his two *Quodlibets* in 1312–1313. His *Quaestiones ordinariae* (*Ordinary Questions*) antedate and postdate his *Quodlibets*. Despite his disagreement at times with **Henry of Ghent**, he should generally be listed, along with the Franciscan **Richard of Conington**, as one of Henry's strong followers. One place where he closely follows Henry is in his portrait of the role of the Uncreated Cause (God) in all productions. Like Henry, he stresses God's universal creative power. Secondary causes affect nothing as far as the creation of creatures itself is concerned. They merely serve as channels for causing the specific kind of existence effects have through the creative action of God. Though a close follower of Henry of Ghent, he at times disagreed with him and also with Richard of Conington, Henry's Franciscan disciple. In short, Robert follows Henry of Ghent, but with some independence. This independence also exists in relation to **Gerard of Bologna** and **Guido Terrena**, his fellow Carmelites, whom he also criticizes.

**ROGER BACON (ca. 1215–ca. 1292).** Bacon received his degree in arts from Paris before 1237 and taught in the **Arts Faculty** from 1237 to 1247. He dedicated the next decade (1247–1256) to private study and research. He joined the **Franciscans** in 1256 in Paris, where he stayed until 1280. He moved to the Franciscan convent in Oxford in 1280 and lived there until his death in 1292. Bacon lectured on **Aristotle**'s works from 1237 to 1247 at Paris and so was the one who lectured longest on the texts of the Philosopher during the time when prohibitions against reading Aristotle were still on the books. When he began to do his private research, he started to broaden his approach with new sources, Seneca's *Quaestiones naturales* (*Questions on Natural Philosophy*) and the works on optics and natural philosophy coming from **Alhacen, Al-Kindi,** and **Albumasar.** He also began to aim at developing a more experiential-experimental approach to the study of nature.

In **theology**, Bacon very much opposed the *Commentaries on **Peter Lombard*** and the errors in method found in most works of theology after Alexander of Hales. He was a man with a unique viewpoint on almost every philosophical and theological issue.

**ROGER MARSTON (ca. 1235–ca. 1303).** A **Franciscan** friar and **theologian**, Marston was a student of **John Peckham** at Paris from 1269 to 1271. He followed Peckham back to England by 1276 and lectured on the *Sentences* of **Peter Lombard** at Cambridge, where he is recorded as the 13th Franciscan **lector**. He later became the 16th Franciscan regent master at Oxford, probably incepting in 1281. In 1292, he was elected provincial of the English Franciscans, an office he held until 1298. Marston is said to have died and been buried at Norwich in 1303. Of his writings, only four *Quodlibets* and his *Disputed Questions* from the period of his Oxford regency survive. The strongest influence on him is surely John Peckham, though he also borrows from **Thomas Aquinas** and **Henry of Ghent**. Lesser sources are **William de la Mare** and **Matthew of Aquasparta**. In his 1282 *Disputed Question on the Fall of Human Nature*, he disagrees with Aquinas, but only in a moderate way. In his *Disputed Question on the Soul*, assigned to 1283–1284, he criticizes Aquinas in a very detailed way and accuses him of being a "philosophizing theologian." In this later work of Marston, the Franciscan order at Oxford has begun its open war against the thought of Aquinas.

**ROLAND OF CREMONA (ca. 1200–1259).** The first **Dominican** master of **theology** at Paris, Roland became a master of the **liberal arts** in Bologna and entered the Dominican order there in 1219. Licensed at Paris, he served as master of theology from 1229 to 1233. From 1233 to 1244, he was often called upon by Popes Gregory IX and Innocent IV, as well as by many bishops, to investigate those suspected of **heresies**. In his later years, he served as **lector** in theology at the convent of Bologna and died there in 1259. His surviving works include his *Postilla on the Book of Job*, his *Quaestiones in libros Sententiarum* (*Questions related to Lombard's **Sentences***), and a *Sermon on the Lord's Supper*.

**ROSCELIN (ca. 1050–ca. 1120).** Born at Compiègne, this prominent scholar of logic or **dialectics** was famous for his doctrine that universal concepts are words. In this, he went against the majority of contemporary logicians, who viewed generic and specific concepts as referring to corresponding universal realities. For Roscelin, as Aristotle teaches, only individuals exist; therefore, he concludes that universal concepts (as referring to an existing thing) are real only as the word physically expresses it. This position was countered by **Anselm** and others, such as **Adelard of Bath** and **William of Champeaux**, who sought in their own ways to ground universal concepts in universal realities. Thus, 12th-century philosophy is dominated by the so-called problem of universals. Against this background, **Peter Abelard** (a student and critic of Champeaux), the major figure among 12th-century logicians, develops some of his influential positions.

**RUPERT OF DEUTZ (1075/80–1129).** Probably a native of Liège, this **Benedictine** monk, priest, and theologian was appointed Abbot of Deutz in 1120 by the archbishop of Cologne (Frederick I), an office he held until his death. He developed **Augustinian** theological themes, such as the **Trinity** and history understood as a divinely ordained moral process. *On the Trinity and Its Works* and *On the Victory of the Word of God* treat these themes, respectively. At a time when classical learning (especially the **liberal art** of logic or **dialectics**) increasingly influenced **theology**, a process that led to **Scholasticism**, Rupert (like **Peter Damian** and some of the other representatives of so-called **monastic theology**) was suspicious of the use of logic in theology (*see also* EXEGESIS). Among other works, such as biblical commentaries and saints' lives, his *Anulus or Dialogue between a Christian and a Jew* provides insight into relations among Jews and Christians at the time. Rupert is also associated with doctrinal controversies, such as his dispute against **Anselm of Laon**'s view of predestination.

**RUSHD, IBN.** *See* AVERROES (IBN RUSHD) (ca. 1126–1198).

**RUYSBROECK, JAN VAN, BL. (1293–1381).** He led a retired and austere life with his uncle, a holy priest and a canon of St. Gudules in Brussels. In 1317, he was ordained a priest. Another canon, a friend of his uncle, joined them in their desire for a more contemplative life. They formed a community of the **Canons Regular of St. Augustine** in 1349, and though staying independent, they decided to follow the rule of the canons of Saint-Victor. His spiritual writings began with *The Spiritual Espousals*, followed by two longer treatises, *The Kingdom of Lovers* and *The Tabernacle*. Some Carthusian friends asked him for a gloss on *The Kingdom of Lovers*, and Jan fulfilled their request with *The Little Book of Enlightenment*. In a more popular vein, Ruysbroeck also produced *The Book of the Twelve Beguines*. In his early days, Ruysbroeck preached against a heretical sect in Brussels that claimed to achieve by their own efforts a state in which they could no longer sin. He argued that the true elevation of the contemplative to a higher way of life does not come from his own effort but from the grace of God. The three books of *The Spiritual Espousals* provide an ascent to God that begins first by meeting Christ in others in an active life, then in an interior life that yearns for God through the practice of virtue and grace, and finally in a contemplative life enjoying the vision of God. Such union is a grace, and it can be withdrawn. The ascent is an ever-repeating rhythm of this threefold or Trinitarian life, reflecting, as St. Augustine portrayed him, man's true nature as an image of God.

# S

SAADIAH GAON (882–942). Appointed as head (*gaon*) of the Talmudic academies at Babylon in 928, Saadiah ben Joseph, generally considered the father of medieval Jewish philosophy, received his early education in Egypt, where he was born, and then in Palestine. In 930, when he disagreed with a decision of the court of the head of Babylonian Jewry (the Exilarch), Saadiah had to abandon his office as *gaon*, which he only regained after seven years of exile in Baghdad. He contributed to practically all fields of Jewish learning, such as **exegesis**, **law**, poetry, grammar, lexicography, philosophy, **theology**, chronology, biblical translation (into Arabic), and commentary. He is famous for his successful role in a dispute (started in 921) concerning the Jewish calendar, when the opinion of Babylonian authorities (and Saadiah's) prevailed over that of Palestinian authorities. As a polemicist, he devoted much energy to the defense of traditional Judaism against the **Karaites** (Jews accepting only the **Bible** as authority, not rabbinic tradition) and other religions.

Aside from Greek philosophy (including **Platonic**, **Aristotelian**, **Stoic**, and **Neoplatonic** ideas), Saadiah's approach was most indebted to Muslim *kalam* or dialectical theology (which already used Greek ideas), specifically the **Mu'tazilite** school, an approach he appropriated in creating the first version of Jewish *kalam*. Occupied primarily with the reconciliation of reason and revelation (the characteristically medieval intellectual tension) and not with the erection of a philosophic system, Saadiah engaged in dialectical theology, using philosophical ideas to clarify revelation. It is in this sense that he is the first medieval thinker to create a Jewish philosophy, a philosophy guided by Scripture. Saadiah, like **Philo of Alexandria** (30 B.C.–40 A.D.) before him (*see* JEWISH PHILOSOPHY AND THEOLOGY), adhered to the principle of the unity of truth, a basic principle of later medieval Jewish philosophers: disagreements between reason and revelation (and among passages of revelation), the human and divine sources of truth, are only apparent, not real. Thus, the proper approach is to interpret revelation in terms of what is most evidently true according to reason; and reason itself must likewise be guided in terms of what are most evidently the true teachings of Scripture. For example, biblical passages saying that God is eternal, all powerful, and unlike anything of this world (which may be clarified with proper philosophical explanation) seem in contradiction with passages describing God in corporeal terms. Since divine eternity, omnipotence, and transcendence are basic principles to all revelation (and compatible with reason), passages describing God in corporeal terms must not be taken literally.

Saadiah's central ideas can be found in his *Book of Doctrines and Beliefs*, reputedly the first major medieval work in Jewish philosophy and theology, as well as in his *Commentary on the Book of Creation*, both of which were written in Arabic and translated into Hebrew. The former (which is still a standard in Jewish thought), follows a Mu'tazilite structure. Divided into two major sections, the first on divine unity and the second on divine justice, the two central *kalamic* topics, it begins with a characteristically *kalamic* goal: proving the creation of the world. To Saadiah, proving the creation of the world (in time and ex nihilo) is proving the existence of the Creator or God, as well as some of his essential attributes (such as unity and simplicity), the topic to which he next turns. Finally, in the section on divine unity, Saadiah discusses prophecy (God's communication with human beings) and law, dividing the commandments of the Torah into rational and traditional, the former discoverable through reason and the latter as solely dependent on God's will—an influential distinction subsequent thinkers either followed or rejected (e.g., **Moses Maimonides**). Reason's capacity to prove creation was a source of debate among medieval thinkers. Maimonides and **Thomas Aquinas**, for example, argued that reason could not prove creation, while others like **Gersonides** considered it demonstrable. The portion on divine justice deals with human action, freedom, and nature and their compatibility with divine omniscience and omnipotence, as well as with Jewish eschatology. To Saadiah, God willed human beings to have free will, and his all-encompassing foreknowledge is not the trigger of human action.

The intent of the prologue to the whole work reflects the intellectual context of the author: at a time when the divergent opinions among various religious and philosophic sects resulted in confusion and even skepticism among Jews, it became necessary to strengthen Jewish belief with reason. Thus in the prologue, Saadiah argues, against skeptics, for the sources of certain truth: sense perception, self-evident first principles, inferential knowledge, and tradition based on historical evidence. Saadiah's fundamental project, the explication and defense of traditional Judaism (demanding a synthesis of reason and revelation) is seminal for later philosophical accounts of Jewish beliefs, such as human freedom, creation, God's existence, unity, and justice. Refer to the introduction, "The Beginning and Development of Medieval Arabian and Jewish Philosophy and Theology."

**SABELLIANISM.** One of the heresies regarding the Christian teaching that there are three persons in one God. For Sabellius, a third-century thinker, the three persons of the **Trinity** are not really distinct but rather are only different modes of God. Unlike the heresy of **Arianism**, which stresses the distinction among the persons to the point that the Son is considered a creature, Sabellianism does not sufficiently recognize the distinction among the persons. A synod of Rome condemned this doctrine in 262. *See also* TRINITY (TRINITARIAN DOCTRINE).

**SACRAMENTS.** The Latin word *sacramentum* was used to signify the oath taken by soldiers binding themselves to service for their country, and it became a fit analogy to speak of the sacrament of baptism, since the baptized become soldiers of Christ and the Church. However, the Latin term had the broader and more fundamental meaning of "consecrated" or "dedicated," and in this way whatever is consecrated or dedicated to God could be called a sacrament. If we study the original languages further, we would discover that *sacramentum* was also a translation of the Greek *mysterion*, meaning "mystery." Sacrament, when linked to mystery, focuses on God's revelation through word and deed of His presence to His chosen people and the ritual remembrance of these divine words and actions. A sacrament in its more fundamental sense, then, is not limited to the seven sacraments of baptism, confirmation, penance, Eucharist, matrimony, holy orders, and extreme unction, named by **Peter Lombard** in his *Sentences*. Before the 12th century, and even down to today, *sacrament* had and has a broader meaning: any sign revealing the presence of God. In this broad sense, Christ as the supreme divine revelation is the primary sacrament. The Church, as the mystical body of Christ, is also a fundamental sacrament.

One can also sense this broader meaning of the term *sacrament* in the medieval period. **Hugh of Saint-Victor**'s *Sacraments of the Christian Faith* deals with the whole mystery of God's relationship with the world in its creation, its fall, and its redemption. Yet *sacrament* did take on with Hugh's contemporary, Peter Lombard, its special meaning related to the rituals that "caused" God's grace to come into man's soul. Although the reality of baptism, the Eucharist, and the other five sacraments was a causal reality, Lombard was the first to use the term *cause* in his treatises describing the effects of these sacraments. The seven sacraments are unique among all the signs of God's presence, because they cause grace in accord with their nature as signs. Baptism is a washing, and it is not only a symbol of spiritual cleansing; it actually, as a grace or a gift of God, cleanses the soul.

In medieval treatises on the seven sacraments, what was implicitly said of these sacraments by the Scriptures and **Fathers of the Church** is brought out in detail and explained at greater length. Under the influence of **Aristotelian** models, such as the hylomorphic composition of material things, the earlier

Patristic language of *element* and *word* was replaced by speaking of the *matter* and *form* of each sacrament. Greater precision regarding the seven sacraments arose during the medieval period, and this improvement is quite evident in the *Summa theologiae* of **Thomas Aquinas**, when he explains the ways in which the sacraments are both signs and causes, and causes in the way they are signs.

**SALERNO.** *See* MEDICINE.

**SCHOLASTICISM.** This is the style of thought, principally in medieval **universities**, that had schoolroom qualities about it. *Scholasticism* comes from the word *schola*, which means "**school**." In a very basic sense, the method of study in the schools, even those that existed before the universities, or in the case of the Islamic and Jewish worlds, those that existed outside the university context, had set procedures. Usually one began with the study of texts, so *lectio* or reading was the first step in learning. Along with the reading was an explanation every time there seemed to be a need for one, for example, when dealing with a technical term or the mention of a person in the text who might not be familiar. The next step was to attempt to dig a little deeper than the surface, so *quaestiones* or questions were asked and they were the kind of questions that aimed at getting more than just information. They were questions that attempted to push the student to a deeper understanding. The next or third step was to look into different understandings of the original text and see how disputes among well-informed people might take place. Seeing the disagreements pushed students to dig even deeper in an effort to find a more fundamental understanding (refer to the introduction, "Methods of Study").

These general study procedures are well illustrated in any question of **Thomas Aquinas**'s *Summa theologiae*. He asks a question and gives responses that answer yes and no. This maneuver makes one see that there is a problem or conflict. The teachers and students have to try to resolve the difficulty. Aquinas, in his works, gives the answer to the question and also provides reasons or grounds for choosing the answer he does. He then tells why the arguments favoring the opposite answer are not strong enough to convince him to hold the opposite position. He thus has an answer to the question and the arguments to back it up.

Scholasticism in a more technical sense is not only the method followed in the medieval schools and universities; it also signifies a certain content. In general, the content has its origin in the Bible and in a philosophical text. The answer the Scholastic gives will in some way be a synthesis of what the Bible says and what the philosophers say. The most influential philosopher Scholastics use to help answer the questions is often **Aristotle**, along with his commentators, especially **Avicenna** and **Averroes**. One of **Plato**'s followers, however, might also be the philosopher of choice. A Scholastic might prefer **Proclus**, **Plotinus**, **Dionysius the Pseudo-Areopagite**, or another **Neoplatonic** author as his guide. Scholasticism, then, offers a content that is biblical and also **Aristotelian** and/or Neoplatonic. The philosophy, whether from the Aristotelian or Neoplatonic traditions, is generally subordinated to the Bible. Scholasticism, then, is the method and the philosophy and theology of the universities, or the schools within or outside the university, that function in these ways.

**SCHOOLS.** After the death of the schools of antiquity in the sixth century, Medieval Western schools began with Charlemagne's effort (expressed in documents such as his *Admonitio generalis* or *General Admonition* of 789) to prepare clerics and monks for the study of Scripture and for correct liturgical practices. At some of the Carolingian ecclesiastical centers, however, there was already some tradition of studies. Prior to Charlemagne's reform, a chief center for formal learning was the palace school. Many received their early education at the different courts, and Charlemagne's court was the best known. The leading figure in Charlemagne's effort to disseminate instruction, starting a growing educational tradition leading to the **universities** of the 13th century, was an English scholar of his palace school, **Alcuin** (735–804), who, together with students such as **Rhabanus Maurus** (776–856), compiled earlier sources for the teaching of the **liberal arts**. Schools, particularly of grammar, were established at different ecclesiastical centers.

This marks the beginning of the growth of palace, monastic, and cathedral schools. Originally each stressed a distinct function. Palace schools focused on training people for the diverse roles necessary for the efficient functioning of the kingdom; monastic schools centered on training for religious life and on the knowledge required for contemplation; and cathedral schools trained the various people necessary for the many functions that were under church jurisdiction. The monastic school, a broad term designating the cultivation of learning by monks, was also the setting of what is today called **monastic theology**. By the 10th century, monastic and cathedral schools cultivated not only grammar but the whole trivium, including rhetoric and **logic**, and the quadrivium (arithmetic, geometry, music, and astronomy). In the 11th and 12th centuries, monastic schools began to decline while cathedral schools flourished and benefited from the reception of previously unavailable works of classical learning. Some of the cathedral schools, notably the one at Paris, developed into universities with faculties of **arts**, **medicine**, and **theology**. The cathedral school at Chartres was also a leading intellectual center. Beginning with its first known master, Fulbert (ca. 970–1028), it is associated with important philosophers and theologians, such as **Bernard of Chartres, William of Conches, Thierry of Chartres**, and **Gilbert of Poitiers**.

In the ninth century, Muslim colleges originated in the everyday mosques called *masjid*, as opposed to the great or Friday mosques (*al-masjid al-jami*). Their focus was on the Islamic disciplines (as opposed to "foreign" Greco-Roman learning), namely the **Koran, law**, and Arabic language and litera-ture. In the 10th century, lodging complexes for students, usually close to the *masjid*, emerged. The madrasa, which flourished in the 11th century, repre-sents the final stage of the Muslim college, combining housing and learning. Other places of Islamic learning also existed, such as study circles associated with the great mosques and with monasteries.

In Jewish communities, the school was embedded in tradition, since ac-cording to Judaism fathers have the duty to educate their children in the **Torah**. Thus, various private and community-sponsored institutions of learn-ing existed. Two predominant models of Jewish education were the Ashke-nazic and the Sephardic approaches. As is to be expected, these models, though different, shared a great deal since they were both grounded in Jewish tradition. Their differences depended in part on the differences between the two main cultural worlds wherein medieval Jews lived, namely Christian Europe and Islam (particularly in Spain). The Ashkenazic model was gener-ally dominant in England and in northern Europe, as well as in various countries of eastern Europe. The Sephardic model was generally dominant in Islamic lands (and in Italy in the late Middle Ages). In addition to their different emphases concerning traditional Jewish subjects (Bible, Talmud, Hebrew grammar, etc.), the Sephardic model was distinct in its inclusion of the scientific and philosophical works of non-Jews. *See also* ARTS FACUL-TY; EXEGESIS; KARAITES; UNIVERSITIES.

**SCIENCE.** In the Middle Ages, the Latin term *scientia* (*scire*: to know) and its Syriac, Arabic, and Hebrew counterparts had diverse connotations. Gener-ally, it meant all learning through reason. In philosophical discussions, *scien-tia* or *science* had a more restricted meaning largely dependent on **Aristotle** (in, e.g., *Nicomachean Ethics* VI, 3; *Posterior Analytics* I, 2), referring to a distinct type of knowledge. For Aristotle, science (*episteme*) is demonstrative knowledge. This is necessary knowledge through causes or, in terms of logic (**dialectics**), a conclusion proceeding from necessary premises through valid reasoning. This Aristotelian conception of science presupposes a twofold dimension, a formal and an objective one. In the former, the term *science* emphasizes an operation and method of the mind. As such it pertains to logic, and medieval thinkers of the three religions appropriated and developed this dimension of science to the extent that they used Aristotelian logic. In the latter dimension, the term *science* emphasizes what is known, and medieval thinkers of the three religions appropriated and developed this Aristotelian dimension of science to the extent that they used Aristotelian philosophy, applying scientific methodology to different subjects (or sciences), such as **ethics**, **politics**, physics, the heavens, the soul, and so on.

Accordingly, the transmission of Aristotle's works (and their commentaries) through translations was instrumental in the development of medieval science. Aristotle's writings became especially significant (and at points controversial) in the application of methodologies to the study of Scripture and in discussions concerning the scientific status of **theology**. Moreover, the Aristotelian conception was also adapted and developed in various ways within theologies influenced by the **Platonic** tradition. Although practically all medieval thinkers adopted Aristotelian logic as a neutral tool for scientific investigation, and to this extent agreed to this formal aspect of science, they differed in regard to the more properly philosophical issues of science. Depending on their philosophical and theological orientations, medieval thinkers differed in their accounts of the extent and nature of knowledge and what is knowable. *See also FALSAFAH, AL-*; LIBERAL ARTS; MEDICINE; OPTICS.

**SCOTISM.** Scotism is the intellectual movement that in varying degrees has continued, especially in the **Franciscan** order, since the time of **John Duns Scotus** himself. This movement assimilated, developed, and defended the principal philosophical and theological positions of Scotus, especially defending his theory of the univocity of the concept of being, *haecceitas* (*thisness*) as the principle of individuation, the formal distinction between the soul and its faculties, the supremacy of God's freedom and love, God's love as the primary motive for the Incarnation, and the meritorious character of man's morally good acts due to God's acceptance of them as meritorious. Among the chief early Scotists were **William of Alnwick**, **Antonius Andreas**, **Anfredus Gonteri**, **John of Bassolis**, **Landulf of Caracciola**, **Francis of Marchia**, and **Francis of Meyronnes**. Scotistic resurgences occurred in the 16th and 17th centuries, culminating in the publication of Duns Scotus's *Opera omnia*, which contained commentaries by Hugh Caughwell (d. 1626), **Maurice O'Fihely**, John Ponce (d. 1670), and Luke Wadding (d. 1657), and more recently in the 20th-century effort, begun by the Franciscan order, to produce a critical edition of the theological and philosophical works of the Subtle Doctor.

**SEMI-PELAGIANISM.** *See* PELAGIANISM.

**SENTENCES (*SENTENTIAE*).** *See COMMENTARY ON THE SENTENCES*; *MAGISTER*; PETER LOMBARD (ca. 1095–1160).

**SHEM TOV IBN FALAQUERA (ca. 1225–ca. 1295).** Little is known about the life of this poet, translator, compiler, exegete, and commentator. Even the general opinion that he was born and lived in Spain is only probable. One of the chief scholars of his time, Falaquera did not aim at producing an original system of thought. He made special efforts to make the works of Arabic and Greek philosophers accessible in Hebrew to the Jewish reader and to show that the study of philosophy and science can be helpful (for those with the requisite education) in understanding the deeper meanings of Scripture. A good example of his efforts at transmission is the encyclopedic work *De'ot ha-Filosofim* (*The Opinions of the Philosophers*). He rarely translated entire works but organized selections, abridgements, and comments according to the various themes he presented. However, he is not simply a mediator of the philosophical tradition. In his commentary on **Maimonides**'s *The Guide of the Perplexed*, titled *Moreh ha-Moreh* (*The Guide of the Guide*), one sees his independent judgment as he both defends and criticizes Maimonides on given issues. His philosophical outlook is heavily **Aristotelian** and especially indebted to **Averroes** and Maimonides. Yet there is also some influence of **Neoplatonism**, specifically **Ibn Gabirol**. He wrote a considerable amount; many of his prose works survive, but a good deal of poetry written in his youth is lost. As he matured as a thinker, his attitude toward poetry became less favorable, since (as he claimed) poetry can persuade on aesthetic rather than on epistemic or philosophical grounds. A similar suspicion toward poetry can already be found in Book X of **Plato**'s *Republic*.

**SHI'ITES.** *See* ISLAM.

**SIBERT OF BEKA (ca. 1260–1332).** Sibert, born in the lower Rhineland town of Beka ca. 1260, entered the **Carmelites** in Cologne ca. 1280, founded the Carmelite house in Geldern and was the prior there from 1312 to 1315. Thereafter, he studied theology in Paris, and in his inaugural question and in question 11 of his *Quodlibet* he argued against **Thomas Wylton**'s position concerning the ultimate cause of beatific vision. He himself defended the Council of Vienne's 1312 determination that beyond man's intellectual nature in itself and by its very nature there was the need for the *lumen gloriae* (light of glory) in order to see and enjoy God in bliss. Sibert is also credited with influencing the tone and character of the Carmelites' spiritual life in the Middle Ages through his authorship of his *Ordinal* or guide to the community's religious celebrations.

**SIGER OF BRABANT (ca. 1240–ca. 1284).** The most prominent among the Latin proponents of **Averroism** (some were called "secular," "heterodox," "radical," or "integral" **Aristotelians**), Siger became in 1266 a master in the Parisian **Arts Faculty**, where most Latin Averroists taught and studied. Their decision to pursue philosophy for its own sake turned the Arts Faculty, once a preparatory faculty for the higher studies of **theology, medicine**, or **law**, into an Aristotelian philosophy faculty. This basic attitude to seek a life and wisdom significantly independent of revelation, aside from their conclusions, made them the source of controversies. Siger's chief goal was philosophic truth, which to him existed primarily in the genuine teachings of Aristotle and his Commentator **Averroes**. In regard to central issues such as the temporal creation of the world, the distinction between essence and existence, and the nature of the intellect, Siger generally followed Averroes against **Avicenna** (the other chief interpreter of Aristotle received by 13th-century Latin thinkers). Unlike theologians like **Albert the Great** and **Thomas Aquinas**, who interpreted Aristotle in light of Christian faith, Siger and other Averroists like **Boethius of Dacia** were pure philosophers who became convinced of the rational necessity of certain philosophical conclusions that conflicted with tenets of Christianity. This did not mean that they necessarily saw these Christian tenets as false, but rather that for them in some cases faith and reason may appear to contradict each other and it is not always possible to resolve the conflict. Thus, the so-called theory of double truth became a feature often associated with Latin Averroism. Interestingly, for Averroes, reason and Muslim faith always agree.

For Siger, philosophy necessarily leads to conclusions such as that the world is eternal and the intellect is unique to mankind. Since the philosopher can approach the world only as already in existence and the question of becoming only as from something, reason affirms the eternity of the world and rejects creation out of nothing. Drawing from **Proclus** and Averroes, Siger notes that God may be understood as Creator, since as first cause He is the ultimate cause of the production of things. However, the Christian notion of creation (i.e., creation out of nothing and in time), is contradictory to philosophy and may be affirmed only as a miracle on the basis of faith. Siger's teaching on the intellect (also based on Averroes) implied a denial of individual afterlife, thus removing individual moral responsibility. To Siger, personal immortality can be held on the basis of faith alone. Another one of Siger's controversial positions concerns happiness. Unlike the theologians who understood true happiness as possible only through revelation, Siger as a philosopher (like Aristotle and his own contemporary, Boethius of Dacia) maintained that beatitude consisted primarily in the life of philosophic wisdom.

Influenced by **Étienne Tempier**'s first **condemnation** in 1270, as well as by opposing arguments such as Aquinas's, Siger became orthodox in later writings, although scholars disagree as to the extent of the actual change of his views. In 1277, Tempier launched a second, more comprehensive condemnation of 219 theological and philosophical propositions, the majority of which were Aristotelian-Averroistic and were associated with Siger, Boethius of Dacia, and other Averroists (although even some of Aquinas's Aristotelian theses were alluded to). This same year the chief **inquisitor** of France summoned Siger, but he had already left France. He was eventually acquitted of heresy by Pope Nicholas III, although he was kept under house arrest. He died tragically at Orvieto, murdered by his secretary. Among his chief works are *De aeternitate mundi* (*On the Eternity of the World*), *De anima intellectiva* (*On the Intellective Soul*), *Liber de felicitate* (*The Book on Happiness*), and *De necessitate et contingentia causarum* (*On the Necessity and Contingency of Causes*).

**SIGER OF COURTRAI (ca. 1283–1341).** Siger was a Parisian master of arts in 1309 and a master of theology at Paris in 1315. From 1308 to 1323, he was a canon of the Cathedral of Notre Dame in Courtrai. He is known especially for his *Grammatica Speculativa* (*Speculative Grammar*) and for expanding the scope of the *Perihermeneias* (*On Interpretation*) of **Aristotle** to a broader consideration, namely, extending modal propositions beyond the more traditional modes of necessary, contingent, possible, and impossible. He introduced research into other modal forms, due mainly to the influence of the ancient Greek commentator Ammonius, whose commentary on the *Perihermeneias* had recently been translated. In writing much of his *Perihermeneias* commentary, he follows **Thomas Aquinas**, whom he refers to as *Commentator* (the Commentator).

**SIMON OF FAVERSHAM (ca. 1245–1306).** Presumably born at Faversham in Kent around 1245, he appears to have trained in **theology** at Oxford. His *Questions on the Posterior Analytics* were disputed at Paris, and since they quote **Thomas Aquinas**'s *Commentary on the "Perihermeneias" of Aristotle*, Simon was probably there in the middle of the 1270s. He was a participant at the *vesperies*, or evening disputation that was part of a master's inception ceremony, of the **Franciscan** Peter of Baldeswell in 1301. He became chancellor of the university in 1304 and held that office until 1306. His extant writings are all works in philosophy, and for the most part in **logic**. Simon has left *Quaestiones* on all the logic treatises of **Aristotle**, as well as on **Porphyry**'s *Isagoge* (*Introduction*). He wrote a *Commentary on the "Summulae logicales"* of **Peter of Spain**. Among his nonlogic works are a number of *Dictata* (*Lessons*) on various treatises of natural philosophy that incorporate the positions of a host of ancient and medieval commentators, including Themistius, Alexander, **Avicenna**, **Averroes**, and **Ghazali**. These comments, however, seem to be derived from **Albert the Great** and Thomas Aquinas, not directly from the ancient and medieval commentators themselves. The main contemporary sources for his thought are Albert, Thomas, and **Giles of Rome**. In logic, he seems to derive help from **Peter of Auvergne**. Simon himself plays the role of the opponent in a number of the logical works of **Radulphus Brito**.

**SIMON OF HINTON (ca. 1210–1262).** Simon received his bachelor's degree at Oxford in 1239. After the death of both **Robert Bacon** and **Richard Fishacre** in 1248, he became the regent master at the **Dominican** *studium* (house of studies) in Oxford, a position he held probably until 1254, when he was elected provincial of the English Dominicans. He held this title until 1261, when he and his whole *definitorium* (provincial council) were deposed by a general chapter of the Dominicans for refusing to accept foreign students at Oxford. Simon was deposed in 1261 and was sent to the *studium generale* (international house of studies) in Cologne, where he served as a successor to Albert the Great. He returned to England in 1262 and died in the same year. Simon is not known as a strong philosophical author, but more for his practical **theology**. He also wrote two commentaries on Scripture that survive, one on the Minor Prophets, the other on Matthew's Gospel. Quite likely he also wrote other Scriptural commentaries for beginners, one on Job and another on the whole of the Old Testament, not including the Psalms. His most widely accepted work, however, was his *Summa iuniorum* (*Summa for the Young*), written between 1250 and 1260 and dealing with the articles of the Creed, the Ten Commandments, the petitions of the Lord's Prayer, the sacraments, the virtues, the gifts of the Holy Spirit, and the principal vices.

**SIMON OF TOURNAI (ca. 1130–ca. 1201).** Simon is one of the first theologians at Paris who benefited from new Latin translations of Greek and Arabic learning (notably those from the Arabic of **Aristotle**'s *Physics*, *Metaphysics*, and *De anima*). Thus he stands at the beginning of that seminal encounter with Aristotle that was to transform Christian theology in the **Scholastic** period. Before teaching theology, he taught the **liberal arts** for about 10 years and distinguished himself in **dialectics**, thereafter applying it enthusiastically in **theology** after the manner of **Peter Abelard** and **Gilbert of Poitiers**. His works include *Disputationes* (*Disputations*), *Expositio super Symbolum* (*Exposition on the Creed*), *Expositio Symboli S. Athanasii* (*Exposition on the Athanasian Creed*), and *Institutiones in sacram paginam* (*Introduction to Sacred Scripture*). The precise historical significance of his work is still to be established.

**SIN.** In Judaism and **Islam**, sin is essentially a breach of God's **law** for mankind, either by omission or by commission. This law was first established through God's covenant with Abraham and then developed in the (different) legal traditions of Judaism and Islam. This concept of sin as the breach of covenantal law is also true in Christianity, although the Christian doctrine of **original sin** as mankind's inherited guilt for the sin of its first parents adds a different dimension to the Christian understanding of sin. The three traditions stress man's free will to obey or disobey God's commands; on the basis of free will, man is held accountable for his actions. In the three traditions, there are also different categories and degrees of sin, with concomitant punishments. In medieval **ethics**, religious tradition and philosophy inform discussions on sin.

**SINA, IBN.** *See* AVICENNA (980–1037).

**SOLOMON BEN ISAAC (RASHI) (ca. 1040–1105).** Rashi, as he is commonly known, was a native of Troyes, France. After studying at the rabbinical academies of Worms and Mainz, he returned to his native city and dedicated his life to writing commentaries on the Talmud and the Bible. Known for his lucid, profound, and erudite **exegesis**, his commentaries have become standard companions to these religious texts and have themselves generated various super-commentaries. Even though his interpretations are not without critics, his writings remain an essential part of contemporary Talmudic and biblical scholarship. His extensive work was left unfinished and completed by his scribe and grandson, Samuel ben Meir. His commentaries have flourished over the centuries in the liturgical role they play in the world's synagogues on the Sabbath, throughout the whole year. Rashi's biblical commentaries were also influential on Christian exegesis, especially through the commentaries of **Nicholas of Lyra**. *See also* EXEGESIS.

**SOLOMON BEN JUDAH IBN GABIROL.** *See* AVICEBRON.

**SOUL.** For the most part, medieval accounts of the soul, the principle of life, were generally either **Platonic** or **Aristotelian**. To medieval thinkers, Plato saw the soul as a complete and individual entity, by nature immortal, which rules the **body** (as may be gathered, e.g., from Plato's *Phaedo*). Aristotle, on the other hand, describes it as a form or principle of actualization inseparable from the body it actualizes, although in the case of the human soul he speaks of the intellect as in a sense incorruptible (*De anima* III, 5). Although Aristotle's discussion of the immortal part of the soul is one of his most obscure passages, his meaning is most likely that the intellect is universally, not individually, immortal, since to him individuality is proper to the composite of matter (body) and form (soul), which is perishable.

Neither of these two accounts, however, strictly on their own, was satisfactory to the vast majority of medieval thinkers, who sought to account for the soul in the context of revelation, namely as something created and able to be either saved or destroyed by an all-powerful God. Accordingly, even though thinkers generally favored at a fundamental level either the Platonic or the Aristotelian approach, these approaches were often combined with each other and with revelation. Those who fundamentally followed the Platonic account revised this account to show how the soul is dependent on God and not by nature immortal. Those who fundamentally followed the Aristotelian account revised this account to show how the soul is not by nature individually mortal but rather is capable of individual immortality through God. **Averroes** and those who followed him in conceiving of immortality in terms of the absorption of the human intellect into one universal intellect (i.e., **monophychism**) are important exceptions to the medieval Aristotelian attitude. The approach to other issues regarding the soul, such as knowledge, **freedom** of the will, sense perception, and the unity between soul and body and among the levels of soul (i.e., nutritive, sentient, etc.), generally flowed from a thinker's attitude in regard to the Aristotelian and Platonic conceptions of the nature of the soul in light of revelation. Moreover, since the soul organizes the body, medieval accounts of the body generally depend on accounts of the soul.

**SPINOZA, BARUCH (1632–1677).** A native of Amsterdam, Spinoza still grappled with some of the problems that occupied medieval Jewish philosophers, notably the interpretation of Scripture in light of philosophy. In this regard, he may be seen as embodying the transition from medieval to modern Jewish philosophy. Some of his doctrines were considered radical and caused his excommunication from his Jewish community, such as his rejection of the traditional notion of divine providence and the immortality of the soul. His work, however, exerted profound influence in modern philosophy, for instance in the work of G. W. F. Hegel, and continues to hold a very important place in the history of philosophy. Refer to the introduction, "Modern Criticisms of Medieval Philosophy and Theology."

**STOICISM (IN THE MIDDLE AGES).** Stoic teachings, in the forms passed down by the **Fathers of the Church** and received by medieval authors, were almost exclusively focused on their ethical writings. These *dicta* were drawn from Epictetus, Seneca, and **Cicero**, or from their doctrines as reported by Varro. The *Moralium dogma philosophorum* (*The Teachings of* *the Moral Philosophers*), a florilegium of citations taken from Cicero, from Seneca, and from Christian adaptations of Stoic teachings found especially in the writings of St. Ambrose and St. **Augustine**, was most likely gathered together by **William of Conches**. This collection, along with many of the works of Cicero and Seneca themselves, provided the core Stoic moral philosophy for medieval writers. Many of these moral and political aphorisms were employed in the ***Commentaries on the Sentences*** of **Peter Lombard** produced in the mid-13th century and much less in later commentaries. Commentaries on Aristotle's *Nicomachean Ethics* continued to cite them, but to a lesser degree and generally in a manner subordinated to Aristotle's moral teachings.

**STRODE, RALPH (fl. 2ND HALF OF 14TH CENTURY).** Little is known about the life of this English **theologian** and philosopher. His most important writings are treatises from a logical collection, known as his *Logica*, which he prepared as a textbook for students. The logical treatises *Consequentiae* and *Obligationes* were his most influential works. They formed part of the curriculum at various **universities** and were published in several Renaissance editions. **John Wycliffe**, Strode's contemporary at Oxford, wrote a response to his criticisms, *Responsiones ad Radulphum Strodum* (*Responses to Ralph Strode*), where some of Strode's theological positions may be gathered (e.g., against predestination), though the context demands cautious interpretation. Geoffrey Chaucer dedicated his *Troylus and Cryseyde* to Strode, apparently his friend, and to the poet John Gower.

***STUDIUM GENERALE.*** Different religious **orders** had their houses of study. Some of these houses were for members of their own particular province, as was the *studium* in London or Newcastle, for the **Franciscans**. Other houses of study were international, attracting students from the various provinces of the particular order. Paris, Oxford, and Cologne had such general houses of study. A general *studium* was part of a **university**, which was a community of masters and students. A provincial *studium* was more like a **school** with a master. A *studium generale* was part of a university where there was a collection of masters with different viewpoints.

**SUÁREZ, FRANCISCO (1548–1617).** He joined the Society of Jesus in Salamanca in 1564 and studied philosophy and **theology** there until 1571 and was ordained a priest the next year. His teaching career began in Avila and Segovia, in both places teaching philosophy from 1571 to 1574 and theology from 1574 to 1580. From 1580 to 1585 he taught at the Collegio Romano and then returned to Spain, teaching first at Alcalá (1585–1593) and then at

Salamanca (1583–1597). In 1597, he received his doctorate in theology and was appointed to the chair of theology at Coimbra, a position he held until 1615.

Suárez's writings are extensive and have had wide distribution—printed in Lyons, Mainz, Cologne, and Geneva before the 23-volume edition of Venice in 1747 and the 28-volume edition of Paris in 1856. While at Alcalá and Salamanca, he wrote large commentaries on **Thomas Aquinas**'s *Summa theologiae*. In Coimbra, he wrote extensive works: *De religione* (*On Religion*), *De gratia* (*On Grace*), and *De legibus* (*On Laws*). Realizing he could not continue these long exposés, he adopted a more succinct style for his *On the Triune God*, *On Faith, Hope, and Charity*, and *On Our Ultimate End*. His commentaries on **Aristotle**'s *Organon* and *Physics*, parts of the regular routine of teaching philosophy for Jesuits at that time, have never been found. However, his *Metaphysical Disputations* well illustrate his strong grasp and reworking of the themes of his Scholastic predecessors. He had a wide acceptance in the newly thriving Jesuit system of education (*ratio studiorum*) and influenced some of its renowned students, such as René Descartes at La Flèche.

**SUBSTANCE.** *See* ACCIDENT.

**SUFISM.** (Arabic: *tasawwuf.*) The term *Sufism*, which refers to the **mysticism** of **Islam**, is etymologically derived from *sufi* (one wears a woolen robe or *suf*), apparently because wearing wool was part of early ascetic practices. Groups of mystics began to appear in the ninth century, when they were first designated as Sufis. It was not until later, however, beginning with Al-Qushiari (d. 1072), that Sufism developed a more systematic formulation of its approach to the search for God. In general terms, Islamic mysticism aims at the experience of personal union with Allah, who, according to the **Koran**, is unlike anything else and absolutely one. This experience consists in knowledge and is the product of illumination. Allah's uniqueness implies transcendence, and so union with Him remains at the psychic level. To achieve their goal, Sufis follow a path or discipline of mystical devotion, consisting of an ascending order of teachings, techniques, and initiations; the last stage is that of an adept. Basic to Sufism is the general idea or belief, also common in the **Neoplatonic** tradition, that God is the source of all and that all aim at its source, its true home and beatitude. In fact, for its formulations, Sufism drew significantly from philosophy or *falsafah*. Mystical life and practices are meant to facilitate the **soul**'s search for God. Though there are differences among Sufi writers, the emptying of consciousness of all but God, moral transformation, and the intuitive vision of God and of God in all things are generally part of Sufism.

Some of the important contributors to medieval Sufi writing are Al-Junayd (d. ca. 910), Ibn al-'Arabi (1165–1240), Al-Farid (1181–1235), **Al-Ghazali**, and the 13th-century Persian poets Rumi (d. 1273), Sa'di (d. ca. 1292), and Hafiz (d. ca. 1388). In the case of some Sufi thinkers, stress on union with God became controversial in that it appeared inconsistent with the orthodox view of God's absolute transcendence. In 922, the Persian Al-Hallaj's utterance "I am The Real" earned him execution. Also controversial was Sufism's insight independent of revelation. Al-Ghazali, the great exponent of *kalam* and critic of *falsafah*, sought to reconcile Sufism with orthodoxy by accentuating, among other things, the contingency and dependence of creation, as well as the way in which mystical knowledge is already contained in revelation.

**SUMMA AND *SUMMULA*.** For medieval philosophers and theologians, the term *summa*, and its diminutive *summula*, had a number of meanings. At times, it might point simply to a compilation or collection of *quaestiones* that had some kind of unity, whether from the same author, connected with a particular text, or treating the same subject matter. It might, however, also signify an abbreviation of a text. It could likewise, and with a more elevated meaning, indicate an organized treatise centered on one theme or one subject. That the word *summa* did not necessarily mean an abbreviation or a short treatise becomes evident when we look at a work called a *brevis summa* (brief summa), as we do in the case of **William of Ockham**'s *Brevis summa libri Physicorum* (*A Brief Summa of the Book of the Physics*). As a "brief summa," it is a much shorter treatise than Ockham's *Expositio in libros Physicorum* (*Exposition on the Book of the Physics*) and much more compact than his incomplete *Summula philosophiae naturalis* (*Summula of Natural Philosophy*).

Certainly, Ockham's *Summa logicae* (*Summa of Logic*) is not a short or abbreviated work. It is a more unified work than **Peter of Spain**'s *Summulae logicales*, which appears to be more of a compilation or collection of different treatises on various logical issues. The most famous summa is the *Summa theologiae* of **Thomas Aquinas**, which is a summa in its highest form. It is a well-organized treatise for beginning students in the Theology Faculty on all the themes of **theology**, placed in an order that attempts as well as possible to approach the divine order of knowledge. In his explanation of the need for such a work, Aquinas criticizes the ***Sentences*** *of* **Peter Lombard** for its lack of a proper theological order, since the *Sentences* has repetitious questions and has questions organized at times by the order found in the Scriptures rather than in a logical order. For Aquinas, *summa* in this case expresses a methodological ideal: a unified body of knowledge that puts all its contents in the place of importance that each deserves and in a proper relation to each other.

**SUSO, HEINRICH (1303–1366).** This German mystic was born in Constance and entered the **Dominicans** there at an early age. He did his philosophical and **theological** studies in Constance before going to the *studium generale* of the Dominicans in Cologne, where along with **Johannes Tauler** he studied under **Meister Eckhart** from 1324 to 1327. Suso returned to Constance, where he became a **lector**, but in the early 1330s he was removed from teaching. He was elected prior of the Dominican priory in Dissenhofen in 1343, where he stayed until he retired to the Dominican house in Ulm in 1348. It was in Ulm that he died. He was beatified by Pope Gregory XVI in 1831.

Although he was known to have given a scholarly defense of Eckhart, Suso is better known for his mystical writings. He wrote his *Little Book on Truth* in German while in Cologne. It is a work aimed at a high spiritual level and also marked by a strong accent on asceticism and an equally strong opposition to the pantheistic tendencies in the Beghards and antinomianism of the Brethren of the Free Spirit. In 1328, back in Constance, he wrote, also in German, *The Little Book on Eternal Truth*, a guidebook for ordinary people with faults, noteworthy for its tempered asceticism and emphasis on detachment as the key to a richer spiritual life. This work he expanded and extended appreciably in 1334 under the Latin title *Horologium sapientiae* (*Wisdom's Watch upon the Hours*). His *Life of the Servant* is an autobiographical account of his spiritual journey, recounted to one of his spiritual charges and not meant for publication. Suso, like Johannes Tauler, worked with the religious movement Friends of God, which began in Basle around 1340 to promote religious life among all Catholics. Known as a preacher, Heinrich Suso really had his greatest impact on the restoration of religious discipline in convents through involvement in this movement and also in his spiritual direction of individuals at all level of society. His various books had enormous influence on the spiritual lives of many in the 14th and 15th centuries and thereafter.

**SUTTON, THOMAS.** *See* THOMAS SUTTON (ca. 1250–ca. 1315).

**SWINESHEAD.** *See* RICHARD SWINESHEAD (fl. ca. 1344–1354).

# T

**TALMUD.** *See* TORAH.

**TAULER, JOHANNES (1300–1361).** Tauler was a **Dominican** who entered the order in Strasbourg in 1315. **Meister Eckhart** had been lecturing there since 1312. Johannes followed him to Cologne around 1324 and was joined there by **Heinrich Suso** as a fellow student. Both were heavily influenced by Eckhart. It was at the *studium generale* (international house of studies) of the Dominicans in Cologne in 1326 that Eckhart was accused of heresy, so both Johannes and Henry lived through the experience of a master who went through an agonizing time. Eckhart died a year later, after submitting to the Holy See. Certain of his propositions, however, were condemned shortly after his death by Pope John XXII.

This troublesome experience is not visible in the writings of Tauler. Tauler's sermons, simple and direct, were usually delivered to Dominican nuns in the Rhineland. They have a commonsense character to them, urging the proper blend of the contemplative and the active life. In the life of activity he praises those who spend what they have received in prayer and silence. He is certainly critical of those who are overly anxious, but, in contrast to the Brethren of the Common Life, he encourages the activity that reveals the riches given by God in the quiet of contemplation. He also preached a welcoming attitude toward suffering, encouraging his audience to join their sufferings to the suffering of Christ, thereby helping him to carry his cross to Calgary.

**TEMPIER, ÉTIENNE (d. 1279).** A native of Orléans, Tempier became chancellor of the University of Paris in 1263 and bishop of Paris in 1268. He is best known for his **condemnations** in 1270 and 1277 of philosophical propositions being debated at the **university**. Certain **Aristotelian** and **Averroist** tenets had come to be seen by many as incompatible with Christian doctrine. Already in 1210, 1215, and 1231 the teaching of certain Aristotelian works had been prohibited by the bishop, the cardinal, and the pope, respectively. **William of Auvergne** before 1240 criticized Aristotle and Avicenna on a number of points. In 1267, **Bonaventure** in the same vein protested against **Averroists**. Tempier, in 10 December 1270, condemned 13 propositions, most of which explicitly or implicitly espoused monopsychism (the doctrine that there is one intellect for all humans), the necessity of events, the eternity of the world, and limitations on God's power. Paris was the leading theological center in Christendom, and thus developments at the **university** were very important to the new pope, John XXI (elected in 1276), who had taught at Paris and, as **Peter of Spain**, had written an important **logic** textbook.

Tempier's great condemnation took place on 7 March 1277, when he condemned 219 propositions. (Soon thereafter the **Dominican** friar **Robert Kilwardby**, archbishop of Canterbury and former theologian at Paris, condemned 30 propositions.) Most of the propositions were associated with doctrines held by masters and students at the Arts Faculty, such as **Siger of Brabant** and **Boethius of Dacia**, and were reflective of the influence of Aristotle and **Averroes**, in regard to, for example, the role of philosophy, the eternity of the world, necessity in regard to God's act of creation, and the unity of intellect. Some doctrines held by **Thomas Aquinas**, mainly on individuation by matter and on the relation between the intellect and the will, were also included (though these propositions as Thomas understood them were removed from the list after his canonization in 1325). For Thomas's disciple **Giles of Rome**, the condemnation meant an eight-year suspension from the university. **Henry of Ghent** played an important role in drafting certain propositions, even ones associated with Aquinas, mainly individuation by matter and the relation of intellect and will.

This great condemnation had a profound influence on the development of medieval thought, but its full significance is still being debated. It is certainly a significant landmark in the developing relation between **Augustinianism** and Aristotelianism in Christian thought. Although the condemnation seems to point to the victory of the former over the latter, Aristotle continued to flourish thereafter, even among Augustinians, who ever more critically appropriated and used Aristotle within their theologies. The condemnation ushered in a much more critical period of synthesis and analysis. Its influence is seen in later writings, which refer to the condemned propositions as the "Parisian articles." Refer to appendix 2.

**THEOLOGY.** The term *theology* in the Latin West was set aside by **St. Augustine** in his *De civitate Dei* (*City of God*), since he criticized the association it had in the ancient world. Varro had spoken of three types of theology: one portraying the gods of the poets, a second defending the gods of the philosophers, and a third supporting the gods of the city. Since Christians rejected each of these senses of *theology*, Augustine avoided the expression. **Peter Abelard** resurrected the term in the 12th century and gave it a Christian understanding as he referred to the study of a number of Christian truths as "our theology." Around the same time, **Hugh of Saint-Victor** mentions "theology" and explains the meaning of its nominal definition. A major change took place in the mid-13th century when Christian teachers realized that Aristotle had spoken of his first philosophy or **metaphysics** as "theological." They took up the challenge to produce a Christian version of the primary science and likewise called it theology.

The meanings of the word *theology* vary among the different medieval Latin authors. For them, *theology* sometimes is a synonym for "sacred Scripture"; at other times, it means some form of logically ordered study of all things as the Scriptures represent them. In its ideal, theology attempts to see all reality according to the way God sees it and has revealed it to men in the sacred Scriptures. The prologues of all the *Commentaries on the Sentences* and *Summae theologiae* try to describe their author's view of what exactly theology is and does.

**THIERRY OF CHARTRES (ca. 1100–ca. 1155).** Possibly a brother of **Bernard of Chartres**, this **theologian**, learned in **liberal arts** (most of the philosophy and science at the time), first taught at Chartres and then at Paris (where **John Salisbury** and **Clarembald of Arras** studied under him) before succeeding **Gilbert of Poitiers** in 1141 as chancellor of Chartres. A native of Brittany, he possibly participated in 1121 at the Council of Soissons, which condemned **Peter Abelard**, in which case he would be the Thierry mentioned in Abelard's *History of My Calamities*. He participated in the Council of Rheims in 1148, which deemed heretical certain **Trinitarian** views of his predecessor Gilbert, and served as archdeacon at Dreux. In a **Platonic** vein, he speaks of God as the transcendent, simple One or Unity, from which all beings derive their formal unity. He also ascribes to the human soul an intellectual capacity for a direct **mystical** vision of God.

Aside from his wide recognition among contemporaries as a prominent Platonist and liberal arts master, Thierry's fame in intellectual history comes primarily from his original use of the arts and **science** in **theology**. Drawing from Chalcidius's translation of **Plato**'s *Timaeus*, his *Tractatus de sex dierum operibus (Treatise on the Works of the Six Days of Creation)* uses mathematics to prove God's existence and triune nature and provides a physical interpretation of the literal text of Genesis that originally relies on mechanistic explanations of motion. This mechanism is noteworthy considering his ignorance of **Aristotle**'s *Physics*. His other works include glosses on **Boethius**'s theological works and on Cicero's *De inventione (On Rhetoric)*, and his *Heptateuchus (Seven Branches of the Mathematical Arts)*, a work that discusses the liberal arts as the only path to wisdom.

**THOMAS AQUINAS (1225–1274).** The most famous of the medieval Christian philosophers and theologians, Aquinas was born into a noble family in Rocca Secca in the kingdom of Naples around 1225. He began his education at the Benedictine monastery of Monte Cassino, but the abbot soon decided that he was worthy of higher challenges and sent him to the new University of Naples in 1226. He studied the **liberal arts** there under Peter of Ireland, and sometime between 1240 and 1243 he joined the **Dominicans**. His family was unhappy with this decision and kept him from following this vocation by incarcerating him for a time, but they finally relented and allowed him to go to Rome and then to Cologne, where in 1244 or 1245 he began his studies with **Albert the Great**. In 1245, Thomas went with Albert to Paris, staying there with him until both returned to the new *studium generale* (international house of studies) at Cologne in 1248. In the early 1250s, he was ordained a priest and also commented on the *Sentences* of **Peter Lombard**. Because of turmoil at the University of Paris, he was not able to become regent master until 1257. His whole life was dedicated to teaching and writing, giving his services at various Dominican *studia*: Anagni, Rome, Bologna, Orvieto, Perugia, Paris, and Naples. He died on his way to the Council of Lyons in 1274.

The number and diversity of Aquinas's writings is very impressive. His commentaries on the works of **Aristotle** reveal an extensive and deep understanding of the **logical** treatises, such as the *Perihermeneias* (*On Interpretation*) and the chief work dealing with the nature of science, the *Posterior Analytics*. In regard to the more properly philosophical works, he studied both the theoretical and practical aspects of Aristotle's philosophy. In the theoretical realm, he commented in detail on the *Physics*, *On the Heavens*, *On Meteorology*, and the *Metaphysics*. In the practical areas of Aristotle's philosophy, he wrote a lengthy commentary on the *Nicomachean Ethics* and on the first part of the *Politics*. He spoke in such depth and detail in his Aristotelian commentaries that he was not able to finish some of them, and they had to be completed by others, as was the case, for example, with the *Politics*, which was completed by **Peter of Auvergne**.

Thomas also left behind a large collection of Scripture commentaries: a long *Literal Commentary on Job* and lectures on the Gospel of John and on many Pauline epistles (Ephesians, Galatians, Hebrews, Philippians, and Thessalonians). He also gathered an extensive *Catena aurea*: a commentary on the four Gospels collected from the works of the **Fathers of the Church**. His basic portrait of **theology** can be found in his *Compendium theologiae* (*Compendium of Theology*), but it is little more than an outline in comparison to his two summae: the *Summa theologiae* (*Summa of Theology*) and his *Summa contra Gentiles* (*On the Truth of the Catholic Faith*). The *Summa theologiae* is his substitute for a commentary on the *Sentences* of Peter Lombard. Thomas, in fact, wrote a *Commentary on the Sentences* and even tried to do so a second time. He gave up, finding Peter Lombard's work repetitious, not well ordered enough, and plagued by a series of useless questions. As a master, Aquinas debated in 12 *Quodlibet* disputations and in an impressive number of specific *Disputed Questions*: *On Virtues*, *On Truth*, *On God's Power*, *On Evil*, *On Spiritual Creatures*, *On the Incarnate Word*, *On Hope*, and *On Fraternal Correction*. He also wrote commentaries on two of **Boethius**'s theological tractates: *On the Hebdomads* and *On the Trinity*. In addition, he produced a collection of smaller philosophical and theological treatises, sermons, and letters.

Aquinas took philosophy more seriously than anyone else, even more seriously than the Averroists. When he argued with them, his main point was that philosophy is not knowing what Aristotle or Averroes said. Philosophy is using reason to know the way things are. It is not principally a study of texts; it is a study of reality. As he dealt with some of the main concerns in the **Arts Faculty**, the eternity of the world or the unicity of the intellect, Thomas was not satisfied to say that a philosophical authority was wrong. He made the effort to show why, on his own terms of using reason alone, he was wrong, if it was possible to do so. At times, he might admit that he could not prove philosophically that a position contrary to the revelation of Scripture was wrong. Yet, his philosophical efforts bore fruit. He made the radical or Averroistic Aristotelian, Siger of Brabant, on philosophical grounds change his position, especially in regard to the unicity of the intellect. Thomas's philosophical positions also got him into difficulties with Church authorities, as can be seen when some of the 219 propositions included in the **condemnation of 1277** are examined. Some propositions that relate to him are also included.

In theology, Aquinas's *Summa theologiae* is considered one of the great treatises in the history of Christian theology. He attempted in this work to make the human effort to try to see things theologically, that is, according to the divine order of reality. That is why he speaks of theology as a subordinated science, an ideal portrayal of reality achieved in subordination to God's knowledge and revelation, and an ideal that is fulfilled only in the enjoyment experienced in the vision of the blessed. For Aquinas, the great synthetic work of Peter Lombard, for all its achievements, had fallen short: unimportant issues received more attention than they deserved, and the ordering at times seemed subordinated to the contingent order of the individual passages of Scripture rather than to the wisdom of God revealed in its whole message.

In organizing a science of theology, that is, trying to map out what we can know of God and His relation to everything else, Thomas had to find a starting point or set of principles for his science. He found them in the Church's digest of the main points of the teaching of the Scriptures, in the Creed. Beginning with the Creed, which provided him with the principal points of God's revelation, he could go, and actually did go, in two directions. He could draw out or deduce further specific teachings of the Scriptures. He could also focus on the articles of the Creed themselves and try to bring a deeper understanding to these main truths of the Christian faith.

In the first approach, that of deductive theology, he was effectively attempting to show how all the elements of theology, the principles and the further conclusions, held together or formed a cohesive unit. Such an effort was the human attempt to see God's order of things. The second procedure, declarative theology, centered attention principally on the articles of the faith and tried to bring a clearer understanding of them. A theologian, like Thomas, could do this by focusing on the doctrine of the **Trinity**, for example, and with the help of the Scriptures and the Fathers of the Church attempt to find the language that best expresses this doctrine of three persons in the one God. The traditional Patristic language spoke of persons and essence. What is meant by *person*? Do we have a definition of *person* that can be applied to God? What is that definition? Is it a good one, or can we get one that brings better understanding? The same holds for *essence*. How is the essence of a person different from what makes a person a person?

In trying to bring understanding to an article of the faith such as the Trinity, Thomas could and did look at the long tradition of theological attempts to bring understanding. He could search Patristic works for analogies that might help. There are many books on the Trinity: the *De Trinitate* of St. Ambrose, the *De Trinitate* of **St. Augustine**, the *De Trinitate* of Boethius, and the *De Trinitate* of **Richard of Saint-Victor**. Which of these works presents the best analogies that might help us understand somewhat this mystery of the faith?

Another source for bringing understanding that Aquinas used to great positive effect was the examination of **heresies**. At first sight, heresies might seem to provide negative feedback, but this is far from the case. The defenses against heresies in the Christian tradition have been a great positive source for understanding, since often in refuting heresies, the Fathers of the Church had to explain why the heretical position was wrong. Aquinas especially shows the positive understanding that comes from defending the faith against heresies in his *Lectures on the Gospel of John* and the *Catena aurea*, where he examines all the heresies related to the Trinity and the Incarnation of Christ as the Son of God.

In developing his theological treatises, Aquinas in his deductive theology is following the course the Church has followed in making the basic truths of the Christian faith more explicit by deducing or leading out what is implicit in the Scriptures and earlier Church credal statements. In practicing declarative theology, he followed the lead of St. Augustine, who in the opening chapter of Book XIV of the *De Trinitate* urged Christians to pursue the kind of knowledge by which "our most wholesome faith . . . is begotten, nourished, strengthened and defended." *See also* ORDERS (RELIGIOUS).

**THOMAS BRADWARDINE.** *See* BRADWARDINE, THOMAS (ca. 1290–1349).

**THOMAS GALLUS (ca. 1200–1246).** Thomas became a **Canon Regular of St. Augustine** at the monastery of Saint-Victor and later assisted in the founding of the Victorine abbey and hospital of Saint-Andrea in Vercelli. He became its first prior and later its first abbot. Most of his writings were done there. His writings are well cataloged, since he provides very helpful information in them that allows for their dating and place of composition. His *Commentary on Isaiah* was completed at Saint-Victor in 1218. A bit earlier he had already made a chart providing the divisions and subdivisions of the works of **Dionysius the Pseudo-Areopagite**, so he had even at this early time a basic sense of how he would write his commentaries on the Scriptures and on the Dionysian corpus. His commentaries on the Song of Songs stretched out over most of his adult life. The first, now lost, was completed at Vercelli around 1224. A second, incomplete, commentary was done either at Vercelli or when he was visiting Chesterton in England in 1237–1238. The third commentary was done while he was in exile in Ivrée in 1243.

While at Vercelli in 1224, Thomas followed up on the outlines he had made of Dionysius's works with short glosses on two of them, the *Celestial Hierarchy* and *Mystical Theology*. Next he made *Extractiones* (*Extracts*) of all of Dionysius's works. These extracts were not paraphrases, commentaries, or translations properly speaking; they provided a more understandable text than the ones offered by the translations of Saracen or **John Scotus Eriugena** by abridging the text, giving a short paraphrase, or leaving aside secondary ideas. Some medievals, for example, **Francis of Meyronnes**, treated these extracts as though they were a new translation. Thomas also made in his later years (1241–1244) *Expositions* or *Explanations* of all four works of Dionysius: *Mystical Theology*, *Divine Names*, *Angelic* or *Celestial Hierarchy*, and *Ecclesiastical Hierarchy*. In these grand-scale commentaries, he explains each word or expression in a few lines, supporting his explanation with citations from the Scriptures and other Dionysian works. Thomas's purpose in all his treatises is to fulfill the words of the prophet Jeremiah (9:24): "Let him who will glory glory in this: to come to a knowledge of (*scire*) and really to know (*nosse*) me." For Gallus, we come to a knowledge of (*scire*) God when we know God through the contemplation of creatures, or the teachings of men, or personal reflection of a rational or intellectual kind. This is the kind of divine knowledge gained by the philosophers. But we come really to know (*nosse*) God when we know Him in a way that is incomparably deeper. This is a knowledge that he describes as supra-intellectual, in that it is associated with *affectus* and thus transcends the philosophical intellect in the way that the philosophical intellect transcends reason and reason transcends imagination. *See also* ORDERS (RELIGIOUS).

**THOMAS OF ERFURT (fl. ca. 1300).** Like the earlier **Martin of Dacia**, Thomas is one of the principal authors of speculative grammar. Grammar was taught at a different level in the Arts Faculty than in pre-university courses. In the **Arts Faculty**, one studied Priscian's *Institutiones grammaticae* (*Grammatical Foundations*), but, as in other fields such as logic or dialectics, from a careful reading or *lectio*, questions developed. Later, at a more advanced level, disputations regarding the issues raised by the questions followed. These methodical developments led in the area of grammar to treatises called *De modis significandi* (*On the Modes of Signifying*). Among the best-known treatises of this kind are the works of Martin of Dacia and Thomas of Erfurt (whose treatise was long published under the works of John Duns Scotus). Thomas's work was probably written at Paris around the end of the 13th century. Eventually, these university materials were digested and were filtered down into the pre-university grammar courses. A text that shows this is John of Cornwall's *Speculum* (*Mirror*), whose technical terminology seems to depend more on Thomas of Erfurt than Martin of Dacia.

**THOMAS OF STRASBOURG (ca. 1275–1357).** Thomas had already completed his **liberal arts** and **theology** studies when he joined the **Hermits of St. Augustine**. We know he taught at Strasbourg from about 1330 to 1345. His *Commentary on the Sentences*, the first by an Augustinian on all four books of the *Sentences*, probably dates from 1335–1337. He was elected general prior in 1345 and held this office until his death in 1357. Thomas still followed the tradition of his fellow Augustinian Hermit **Giles of Rome**, staying close to the teachings of **Thomas Aquinas**. Later Augustinian Hermits, for example, **Gregory of Rimini**, pursued a new direction, more related to Oxford theology.

**THOMAS OF YORK (ca. 1210–ca. 1260).** Prior to his appointment as the sixth master of the **Franciscan** *studium* at Cambridge, Thomas was master in theology at Oxford from 1253 to 1256. Concerning central issues, such as his theory of knowledge and the relation between philosophy and **theology**, he follows the **Augustinian** tradition of **Bonaventure** rather than **Thomas Aquinas**'s **Aristotelianism**. However, his style is rather synthetic and conciliatory, as reflected by his encyclopedic work *Sapientiale* (*A Wisdom Collection*), which is made up of seven books. It carefully recognizes a great variety of sources from philosophical and theological traditions, including Jewish and Islamic ones, and tends to bring them together harmoniously in relation to different questions. If *Manus quae contra omnipotentem* (*The Hand Raised against the Omnipotent God*) is correctly attributed to Thomas, he wrote in favor of the mendicant **orders** against seculars, such as **William of St. Amour**.

**THOMAS SUTTON (ca. 1250–ca. 1315).** Thomas was born near Lincoln. He was a *socius* at Merton College, and his study of the **liberal arts** gave him a predilection for a pure **Aristotle**. He was ordained a deacon by Walter Giffard, the bishop of York, in 1274. In 1282, he joined the **Dominicans** and incepted as regent master about 1285. He was a master of **theology** from around 1290 until about 1300, but there are signs that he was still teaching up to 1315. He was considered very Thomistic in his teachings, and some of his writings were so close in their teachings to the positions of **Thomas Aquinas** that they were considered to be authentic works of Aquinas himself. Sutton was an early defender of Aquinas, especially concerning metaphysics and epistemology, against the alternative projects of **Henry of Ghent** and **Duns Scotus**. He defended the doctrine, held by Aquinas, that there is only one substantial form in composite beings in his treatises *Contra pluralitatem formarum* (*Against the Plurality of Forms*) and *De productione formae substantiarum* (*On the Production of the Form of Substances*), and in his question *Utrum forma fiat ex aliquo* (*Whether the Form Comes into Existence from Something*). Among other works, he completed some of Aquinas's commentaries on Aristotle, namely his *Perihermenias* (*On Interpretation*), *De generatione et corruptione* (*On Generation and Corruption*), and *Quaestiones super librum sextum metaphysicorum* (*Questions on Book VI of the Metaphysics*). In addition, he composed four *Quodlibets* and 36 disputed questions. His first two *Quodlibets* are dated after 1287, since they quote certain later works of Henry of Ghent. His references to Duns Scotus place his last two *Quodlibets* and questions 27–35 of his disputed questions in the early 14th century.

**THOMAS WYLTON (WILTON) (ca. 1265–1327).** This secular priest received his master of arts at Oxford and was a fellow of Merton College from 1288 to 1301. He was granted permission to study **theology** in England or elsewhere in 1304. He chose Paris, since we know that he taught as a bachelor of theology at Paris in 1311. Thomas was master of theology there from 1312 to 1322 and counted **Walter Burley** as one of his students. Burley is also an author with whom he often argued. Very independent in his thinking, Wylton was at times influenced by **John Duns Scotus**. This is especially noticeable in his *Quodlibet*, probably disputed around 1315, where he explains in a very detailed way Scotus's formal distinction in the context of his discussion of the divine attributes. He left Paris in 1322 to become chancellor of St. Paul's in London, a position he held until his death in 1327.

**THOMISM.** The term *Thomistic* might refer to a particular teaching of **Thomas Aquinas** or to the Thomistic school of philosophy and **theology** that is named after him. In the latter sense, *school* might be multiplied, since historians speak of the early Thomistic school at Oxford or the early Thomistic school of Paris. Some of Aquinas's philosophical and theological positions were attacked even in the 13th century. He was one of the focuses of the **condemnation of 1277** at Paris, which was extended to Oxford by **Robert Kilwardby**, himself a **Dominican** like Aquinas. However, Thomas was mostly attacked in Oxford by **Franciscans**. Among the early Thomists at Oxford were those who came to his defense: **Robert of Orford**, **Richard Knapwell**, and **Thomas Sutton**. Aquinas's chief opponent at Paris quite likely was **Henry of Ghent**. Early Parisian Thomists who attempted to respond to various challenges from Henry were **John of Paris** and **William Peter of Godino**. In the next generation, the leading Thomist was **Hervaeus Natalis**, who was the chief force in the effort to have Thomas canonized. More famous later Thomists were Ioannes Capreolus (d. 1444), called "the Prince of the Thomists"; Thomas de Vio or Cardinal Cajetan (d. 1534), renowned for his commentary on the *Summa theologiae*; and Sylvester of Ferrara (d. 1528), the famous commentator for the *Summa contra Gentiles*. The 20th century also had well-known Thomistic theologians, such as Reginald Garrigou-Lagrange, and respected historians of Thomistic philosophy, such as Étienne Gilson.

**TORAH.** As a term, *Torah* comes from the Hebrew root *yaroh*, which means "to teach." As an entity, the Torah is the sacred revelation of the Jews, their holy teaching. Though *Torah* is commonly translated as "law," the teaching of the Torah goes far beyond purely legal matters. According to the Jewish tradition, the prophet Moses received from God both the written law (the Pentateuch) and the oral law, passed on through the rabbinic tradition and viewed as necessary for the proper understanding of the written law. Thus, as a term, *Torah* can mean not only the Pentateuch but the whole Scriptural tradition. This includes the 24 books of the Hebrew Bible and their commentaries, as well as the oral legal tradition embodied in the Talmud. The Talmud includes the Mishnah, codified in the second century A.D., and the Gemara, which elaborates and comments on the Mishnah from the second to the sixth centuries. **Karaite** Jews, who rejected the rabbinic tradition and accepted only the written text of the Bible as authoritative, are the exception to those accepting this broader sense of the Torah.

**TRANSUBSTANTIATION.** *See* EUCHARIST.

**TRINITY (TRINITARIAN DOCTRINE).** The Trinity and the Incarnation constitute the two fundamental truths of Christianity. The central Christian teaching about God is that He is triune, and the traditional formula is one God in three persons, the Father, the Son, and the Holy Spirit. Its basis is found in revelation, in both the Old and New Testaments, especially in St. John's Gospel and in the writings of St. Paul. The Trinity did not become an officially declared doctrine of the Church until the fourth century. Questions about the divinity of God's Word, incarnate in Jesus, and of God's Spirit prompted the Church to elaborate an official doctrine about God that also served as the criterion for **heresies**. **Sabellianism**, initiated by Sabellius in the third century, and **Arianism**, initiated by Arius (ca. 256–ca. 336), were then the two most significant heresies. Sabellianism asserted that the three persons are only modes or aspects of God, without being really distinct persons, while Arianism stated that the Father, who alone is God, is a different being from the creatures that come from him, the first creature being the Son.

In its first ecumenical council, the First Council of Nicaea (325), the Father and the Son were officially identified as God. The three persons were explicitly declared to be three divine persons in the creed of the First Council of Constantinople (381) (the "Nicene Creed"), after theological reflections by Athanasius and the Cappadocian Fathers, portraying them as distinct divine persons according to origin or procession. The Latin or Catholic Church's official *Filioque* doctrine, that the Holy Spirit proceeds from both the Father and the Son and not from the former only, as is taught by the Eastern Orthodox Church, was added to the Nicene Creed in the sixth century, chiefly due to **Augustine**'s influential teaching. The popes resisted the official inclusion of the *Filioque* until the 11th century, although Charlemagne wanted to impose it on the whole church as far back as the late eighth century.

Medieval Christian theologians provided accounts of the Trinity. Though they generally treated the Trinity as a revealed article of faith, not subject to demonstration, they still sought to clarify this belief, their central tenet about God. In so doing, they drew from the various areas of learning, especially philosophy. **Anselm**, **Peter Abelard**, **Peter Lombard**, and **Gilbert of Poitiers** are well known for their use of **dialectics** in Trinitarian speculation, while others distinguish themselves through their use of other branches of learning, particularly metaphysics. Some of the most elaborate philosophical treatments in medieval thought, which is fundamentally God oriented, are found in Trinitarian discussions. What follows is a brief statement of salient points in the tradition of Trinitarian speculation.

Medieval Christian thinkers generally agree with **Aristotle**'s view that God is essentially mind, thought thinking itself, and they stress that God's thinking also includes willing or love. However, they disagree with Aristotle because for them the First Cause is not merely a final cause of the world, but also an efficient cause, the Creator of the world. In turn, they agree with the father of **Neoplatonism**, Plotinus, who holds that God is the One from which all emanates. However, they disagree with Plotinus because for them the One is not beyond being but rather is the highest and transcendent being, and the One is *not absolutely* one, because the first emanations of the One, namely the Son and the Holy Spirit, are not transitive but immanent to the One.

Despite these disagreements with Plotinus, most Christian thinkers, some to a larger extent than others, have derived inspiration from the Neoplatonic tradition when speculating about the Trinity. For example, **Dionysius the Pseudo-Areopagite**, **Bonaventure**, **Richard of Saint-Victor**, and **Henry of Ghent** draw from **Plato**'s *Timaeus* and take it one step further. Whereas Plato describes the Good as diffusive of itself toward the created world, they understand the Good as an essentially self-diffusive Love. Since love or charity is the most perfect goodness, and love is by nature diffusive of itself, then God, who is the most perfect Love, must be essentially self-diffusive. His first act of diffusion cannot be transitive or creative, which would be an imperfect diffusion, created goodness being less perfect than Love or God Himself. Rather, God's first self-diffusion, as most perfect, must be constitutive of and identical with Himself: a most perfect self-communication in one singularity of essence, whereby that which receives what is given and that which gives it share the same singular nature. However, since God is mind, rationally distinguished into intellect and will, there are two emanations within the Godhead and three consubstantial persons. Thus, the Son is the Word generated by the divine intellect or Father, and the Holy Spirit is the love between the Father and Son. Through these emanations, God communicates himself to himself, by knowing and loving himself. But how can these tenets be understood in a way that elucidates God's triune nature?

Aristotle, through his categories of substance and relation, is also present in medieval speculation on the Trinity. Relation, which is not an absolute thing but a circumstance of an absolute thing, can explain how God is one substance in three distinct persons, the official Christian position. For example, the Father is the divine substance as related to and distinct from the Son, who is this same substance as related to and distinct from the Father. Thus, there is substantial unity and relative or personal plurality in God: the heresies of Sabellius (the divine persons are distinct only nominally) and of Arius (the Son and the Holy Spirit are creatures because they are not substantially one with the Father) can be avoided.

Most medieval Christian theologians, whether of a more Aristotelian or Neoplatonic inspiration, grant the two immanent emanations, as well as the relations, of the Trinity. However, even though they see the Trinity in itself as eternal and necessary, the question for them still is, what is the right *conception* of the ultimate reason for God being triune? Is it emanation or is it relation? For example, one may ask of the Father, is he the Father because he generates, or does he generate because he is the Father? These are two chief Latin accounts of the Trinity received by thinkers in the latter half of the 13th century: the relations account originated by Augustine (354–430) and Boethius (ca. 480–ca. 525) in their respective treatises *De Trinitate* and developed by **Thomas Aquinas** (influenced by his teacher **Albert the Great**), and the emanation account originated in the 12th century by Richard of Saint-Victor (influenced by his teacher **Hugh of Saint-Victor**) and developed by Bonaventure. For Thomas Aquinas, the Father generates because he is the Father; relation accounts for the subsistence of the Father, which relative subsistence is presupposed by the Father's proper activity of generating. For Bonaventure, the Father is Father because he generates: generation accounts for, and thus is rationally prior to, the Father's relative subsistence as Father. In turn, **Giles of Rome**'s account modifies St. Thomas's. Finally, Henry of Ghent, though more in line with Bonaventure's tradition, is rather innovative in his development of both traditions, especially in his use of Augustine's psychology of the Trinity. For Henry, the ultimate reason why the persons are distinct is not emanation or relation (though he grants the reality of both) but the divine nature's intellectual and willing dimensions.

These 13th-century positions were then developed variously. **Duns Scotus** developed many of his positions against the background of Henry of Ghent and drew from, among others, the Victorines and his fellow **Franciscan** Bonaventure. Scotus produced many immediate followers, such as **Peter Aureoli** and **William of Ockham**. His influence was still strong at the Council of Trent (1545–1563), where roughly one-half of the representatives were Scotists. Thomas Aquinas also generated many medieval followers, such as **Ulrich of Strasbourg** and **Godfrey of Fontaines**. **Meister Eckhart** (1260–1328) and **Nicholas of Cusa** in the 15th century provided accounts that synthesize the Aristotelian tradition of Aquinas and the Neoplatonic tradition of Henry of Ghent and Bonaventure.

**TRIVIUM.** *See* LIBERAL ARTS.

# U

**ULRICH OF STRASBOURG (ca. 1220–1277).** Ulrich is well known as a student and close friend of **Albert the Great**, under whom he studied in Cologne from 1248 to 1252. His best-known work is his *Summa de summo bono* (*Summa on the Highest Good*), which does not limit itself to a study of the Highest Good but of the Highest Good and all that comes forth and returns to the Highest Good or God. The work is more adequately described by its adjusted title, *Summa de bono* (*Summa on the Good*). Ulrich spares **Aristotle** rejection by treating him as a natural philosopher, not a metaphysician. On the question of the eternity of the world, he interprets the Philosopher as a person who does not raise the question of creation or answer it. Aristotle, according to him, simply assumes the existence of the world and dedicates himself to explaining its nature and laws, not its origin. His principal sources are **Neoplatonic**, as is evident from his extensive use of **Dionysius the Pseudo-Areopagite**'s *On the Divine Names* for the earlier parts of his *Summa*.

**UNIVERSALS.** Since **Plato** and **Aristotle**, the biggest philosophical influences on medieval thought, described the objects of science as universal, necessary, and eternal, scientific studies like philosophy and **theology** must have as their objects of study something universal, necessary, and eternal if they are going to be sciences. Plato argued that the objects of sense are particular, contingent, and temporal. To have science, then, we must have, or must have had, some contact with the world of pure forms that are universal, necessary, and eternal. Aristotle rejected any knowledge of pure forms and argued that we can still have science of particular, contingent, and temporal things because these objects have in them dimensions of universality, necessity, and eternity. An individual man like Socrates is particular, contingent, and temporal, but for him to be a man he must have certain characteristics that make him to be a man. These essential characteristics are universally, necessarily, and eternally found in every man as long as he is a man. In short, there is in each particular a universal dimension that makes it to be the kind of thing it is. It has to always have such essential traits if it is to be not just an individual but to be an individual of a particular type or class.

Medieval thinkers will consider these Platonic and Aristotelian answers to the question of how science is possible and develop their own ways of nuancing a solution. In general, throughout the medieval period, people will follow one or the other solution to the problem of universals. Some might say that the universality is found only in the words or names we use, since we do use class names, such as *man*, *animal*, and *lion*. These will be called **nominalists**. Others will say that not only are our written or spoken words for classes of things universal, but we also have interior words or concepts that are universal. These are conceptualists, and in their case, our written or spoken class names correspond to our universal concepts. We do not just simply make up classes; we think in terms of classes of things. Another group of philosophers goes even further. This group will say that we think universally because the objects we think about are, independently of our thinking of them, universal. These will be called **realists**, since they believe universals are real. These are three classical explanations for universals, but they will be understood and presented with different nuances. *See also* BURLEY, WALTER (ca. 1274–1344); WILLIAM OF OCKHAM (ca. 1285–1347).

**UNIVERSITIES.** In the Middle Ages, the Latin term *universitas*, which at first simply meant humanity (Cicero), and later on a body or society of individuals, acquired its academic significance when it first designated a unified body of masters and students. This was in 1221 in documents referring to the young University of Paris. *Studium* or *studium generale* was another common designation for university. Universities emerged as a third power, representing "wisdom," which was granted rights and privileges (and sought out for support) by the other two powers, the empire and the papacy. The guild model of urban organization, an established tradition of scholarship at (canonical and cathedral **schools**), and the translation of classical texts (in, e.g., **liberal arts** and Roman law) all prepared the ground for the development of European universities, which were originally grounded in Catholic doctrine. Some universities became organized into **colleges**; originally, before becoming relatively autonomous centers of teaching and learning within universities, colleges were simply endowed institutions providing room and board for students.

The inauguration of the first universities (such as Paris, Bologna, Oxford, and Orléans) generally meant the formalization of school traditions that already existed in the 12th century, and so it is difficult to determine their exact time of origin; Cambridge (1209) and Padua (1222) were among the first to be created strictly as universities. Paris, a model for other universities, consisted of four faculties: arts, **law**, **medicine**, and **theology**. The **Arts Faculty**, focusing mainly on **Aristotelian** philosophy, was originally a preparatory faculty for higher studies in the other three faculties (although its preparatory status changed when **Averroists** decided to remain in this faculty, pursuing philosophy for its own sake). The Theology Faculty held the highest authority. Drawing from the philosophical tradition in its efforts to synthesize reason and revelation, it focused on Holy Scripture, texts from the Church Fathers, and standard textbooks (especially **Peter Lombard**'s *Sentences*). Across Europe at the time, theology faculties attracted the greatest intellectual talent.

Teaching and learning were based on the critical study of these traditional texts embodying secular and Christian wisdom. A logical or **dialectical** method, emphasizing clear definitions, distinctions, and inferences, was rigorously applied. Questions arising from the curriculum were posed and systematically handled; the question became the commonest mode of intellectual activity. Disputed questions (*quaestiones disputatae*), posed and developed by masters in class discussion with students, and "**quodlibetal**" questions (questions from the audience on whatsoever: *quaestiones de quolibet*), publicly handled by masters at fixed times during the academic year, were not only central to academic life but also the basis, after revisions and at the discretion of the master, of publications. The resolution of a question usually followed upon analysis of relevant contemporary and traditional arguments. *Quaestiones disputatae* (called "reports" or *reportationes* when a listener wrote them for the master), *quaestiones quodlibetales*, and other works based on questions were standard works by medieval masters. Another genre (less common due to its monumental nature) was the theological summa (summation or summary), a long systematic exposition of an author's doctrines (also usually arranged by questions), such as **Thomas Aquinas**'s *Summa theologiae* or **Henry of Ghent**'s *Summa quaestionum ordinariarum*. The commentary on an authority (such as biblical texts, Aristotle, or Lombard), often very detailed treatments, was another important mode of scholarly writing; its classroom counterpart was the lecture, an explanatory reading by the master. Finally, treatises of various kinds were produced. At the Parisian Theology Faculty, some of the greatest minds of medieval Europe (not just France) taught and studied, such as **Albert the Great**, Aquinas, **Bonaventure**, and **Duns Scotus**. This method of teaching, learning, and writing associated with medieval universities is often referred to as the Scholastic method, and the philosophical and theological doctrines it produced as Scholastic philosophy and Scholastic theology, respectively; **Scholasticism** refers to the whole.

The duties of a master of theology at the university included other offices besides those of lecturing. One of these principal duties was to preach. Among the more famous university sermons were, for example, the series of sermons delivered during Lent. Noteworthy instances of such serial sermons are the conferences delivered by St. Bonaventure during the crisis times of the late 1260s: *Conferences on the Six Days of Creation, Conferences on the Gifts of the Holy Spirit*, and *Conferences on the Ten Commandments*. However, among the works of St. Bonaventure are found many other sermons on the different feasts and the temporal cycle of the Church year. Many theologians of the Middle Ages, like Bonaventure, have left long lists of sermons: some of them, such as inaugural sermons, connected with their classroom duties; others related to their duties as priests.

Among the various centers, schools, sponsors, and traditions of learning in the medieval Byzantine, **Islamic**, and **Jewish** worlds, there is no precise analogue to the university, a medieval inheritance still providing the resources for much of intellectual life around the world.

# V

*VIA ANTIQUA* **AND** *VIA MODERNA.* *Via antiqua* means "the old way"; *via moderna* means "the new way." In many cases, these are primarily or even exclusively temporal designations. Medievals spoke of the Old Logic (the logical texts and commentaries dating from the time of **Boethius**) and the New Logic (the rest of **Aristotle**'s logical works that were translated in the 12th century).

However, *via antiqua* and *via moderna* became more than temporal designations when Walter Burley in his *De puritate artis logicae* (*On the Purity of the Art of Logic*), written around 1325, accused **William of Ockham** of being out of accord with the ancients. Burley wanted to go back to the old way of representing things, the way of Aristotle, Boethius, **Priscian**, and **Averroes**. Before they were contaminated by the nominalistic interpretation of Ockham, the ancients were in Burley's eyes realists. When Ockham used the word *man* in a meaningful sentence, such as "Man is an animal," he thought that *man* stood for Peter or John. But Burley said something quite different. In the sentence "Man is an animal," *man* stands not for Peter or John but for the universal man that is found in Peter or John. In brief, Burley is a **realist**; Ockham is a **nominalist**. Burley claims to belong to the old way (*via antiqua*); Ockham, in Burley's judgment, belongs to the new way (*via moderna*).

There are many other things that will become characteristic of the *via antiqua*. For one, Burley explains Aristotle's 10 categories as 10 different types of realities. Ockham paints a different portrait of the 10 categories. There are individual substances, and there are also some individual qualities inhering in substances. When a man is white, whiteness is an inhering quality in the man. However, if there are two white men, then they are alike according to both Burley and Ockham. But for Ockham, likeness or similarity is not an inhering quality in each man, as it is for Burley. For Ockham, the men are alike in their color because they are both white, not because of any extra "likeness" that is added to them. It is according to this pattern that Burley and Ockham build their different explanations of Aristotle's categories and thus their different systems of realism and nominalism.

Later, similar new explanations will arise in **theology** so that certain authors and their explanations will be portrayed as representing the *via moderna*. Their opponents will be said to belong to the *via antiqua*. There is no one meaning or one collection of positions that belongs to these terms. In dealing with each author, we have to discover concretely what he means by the label when he applies it to another or claims it for himself.

**VITALIS DE FURNO (VITAL DU FOUR) (ca. 1260–1327).** This Franciscan author taught theology at Paris from 1285 to 1291. A general portrait of his teachings would link him to other **Franciscan** authors preceding him: **John Peckham, William de la Mare, Matthew of Aquasparta,** and **Peter John Olivi**. Vitalis, however, did not spend his life teaching in Paris. His commentaries on Books I and IV of Peter Lombard's *Sentences* date from his teaching at the *studium generale* of the Franciscans in Montpellier (1292–1296). Later, he also taught at Toulouse (1296–1307). In 1307, he was elected provincial of the Franciscan province of Aquitaine, a position he held until he was made a cardinal in 1312. He was consecrated bishop of Albano in 1321 and served in many capacities at the papal court, where he died in 1327. Vitalis is known especially for his treatment of the doctrine of divine illumination, attempting to reconcile the **Augustinian** tradition concerning intellectual knowledge with **Aristotle**'s doctrine of the agent intellect. In metaphysics, he is known for opposing the real distinction between essence and existence in creatures, admitting, as does **Henry of Ghent**, only an intentional distinction.

**VULGATE.** *See* BIBLE.

**WALAFRID STRABO (ca. 808–849).** A native of Swabia, he studied under **Alcuin**'s students **Hilduin** and **Rhabanus Maurus**, who with Alcuin contributed greatly to the Carolingian Renaissance of classical learning and **liberal arts**. Walafrid's writings include saints' lives, summaries of writings of Rhabanus, and a revision of Alcuin's student, the Benedictine monk Einhard's *Vita Caroli Magni* (*Life of Charlemagne*). A tutor of Charles the Bald from 829 to 838, Walafrid became abbot of Reichenau in 838. One of the most accomplished Latin poets of his time, his fame in liberal arts lies with the trivium. His poetry includes *Visio Wettini* (*The Vision of Wettin*), his teacher, which lyrically describes heaven, hell, and purgatory, and *De cultura hortorum* (*On the Cultivation of Gardens*), a piece on herbs and plants. His **theological** writings include *Liber de exordiis et incrementis quarundam in observationibus ecclesiasticis* (*A Book on the Beginnings and Developments of Certain Church Rituals*) dealing chiefly with ecclesiastical rites and norms.

**WALDENSIANS.** The Waldensians were the largest **heretical** group in medieval Christianity. Their founder, Waldes, was a merchant of Lyons who experienced a Christian conversion that prompted him to live a life of poverty, begging and preaching. What earned them condemnation, however, was not their way of life, which some Church officials found objectionable, but their unlicensed preaching. After resisting orders by the archbishop of Lyons to stop preaching publicly, they brought their case in 1179 to Alexander III in Rome at the Third Lateran Council. Their chief goal was becoming official preachers against the Albigensians or Cathar heretics, but they were refused, chiefly for being unprepared laypeople. They continued to preach, however, and around 1182 they were excommunicated and expelled from Lyons. Condemned by Pope Lucius III in 1184 (mainly for preaching without authorization), they continued to grow in western Europe. Later on, they formulated a set of truly **heretical** teachings, such as rejecting the authority of priests, denying purgatory, and espousing a completely evangelical way of life. They increasingly began to see the Church as sinful and poisoned by wealth and finally rejected its entire structure, focusing only on what they saw as literally contained in the Gospels.

**WALTER BURLEY.** *See* BURLEY, WALTER (ca. 1274–1344).

**WALTER CHATTON (ca. 1285–1343).** This English **Franciscan** philosopher and **theologian**, born in Catton, west of Durham, was a contemporary of **William of Ockham** and **Adam of Wodeham** at the Franciscan custodial school in London from 1321 to 1323. There he delivered his custodial lectures on all four books of **Peter Lombard**'s *Sentences* in the form of *Reportationes* in preparation for his later *Lectura* on the *Sentences* at Oxford given sometime between 1324 and 1330, but more likely in 1328–30. He was such a detailed critic of Ockham that it is impossible to follow many arguments in the latter's **Quodlibets** without having Chatton's *Reportatio* at hand, since Ockham sometimes did not write out Chatton's objections to which he responded. Ockham presumed that the audience knew Chatton's objections. Chatton was also at times an opponent of **Peter Aureoli** and **Richard of Campsall**; he generally, though not always, followed **John Duns Scotus** and responded to his critics. He was also one of the examiners of the works of **Durandus of Saint-Pourçain** at the papal court in Avignon and is believed to have died there in 1343.

Ockham's famous razor was sharpened partly in response to Chatton's critique (*see* OCKHAM'S RAZOR). Its early formulation ("Beings should not be multiplied without necessity") was challenged by Walter, who countered with an anti-razor that he called "my proposition": "When a proposition is made true by things, if two things are not sufficient for its truth, then it is necessary to posit a third, and so on." In response, Ockham in his later works reformulated his razor to say, "When a proposition is made true by things, if two things are sufficient for its truth, then it is superfluous to posit a third, and so on."

Walter also attacked Ockham's view of concepts, at least the view Ockham held in the first redaction of his *Sentences* commentary, where he defends the *fictum* theory, which holds that the concept does not exist in the mind as in a subject, but that it only has the reality of an object created by an act of understanding. Walter himself held the *intellectio* theory, which contends that the concept is nothing other than the very act of knowing. Such an act of knowing is a true quality existing in the soul as in a subject, and it is also a natural sign of the object that is immediately understood by means of it. Ockham not only did not despise Chatton's critique of the *fictum* theory;

he incorporated his opponent's *intellectio* theory into his later treatments of concepts, at first reducing the *fictum* theory to a less probable opinion and then finally abandoning it.

The Ockham-Chatton exchange, however, is not limited to the period when both were in London. In discussing the dependence of a second cause on the first cause in essentially ordered causes, Chatton, in his *Lectura*, defends Scotus's position against Ockham's challenges, quoting verbatim from Ockham's last philosophical work, the *Quaestiones in libros Physicorum Aristotelis* (*Questions on Aristotle's "Physics"*), probably written at Oxford about 1324.

Chatton, in dealing with his own questions concerning **Aristotle**'s *Physics*, is known especially for joining the early 14th-century minority of **Henry of Harclay**, **Gerard Odon**, and Nicholas Bonet—thinkers who opposed Aristotle's claim that *continua* cannot be composed of indivisibles. Although Chatton had contemporary allies among the atomists, he seems to be alone in holding that *continua* are composed of finite numbers of indivisibles. **Thomas Bradwardine**, in his *Tractatus de continuo* (*Treatise on the Nature of a Continuum*), makes Walter a follower of Pythagoras and **Plato**, who held the same position.

Besides Ockham, Chatton had a number of other debating partners. When Peter Aureoli attacked Scotus's theory of the univocity of being, Chatton came to its defense. Aureol attacked Duns Scotus for claiming that we can have a univocal concept of being, a concept that is predicable in the same sense both of God and of creatures. Scotus achieved this univocal concept at a price, since his concept of being leaves outside its ambit the modes "infinite" and "finite," which, if they were included, would impede "being" from being predicable both of God and creatures. Chatton grants this objection but considers it irrelevant. If Aureoli, he argues, wants to include modes and differences in his concept of being, then "being" becomes a most general concept of all that is opposed to nothing, and this is merely a logical and not a metaphysical concept. It is the latter, according to Chatton, that Scotus had in mind.

Richard Campsall became Chatton's opponent when he argued that intuitive and abstractive cognition are not really distinct, "since numerically the same knowledge is intuitive when the object is present and abstractive when it is absent, because plurality should not be admitted without necessity." Against this position, Chatton raised 12 difficulties and then refuted Campsall by appealing to his anti-razor, arguing that it is not impossible that God conserve in existence the intellect with its abstractive cognition and make the object present without the intellect grasping it as present. Thus, for the proposition "He sees that object" to be true, it is not enough to have his intellect, its abstractive cognition, and the object present. A distinct thing has to be added, intuitive cognition. He clashed with Campsall also over the logic involved in statements of nonidentity related to the Christian teaching on the **Trinity**.

Chatton's treatment of the Trinity had its own logical and metaphysical problems, turning the divine essence into a collection of persons. He was severely ridiculed and criticized for such Trinitarian views by Adam Wodeham, who was quite likely the student who wrote down Chatton's *Reportatio*. In the margin of Chatton's text, Wodeham wrote. "In all this discussion the report is not in accord with the mind of the speaker. Nor is there any wonder, since when the author said these things he was not quite sane. Later on he thought things out better and had another go at it. And then the reporter naturally expressed things in a better way." Wodeham was Chatton's chief critic, often accusing him of misunderstanding or misrepresenting Ockham, or of accepting Ockham's views but pretending, by petty quibbles, that he was differing. Despite Wodeham's frequent attacks on him, the influence Chatton had on both Ockham and Wodeham shows his philosophical importance.

**WALTER OF BRUGES (ca. 1235–1307).** Walter is a **Franciscan** author who probably lectured on **Peter Lombard**'s *Sentences* at Paris between 1260 and 1265. He was regent master there from 1267 to 1268. Books I and II of his *Sentences* are from the early years when he was a bachelor of the *Sentences*, but Book IV, which refers back to Book I, was presumably written around 1270, since it cites **Peter of Tarantaise**, probably from the *Sentences* commentary Peter produced during his second regency at Paris (1267–1269). There is evidence, particularly in regard to his treatment of the Trinity, that he continued in the tradition of St. **Bonaventure**. However, he also shows quite an independent spirit and sides with St. **Thomas Aquinas** on some positions, so it is only with qualification that he can be associated with the tradition of St. Bonaventure.

**WALTER OF MORTAGNE (ca. 1090–1174).** Walter began his studies at the cathedral **school** of Tournai and then moved to Reims, where he studied under Alberic. Dissatisfied with Alberic's mechanical style of teaching, he opened his own school at the abbey of Saint-Remy, drawing away some of his fellow students from Alberic. Shortly thereafter, he was working with Ralph at Laon who taught Walter the importance of mathematics, geometry, and astronomy. Upon Ralph's death, Walter became master of the school and, like him, kept it at the high level set by Anselm of Laon.

Walter has left a series of letters on various subjects: on the validity of baptism performed by heretics; on the Incarnation; on God's presence in all things by his essence; on the human feelings of Christ; and, finally, a letter to

Abelard about his proofs for the **Trinity** and his making the Father more powerful than the Son. Some works attributed to others have found him as their original author: a *Tractatus de coniugio* (*A Treatise on Marriage*), once assigned to Hugh of Saint-Victor, and a *Liber de Trinitate* (*A Book on the Trinity*), at times thought to belong to Walter of Chatillon. In 1150, he was named dean of the Cathedral of Laon, and in 1155 he was elected bishop. He died in 1174 at Plaisance while on a royal mission to Rome.

**WALTER OF SAINT-VICTOR (ca. 1120–1190).** Most likely of English origin, this successor of **Richard of Saint-Victor** as prior of the monastery of the Canons Regular of St. Augustine is most famous for his ferocious attack on the 12th-century Scholastics. In his pamphlet titled *Contra quattuor labyrinthos Franciae* (*Against the Four Labyrinths of France*), he envisioned within the four labyrinths of heresy the four minotaurs who aim, according to him, to destroy the Christian faith: **Peter Lombard**, **Peter Abelard**, Peter of Poitiers, and **Gilbert of Poitiers**. According to Palémon Glorieux, who edited the text, it is a work "badly put together and badly written." Walter's reputation, however, has been somewhat redeemed by recently edited letters and the discovery that the work titled *Quaestiones et decisiones in Epistolas S. Pauli* (*Questions and Answers regarding the Letters of St. Paul*) that had been attributed to **Hugh of Saint-Victor** comes from Walter's pen.

**WILLIAM DE LA MARE (ca. 1235–ca. 1290).** This English **Franciscan** follower of **Bonaventure** and critic of the **Dominican Thomas Aquinas** became a master of theology at Paris in 1274 (the year of Aquinas's death) or 1275—*see also* ORDERS (RELIGIOUS). One of the outstanding 13th-century biblical scholars, he wrote a revered *Correctio textus Bibliae* (*Correction of the Text of the Bible*) and an aid to biblical study expounding upon Hebrew and Greek terms (*De Hebraeis et Graecis vocabulis glossarium Bibliae*). At a time when **Aristotelianism** (including **Averroism** and even **Thomism**) generated much controversy among Parisian theologians, a process leading to the **condemnation of 1277**, William sought to revive the **Augustinian** spirit of Bonaventure as the true expression of the Christian faith. (In this respect, his **theological** efforts may be likened to those of his influential contemporary **Henry of Ghent**.) Aside from a series of *Quaestiones disputatae* (*see* UNIVERSITIES), he composed a commentary on **Peter Lombard**'s *Sentences*. William amply engaged in debates against Dominicans, particularly in ones generated by his influential *Correctorium Fratris Thomae* (1278) (later expanded and revised), where he concludes the inconsistency between some of Aquinas's doctrines and Scripture and the **Fathers of the Church**, notably **Augustine**.

**WILLIAM OF ALNWICK (ca. 1275–1333).** William took his name from Alnwick in Northumberland and probably began his studies at the Franciscan *studium* (house of studies) in Newcastle. By 1303, he was a master of theology at the University of Paris, following in the long tradition, since the 1260s, of English **Franciscans** who became masters of theology at Paris. He taught at Montpellier, Bologna, and Naples before returning to England, where he is listed as the 42nd Franciscan regent master at Oxford. The marginal notes to his manuscripts indicate that he was in lively discussions with **Thomas Aquinas, Bonaventure, Henry of Ghent, Peter Aureoli, Godfrey of Fontaines, Henry Harclay,** and **Thomas Wylton.** William was chiefly associated with **John Duns Scotus** and collaborated with him in the production of the latter's *Ordinatio* (*Oxford Commentary on the Sentences*). He was the *reportator* (student recorder) for one of Scotus's *Collationes* and is especially known as the author of the long additions (*Additiones magnae*), which were meant to fill the lacunae left in Books I and II of Scotus's *Ordinatio*.

William's own works include a *Commentary on the **Sentences*** of **Peter Lombard,** a *Quodlibet,* a sermon on the beatific vision, 12 questions that make up his *Determinationes,* some questions on Aristotle's *De anima,* and a collection of *Quaestiones de esse intelligibili* (*Questions on Intelligible Being*). In question 14 of his *Determinationes,* defended in Bologna in 1322, he provided a strong defense of the formal distinction of Scotus. But more noted in this work is his public defense of the stance he took with other Franciscan theologians in their decree *De paupertate Christi* (*On the Poverty of Christ*), which attacked the position on apostolic poverty maintained by Pope John XXII. There, he argued that Christ and his apostles possessed nothing either personally or in common. When the pope initiated a process against him, he fled to Naples where he was protected by King Robert of Sicily. In 1330, he was made bishop of Giovinazzo. He died three years later in Avignon.

**WILLIAM OF AUVERGNE (ca. 1190–1249).** After obtaining the degree of master of **theology** (1223) at Paris, William then taught in that faculty (1225) and became bishop of Paris in 1228, an office he held until his death. Benefiting from the new Latin translations of **Aristotelian** philosophy, he was one of the first major **theologians** at Paris to develop an **Augustinian** theology that addresses (and criticizes) Aristotle and his commentators, especially **Avicenna.** In this sense, he was a forerunner of later similar attempts by thinkers such as **Bonaventure** and **Henry of Ghent.** Aside from various sermons and treatises, the *Magisterium divinale* (*The Teaching concerning God*) is his comprehensive philosophical and theological work. It is made up of seven sections: *On the Trinity* or *On the First Principle*; *Why the God-Man*; *On the Sacraments in General and in Particular*; *On Faith and Laws*; *On Merits and Punishments*; *On the Universe*; and *On the Soul.*

**WILLIAM OF AUXERRE (ca. 1140–1231).** Although William has at times, both ancient and recent, been confused with a bishop of the same name, there are some facts of his life that are clear. He lived in Auxerre and even made arrangements for an annual memorial mass to be offered there after his death. His *Summa theologica*, traditionally called the *Summa aurea* or *Golden Summa*, and other documents of the time, verify that he taught theology in Paris. Salimbene, in 1247, claimed that when William carried on a disputation at Paris, no one could do it better; and when he preached, no one would be ignorant about what he said. One of the copies of his *Summa* and a letter of Pope Gregory IX indicate that William was also an archdeacon of Beauvais. We have evidence, furthermore, of two visits to Rome and that he was also named by Pope Gregory IX in 1231 to head a three-person commission to examine carefully and with prudence the books of **Aristotle** that had been prohibited at Paris in 1210. He was asked to see if they were erroneous and could be the cause of scandal for their readers. William, however, died in Rome in the same year, so the committee was never convened. Some works attributed to him, for example, a gloss on the *Anticlaudianus* of **Alan of Lille** and a gloss on **Porphyry**'s *Isagoge* (*Introduction to Aristotle's Logic*), have had their authenticity challenged, but uncontested is his authorship of the *Summa aurea* and also his *Summa de officiis ecclesiasticis* (*Summa of Ecclesiastical Offices*).

**WILLIAM OF CHAMPEAUX (1070–1132).** A student of **Roscelin** and **Anselm of Laon**, William taught **dialectics** and **theology** at Paris. In the field of **liberal arts**, he is respected for his commentaries on Cicero's *De inventione* (*On Rhetoric*) and *Rhetorica ad Herennium* (*On Rhetoric for Herennius*) and on **Boethius**'s *Topics*. In theology, he and Anselm of Laon are the early authors organizing theological discussions according to a logical order or theme (called *Sententiae* or *Sentences*) rather than according to the order of the biblical text. Among his students was **Peter Abelard**, who so strongly criticized William's extreme realism theory of universals that he was forced to change his account. In 1108, he withdrew from teaching and retired to the hermitage of Saint-Victor. There he reorganized the community according to the new rule of the **Canons Regular of St. Augustine**. The Abbey of Saint-Victor flourished under his care. He had similar success in reforming the clergy under his charge when he was consecrated bishop of Chalons-sur-Marne in 1113. His surviving works are his *Sententiae*, his treatise *De essentia et substantia Dei et de tribus eius personis* (*On the Essence and Substance of God and His Three Persons*), and a fragment of his *De sacramento altaris* (*On the Eucharist*).

**WILLIAM OF CONCHES (ca. 1090–ca. 1155).** A native of Normandy, this leading figure of the so-called renaissance of the 12th century started teaching at the **school** of Chartres around 1125, where he was a student of **Bernard of Chartres** and teacher of **John of Salisbury**. Learned in **theology**, the sciences, and the seven **liberal arts**, his writings include glosses on **Boethius**'s *De consolatione philosophiae* (*On the Consolation of Philosophy*), **Priscian**'s *Institutiones grammaticae* (*Foundations of Grammar*), Martianus Capella's *De nuptiis Philologiae et Mercurii* (*On the Marriage of Philology and Mercury*), Macrobius's *De somnio Scipionis* (*On the Dream of Scipio*), and **Plato**'s *Timaeus* (translated by Chalcidius). His chief works are *Dragmaticon* and *Philosophia mundi* (*Philosophy of the World*).

As with other teachers at Chartres, one of his fundamental concerns was cosmology; the *Philosophia mundi* deals with the **Trinity** and creation and attempts a reconciliation of *Genesis* with Plato's *Timaeus*. The *Dragmaticon* (written around 1148), displaying knowledge of many sources (a chief one is Constantinus of Africa), develops some of the themes of the *Philosophia* as well as other scientific topics. Both works evidence the state and development of science at the time, largely occasioned by the assimilation of Greek and Arabic learning. William also had a strong interest in the **ethical** writings of Seneca and **Cicero**, gathering a number of their sayings from their works and from those of Christian authors who reported their teachings into his *Moralium dogma philosophorum* (*The Teaching of the Moral Philosophers*). In *De erroribus Guillelmi a Conchis* (*Concerning the Errors of William of Conches*), **William of Saint-Thierry** (a previous critic of **Peter Abelard**) attacked William's view of the Trinity (as an example of modalism), as well as his view of the Trinity's relation to creation (for being materialistic). Partly because of this, William of Conches left the schools and went to the court of Geoffrey Plantagenet (Duke of Normandy and Count of Anjou), where he became tutor to his sons, including the future English king, Henry II.

**WILLIAM OF HEYTESBURY.** *See* HEYTESBURY, WILLIAM (ca. 1313–ca. 1373).

**WILLIAM OF HOTHUM (ca. 1245–1298).** William was probably born in Yorkshire and joined the **Dominicans** at an early age. He studied **theology** in Paris and began his teaching career lecturing *cursorie* on the **Sentences** of **Peter Lombard** at Oxford in 1269. He returned to Paris to teach in the Theology Faculty as regent master between 1280 and 1282, but possibly even as early as 1275. Frequently he performed political missions for King Edward I. In 1282, William was elected to serve as the provincial of the Dominican friars in England. At times he attended academic ceremonies at

Oxford, but his main work was the administration of the English province and service to the king. On 24 November 1284, he defended **Thomas Aquinas** against the attack of Archbishop **John Peckham**. In 1287, the General Chapter of the Order at Bordeaux appointed him for a second time as *magister regens* at Paris, though he never exercised this appointment. Boniface VIII appointed him archbishop of Dublin in 1296. William died on 27 August 1298 at Dijon while on a diplomatic mission to secure peace between Edward I and Philip IV. He was buried at the Dominican church in London, near Ludgate.

**WILLIAM OF MACCLESFIELD (ca. 1260–1303).** William was born in the diocese of Coventry, so it is a simple inference to believe that his association with the **Dominicans** began in Chester. He was a bachelor in theology at Paris in 1293–1294. It was about 1298 that he became a master in theology at Oxford and was regent master from 1299 to 1301. William, along with **Richard Knapwell**, **Thomas Sutton**, and **William Hothum**, was among the group of Dominicans who defended **Thomas Aquinas**'s teachings and thus came to form the early Oxford **Thomistic** school. In 1300, he received permission to hear confessions in the diocese of Lincoln, and in February 1302, he served, along with one of his confreres, as an arbiter in a dispute between the Exeter priory and the chapter of Exeter. In the same year, William was elected at the provincial chapter to be a *definitor* for the General Chapter to be held in Besançon in 1303. He died upon his return from the General Chapter sometime between May and December 1303. On 18 December 1303, he was created a cardinal priest of St. Sabina by Pope Benedict XI, who was unaware of his death.

**WILLIAM OF MOERBEKE (ca. 1215–1286).** William entered the **Dominicans** at Ghent and then studied with **Albert the Great** at Cologne. Quite likely, he also studied at Paris before being sent in 1260 to Thebes and later to Nicaea. He served many years as chaplain and confessor at the papal court, first probably under Pope Clement IV and later under Pope Gregory X. As an advisor to Gregory, he attended the Council of Lyons (1274), where he sang the *Credo* in Greek. He was named archbishop of Corinth in 1278 by Nicholas III, and he died there in 1286. William's knowledge of Greek and his training at Cologne and Paris provided him with the tools that allowed him "at the request of Friar **Thomas Aquinas**" to translate or retranslate many works of **Aristotle** and his Greek commentators, as well as **Proclus**, Archimedes, Galen, and **Ptolemy**. His translations were quite literal, but this allowed authors like Aquinas to grasp more exactly the philosophical thought of Aristotle and the **Neoplatonic** thought of Proclus. His translation of Aristotle's Greek commentators (Ammonius, Simplicius, Alexander of Aphrodisias, Themistius, and **Philoponus**) added much to the understanding of the Philosopher, and his translation of Proclus's *Elementatio Theologica* (*Elements of Theology*) allowed Aquinas to realize that the *Liber de causis* (*The Book of Causes*), which depended on it, was not rightly attributed to Aristotle.

**WILLIAM OF NOTTINGHAM (ca. 1280–1336).** William is one of the English **Franciscans** who did his studies at Oxford, not at Paris, as had been the tradition for the most talented English Franciscans from the time of **John Peckham** up to William's near contemporaries, **William of Alnwick** and **Robert Cowton**. He was the 39th Franciscan regent master at Oxford from 1312 to 1314, so he would have completed his theological studies before this appointment. His *Commentary on the Sentences* survives in only one manuscript, so it is likely that he did not have a great deal of influence on his contemporaries. His *Sentences*, however, provides a great deal of information about them, since he names many of his contemporaries and reports their positions. Like **Richard Conington** and Robert Cowton, William differed with **John Duns Scotus** on many points, seeming to favor the positions of **Henry of Ghent**. In 1316, he was elected provincial of the English province of the Franciscans and carried out this office until 1330. As provincial, he participated in the General Chapters of 1322 in Perugia and of 1325 in Lyon. He died in 1336 and is buried at the Franciscan convent of Leicester.

**WILLIAM OF OCKHAM (ca. 1285–1347).** Born in Ockham, a village in county Surrey, southwest of London, William joined the **Franciscans** before the age of 14 and quite likely studied philosophy at the friars' school in London. He studied **theology** at Oxford, and as a bachelor of the *Sentences*, he commented on **Peter Lombard**'s work there between 1317 and 1319. Because of the long line of Franciscan candidates before him, he never became a presiding master at Oxford. His fame was thus achieved under the title Venerable Inceptor, although some records refer to him as the Invincible Doctor or the Singular Doctor. Although William lectured on the four books of Peter Lombard's *Sentences* at Oxford, his chief academic work was done between 1319 and 1324 at the Franciscan house of studies in London, where he had close association with **Walter Chatton** (a chief opponent) and **Adam Wodeham** (a frequent follower). There he made a modest revision of his *Commentary on Book I of Lombard's Sentences* that is called the *Scriptum* or *Written Commentary* in contrast to the *Reportationes* or *Quaestiones* that are the records of his Oxford lectures on Books II–IV of the *Sentences*. During these London years he wrote expositions on Porphyry's *Isagoge* and on **Aristotle**'s *Categories* and *On Interpretation*. His theological treatises, such as *De sacramento altaris* (*On the Eucharist*) and his well-organized *Summa* *logicae* also date from this period at London, which ended in 1323–1324 with the disputation of his *Quodlibets* and the crafting of his final philosophical work, the *Questions on the Physics*.

In 1324, Ockham was called to Avignon by Pope John XXII to answer charges against him contained in the *Libellus* or *Pamphlet against the Teaching of William of Ockham* drawn up by **John Lutterell**, the chancellor of Oxford who was deposed two years earlier. The commission appointed to investigate the propositions presented 51 of them as worthy of censure, but no formal condemnation was ever made by the pope. On 26 May 1328, Ockham fled with Michael of Cesena and Bonagratia de Bergamo, the general minister and vicar of the Franciscans, to Pisa. There they sought the protection of Louis of Bavaria, emperor of the Holy Roman Empire. Two years later, they journeyed with Louis to Munich, where during the next 17 years Ockham wrote on the proper extent of papal power. Although he continually expressed a willingness to submit to the legitimate authorities of the Church and the Franciscan order, he died unrepentant on 10 April 1347 in Munich, where he was buried in the Franciscan church.

William of Ockham has been portrayed in modern times as an innovator, a **nominalist**, and the leading figure of the *via moderna*. Since the recent critical edition of his works, however, and the studies it has spurred, more tempered judgments of the innovative character of his work have been passed. As a better knowledge of his sources has developed, the influences of earlier writers and contemporaries (**John Duns Scotus**, **Walter Burley**, **Hervaeus Natalis**, **Henry of Harclay**, **William of Alnwick**, **William of Nottingham**, **Richard of Conington**, **Robert Cowton**, **John of Reading**, **Peter Aureoli**, and others) on his thought have become more visible.

One ruling principle of his philosophy and theology is his famous "razor" (i.e., the principle of parsimony: "Beings should not be multiplied without necessity"). In philosophy, for example, he speaks of substances and certain inhering qualities, such as whiteness, as realities, while other qualities, such as curvedness and straightness, and the other categories, are names, that is, concepts or words. The latter categories, he argues, do not require an extra reality beyond substances and real qualities. Curvedness is not an inhering real quality but can be explained more economically by local motion; that is, when the ends of something are bent up or down and are thus closer to one another, then the substance is curved, but not by a curvedness inhering in it. In a parallel way in theology, due to Ockham's denial that quantity is a reality distinct from substances and real **accidents**, his discussions of the Eucharist (e.g., in *De sacramento altaris* [*On the Eucharist*]) vary significantly from those who take a more **realist** view of the categories.

Another ruling principle for Ockham is the distinction between God's absolute and ordained power. Although there is in God only one power that actually creates—that is, God's ordained power, which causes the created order chosen by the divine will—still, God could have chosen other orders that creation might have followed. This collection of possible worlds is the domain of God's absolute power. This distinction in effect stresses the contingency of the chosen order. For example, absolutely speaking, grace is not necessary for salvation, according to Ockham, but in the contingent order established by God's ordained will, it is required (*I Sent.*, d. 17, q. 1). Although Christian theologians, who hold that God freely created the world, must admit a distinction of two powers, its use in Ockham's case underscored the contingency of the natural order and gave rise to a large number of hypothetical considerations. *See also* OCKHAM'S RAZOR.

**WILLIAM OF SAINT-AMOUR (ca. 1200–1272).** Best known historically for his intense opposition to the mendicant **orders** and their representatives at the Parisian Theology Faculty (notably **Thomas Aquinas** and **Bonaventure** of the **Dominican** and **Franciscan** orders, respectively), William studied the **liberal arts** and canon **law** at Paris and became there regent master in **theology** around 1250. He actively sought to restrict mendicant **university** and ecclesiastical privileges and contributed to the suspension and excommunication of Dominican masters on 4 February 1254, on account of their refusal to participate in the previous year's suspension of classes. After some success with Pope Innocent IV (d. 1254), William's efforts against the mendicants increasingly backfired with Innocent's successor, Pope Alexander IV, who defended the mendicants to the point of having William and his followers (who never desisted) expelled from France in 1257 at the request of the king. His antimendicant writings include *Liber de antichristo et eiusdem ministris* (*The Book of the Antichrist and His Ministers*), making the case that the Dominicans are the forerunners of the Antichrist), and *De periculis novissimorum temporum* (*The Dangers of Our Age*), which was condemned twice in 1256 and once in 1257. He was eventually allowed to return from exile, though he never regained his former powers and was never allowed back into university circles. However, William's followers at Paris, such as **Nicholas of Lyra** and **Gerard of Abbeville**, reintroduced antimendicant efforts.

**WILLIAM OF SAINT-THIERRY, BL. (ca. 1080–1148).** Born in Liège, William most likely received his early education in this center of culture rather than at Laon, as some have suggested. He entered the Benedictines in 1113 in Reims. Between 1116 and 1118, he became a close friend of **St. Bernard**, and they exchanged dedications of their works during these years and thereafter. In 1119, he was elected Abbot of Saint-Thierry, and his first works were written in his early days as abbot. His *De natura et dignitate amoris* (*On the Nature and Dignity of Love*) and *De contemplando Deo* (*On

*Contemplating God*) were written between 1119 and 1122. He took an active part in the General Chapter of the Benedictines in 1130, but in 1135 he resigned as abbot of Saint-Thierry and sought a more contemplative life as a Cistercian monk at Signy.

During the next decade, William wrote his *Speculum fidei* (*The Mirror of Faith*) and *Aenigma fidei* (*The Enigma of Faith*), deep reflections on the nature of supernatural faith. He also wrote criticisms of those who seemed to him to be reducing the primacy of faith: his *Disputatio adversus Abelardum* (*A Challenge against Abelard*) and his *De erroribus Guillelmi de Conchis* (*On the Errors of William of Conches*). After visiting the charterhouse of Mont-Dieu in 1144, he wrote for these **Carthusians** his *Golden Epistle* or *Epistola ad fratres de Monte Dei* (*Letter to the Brothers of Mont-Dieu*). William's early work *On the Nature and Dignity of Love* provides the key to union with God as he portrays the animal, rational, and spiritual stages of the soul's journey.

**WILLIAM OF SHERWOOD (ca. 1200–ca. 1267).** Quite likely William was born shortly after 1200 in Nottinghamshire. It is probable that he studied at Paris and Oxford. He became a master of arts at Oxford in 1252. Around 1257, he was made treasurer of Lincoln Cathedral, a position he held until his death about a decade later. William is best known for his outstanding work in logic or **dialectics**. His *Introductiones in logicam* and *Syncategoremata*, the only two works determined with certainty as his, earned him the admiration of **Roger Bacon** and have led some to think he was a teacher of **Peter of Spain** (Pope John XXI) at Paris, due to the resemblance of these works to the latter's better-known *Summulae logicales*.

**WILLIAM PETER OF GODINO (ca. 1260–1336).** This **Dominican** philosopher and theologian joined the Dominicans about 1281 and studied in various schools of the order. He commented on the *Sentences* of **Peter Lombard** at Paris between 1299 and 1301, and in this work he defended the teachings of **Thomas Aquinas**, particularly against the challenges of **Henry of Ghent**. It earned his commentary the title *Lectura Thomasina*. He was elected provincial of the Toulouse province of the Dominicans in 1303. We know that he lectured at Paris in 1304 and at Avignon in 1306. William Peter was named a cardinal in 1312 and did various missions for the popes until his death in 1336. Besides his *Lectura Thomasina*, he is also known for a disputed question on individuation and a treatise titled *De causa immediata ecclesiasticae potestatis* (*On the Immediate Cause of Church Power*).

**WYCLIFFE, JOHN (ca. 1335–1384).** Wycliffe became a master of theology at Oxford around 1372. He was a prolific writer in philosophy, the **Bible**, and **law**. His early philosophical works include a *Logica* that well spells out in its treatment of universals his opposition to extreme **nominalism (Ockhamism)** and mitigated nominalism (conceptualism). He is a **realist** who, in his other philosophical writings, strongly criticized his nominalistic opponents in whatever form they took or in whatever area they invaded. His chief biblical works are his *Postilla super totam Bibliam* (*Commentary on the Whole Bible*) (1372–1376) and his 1378 *De veritate sacrae Scripturae* (*On the Truth of the Sacred Scriptures*). In this latter treatise, he defended the thesis that the Bible presents the sole and immediate source of Christian teaching. In the field of law, he wrote, in quick order, a number of treatises: *De dominio divino* (*On Divine Dominion*) (1372), *De mandatis divinis* (*On the Divine Commandments*) (1373–1374), *De statu innocentiae* (*On the State of Innocence*) (1373–1375), and *De civili dominio* (*On Civil Dominion*) (1376–1378).

Borrowing from **Marsilius of Padua** and **Richard Fitzralph**, Wycliffe argued that only man in the state of grace or righteousness can properly exercise authority. Authority, thus, is not found in an office, and the clergy and the pope cannot claim jurisdiction solely by occupying their positions. They receive jurisdiction only if they are truly righteous. Although this theory has a broader realm of application, Wycliffe applied his theory of dominion most often to Church authority, criticizing the pope, bishops, clergy, and members of the religious orders. His theories of dominion passed over into the realm of the sacraments, as he claimed that absolution by the Church was confirmatory, not causal. His attack on transubstantiation in his *De eucharistia* (1379) caused him the most damage. When he criticized the Church hierarchy and clergy for abuses, he could find a great deal of support, but when he argued that "Christ is not in the sacrament of the Altar identically, truly, and really in his bodily person," his claim to orthodoxy in his teachings lost its power. Wycliffe had already left Oxford by 1382 when Archbishop William Courtenay forced his followers to retract their views and later had 24 propositions attributed to Wycliffe condemned. The Council of Constance condemned his writings and had his books burned and his body removed from consecrated ground. The Lollards became his strong supporters in England. The Hussites called him "the fifth evangelist" and were even called Wycliffites, although they did not follow him in his Eucharistic teachings.

# Appendix 1

## Honorific Titles of Philosophers and Theologians in the University Tradition

This list includes only some of the better-known titles in the European university tradition. In the case of medieval Scholastic doctors, it includes the religious order and year of death when applicable and available. A more comprehensive list may be found in the *New Catholic Encyclopedia* under the entry "Doctor (Scholastic Title)" by J. C. Vansteenkiste. A clear analogue of this university tradition, and of its title-conferring practices, is not found in medieval Judaism or Islam. To be sure, honorific titles of medieval Jewish and Islamic thinkers exist, though not in the same formal context. For example, in Judaism some thinkers were known by the names of their works. Moses Maimonides, known in his culture as Rambam, the acronym of his full name, Rabbi Moses ben Maimon, is even sometimes referred to in the Latin tradition as Dux Perplexorum, on account of his *Guide of the Perplexed*. In a different context, Saadiah is known as Saadiah Gaon because he held the formal title of gaon or "head" of Talmudic academies in Babylon. In Islam, Al-Ghazali became known, remarkably, as "the Proof of Islam" (Hujjat al-Islam), and Al-Kindi simply as "the Philosopher of the Arabs," titles that go well beyond the academic context.

## MEDIEVAL SCHOLASTIC DOCTORS

| | | |
|---|---|---|
| *Angelicus* (or *Communis* or *Sanctus*) | St. Thomas Aquinas, O.P. | 1274 |
| *Authenticus* | Gregory of Rimini, O.E.S.A. | 1358 |
| *Christianissimus* (or *Venerabilis*) | Jean Gerson | 1429 |
| *Christianus* | Nicholas of Cusa | 1464 |
| *Columna doctorum* | William of Champeaux, O.S.B. | 1121 |
| *Correctivus* | William de la Mare, O.F.M. | 1290 |
| *Dulcifluus* and *Scotellus* | Antonius Andreas, O.F.M. | ca. 1335 |

| | | |
|---|---|---|
| *Ecstaticus* | Denys the Carthusian | 1471 |
| | Jan Van Ruysbroeck | 1381 |
| *Expertus* | Albert the Great | 1280 |
| *Facundus* (or *Ingeniosus*) | Peter Aureoli, O.F.M. | 1322 |
| *Fundatus* | William de la Ware, O.F.M. | 1270 |
| *Fundatissimus* (or *Beatus* or *Verbosus*) | Giles of Rome, O.E.S.A. | 1316 |
| *Illuminatus* | Francis of Meyronnes, O.F.M. | 1325–27 |
| | Raymond Lull, O.F.M. | 1315 |
| *Illustratus* | Adam Marsh, O.F.M. | 1259 |
| | Francis of Marchia, O.F.M. | 1345 |
| *Invincibilis* (or *Singularis* or *Venerabilis Inceptor*) | William of Ockham, O.F.M. | 1349 |
| *Irrefragibilis* (or *Doctor Doctorum* or *Primus*) | Alexander of Hales, O.F.M. | 1245 |
| *Magister historiarum* | Peter Comestor | 1180 |
| *Magister sententiarum* (in the *Sentences*, simply *Magister*) | Peter Lombard | 1164 |
| *Magnus* (or *Universalis* or *Venerabilis* or *Expertus*) | Albertus Magnus, O.P. | 1280 |
| *Marianus* | St. Anselm of Canterbury, O.S.B. | 1109 |
| | John Duns Scotus, O.F.M. | 1308 |
| *Mellifluus* | Bernard of Clairvaux, O. Cist. | 1153 |
| *Mirabilis* (or *Admirabilis*) | Roger Bacon, O.F.M. | 1294 |
| *Nominatissimus* | Stephen Langton | 1228 |
| *Ornatissimus* (or *Sufficiens*) | Peter of Aquila, O.F.M. | 1344 |
| *Peripateticus palatinus* | Peter Abelard | 1142 |
| *Planus* | Walter Burley | 1344 |
| | Nicolas of Lyra, O.F.M. | 1340 |
| *Praecellentissumus philosophiae* | Siger of Brabant | 1274 |

| | | |
|---|---|---|
| *Praeceptor Germaniae* | Rhabanus Maurus | 856 |
| *Profundus* | Thomas Bradwardine | 1349 |
| *Providus* | Aufredus or Anfredus Gonteri | 1325 |
| *Refulgens* (or *Refulgidus*) | Peter of Candia, O.F.M. | 1410 |
| *Relucens* | Francis of Marchia, O.F.M. | 1345 |
| *Resolutissimus* | Durandus of Saint-Pourçain, O.P. | 1334 |
| *Scholasticus* | Anselm of Laon | 1117 |
| | Peter Abelard | 1142 |
| | Gilbert de la Porrée | 1154 |
| | Peter Lombard | 1164 |
| | Peter of Poitiers | 1205 |
| | Hugh of Newcastle, O.F.M. | 1322 |
| *Seraphicus* | St. Bonaventure, O.F.M. | 1274 |
| *Solemnis* | Henry of Ghent | 1293 |
| *Solidus* (or *Copiosus*) | Richard of Middleton, O.F.M. | 1300 |
| *Speculativus* | James of Viterbo, O.E.S.A. | 1307 |
| *Sublimis* (or *Illuminatus*) | Joannes Tauler, O.P. | 1361 |
| *Subtilis* | John Duns Scotus, O.F.M. | 1308 |
| *Supersubtilis* | John of Ripa, O.F.M. | 1368 |
| *Universalis* | Alan of Lille, 1202; Albert | 1280 |
| *Utilis* (or *Planus*) | Nicholas of Lyra, O.F.M. | 1340 |
| *Venerabilis Inceptor* | William of Ockham, O.F.M. | 1347 |
| *Venerandus* | Godfrey of Fontaines | 1240 |

## OTHER TITLES

| | |
|---|---|
| *Apostolus* (or *Doctor Gentium*) | St. Paul |
| *Commentator* | Averroes; before 1250 sometimes Avicenna |
| *Doctor Doctorum* | Alexander of Hales |

| | |
|---|---|
| *Doctor Gratiae* (or *Theologus* or *Magister*) | Augustine |
| *Philosophus* | Aristotle |

# Appendix 2

## *Condemnations of 1277*

The list of condemnations contained in the *Chartularium Universitatis Parisiensis* is found in its original unordered form. A second presentation of the condemnations, in an orderly logical collection made by the respected historian of medieval thought, Pierre Mandonnet, gives a topical structure to the list in *Siger de Brabant et l'averroïsme latin au XIIIe siècle* (Les Philosophes Belges 7 [Louvain: Institut Supérieur de Philosophie de l'Université, 1908]), 175–91. This latter numbering and also the logical grouping are followed in our representative list of condemned propositions.

### ERRORS RELATED TO THE NATURE OF PHILOSOPHY

1. That there is no more excellent state than to study philosophy.
2. That the only wise men in the world are the philosophers.
3. That in order to have some certitude about any conclusion, man must base himself on self-evident principles.—The statement is erroneous because it refers in a general way both to the certitude of apprehension and to that of adherence.
4. That one should not hold anything unless it is self-evident or can be manifested from self-evident principles.
5. That man should not be content with authority to have certitude about any question.
6. That there is no rationally disputable question that the philosopher ought not to dispute and determine, because reasons are derived from things. It belongs to philosophy under one or another of its parts to consider all things.
7. That besides the philosophical disciplines, all the sciences are necessary, but that they are necessary only on account of human custom.

### ERRORS RELATED TO GOD'S KNOWLEDGE

13. That God does not know things other than Himself.
14. That God cannot know contingent beings immediately except through their particular and proximate causes.

15. That the First Cause does not have science of future contingents. The first reason is that future contingents are not beings. The second is that future contingents are singulars, but God knows by means of an intellectual power, which cannot know singulars. Hence, if there were no senses, the intellect would perhaps not distinguish between Socrates and Plato, although it would distinguish between a man and an ass. The third reason is the relation of cause to effect; for the divine foreknowledge is a necessary cause of the things foreknown. The fourth reason is the relation of science to the known, for even though science is not the cause of the known, it is determined to one of two contradictories by that which is known; and this is true of divine knowledge much more than of ours.

## ERRORS RELATED TO THE ETERNITY OF THE WORLD

83. That the world, although it was made from nothing, was not newly made, and, although it passed from nonbeing to being, the nonbeing did not precede being in duration but only in nature.

84. That the world is eternal because that which has a nature by which it is able to exist for the whole future has a nature by which it was able to exist in the whole past.

85. That the world is eternal as regards all the species contained in it, and that time, motion, matter, agent, and receiver are eternal, because the world comes from the infinite power of God and it is impossible that there be something new in the effect without there being something new in the cause.

86. That eternity and time have no existence in reality but only in the mind.

89. That it is impossible to refute the arguments of the Philosopher concerning the eternity of the world unless we say that the will of the first being embraces incompatibles.

## ERRORS RELATED TO THE AGENT INTELLECT

117. That the intellect is numerically one for all, for although it may be separated from this or that body, it is not separated from every body.

118. That the agent intellect is a certain separated substance superior to the possible intellect, and that it is separated from the body according to its substance, power, and operation and is not the form of the human body.

120. That the form of man does not come from an extrinsic source but is educed from the potency of matter, for otherwise generation would not be univocal.

121. That no form coming from an extrinsic source can form one being with matter; for that which is separable does not form one being with that which is corruptible.

122. That from the sensitive and intellectual parts of man there does not result a unity in essence, unless it be a unity such as that of an intelligence and a sphere, that is, a unity in operation.

123. That the intellect is not the form of the body, except in the manner in which a helmsman is the form of a ship, and that it is not an essential perfection of man.

126. That the intellect, which is man's ultimate perfection, is completely separated.

129. That the substance of the soul is eternal, and that the agent intellect and the possible intellect are eternal.

130. That the human intellect is eternal because it comes from a cause that is always the same and because it does not have matter by means of which it is in potency prior to being in act.

131. That the speculative intellect is simply eternal and incorruptible; with respect to this or that man, however, it is corrupted when the phantasms in him are corrupted.

132. That the intellect casts off the body when it so desires and puts it on when it so desires.

133. That the soul is inseparable from the body, and that the soul is corrupted when the harmony of the body is corrupted.

## ERRORS RELATED TO ETHICS OR MORAL MATTERS

172. That happiness is had in this life and not in another.

173. That happiness cannot be infused by God immediately.

174. That after death man loses every good.

175. That since Socrates was made incapable of eternity, if he is to be eternal, it is necessary that he be changed in nature and species.

177. That raptures and visions are caused only by nature.

## ERRORS RELATED TO CHRISTIAN FAITH

180. That the Christian law impedes learning.

181. That there are fables and falsehoods in the Christian law just as in others.

182. That one does not know anything more by the fact that he knows theology.

183. That the teachings of the theologian are based on fables.

184. That what is possible or impossible absolutely speaking, that is, in every respect, is what is possible or impossible according to philosophy.

## ERRORS RELATED TO SPECIFIC CHRISTIAN TEACHINGS

185. That God is not triune because Trinity is incompatible with the highest simplicity; for where there is a real plurality there is necessarily addition and composition. Take the example of a pile of stones.

186. That God cannot beget his own likeness, for what is begotten has its beginning from something on which it depends; and that in God to beget would not be a sign of perfection.

187. That creation should not be called a change to being.—This is erroneous if understood of every kind of change.

188. That it is not true that something comes from nothing or was made in a first creation.

189. That creation is not possible, even though the contrary must be held according to the faith.

195. That without a proper agent, such as a father and a man, God could not make a man.

196. That to make an accident exist without a subject has the nature of an impossibility implying contradiction.

## ERRORS RELATED TO CHRISTIAN VIRTUES

200. That no other virtues are possible except the acquired or the innate virtues.

201. That one should not be concerned about the faith if something is said to be heretical because it is against the faith.

202. That one should not pray.

203. That one should not confess except for the sake of appearance.

205. That simple fornication, namely, that of an unmarried man with an unmarried woman, is not a sin.

208. That continence is not essentially a virtue.

211. That humility, in the degree to which one does not show what he has but depreciates and lowers himself, is not a virtue.—This is erroneous if what is meant is: neither a virtue nor a virtuous act.

212. That one who is poor as regards the goods of fortune cannot act well in moral matters.

## ERRORS RELATED TO MAN'S LAST END

214. That God cannot grant perpetuity to a changeable and corruptible thing.

216. That a philosopher must not concede the resurrection to come, because it cannot be investigated by reason.—This is erroneous because even a philosopher must "bring his mind into captivity to the obedience of Christ" (2 Corinthians 10:5).

## SOME ERRORS ASSOCIATED WITH THOMAS AQUINAS, AS SUGGESTED BY GODFREY OF FONTAINES

42. That God cannot multiply individuals of the same species without matter.

43. That God could not make several intelligences of the same species because intelligences do not have matter.

147. That it is improper to maintain that some intellects are more noble than others because this diversity has to come from the intelligences, since it cannot come from the bodies; and thus noble and ignoble souls would necessarily be of different species, like the intelligences.—This is erroneous, for thus the soul of Christ would not be more noble than that of Judas.

54. That the separated substances are nowhere according to their substance.—This is erroneous if so understood as to mean that substance is not in a place. If, however, it is so understood as to mean that substance is the reason for being in a place, it is true that they are nowhere according to their substance.

55. That the separated substances are somewhere by their operation and that they cannot move from one extreme to another or to the middle except insofar as they can will to operate either in the middle or in the extremes.—This is erroneous if so understood as to mean that without operation a substance is not in a place and that it does not pass from one place to another.

163. That the will necessarily pursues what is firmly held by reason, and that it cannot abstain from that which reason dictates. This necessitation, however, is not compulsion but the nature of the will.

# Bibliography

## CONTENTS

## INTRODUCTION

This bibliography is lengthy, but still very selective and, in fact, quite limited. The works listed are for the most part in English, but since we have depended on encyclopedias published in different languages for some of our information and because English articles concerning many of the authors mentioned are at times in foreign-language books and journals, we have included these foreign-language titles, particularly in the case of those encyclopedias and journals that we would especially recommend.

Among the general and special bibliographies listed below, readers could become lost in the forest of books and articles recommended. For general bibliographic information, a good place to begin would be with Marcia Colish's "Medieval Europe: Church and Intellectual History," an article in *The American Historical Association's Guide to Historical Literature*. Its selections show the sweeping vision of a trained historian and the focus of a specialist in the history of Christian thought. A very thorough selection of works relating to Islamic philosophy and theology can be found in Hans

Daiber's two-volume *Bibliography of Islamic Philosophy*. A more specific direction, relating Islamic philosophy to the universities of the Latin West, is provided in the "Special Bibliographies" section by the articles of Charles Butterworth and Thérèse-Anne Druart. For solid introductions to medieval Jewish philosophy and theology, a better place to begin than in the bibliographical sections would be with the titles provided in the bibliographies contained in *A History of Jewish Philosophy in the Middle Ages* by Collette Sirat or the more recent *History of Jewish Philosophy* edited by Daniel H. Frank and Oliver Leaman.

Introductory and advanced articles on philosophers and theologians and on various topics of medieval thought can be found in numerous encyclopedias and biographical dictionaries. Very helpful as introductions are the articles in *The New Catholic Encyclopedia*, the *Encyclopedia of Islam*, and the *Encyclopedia Judaica*.

*A Companion to Philosophy in the Middle Ages*, edited by Jorge Gracia and Timothy Noone, provides a more advanced introduction to many of the philosophers of the medieval world, with articles written by scholars who have worked seriously on the particular authors they treat. *The Dictionnaire de Théologie Catholique* has very long and learned contributions on the themes of theology and the contributions of individual theologians, though many need to be updated. This work is complemented in the area of Christian mysticism and spirituality by the more modern and still incomplete *Dictionnaire de Spiritualité ascétique et mystique*. A comparison of their different presentations on Richard of Saint-Victor or St. Bonaventure reveals the different sides, doctrinal and spiritual, of these authors and the need for complementary treatments of them.

There are no general histories of medieval theology that can compete with the many histories of philosophy. *The History of Christian Philosophy in the Middle Ages* by Étienne Gilson is a classic. Much of its content can be found in an updated form in Armand Maurer's *Medieval Philosophy*, but this also needs a further update. A number of recent histories of medieval philosophy concentrate on particular eras. For the early Middle Ages (480–1150), John Marenbon's work is a good introduction, as is his work on late medieval thought (1150–1350). William Courtenay's *Schools and Scholars in Fourteenth-Century England* brings a more particularized vision, but argues convincingly for a major shift of focus from Paris to Oxford and Cambridge and their influence on later Parisian philosophy and theology. James Hankins's two-volume work, *Plato in the Italian Renaissance*, is a scholarly invitation to hear the other ancient voice that challenged the dominance of Aristotle in the later Middle Ages. *The Columbia History of Western Philosophy*, edited by Richard Popkin and a collection of assistants, stretches beyond the medieval period, but it is especially strong on the Jewish and Arabic authors of the Middle Ages.

The list of specialized and related histories sounds an alert. Medieval philosophy and theology need to be understood in terms of educational contexts: a school with one master is not the same as a university with many masters. Michèle Mulchahey's detailed work on Dominican education and Olaf Pederson's history of the medieval education movements that prepared the first universities place many of the medieval philosophers and theologians in their institutional contexts. A large amount of study in American and British universities has focused on medieval logic. *The Cambridge History of Later Medieval Philosophy*, edited by Norman Kretzman, Anthony Kenny, Jan Pinborg, and Eleanore Stump, provides biographies, bibliographies, and detailed articles on many authors who contributed to this special area of study. Other authors remind us that there is more to the medieval world of thought than logic. Anthony Black stresses the development of political thought in Europe from 1250 to 1450; Edward Grant accentuates the ways in which the foundations of modern science are found in medieval sources; Beryl Smalley, in her classic, *The Study of the Bible in the Middle Ages*, restores the religious and biblical context of medieval intellectual pursuit; and Bernard McGinn, in three volumes, turns attention to medieval spirituality in his mature presentation of the foundations, growth, and flourishing of mysticism.

The remainder of the bibliographical selections are attempts to put readers in contact with the large, though very partial, selection of primary medieval philosophical and theological texts that exist in English. The titles listed, for the most part, are works belonging to individual authors. Access to English text collections introducing various authors are also provided by some classical anthologies, such as that of John F. Wippel and Alan B. Wolter. Another classic, that of Arthur Hyman and James Walsh, likewise offers a wonderful collection of texts and has the particular attraction of including Arabian and Jewish authors. There are also thematic collections that carry the texts of a good selection of authors, such as the hearty three-volume set *The Cambridge Translations of Medieval Philosophical Texts*, which deals with logic and philosophy of language, ethics and political philosophy, and mind and knowledge.

The bibliographies suggested for Arabic and Jewish authors provide lists of works available in their original language. The *Repertorium edierter Texte des Mittelalters*, edited by Rolf Schoenberger and Brigitte Kible, offers a detailed listing of all the editions of the original Latin works of the authors listed in this Dictionary. Its vastly expanded second edition appeared in 2011.

Finally, in connection with each of the medieval authors described in this present volume, there is listed at least one book or article that offers an introduction to the philosophical and theological thought of that author. Preference has been given to English books and articles. They should help those who want to begin study on a particular author. These suggested introductory books and articles will also provide references to other works connected to the same author, his sources, and his critics.

Of course, scholars who want to go further in their studies would quickly realize that except in the very few cases of famous authors, such as St. Anselm, St. Bonaventure, St. Thomas Aquinas, Moses Maimonides, Avicenna, and Averroes, most works of medieval philosophers and theologians still remain in handwritten copies in shorthand Latin, Arabic, and Hebrew. Medieval works in all three languages can be found mostly in the great manuscript libraries of the world: the Bibliothèque Nationale and the Bibliothèque Mazarine in Paris, the many college libraries of Oxford, the Cambridge University Library that houses the manuscripts of most of the Cambridge colleges, the British Library in London, and the Vatican Library in Rome. Many of the libraries of the old university cities of Europe have large collections: Bologna, Padua, Naples, Munich, Erfurt, Vienna, Prague, and Cracow. Capital cities, like Brussels and Berlin, and former capital cities, like St. Petersburg, also have large collections. A few religious houses kept sizeable libraries, such as that of the Dominikanerkloster in Vienna. Others had their collections reduced or removed by armies: many of these manuscripts were lost; many were merely transferred. Clues to these changes can be found in the collection names of libraries, such as the *Fondo dei conventi soppressi* in the Biblioteca Nazionale Centrale and the Biblioteca Medicea Laurenziana in Florence and the collection of *nouvelles acquisitions* in the Bibliothèque Nationale in Paris. Famous Benedictine monasteries (Monte Cassino, Melk, Klosterneuburg) still have noteworthy collections, but most monastic collections have moved on to the Staatsbibliothek of Munich or the Bibliothèque Nationale of Paris. Their original homes are simply noted on the inside front or back covers.

## BIBLIOGRAPHIES

### General Bibliographies

Boyce, G. C. *Literature of Medieval History, 1930–1975: A Supplement to Louis J. Paetow's A Guide to the Study of Medieval History.* 5 vols. Millwood, N.Y.: Kraus International Publications, 1981.
Caenegem, R. C. van, and F. L. Ganshof. *Guide to the Sources of Medieval History.* Amsterdam: North Holland Publishing, 1978.
Carlson, J. W. *Words of Wisdom: A Philosophical Dictionary of the Perennial Tradition.* Notre Dame, Ind.: University of Notre Dame Press, 2012.

Case, S. J., et al. *A Bibliographical Guide to the History of Christianity*. New York: P. Smith, 1951.

Chadwick, O. *The History of the Church: A Select Bibliography*. London: Historical Association, 1962.

Colish, M. L. "Medieval Europe: Church and Intellectual History." In *The American Historical Association's Guide to Historical Literature*, ed. M. B. Norton and P. Gerardi, 617–703. New York: Oxford University Press, 1995.

Daiber, H. *Bibliography of Islamic Philosophy*. 2 vols. Leiden: Brill, 1999.

Fallon, J., ed. *Guide Bibliographique des Études de Philosophie*. Paris: J. Vrin-Librairie Peeters, 1993.

Fisher, J. H., ed. *The Medieval Literature of Western Europe: A Review of Research, Mainly 1930–1960*. New York: New York University Press, 1966.

Menasce, J. de. *Arabische Philosophie*. Bibliographische Einführungen in das Studium der Philosophie 6. Bern: A. Francke, 1948.

Paetow, L. J. *A Guide to the Study of Medieval History*. Rev. by G. C. Boyce with an addendum by L. Thorndike. New York: Kraus Reprint, 1959.

Synan, E. A. "Latin Philosophies of the Middle Ages." In *Medieval Studies: An Introduction*, ed. J. M. Powell, 277–311. Syracuse, N.Y.: Syracuse University Press, 1976.

Vajda, G. *Jüdische Philosophie*. Bibliographische Einführungen in das Studium der Philosophie 19. Bern: A. Francke, 1950.

Van Steenberghen, F. *Philosophie des Mittelaters*. Bibliographische Einführungen in das Studium der Philosophie 17. Bern: A. Francke, 1950.

## Special Bibliographies

Anawati, G. C. *Bibliographie d'Averroès (Ibn Rushd)*. Algiers: Organisation Arabe pour l'Éducation, la Culture et les Sciences, 1978.

Ashworth, E. J. *The Tradition of Medieval Logic and Speculative Grammar from Anselm to the End of the Seventeenth Century: A Bibliography from 1836 Onwards*. Toronto: Pontifical Institute of Mediaeval Studies, 1978.

Beckmann, J. P. *Ockham-Bibliographie, 1900–1990*. Hamburg: Felix Meiner Verlag, 1992.

Benakis, L. G. *Byzantine Philosophy B'*. Athens: Parousia, 2013.

Bougerol, J. G. *Bibliographia Bonaventuriana (c. 1850–1973)*. In *San Bonaventura 1274–1974*, vol. 5. Grottaferrata: Quaracchi, 1974.

Bourke, V. J. *Thomistic Bibliography, 1920–1940*. St. Louis, Mo.: The Modern Schoolman, 1945.

Brennan, M. *Guide des Études Erigeniennes—A Guide to Eriugenian Studies, 1930–1987*. Paris: Éditions du Cerf-Édition Universitaires, 1989.

Brummer, R. *Bibliographia Lulliana: Ramon-Llull-Schrifttum, 1870–1973.* Hildesheim: Verlag Dr. H. A. Gerstenberg, 1976.

Burton, P.-A. *Bibliotheca Aelrediana Secunda: Une Bibliographie Cumulative (1962–1996).* Louvain-la-Neuve: Fédération Internationale des Instituts d'Études Médiévales, 1997. Refer to Hoste, A.

Butterworth, C. E. "The Study of Arabic Philosophy Today." In *Arabic Philosophy and the West: Continuity and Interaction,* 55–140. Washington, D.C.: Georgetown University Press, 1988.

Bydén, B., and K. Ierodiakonou, eds. *The Many Faces of Byzantine Philosophy.* Athens: Norwegian Institute at Athens, 2012.

Cacourosk, M., and M.-H. Congourdeau, eds. *Philosophies et Sciences à Byzance de 1204 à 1453.* Leuven: Peeters, 2006.

Cordonier, V., and T. Suarez-Nani, eds. *L'aristotelisme exposé: Aspects du débat philosophique entre Henri de Gand et Gilles de Rome.* Fribourg: J. Vrin, 2014.

Danan, G., and I. Rosier-Catach, eds. *La Rhétorique d'Aristote. Tradition et commentaires de l'Antiquité au XVIIeme siècle.* Paris: J. Vrin, 1998.

Doucet, V. "Notulae bibliographicae de quibusdam operibus Fr. Ioannis Pecham, OFM." *Antonianum* 8 (1933): 425–59.

Druart, T.-A. *Arabic Philosophy and the West: Continuity and Interaction,* 55–140. Washington, D.C.: Catholic University of America Press, 1988.

Galle, G. "A Comprehensive Bibliography of Peter of Auvergne." *Bulletin de Philosophie Médiévale* 42 (2000): 53–79.

Hillgarth, J. N. "Isidorian Studies, 1976–1985." *Studi Medievali,* 3rd. ser., 31 (1990): 925–73.

———. "The Position of Isidorian Studies: A Critical Review of the Literature 1936–1975." *Studi medievali,* 3rd. ser., 24 (1983): 817–905.

Hoste, A. *Bibliotheca Aelrediana: A Survey of the Manuscripts, Old Catalogues, Editions, and Studies concerning St. Aelred of Rievaulx.* The Hague: Nijhoff, 1942.

Ierodiakonou, K., and D. O'Meara. "Byzantine Philosophy." In *The Oxford Handbook of Byzantine Studies,* ed. E. Jeffreys et al., 711–20. Oxford: Oxford University Press, 2008.

Ingardia, R. *Thomas Aquinas: International Bibliography, 1977–1990.* Bowling Green, Ohio: Philosophy Documentation Center, 1993.

Janssens, J. L. *An Annotated Bibliography on Ibn Sina, 1970–1989.* Leuven: Leuven University Press, 1991.

———. *An Annotated Bibliography on Ibn Sina (First Supplement, 1990–1994).* Louvain-la-Neuve: Presse Universitaire, 1999.

Kaufhold, M. *Reflexion in der Welt des späten Mittelalters—Political Thought in the Age of Scholasticism. Essays in Honour of Jürgen Miethke.* Leiden: Brill, 1992.

Kellner, M. "Bibliographia Gersonideana: An Annotated List of Writings by and about R. Levi ben Gershom." In *Studies on Gersonides: A Fourteenth-Century Jewish Philosopher-Scientist*, ed. G. Freudenthal, 367–414. Leiden: Brill, 1992.

Kienzler, K. *International Bibliography: Anselm of Canterbury*. Lewiston, N.Y.: Mellen, 1999.

Krieger, G. "Studies on Walter Burley." *Vivarium* 37 (1999): 94–100.

Largier, N. *Bibliographie zu Meister Eckhart*. Freiburg: Universitätsverlag, 1989.

———. "Recent Work on Meister Eckhart: Positions, Problems, New Perspectives, 1990–1997." *Recherches de Théologie et Philosophie Médiévales* 65 (1998): 147–67.

Leaman, O. "A Guide to Bibliographical Resources (Islamic Philosophy)." In *History of Islamic Philosophy*, ed. S. H. Nasr and O. Leaman, 1173–76, Routledge History of World Philosophies 1. London: Routledge, 1996.

Manning, E. *Bibliographie bernardine, 1957–1970*. Documentation Cistercienne 6. Rochefort: Abbaye Saint-Rémy, 1972.

Miethe, T. L., and V. J. Bourke. *Thomistic Bibliography, 1940–1978*. Westport, Conn.: Greenwood Press, 1980.

Nasr, S. A., and W. C. Chittick. *An Annotated Bibliography of Islamic Science*. 3 vols. Tehran: Imperial Iranian Academy of Philosophy, 1975–1994.

Parodi, M. "Recenti studi su Giovanni di Mirecourt." *Rivista Critica di Storia della Filosofia* 33 (1978): 297–307.

Perreiah, A. R. *Paul of Venice: A Bibliographical Guide*. Bowling Green, Ohio: Philosophy Documentation Center, 1986.

Pironet, F. *The Tradition of Medieval Logic and Speculative Grammar: A Bibliography, 1977–1994*. Turnhout: Brepols, 1995.

Porro, P. "Bibliography." In *Henry of Ghent*, ed. W. Vanhamel, 405–34. Leuven: Leuven University Press, 1996.

———. "Bibliography on Henry of Ghent (1994–2002)." In *Henry of Ghent and the Transformation of Scholastic Thought*, ed. G. Guldentops and C. Steel, 409–26. Leuven: Leuven University Press, 2003.

Rescher, N. *Al-Kindi: An Annotated Bibliography*. Pittsburgh: University of Pittsburgh Press, 1964.

Rigo, A., ed. *Byzantine Theology and Its Philosophical Background*. Turnhout: Brepols, 2011.

Rosemann, P. "Averroes: A Catalogue of Editions and Scholarly Writings from 1821 Onwards." *Bulletin de la Philosophie Médiévale* 30 (1988): 153–215.

Schabel, C. *Theological Quodlibeta in the Middle Ages: The Thirteenth Century*. Leiden: Brill, 2006.

———. *Theological Quodlibeta in the Middle Ages: The Fourteenth Century*. Leiden: Brill, 2007.

Schaefer, O. *Bibliographia de vita, operibus et doctrina Iohannis Duns Scoti*. Rome: Herder, 1955.

Schoepfer, J. "Bibliographie." In *Albertus Magnus-Doctor Universalis, 1280/1980*, ed. G. Meyer and A. Zimmermann, 495–508. Mainz: Matthias-Grünewald Verlag, 1980.

West, D. C. "Bibliography of Joachim Studies since 1954." In *Joachim of Fiore in Christian Thought*, xix–xxiv. New York: Burt Franklin, 1975.

Wood, R. "Studies on Walter Burley, 1968–1988." *Bulletin de Philosophie Médiévale* 30 (1988): 233–50.

## ENCYCLOPEDIAS AND BIOGRAPHICAL DICTIONARIES

*Biographical Dictionary of Christian Theologians*. Ed. P. Carey and J. T. Lienhard. Westport, Conn.: Greenwood, 2000.

*Companion to Philosophy in the Middle Ages*. Ed. J. J. E. Gracia and T. B. Noone. Malden, Mass.: Blackwell, 2003.

*Dictionary of the Middle Ages*. Ed. J. R. Strayer. 13 vols. New York: Scribner, 1982–1989.

*Dictionnaire de Spiritualité ascétique et mystique*. Ed. M. Viller, F. Cavalleva, and André Derville. 17 vols. Paris: Beauchesne, 1932–1995.

*Dictionnaire de Théologie Catholique*. Ed. A. Vacant, E. Mangenot, and E. Amann. 15 vols. Paris: Letouzez et Ané, 1899–1950.

*Dictionnaire d'histoire et de géographie ecclésiastiques*. Ed. A. Baudrillart, A. Vogt, U. Rouziés, A. De Meyer, and R. Aubert. 28 vols. Paris: Letouzey et Ané, 1912–.

*Enciclopedia Cattolica*. Ed. G. Pizzardo. 12 vols. Rome: Città del Vaticano, 1949–1954.

*Encyclopaedia Judaica*. Ed. C. Roth et al. 16 vols. New York: Macmillan, 1972–2003.

*Encyclopaedia of Islam*. New ed. Ed. H. A. R. Gibb, J. H. Kramers, E. Lévi-Provençal, and J. Schacht. 9 vols. Leiden: Brill, 1960–1995.

*Encyclopedia of Medieval Philosophy: Philosophy between 500 and 1500*. Ed. H. Lagerhand. Dordrecht: Springer, 2011.

*The Encyclopedia of Philosophy*. Ed. P. Edwards. 8 vols. New York: Macmillan, 1967; supplement, 1996.

*Lexikon des Mittelalters*. Ed. R. Auty. 10 vols. Munich: Artemis Verlag, 1980–1999.

*Lexikon für Theologie und Kirche*. Ed. K. Baumgartner. 11 vols. Freiburg: Herder, 1993–2001.

*The Medieval Hebrew Encyclopedias of Science and Philosophy*. Ed. S. Harvey. Dordrecht: Springer, 2000.

*New Catholic Encyclopedia*. 2nd ed. Ed. B. L. Marthaler. 14 vols. Detroit, Washington, D.C.: Thomson Gale, Catholic University of America Press, 2003.

*Routledge Encyclopedia of Philosophy*. Ed. E. Craig. 10 vols. London: Routledge, 1998.

*Theologische Realenzyklopädie*. Ed. H. R. Balz et al. 36 vols. Berlin: De Gruyter, 1997–2003.

## HISTORIES OF MEDIEVAL PHILOSOPHY AND THEOLOGY

### General Histories

Adamson, P., and R. Taylor. *Cambridge Companion to Arabic Philosophy*. Cambridge: Cambridge University Press, 2005.

Caponigri, A. R., and R. McInerny. *A History of Western Philosophy*. Vols. 2–3. Notre Dame, Ind.: University of Notre Dame Press, 1969–1970.

Clark, G. H. *Thales to Dewey: A History of Philosophy*. Boston: Houghton Mifflin, 1957.

Colish, M. L. *Medieval Foundations of the Western Intellectual Tradition, 400–1400*. New Haven, Conn.: Yale University Press, 1997.

Copelston, F. C. *A History of Philosophy*. Vols. 2–3. New York: Doubleday, 1985.

———. *Medieval Philosophy*. New York: Harper Torchbooks, 1961.

Corbin, H. *History of Islamic Philosophy*. Trans. L. Sherrard and P. Sherrard. London: Kegan Paul, 1993.

Fakhry, M. *A History of Islamic Philosophy*. 3rd ed. New York: Columbia University Press, 2004.

Forest, A., Van Steenberghen, F., and M. de Gandillac. *Le mouvement doctrinal du IXe au XIVe siècle*. Histoire de l'Église depuis les origines jusqu'à nos jours 13. Paris: Bloud et Gay, 1951.

Frank, D. H., and O. Leaman. *History of Jewish Philosophy*. Routledge History of World Philosophies 2. London: Routledge, 1997.

Gerson, L., ed. *The Cambridge History of Philosophy in Late Antiquity*. 2 vols. Cambridge: Cambridge University Press, 2011.

Gilson, E. *Christian Philosophy: An Introduction*. Trans. A. Maurer. The Étienne Gilson Series 17. Toronto: Pontifical Institute of Mediaeval Philosophy, 1993.

———. *The History of Christian Philosophy in the Middle Ages*. New York: Random House, 1956.

————. *The Spirit of Medieval Philosophy (The Gifford Lectures, 1931–1932)*. Trans. A. H. C. Downes. London: Sheed and Ward, 1936.

Guttmann, J. *Philosophies of Judaism*. Trans. D. Silverman. New York: Schocken, 1973.

Hägglund, B. *History of Theology*. St. Louis, Mo.: Concordia Publishing House, 1968.

Jones, W. T. *A History of Western Philosophy*. New York: Harcourt, Brace and World, 1952.

Jospe, R. *Jewish Philosophy in the Middle Ages*. Brighton, Mass.: Academic Studies Press, 2000.

Lamprecht, S. P. *Our Philosophical Traditions: A Brief History of Philosophy in Western Civilization*. New York: Appleton-Century-Crofts, 1955.

Leaman, O. *An Introduction to Medieval Islamic Philosophy*. 2nd ed. Cambridge: Cambridge University Press, 2002.

Leff, G. *Medieval Thought from Saint Augustine to Ockham*. Harmondsworth, UK: Penguin, 1958.

Luscombe, D. *Medieval Thought*. A History of Philosophy 2. New York: Oxford University Press, 1997.

Marenbon, J., ed. *Medieval Philosophy*. Routledge History of Philosophy 3. London: Routledge, 1998.

Maurer, A. *Mediaeval Philosophy*. 2nd ed. The Étienne Gilson Series 4. Toronto: Pontifical Institute of Mediaeval Studies, 1982.

Mascia, C., and T. Edwards. *A History of Philosophy*. Paterson, N.J.: Saint Anthony Guild Press, 1957.

Pasnau, R., ed. *The Cambridge History of Medieval Philosophy*. 2 vols. Cambridge: Cambridge University Press, 2010.

Pelikan, J. *The Christian Tradition: A History of the Development of Doctrine*. 4 vols. Chicago: University of Chicago Press, 1971–1989.

————. *The Growth of Medieval Theology, 600–1300*. Chicago: University of Chicago Press, 1978.

Popkin, R. H. *The Columbia History of Western Philosophy*. New York: Columbia University Press, 1999.

Price, B. B. *Medieval Thought: An Introduction*. Oxford: Oxford University Press, 1992.

Rudavsky, T., and S. Nadler, eds. *The Cambridge History of Jewish Philosophy: From Antiquity to the Seventeenth Century*. Cambridge: Cambridge University Press, 2009.

Sharif, M., ed. *A History of Muslim Philosophy*. 2 vols. Wiesbaden: Harrassowitz, 1963–1966.

Sirat, C. *A History of Jewish Philosophy in the Middle Ages*. Cambridge: Cambridge University Press, 1985.

Thilly, F. *A History of Philosophy*. 3rd ed. New York: Holt, 1957.

Weinberg, J. *A Short History of Medieval Philosophy*. Princeton, N.J.: Princeton University Press, 1964.


## Special and Related Histories

Abrahamov, B. *Studies in Arabic and Islamic Culture*. Ramut Gan: Ben Ilan University, 2006.

Adamson, P., and R. Taylor, eds. *The Cambridge Companion to Arabic Philosophy*. Cambridge: Cambridge University Press, 2005.

———. *Classical Arabic Philosophy: Sources and Reception*. London: Warburg Institute/Nino Aragno, 2007.

Aertsen, J., ed. *Averroes and the Aristotelian Tradition*. Leiden: Brill, 1999.

———. *Medieval Philosophy as Transcendental Thought*. Leiden: Brill, 2012.

Akasoy, A., and G. Giglioni, eds. *Islamic Thought in the Middle Ages: Studies in Text, Transmission and Translation, in Honour of Hans Daiber*. Leiden: Brill, 2008.

———, eds. *Renaissance Averroism and Its Aftermath: Arab Philosophy in Early Modern Europe*. Dordrecht: Springer, 2013.

Arnzen, R. *Platonische Ideen in der arabischen Philosophie: Texte und Materialien zur Begriffsgeschichte von* suwar aflatuniyya *und* muthul aflatuniyya. Berlin-Boston: De Gruyter, 2011.

Black, A. *Political Thought in Europe, 1250–1450*. Cambridge: Cambridge University Press, 1992.

Boehner, P. *The History of the Franciscan School*. St. Bonaventure, N.Y.: Franciscan Institute, 1943–1944.

Brenet, J. B., ed. *Averroes et Averroismes juif et latin*. Turnhout: Brepols, 2007.

Brundage, J. A. *Medieval Canon Law*. London: Longman, 1995.

Burrell, D., C. Cogliati, J. M. Soskice, and W. R. Stoeger, eds. *Creation and the God of Abraham*. Cambridge: Cambridge University Press, 2010.

Butterworth, C., and B. A. Kessel, eds. *The Introduction of Arabic Philosophy into Europe*. Leiden: Brill, 1994.

Bydén, B., and K. Ierodishanon, eds. *The Many Faces of Byzantine Philosophy*. Athens: Norwegian Institute of Athens, 2012.

Calma, D. *Études sur le premier siècle de l'averroisme latin: approches et textes inédits*. Turnhout: Brepols, 2010.

Cameron, M., and J. Marenbon, eds. *Methods and Methodologies: Aristotelian Logic East and West, 500–1500*. Leiden: Brill, 2011.

Celia, F., and A. Ulacco, eds. *Il Timeo: Esegesi greche, arabe, latine*. Pisa: Pisa University Press, 2012.

Cessario, R. *A Short History of Thomism*. Washington, D.C.: Catholic University of America Press, 2005.

Clanchy, M. T. *From Memory to Written Record: England, 1066–1307*. 2nd ed. Oxford: Blackwell, 1993.

Cobban, A. B. *The Medieval Universities: Their Development and Organization*. Berkeley: University of California Press, 1988.

Colish, M. L. *The Stoic Tradition from Antiquity to the Early Middle Ages*. Leiden: Brill, 1985.

Contreni, J. J. "The Carolingian Renaissance: Education and Literary Culture." In *The New Cambridge Medieval History*, 2 vols., 2:709–57. Cambridge: Cambridge University Press, 1996.

Courtenay, W. J. *Schools & Scholars in Fourteenth-Century England*. Princeton, N.J.: Princeton University Press, 1987.

Crossley, J. N., and C. J. Mews, eds. *Communities of Learning: Networks and the Shaping of Intellectual Identity in Europe 1100–1450*. Turnhout: Brepols, 2011.

D'Ancona, C., ed. *The Libraries of the Neoplatonists*. Leiden: Brill, 2007.

Dronke, P., ed. *A History of Twelfth-Century Western Philosophy*. Cambridge: Cambridge University Press, 1988.

———. *Women Writers of the Middle Ages: A Critical Study of Texts from Perpetua (d. 203) to Marguerite Porete (d. 1310)*. Cambridge: Cambridge University Press, 1984.

El-Rouayheb, K. *Relational Syllogisms and the History of Arabic Logic, 900–1900*. Leiden: Brill, 2010.

Emery, K. A. Speer, and R. Friedman, eds. *Philosophy and Theology in the Long Middle Ages: A Tribute to Stephen F. Brown*. Leiden: Brill, 2011.

Evans, G. R. *Old Arts and New Theology: The Beginning of Theology as an Academic Discipline*. Oxford: Oxford University Press, 1980.

Fidora, A. J. Fried, and M. Lutz-Bachmann, eds. *Politischer Aristotelismus und Religion in Mittelalter und Früher Neuzeit*. Berlin: Akademie Verlag, 2007.

Frankel, C., R. Wisnovsky, F. Wallis, and J. Furno, eds. *Vehicles of Transmission, Translation and Transformation in Medieval Cultures*. Turnhout: Brepols, 2011.

Friemuth, M. E., and J. M. Dillon, eds. *The Afterlife of the Platonic Soul: Reflections on Platonic Psychology in the Monotheistic Religions*. Leiden: Brill, 2009.

Gilchrist, J. T. *The Church and Economic Activity in the Middle Ages*. London: Routledge, 1969.

Gilson, E. *Greco-Arabic Sources of Avicennist Augustinism*. Trans. J. G. Colbert. New York: Global Scholarly Publications, 2003.

Goldziher, I. *Introduction to Islamic Theology and Law*. Trans. A. Hamori and R. Hamori. Princeton, N.J.: Princeton University Press, 1981.

Grant, E. *The Foundations of Modern Science in the Middle Ages: The Religious, Institutional, and Intellectual Contexts*. Cambridge: Cambridge University Press, 1996.

Hankins, J. *Cambridge Companion to Renaissance Philosophy*. Cambridge: Cambridge University Press, 2007.

———. *Plato in the Italian Renaissance*. 2 vols. Leiden: Brill, 1990.

Haskins, C. H. *The Rise of Universities*. Ithaca, N.Y.: Cornell University Press, 1979.

Hasse, D. N., and A. Bertolacci, eds. *The Arabic, Hebrew and Latin Reception of Avicenna's Metaphysics*. Berlin: De Gruyter, 2012.

Hause, J. *Debates in Medieval Philosophy*. London: Routledge, 2016.

Hesse, P., and P. Schulte, eds. *Reichtum im späten Mittelalter*. Stuttgart: Franz Steiner Verlag, 2015.

Holopainen, T. *Dialectic and Theology in the Eleventh Century*. Leiden: Brill, 1996.

Holt, P. M., A. K. S. Lambton, and E. Lewis, eds. *The Cambridge History of Islam*. 2 vols. Cambridge: Cambridge University Press, 1970.

Jayyusi, S., ed. *The Legacy of Muslim Spain*. 2nd ed. Leiden: Brill, 1994.

Knuuttila, S., and P. Kärkkäinen, eds. *Theories of Perception in Medieval and Early Modern Philosophy*. Dordrecht: Springer, 2008.

Kretzmann, N., A. Kenny, J. Pinborg, and E. Stump, eds. *The Cambridge History of Later Medieval Philosophy from the Rediscovery of Aristotle to the Disintegration of Scholasticism, 1100–1600*. Cambridge: Cambridge University Press, 1982.

Laistner, M. L. W. *Thought and Letters in Western Europe, AD 500–900*. Ithaca, N.Y.: Cornell University Press, 1966.

Lampe, G. W. H., ed. *The Cambridge History of the Bible*. 3 vols. Cambridge: Cambridge University Press, 1969.

Lawrence, C. H. *Medieval Monasticism: Forms of Religious Life in the Middle Ages*. 3rd ed. London: Longman, 2001.

Leclercq, J. *The Love of Learning and the Desire for God: A Study of Monastic Culture*. Trans. C. Misrahi. New York: Fordham University Press, 1982.

Lewry, O. "Grammar, Logic, and Rhetoric: 1220–1320." In *The History of the University of Oxford*, ed. J. I. Catto, R. Evans, and T. H. Astor, 401–33. Oxford: Clarendon Press, 1984.

Lindberg, D. C. *The Beginnings of Western Science: The European Scientific Tradition in Philosophical, Religious, and Institutional Context, 800 B.C. to A.D. 1450*. Chicago: University of Chicago Press, 1992.

McGinn, B. *The Flowering of Mysticism: Men and Women in the New Mysticism, 1200–1350*. Vol. 3 of *The Presence of God: A History of Western Christian Mysticism*. New York: Crossroad, 1998.

———. *The Foundations of Mysticism: Origins to the Fifth Century* (*The Presence of God: A History of Western Christian Mysticism,* 1). New York: Crossroad, 2002.

———. *The Growth of Mysticism: Gregory the Great through the 12th Century* (*The Presence of God: A History of Western Christian Mysticism,* 2). New York: Crossroad, 1999.

Marenbon, J. *Early Medieval Philosophy (480–1150): An Introduction.* London: Routledge and Kegan Paul, 1983.

———. *From the Circle of Alcuin to the School of Auxerre.* Cambridge: Cambridge University Press, 1981.

———. *Later Medieval Philosophy (1150–1350): An Introduction.* London: Routledge and Kegan Paul, 1987.

Meyendorff, J. *Byzantine Theology: Historical Trends and Doctrinal Theories.* 2nd ed. New York: Fordham University Press, 1987.

Morewedge, P.. *Islamic Philosophy and Mysticism.* Delmar, N.Y.: Caravan Books, 1981.

———, ed. *Neoplatonism and Islamic Thought.* Albany: State University of New York Press, 1992.

Morrison, K. F. *Tradition and Authority in the Western Church.* Princeton, N.J.: Princeton University Press, 1966.

Mulchahey, M. Michèle. *"First the Bow Is Bent . . . ," Dominican Education before 1350.* Toronto: Pontifical Institute of Mediaeval Studies, 1998.

Nasr, S. A. *Islamic Life and Thought.* Albany: State University of New York Press, 1982.

Nielsen, L. O. *Theology and Philosophy in the Twelfth Century.* Leiden: Brill, 1982.

Osborne, K. B. *The History of Franciscan Theology.* St. Bonaventure, N.Y.: Franciscan Institute Publications, 1994.

Pedersen, O. *The First Universities: "Studium Generale" and the Origins of University Education in Europe.* Cambridge: Cambridge University Press, 1997.

Peters, F. *Aristotle and the Arabs.* New York: New York University Press, 1968.

Roest, B. *Reading the Book of History: Intellectual Contexts and Educational Functions of Franciscan Historiography, 1226–ca. 1350.* Leiden: Brill, 1996.

Rosenthal, E. I. J. *Political Thought in Medieval Islam: An Introductory Outline.* Cambridge: Cambridge University Press, 2015.

Sharp, D. E. *Franciscan Philosophy at Oxford in the Thirteenth Century.* New York: Russell and Russell, 1964.

Smalley, B. *The Study of the Bible in the Middle Ages.* 3rd ed. Oxford: Oxford University Press, 1983.

Thijssen, J. M. M. H. *Censure and Heresy at the University of Paris, 1200–1440*. Philadelphia: University of Pennsylvania Press, 1998.

Tischler, M. M., and A. Fidora, eds. *Christliche Norden: Muslimischer Süden: Ansprüche und Wirklichkeiten von Christen, Juden und Muslimen auf der Iberischen Halbinsel im Hoch—und Spägtmittelalter*. Münster: Aschendorff, 2011.

Tuozzo, T. M. *Efficient Causation: A History*. Oxford: Oxford University Press, 2014.

Van der Lugt, M. *La nature comme source de la morale au moyen âge*. Firenze: Edizioni del Galluzzo, 2014.

Van Steenberghen, F. *Aristotle in the West: The Origins of Latin Aristotelianism*. Trans. L. Johnston. Louvain: Nauwelaerts, 1970.

———. *The Philosophical Movement in the Thirteenth Century*. London: Nelson, 1955.

## SOURCEBOOKS FOR PRIMARY TEXTS

### In Medieval Languages

Doucet, V. *Commentaires sur les Sentences: Supplément au Répertoire de M. Frédéric Stegmüller*. Quaracchi: Collegium S. Bonaventurae, 1954.

Fidora, A., and D. Werner. *Dominicus Gundissalinus: De divisione philosophiae: Lateinisch/Deutsch: Über die Einteilung der Philosophie*. Freiburg im Breisgau: Herder, 2007.

Ierodiakonou, K., ed. *Byzantine Philosophy and Its Ancient Sources*. Oxford: Oxford University Press, 2002.

Lohr, C. "Medieval Latin Aristotle Commentaries." *Traditio* 23–30 (1967–1974).

———. *Latin Aristotle Commentaries*. Vol. 2 of *Renaissance Authors*. Florence: L. S. Olschki, 1988.

———. *Latin Aristotle Commentaries*. Vol. 3 of *Index initiorum–Index finium*. Florence: L. S. Olschki, 1995.

Schneyer, J. B. *Repertorium der lateinischen Sermones des Mittelalters für die Zeit von 1150 bis 1350*. 11 vols. Beiträge zür Geschichte der Philosophie und Theologie des Mittelalters 43. Münster (Westf.): Aschendorffsche Verlagsbuchhandlung, 1969–1990.

Schoenberger, R., and B. Kible, eds. *Repertorium edierter Texte des Mittelalters aus dem Bereich der Philosophie und angrenzender Gebiete*. Berlin: Akademie Verlag, 1994.

Stegmüller, F. *Repertorium Biblicum Medii Aevi*. 10 vols. Madrid: Graficas Clavileno, 1949–1979.

————. *Repertorium Commentariorum in Sententias Petri Lombardi.* 2 vols. Würzburg: F. Schöningh, 1947.

## In Modern Languages

### Volumes of Collected Texts

Benakis, L. G. *Texts and Studies on Byzantine Philosophy.* Athens: Parousia, 2002.

Bond, H. L. *Selected Spiritual Writings.* New York: Paulist Press, 1997.

Bosley, R. N., and M. Tweedale. *Basic Issues in Medieval Philosophy.* Peterborough (Canada): Broadview, 1997.

Cassirer, E., P. O. Kristeller, and J. H. Randall. *The Renaissance Philosophy of Man.* Chicago: University of Chicago Press, 1945.

Clagett, M. *Archimedes in the Middle Ages.* 5 vols. Philadelphia, Pa.: American Philosophical Society, 1964–1984.

————. *The Science of Mechanics in the Middle Ages.* Madison: University of Wisconsin Press, 1961.

Colledge, E. *The Mediaeval Mystics of England.* London: John Murray, 1962.

Collins, J. D., ed. *Readings in Ancient and Medieval Philosophy.* Westminster, Md.: Newman Press, 1960.

Coolman, B. T., and D. M. Coulton. *Trinity and Creation: A Selection of Works of Hugh, Richard and Andrew of St.-Victor.* Turnhout: Brepols, 2010.

Ezzaher, L. E. *Three Arabic Treatises on Aristotle's Rhetoric.* Carbondale: Southern Illinois University Press, 2015.

Fairweather, E. R., ed. *A Scholastic Miscellany: Anselm to Ockham.* New York: Macmillan, 1970.

Frank, D. H., O. Leaman, and C. H. Manekin, eds. *The Jewish Philosophy Reader.* London: Routledge, 2000.

Freeland, J. P. *Lives of Northern Saints.* Kalamazoo, Ind.: Cistercians Publications, 2006.

Houser, R. E. *The Cardinal Virtues: Aquinas, Albert and Philip the Chancellor.* Toronto: Pontifical Institute of Mediaeval Studies, 2009.

Howell, W. S. *The Rhetoric of Alcuin and Charlemagne.* Princeton, N.J.: Princeton University Press, 1941.

Hyman, A., and J. Walsh, eds. *Philosophy in the Middle Ages: The Christian, Islamic, and Jewish Traditions.* 3rd ed. Indianapolis, Ind.: Hackett, 2010.

Katz, J., and R. Weingartner, eds. *Philosophy in the West: Readings in Ancient and Medieval Philosophy.* New York: Harcourt, Brace and World, 1965.

Kaufmann, W., and F. E. Baird, eds. *Medieval Philosophy.* Englewood Cliffs, N.J.: Prentice Hall, 1994.

Klima, G. I., et al., eds. and trans. *Medieval Philosophy: Essential Readings with Commentary.* Oxford: Blackwell, 2007.

Kretzmann, N., and E. Stump. *The Cambridge Translations of Medieval Philosophical Texts.* Vol. 1, *Logic and the Philosophy of Language.* Cambridge: Cambridge University Press, 1988.

Lerner, R., M. Mahdi, and E. Fortin. *Medieval Political Philosophy: A Sourcebook.* New York: Free Press of Glencoe, 1963.

Lettinck, P. *Aristotle's Meteorology and Its Reception in the Arabian World with an Edition and Translation of Ibn Suwar's "Treatise on Meteorological Phenomena" and Ibn Bâjja's "Commentary on the Meteorology."* Leiden: Brill, 1999.

Manekin, C., ed. *Medieval Jewish Philosophical Writings.* Cambridge: Cambridge University Press, 2008.

McEvoy, J. *Mystical Theology: The Glosses by Thomas Gallus and the Commentary of Robert Grosseteste on "De mystica theologia."* Paris: Peeters, 2003.

McGinnis, J., and D. C. Reisman. *Classical Arabian Philosophy: An Anthology of Sources.* Indianapolis, Ind.: Hackett, 2007.

McGrade, A. S., J. Kilcullen, and M. Kempshall, ed. *The Cambridge Translations of Medieval Philosophical Texts.* Vol. 2, *Ethics and Political Philosophy.* Cambridge: Cambridge University Press, 2001.

McKeon, R., ed. *Selections from Medieval Philosophers.* 2 vols. New York: Schribner, 1929.

Nederman, C. J., and K. L. Forhan. *Medieval Political Theory—a Reader: The Quest for the Body Politic, 1100–1400.* London: Routledge, 1993.

Pasnau, R. *The Cambridge Translations of Medieval Philosophical Texts.* Vol. 3, *Mind and Knowledge.* Cambridge: Cambridge University Press, 2002.

Peters, E. *Heresy and Authority in Medieval Europe.* Philadelphia: University of Pennsylvania Press, 1980.

Rosemann, P. W. *Henry of Harclay and Aufredo Gonteri Brito: Mediaeval Commentaries on the "Sentences" of Peter Lombard.* Trans. W. Duba, R. L. Friedman, and C. Schabel. Leiden: Brill, 2010.

Schoedinger, A. B., ed. *Readings in Medieval Philosophy.* Oxford: Oxford University Press, 1996.

Shapiro, H. *Medieval Philosophy: Selected Readings from Augustine to Buridan.* New York: Modern Library, 1964.

Volert, C., L. H. Kindzierski, and P. M. Byrne, ed. *On the Eternity of the World (Thomas Aquinas, Siger of Brabant and St. Bonaventure).* Milwaukee, WI: Marquette University Press, 1964.

Wippel, J. F., and A. B. Wolter, eds. *Medieval Philosophy: From St. Augustine to Nicholas of Cusa.* New York: Macmillan, 1969.

Series of Medieval Philosophical and Theological Texts

*Amsterdam Studies in the Theory and History of Linguistic Science*
*Ancient Christian Writers*
*The Ancient Commentators on Aristotle*
*The Archbishop Iakovos Library of Ecclesiastical and Historical Sources*
*Boston Studies in the Philosophy of Science*
*Cambridge Texts in the History of Political Thought*
*Cambridge Translations of Medieval Philosophical Texts*
*Center for Muslim Contributions to Civilization*
*Cistercian Fathers Series*
*Cistercian Studies Series*
*Classical and Medieval Logic Texts*
*Classics of the Contemplative Life*
*Classics of Western Spirituality*
*Cross and Crown Series of Spirituality*
*Dallas Medieval Texts and Translations*
*Duckworth Classical, Medieval, and Renaissance Editions*
*English Recusant Literature*
*Fathers of the Church, Medieval Continuation*
*The Fleur de Lys Series*
*The I Tatti Renaissance Library*
*Islamic Philosophy and Theology: Texts and Studies*
*Library of Christian Classics*
*Loeb Classical Library*
*Mediaeval Academy of America*
*Mediaeval Philosophical Texts in Translation*
*Mediaeval Sources in Translation*
*Medieval and Renaissance Texts and Studies*
*Medieval Philosophy, Mathematics and Science*
*Moreshet*
*The New Synthese Historical Library*
*Notre Dame Texts in Medieval Culture*
*Persian Heritage*
*Publications in Mediaeval Studies*
*Renaissance Text Studies*
*Studies in Classical Antiquity*
*Studies in Islamic Philosophy and Science*
*Studies in Medieval Moral Teaching*

*Synthese Historical Library*
*Texts in Medieval Culture*
*Yale Library of Medieval Philosophy*

## PERIODICALS PROVIDING SOURCES FOR STUDYING MEDIEVAL PHILOSOPHY AND THEOLOGY

*Acta Philosophica Fennica*
*Alif*
*American Catholic Philosophical Quarterly*
*Angelicum*
*Antonianum*
*Aquinas*
*Archa Verbi*
*Archives d'Histoire Doctrinale et Littéraire du Moyen Âge*
*Archivum Franciscanum Historicum*
*Archivum Fratrum Praedicatorum*
*Archivum Latinitatis Medii Aevi*
*Augustinian Studies*
*Augustininana*
*Bijdragen*
*British Journal of the History of Philosophy*
*Bulletin de Philosophie Médiévale*
*Bulletin de Théologie Ancienne et Médiévale*
*Bulletin of the John Rylands Library*
*Cahiers de l'Institut du Moyen-Âge Grec et Latin*
*Carmelus*
*Ciencia Tomista*
*Classica et Mediaevalia*
*Collectanea Francescana*
*Collectanea Ordinis Ciscerciensium Reformatorum*
*Dionysius*
*Divus Thomas*
*Doctor Communis*
*Doctor Seraphicus*
*Documenti e Studi sulla tradizione filosofica*
*Ephemerides Theologicae Lovanienses*
*Filosofia Medievale*
*Franciscan Studies*
*Franciscanum*
*Franziskanische Studien*

*Freiburger Zeitschrift für Philosophie und Theologie*
*Gregorianum*
*Heythrop Journal: A Bimonthly Review of Philosophy and Theology*
*International Journal for the Philosophy of Religion*
*International Philosophical Quarterly*
*Iqbad*
*Isis*
*Journal of Philosophy*
*Journal of the American Oriental Society*
*Journal of the History of Philosophy*
*Laval Théologique et Philosophique*
*Manuscripta*
*Mediaeval Studies*
*Mediaevalia Philosophica Polonorum*
*Medieval Philosophy and Theology*
*Medioevo*
*Mind*
*Miscellanea Francescana*
*Miscellanea Medievalia*
*Mitteilungen und Forschungsbeitraege der Cusanus-Gesellschaft*
*The Modern Schoolman*
*Monist*
*Münchener Theologische Zeitschrift*
*Naturaleza y Gracia*
*New Scholasticism*
*Notre Dame Journal of Formal Logic*
*Nouvelle Revue Théologique*
*Nova et Vetera*
*Osiris*
*Patristica et Mediaevalia*
*Philosophisches Jahrbuch*
*Proceedings of the American Catholic Philosophical Association*
*Proceedings of the British Academy*
*Recherches de Théologie et Philosophie Médiévales*
*Renaissance Quarterly*
*Res Philosophica*
*Review of Metaphysics*
*Revista di Storia della Filosophia*
*Revue Benedictine*
*Revue de Synthese*
*Revue de Théologie et de Philosophie*
*Revue des Études Augustiniennes*
*Revue des Études Islamiques*

*Revue des Sciences Religieuses*
*Revue d'Histoire Ecclésiastique*
*Revue du Moyen-Âge Latin*
*Revue Philosophique de Louvain*
*Revue Théologique de Louvain*
*Revue Thomiste*
*Sacris Erudiri*
*Salesianum*
*Salmanticensis*
*Schede Medievali*
*Speculum*
*Studi Mediaevali*
*Studia Lulliana*
*Studies in Medieval Thought*
*Studies in Spirituality*
*Theologie und Philosophie*
*The Thomist*
*Tijdschrift voor Filosofie*
*Tijdschrift voor Theologie*
*Topoi*
*Traditio*
*Verdad y Vida*
*Vigiliae Christianae*
*Vivarium*
*Zeitschrift für Katholische Theologie*

## PRIMARY PHILOSOPHICAL AND THEOLOGICAL TEXTS IN ENGLISH TRANSLATION

Abelard, Peter. *Abelard's Christian Theology* (partial text of *Theologia Christiana*). Trans. J. R. McCallum. Oxford: Blackwell, 1948.
———. "Commentary on St. Paul's *Epistle to the Romans*: Prologue and Beginning of Commentary." In *Medieval Literary Theory and Criticism, c. 1100–c. 1375: The Commentary Tradition*, ed. A. J. Minnis and A. B. Scott, 100–105. Oxford: Clarendon Press, 1988.
———. *A Dialogue of a Philosopher with a Jew and a Christian*. Trans. P. J. Payer. Toronto: Pontifical Institute of Mediaeval Philosophy, 1979.
———. *Ethical Writings: "Ethics" and "Dialogue between a Philosopher, a Jew and a Christian."* Trans. P. Spade. Indianapolis, Ind.: Hackett, 1995.

————. *Five Texts on the Medieval Problem of Universals* (Abelard's *Logica "Ingredientibus"*). Trans. P. V. Spade. Indianapolis, Ind.: Hackett, 1994.

————. *The Hymns of Abelard in English Verse*. Trans. Sr. Jane Patricia Freeland. Lanham, Md.: University Press of America, 1986.

————. *The Letters of Abelard and Heloise*. Trans. B. Radice. London: Penguin, 2003.

————. *Peter Abelard: Collationes* (Abelard's *Dialogus*). Trans. J. Marenbon. Cambridge: Cambridge University Press, 2001.

————. "Prologue to the *Yes and No*." Trans. A. J. Minnis. In *Medieval Literary Theory and Criticism, c. 1100–c. 1375: The Commentary Tradition*, ed. A. J. Minnis and A. B. Scott, 87–100. Oxford: Clarendon Press, 1988.

————. *The Story of Abelard's Adversities*. Trans. J. T. Muckle. Toronto: Pontifical Institute of Medieval Philosophy, 1964.

Abraham ibn Daud. *A Critical Edition with Translation and Notes of the "Book of Tradition" (Sefer ha-qabbalah)*. Trans. G. D. Cohen. London: Routledge and Regan, 1967.

————. *The Exalted Faith, Abraham ibn Daud*. Trans. with commentary by N. M. Samuelson. Rutherford, N.J.: Fairleigh Dickinson University Press, 1986.

Abu Ma'shar. *The Abbreviation of "The Introduction to Astrology": Together with the Medieval Latin Translation of Adelard of Bath*. Trans. C. Burnett, K. Yamamoto, and M. Yano. Islamic Philosophy, Theology, and Science 15. Leiden: Brill, 1994.

Adam Marsh. *The Letters of Adam Marsh*. Trans. C. H. Lawrence. Oxford: Clarendon Press, 2006.

Adam of Buckfield. *Adam of Bockenfield, Glossae super de vegetalibus et plantis: A Critical Edition with Introduction*. Ed. R. J. Long. Leiden: Brill, 2013.

Adam of St. Victor. *The Liturgical Poetry of Adam of St. Victor*. Trans. D. S. Wrangham. London: Kegan Paul, 1881.

Adam Wodeham. "The Objects of Knowledge." In *The Cambridge Translations of Medieval Philosophical Texts*, ed. and trans. R. Pasnau, 3:320–51. Cambridge: Cambridge University Press, 2002.

————. "The Objects of Knowledge (*Lectura Secunda*, I, 1, 1)." In *Cambridge Translations of Medieval Philosophical Texts*, vol. 3, *Mind and Knowledge*, ed. and trans. Robert Pasnau, 318–51. Cambridge: Cambridge University Press, 2002.

————. *Tractatus de indivisibilibus: A Critical Edition with Introduction, Translation, and Textual Notes*. Trans. R. Wood. Synthese Historical Library 31. Dordrecht: Kluwer Academic Publishers, 1988.

Adelard of Bath. *Conversations with His Nephew: On the Same and the Different; Questions on Natural Science, and On Birds.* Trans. Charles Burnett. Cambridge Medieval Classics 9. Cambridge: Cambridge University Press, 1998.

Aelred of Rievaulx. *Dialogues on the Soul.* Trans. C. H. Talbot. Kalamazoo, Mich.: Cistercian Publications, 1981.

———. *For Your Own People: Aelred of Rievaulx's Pastoral Prayer.* Trans. M. Del Cogliano. Kalamazoo, Mich.: Cistercian Publications, 2008.

———. *The Historical Works of Aelred of Rievaulx.* Trans. J. P. Freeland. Cistercian Fathers Series 56. Kalamazoo, Mich.: Cistercian Publications, 1998.

———. *The Liturgical Sermons.* Trans. T. Berkeley et al. Kalamazoo, Mich.: Cistercian Publications, 2001.

———. *Lives of the Northern Saints.* Trans. J. P. Freeland. Kalamazoo, Mich.: Cistercian Publications, 2006.

———. *Mirror of Charity.* Trans. E. Connor. Kalamazoo, Mich.: Cistercian Publications, 1990.

———. "Sermons on the Feast of Saint Mary." Trans. A. Sulavik. *Cistercian Studies* 32 (1997): 37–125.

———. *Spiritual Friendship.* Trans. M. F. Williams. Scranton, Pa.: University of Scranton Press, 1994.

———. "St. Aelred's Sermons for the Feast of St. Benedict. With an Introduction." Trans. B. Pennington. *Cistercian Studies* 4 (1969): 62–89.

———. *Treatises. The Pastoral Prayer.* Trans. T. Berkeley, D. Knowles, and R. P. Lawson. Kalamazoo, Mich.: Cistercian Publications, 1988.

Alan of Lille. *Alan of Lille: Literary Works.* Trans. W. Wetherbee. Cambridge, Mass.: Harvard University Press, 2013.

———. *Anticlaudianus or The Good and Perfect Man.* Trans. J. J. Sheridan. Toronto: Pontifical Institute of Mediaeval Studies, 1973.

———. *The Art of Preaching.* Trans. G. R. Evans. Cistercian Fathers Series 23. Kalamazoo, Mich.: Cistercian Publications, 1981.

———. *The Plaint of Nature.* Trans. J. J. Sheridan. Mediaeval Sources in Translation 26. Toronto: Pontifical Institute of Mediaeval Studies, 1980.

Albert of Saxony. "Insolubles (*Perutilis Logica*, VI, 1)." In *The Cambridge Translations of Medieval Philosophical Texts*, ed. and trans. N. Kretzmann and E. Stump, 1:338–68. Cambridge: Cambridge University Press, 1999.

———. *Quaestiones super logicam: Twenty-Five Disputed Questions on Logic.* Trans. M. J. Fitzgerald. Paris: Peeters, 2010.

Albert the Great. *Book of Minerals.* Trans. D. Wyckoff. Oxford: Clarendon Press, 1967.

———. *The Book of Secrets of Albertus Magnus, of the Virtues of Herbs, Stones and Certain Beasts*; also *A Book of the Marvels of the World.* Trans. M. B. Best and F. H. Brightman. Oxford: Clarendon Press 1973.

———. *The Cardinal Virtues: Aquinas, Albert and Philip the Chancellor.* Trans. R. E. Houser. Mediaeval Sources in Translation 39. Toronto: Pontifical Institute of Mediaeval Studies, 2004.

———. *The Commentary of Albertus Magnus on Book 1 of Euclid's "Elements of Geometry."* Trans. Anthony Lo Bello. Medieval Philosophy, Mathematics, and Science 3. Leiden: Brill Academic Publishers, 2003.

———. *Commentary on Dionysius' "Mystical Theology."* In *Albert & Thomas: Selected Writings*, trans. S. Tugwell, Classics of Western Spirituality. New York: Paulist Press, 1988.

———. *Man and the Beasts* (*De animalibus, Books 22–26*). Trans. J. J. Scanlan. Medieval and Renaissance Texts and Studies 47. Binghamton, N.Y.: Center for Medieval and Early Renaissance Studies, 1987.

———. *Mirror of Astronomy.* In *The Speculum astronomiae and Its Enigma*, trans. P. Zambelli, Boston Studies in the Philosophy of Science 135. Dordrecht: Kluwer Academic, 1992.

———. *On Animals: A Medieval Summa Zoologica.* 2 vols. Trans. K. F. Kitchell Jr. and I. M. Resnick. Baltimore, Md.: Johns Hopkins University Press, 1999.

———. *On the Causes of the Properties of the Elements.* Trans. I. M. Resnick. Milwaukee, Wisc.: Marquette University Press, 2010.

———. *On the Six Principles.* In *Medieval Philosophy: Selected Readings from Augustine to Buridan*, ed. and trans. H. Shapiro, 265–92. New York: Modern Library, 1964.

———. *On Union with God.* Trans. Anon. New York: Continuum, 2000.

———. *Pamphlet on Alchemy.* Trans. V. Heines. Berkeley: University of California Press, 1958.

———. *The Paradise of the Soule* (1617). Trans. Anon. English Recusant Literature 96. Menston: Scolar Press, 1972.

———. "Questions on Book X of the '*Ethics.*'" In *The Cambridge Translations of Medieval Philosophical Texts*, ed. and trans. A. S. McGrade, J. Kilcullen, and M. Kempshall, 2:12–168. Cambridge: Cambridge University Press, 2001.

Alcher of Clairvaux. *On the Soul and Spirit.* In *Three Treatises of Man*, trans. B. McGuinn, Cistercian Fathers Series 24. Kalamazoo, Mich.: Cistercian Publications, 1977.

Alcuin. "Against the Adoptionist Heresy of Felix." Trans. B. V. N. Edwards. In *Heresy and Authority in Medieval Europe*, ed. E. Peters, 53–56. Philadelphia: University of Pennsylvania Press, 1980.

———. *The Bishops, Kings, and Saints of York.* Trans. P. Goodman. Oxford: Clarendon Press, 1982.

———. *Disputation on Rhetoric and the Virtues.* In *The Rhetoric of Alcuin and Charlemagne*, trans. W. S. Howell, Princeton Studies in English 23. Princeton, N.J.: Princeton University Press, 1941.

————. *Letters*. In *Alcuin of York, c. A.D. 732 to 804: His Life and Letters*, trans. S. Allott. York, UK: William Sessions, 1974.

Alexander of Hales. "*Alexander's Sum of Theology* (Q. 1, c. 4, a. 1–4)." In *Medieval Literary Theory and Criticism, c. 1100–c. 1375: The Commentary Tradition*, ed. A. J. Minnis and A. B. Scott, 212–23. Oxford: Clarendon Press, 1988.

Alhacen. *The Optics of Ibn al-Haytham; Books I–III, on Direct Vision*. 2 vols. Trans. A. I. Sabra. London: Warburg Institute, 1989.

Alphonsus Vargas of Toledo. "The Commentary on Aristotle's *De anima* by Alphonsus Vargas Toletanus, OESA." In *Bulletin de Philosophie Médiévale* 52 (2010): 201–34.

Al-Razi, Abu Bakr. "*The Book of the Philosophic Life*." Trans. C. E. Butterworth. *Interpretation* 20 (1993): 227–236.

————. "On the Five Eternals." Selections in *Classical Arabic Philosophy: An Anthology of Sources*, trans. J. McGinnis and D. C. Reisman. Indianapolis, Ind.: Hackett, 2007.

————. *The Spiritual Physick of Rhazes*. Trans. A. J. Arberry. London: John Murray, 1950.

Andrew of Saint-Victor. *Andrew of Saint-Victor: Commentary on Samuel and Kings*. Trans. F. A. van Liere. Turnhout: Brepols, 2009.

————. *Trinity and Creation: A Selection of Works of Hugh, Richard and Andrew of St.-Victor*. Trans. B. T. Coolman and D. M. Coulter. Turnhout: Brepols, 2010.

Anselm. *Anselm: Basic Writings*. Trans. T. Williams. Indianapolis, Ind.: Hackett, 2007.

————. *Anselm of Canterbury: The Major Works*. Trans. B. Davies and G. R. Evans. New York: Oxford University Press, 1998.

————. *Complete Philosophical and Theological Treatises of Anselm of Canterbury*. Trans. J. Hopkins and H. Richardson. Minneapolis, Minn.: A. J. Banning Press, 2000.

————. *The Letter Collection of Anselm of Canterbury*. Ed. S. Niskanen. Turnhout: Brepols, 2011.

————. *The Letters of Saint Anselm of Canterbury*. Trans. W. Fröhlich. Cistercian Studies Series 96, 97, and 142. Kalamazoo, Mich.: Cistercian Publications, 1990–.

————. *The Prayers and Meditations of St. Anselm*. Trans. B. Ward. Harmondsworth, UK: Penguin, 1973.

Anselm of Laon. "A Fragment on Original Sin." In *A Scholastic Miscellany: Anselm to Ockham*, ed. and trans. E. R. Fairweather, 261–63, Library of Christian Classics 10. New York: Macmillan, 1956.

————. *Glossa ordinaria, Pars 22, In Canticum canticorum* (*English & Latin*). Trans. M. Dove. Turnhout: Brepols, 1997. (Attributed to Anselm of Laon)

Aristotle. *The Complete Works of Aristotle.* 2 vols. Ed. J. Barnes. Princeton, N.J.: Princeton University Press, 1984.

Aufredus Gonteri. "Henry of Harclay and Aufredo Gonteri Brito." In *Mediaeval Commentaries on the "Sentences" of Peter Lombard*, vol. 2, ed. P. W. Rosemann, trans. W. Duba, R. L. Friedman, and C. Schabel, 263–368. Leiden: Brill, 2010.

Augustine, St. *Augustine: Against the Academicians and The Teacher.* Trans. P. King. Indianapolis, Ind.: Hackett, 1995.

———. *Augustine: Confessions.* Trans. H. Chadwick. Oxford: Oxford University Press, 1991.

———. *Augustine: The City of God against the Pagans.* Trans. R. W. Dyson. Cambridge: Cambridge University Press, 1998.

———. *St. Augustine: The Literal Meaning of Genesis.* Trans. J. H. Taylor. Washington, D.C.: Newman Press, 1982.

———. *The Works of Saint Augustine: A Translation for the 21st Century.* New York: New City Press, 1990–.

Augustine of Ancona (Augustinus Triumphus). "Summa on Ecclesiastical Power (selections)." In *The Cambridge Translations of Medieval Philosophical Texts*, ed. and trans. A. S. McGrade, J. Kilcullen, and M. Kempshall, 2:419–83. Cambridge: Cambridge University Press, 2001.

Avempace. *Commentary on Aristotle's Physics, Selections.* In *Aristotle's Physics and Its Reception in the Arabic World (Aristoteles Semitico-latinus).* Trans. P. Lettinck. Leiden: Brill, 1994.

———. *Aristotle's Meteorology and its reception in the Arabian world with an edition and translation of Ibn Suwar's "Treatise on Meteorological Phenomena" and Ibn Bâjja's "Commentary on the Meteorology."* Trans. P. Lettinck. Leiden: Brill, 1999.

Averroes. *Averroes (Ibn Rushd) of Cordova: Long Commentary on the "De anima" of Aristotle.* Trans. R. C. Taylor. New Haven, Conn.: Yale University Press, 2009.

———. *Averroes' Middle Commentaries on Aristotle's Categories and De interpretatione.* Trans. C. E. Butterworth. Princeton, N.J.: Princeton University Press, 1983.

———. *Averroes' Middle Commentaries on Aristotle's Poetics.* Trans. C. E. Butterworth. Princeton, N.J.: Princeton University Press, 1986.

———. *Averroës Three Short Commentaries on Aristotle's Topics, Rhetoric, and Poetics.* Trans. C. E. Butterworth. Studies in Islamic Philosophy and Science. Albany: State University of New York Press, 1977.

———. *The Book of the Decisive Treatise Determining the Connection between the Law and Wisdom.* Trans. C. E. Butterworth. Provo, Utah: Brigham Young University Press, 2001.

———. *The Distinguished Jurist's Primer.* 2 vols. Trans. I. A. K. Nyazee and M. A. Rauf. Reading, UK: Center for Muslim Contributions to Civilization, 1994.

———. *The Epistle on the Possibility of Conjunction with the Active Intellect, with the Commentary of Moses Narboni.* Trans. K. P. Bland. Moreshet Series 7. New York: Jewish Theological Seminary of America, 1982.

———. *Epitome of Parva naturalia.* Trans. H. Blumberg. Mediaeval Academy of America 71. Cambridge, Mass.: Mediaeval Academy of America, 1961.

———. *Faith and Reason in Islam: Averroes' Exposition of Religious Arguments.* Trans. I. Y. Naijar. Oxford: Oneworld, 2001.

———. *"The Governance of the Solitary* (Selections)." Trans. L. Berman. In *Medieval Political Philosophy: A Sourcebook*, ed. R. Lerner, M. Mahdi, and E. Fortin, 123–33. Ithaca, N.Y.: Cornell University Press, 1963.

———. *Middle Commentary on Aristotle's De anima.* Trans. A. L. Ivry. Provo, Utah: Brigham Young University Press, 2002.

———. *Middle Commentary on Porphyry's Isagoge.* Trans. H. A. Davidson. Mediaeval Academy of America 79. Cambridge, Mass.: Mediaeval Academy of America, 1969.

———. *Middle Commentary on the Republic.* In *Averroes on Plato's Republic*, trans. R. Lerner. Ithaca, N.Y.: Cornell University Press, 1974.

———. *On Aristotle's Metaphysics: An Annotated Translation of the So-Called "Epitome."* Ed. and trans. R. Arnzen. Berlin: De Gruyter, 2010.

———. *Tahafut al-tahafut (The Incoherence of the Incoherence).* Trans. S. van den Bergh. E. J. W. Gibb Memorial, n.s., 19. London: Luzac, 1969.

———. "A Treatise Concerning the Substance of the Celestial Sphere." In *Philosophy in the Middle Ages: The Christian, Islamic, and Jewish Traditions*, ed. and trans. A. Hyman and J. J. Walsh, 307–13. New York: Harper and Row, 1967.

Avicenna. *Avicenna on Philosophy.* Trans. A. J. Arberry. The Wisdom of the East Series. London: Murray, 1951.

———. *Avicenna's Commentary on the Poetics of Aristotle.* Trans. I. M. Dahiyat. Leiden: Brill, 1974.

———. *Avicenna's Poem on Medicine.* Trans. H. C. Krueger. Springfield, Ill.: Thomas, 1963.

———. *Avicenna's Psychology Book II, Chap. 6.* Trans. F. Rahman. London: Oxford University Press, 1952.

———. *Avicenna's Treatise on Logic.* Trans. F. Zabeeh. The Hague: Nijhoff, 1971.

———. *The Book of the Prophet Muhammad's Ascent to Heaven.* In *Allegory and Philosophy in Avicenna*, trans. P. Heath. Philadelphia: University of Pennsylvania Press, 1992.

————. "Essay on the Secret of Destiny." In *Medieval Philosophy: From St. Augustine to Nicholas of Cusa*, ed. and trans. J. F. Wippel and A. B. Wolter, 229–32. New York: Free Press, 1969.

————. *The Life of Ibn Sina*. Trans. W. E. Gohlman. Studies in Islamic Philosophy and Science. Albany: State University of New York Press, 1974.

————. *The Metaphysica of Avicenna*. Trans. P. Morewedge. Persian Heritage Series 13. London: Routledge and Kegan Paul, 1973.

————. *The Metaphysics of "The Healing."* Trans. M. E. Marmura. Provo, Utah: Brigham Young University Press, 2005.

————. "On the Divisions of the Rational Sciences (Selections)" and "On the Proof of Prophecies and the Interpretation of the Prophets' Symbols and Metaphors." Trans. M. Mahdi and M. E. Marmura. In *Medieval Political Philosophy: A Sourcebook*, ed. R. Lerner, M. Mahdi, and E. Fortin, 96–97, 113–33. Ithaca, N.Y.: Cornell University Press, 1963.

————. *The Physics of "The Healing."* Trans. J. McGinnis. Provo, Utah: Brigham Young University Press, 2009.

————. *The Propositional Logic of Avicenna*. Trans. N. Shehaby. Dordrecht: Reidel, 1973.

————. *Remarks and Admonitions*. Trans. S. C. Inati. Mediaeval Sources in Translation 28. Toronto: Pontifical Institute of Mediaeval Studies, 1984.

————. *Selections*. Trans. Anon. In *Avicenna and the Visionary Recital*, Bollingen Series 66. New York: Pantheon Books, 1960.

Bahya ibn Paquda. *The Guide to the Duties of the Heart*. Trans. D. Haberman. Nanuet, N.Y.: Feldheim Publications, 1996.

Bede the Venerable. *The Commentary on Revelation*. Trans. F. Wallis. Liverpool: Liverpool University Press, 2013.

————. *Commentary on the Acts of the Apostles*. Trans. L. T. Martin. Kalamazoo, Mich.: Cistercian Publications, 1989.

————. *Ecclesiastical History*. Trans. J. E. King. Cambridge, Mass.: Harvard University Press, 2014.

————. *The Lives of the Abbots of Wearmouth*. Trans. P. Wilcock. Newcastle upon Tyne: F. Graham, 1973.

————. *On Ezra and Nehemiah*. Trans. S. DeGregorio. Liverpool: Liverpool University Press, 2006.

————. *On Genesis*. Trans. G. B. Kendall. Liverpool: Liverpool University Press, 2008.

————. *On the Nature of Things*. Trans. G. B. Kendall and F. Wallis. Liverpool: Liverpool University Press, 2010.

————. *The Reckoning of Time*. Trans. F. Wallis. Liverpool: Liverpool University Press, 1999.

————. *Two Lives of Saint Cuthbert*. Trans. B. Colgrave. New York: Greenwood Press, 1969.

Bernard of Clairvaux, St. "*Apologia ad Guillelmum Abbatem.*" In *The Things of Greater Importance*, ed. and trans. C. Rudolph, 232–87. Philadelphia: University of Pennsylvania Press, 1990.

———. *Bernard of Clairvaux: The Parables* and *The Sentences*. Trans. M. Casey and F. R. Swietek. Cistercian Fathers Series 55. Kalamazoo, Mich.: Cistercian Publications, 2000.

———. "Letter to Pope Eugenius III." Trans. K. L. Forhan. In *Medieval Political Theory: A Reader*, ed. C. J. Nederman and K. L. Forhan, 22–23. London: Routledge, 1993.

———. *The Letters*. Trans. B. S. James. Kalamazoo, Mich.: Cistercian Publications, 1998.

———. *The Life and Death of St. Malachy, the Irishman*. Trans. R. T. Meyer. Cistercian Fathers Series 10. Kalamazoo, Mich.: Cistercian Publications, 1978.

———. *The Nativity*. Trans. L. Hickey. Chicago: Scepter, 1959.

———. *On Grace and Free Choice*. Trans C. Greenia. Cistercian Fathers Series 19. Kalamazoo, Mich.: Cistercian Publications, 1977.

———. *On Loving God*. Trans. E. Stiegman. Cistercian Fathers Series 13B. Kalamazoo, Mich.: Cisterican Publications, 1995.

———. *On Loving God*. Trans. K. Walsh. Cistercian Fathers Series 4, 7, 31, 40. Spencer, Mass.: Cistercian Publications, 1971–1980.

———. *Sermons for the Summer Season; Liturgical Sermons from Rogationtide and Pentecost*. Trans. B. M. Kienzle and J. Marzembowski. Cistercian Fathers Series 53. Kalamazoo, Mich.: Cistercian Publications, 1991.

———. *Sermons of St. Bernard on Advent and Christmas, including the Famous Treatise on the Incarnation called "Missus Est."* Trans. Anon. London: Washbourne and Benziger Brothers, 1909.

———. *Sermons on Conversion*. Trans. M.-B. Said. Cistercian Fathers Series 25. Kalamazoo, Mich.: Cistercian Publications, 1981.

———. *St. Bernard's Sermons for the Seasons and Principal Festivals of the Year*. Trans. A. J. Luddy. Westminster, Md.: Carrol Press, 1950.

———. *St. Bernard's Sermons on the Blessed Virgin Mary*. Trans. Anon. Chumleigh, UK: Augustine Publishing, 1984.

———. *The Steps of Humility and Pride*. Trans. G. B. Burch. Cistercian Fathers Series 13A. Kalamazoo, Mich.: Cisterican Publications, 1989.

Boethius. *Boethian Number Theory*. Trans. M. Mast. Studies in Classical Antiquity 6. Amsterdam: Rodopi, 1983.

———. *Boethius: Consolation of Philosophy*. Trans. J. C. Relihan. Indianapolis, Ind.: Hackett, 2001.

———. *Boethius: De divisione*. Trans. J. Magee. Leiden: Brill, 1998.

———. *Boethius's "De topicis differentiis."* Trans. E. Stump. Ithaca, N.Y.: Cornell University Press, 1978.

———. *Boethius's "In Ciceronis Topica."* Trans. E. Stump. Ithaca, N.Y.: Cornell University Press, 1988.

———. *Fundamentals of Music.* Trans. C. M. Bower. New Haven, Conn.: Yale University Press, 1989.

———. *On Aristotle "On Interpretation 9."* Trans. N. Kretzman. London: Duckworth, 1998.

———. "The Second Edition of the Commentaries on the Isagoge of Porphyry (in part)." Trans. W. Kaufmann. In *Medieval Philosophy*, ed. W. Kaufmann and F. E. Baird, 142–45. Englewood Cliffs, N.J.: Prentice Hall, 1980.

———. *Theological Tractates.* Trans. H. F. Stewart, E. K. Rand, and S. J. Tester. Loeb Classical Library 74. Cambridge, Mass.: Harvard University Press, 1918.

Boethius of Dacia. *Godfrey of Fontaine's Abridgement of Boethius of Dacia's "Modi significandi sive Quaestiones super Priscianum Maiorem."* Trans. A. Ch. Senape McDermott. Amsterdam Studies in the Theory and History of Linguistic Science 22. Amsterdam: Benjamins, 1980.

———. *On the Supreme Good, On the Eternity of the World, On Dreams.* Trans. J. F. Wippel. Mediaeval Sources in Translation 30. Toronto: Pontifical Institute of Mediaeval Studies, 1987.

Bonaventure, St. *Bonaventure: The Soul's Journey into God, The Tree of Life, The Life of St. Francis.* Trans. E. Cousins. New York: Paulist Press, 1978.

———. "Commentary on Peter Lombard's Sentences: Extracts from Exposition of the Prologue." In *Medieval Literary Theory and Criticism, c. 1100–c. 1375: The Commentary Tradition*, ed. A. J. Minnis and A. B. Scott, 223–28. Oxford: Clarendon Press, 1988.

———. "Commentary on the Four Books of Sentences of Peter Lombard (Book I, d. 3, p. 1)." In *Selections from Medieval Philosophers*, 2 vols., ed. and trans. R. McKeon, 2:118–48. New York: Scribner, 1930.

———. "Conscience and Synderesis." In *The Cambridge Translations of Medieval Philosophical Texts*, ed. and trans. A. S. McGrade, J. Kilcullen, and M. Kempshall, 2:170–99. Cambridge, Mass.: Cambridge University Press, 2001.

———. *The Disciple and the Master.* Trans. E. Doyle. St. Bonaventure, N.Y.: Franciscan Institute, 1983.

———. *Disputed Questions on the Knowledge of Christ.* Trans. Z. Hayes. St. Bonaventure, N.Y.: Franciscan Institute Publications, 1992.

———. *Disputed Questions on the Mystery of the Trinity.* Trans. Z. Hayes. St. Bonaventure, N.Y.: Franciscan Institute Publications, 1979.

———. *The Journey of the Mind to God.* Trans. P. Boehner. Indianapolis, Ind.: Hackett, 1993.

————. "Major and Minor Life of St. Francis." Trans. B. Fahey. In *St. Francis of Assisi: Writings and Early Biographies; English Omnibus of the Sources for the Life of St. Francis*, ed. M. A. Habig, 627–51. Chicago: Franciscan Herald Press, 1974.

————. *On the Eternity of the World* (*Thomas Aquinas, Siger of Brabant, and St. Bonaventure*). Trans. C. Volert, L. H. Kendzierski, and P. M. Byrne. Milwaukee, Wisc.: Marquette University Press, 1964.

————. *On the Reduction of the Arts to Theology*. Trans. Z. Hayes. St. Bonaventure, N.Y.: Franciscan Institute, 1996.

————. *Rooted in Faith: Homilies to a Contemporary World by St. Bonaventure*. Trans. M. Schumacher. Chicago: Franciscan Herald Press, 1974.

————. *St. Bonaventure as a Biblical Commentator: Commentary on Luke 18, 34–19, 42*. Trans. T. Reist. Lanham, Md.: University Press of America, 1985.

————. *St. Bonaventure's Collations on the Ten Commandments*. Trans. P. J. Spaeth. St. Bonaventure, N.Y.: Franciscan Institute Publications, 1995.

————. *St. Bonaventure's Writings concerning the Franciscan Order*. Trans. D. Monti. St. Bonaventure, N.Y.: Franciscan Institute, 1994.

————. *What Manner of Man? Sermons on Christ by St. Bonaventure*. Chicago: Franciscan Herald Press, 1974.

————. *The Works of Bonaventure*. 5 vols. Trans. J. de Vinck. Patterson, N.J.: St. Anthony's Guild Press, 1960–1970.

Bradwardine, Thomas. *Geometria speculativa*. Trans. G. Molland. Stuttgart: Steiner Verlag, 1989.

————. *Tractatus de proportionibus*. In *Thomas of Bradwardine: His Tractatus de proportionibus and Its Significance for the Development of Mathematical Physics*, trans. H. L. Crosby Jr. Madison: University of Wisconsin Press, 1955.

Bruno the Carthusian. *Bruno the Carthusian and His Mortuary Roll*. Ed. H. Beyer, G. Signon, and S. Steckel. Turnhout: Brepols, 2014.

————. *Early Carthusian Writings*. Leominster, Hereforshire: Gracewings Publishing, 2009.

Buridan, John. "Commentary on Aristotle's *De anima* (Book II, qq. 9–11)." In *Readings in Medieval Philosophy*, ed. and trans. A. B. Schoedinger, 495–513. New York: Oxford University Press, 1996.

————. "The Impetus Theory of Projective Motion (Qq. on *Physics*, VIII, q. 12)," "On the Free Fall of Bodies (Qq. on *De caelo et mundo*, II, q. 12)," and "On the Diurnal Rotation of the Earth (Qq. on *De caelo et mundo*, II, q. 22)." In *Medieval Philosophy: Selected Readings from Augustine to Buridan*, ed. and trans. H. Shapiro, 530–56. New York: Modern Library, 1964.

—————. *John Buridan on Self-Reference: Chapter Eight of Buridan's "Sophismata."* Trans. G. E. Hughes. Cambridge: Cambridge University Press, 1982.

—————. "Questions on Aristotle's *Metaphysics* (Book II, q. 1 and Book IV, q. 8–9." In *Philosophy in the Middle Ages: The Christian, Islamic, and Jewish Traditions*, ed. and trans. A. Hyman and J. J. Walsh, 702–5, 711–15. New York: Harper and Row, 1967.

—————. "Questions on Book X of the 'Ethics.'" In *The Cambridge Translations of Medieval Philosophical Texts*, ed. and trans. A. S. McGrade, J. Kilcullen, and M. Kempshall, 2:500–86. Cambridge: Cambridge University Press, 2001.

—————. *Sophisms on Meaning and Truth.* Trans. T. K. Scott. New York: Appleton-Century-Crofts, 1966.

—————. *Summulae de dialectica.* Trans. G. Klima. New Haven, Conn.: Yale University Library, 2001.

—————. *Treatise on Supposition and Treatise on Consequences.* In *Jean Buridan's Logic: The Treatise on Supposition, the Treatise on Consequences*, trans. P. King. Synthese Historical Library 27. Dordrecht: Kluwer Academic Publishers, 1985.

Burley, Walter. "Consequences" and "Obligations." In *The Cambridge Translations of Medieval Philosophical Texts*, ed. and trans. N. Kretzmann and E. Stump, 284–311, 482–510. Cambridge: Cambridge University Press, 1988.

—————. *On the Purity of the Art of Logic: The Shorter and the Longer Treatises.* Trans. P. V. Spade. Yale Library of Medieval Philosophy. New Haven, Conn.: Yale University Press, 2000.

—————. "On Universals." In *Readings in Medieval Philosophy*, ed. and trans. A. B. Schoedinger, 619–44. New York: Oxford University Press, 1996.

Capreolus, John. *On the Virtues.* Trans. K. White and R. Cessario. Washington, D.C.: Catholic University of America Press, 2001.

Cicero. *Works.* Ed. W. A. Falconer and H. Rackham. Loeb Classical Library, vols. 154 (1923) and 349 (1942). Cambridge, Mass.: Harvard University Press.

Clarembald of Arras. *The Boethian Commentaries of Clarembald of Arras.* Trans. D. B. George and J. R. Fortin. Notre Dame Texts in Medieval Culture 7. Notre Dame, Ind.: University of Notre Dame Press, 2002.

Clement of Alexandria. *Ante-Nicene Christian Library.* Vol. 4, *Clement of Alexandria*, ed. J. Donaldson. Edinburgh: T. and T. Clark, 1871.

Crescas, Hasdai. *The Refutation of the Christian Principles.* Trans. D. J. Lasker. Albany, N.Y.: State University of New York Press, 1992.

—————. *Sermon on the Passover.* Trans. A. Ravitzky. Jerusalem: Israel Academy of Sciences and Humanities, 1998.

———. *"Twenty-five Propositions of Book I of the 'Or Adonai.'"* In *Crescas' Critique of Aristotle: Problems of Aristotle's Physics in Jewish and Arabic Philosophy*, trans. H. A. Wolfson, 130–315. Cambridge, Mass.: Harvard University Press, 1971.

Damascene, John. *Barlaam and Joasaph*. Trans. G. R. Woodward and H. Mattingly. Loeb Classical Library 34. London: Heinemann, 1914.

———. *Three Treatises on the Divine Images*. Trans. A. Louth. Crestwood, N.Y.: St. Vladimir's Seminary Press, 2003.

———. *Writings*. Trans. F. H. Chase Jr. Washington, D.C.: Catholic University of America Press, 1958.

Dante. *The Divine Comedy*. 6 vols. Trans. C. S. Singleton. Princeton, N.J.: Princeton University Press, 1970–1975.

———. *Monarchia*. Trans. R. Kay. Toronto: Pontifical Institute of Mediaeval Studies, 1998.

———. *Poems and Translations, including Dante's "Vita nuova."* Trans. D. G. Rossetti. New York: E. P. Dutton.

David de Dinant. *Autour de Décret de 1210: David de Dinant*. Ed. G. Théry. Le Saulchoir: Kain, 1923.

Dietrich of Freiberg. *Treatise on the Intellect and the Intelligible*. Trans. M. L. Fuehrer. Milwaukee, Wisc.: Marquette University Press, 1992.

Dionysius the Pseudo-Areopagite. *The Complete Works*. Trans. C. Luibheid. Classics of Western Spirituality. London: SPCK, 1897.

———. *Thirteenth-Century Textbook of Mystical Theology at the University of Paris: The Mystical Theology of Dionysius the Areopagite in Eriugena's Latin Translation with the Scolia Translated by Anastasius the Librarian and Excerpts from Eriugena's Periphysion*. Trans. L. M. Harrington. Dallas Medieval Texts and Translations 4. Paris: Peeters, 2004.

Duns Scotus, John, Bl. *Contingency and Freedom: Lectura I 39*. Trans. A. Vos Jaczn et al. New Synthese Historical Library 42. Dordrecht: Kluwer Academic Publishers, 1994.

———. *Duns Scotus on the Will and Morality*. Trans. A. B. Wolter. Washington, D.C.: Catholic University of America Press, 1986.

———. *Duns Scotus on Time and Existence: The Questions on "De interpretatione."* Trans. E. Buckner and J. Zupko. Washington, D.C.: Catholic University of America Press, 2014.

———. *The Examined Report of the Paris Lecture: Reportatio I-A*. Trans. A. B. Wolter and O. V. Bychkov. St. Bonaventure, N.Y.: Franciscan Institute, 2004.

———. *God and Creatures: The Quodlibetal Questions*. Trans. F. Alluntis and A. B. Wolter. Princeton, N.J.: Princeton University Press, 1975.

———. *John Duns Scotus' Political and Economic Philosophy*. Trans. A. B. Wolter. St. Bonaventure, N.Y.: Franciscan Institute, 2001.

———. *John Duns Scotus: Selected Writings on Ethics*. Trans. T. Williams. Oxford: Oxford University Press, 2017.

———. "The Oxford Commentary on the Four Books of the Master of the Sentences (Book I, d. 3, q. 4)." In *Selections from Medieval Philosophers*, 2 vols., ed. and trans. R. McKeon, 2:313–50. New York: Scribner, 1930.

———. *Philosophical Writings*. Trans. A. B. Wolter. New York: Nelson, 1962.

———. *Questions on Aristotle's Categories*. Trans. L. Newton. Washington, D.C.: Catholic University of America Press, 2014.

———. *Questions on the Metaphysics of Aristotle by John Duns Scotus*. 2 vols. Trans. G. J. Etzkorn and A. B. Wolter. St. Bonaventure, N.Y.: Franciscan Institute Press, 1997–1998.

———. *Scotus and Ockham: a Medieval Dispute over Universals*. 2 vols. Trans. M. Tweedale. Lewiston, N.Y.: Mellen, 1999.

———. *A Treatise on God as First Principle*. Trans. A. B. Wolter. Chicago: Franciscan Herald Press, 1982.

———. *A Treatise on Potency and Act: Questions on the Metaphysics of Aristotle, Book IX*. Trans. A. B. Wolter. St. Bonaventure, N.Y.: Franciscan Institute, 2000.

Eadmer of Canterbury. *The Life of St. Anselm, Archbishop of Canterbury*. Trans. R. W. Southern. Oxford: Clarendon Press, 1972.

Eckhart, Meister. *The Essential Sermons, Commentaries, Treatises, and Defense*. Trans. E. Colledge and B. McGinn. Classics of Western Spirituality. New York: Paulist Press, 1981.

———. *German Sermons and Treatises*. 2 vols. Trans. M. O'C. Walshe. London: Dulverton Watkins, 1979–1981.

———. *Meister Eckhart: A Modern Translation*. Trans. R. B. Blakney. New York: Harper Perennial, 1941.

———. *Meister Eckhart: Teacher and Preacher*. Trans. B. McGinn, F. Tobin, and E. Borgstaedt. Classics of Western Spirituality. New York: Paulist Press, 1986.

———. *Parisian Questions and Prologues*. Trans. A. A. Maurer. Toronto: Pontifical Institute of Mediaeval Studies, 1974.

———. *Selected Writings*. Trans. O. Davies. London: Penguin, 1994.

———. *Sermons and Treatises*. 3 vols. Trans. M. O'C. Walshe. Longmead, UK: Element Books, 1987–1991.

Farabi, al-. *Al-Farabi on the Perfect State*. Trans. R. Walzer. Oxford: Clarendon Press, 1985.

———. *Alfarabi, The Political Writings: "Political Regime" and "Summary of Plato's Laws."* Trans. C. E. Butterworth. Ithaca, N.Y.: Cornell University Press, 2015.

———. *Alfarabi, The Political Writings: "Selected Aphorisms" and Other Texts*. Vol. 1. Trans. C. E. Butterworth. Ithaca, N.Y.: Cornell University Press, 2001.

———. *Alfarabi's Book of Rhetoric*. Trans. L. E. Ezzaher. *Rhetorica* 26 (2008): 347–91.

———. *Alfarabi's Commentary and Short Treatise on Aristotle's "De interpretatione."* Trans. F. W. Zimmermann. Classical and Medieval Logic Texts 3. Oxford: Oxford University Press, 1981.

———. *Alfarabi's Philosophy of Plato and Aristotle*. Trans. M. Mahdi. New York: Free Press, 1962.

———. *Alfarabi's Short Commentary on Aristotle's "Prior Analytics."* Trans. N. Rescher. Pittsburgh, Pa.: University of Pittsburgh Press, 1963.

———. "The Enumeration of the Sciences (c. 5)," "*The Political Regime*," and "*Plato's Laws* (Intro. and 2 Discourses)." Trans. F. M. Naijar, M. E. Marmura, and M. Mahdi. In *Medieval Political Philosophy: A Sourcebook*, ed. R. Lerner, M. Mahdi, and E. Fortin, 23–57, 83–94. Ithaca, N.Y.: Cornell University Press, 1963.

———. "The Letter Concerning the Intellect." In *Philosophy in the Middle Ages: The Christian, Islamic, and Jewish Traditions*, ed. and trans. A. Hyman and J. J. Walsh, 215–21. New York: Harper and Row, 1967.

———. "*On the Aims of Aristotle's 'Metaphysics.'*" In *Avicenna and the Aristotelian Tradition*, trans. D. Gutas, 240–42. Leiden: Brill, 1988.

———. *Three Arabic Treatises on Aristotle's "Rhetoric."* Trans. L. E. Ezzaher. Carbondale: Southern Illinois University Press, 2015.

Ficino, Marsilio. *Ficino: Commentaries on Plato (Phaedrus and Ion)*. Trans. M. J. B. Allen. Cambridge, Mass.: Harvard University Press, 2008.

———. "Five Questions concerning the Mind." Trans. J. L. Burroughs. In *The Renaissance Philosophy of Man*, ed. E. Cassirer, P. O. Kristeller, and J. H. Randall. Chicago: University of Chicago Press, 1948.

———. *Icastes: Marsilio Ficino's Interpretation of Plato's "Sophist."* Trans. M. J. B. Allen. Berkeley: University of California Press, 1989.

———. *The Letters of Marsilio Ficino*. 8 vols. London: Shepherd-Walwyn, 1975–2010.

———. *Nuptial Arithmetic: Marsilio Ficino's Commentary on the Fatal Number in Book VIII of Plato's Republic*. Trans. M. J. B. Allen. Berkeley: University of California Press, 1994.

———. *The Philebus Commentary*. Trans. M. J. B. Allen. Berkeley: University of California Press, 1975.

———. *Platonic Theology*. 4 vols. Trans. M. J. B. Allen and J. Warden. The I Tatti Renaissance Library, 2, 4, 7, and 13. Cambridge, Mass.: Harvard University Press, 2001–2004.

———. *Three Books on Life*. Trans. C. V. Kaske and J. R. Clark. Renaissance Text Studies 11. Binghamton, N.Y.: Medieval and Renaissance Texts and Studies, 1989.

Fridugisius. *Letter on Nothing and Darkness*. In *Medieval Philosophy: From St. Augustine to Nicholas of Cusa*, ed. and trans. J. F. Wippel and A. B. Wolter, 104–8. New York: Free Press, 1969.

Gabirol, Ibn (Avicebron). *Fountain of Life*. Trans. H. E. Wedeck. London: Owen, 1962.

———. *The Improvement of Moral Qualities*. Trans. S. Wise. New York: Columbia University Press, 1902.

———. *The Kingly Crown*. Trans. B. Lewis. Notre Dame, Ind.: University of Notre Dame Press, 2003.

———. "Solomon ibn Gabirol and Shem Tov ben Joseph Falaquera: Excerpts from 'The Source of Life.'" In *Medieval Jewish Philosophical Writings*, ed. C. Manekin, 23–87. Cambridge: Cambridge University Press, 2008.

Gabriel Biel. *Defensorium obedientiae apostolicae et alia documenta*. Trans. H. A. Oberman, D. E. Zerfoss, and W. J. Courtenay. Cambridge, Mass.: Harvard University Press, 1968.

Gerard of Cremona. *Gerard of Cremona's Translation of the Commentary of Al-Nayrizi on Book I of Euclid's Elements of Geometry*. Trans. A. Lo Bello. Leiden: Brill, 2003.

Gerson, Jean. *The Consolation of Theology*. Trans. C. L. Miller. New York: Abaris Books, 1998.

———. *Jean Gerson: Early Works*. Trans. B. P. McGuire. Classics of Western Spirituality. New York: Paulist Press, 1998.

———. *Selections from "A Deo Exivit," "Contra curiositatem studentium," and "De mystica theologia speculative."* Trans. S. E. Ozment. Leiden: Brill, 1969.

———. *A Treatise on Bringing Children to Jesus Christ*. Trans. W. Whitty. Dublin: M. H. Gill, 1899.

Gersonides (Gershom, Levi ben). *Commentary on Song of Songs*. Trans. M. Kellner. Yale Judaica Series 28. New Haven, Conn.: Yale University Press, 1998.

———. *Commentary on the "Book of Job."* Trans. A. I. Lassen. New York: Bloch, 1946.

———. *Creation of the World according to Gersonides*. Trans. J. Staub. Chico, Calif.: Scholars Press, 1982.

———. *The Logic of Gersonides: A Translation of Sefer ha-Heqqesh ha-Yashar (The Book of the Correct Syllogism)*. Trans. C. H. Manekin. New Synthese Historical Library 40. Dordrecht: Kluwer Academic Publishers, 1992.

————. *The Wars of the Lord*. 3 vols. Trans. S. Feldman. Philadelphia, Pa.: Jewish Publications Society of America, 1984–1999.

Ghazali, al- (Algazel). *Al-Ghazali: On the Manners relating to Eating*. Trans. D. Johnson-Davies. Cambridge, UK: Islamic Texts Society, 2000.

————. *Al-Ghazali's Book of Fear and Hope*. Trans. W. McKane. Leiden: Brill, 1962.

————. *Al-Ghazali's Tract on Dogmatic Theology*. Trans. A. L. Tibawi. London: Luzac, 1965.

————. *The Alchemy of Happiness*. Trans. E. L. Daniel. London: Sharpe, 1991.

————. *The Book of Knowledge*. Trans. N. A. Faris. Lahore: Sh. Muhammad Ashraf, 1962.

————. *Deliverance from Error and Mystical Union with the Almighty*. Trans. J. Ab'ulayah. Washington, D.C.: Council for Research in Values and Philosophy, 2001.

————. *Freedom and Fulfillment: An Annotated Translation of "Al-Munqidh min al-Dalal" and Other Relevant Works*. Trans. R. J. McCarthy. Boston, Mass.: Twayne, 1980.

————. *The Incoherence of the Philosophers: A Parallel English-Arabic Text*. Trans. M. E. Marmura. Provo, Utah: Brigham Young University Press, 1997.

————. *Invocations & Supplications: Book IX of The Revival of the Religious Sciences*. Trans. K. Nakamura. Cambridge, UK: Islamic Texts Society, 1990.

————. *The Jewels of the Quran: Al-Ghazzali's Theory*. Trans. M. A. Quasem. Bangi: University Kebansaan Mayalysia: 1977.

————. *The Niche of Lights: A Parallel English-Arabic Text*. Trans. D. Buchman. Provo, Utah: Brigham Young University Press, 1998.

————. *On the Boundaries of Theological Tolerance in Islam*. Trans. S. A. Jackson. Karachi: Oxford University Press, 2002.

————. *The Remembrance of Death and the Afterlife*. Trans. T. J. Winter. Cambridge, UK: Islamic Texts Society, 1989.

Giles of Rome. "Commentary on the Song of Songs: Prologue." In *Medieval Literary Theory and Criticism, c. 1100–c. 1375: The Commentary Tradition*, ed. A. J. Minnis and A. B. Scott, 243–47. Oxford: Clarendon Press, 1988.

————. *Errores Philosophorum*. Trans. J. O. Riedl. Milwaukee, Wisc.: Marquette University Press, 1944.

————. *Giles of Rome's On Ecclesiastical Power: A Medieval Theory of World Government*. Trans. R. W. Dyson. New York: Columbia University Press, 2004.

———. "On Civil Government (*De regimine principum*, Book III, cc. 33, 36)." Trans. K. L. Forhan. In *Medieval Political Theory—A Reader*, ed. C. J. Nederman and K. L. Forhan, 150–52. London: Routledge, 1993.

———. "On the Rule of Princes" (selections). In *The Cambridge Translations of Medieval Philosophical Texts*, ed. and trans. A. S. McGrade, J. Kilcullen, and M. Kempshall, 2:203–15. Cambridge: Cambridge University Press, 2001.

———. *Theorems on Existence and Essence*. Trans. M. V. Murray. Milwaukee, Wisc.: Marquette University Press, 1952.

Godfrey of Fontaines. "Are Subjects Bound to Pay a Tax When the Need for It Is Not Evident?," "Does a Human Being Following the Dictates of Natural Reason Have to Judge That He Ought to Love God More than Himself?," and "Reply to James of Viterbo on Love of God and Self." In *The Cambridge Translations of Medieval Philosophical Texts*, ed. and trans. A. S. McGrade, J. Kilcullen, and M. Kempshall, 2:272–84, 302–6, 316–20. Cambridge: Cambridge University Press, 2001. Refer to Boethius of Dacia.

Gratian. "The Concord of Discordant Canons (Excerpt)." In *A Scholastic Miscellany: Anselm to Ockham*, ed. and trans. E. R. Fairweather, 243–46. Library of Christian Classics 10. New York: Macmillan, 1970.

———. *The Treatise on Laws (Decretum, DD. 1–20)*. Trans. A. Thompson. Washington, D.C.: Catholic University of America Press, 1993.

Gregory Palamas. *Dialogue between an Orthodox and a Barlaamite*. Trans. S. J. Denning-Bolle. Binghamton, N.Y.: Global Publications, 1999.

———. *The One Hundred and Fifty Chapters*. Trans. R. E. Sinkewicz. Studies and Texts 83. Toronto: Pontifical Institute of Mediaeval Studies, 1988.

———. *The Triads*. Trans. N. Gendle. Classics of Western Spirituality. New York: Paulist Press, 1983.

Grosseteste, Robert. "Commentary on 'The Celestial Hierarchy,' Chapter XV: Extracts." In *Medieval Literary Theory and Criticism, c. 1100–c. 1375: The Commentary Tradition*, ed. A. J. Minnis and A. B. Scott, 192–96. Oxford: Clarendon Press, 1988.

———. *The Letters of Robert Grosseteste, Bishop of Lincoln*. Trans. J. Goering and F. A. C. Mantello. Toronto: University of Toronto Press, 2010.

———. *Moralities on the Gospels: A New Source of "Ancrene Wisse."* Trans. E. J. Dobson. Oxford: Clarendon Press, 1975.

———. *On Light*. Trans. C. C. Riedl. Milwaukee, Wisc.: Marquette University Press, 1978.

———. *On the Cessation of Laws*. Trans. S. M. Hilderbrand. Washington, D.C.: Catholic University of America Press, 2012.

———. *On the Six Days of Creation*. Trans. C. F. J. Martin. Oxford: Oxford University Press, 1996.

———. "On Truth (*De veritate*), On the Truth of Propositions (*De veritate propositionis*), On the Knowledge of God (*De scientia Dei*)." In *Selections from Medieval Philosophers*, 2 vols., ed. and trans. R. McKeon, 1:263–87. New York: Scribner, 1930.

———. *Robert Grosseteste's Commentary on Aristotle's "Posterior Analytics."* Trans. S. MacDonald. New Haven, Conn.: Yale University Press, 2004.

Halevi, Jehudah. *Kuzari: The Book of Proof and Argument*. Trans. I. Heinemann. Oxford: East and West Library, 1948. Reprinted in *Three Jewish Philosophers*. New York: Atheneum, 1977.

———. *Selected Poems of Jehudah Halevi*. Trans. N. Salaman. Philadelphia, Pa.: Jewish Publication Society of America, 1974.

Henry of Ghent. "Can a Human Being Know Anything?" and "Can a Human Being Know Anything without Divine Illumination?" In *The Cambridge Translations of Medieval Philosophical Texts*, ed. and trans. R. Pasnau, 3:95–102, 110–35. Cambridge: Cambridge University Press, 2002.

———. *Henry of Ghent's Summa of Ordinary Questions: Articles Six to Ten on Theology*. Trans. R. J. Teske. Milwaukee, Wisc.: Marquette University Press, 2011.

———. *Henry of Ghent's Summa of Ordinary Questiones: Articles Thirty One and Thirty Two on God's Eternity and the Divine Attributes in General*. Milwaukee, Wisc.: Marquette University Press, 2012.

———. "Is It Rational for Someone without Hope of a Future Life to Choose to Die for the Commonwealth?" and "Is a Subject Bound to Obey a Statute When It Is Not Evident?" In *The Cambridge Translations of Medieval Philosophical Texts*, ed. and trans. A. S. McGrade, J. Kilcullen, and M. Kempshall, 2:259–70, 310–14. Cambridge: Cambridge University Press, 2001.

———. *Quodlibetal Questions on Free Will*. Trans. R. J. Teske. Mediaeval Philosophical Texts in Translation 32. Milwaukee, Wisc.: Marquette University Press, 1993.

———. "The Sum of Ordinary Questions: Extracts from Articles 14 and 16." In *Medieval Literary Theory and Criticism, c. 1100–c. 1375: The Commentary Tradition*, ed. A. J. Minnis and A. B. Scott, 250–66. Oxford: Clarendon Press, 1988.

———. *Summa of Ordinary Questions: Articles 35, 36, 42 & 45*. Trans. with intro. and notes by R. J. Teske. Milwaukee, Wisc.: Marquette University Press, 2013.

Henry of Zomeren. *The Quarrel over Future Contingents (Louvain, 1465–1475): Unpublished Texts Collected by L. Baudry*. Trans. R. Guerlac. Dordrecht: Kluwer Academic Publishers, 1989.

Hervaeus Natalis (Harvey Nedellec). *The Poverty of Christ and the Apostles.* Trans. J. D. Jones. Studies in Medieval Moral Teaching 2. Toronto: Pontifical Institute of Mediaeval Studies, 1999.

Heytesbury, William. *"The Compounded and Divided Senses"* and *"The Verbs 'Know' and 'Doubt.'"* In *The Cambridge Translations of Medieval Texts*, ed. and trans. N. Kretzmann and E. Stump, 1:413–79. Cambridge: Cambridge University Press, 1988.

———. *On "Insoluble" Sentences: Chapter One of His Rules for Solving Sophisms.* Trans. P. V. Spade. Toronto: Pontifical Institute of Mediaeval Studies, 1979.

———. *On Maxima and Minima: Chapter 5 of Rules for Solving Sophismata.* Trans. J. Longeway. Synthese Historical Library 26. Dordrecht: Reidel, 1984.

Hildegard of Bingen. *Book of Divine Works, with Letters and Songs.* Trans. B. Milem. Santa Fe, N.M.: Bear and Company, 1987.

———. *Hildegard of Bingen, On Natural Philosophy and Medicine: Selections from "Cause and Cure."* Trans. M. Berger. Cambridge, UK: Brewer, 1999.

———. *Mystical Writings.* Trans. R. Carver. New York: Crossroads, 1995.

———. *Scivias.* Trans. C. Hart and J. Bishop. Classics of Western Spirituality. New York: Paulist Press, 1990.

———. *Symphonia.* Trans. B. Newman. Ithaca, N.Y.: Cornell University Press, 1988.

Honorius of Autun. "A Picture of the World." In *Medieval Philosophy: From St. Augustine to Nicholas of Cusa*, ed. and trans. J. F. Wippel and A. B. Wolter, 177–86. New York: Free Press, 1968.

Hugh of Saint-Victor. *The Didascalicon of Hugh of Saint-Victor.* Trans. J. Taylor. New York: Columbia University Press, 1991.

———. *The Divine Love: The Two Treatises "De laude caritatis" and "De amore sponsi ad sponsam."* Trans. Anon. Fleur de Lys Series 9. London: A. R. Mowbray, 1956.

———. *On the Sacraments of the Christian Faith.* Trans. R. J. Deferrari. Cambridge, Mass.: Mediaeval Academy of America, 1951.

———. "On the Trinity (selections, Book I)." In *Medieval Philosophy: From St. Augustine to Nicholas of Cusa*, ed. and trans. J. F. Wippel and A. B. Wolter, 212–22. New York: Free Press, 1968.

———. *Practical Geometry, attributed to Hugh of Saint-Victor.* Trans. F. A. Homann. Mediaeval Philosophical Texts in Translation 29. Milwaukee, Wisc.: Marquette University Press, 1991.

———. *Selected Spiritual Writings.* Trans. Anon. Classics of the Contemplative Life. New York: Harper and Row, 1962.

―――. *Soliloquy on the Earnest Money of the Soul*. Trans. K. Herbert. Mediaeval Philosophical Texts in Translation 9. Milwaukee, Wisc.: Marquette University Press, 1956.

―――. *The Soul's Betrothal-Gift* (*De arrha animae*). Trans. F. S. Taylor. Westminster: Dacre, 1945.

Isaac Israeli. *The Fragments of Isaac Israeli's Book of Substances*. Trans. S. M. Stern. *Journal of Jewish Studies* 7 (1956): 13–29.

―――. *Isaac Israeli: A Neoplatonic Philosopher of the Tenth Century; His Works Translated with Comments and an Outline of His Philosophy*. Trans. A. Altmann and S. M. Stern. Oxford: Oxford University Press, 1958.

―――. "Isaac Israeli's 'Book on Definitions. Some Fragments of a Second Hebrew Translation." Trans. A. Altmann. *Journal of Semitic Studies* 2 (1957): 232–42.

―――. "Isaac Israeli's Book of Substances." Trans A. Altmann. *Journal of Jewish Studies* 6 (1955): 133–45.

Isidore of Seville, St. *Isidore of Seville's History of the Goths, Vandals and Suevi*. Trans. G. Donini and G. B. Ford Jr. Leiden: Brill, 1970.

―――. *The Letters of St. Isidore of Seville*. Trans. G. B. Ford Jr. Amsterdam: Hakkert, 1970.

―――. "On the Church and the Sects (*Etymologies*, VII, 14 and VIII, I, 3, 5)." In *Heresy and Authority in Medieval Europe*, ed. and trans. E. Peters, 47–50. Philadelphia: University of Pennsylvania Press, 1980.

James of Viterbo. *De regimine christiano* (*On Christian Government*). Trans. R. W. Dyson. Leiden: Brill, 2009.

―――. "Does a Human Being Have a Greater Natural Love for God than for Himself, or Vice Versa?" and "Is It Better to Be Ruled by the Best Man than by the Best Laws?" In *The Cambridge Translations of Medieval Philosophical Texts*, ed. and trans. A. S. McGrade, J. Kilcullen, and M. Kempshall, 2:286–300, 322–25. Cambridge: Cambridge University Press, 2001.

Joachim of Fiore. *Two Poems Attributed to Joachim of Fiore*. Trans. M. Reeves and J. V. Fleming. Princeton, N.J.: Pilgrim Press, 1978.

John of Naples. "Should a Christian King Use Unbelievers to Defend His Kingdom?" In *The Cambridge Translations of Medieval Philosophical Texts*, ed. and trans. A. S. McGrade, J. Kilcullen, and M. Kempshall, 2:328–48. Cambridge: Cambridge University Press, 2001.

John of Paris. *On Royal and Papal Power*. Trans. A. P. Monahan. New York: Columbia University Press, 1974.

―――. "On Royal and Papal Power (Prologue, cc. 1–9)." Trans. C. J. Nederman. In *Medieval Political Theory—A Reader*, C. J. Nederman and K. L. Forhan, 158–72. London: Routledge, 1993.

John of Salisbury. *Anselm and Becket: Two Canterbury Saints' Lives by John of Salisbury*. Trans. R. E. Pepin. Toronto: Pontifical Institute of Mediaeval Studies, 2009.

———. *John of Salisbury's "Entheticus maior" and "minor."* Trans. J. van Laarhoven. Leiden: Brill, 1987.

———. *John of Salisbury's Memoirs of the Papal Court*. Trans. M. Chibnall. London: Nelson, 1956.

———. *The Letters of John of Salisbury: The Early Letters (1153–1161)*. Ed. W. J. Millor, H. E. Butler, and C. N. L. Brooke. Edinburgh: Thomas Nelson and Sons, 1955.

———. *The Letters of John of Salisbury: The Later Letters*. Ed. W. J. Millor and C. N. L. Brooke. Oxford: Oxford University Press, 1979.

———. *The Metalogicon of John of Salisbury: A Twelfth-Century Defense of the Verbal and Logical Arts of the Trivium*. Trans. D. D. McGarry. Berkeley: University of California Press, 1962.

———. *Policraticus: Of the Frivolities of Courtiers and the Footprints of Philosophers*. Trans. C. J. Nederman. Cambridge Texts in the History of Political Thought. Cambridge: Cambridge University Press, 1990.

John of St. Thomas (John Poinsot). *Outlines of Formal Logic*. Trans. F. C. Wade. Mediaeval Philosophical Texts in Translation 8. Milwaukee, Wisc.: Marquette University Press, 1955.

———. *Tractatus de signis: The Semiotic of John Poinsot*. Trans. J. N. Deely. Berkeley: University of California Press, 1985.

John Scotus Eriugena. *Periphyseon: (The Division of Nature)*. Trans. I. P. Sheldon-Williams. Rev. J. O'Meara. Washington, D.C.: Dumbarton Oaks, 1987.

———. *Treatise on Divine Predestination*. Trans. M. Brennan. Notre Dame, Ind.: University of Notre Dame Press, 1998.

Julian of Norwich. *Showings*. Ed. E. Colledge and J. J. Walsh. Classics of Western Spirituality. New York: Paulist Press, 1978.

Kindi, al-. *Al-Kindi's "Metaphysics."* Trans. A. L. Ivry. Albany: State University of New York Press, 1971.

———. *The Medical Formulary or Aqrabadhin of al-Kindi*. Trans. M. Levy. Madison: University of Wisconsin Press, 1966.

———. *The Philosophical Works of al-Kindi*. Trans. P. Adamson and P. E. Pormann. Karachi: Oxford University Press, 2012.

Lambert of Auxerre. "Properties of Terms." In *The Cambridge Translations of Medieval Philosophical Texts*, ed. and trans. N. Kretzmann and E. Stump, 104–62. Cambridge: Cambridge University Press, 1988.

Lanfranc of Bec. *The Letters of Lanfranc, Archbishop of Canterbury*. Trans. H. Clover and M. Gibson. Oxford: Clarendon Press, 1979.

———. *The Monastic Constitutions of Lanfranc*. Trans. D. Knowles. London: Nelson, 1951.

Langton, Stephen. "A Question on Original Sin" and "Fragments on the Morality of Human Acts." In *A Scholastic Miscellany*, ed. E. Fairweather, 352–58. New York: Macmillan, 1970.

Lull, Raymond. *The Book of the Lover and the Beloved*. Trans. E. A. Peers. London: Society for Promoting Christian Knowledge, 1928.

―――. *The Book of the Ordre of Chyvalry*. Trans. A. T. P. Byles. London: Oxford University Press, 1926.

Maimonides, Moses. *The Book of Knowledge* (*Mishneh Torah*, 1–2). Trans. M. Hyamson. Jerusalem: Feldheim Publishers, 1981.

―――. *The Code of Maimonides, Book Fourteen: The Book of Judges*. Trans. A. Hershman. New Haven, Conn.: Yale University Press, 1949.

―――. *Ethical Writings of Maimonides*. Trans. R. L. Weiss and C. Butterworth. New York: New York University Press, 1975.

―――. *The Guide of the Perplexed*. 2 vols. Trans. S. Pines. Chicago: University of Chicago Press, 1963–1974.

―――. *Letters of Maimonides*. Trans. L. D. Stitskin. New York: Yeshiva University Press, 1977.

―――. *Maimonides' Commentary on the Mishnah, Tractate "Sanhedrin."* Trans. F. Rosner. New York: Sepher-Hermon, 1981.

―――. *A Maimonides Reader*. Ed. I. Twersky. West Orange, N.J.: Behrman, 1972.

―――. *Maimonides: The Book of Knowledge*. Trans. M. Hyamson. Jerusalem: Feldheim, 1974.

―――. *Maimonides' Treatise on Logic*. Trans. I. Efros. New York: American Academy for Jewish Research, 1938.

―――. *The Medical Writings of Moses Maimonides*. 3 vols. Trans. F. Rosner and S. Muntner. Philadelphia, Pa.: Lippincott, 1963–1969.

―――. *Mishneh Torah: The Book of Knowledge*. Trans. M. Hyamson. Jerusalem: Boys Town, 1965.

―――. *Moses Maimonides' Commentary on the Mishnah: Introduction to "Seder Zeriam" and Commentary on Tractate "Berahcoth."* Trans. F. Rosner. New York: Feldheim, 1975.

―――. *Six Treatises Attributed to Maimonides*. Trans. F. Rosner. Northvale, N.J.: Aronson, 1991.

―――. *Treatise on Asthma*. Trans. S. Muntner. Philadelphia, Pa.: Lippincott, 1963.

―――. *Treatise on Hemorrhoids*. Trans. F. Rosner and S. Muntner. Philadelphia, Pa.: Lippincott, 1969.

―――. *Treatise on Poisons and Their Antidotes*. Trans. S. Muntner. Philadelphia, Pa.: Lippincott, 1966.

Marsilius of Inghen. *Treatises on the Properties of Terms*. Trans. E. P. Bos. Synthese Historical Library 22. Dordrecht: Reidel, 1983.

Marsilius of Padua. *The Defensor Pacis*. In *Marsilius of Padua, the Defender of Peace*, 2 vols., trans. A. Gewirth. New York: Columbia University Press, 1951–1956.

———. *Writings on the Empire: "Defensor minor" and "De translatione imperii."* Trans. C. J. Nederman and F. Watson. Cambridge Texts in the History of Political Thought. Cambridge: Cambridge University Press, 1993.

Martianus Capella. *Martianus Capella and the Seven Liberal Arts*. 2 vols. Trans. W. H. Stahl, R. Johnson, and E. L. Burge. New York: Columbia University Press, 1971–1977.

Matthew of Aquasparta. "Disputed Questions on Faith." In *A Scholastic Miscellany: Anselm to Ockham*, trans. R. D. Crouse, 402–27, Library of Christian Classics 10. New York: Macmillan, 1956.

———. "Ten Disputed Questions on Knowledge (Qq. 1–2)." In *Selections from Medieval Philosophers*, 2 vols., ed. and trans. R. McKeon, 2:240–302. New York: Scribner, 1930.

Maximus the Confessor. *The Ascetic Life: The Four Centuries on Charity*. Trans. P. Sherwood. Westminster, Md.: Newman Press, 1955.

———. *The Church, the Liturgy, and the Soul of Man: the "Mystagogia" of St. Maximus the Confessor*. Trans. J. Stead. Still River, Mass.: St. Bede's Publications, 1982.

———. *Maximus Confessor: Selected Writings*. Trans. G. C. Berthold. Classics of Western Spirituality. New York: Paulist Press, 1985.

———. *Maximus the Confessor and His Companions: Documents from Exile*. Trans. P. Allen and B. Neil. Oxford: Oxford University Press, 2002.

———. *On the Cosmic Mystery of Jesus Christ: Selected Writings from St. Maximus the Confessor*. Trans. P. M. Blowers and R. L. Wilken. Crestwood, N.Y.: St. Vladimir's Seminary Press, 2003.

Nicholas of Autrecourt. "Critique of Causality and Substance." In *Medieval Philosophy: Selected Readings from Augustine to Buridan*, ed. and trans. H. Shapiro, 509–17. New York: Modern Library, 1964.

———. *Nicholas of Autrecourt: His Correspondence with Master Giles and Bernard of Arezzo*. Trans. L. M. de Rijk. Leiden: Brill, 1994.

———. *The Universal Treatise of Nicholas of Autrecourt*. Trans. L. A. Kennedy. Mediaeval Philosophical Texts in Translation 20. Milwaukee, Wisc.: Marquette University Press, 1971.

Nicholas of Cusa. *The Catholic Concordance*. Trans. P. E. Sigmund. Cambridge: Cambridge University Press, 1991.

———. *Complete Philosophical and Theological Treatises of Nicholas of Cusa*. Trans. J. Hopkins. Minneapolis, Minn.: Banning, 2001.

———. *A Concise Introduction to the Philosophy of Nicholas of Cusa*. Trans. J. Hopkins. Minneapolis: University of Minnesota Press, 1980.

———. *De coniecturis (On Conjectures)*. In *Toward a New Council of Florence: "On the Peace of Faith" and Other Works of Nicholas of Cusa*, trans. W. F. Wertz. Washington, D.C.: Schiller Institute, 1993.

———. *Directio speculantis seu de non aliud (On God as Not-Other)*. In *Nicholas of Cusa on God as Not-Other: A Translation and Appraisal of De li non aliud*, trans. J. Hopkins. Minneapolis: University of Minnesota Press, 1981.

———. *The Layman on Wisdom and the Mind*. Trans. M. L. Führer. Ottawa: Dovehouse Editions, 1989.

———. *A Miscellany on Nicholas of Cusa*. Trans. J. Hopkins. Minneapolis, Minn.: Banning Press, 1998.

———. *Nicholas of Cusa on Wisdom and Knowledge*. Trans. J. Hopkins. Minneapolis, Minn.: Banning Press, 1996.

———. *Nicholas of Cusa: Selected Spiritual Writings*. Trans. H. L. Bond. New York: Paulist Press, 1997.

———. *Nicholas of Cusa's Debate with John Wenck: A Translation and an Appraisal of "De ignota litteratura" and "Apologia doctae ignorantiae."* Trans. J. Hopkins. Minneapolis, Minn.: Banning Press, 1981.

———. *Nicholas of Cusa's "De pace fidei" and "Cribratio Alkorani": Translation and Analysis*. Trans. J. Hopkins. Minneapolis, Minn.: Banning Press, 1990.

———. *Nicholas of Cusa's Dialectical Mysticism: Text, Translation, and Interpretative Study of "De visione Dei."* Trans. J. Hopkins. Minneapolis, Minn.: Banning Press, 1985.

———. *Nicholas of Cusa's Metaphysics of Contraction (De dato Patris luminum)*. Trans. J. Hopkins. Minneapolis, Minn.: Banning Press, 1983.

Nicholas of Lyra. "Literal Postill on the Bible: Extracts from the General and Special Prologues, and from the Commentary on the Psalter." In *Medieval Literary Theory and Criticism, c. 1100–c. 1375: The Commentary Tradition*, ed. A. J. Minnis and A. B. Scott, 266–76. Oxford: Clarendon Press, 1988.

———. *Nicholas of Lyra's Apocalypse Commentary*. Trans. P. D. W. Krey. Kalamazoo, Mich.: Medieval Institute Publications, 1997.

Nicholas Trevet. "Commentary on Boethius' 'On the Consolation of Philosophy': Extracts." In *Medieval Literary Theory and Criticism, c. 1100–c. 1375: The Commentary Tradition*, ed. A. J. Minnis and A. B. Scott, 336–40. Oxford: Clarendon Press, 1988.

———. "Commentary on Seneca's Tragedies: Extracts." In *Medieval Literary Theory and Criticism, c. 1100–c. 1375: The Commentary Tradition*, ed. A. J. Minnis and A. B. Scott, 340–44. Oxford: Clarendon Press, 1988.

———. "Exposition of 'Agamemnon,' Act V." In *Medieval Literary Theory and Criticism, c. 1100–c. 1375: The Commentary Tradition*, ed. A. J. Minnis and A. B. Scott, 346–49. Oxford: Clarendon Press, 1988.

———. "Exposition of 'Hercules Furens': Prologue and Beginning of the Commentary." In *Medieval Literary Theory and Criticism, c. 1100–c. 1375: The Commentary Tradition*, ed. A. J. Minnis and A. B. Scott, 345–46. Oxford: Clarendon Press, 1988.

Odo Rigaud. "Is Theology a Science?" In *Medieval Philosophy: From St. Augustine to Nicholas of Cusa*, ed. and trans. J. F. Wippel and A. B. Wolter, 265–72. New York: Free Press, 1969.

Oresme, Nicole. *The "De moneta" of Nicholas Oresme and English Mint Documents*. Trans. C. Johnson. London: Nelson, 1956.

———. *Nicole Oresme and the Kinematics of Circular Motion*. Trans. E. Grant. Publications in Mediaeval Studies 15. Madison: University of Wisconsin Press, 1971.

———. *Nicole Oresme and the Marvels of Nature: A Critical Edition of his Quodlibeta with English Translation and Commentary*. Trans. B. Hansen. Ann Arbor, Mich.: University Microfilms International, 1974.

———. *Nicole Oresme and the Medieval Geometry of Qualities and Motions*. Trans. M. Clagett. Madison: University of Wisconsin Press, 1968.

———. *Nicole Oresme, "De proportionibus proportionum" and "Ad pauca respicientes."* Trans. E. Grant. Madison: University of Wisconsin Press, 1966.

———. *Nicole Oresme on Light, Color, and the Rainbow*. Trans. S. C. McCluskey. Ann Arbor, Mich.: University Microfilms, 1974.

———. *Nicole Oresme's "On Seeing the Stars" (De visione stellarum)*. Trans. D. E. Burton. Leiden: Brill, 2007.

———. "The Questiones super De Celo of Nicole Oresme." Trans. C. Kren. Ph.D. diss., University of Wisconsin, 1966.

Otto of Freising. *The Deeds of Frederick Barbarossa*. Trans. C. C. Mierow. Toronto: University of Toronto Press, 1994.

Paschasius Radbertus. *Charlemagne's Cousins: Contemporary Lives of Adalard and Wala*. Trans. A. Cabaniss. Syracuse, N.Y.: Syracuse University Press, 1967.

Paul of Venice. *Logica Magna*, attributed to Paul of Venice. 8 vols. Trans. N. Kretzmann et al. Classical and Medieval Logical Texts 1–8. Oxford: Oxford University Press, 1978–1991.

———. *Logica Parva*. Trans. A. R. Perreiah. Washington, D.C.: Catholic University of America Press, 1984.

Peckham, John. *A Critical Edition and Translation, with Commentary, of John Peckham's "Tractatus de Sphera."* Trans. B. R. MacLaren. Ann Arbor, Mich.: Xerox University Microfilms, 1978.

———. *John Peckham and the Science of Optics: Perspectiva communis*. Trans. D. C. Lindberg. Publications in Mediaeval Studies 14. Madison: University of Wisconsin Press, 1970.

———. *Questions concerning the Eternity of the World.* Trans. V. G. Potter. New York: Fordham University Press, 1997.

Peter Aureoli (Auriol). "Intuition, Abstraction, and Demonstrative Knowledge." In *The Cambridge Translations of Medieval Philosophical Texts*, ed. and trans. C. Bolyard, 3:179–218. Cambridge: Cambridge University Press, 2002.

Peter Damian. *Book of Gomorrah: An Eleventh-Century Treatise against Clerical Homosexual Practices.* Trans. P. J. Payer. Waterloo: Wilfrid Laurier University Press, 1982.

———. *Letters.* 5 vols. Trans. O. J. Blum and I. M. Resnick. Fathers of the Church: Mediaeval Continuation 1–5. Washington, D.C.: Catholic University of America Press, 1989–2004. [Letter 119 = *De divina omnipotentia*].

———. *On Divine Omnipotence.* In *Medieval Philosophy: From St. Augustine to Nicholas of Cusa*, ed. and trans. J. F. Wippel and A. B. Wolter, 143–52. New York: Free Press, 1969.

———. *Selected Writings on the Spiritual Life.* Trans. P. McNulty. London: Faber and Faber, 1959.

Peter John Olivi. *Commentary on the Gospel of Mark.* Trans. R. J. Karris. St. Bonaventure, N.Y.: Franciscan Institute Publications, 2011.

———. "The Mental Word." In *The Cambridge Translations of Medieval Philosophical Texts*, ed. and trans. R. Pasnau, 3:137–51. Cambridge: Cambridge University Press, 2002.

———. *The Sum of Questions on The Sentences [of Peter Lombard].* Trans. D. Flood and O. Bychkov. *Franciscan Studies* 66 (2008): 67–97. [*Summa* I, q. 1].

———. *Treatise on Contracts (Tractatus de contractibus).* Trans. R. Thorton and M. Cusato. St. Bonaventure, N.Y.: Franciscan Institute Publications, 2016.

Peter Lombard. "Commentary on the Psalter: Prologue." In *Medieval Literary Theory and Criticism, c. 1100–c. 1375: The Commentary Tradition*, ed. A. J. Minnis and A. B. Scott, 110–12. Oxford: Clarendon Press, 1988.

———. "How Creatures Manifest God as One and Triune." In *Medieval Philosophy: From St. Augustine to Nicholas of Cusa*, ed. and trans. J. F. Wippel and A. B. Wolter, 206–9. New York: Free Press, 1969.

———. *The Sentences.* 4 vols. Trans. G. Silano. Toronto: Pontifical Institute of Mediaeval Philosophy, 2007–2010.

Peter of Auvergne. "Commentary and Questions on Book III of Aristotle's 'Politics.'" In *The Cambridge Translations of Medieval Philosophical Texts*, ed. and trans. A. S. McGrade, J. Kilcullen, and M. Kempshall, 2:219–56. Cambridge: Cambridge University Press, 2001.

Peter of Spain. *On Composition and Negation.* Trans. Joke Spruyt. Nijmegen: Ingenium Publishers, 1989.

————. "On Supposition (*Summulae logicales*, tr. 6)." In *Medieval Philosophy: Selected Readings from Augustine to Buridan*, ed. and trans. R. Shapiro, 294–303. New York: Modern Library, 1964.

————. "Predicables" and "Categories." In *The Cambridge Translations of Medieval Philosophical Texts*, ed. and trans. N. Kretzmann and E. Stump, 1:78–101. Cambridge: Cambridge University Press, 1988.

————. *Summaries of Logic*. Trans. B. P. Coperhaven et al. Oxford: Oxford University Press, 2014.

————. *Syncategoreumata*. Trans. Joke Spruyt. Leiden: Brill, 1992.

Peter the Chanter. *The Christian at Prayer: An Illustrated Prayer Manual Attributed to Peter the Chanter*. Trans. R. C. Trexler. Binghamton, N.Y.: Center for Medieval and Early Renaissance Studies, 1987.

Philip the Chancellor. *The Cardinal Virtues: Aquinas, Albert, and Philip the Chancellor*. Trans. R. E. Houser. Mediaeval Sources in Translation 39. Toronto: Pontifical Institute of Mediaeval Studies, 2004.

Philoponus, John. *Against Aristotle: On the Eternity of the World*. Trans. C. Wildberg. Ancient Commentators on Aristotle. Ithaca, N.Y.: Cornell University Press, 1987.

————. *The Astrolabes of the World*. Trans. H. W. Green. London: Holland Press, 1976.

————. *Corollaries on Place and Void*. Trans. D. Furley and C. Wildberg. Ancient Commentators on Aristotle. London: Duckworth, 1991.

————. *John Philoponus and the Controversies over Chalcedon in the Sixth Century: A Study with translation of the Arbiter*. Trans. E. M. Lang. Spicilegium sacrum Lovaniense, Etudes et documents, 47. Leuven: Peeters, 2001.

————. *On Aristotle: On Coming-to-Be and Perishing, 1.1–5*. Trans. C. J. F. Williams. Ancient Commentators on Aristotle. London: Duckworth, 1999.

————. *On Aristotle: On Coming-to-Be and Perishing, 1.6–2.4*. Trans. C. J. F. Williams. Ancient Commentators on Aristotle. London: Duckworth, 1999.

————. *On Aristotle: On the Intellect [De anima 3.4–8]*. Trans. W. Charlton and F. Bossier. Ancient Commentators on Aristotle. London: Duckworth, 1991.

————. *On Aristotle: On the Soul, 3.1–8*. Trans. W. Charlton. Ancient Commentators on Aristotle. London: Duckworth, 2000.

————. *On Aristotle: On the Soul, 3.9–13*. Trans. W. Charlton. Ancient Commentators on Aristotle. Ithaca, N.Y.: Cornell University Press, 2000.

————. *On Aristotle: Physics, 2*. Trans. A. R. Lacey. Ancient Commentators on Aristotle. London: Duckworth, 1993.

————. *On Aristotle: Physics, 3*. Trans. M. J. Edwards. Ancient Commentators on Aristotle. London: Duckworth, 1994.

————. *On Aristotle: Physics, 5–8.* Trans. P. Lettinck and J. O. Urmson. Ancient Commentators on Aristotle. London: Duckworth, 1994.

Photius. *The Homilies of Photius, Patriarch of Constantinople.* Trans. C. Mango. Dumbarton Oaks Studies 3. Cambridge, Mass.: Harvard University Press, 1958.

————. *The Library of Photius.* Trans. J. H. Freese. London: Macmillan, 1920.

————. *The Patriarch and the Prince: The Letter of Patriarch Photios of Constantinople to Khan Boris of Bulgaria.* Trans. D. S. White and J. R. Berrigan Jr. Archbishop Iakovos Library of Ecclesiastical and Historical Sources 6. Brookline, Mass.: Holy Cross Orthodox Press, 1982.

————. *The Patriarch Photios of Constantinople: His Life, Scholarly Contributions, and Correspondence, together with a Translation of Fifty-Two of His Letters.* Trans. D. S. White. Archbishop Iakovos Library of Ecclesiastical and Historical Sources 5. Brookline, Mass.: Holy Cross Orthodox Press, 1981.

Pico della Mirandola, Giovanni. *Commentary on a Poem of Platonic Love.* Trans. D. Carmichael. Lanham, Md.: University Press of America, 1986.

————. *Commentary on a Canzone of Benivieni.* Trans. S. Jayne. New York: Lang, 1984.

————. *On Being and Unity.* Trans. V. M. Hamm. Mediaeval Philosophical Texts in Translation 3. Milwaukee, Wisc.: Marquette University Press, 1943.

————. *On the Dignity of Man.* Trans. P. J. W. Miller. Indianapolis, Ind.: Hackett, 1998.

————. *On the Imagination.* Trans. H. Caplan. Westport, Conn.: Greenwood Press, 1971.

————. *Syncretism in the West: Pico's 900 Theses (1486): The Evolution of Traditional Religious and Philosophical Systems.* Trans. S. A. Farmer. Medieval and Renaissance Texts and Studies 167. Tempe, Ariz.: Medieval and Renaissance Texts and Studies, 1998.

Proclus. *A Commentary on the First Book of Euclid's "Elements."* Trans. G. R. Morrow. Princeton, N.J.: Princeton University Press, 1970.

————. *The Elements of Theology.* Trans. E. R. Dodds. Oxford: Clarendon Press, 1963.

————. *Proclus: On the Existence of Evils.* Trans. J. Opsomer and C. Steel. London: Duckworth, 2003.

————. *Proclus: On Providence.* Trans. C. Steel. London: Duckworth, 2007.

————. *Proclus: Ten Doubts concerning Providence.* Trans. J. Opsomer and C. Steel. London: Duckworth, 2012.

————. *Proclus' Commentary of Plato's "Parmenides."* Trans. G. R. Morrow and J. M. Dillon. Princeton, N.J.: Princeton University Press, 1987.

———. *Proclus Diadochus: Commentary on the First Alcibiades*. Trans. L. G. Westerlink. Amsterdam: North Holland Publishing, 1954.

Prosper of Aquitaine. *The Call of All Nations*. Trans. P. De Letter. Ancient Christian Writers 14. Westminster, Md.: Newman, 1952.

———. *Defense of St. Augustine*. Trans. P. De Letter. Westminster, Md.: Newman, 1963.

———. *Grace and Free Will*. Trans. J. R. O'Donnell. In *Writings: Niceta of Remesiana, Sulpicius Severus, Vincent of Lerins, and Prosper of Aquitaine*. New York: Fathers of the Church, 1949.

Psellus, Michael. *The "Chronographia" of Michael Psellus*. Trans. E. R. A. Sewter. London: Routledge and Kegan Paul, 1953.

Ptolemy. *Ptolemy's "Almagest."* Trans. G. J. Toomer. Duckworth Classical, Medieval, and Renaissance Editions. London: Duckworth, 1984.

———. *Ptolemy's The Criterion of Truth: Essays in Honour of George Kerferd together with a Text and Translation (with Annotations) of Ptolemy's "On the Kriterion and Hegemonikon."* Trans. G. Kerferd. Liverpool: Liverpool University Press, 1989.

———. *Ptolemy's Theory of Visual Perception: An English Translation of the "Optics."* Trans. A. M. Smith. Philadelphia, Pa.: American Philosophical Society, 1996.

Ptolemy of Lucca. *On the Government of Rulers: "De Regimine Principum," with portions attributed to Thomas Aquinas*. Trans. J. M. Blythe. Philadelphia: University of Pennsylvania Press, 1997.

Radulphus Ardens. *The Questions on the Sacraments=Speculum Universale 8.31–92*. Ed. and trans. C. P. Evans. Toronto: Pontifical Institute of Mediaeval Studies, 2015.

Richard Brinkley. *Richard Brinkley's Theory of Sentential Reference: "De significato propositionis" from Part V of His "Summa nova de Logica."* Trans. M. J. Fitzgerald. Leiden: Brill, 1987.

Richard Fitzralph. *Sermon "Defensio curatorum."* In *Dialogus inter militem et clericum*, trans. A. J. Perry. Early English Text Society 167. London: Oxford University Press, 1925.

Richard Kilvington. *The "Sophismata" of Richard Kilvington*. Trans. N. Kretzmann and B. E. Kretzmann. Cambridge: Cambridge University Press, 1990.

Richard of Saint-Victor. "Mystical Comments on the Psalms" and "On Ezechiel's Vision." In *A Scholastic Miscellany: Anselm to Ockham*, ed. and trans. E. R. Fairweather, 319–23. Library of Christian Classics X. New York: Macmillan, 1956.

———. *On the Interpretation of Scripture: Theory: [The Book of Notes and On the Apocalypse of John]*, trans. H. Feiss, 297–370. Turnhout: Brepols, 2012.

————. *On the Interpretation of Scripture: Practice*: [*On the Concordance of the Times of the Kings Co-ruling over Judah and Israel; On Isaiah: Interpreting "He calls to me from Seir"; Explanations of Several Difficulties of Scripture; On Emmanuel; The Book of Notes II.12.5; Sermon 70*], trans. H. Feiss, 147–60, 227–58, 259–75, 357–439, 455–60. Turnhout: Brepols, 2015.

————. *Richard of Saint Victor, On the Trinity*. Trans. A. Ruben. Eugene, Ore.: Cascade Books, 2011.

————. *Richard of Saint-Victor: Selected Writings on Contemplation*. Trans. C. Kirchberger. New York: Harper and Brothers, 1957.

————. *The Twelve Patriarchs, The Mystical Ark: Book Three of The Trinity*. Trans. G. A. Zinn. Classics of Western Spirituality. New York: Paulist Press, 1979.

Robert Holcot. "Can God Know More than He Knows?" In *The Cambridge Translations of Medieval Philosophical Texts*, ed. and trans. R. Pasnau, 3:303–17. Cambridge: Cambridge University Press, 2002.

————. *"Super libros Sapientiae"* [chap. 3, lects. 35 and 52; chap. 12, lect. 145]. In *Forerunners of the Reformation: The Shape of Late Medieval Thought Illustrated by Key Documents*, trans. H. Oberman, 142–50. Philadelphia, Pa.: Holt, Rinehart and Winston, 1981.

Robert Kilwardby. "The Nature of Logic" and "Dialectic and Demonstration." In *The Cambridge Translations of Medieval Philosophical Texts*, ed. and trans. N. Kretzmann and E. Stump, 264–82. Cambridge: Cambridge University Press, 1988.

————. *On Time and Imagination, Parts 1–2*. Trans. P. O. Lewry. Auctores Britannici Medii Aevi 9. Oxford: Oxford University Press, 1987–1993.

Roger Bacon. *Compendium of the Study of Theology*. Trans. T. S. Maloney. Leiden: Brill, 1988.

————. *"De multiplicatione specierum"* and *"De speculis comburentibus."* In *Roger Bacon's Philosophy of Nature: A Critical Edition, with English Translation, Introduction, and Notes of "De multiplicatione specierum" and "De speculis comburentibus,"* ed. and trans. D. C. Lindberg. Oxford: Clarendon Press, 1983.

————. *The Mirror of Alchemy*. Trans. S. J. Linden. New York: Garland Press, 1992.

————. *The "Opus Majus" of Roger Bacon*. Trans. R. B. Burke. Philadelphia: University of Pennsylvania Press, 1923.

————. *Perspectiva*. In *Roger Bacon and the Origins of "Perspectiva" in the Middle Ages: A Critical Edition and English Translation of Bacon's "Perspectiva" with Introduction and Notes*, trans. D. C. Lindberg. Oxford: Oxford University Press, 1996.

————. *Roger Bacon: The Art and Science of Logic*. Trans. T. S. Maloney. Toronto: Pontifical Institute of Mediaeval Philosophy, 2009.

————. *Roger Bacon: On Signs*. Trans. T. S. Maloney. Toronto: Pontifical Institute of Mediaeval Philosophy, 2013.

————. *Roger Bacon's "Geometria speculativa."* In *Vestigia mathematica*, ed. M. Folkerts and J. P. Hogendijk, trans. G. Molland. Amsterdam: Editions Rodolpi, 1993.

————. *Three Treatises of Universals by Roger Bacon*. Trans. T. S. Maloney. Binghamton: State University of New York Press, 1994.

Roland of Cremona. *The Tract on Holy Orders in the "Summa" of Roland of Cremona*. Trans. C. R. Hess. Rome: Officium libri Catholici, 1969.

Ruysbroeck, Jan van, Bl. *"The Chastising of God's Children" and "The Treatise of Perfection of the Sons of God."* Trans. J. Bazire and E. Colledge. Oxford: Basil Blackwell, 1957.

————. *The Complete Ruusbroec: English Translation with the Original Dutch Text*. Trans. T. Mertens et al. Turnhout: Brepols. 2014.

————. *Flowers of a Mystic Garden*. Trans. Anon. Felinfach: Llanerch Publishers, 1994.

————. *The Spiritual Expousals*. Trans. E. Colledge. Westminster, Md.: Christian Classics, 1983.

Saadiah Gaon. *Book of Doctrines and Beliefs*. In *Three Jewish Philosophers*. Trans. A. Altmann. New York: Atheneum, 1976.

————. *The Book of Theodicy (Commentary on the "Book of Job")*. Trans. L. E. Goodman. New Haven, Conn.: Yale University Press, 1988.

Shem Tov ibn Falaquera. *Iggeret ha-Vikkuah (The Epistle of the Debate)*. In *Falaquera's Epistle of the Debate: An Introduction to Jewish Philosophy*. Cambridge, Mass.: Harvard University Press, 1987.

————. "On Plants." In *Nicholas Damascenus, De Plantis: Five Translations*. Trans. H. J. Drossaart Lulofs and E. L. J. Poortman. Leiden: Brill, 1989.

Sibert of Beka. *Ordinaire de l'Ordre de Notre Dame du Mont-Carmel*. Paris: Picard, 1910.

Siger of Brabant. *On the Eternity of the World*. In *On the Eternity of the World: St. Thomas Aquinas, Siger of Brabant, St. Bonaventure*. Trans. C. Vollert. Milwaukee, WI: Marquette University Press, 1984.

————. "On the Intellective Soul." In *Medieval Philosophy: From St. Augustine to Nicholas of Cusa*, ed. and trans. J. F. Wippel and A. B. Wolter, 360–65. New York: Free Press, 1969.

————. "On the Necessity and Contingency of Causes." In *Medieval Philosophy: Selected Readings from Augustine to Buridan*, ed. and trans. H. Shapiro, 414–39. New York: Modern Library, 1965.

Solomon ben Isaac (Rashi). *Rashi 'al ha-Torah: The Torah with Rashi's Commentary*. Trans. Y. I. Z. Herczeg et al. Brooklyn, N.Y.: Mesorah Publications, 1994.

———. Rashi's Commentary on Psalms. Trans. M. I. Gruber. Atlanta, Ga.: Scholars Press, 1998.

Suárez, Francisco. *The Metaphysics of Good and Evil according to Suárez: Metaphysical Disputations X and XI, and Selected Passages from Disputation XXIII and Other Works*. Trans. J. J. E. Gracia and D. Davis. München: Philosophia Verlag, 1989.

———. *On Beings of Reason: Metaphysical Disputation XIV*. Trans. J. P. Doyle. Mediaeval Philosophical Texts in Translation 33. Milwaukee, Wisc.: Marquette University Press, 1995.

———. *On Efficient Causality: Metaphysical Disputations 17, 18, and 19*. Trans. A. J. Freddoso. Yale Library of Medieval Philosophy. New Haven, Conn.: Yale University Press, 1994.

———. *On Formal and Universal Unity*. Trans. J. F. Ross. Mediaeval Philosophical Texts in Translation 15. Milwaukee, Wisc.: Marquette University Press, 1964.

———. *On the Essence of Finite Being as Such, on the Existence of that Essence and Their Distinction*. Trans. N. J. Wells. Mediaeval Philosophical Texts in Translation 24. Milwaukee, Wisc.: Marquette University Press, 1983.

———. *On the Various Kinds of Distinction: Disputatio Metaphysicae, Disputatio VII*. Trans. C. Voller. Mediaeval Philosophical Texts in Translation 4. Milwaukee, Wisc.: Marquette University Press, 1947.

———. *Suarez in English Translation*. Ed. Sydney Penner. (electronic)

———. *Suarez on Individuation: Metaphysical Disputation V: Individual Unity and Its Principle*. Trans. J. J. E. Gracia. Mediaeval Philosophical Texts in Translation 23. Milwaukee, Wisc.: Marquette University Press, 1982.

Suso, Heinrich. *The Exemplar, with Two German Sermons*. Trans. F. Tobin. Classics of Western Spirituality. New York: Paulist Press, 1989.

———. *The Life of Blessed Heinrich Suso by Himself*. Trans. T. F. Knox. London: Methuen, 1913.

———. *Little Book of Eternal Wisdom and Little Book of Truth*. London: Faber and Faber, 1953.

———. *Sermons*. Trans. M. Shrady. Classics of Western Spirituality. New York: Paulist Press, 1985.

———. *Wisdom's Watch upon the Hours*. Trans. E. College. Fathers of the Church, Mediaeval Continuation 4. Washington, D.C.: Catholic University of America Press, 1994.

Tauler, Johannes. *The Following of Christ*. Trans. J. R. Morrell. London: John M. Watkins, n.d.

———. *Sermons*. Trans. Maria Shrady. New York: Paulist Press, 1985.

———. *Spiritual Conferences*. Trans. E. College and Sr. Mary Jane. Cross and Crown Series of Spirituality. St. Louis, Mo.: Herder Book, 1961.

Thomas Aquinas. *Aquinas on Creation: Writings on the "Sentences" of Peter Lombard, Book 2, Distinction 1, Question 1*. Trans. S. E. Baldner and W. E. Carroll. Toronto: Pontifical Institute of Mediaeval Studies, 1997.

———. *Catena aurea: Commentary on the Four Gospels*. 4 vols. Trans. M. Pattison, J. D. Dalgairns, and T. T. Ryder. Oxford: J. Parker, 1874.

———. *Collationes in decem praecepta: The Commandments of God*. Trans. L. Shapcote. London: Blackfriars, 1937.

———. *Collationes in orationem dominicam, in Symbolum Apostolorum, in salutationem angelicam: Three Great Prayers*. Trans L. Shapcote. Manchester, N.H.: Sophia Institute Press, 1990.

———. *Compendium theologiae: Compendium of Theology*. Trans. C. Vollert. St. Louis, Mo.: Herder, 1952.

———. *De anima: Aristotle's "De anima" with the Commentary of St. Thomas Aquinas*. Trans. K. Foster and S. Humphries. New Haven, Conn.: Yale University Press, 1951; repr. Notre Dame, Ind.: Dumb Ox Books, 1994.

———. *De anima: Saint Thomas Aquinas, Questions on the Soul*. Trans. J. H. Robb. Milwaukee, Wisc.: Marquette University Press, 1984.

———. *De articulis fidei*. Partial trans. J. B. Collins. Part 2, *"On the Sacraments," Catechetical Instruction on St. Thomas*. New York: Wagner, 1953.

———. *De caritate: On Charity*. Trans L. H. Kenzierski. Milwaukee, Wisc.: Marquette University Press, 1960.

———. *"De emptione et venditione ad tempus*: 'On Buying and Selling on Credit.'" *Irish Ecclesiastic Record* 31 (1928): 159–65.

———. *De ente et essentia: Aquinas on Being and Essence*. Trans. A. A. Maurer. Toronto: Pontifical Institute of Mediaeval Studies, 1968.

———. *De malo: Saint Thomas Aquinas, Disputed Questions on Evil*. Trans. J. Osterle and J. Osterle. Notre Dame, Ind.: University of Notre Dame Press, 1983.

———. *"De mixtione elementorum*: 'On the Combining of the Elements.'" Trans. V. R. Larking. *Isis* 51 (1960): 67–72.

———. *"De motu cordis*: 'On the Movement of the Heart.'" Trans. V. R. Larking. *Journal of the History of Medicine* 15 (1960): 22–30.

———. *De operationibus occultis naturae: The Letter of St. Thomas Aquinas "De occultis operibus naturae."* Trans. J. B. McAllister. Washington, D.C.: Catholic University of America Press, 1939.

———. *De potentia: Saint Thomas Aquinas, On the Power of God*. 3 vols. Trans. L. Shapcote. London: Blackfriars, 1932–1934.

———. *De principiis naturae*. In *The Pocket Aquinas*, trans. V. J. Bourke. New York: Pocket Books, 1973.

————. *De quolibet I–XII: Saint Thomas Aquinas, Quodlibetal Questions 1 and 2*. Trans. S. Edwards. Mediaeval Sources in Translation 27. Toronto: Pontifical Institute of Mediaeval Studies, 1983.

————. *De rationibus fidei ad Cantorem Antiochenum*. Partial trans. H. Nash, "Why Did God the Son Become Man?" In chapter 5 of *Life of the Spirit*. London: Blackfriars, 1952.

————. *De regno: On Kingship, to the King of Cyprus*. Trans. G. B. Phelan and J. T. Eschmann. Toronto: Pontifical Institute of Mediaeval Studies, 1949.

————. *De secreto*. In *Aquinas's Search for Wisdom*, trans. V. J Bourke, 143–46. Milwaukee, Wisc.: Bruce Publishing, 1965.

————. *De spiritualibus creaturis: Saint Thomas Aquinas, On Spiritual Creatures*. Trans. M. C. Fitzpatrick and J. J. Wellmuth. Milwaukee, Wisc.: Marquette University Press, 1949.

————. *De substantiis: Treatise on Separate Substances*. Trans. F. J. Lescoe. West Hartford, Conn.: St. Joseph's College, 1959.

————. *De veritate*: *Saint Thomas, On Truth*. 3 vols. Trans. R. W. Mulligan, J. V. McGlynn, and R. W. Schmidt. Chicago: Henry Regnery, 1952–1954.

————. *De virtutibus in communi* and *De virtutibus cardinalibus*: *Disputed Questions on Virtue*. Trans. R. McInerny. South Bend, Ind.: St. Augustine Press, 1999.

————. *Epistola ad Bernardum*. Partial trans. V. J. Bourke. In *Aquinas's Search for Wisdom*, 114–15. Milwaukee, Wisc.: Bruce Publishing, 1965.

————. "*Epistola ad ducissam Brabantiae*: 'On the Government of Jews in Aquinas.'" In *Aquinas: Selected Political Writings*, trans. J. G. Dawson, 84–95. Oxford: B. Blackwell, 1948.

————. "Inaugural Sermon on Scripture: 'Rigans montes de superioribus.'" In *Albert and Thomas: Selected Writings*, ed. and trans. S. Tugwell. Mahwah, N.Y.: Paulist Press, 1988.

————. *Saint Thomas Aquinas: A Literal Exposition on Job: A Scriptural Commentary concerning Providence*. Trans. A. Damico. Atlanta, Ga.: Scholars Press.

————. *Saint Thomas Aquinas: Commentary on Saint Paul's Epistle to the Ephesians*. Trans. M. L. Lamb. Albany, N.Y.: Magi Books, 1966.

————. *Saint Thomas Aquinas: Commentary on Saint Paul's Epistle to the Galatians*. Trans. F. R. Larcher. Albany, N.Y.: Magi Books, 1966.

————. *Saint Thomas Aquinas: Commentary on Saint Paul's Letter to the Philippians*. Trans. F. R. Larcher. Albany, N.Y.: Magi Books, 1969.

————. *Saint Thomas Aquinas: Commentary on Saint Paul's Letter to the Thessalonians*. Trans. F. R. Archer and M. Duffy. Albany, N.Y.: Magi Books, 1969.

————. *Saint Thomas Aquinas: Commentary on the Gospel of Saint John.* Part 1. Trans. J. A. Weisheipl and F. R. Larcher. Albany, N.Y.: Magi Books, 1980.

————. *St. Thomas Aquinas on Politics and Ethics.* Trans. P. E. Sigmund. New York: Norton, 1988.

————. *Summa theologiae.* 61 vols. Trans. T. Gilbey, T. C. O'Brien, et al. London: Eyre and Spottiswoode, 1964–1986.

————. *Super Analytica Posteriora: Saint Thomas Aquinas, Exposition of the Posterior Analytics of Aristotle.* Trans. F. R. Archer. Albany, N.Y.: Magi Books, 1970.

————. *Super Boethium De hebdomadibus: The Exposition of the "On the Hebdomads" of Boethius.* Trans. J. L. Schultz and E. A. Synan. Washington, D.C.: Catholic University of America Press, 2001.

————. *Super Boethium De Trinitate: Saint Thomas Aquinas, Faith, Reason, and Theology: Questions I–IV of His Commentary on the "De Trinitate" of Boethius* and *Saint Thomas Aquinas, The Division and Methods of the Sciences: Questions V and VI of His Commentary on the "De Trinitate" of Boethius.* Trans. A. A. Maurer. Mediaeval Sources in Translation 3 and 32. Toronto: Pontifical Institute of Mediaeval Studies, 1986–1987.

————. *Super De Caelo et mundo: Exposition of Aristotle's Treatise on the Heavens.* Trans. P. Conway and F. R. Larcher. Columbus, Ohio: College of St. Mary of the Springs, photocopy, 1963–1964.

————. *Super De generatione et corruptione: On Generation and Corruption.* Trans. P. Conway and W. H. Kane. Columbus, Ohio: College of St. Mary of the Springs, photocopy, n.d.

————. *Super libros Ethicorum: Saint Thomas Aquinas, Commentary on the Nicomachean Ethics.* 2 vols. Trans C. I. Litzinger. Chicago: Henry Regnery, 1964; repr. Notre Dame, Ind.: Dumb Ox Books, 1993.

————. *Super Librum de causis: St. Thomas Aquinas, Commentary on the "Book of Causes."* Trans. V. A. Guagliaro, C. R. Hess, and R. C. Taylor. Washington, D.C.: Catholic University of America Press, 1996.

————. *Super Metaphysicam: Saint Thomas Aquinas, Commentary on the Metaphysics of Aristotle.* 2 vols. Trans. J. P. Rowan. Chicago: Henry Regnery, 1964; repr. Notre Dame, Ind.: Dumb Ox Books, 1995.

————. *Super Meteora: On Meteorology.* Trans. P. Conway and F. R. Larcher. Columbus, Ohio: College of St. Mary of the Springs, photocopy, 1964.

————. *Super Perihermenias: Aristotle on Interpretation.* Commentary by St. Thomas and Cajetan. Trans. J. T. Oesterle. Milwaukee, Wisc.: Marquette University Press, 1963.

————. *Super Physicam: Thomas de Aquino: Commentary on Aristotle's "Physics."* Trans. R. J. Blackwell et al. New Haven, Conn.: Yale University Press, 1963.

Thomas Bradwardine. *Thomas Bradwardine: Geometria speculativa.* Trans. G. Molland. Stuttgart: Steiner Verlag, 1989.

———. *Tractatus de proportionibus.* In *Thomas of Bradwardine: His Tractatus de proportionibus*, ed. and trans H. L. Crosby. University of Wisconsin Publications in Medieval Science 2. Madison: University of Wisconsin Press, 1955.

Thomas Gallus. "Extraction of 'The Celestial Hierarchy': Chapters i, ii, xv." In *Medieval Literary Theory and Criticism, c. 1100–c. 1375: The Commentary Tradition*, ed. A. J. Minnis and A. B. Scott, 171–92. Oxford: Clarendon Press, 1988.

———. *Mystical Theology: The Glosses by Thomas Gallus and the Commentary of Robert Grosseteste on "De mystica theologia."* Trans. J. McEvoy. Dallas Medieval Texts and Translations 3. Paris: Peeters, 2003.

Thomas of Erfurt. *Grammatica Speculativa of Thomas of Erfurt.* Trans. G. L. Bursill-Hall. London: Longman, 1972.

Walafrid Strabo. *Hortulus.* Trans. R. Payne. Pittsburg, Pa.: Hunt Botanical Library, 1966.

William of Alnwick. "Intelligible Being." In *The Cambridge Translations of Medieval Philosophical Texts*, ed. and trans. R. Pasnau, 3:153–77. Cambridge: Cambridge University Press, 2002.

William of Auvergne. *The Immortality of the Soul.* Trans. R. J. Teske. Medieval Philosophical Texts in Translation 30. Milwaukee, Wisc.: Marquette University Press, 1991.

———. *On Morals: De moribus.* Trans. R. J. Teske. Mediaeval Sources in Translation 55. Toronto: Pontifical Institute of Mediaeval Studies, 2013.

———. *On the Virtues.* Trans. R. J. Teske. Medieval Philosophical Texts in Translation 45. Milwaukee, Wisc.: Marquette University Press, 2009.

———. *The Providence of God regarding the Universe: De universo.* Trans. R. J. Teske. Medieval Philosophical Texts in Translation 43. Milwaukee, Wisc.: Marquette University Press, 2007.

———. *Selected Spiritual Writings*: *Cur Deus Homo, De gratia and De fide.* Trans. R. J. Teske. Mediaeval Sources in Translation 50. Toronto: Pontifical Institute of Mediaeval Studies, 2011.

———. *The Soul.* Trans. R. J. Teske. Medieval Philosophical Texts in Translations 37. Milwaukee, Wisc.: Marquette University Press, 2000.

———. *The Trinity, or the First Principle.* Trans. R. J. Teske and F. C. Wade. Medieval Philosophical Texts in Translations 28. Milwaukee, Wisc.: Marquette University Press, 1989.

William of Conches. "Commentary on Boethius, 'The Consolation of Philosophy': Second Redaction: Exposition of Book IV, metre iii." In *Medieval Literary Theory and Criticism, c. 100–c. 1375: The Commentary Tradition*, ed. A. J. Minnis and A. B. Scott, 126–34. Oxford: Clarendon Press, 1988.

―――. *A Dialogue on Natural Philosophy* [*Dragmaticon Philosophiae*]. Trans. I. Ronca and M. Curr. Notre Dame Texts in Medieval Culture 2. Notre Dame, Ind.: University of Notre Dame Press, 1997.

William of Ockham. "Apparent Beings." In *The Cambridge Translations of Medieval Philosophical Texts*, ed. and trans. R. Pasnau, 220–44. Cambridge: Cambridge University Press, 2002.

―――. *A Compendium of Ockham's Teachings: A Translation of the "Tractatus de principiis theologiae."* Trans. J. Davies. Franciscan Institute Publications, Text Series, 20. St. Bonaventure, N.Y.: Franciscan Institute Publications, 1998.

―――. *De sacramento altaris* [*On the Body of Christ*]. Trans. T. B. Birch. Burlington, Iowa: Lutheran Literary Board, 1930.

―――. *A Letter to the Friars Minor, and Other Writings.* Trans. J. Kilcullen. Cambridge Texts in the History of Political Thought. Cambridge: Cambridge University Press, 1995.

―――. "Modal Consequences." In *The Cambridge Translations of Medieval Philosophical Texts*, ed. and trans. N. Kretzmann and E. Stump, 167–82. Cambridge: Cambridge University Press, 1988.

―――. *Ockham on Aristotle's "Physics": A Translation of Ockham's "Brevis Summa libri Physicorum."* Trans. J. Davies. Franciscan Institute Publications, Text Series, 17. St. Bonaventure, N.Y.: Franciscan Institute Publications, 1989.

―――. *Ockham: On the Virtues.* Trans. R. Wood. West Lafayette, Ind.: Purdue University Press, 1997.

―――. *Ockham's Theory of Propositions: Part II of the "Summa logicae."* Trans. A. J. Freddoso. Notre Dame, Ind.: University of Notre Dame Press, 1980.

―――. *Ockham's Theory of Terms: Part I of the "Summa logicae."* Trans. M. J. Loux. Notre Dame, Ind.: University of Notre Dame Press, 1974.

―――. "On the Eternity of the World." In *Basic Issues in Medieval Philosophy*, ed. and trans. R. N. Bosley and M. Tweedale. Peterborough (Canada): Broadview, 1997.

―――. *Philosophical Writings: A Selection.* Trans. Ph. Boehner. Rev. S. F. Brown. Indianapolis, Ind.: Hackett, 1990.

―――. *Predestination, God's Foreknowledge, and Future Contingents.* Trans. M. McCord Adams and N. Kretzmann. New York: Appleton-Century-Crofts, 1969.

―――. *Quodlibetal Questions.* 2 vols. Trans. A. J. Freddoso. Yale Library of Medieval Philosophy. New Haven, Conn.: Yale University Press, 1991.

―――. *A Short Discourse on the Tyrannical Government over Things Divine and Human, but especially over the Empire and Those Subject to the Empire.* Trans. J. Kilcullen. Cambridge Texts in the History of Political Thought. Cambridge: Cambridge University Press, 1992.

————. "Using and Enjoying" and "Is an Errant Individual Bound to Recant at the Rebuke of a Superior." In *The Cambridge Translations of Medieval Philosophical Texts*, ed. and trans. A. S. McGrade, J. Kilcullen, and M. Kempshall, 2:351–48, 485–97. Cambridge: Cambridge University Press, 2001.

————. "Whether the Ruler Can Receive the Goods of the Church for his own Needs, namely, in the case of War, even against the Wishes of the Pope." In *Political Thought in Early Fourteenth-Century England*, ed. and trans. C. J. Nederman. Medieval and Renaissance Texts and Studies 250. Tempe: Arizona Center for Medieval and Renaissance Studies, 2002.

William of Saint-Thierry. *The Works of William of Saint-Thierry.* 4 vols. Trans. Sister Penelope et al. Cistercian Fathers Series. Spencer, Mass.: Cistercian Publications, 1970.

William of Sherwood. *Introduction to Logic.* In *William of Sherwood's Introduction to Logic*, trans. N. Kretzmann. Minneapolis: University of Minnesota Press, 1966.

————. *William of Sherwood's Treatise on Syncategorematic Words.* Trans. N. Kretzmann. Minneapolis: University of Minnesota Press, 1968.

Wycliffe, John. *The English Works of Wyclif.* Ed. F. D. Matthew. Early English Text Society 74. London: Trübner, 1880.

————. *English Wycliffite Sermons.* 5 vols. Ed. A Hudson and P. O. E. Gradon. Oxford: Clarendon Press, 1983–1996.

————. "On Civil Lordship (selections)." In *The Cambridge Translations of Medieval Philosophical Texts*, ed. and trans. A. S. McGrade, J. Kilcullen, and M. Kempshall, 591–654. Cambridge: Cambridge University Press, 2001.

————. *On Simony.* Trans. T. A. McVeigh. New York: Fordham University Press, 1992.

————. "On the Duty of the King (cc. 3 and 5)." Trans. C. J. Nederman. In *Medieval Political Theory—A Reader*, ed. C. J. Nederman and K. L. Forhan, 222–29. London: Routledge, 1993.

————. *On the Truth of Holy Scripture.* Trans. I. C. Levy. Kalamazoo, Mich.: Medieval Institute Publications, 2001.

————. *On Universals.* Trans. P. V. Spade. Oxford: Clarendon Press, 1985.

## SECONDARY SOURCES FOR THE STUDY OF MEDIEVAL AUTHORS

[Secondary sources for the study of medieval philosophers and theologians can be found listed in bibliographies, the encyclopedias and biographical dictionaries, and the histories of medieval philosophy and theology just presented. A first approach to a particular author can also be found in the bibliography below. The order pursued in this bibliography is the order according to the Dictionary proper. It attempts to provide works that will lead the reader into the study of each author treated there and thus to provide a more direct bibliographical resource.]

Clanchy, M. *Abelard: A Medieval Life*. Oxford: Blackwell, 1999. (Abelard, Peter)

Sweeney, E. *Logic, Theology, and Poetry in Boethius, Abelard, and Alan of Lille*. New York: Palgrave Macmillan, 2006. (Abelard, Peter)

Marenbon, J. *The Philosophy of Peter Abelard*. Cambridge: Cambridge University Press, 1997. (Abelard, Peter)

Bertolacci, A. "A Community of Translators: The Latin Medieval Versions of Avicenna's 'Book of the Cure.'" In *Communities of Learning: Networks and the Shaping of Intellectual Identity in Europe, 1100–1500*, ed. C. J. Mews and J. N. Crossley, 37–54. Turnhout: Brepols, 2011. (Abraham ibn Daud)

Fidora, A. "Religious Diversity and the Philosophical Translations of 12th-Century Toledo." In *Communities of Learning: Networks and the Shaping of Intellectual Identity in Europe, 1100–1500*, ed. C. J. Mews and J. N. Crossley. Turnhout: Brepols, 2011. (Abraham ibn Daud)

Twersky, I., and J. M. Harris, eds. *Rabbi Abraham ibn Ezra: Studies in the Writings of a Twelfth-Century Jewish Polymath*. Cambridge, Mass.: Harvard University Press, 1993. (Abraham ibn Ezra)

Lemay, R. *Abu Ma'shar and Latin Aristotelianism in the Twelfth Century: The Recovery of Aristotle's Natural Philosophy through Arabic Astrology*. Beirut: American University of Beirut, 1962. (Abu Ma'shar *or* Albumasar)

Lawrence, C. H. "The Letters of Adam Marsh and the Franciscan School at Oxford." *Journal of Ecclesiastical History* 42 (1991): 218–38. (Adam Marsh)

McEvoy, J. *Robert Grosseteste*. Oxford: Oxford University Press, 2000. (Adam Marsh and Adam of Buckfield)

Sharp, D. E. *Franciscan Philosophy at Oxford in the Thirteenth Century*. New York: Russell and Russell, 1964. (Adam Marsh and Adam of Buckfield)

Courtenay, W. *Adam Wodeham*. Leiden: Brill, 1978. (Adam Wodeham)

Gal, G. "Adam Wodeham's Question on the *Complexum significabile*." *Franciscan Studies* 37 (1977): 66–102. (Adam Wodeham)

Perler, D. "Seeing and Judging: Ockham and Wodeham on Sensory Cognition." In *Theories of Perception in Medieval and Early Modern Philosophy*, eds. S. Knuuttila and P. Kärkkäinen, 151–69. Dordrecht: Springer, 2008. (Adam Wodeham)

Zupko, J. "How It Played in the Rue de Fouarre: The Reception of Adam Wodeham's Theory of the Complexum Significabile in the Arts Faculty at Paris in the Mid-Fourteenth Century." *Franciscan Studies* 54 (1994–1997): 211–25. (Adam Wodeham)

Burnett, C., ed. *Adelard of Bath: An English Scientist and Arabist of the Early Twelfth Century*. London: Warburg Institute, 1987. (Adelard of Bath)

Cochrane, L. *Adelard of Bath: The First English Scientist*. London: British Museum Press, 1994. (Adelard of Bath)

Murdoch, J. E. "The Medieval Euclid: Salient Aspects of the Translations of the 'Elements' by Adelard of Bath and Campanus of Novara." *XIIe Congres internationale d'histoire des sciences. Colloques* in *Revue de Synthese* 49–52 (1968): 67–94. (Adelard of Bath)

Daniel, W. *The Life of Ailred of Rievaulx*. Trans. F. M. Powicke. Oxford: Clarendon Press, 1978. (Aelred *or* Ethelred of Rievaulx)

Hallier, A. *The Monastic Theology of Aelred of Rievaulx*. Trans. C. Heaney. Spencer, Mass.: Cistercian Publications, 1969. (Aelred *or* Ethelred of Rievaulx)

McGuire, B. P. *Brother and Lover: Aelred of Rievaulx*. New York: Crossroads, 1994. (Aelred *or* Ethelred of Rievaulx)

Evans, G. R. *Alan of Lille: The Frontiers of Theology in the Later Twelfth Century*. Cambridge: Cambridge University Press, 1983. (Alan of Lille)

Walsh, P. G. "Alan of Lille as a Renaissance Figure." In *Renaissance and Renewal in Christian History*, ed. D. Baker, 117–35. Oxford: Oxford University Press, 1977. (Alan of Lille)

Biard, J. *Paris-Vienne au XIVe siècle: Itineraires d'Albert de Saxe*. Paris: Vrin, 1991. (Albert of Saxony)

Fitzgerald, M. "Unconfusing Merely Confused Supposition in Albert of Saxony." *Vivarium* 50 (2012): 161–89. (Albert of Saxony)

Blankenhorn, B. *The Mystery of Union with God in Albert the Great and Thomas Aquinas*. Washington, D.C.: Catholic University of America Press, 2015. (Albert the Great)

Cunningham, S. B. *Reclaiming Moral Agency: The Moral Philosophy of Albert the Great*. Washington, D.C.: Catholic University of America, 2008. (Albert the Great)

de Libera, A. *Albert le Grand et la philosophie*. Paris: J. Vrin, 1990. (Albert the Great)

Honnefelder, L., H. Möhle, and S. Bullido del Barrio, eds. *Via Alberti. Texte—Quellen—Interpretationen*. Münster: Aschendorff, 2009. (Albert the Great)

Kovach, F. J., and R. W. Shahan, eds. *Albert the Great: Commemorative Essays*. Norman: University of Oklahoma Press, 1980. (Albert the Great)

Weisheipl, J. A. ed. *Albertus Magnus and the Sciences: Commemorative Essays 1980.* Toronto: Pontifical Institute of Mediaeval Studies, 1980. (Albert the Great)

McGinn, B. Introduction to *Three Treatises on Man: A Cistercian Anthropology.* Cistercian Fathers Series 24. Kalamazoo, Mich.: Cisterican Publications, 1977. (Alcher of Clairvaux)

Wallach, L. *Alcuin and Charlemagne. Studies in Carolingian History and Literature.* Ithaca, N.Y.: Cornell University Press, 1959. (Alcuin)

Hunt, R. W. *The Schools and the Cloister: The Life and Writings of Alexander Nequam (1157–1217).* Rev. M. T. Gibson. Oxford: Oxford University Press, 1984. (Alexander Nequam)

Doucet, V. "A New Source of the *Summa fratris Alexandri.*" *Franciscan Studies* 6 (1946): 403–417. (Alexander of Hales)

Principe, W. *Alexander of Hales' Theology of the Hypostatic Union.* Toronto: Pontifical Institute of Mediaeval Studies, 1967. (Alexander of Hales)

Sabra, A. I., ed. *The Optics of Ibn al-Haytham, Books I–III, on Direct Vision.* 2 vols. London: Warburg Institute, 1989. (Alhacen *or* Hasan, al-)

Trapp, D. "Augustinian Theology of the 14th Century." *Augustiniana* 6 (1956): 213–23. (Alphonsus Vargas of Toledo)

Druart, T.-A. "Al-Razi's Conception of the Soul: Psychological Background to His Ethics." *Medieval Philosophy and Theology* 5 (1996): 245–63. (Al-Razi)

———. "The Ethics of al-Razi (865–925)." *Medieval Philosophy and Theology* 6 (1997): 47–71. (Al-Razi)

dal Pra, Mario. *Amalrico di Bene.* Milano: Fratelli Bocca Editori, 1951. (Amalric of Bène)

Berndt, R. *André de Saint-Victor: Exégète et Théologien.* Turnhout: Brepols, 1991. (Andrew of Saint-Victor)

Zier, M. "Andrew of Saint-Victor." In *Selected Christian Hebraists,* ed. W. McKane, 42–75. Cambridge: Cambridge University Press, 1989. (Andrew of Saint-Victor)

Davies, B., and B. Leftow. *The Cambridge Companion to Anselm.* Cambridge: Cambridge University Press, 2004. (Anselm of Canterbury)

Gasper, G. E. M., and I. Logan. *Saint Anselm of Canterbury and His Legacy.* Toronto: Pontifican Institute of Medieval Studies, 2012. (Anselm of Canterbury)

Luscombe, D. E., and G. R. Evans, eds. *Anselm: Aosta, Bec and Canterbury.* Sheffield: Sheffield Academic Press, 1996. (Anselm of Canterbury)

Southern, R. W. *Saint Anselm: A Portrait in a Landscape.* New York: Cambridge University Press, 1990. (Anselm of Canterbury)

Sweeney, E. *Anselm of Canterbury and the Desire for the Word.* Washington, D.C.: Catholic University of America Press, 2012 (Anselm of Canterbury)

Dove, M. Introduction to *Glossa ordinaria, Pars 22, In Canticum Canticorum.* Corpus Christianorum, Continuatio Mediaevalis, 170. Turnhout: Brepols, 1997. (Anselm of Laon)

Kassim, H. *Aristotle and Aristotelianism in Medieval Muslim, Jewish, and Christian Philosophy.* Lanham, Md.: Austin and Winfield Publishers, 2000. (Aristotle and Aristotelianism)

Mahoney, E. P. "Aristotle as 'The Worst Natural Philosopher' and 'The Worst Metaphysician': His Reputation among Some Franciscan Philosophers (Bonaventure, Francis of Meyronnes, Antonius Andreas, and Joannes Canonicus) and Later Reactions." In *Die Philosophie im 14. und 15. Jahrhundert, in memoriam Konstanty Michalski (1879–1947)*, ed. O. Pluta. Amsterdam: Verlag B. R. Grüner, 1988. (Aristotle and Aristotelianism)

Van Steenberghen, F. *Aristotle in the West: The Origins of Latin Aristotelianism.* Trans. L. Johnston. Louvain: Nauwelaerts, 1955. (Aristotle and Aristotelianism)

McCarthy, R. J. Appendices in *The Theology of al-Ash'ari.* Beirut: Imprimerie Catholique, 1953. (Ashari, Al- and Asharites)

Wicks, M. J. *"Papa est nomen jurisdictionis*: Augustinus Triumphus and the Papal Vicariate of Christ." *Journal of Theological Studies* 8 (1957): 71–88. (Augustine of Ancona)

Ayers, L. *Augustine and the Trinity.* Cambridge: Cambridge University Press, 2010. (Augustine, St. and Augustinianism)

Fitzgerald, A. D. *Augustine through the Ages: An Encyclopedia.* Grand Rapids, Mich.: Eerdmans, 1999–. (Augustine, St. and Augustinianism)

Gilson, E. *The Christian Philosophy of St. Augustine.* New York: Random House, 1960. (Augustine, St. and Augustinianism)

Hollingworth, M. *Saint Augustine of Hippo: An Intellectual Biography.* London: Bloomsbury, 2009. (Augustine, St. and Augustinianism)

Teske, R. J. *To Know God and the Soul: Essays on the Thought of Saint Augustine.* Washington, D.C.: The Catholic University of America, 2008. (Augustine, St. and Augustinianism)

Abbès, M. "Le Statut de la raison pratique chez Avempace." *Arabic Sciences and Philosophy* 21 (2011): 85–110. (Avempace *or* Ibn Bajjah)

Forcada, M. "Ibn Bâjja on Medecine and Medical Experience." *Arabic Sciences and Philosophy* 21 (2011): 111–48. (Avempace *or* Ibn Bajjah)

Marcinkowski, C. "A Biographical Note on Ibn Bajjah (Avempace) and an English Translation of His Annotations to al-Farabi's *Isagoge.*" *Iqbal* 43 (2002): 83–99. (Avempace *or* Ibn Bajjah)

Adamson, P., ed. *In the Age of Averroes: Arabic Philosophy in the Sixth/Twelfth Century.* London: Warburg Institute/Nino Aragno, 2011. (Averroes *or* Ibn Rushd and Averroism)

Arnaldez, R. *Averroes: A Rationalist in Islam Arabic Sciences and Philosophy.* Notre Dame, Ind.: Notre Dame University Press, 2000. (Averroes *or* Ibn Rushd and Averroism)

Butterworth, C. "Averroes, Precursor of the Enlightenment." *Alif* 16 (1996): 6–18. (Averroes *or* Ibn Rushd and Averroism)

Davidson, H. A. *Alfarabi, Avicenna, and Averroes on Intellect.* Oxford: Oxford University Press, 1992. (Averroes *or* Ibn Rushd and Averroism)

Hasnawi, A., ed. *La lumière de l'intellect: La pensée scientifique et philosophique d'Averroès dans son temps.* Leuven: Peters, 2011. (Averroes *or* Ibn Rushd and Averroism)

Leaman, O. *Averroes and His Philosophy.* Oxford: Oxford University Press, 1988. (Averroes *or* Ibn Rushd and Averroism)

Urvoy, D. "Ibn Rush." In *History of Islamic Philosophy*, ed. S. H. Nasr and O. Leaman, 1:330–45. London: Routledge, 1996. (Averroes *or* Ibn Rushd and Averroism)

Frank, R. *Creation and the Cosmic System: Al-Ghazali and Avicenna.* Heidelberg: Carl Winter, 1992. (Avicenna *or* Ibn Sina)

Goodman, L. *Avicenna.* London: Routledge, 1992. (Avicenna *or* Ibn Sina)

Goris, H. *Free Creatures of an Eternal God.* Leuven: Peeters, 1996. (Avicenna *or* Ibn Sina)

Gutas, D. *Avicenna and the Aristotelian Tradition: Introduction to Reading Avicenna's Philosophical Works.* Leiden: Brill, 1988. (Avicenna *or* Ibn Sina)

Inati, S. "Ibn Sina." In *History of Islamic Philosophy*, ed. S. H. Nasr and O. Leaman, 1:231–51. London: Routledge, 1996. (Avicenna *or* Ibn Sina)

Koutzarova, T. I. *Das Transzendentale bei Ibn Sina (Avicenna). Zur Metaphysik als Wissenschaften erster Begriffs-und Urteilsprinzipien.* Leiden: Brill, 2009. (Avicenna *or* Ibn Sina)

Langermann, Y. T., ed. *Avicenna and His Legacy: A Golden Age of Science and Philosophy.* Turnhout: Brepols, 2009. (Avicenna *or* Ibn Sina)

Lizzini, O. *Fluxus (fayd): Indagine sui fondamenti della metafisica e della fisica di Avicenna.* Bari: Pagina, 2011. (Avicenna *or* Ibn Sina)

McGinnis, J. *Avicenna.* Oxford: Oxford University Press, 2010. (Avicenna *or* Ibn Sina)

Diana, L. *A Sufi-Jewish Dialogue. Philosophy and Mysticism in Bahya Ibn Paquda's "Duties of the Heart."* Philadelphia: University of Pennsylvania Press, 2007. (Bahya ibn Paquda)

Blair, P. H. *The World of Bede.* London: Secker and Warburg, 1970. (Bede, the Venerable)

Keyes, D. J. *Exploring the Belief in the Real Presence*, 91–93. Bloomington, Ind.: Universe Books, 2005. (Berengarius of Tours)

Radding, C. M., and F. Newton. *Theology, Rhetoric, and Politics in the Eucharistic Controversy, 1078–1079*. New York: Columbia University Press, 2003. (Berengarius of Tours)

Côté, A. "Bernard of Auvergne on James of Viterbo's Doctrine of Possibles." *Augustiniana* 66 (2016): 151–84. (Bernard of Auvergne)

Maurer, A. *Being and Knowing: Studies in Thomas Aquinas and Later Mediaeval Philosophers*, 78–80. Toronto: Pontifical Institute of Mediaeval Studies, 1990. (Bernard of Auvergne)

Dutton, P. E. Introduction to *Bernard of Chartres, "Glosae super Platonem,"* 1–135. Toronto: Pontifical Institute of Mediaeval Studies, 1991. (Bernard of Chartres)

Casey, M. *A Thirst for God: Spiritual Desire in Bernard of Clairvaux's Sermons on the Song of Songs*. Kalamazoo, Mich.: Cistercian Publications, 1988. (Bernard of Clairvaux)

Evans, G. R. *The Mind of St. Bernard of Clairvaux*. Oxford: Clarendon Press, 1982. (Bernard of Clairvaux)

McGuire, B. P. *The Difficult Saint: Bernard of Clairvaux and his Tradition*. Kalamazoo, Mich.: Cistercian Publications, 1991. (Bernard of Clairvaux)

Sturlese, L. "Introduzione." In *Bertoldo di Moosburg "Expositio super Elementationem Theologicam Procli,"* 184–211: *"De animabus,"* 15–83. Rome: Edizioni di Storia e Letteratura, 1974. (Berthold of Moosburg)

Boehm, T., Jurgasch, T., and Kirchner. A., eds. *Boethius as a Paradigm of Late Ancient Thought*. Berlin: De Gruyter, 2014. (Boethius)

Ebbensen, S. "Boethius as an Aristotelian Commentator." In *Aristotle Transformed: The Ancient Commentators and Their Influence*, ed. R. Sorabji, 373–91. Ithaca, N.Y.: Cornell University Press, 1990. (Boethius)

Gibson, M., ed. *Boethius: His Life, Thought, and Influence*. Oxford: Blackwell, 1981. (Boethius)

Magee, J. *Boethius on Signification and Mind*. Leiden: Brill, 1989. (Boethius)

Marenbon, J. *Boethius*. New York: Oxford University Press, 2002. (Boethius)

Sweeney, E. *Logic, Theology, and Poetry in Boethius, Abelard, and Alan of Lille: Words in the Absence of Things*. New York: Palgrave Macmillan, 2006. (Boethius)

Wippel, J. Introduction to *Boethius of Dacia: On the Supreme Good, On the Eternity of the World, On Dreams*, 1–23. Toronto: Pontifical Institute of Mediaeval Studies, 1987. (Boethius of Dacia)

Bougerol, J. G. *Introduction to the Works of Bonaventure*. Trans. J. de Vinck. Paterson, N.J.: Saint Anthony's Guild Press, 1964. (Bonaventure, St.)

Gilson, E. *The Christian Philosophy of Saint Bonaventure*. Trans. Dom. I. Trethowan and F. J. Sheed. Paterson, N.J.: Saint Anthony's Guild Press, 1965. (Bonaventure, St.)

Marrone, S. P. *The Light of Thy Countenance: Science and Knowledge of God in the Thirteenth Century*. 2 vols. Leiden: Brill, 2001. (Bonaventure, St.)

Monti, D. V., and K. Wrisley Shelby, eds. *Bonaventure Revisited: Companion to the Breviloquium*. St. Bonaventure, N.Y.: Franciscan Institute Publications, 2017. (Bonaventure, St.)

Speer, A. "Bonaventure and the Question of a Medieval Philosophy." *Medieval Philosophy and Theology* 6 (1997): 25–46. (Bonaventure, St.)

Wood, C. T., ed. *Philip the Fair and Boniface VIII: State vs. Papacy*. New York: Holt, Rinehart and Winston, 1967. (Boniface VIII, Pope)

Leff, G. *Bradwardine and the Pelagians*. Cambridge: Cambridge University Press, 1962. (Bradwardine, Thomas)

Ravier, A. *Saint Bruno, the Carthusian*. Los Angeles: Ignatius Press, 1995. (Bruno the Carthusian)

Klima, G. *John Buridan*. Oxford: Oxford University Press, 2009. (Buridan, John)

Zupko, J. *John Buridan: Portrait of a 14th-Century Arts Master*. Notre Dame, Ind.: Notre Dame University Press, 2002. (Buridan, John)

Conti, A. D. *A Companion to Walter Burley*. Leiden: Brill, 2016. (Burley, Walter)

Wood, R., and J. Ottman. "Walter of Burley: His Life and Works." *Vivarium* 37 (1999): 1–23. (Burley, Walter)

Bedouelle, G., R. Cessario, and K. White. *Jean Capreolus et son temps*. Paris: Cerf, 1997. (Capreolus, John)

Baron, H. "Cicero and the Roman Civic Spirit in the Middle Ages and the Early Renaissance." In *Bulletin of the John Rylands Library* 22 (1938): 72–97. (Cicero)

Murphy, J. J. "Rhetoric in the Middle Ages." In *Critics and Criticism*, ed. R. S. Crane, 260–96. Chicago: University of Chicago Press, 1952. (Cicero)

Fortin, J. R. *Clarembald of Arras as a Boethian Commentator*. Kirksville, Mo.: Thomas Jefferson University Press, 1995. (Clarembald of Arras)

Van den Hoek, A. *Clement of Alexandria and the Use of Philo in the "Stromateis": An Early Christian Reshaping of a Jewish Model*. Leiden: Brill, 1983. (Clement of Alexandria)

Daiber, H. Introduction and bibliography in *Aetius Arabus: der Vorsokratiker in Arabischer Uberlieferung*, 3–89, 695–789. Wiesbaden: Steiner, 1980. (Trans. of *Placita Philosophorum* attributed to Costa ben Luca). (Costa ben Luca)

Fraenkel, C. "From the Pythatorean Void to Crescas: God as the Place of the World." *Zutot* 5 (2008): 87–94. (Crescas, Hasdai)

Harvey, W. Z. *Physics and Metaphysics in Hasdai Crescas*. Amsterdam: J. C. Gieben, 1998. (Crescas, Hasdai)

Hollander, R. *Dante, a Life in Works*. New Haven, Conn.: Yale University Press, 2001. (Dante Alighieri)

Dronke, P. "Profane Elements in Literature." In *Renaissance and Renewal in the Twelfth Century*, ed. R. L. Benson, G. Constable, and C. D. Lanham, 589–90. Toronto: University of Toronto Press, 1991. (David of Dinant)

Kurdzialek, M. "L'idee de l'homme chez David de Dinant." In *Images of Man in Ancient and Medieval Thought: Studia Gerardo Verbeke ab amicis et collegiis dicata*, ed. F. Bossier et al, 311–22. Leuven: Leuven University Press, 1976. (David of Dinant)

Emery, Kent, Jr. "Cognitive Theory and the Relation between Scholastic and Mystical Modes of Theology: Why Denys the Carthusian Outlawed Durandus of Saint-Pourçain." In *Crossing Borders at Medieval Universities*, ed. S. E. B. Young, 145–76. Leiden: Brill, 2011. (Denys the Carthusian *or* Denys of Rijkel)

Palazzo, A. "Ulrich of Strasbourg and Denys the Carthusian: Textual Analysis and Doctrinal Comments." *Bulletin de Philosophie Médiévale* 46 (2004): 61–113. (Denys the Carthusian *or* Denys of Rijkel)

Ariew R. *Descartes among the Scholastics*. Leiden: Brill, 2011. (Descartes)

Flasch, K. *Dietrich von Freiberg: Philosophie, Theologie Naturforschung zum 1300*. Frankfurt: Klostermann, 2007. (Dietrich of Freiberg)

Wallace, W. A. *The Scientific Method of Theodoric of Freiberg*. Fribourg: Fribourg University Press, 1959. (Dietrich of Freiberg)

Golitzin, A. *Et introibo ad altare Dei: The Mystagogy of Dionysius Areopagita with Special Reference to His Predecessors in the Eastern Christian Tradition*. Thessalonica: Patriarchikon Chidryma Paterikon, 1994. (Dionysius the Pseudo-Areopagite *or* Pseudo-Dionysius)

Perl, E. D. *Theophany: The Neoplatonic Philosophy of Dionysius the Areopagite*. Albany: State University of New York Press, 2008. (Dionysius the Pseudo-Areopagite or Pseudo-Dionysius)

Robins, R. H. *A Short History of Linguistics*. 4th ed. London: Longman, 1997. (Donatus)

Wolter, A. B., ed. *Duns Scotus*. Special issue, *American Catholic Philosophical Quarterly* 47, no. 1 (1993). (Duns Scotus, John, Bl.)

Henniger, M. "Durand of Saint-Pourçain (ca. 1270–ca. 1334)." In *Individuation in Scholasticism: The Later Middle Ages and the Counter-Reformation, 1150–1650*, ed. J. J. E Gracia, 319–32. Albany: State University of New York Press, 1994. (Durandus of Saint-Pourçain)

Schabel, C., R. L. Friedman, and I. Balcoyiannopoulou. "Peter of Palude and the Parisian Reaction to Durand de Saint-Pourçain on Future Contingents." In *Archivum Fratrum Praedicatorum* 71 (2001): 183–300. (Durandus of Saint-Pourçain)

Southern, R. W. *Saint Anselm and His Biographer*. Cambridge: Cambridge University Press, 1963. (Eadmer of Canterbury)

McGinn, B. *The Man from Whom God Hid Nothing: Meister Eckhart's Mystical Thought.* New York: Crossroad, 2001. (Eckhart, Meister)

Mojsisch, B. *Meister Eckhart: Analogy, Univocity and Unity.* Trans. O. F. Summerell. Amsterdam: Gruner, 2001. (Eckhart, Meister)

Flasch, K. *Meister Eckhart. Philosoph des Christentums.* München: C. H. Beck, 2010. (Eckhart, Meister)

McEvoy, J. *Robert Grosseteste*, 13–16. Oxford: Oxford University Press, 2000. (Edmund of Abingdon)

Druart, Th. A. "Al-Farabi, the Categories, Metaphysics and the Book of Letters." *Medioevo* 32 (2007): 15–37. (Farabi, Al- *or* Alfarabi)

Galston, M. *Politics and Excellence: The Political Philosophy of Alfarabi.* Princeton, N.J.: Princeton University Press, 1990. (Farabi, Al- *or* Alfarabi)

Netton, I. R. *Al-Farabi and His School.* London: Routledge, 1989. (Farabi, Al- *or* Alfarabi)

Zonta, M. "Al-Farabi's Long Commentary on Aristotle's Categories in Hebrew and Arabic, a Critical Edition and English Translation of the Newly-Found Extant Fragments." In *Studies in Arabic and Islamic Culture*, ed. B. Abrahamov, 2:185–254. Ramut Gan: Ben Ilan University, 2006. (Farabi, Al- *or* Alfarabi)

Celenza, C. S. "The Platonic Revival." In *The Cambridge Companion to Renaissance Philosophy*, ed. J. Hankins, 72–96. Cambridge: Cambridge University Press, 2007. (Ficino, Marsilio)

Edelheit, A. *Ficino, Pico and Savonarola: The Evolution of Humanist Theology, 1461/2–1498.* Leiden: Brill, 2008. (Ficino, Marsilio)

Kristeller, P. O. "Marsilio Ficino as a Man of Letters and the Glosses Attributed to Him in the Caetani Codex of Dante." *Renaissance Quarterly* 36 (1983): 1–47. (Ficino, Marsilio)

Leitgeb, M. C., S. Toussaint, and H. Bannert, eds. *Platon, Plotin, und Marsilio Ficino: Studien zu den Vorläufern und zur Rezeption des Florentiner Neuplatonismus.* Vienna: Verlag des Österreichischen Akademie der Wissenschaften, 2009. (Ficino, Marsilio)

Long, R. J., and Maura O'Carroll. *The Life and Works of Richard Fishacre.* Bayerische Akademie der Wissenschaften, Bd. 21. Munich: Verlag der Bayerischen Akademie der Wissenschaften, 1999. (Fishacre, Richard)

Dunne, M. "A Fourteenth-Century Example of an *Introitus Sententiarum* at Oxford: Richard FitzRalph's Inaugural Speech in Praise of the *Sentences* of Peter Lombard." *Mediaeval Studies* 63 (2001): 1–29. (Fitzralph, Richard)

Ashworth, E. J. *Language and Logic in the Post-Medieval Period*, passim. Dordrecht: Reidel Publishing Company, 1974. (Fonseca, Petrus)

Friedman, R. L., and C. Schabel. "Francis of Marchia's Commentaries on the Sentences: Question List and State of Research." In *Mediaeval Studies* 63 (2001): 31–106. (Francis of Marchia)

Schabel, C. *Theology at Paris, 1316–1345: Peter Auriol and the Problem of Divine Foreknowledge and Future Contingents*, 149–55. Burlington, Vt.: Ashgate, 2001. (Francis of Meyronnes)

Colish, M. L. "Carolingian Debates over 'Nihil' and 'Tenebrae.'" *Speculum* 59 (1984): 757–95. (Fredegisus *or* Fridugisus)

Lancaster, I. "Ibn Gabirol." In *History of Islamic Philosophy*, ed. S. H. Nasr and O. Leaman, 1:712–17. London: Routledge, 1996. (Gabirol, Ibn *or* Avicebron)

Loewe, R. *Ibn Gabirol*. New York: Grove Weidenfeld, 1989. (Gabirol, Ibn *or* Avicebron)

McGinn, B. "Ibn Gabirol: The Sage among the Schoolmen." In *Neoplatonism and Jewish Thought*, ed. L. E. Goodman, 79–109. Albany: State University of New York Press, 1992. (Gabirol, Ibn *or* Avicebron)

Pessin, S. *Ibn Gabirol's Theology of Desire: Matter and Method in Jewish Medieval Philosophy*. Cambridge: Cambridge University Press, 2013. (Gabirol, Ibn *or* Avicebron)

———. "Matter, Form and the Corporeal World." In *The Cambridge History of Jewish Philosophy: From Antiquity to the Seventeenth Century*, ed. T. Radavsky and S. Nadler. Cambridge: Cambridge University Press, 2009. (Gabirol, Ibn *or* Avicebron)

Farthing, J. L. *Thomas Aquinas and Gabriel Biel: Interpretations of Thomas Aquinas in German Nominalism on the Eve of the Reformation*. Durham, N.C.: Duke University Press, 1988. (Gabriel Biel)

Oberman, H. A. *The Harvest of Medieval Theology: Gabriel Biel and Late Medieval Nominalism*. 3rd ed. Durham, N.C.: Labyrinth Press, 1983. (Gabriel Biel)

Valsanzibio, S. da. *Vita e dottrina di Gaetano di Thiene*. 2nd ed. Padua: Studio Filosofico dei Fratri Minori Cappucinni, 1949. (Gaetano of Thiene)

de Rijk, L. M. Introduction to *Giraldus Odonis OFM, Opera Philosophica*, 1:1–67. Leiden: Brill, 1997. (Gerald *or* Gerard Odon *or* Guiral Ot)

Dubrule, D. E. "Gerard of Abbeville 'Quodlibet XIII, Question 10.'" *Mediaeval Studies* 32 (1970): 128–37. (Gerard of Abbeville)

Brown, S. F. "Gerard of Bologna's 'Quodlibet I, qu. 1,' On the Analogy of Being." *Carmelus* 31 (1984): 143–70. (Gerard of Bologna)

Lemay, R. "Gerard of Cremona." In *Dictionary of Scientific Biography*, vol. 15, supplement 1, 173–92. New York: Scribner. (Gerard of Cremona)

Burrows, M. *Jean Gerson and "De consolatione theologiae."* Beiträge zur Historischen Theologie 78. Tübingen: J. C. B. Mohr, 1991. (Gerson, Jean)

Pascoe, L. *Jean Gerson: Principles of Church Reform*. Leiden: Brill, 1973. (Gerson, Jean)

Feldman, S. *Gersonides: Judaism within the Limits of Reason*. Portland, Ore.: Littman Library of Jewish Civilization, 2010. (Gersonides *or* Gershom, Levi ben)

Kellner, M. *Torah in the Observatory: Gersonides, Maimonides, Song of Songs.* Boston: Academic Studies Press, 2010. (Gersonides *or* Gershom, Levi ben)

Wolfson, H. "Maimonides and Gersonides on Divine Attributes as Ambiguous Terms." In *Mordecai Kaplan Jubilee Volume*, ed. M. Davis, 515–30. New York: Jewish Theological Seminary of America, 1953. (Gersonides *or* Gershom, Levi ben)

Frank, R. M. *Creation and the Cosmic System: Al-Ghazali and Avicenna.* Heidelberg: Carl Winter Universitaetsverlag, 1992. (Ghazali, Al- *or* Algazel)

Griffel, F. *Al-Ghazali's Philosophical Theology.* New York: Oxford University Press, 2009. (Ghazali, Al- *or* Algazel)

Hourani, G. F. "A Revised Chronology of Ghazali's Writings." *Journal of the American Oriental Society* 104 (1984): 289–302. (Ghazali, Al- *or* Algazel)

Marmura, M. E. "Ghazalian Causes and Intermediaries." *Journal of the American Oriental Society* 115 (1995): 89–100. (Ghazali, Al- *or* Algazel)

Shihadeh, A. "New Light on the Reception of al-Ghazali's Doctrines of the Philosophers (Maqâsid Falâsifa)." In *In the Age of Averroes: Arabic Philosophy in the Sixth/Twelfth Century*, ed. P. Adamson, 77–92. London: Warburg Institute/Nino Aragno, 2011. (Ghazali, Al- *or* Algazel)

Treiger, A. *Inspired Knowledge in Islamic Thought: Al-Ghazali's Theory of Mystical Cognition and Its Avicennian Foundation.* London: Routledge, 2012. (Ghazali, Al- *or* Algazel)

Nielsen, L. O. *Theology and Philosophy in the Twelfth Century.* Leiden: Brill, 1982. (Gilbert of Poitiers *or* Gilbert de la Porrée)

De Wulf, M. Introduction to *Le Traité "De unitate formae" de Gilles de Lessines.* Les Philosophes Belges 1. Louvain: Institut Supérieur de Philosophie de l'Université, 1901. (Giles of Lessines)

Nash, P. W. "Giles of Rome on Boethius' 'Diversum est esse et id quod est.'" *Mediaeval Studies* 12 (1959): 57–91. (Giles of Rome)

Pini, G. "Being and Creation in Giles of Rome." In *Nach der Verurteilung von 1277: Philosophie und Theologie an der Universität von Paris im letzten Viertel des 13. Jahrhunderts*, ed. J. A. Aertsen, K. Emery, and A. Speer, 390–409. Miscellanea Mediaevalia 28. Berlin: De Gruyter, 2000. (Giles of Rome)

Tihon, P. *Foi et Théologie selon Godefroid de Fontaines.* Paris: Desclée de Brouwer, 1966. (Godfrey of Fontaines)

Wippel, J. F. *The Metaphysical Thought of Godfrey of Fontaines: A Study in Late Thirteenth-Century Philosophy.* Washington, D.C.: Catholic University of America Press, 1981. (Godfrey of Fontaines)

Gracia, J. J. E. "The Agent and Possible Intellects in Gonsalvus Hispanus' Question XIII." *Franciscan Studies* 29 (1969): 5–36. (Gonsalvus Hispanus *or* Gonsalvo of Spain)

Lambot, C. Introduction to *Oeuvres théologique et grammaticales de Godescalc d'Orbais*. Spicilegium Sacrum Lovaniense. Études et documents 20. Louvain: Spicilegium Sacrum Lovaniense, 1945. (Gottschalk of Orbais)

Christensen, K. Introduction to *Gratian, The Treatise on Laws (Decretum DD. 1–20) with the Ordinary Gloss*. Studies in Medieval and Early Modern Canon Law 2. Washington, D.C.: Catholic University of America Press, 1993. (Gratian)

Denning-Boole, S. J. Introduction to *Dialogue between an Orthodox and a Barlaamite*. Trans. R. Ferwerda. Binghamton, N.Y.: Global Publications, 1999. (Gregory Palamas)

Courtenay, W. J. "John of Mirecourt and Gregory of Rimini on Whether God Can Undo the Past." *Recherches de Theologie Ancienne et Medievale* 39 (1972): 224–56, and 40 (1973): 147–74. (Gregory of Rimini)

Friedman, R. L. *Intellectual Traditions at the Medieval University: The Use of Philosophical Mind in the Trinitatian Theology of the Franciscans and Dominicans, 1250–1350*. 2 vols. Leiden: Brill, 2013. (Gregory of Rimini)

Trapp, A. D. "Augustinian Theology in the Fourteenth Century: Notes on Editions, Marginalia, Opinions, and Booklore" *Augustiniana* 6 (1956): 146–274. (Gregory of Rimini)

Post, R. R. *The Modern Devotion*, 51–196. Leiden: Brill, 1968. (Groote, Geert *or* Gerard)

Cunningham, J. P. *Robert Grosseteste: His Thought and Its Impact*. Toronto: Pontifical Institute of Mediaeval Studies, 2012. (Robert Grosseteste)

Marrone, S. P. *William of Auvergne and Robert Grosseteste: New Ideas of Truth in the Early Thirteenth Century*. Princeton, N.J.: Princeton University Press, 1983. (Robert Grosseteste)

McEvoy, J. *Robert Grosseteste*. Oxford: Oxford University Press, 2000. (Robert Grosseteste)

Brown, S. F. "Guido Terrena and the Unity of the Concept of Being." *Documenti e Studi sulla Tradizione Filosofica Medievale* 3, no. 2 (1992): 599–631. (Guido *or* Guy Terrena)

Turley, T. "Guido Terreni and the 'Decretum.'" *Bulletin of Medieval Canon Law* 8 (1978): 29–34. (Guido *or* Guy Terrena)

d'Alverny, M.-T. "Translations and Translators." In *Renaissance and Renewal in the Twelfth Century*, ed. R. Benson and G. Constable, 444–62. Cambridge, Mass.: Harvard University Press, 1982. (Gundissalinus, Dominicus)

Jospe, R. "Judah La-Levi and the Critique of Philosophy." In *Jewish Philosophy in the Middle Ages*, ed. R. Jospe. Brighton, Mass.: Academic Studies Press, 2009. (Halevi, Judah)

Korobkin, N. D. Introduction to *The Kuzari: In Defense of the Despised Faith*. Northvale, N.J.: J. Aronson, 1998. (Halevi, Judah)

Flores, J. C. *Henry of Ghent: Metaphysics and the Trinity*. Leuven: Leuven University Press, 2006. (Henry of Ghent)

Guldentops, G., and C. Steel. *Henry of Ghent and the Transformation of Scholastic Thought*. Leuven: Leuven University Press, 2003. (Henry of Ghent)

Marrone, S. P. *Truth and Scientific Knowledge in the Thought of Henry of Ghent*. Cambridge, Mass.: Medieval Academy of America, 1985. (Henry of Ghent)

Vanhamel, W., ed. *Henry of Ghent: Proceedings of the International Colloquium on the Occasion of the 700th Anniversary of his Death (1293)*. Louvain: Peeters, 1996. (Henry of Ghent)

Wilson, G. *A Companion to Henry of Ghent*. Leiden: Brill, 2011. (Henry of Ghent)

Murdoch, J. "Henry of Harclay and the Infinite." In *Studi sul XIV Seculo in Memoria di Anneliese Maier*, ed. A. Maieru and A. Paravicini Rabliani, 219–61. Rome: Edizioni de Storia e Letteratura, 1981. (Henry of Harclay)

Pelster, F. "Heinrich von Harclay, Kanzler von Oxford und seine Quaestionem." In *Miscellanea Francesco Ehrle*, 1:307–56. Rome: Biblioteca Apostolica Vaticana, 1924. (Henry of Harclay)

Brown, S. F. "The Treatise 'De arcanis Dei.'" In *Cardinal Bessarion: De arcanis Dei*, ed. G. J. Etzkorn, 16–64. Rome: Miscellanea Francescana, 1997. (Henry of Zomeren)

Schabel, C. *Theology at Paris, 1316–1345: Peter Auriol and the Problem of Divine Foreknowledge and Future Contingents*, 300–302. Aldershot: Ashgate, 2000. (Henry Totting of Oyta)

Conforti, P. "'Naturali cognitione probare': Natural and Theological Knowledge in Hervaeus Natalis." In *Was ist Philosophie im Mittelalter?*, ed. J. A. Aertsen and A. Speer, 614–21. Miscellanea Mediaevalia 26. Berlin: De Gruyter, 1998. (Hervaeus Natalis *or* Harvey Nedellec)

Wengert, R. G. "Three Senses of Intuitive Cognition: A Quodlibetal Question of Harvey of Nedellec." *Franciscan Studies* 43 (1983): 408–31. (Hervaeus Natalis *or* Harvey Nedellec)

Wilson, C. *William Heytesbury: Medieval Logic and the Rise of Mathematical Physics*. Madison: University of Wisconsin Press, 1960. (Heytesbury, William)

Newman, B., ed. *Voice of the Living Light: Hildegard of Bingen and her World*. Berkeley: University of California Press, 1998. (Hildegard of Bingen)

Théry, G. Introduction to *Études Dionysiennes*, vol. 1. Etudes de philosophie médiévale 16. Paris: Vrin, 1932. (Hilduin)

Nachtmann, D. Introduction to *De cavendis vitiis et virtutibus exercendis*, by Hincmar von Reims. Monumenta Germaniae Historica: Quellen zur Geistesgeschichte des Mittelalters 16. Munich: Monumenta Germaniae Historica, 1998. (Hincmar of Reims)

Incandela, J. M. "Robert Holcot, O.P., on Prophecy, the Contingency of Revelation, and the Freedom of God." *Medieval Philosophy and Theology* 4 (1994): 165–88. (Holcot, Robert)

Keele, R. "Oxford Quodlibeta from Ockham to Holcot." In *Theological Quodlibeta in the Middle Ages: The Fourteenth Century*, ed. C. Schabel, 651–92. Leiden: Brill, 2007. (Holcot, Robert)

Kennedy, L. A. *The Philosophy of Robert Holcot, Fourteenth-Century Skeptic*. Lewiston, N.Y.: Mellen, 1993. (Holcot, Robert)

Slotemaker, J. T., and J. C. Witt. *Robert Holcot*. Oxford: Oxford University Press, 2016. (Holcot, Robert)

Crouse, R. D. "Honorius Augustodunensis: Disciple of Anselm?" In *Die Wirkungsgeschichte Anselms von Canterbury. Akten der ersten Internationalen Anselm-Tagung*, ed. H. Kohlenberger, 131–39. Analecta Anselmiana 4. Frankfurt: Minerva, 1975. (Honorius of Autun)

Heynck, V. "Der Skotist: Hugo de Novo Castro." *Franziskanische Studien* 43 (1961): 244–70. (Hugh of Newcastle)

Fisher, J. "Hugh of St. Cher and the Development of Mediaeval Theology." *Speculum* 31 (1956): 57–69. (Hugh of Saint-Cher)

Principe, W. *Hugh of Saint-Cher's Theology of the Hypostatic Union*. Toronto: Pontifical Institute of Mediaeval Studies, 1970. (Hugh of Saint-Cher)

Illich, I. *In the Vineyard of the Text: A Commentary to Hugh's "Didascalicon."* Chicago: University of Chicago Press, 1993. (Hugh of Saint-Victor)

Kleinz, J. P. *The Theory of Knowledge of Hugh of Saint-Victor*. Washington, D.C.: Catholic University of America Press, 1944. (Hugh of Saint-Victor)

Rorem, P. *Hugh of Saint Victor*. Oxford: Oxford University Press, 2009. (Hugh of Saint Victor)

Bashier, S. *The Story of Islamic Philosophy: Ibn 'Arabî, Ibn Tufayl, and Others on the Limit between Naturalism and Tradition*. Albany: State University of New York Press, 2012. (Ibn Arabi)

Pourjavady, R., and S. W. Schmidtke. *A Jewish Philosopher of Baghdad. 'Izz al-Dawla Ibn Kammuna (d. 683/1284) and His Writings*. Leiden: Brill, 2006. (Ibn Kammunah)

Altman, A., and S. M. Stern. *Isaac Israeli: A Neoplatonic Philosopher of the Early Tenth Century*. London: Oxford University Press, 1958. (Isaac Israeli)

Gaggero, L. "Isaac of Stella and the Theology of Redemption." *Collectanea Ordinis Cisterciensium Reformatorum* 22 (1960): 21–36. (Isaac of Stella)

Lear, S. F. "St. Isidore and Medieval Science." *Rice Institute Pamphlets* 23 (1936): 75–105. (Isidore of Seville, St.)

Sharpe, W. D. *Isidore of Seville: The Medical Writings*. Philadelphia: University of Pennsylvania Press, 1964. (Isidore of Seville, St.)

Yokoyama, T. "Zwei Questiones des Iacobus de Aesculo über das Esse obiectivum." In *Wahrheit und Verkündigung. Michael Schmaus zum 70. Geburtstag*, ed. L. Scheffezyk et al., 2 Bd., 1:31–74. Paderborn: Schöningh, 1967. (James of Ascoli)

Friedman, R. L. "The 'Sentences' Commentary, 1250–1320." In *Mediaeval Commentaries on the "Sentences" of Peter Lombard*, ed. G. R. Evans, 1:69–70. Leiden: Brill, 2002. (James of Metz)

Ebbensen, S. "Jacobus Veneticus on the 'Posterior Analytics' and Some Early 13th Century Oxford Masters on the Elenchi." *Cahiers de l'Institut du Moyen-Age Grec et Latin* 21 (1977): 1–9. (James of Venice)

Côté, A. "Bernard of Auvergne on James of Viterbo's Doctrine of Possibles: With a Critical Edition of Bernard's *Reprobatio* of James's Quodlibet 1, Question 5." *Augustiniana* 66 (2016): 151–84. (James of Viterbo)

Gossiaux, M. D. "James of Viterbo on the Relationship between Essence and Existence." *Augustiniana* 49 (1999): 73–107. (James of Viterbo)

Reeves, M. *The Influence of Prophecy in the Later Middle Ages: A Study in Joachimism*. Oxford: Clarendon Press, 1969. (Joachim of Fiore)

Wessley, S. E. *Joachim of Fiore and Monastic Reform*. New York: Peter Lang, 1990. (Joachim of Fiore)

West, D. C., ed. *Joachim of Fiore in Christian Thought*. 2 vols. New York: Burt Franklin & Co., 1975. (Joachim of Fiore)

Wippel, J. F. "Godfrey of Fontaines, Peter of Auvergne, and John Baconthorpe." In *Individuation in Scholasticism: The Later Middle Ages and the Counter-Reformation, 1150–1650*, ed. J. J. E. Gracia, 221–56. Albany, N.Y.: State University of New York Press, 1994. (John Baconthorpe)

Pasiecznik, M. "John de Bassolis, O.F.M." *Franciscan Studies* 13 (1953): 59–77, and 14 (1954): 49–80. (John Bassolis *or* of Bassol)

Callus, D. "The Treatise of John Blund 'On the Soul.'" In *Autour d'Aristotle. Recueil d'etudes de philosophie ancienne et medievale offert a Monseigneur A. Mansion*, 471–95. Louvain: Publications Universitaires de Louvain, 1955. (John Blund)

Courtenay, W. *Schools and Scholars in Fourteenth-Century England*, passim. Princeton, N.J.: Princeton University Press, 1987. (John Lutterell)

Ermatinger, C. J. "John of Jandun in His Relations with Arts Masters and Theologians." In *Arts liberaux et Philosophie au Moyen Age*, 1173–84. Montreal: Institut d'Etudes Medievales, 1969. (John of Jandun)

Mahoney, E. P. "John of Jandun and Agostino Nifo on Human Felicity." In *L'homme et son Univers au Moyen Age*, ed. C. Wenin, 465–77. Louvain-la-Neuve: Éditions de l'Institut Supérieur de Philosophie, 1986. (John of Jandun)

Lynch, K. F., ed. *Ioannes de Rupella, Eleven Marian Sermons*. Paderborn: Schöningh, 1961. (John of La Rochelle *or* of Rupella)

Fries, A. "Cod. Vat. Lat. 1114 und der Sentenzkommentar des Iohannes von Lichtenberg." *Archivum Fratrum Praedicatorum* 7 (1937): 305–19. (John of Lichtenberg *or* Picardy)

Thijssen, J. M. M. H. *Censure and Heresy at the University of Paris, 1200–1400*. Philadelphia: University of Pennsylvania Press, 1998. (John of Mirecourt)

Schabel, C. *Theology at Paris, 1316–1345*, 181–82. Aldershot: Ashgate, 2000. (John of Naples)

Dunbabin, J. "The Commentary of John of Paris (Quidort) on the 'Sentences.'" In *Mediaeval Commentaries on the "Sentences" of Peter Lombard*, ed. G. R. Evans, 1:131–47. Leiden: Brill. (John of Paris *or* Jean Quidort)

Livesey, S. J. *Theology and Science in the Fourteenth Century: Three Questions on the Unity and Subalternation of the Sciences from John of Reading's Commentary on the "Sentences."* Leiden: Brill, 1989. (John of Reading)

Kaluza, Z. "La Nature des Écrits de Jean de Ripa." *Traditio* 43 (1987): 257 98. (John of Ripa)

Courtenay, W. J. *Schools and Scholars in Fourteenth-Century England*, 267–75. Princeton, N.J.: Princeton University Press, 1987. (John of Rodington)

McInerny, R. *Introduction to the "Summa theologiae" of Thomas Aquinas: The Isagoge of John of St. Thomas*. South Bend, Ind.: St. Augustine's Press, 2004. (John of St. Thomas *or* John Poinsot)

Wilks, M., ed. *The World of John Salisbury*. Oxford: Blackwell, 1984. (John of Salisbury)

Friedman, R. L. "The 'Sentences' Commentary, 1250–1320." In *Mediaeval Commentaries on the "Sentences" of Peter Lombard*, ed. G. R. Evans, 1:41–128, esp. 58–59. Leiden: Brill, 2002. (John of Sterngassen)

Senner, W. "Jean de Sterngassen et son Commentaire des 'Sentences.'" *Revue Thomiste* 117 (1997): 83–98. (John of Sterngassen)

Carabine, D. *John Scot Eriugena*. Oxford: Oxford University Press, 2000. (John Scotus Eriugena)

Moran, D. *The Philosophy of John Scottus Eriugena*. Cambridge: Cambridge University Press, 1889. (John Scotus Eriugena)

Mahoney, E. P. "Aristotle as 'The Worst Natural Philosopher' and 'The Worst Metaphysician': His Reputation among some Franciscan Philosophers (Bonaventure, Francis of Meyronnes, Antonius Andreas, and Joannes Canonicus) and Later Reactions." In *Die Philosophie im 14. und 15. Jahrhundert, in memoriam Konstanty Michalski (1879–1947)*, ed. O. Pluta, 261–73. Amsterdam: Verlag B. R. Gruner, 1988. (John the Canon)

Bauerschmidt, F. C. *Julian of Norwich and the Mystical Body Politic of Christ*. Notre Dame, Ind.: University of Notre Dame Press, 1999. (Julian of Norwich)

Gibson, M. *Lanfranc of Bec*. Oxford: Oxford University Press, 1977. (Lanfranc of Bec)

Smalley, B. "Stephen Langton and the Four Senses of Scripture." *Speculum* 6 (1931): 60–76. (Langton, Stephen)

Hornbeck, J. P., II, M. Bose, and F. Somerset. *A Companion to Lollardy*. Leiden-Boston: Brill, 2016. (Lollards)

Hillgarth, J. N. *Ramon Lull and Lullism in Fourteenth-Century France*. Oxford: Oxford University Press, 1971. (Lull, Raymond)

Tuen, K. "Llull (1232–1350): From Theology to Mathematics." *Studies in Logic* 44 (2016): 55–80. (Lull, Raymond)

Nielsen, L. *Theology and Philosophy in the Twelfth Century: A Study of Gilbert Porreta's Thinking and the Theological Expositions of the Doctrine of the Incarnation during the Period 1130–1180*. Leiden: Brill, 1982. (Magister Martinus)

Garvin, J. N. "Magister Udo, a Source of Peter of Poitiers' *Sentences*." *New Scholasticism* 28 (1954): 286–98. (Magister Udo)

Frank, D. H., ed. *Maimonides*. Special issue, *American Catholic Philosophical Quarterly* 76, no. 1 (2002). (Maimonides, Moses)

Ivry, A. "Isma'ili Theology and Maimonides' Philosophy." In *The Jews of Medieval Islam*, ed. D. Frank, 271–99. Leiden: Brill, 1995. (Maimonides, Moses)

Pines, S. "Translator's Introduction." In *Moses Maimonides: The Guide of the Perplexed*, lvii–cxxxiv. Chicago: University of Chicago Press, 1963. (Maimonides, Moses)

Rudavsky, T. M. *Maimonides*. Oxford: Wiley-Blackwell, 2010. (Maimonides, Moses)

Seeskin, K., ed. *The Cambridge Companion to Maimonides*. New York: Cambridge University Press, 2005. (Maimonides, Moses)

Sroumsa, S. *Maimonides in His World*. Princeton, N.J.: Princeton University Press, 2009. (Maimonides, Moses)

Strauss, L. *Philosophy and Law*. Trans. F. Baumann. Philadelphia: Jewish Publication Society, 1987. (Maimonides, Moses)

Hoenen, M. J. F. M. *Marsilius of Inghen: Divine Knowledge in Late Medieval Thought*. Leiden: Brill, 1993. (Marsilius of Inghen)

Gewirth, A. *Marsilius of Padua: The Defender of Peace*. 2 vols. New York: Columbia University Press, 1951. (Marsilius of Padua)

Moreno-Riaño, G., ed. *The World of Marsilius of Padua*. Turnhout: Brepols, 2007. (Marsilius of Padua)

Marno, C. "A Pragmatic Approach to Language Modism." In *Sprachtheorien in Spätantike und Mittelalter*, ed. S. Ebbensen, 169–83. Tübingen: Gunter Narr Verlag, 1995. (Martin of Dacia)

Hayes, Z. *The General Doctrine of Creation in the Thirteenth Century, with Special Emphasis on Matthew of Aquasparta*. Paderborn: F. Schöningh, 1964. (Matthew of Aquasparta)

Marrone, S. "Matthew of Aquasparta, Henry of Ghent and the Augustinian Epistemology after Bonaventure." *Franziskanische Studien* 65 (1983): 252–90. (Matthew of Aquasparta)

Little, A. G. *The Grey Friars in Oxford*, 267–68. Oxford, Oxford University Press, 1892. (Maurice O'Fihely *or* Mauritius de Portu)

Robson, C. A. *Maurice de Sully and the Medieval Vernacular Homily*. Oxford: Oxford University Press, 1952. (Maurice of Sully)

Thumberg, L. *Man and the Cosmos*. Crestwood, N.Y.: St. Vladimir's Seminary Press, 1985. (Maximus the Confessor)

———. *Microcosm and Mediator*. Lund: C. W. K. Gleerup, 1965. (Maximus the Confessor)

Trapp, D. "Augustinian Theology in the 14th Century: Notes on Editions, Marginalia, and Booklore." *Augustiniana* 6 (1965): 146–274. (Michael of Massa)

Thorndike, L. *Michael Scot*. London: Nelson, 1965. (Michael Scot)

Weinberg, J. R. *Nicolaus of Autrecourt: A Study in 14th Century Thought*. Princeton, N.J.: Princeton University Press for University of Cincinnati, 1948. (Nicholas of Autrecourt)

Albertson, D. "Mystical Philosophy in the Fifteenth Century: New Directions in Research on Nicholas of Cusa." *Religion Compass* 4 (2010): 471–85. (Nicholas of Cusa)

Bocken, I., ed. *Conflict and Reconciliation: Perspectives on Nicholas of Cusa*. Leiden: Brill, 2004. (Nicholas of Cusa)

Hopkins, J. *Nicholas of Cusa's Dialectical Mysticism*. Minneapolis: University of Minnesota Press, 1985. (Nicholas of Cusa)

Moran, D. "Nicholas of Cusa (1401 1464): Platonism at the Dawn of Modernity." In *Platonism at the Origins of Modernity: Studies on Platonism and Early Modern Philosophy*, ed. D. Hedley and S. Hutton, 9–29. Dordrecht: Springer, 2008. (Nicholas of Cusa)

———. "Nicholas of Cusa and Modern Philosophy." In *The Cambridge Companion to Renaissance Philosophy*, ed. J. Hankins, 173–92. Cambridge: Cambridge University Press, 2007. (Nicholas of Cusa)

Watanabe, M., G. Christianson, and T. Izbicki, ed. *Nicholas of Cusa: A Companion to His Life and His Times*. Burlington, Vt.: Ashgate, 2011. (Nicholas of Cusa)

Krey, P. D. W., and L. Smith, eds. *Nicholas of Lyra, The Senses of Scripture*. Leiden: Brill, 2000. (Nicholas of Lyra)

Alarcon, S. C. "Nicolas de Ockham OFM (d. ca. 1320): Vida y obras." *Antonianum* 53 (1978): 493–573. (Nicholas of Ockham)

Little, A. G., and F. Pelster. *Oxford Theology and Theologians, c. 1282–1302*, 88–89, 124–26. Oxford: Clarendon Press, 1934. (Nicholas of Ockham)

Dales, R. C., and O. Argerami. *Medieval Latin Texts on the Eternity of the World*, 43–53. Leiden: Brill, 1991. (Odo Rigaud)

Grant, E. "Jean Buridan and Nicole Oresme on Natural Knowledge." *Vivarium* 31 (1993): 84–105. (Oresme, Nicole)

Harvey, W. Z. "Nicole Oresme and Hasdai Crescas on Many Worlds." In *Studies in the History and Culture of Science: A Tribute to Gad Freudenthal*, ed. R. Fontaine et al. Leiden: Brill, 2011. (Oresme, Nicole)

Morrison, K. F. "Otto of Freising's Quest for the Hermeneutic Circle." *Speculum* 55 (1980): 207–36. (Otto of Freising)

Sheedy, C. E. *The Eucharistic Controversy of the Eleventh Century against the Background of Pre-Scholastic Theology*. Washington, D.C.: Catholic University of America Press, 1947. (Paschasius Radbertus)

Perreiah, A. R. *Paul of Venice: A Bibliographical Guide*. Bowling Green, Ohio: Philosophy Documentation Center, 1986. (Paul of Venice)

Douie, D. *Archbishop Pecham*. Oxford: Clarendon Press, 1952. (Peckham, John)

Etzkorn, G. "John Pecham, OFM: A Career of Controversy." In *Monks, Nuns, and Friars in Medieval Society*, 71–82. Sewanee, Tenn.: Press of the University of the South, 1989. (Peckham, John)

Kaeppeli, T. "Guillelmus Peraldus (Peyraut)." In *Scriptores Ordinis Praedicatorum Medii Aevi*, 5 vols., 2:133–52. Rome: S. Sabina, 1975. (Peraldus *or* Peyraud, William)

Friedman, R. L., and L. O. Nielsen, eds. "Peter Auriol." Special issue, *Vivarium* 38, no. 1 (2000). (Peter Aureoli *or* Auriol)

Schabel, C. *Theology at Paris, 1316–1345: Peter Auriol and the Problem of Divine Foreknowledge and Future Contingents*. Aldershot, UK: Ashgate, 2000. (Peter Aureoli *or* Auriol)

Trapp, A. D. "Pierre Ceffons of Clairvaux." *Recherches de Théologie Ancienne et Médiévale* 24 (1957): 101–54. (Peter Ceffons)

Luscombe, D. E. "Peter Comestor." *The Bible in the Medieval World: Essays in Memory of Beryl Smalley*, ed. K. Walsh and D. Wood, 109–29. Oxford: Oxford University Press, 1985. (Peter Comestor)

Gaskin. R. "Peter Damian on Divine Power and the Contingency of the Past." *British Journal for the History of Philosophy* 5 (1997): 229–47. (Peter Damian)

Holopainen, T. *Dialectic and Theology in the Eleventh Century*. Leiden: Brill, 1996. (Peter Damian)

Kneepkens, C. H. "Grammar and Semantics in the Twelfth Century: Petrus Helias and Gilbert de la Porree on the Substantive Verb." In *The Winged Chariot*, ed. M. Kardaun and J. Spruyt. Leiden: Brill, 2000. (Peter Helias)

Colish, M. L. *Peter Lombard*. 2 vols. Leiden: Brill, 1994. (Peter Lombard)

Rosemann, P. W. *Peter Lombard*. Great Medieval Thinkers. Oxford: Oxford University Press, 2004. (Peter Lombard)

Dumont, S. D. "Transcendental Being: Scotus and the Scotists." *Topoi* 11 (1992): 25–38. (Peter of Aquila)

Galle, G. *Peter of Auvergne: Questions on Aristotle's "De caelo," a Critical Edition with an Interpretative Essay*. Leuven: Leuven University Press, 2003 (Peter of Auvergne)

Markowski, M. "Peter of Blois: Writer and Reformer." Ph.D. diss., University of Syracuse, N.Y., 1988. (Peter of Blois)

Brown, S. F. "Peter of Candia's Hundred-Year 'History' of the Theologian's Role." *Medieval Philosophy and Theology* 1 (1998): 156–90. (Peter of Candia)

———. "Peter of Candia's Sermons in Praise of Peter Lombard." In *Studies Honoring Ignatius Charles Brady, Friar Minor*, eds. R. S. Almagno and C. L. Harkins. St. Bonaventure, N.Y.: Franciscan Institute Publications, 1976. (Peter of Candia)

Burr, D. *Olivi and Franciscan Poverty*. Philadelphia: University of Pennsylvania Press, 1989. (Peter of John Olivi)

———. *Olivi's Peaceable Kingdom: A Reading of the "Apocalypse" Commentary*. Philadelphia, Pa.: University of Pennsylvania Press, 1993. (Peter of John Olivi)

Dunbabin, J. *A Hound of God: Pierre de la Palud and the Fourteenth-Century Church*. Oxford: Oxford University Press, 1991. (Peter of la Palu or Palude)

Garvin, J. N. "Magister Udo, a Source of Peter of Poitiers' *Sententiae*." *New Scholasticism* 28 (1954): 286–98. (Peter of Poitiers)

Moore, P. S. *The Works of Peter of Poitiers, Master in Theology and Chancellor of Paris (1193–1205)*. Notre Dame, Ind.: University of Notre Dame Press, 1936. (Peter of Poitiers)

Schabel, C. "Peter de Rivo and the Quarrel over Future Contingents at Louvain: New Evidence and New Perspectives." *Documenti e Studi sulla Tradizione Filosofica Medievale* 6 (1995): 363–473, and 7 (1996): 369–435. (Peter of Rivo)

De Rijk, L. M. Introduction to *Peter of Spain*. Assen: Van Gorcum, 1972. (Peter of Spain)

d'Ors, A. "Petrus Hispanus O.P., Auctor Summularum." *Vivarium* 35 (1997): 21–71. (Peter of Spain)

Courtenay, W. J. "Dominicans and Suspect Opinion in the Thirteenth Century: The Cases of Stephen of Venizy, Peter of Tarentaise, and the Articles of 1270 and 1277." *Vivarium* 32 (1994): 186–95. (Peter of Tarantaise)

Beichner, P. F. Introduction to *Aurora Petri Rigae: Biblia Versificata; A Verse Commentary on the Bible*, 2 vols., 1:vii–lv. Notre Dame, Ind.: University of Notre Dame Press, 1965. (Peter Riga)

Baldwin, J. W. *Masters, Princes, and Merchants: The Social View of Peter the Chanter and His Circle*. Princeton, N.J.: Princeton University Press, 1970. (Peter the Chanter *or* Peter Cantor)

Kritzeck, J. *Peter the Venerable and Islam*. Princeton, N.J.: Princeton University Press, 1964. (Peter the Venerable)

Torrell, J.-P., and D. Bouthillier. *Pierre le Vénérable et sa vision du monde*. Leuven: Spicilegium Sacrum Lovaniense, 1986. (Peter the Venerable)

Dumont. S. D. "The Univocity of the Concept of Being in the Fourteenth Century, II: The *"De ente"* of Peter Thomae." *Mediaeval Studies* 50 (1988): 186–256. (Peter Thomae)

Gál. G. "Petrus de Trabibus on the Absolute and Ordained Power of God." In *Studies Honoring Ignatius Charles Brady, Friar Minor*, 283–92. St. Bonaventure, N.Y.: Franciscan Institute Publications, 1976. (Petrus de Trabibus)

Huning, H. A. "The Plurality of Forms according to Petrus de Trabibus." *Franciscan Studies* 28 (1968): 130–46. (Petrus de Trabibus)

McDonald, S. "Goodness as Transcendental: The Early Thirteenth-Century Recovery of an Aristotelian Idea." *Topoi* 11 (1992): 173–86. (Philip the Chancellor)

Principe, W. *Philip the Chancellor's Theology of the Hypostatic Union*. Toronto: Pontifical Institute of Mediaeval Studies, 1975. (Philip the Chancellor)

Sandmel, S. *Philo of Alexandria: An Introduction*. Oxford: Oxford University Press, 1979. (Philo of Alexandria)

Wolfson, H. A. *Philo: Foundations of Religious Philosophy in Judaism, Christianity and Islam*. 2 vols. Cambridge, Mass.: Harvard University Press, 1947. (Philo of Alexandria)

Sorabji, R. R. K., ed. *Philoponus and the Rejection of Aristotelian Science*. London: Duckworth, 1987. (Philoponus, John *or* John the Grammarian)

Verrycken, K. "The Development of Philoponus' Thought and Its Chronology." In *Aristotle Transformed*, ed. R. R. K. Sorabji, 233–74. London: Duckworth, 1990. (Philoponus, John *or* John the Grammarian)

Mass, M. "Photius' Treatment of Josephus and the High Priesthood." *Byzantion* 60 (1990): 183–94. (Photius)

White, D. S. *Patriarch Photios of Constantinople: His Life, Scholarly Contributions and Correspondence, together with the Translation of Fifty-Two of His Letters*. Archbishop Iakavos Library of Ecclesiastical and Historical Sources 5. Brookline, Mass.: Holy Cross College Press, 1981. (Photius)

Kristeller, P. O. "Giovanni Pico della Mirandola and his Sources." In *L'opera e il pensiero di Giovanni Pico dela Mirandola nella storia dell' Umanesimo*, 2 vols., 1:35–133. Florence: Istituto Nazionale di Studi sul Rinascimento, 1965. (Pico della Mirandola, Giovanni)

Ackerman Smoller, L. *History, Prophecy, and the Stars: The Christian Astrology of Pierre d'Ailly, 1350–1420*. Princeton, N.J.: Princeton University Press, 1994. (Pierre d'Ailly *or* Petrus de Alliaco)

Gerson, L. B., ed. *The Cambridge Companion to Plotinus*. Cambridge: Cambridge University Press, 1996. (Plotinus)

Gregory, T. "The Platonic Inheritance." In *A History of Twelfth-Century Western Philosophy*, ed. P. Dronke, 54–80. Cambridge: Cambridge University Press, 1988. (Plato in the Middle Ages)

Porette, M. *The Mirror of Simple Souls*. Trans. E. Colledge et al. Fwd. K. Emery Jr. Notre Dame, Ind.: University of Notre Dame Press, 1999. (Margaret Porete)

Karamanolis, G. *Plato and Aristotle in Agreement? Platonists on Aristotle from Antiochus to Porphyry*. Oxford: Oxford University Press, 2006. (Porphyry)

Corbett, J. A. Introduction to *Praepositini Cremonensis: Tractatus de Officiis*, xi–xxix. Notre Dame, Ind.: University of Notre Dame Press, 1969. (Praepositinus *or* Prévostin of Cremona)

O'Donnell, R. "Alcuin's Priscian." In *Latin Script and Letters, A.D. 400–900*, ed. J. J. O'Meara and B. Naumann. Leiden: Brill, 1976. (Priscian)

Bos, A., and P. A. Meijer, eds. *Proclus and His Influence in Medieval Philosophy*. Leiden: Brill, 1992. (Proclus)

Chadwick, N. K. *Poetry and Letters in Early Christian Gaul*. London: Bowes and Bowes, 1955. (Prosper of Aquitaine)

Brown, S. F. "'Duo Candelabra Parisiensia': Prosper of Reggio in Emilia's Portrait of the Enduring Presence of Henry of Ghent and Godfrey of Fontaines regarding the Nature of Theological Study." In *Nach der Verurteilung von 1277*, ed. J. A. Aertsen, J. Emery Jr., and A. Speer, 320–56. Miscellanea Mediaevalia 28. Berlin: De Gruyter, 2001. (Prosper of Reggio Emilia)

Kaldellis, A. *The Argument of Psellos's Chronographia*. Leiden: Brill, 1999. (Psellos, Michael)

Papaioannou, S. *Michael Psellos: Rhetoric and Authorship in Byzantium*. Cambridge: Cambridge University Press, 2013. (Psellos, Michael)

Robbins, F. E. Introduction to *Ptolemy: Tetrabiblos*, vii–xxiv. Loeb Classical Library. Cambridge, Mass.: Harvard University Press, 1940. (Psellos, Michael)

Blythe, J. M. Introduction to *On the Government of Rulers: "De Regimine Principum," Ptolemy of Lucca*, 1–59. Philadelphia: University of Pennsylvania Press, 1997. (Ptolemy of Lucca)

Bejczy, I. P. *The Cardinal Virtues in the Middle Ages: A Study in Moral Thought from the Fourth to the Fourteenth Century*, 122–24. Leiden: Brill, 2011. (Radulphus Ardens)

Ebbensen, S., and J. Pinborg. "Gennadios and Western Scholasticism: Radulphus Brito's 'Ars vetus' in Greek Translation." *Classica et Mediaevalia* 33 (1981–1982): 263–319. (Radulphus *or* Ralph Brito)

Pinborg, J. "Radulphus Brito on Universals." *Cahiers de l'Institut du Moyen-Age Grec et Latin* 35 (1980): 56–142. (Radulphus *or* Ralph Brito)

Orth, E. J. "Ralph Strode on Inconsistency in Obligational Disputations." In *Argumentationstheorie, Scholastische Forschungen zu den logischen und semantischen Regeln korrekten Folgerns*, ed. K. Jacobi, 363–86. Leiden: Brill, 1993. (Ralph Strode)

Spade, P. V. "Ralph Strode." In *The Mediaeval Liar: A Catalogue of the "Insolubilia" Literature*, 87–91. Toronto: Pontifical Institute of Mediaeval Studies, 1975. (Ralph Strode)

Fahey, J. J. *The Eucharistic Teaching of Ratramn of Corbie*. Mundelein, Ill.: Our Lady of the Lake Seminary, 1951. (Ratramnus of Corbie)

Bolton, D. K. "Remigian Commentaries in the 'Consolation of Philosophy' and Their Sources." *Traditio* 33 (1977): 381–94. (Remigius of Auxerre)

Gal, G., and R. Wood. "Richard Brinkley and His 'Summa logicae.'" *Franciscan Studies* 40 (1980): 59–101. (Richard Brinkley)

Spade, P. V. "Richard Brinkley's 'De insolubilibus': A Preliminary Assessment." In *Revista di Storia della Filosofia* 46 (1991): 245–56. (Richard Brinkley)

Long, R. J., and M. O'Carroll. *The Life and Works of Richard Fishacre OP: Prolegomena to the Edition of His Commentary on the "Sentences."* Munich: Bavarian Academy of Sciences, 1999. (Richard Fishacre)

Leff, G. *Richard Fitzralph, Commentator on the Sentences*. Manchester: Manchester University Press, 1963. (Richard Fitzralph)

Walsh, K. *Richard Fitzralph in Oxford, Avignon and Armagh*. Oxford: Clarendon Press, 1981. (Richard Fitzralph)

Jung-Palczewska, E. "Works by Richard Kilvington." *Archives d'Histoire Doctrinale et Littéraire du Moyen-Âge* 67 (2000): 181–223. (Richard Kilvington)

Kelley, F. E. Introduction to *Richard Knapwell: "Quaestio disputata de unitate formae,"* 3–23. Paris: Vrin, 1982. (Richard Knapwell)

Synan, E. A. *The Works of Richard of Campsall.* Toronto: Pontifical Institute of Mediaeval Philosophy, 1968. (Richard of Campsall)

Brown, S. F. "Richard of Conington and the Analogy of the Concept of Being." *Franziskanische Studien* 48 (1966): 297–307. (Richard of Conington)

Spade, P. V. "Five Logical Tracts by Richard Lavenham." In *Essays in Honour of Anton Charles, Pegis*, ed. R. O'Donnell, 70–124. Toronto: Pontifical Institute of Mediaeval Studies, 1974. (Richard of Lavenham *or* Lavingham)

Cunningham, F. A. "Richard of Middleton, O.F.M. on 'esse' and 'essence.'" *Franciscan Studies* 30 (1970): 49–76. (Richard of Middleton)

Den Bok, N. *Communicating the Most High: A Systematic Study of Person and Trinity in the Theology of Richard of St. Victor (d. 1173).* Paris: Brepols, 1996. (Richard of Saint-Victor)

Raedts, P. *Richard Rufus of Cornwall and the Tradition of Oxford Theology.* Oxford: Clarendon Press, 1987. (Richard Rufus)

Clagett, M. "Richard Swineshead and Late Medieval Physics." *Osiris* 9 (1950): 131–61. (Richard Swineshead)

McEvoy, J. *Robert Grosseteste*, 13–15, passim. Oxford: Oxford University Press, 2000. (Robert Bacon)

Brown, S. F. "Robert Cowton and the Analogy of the Concept of Being." *Franciscan Studies* 31 (1971): 5–40. (Robert Cowton)

Spade, P. V. "Robert Fland's 'Consequentiae': An Edition." *Mediaeval Studies* 38 (1976): 54–84. (Robert Fland *or* Robert of Flanders)

Judy, A. G. Introduction to *Robert Kilwardby O.P., De ortu scientiarum*, xi–lxi. Oxford: Oxford University Press, 1976. (Robert Kilwardby)

Langholm, O. *Economics in the Medieval Schools*, 37–52. Leiden: Brill, 1992. (Robert of Courçon)

Colish, M. L. *Peter Lombard*, 2 vols., 1:72–77, 108–113, passim. Leiden: Brill, 1994. (Robert of Melun)

Kelley, F. E. "Two Early English Thomists: Thomas Sutton and Robert Orford vs. Henry of Ghent." *The Thomist* 45 (1981): 345–87. (Robert of Orford)

Copsey, R. "The Carmelites in England, 1242–1500: Surviving Writings." *Carmelus* 43 (1996): 213–18. (Robert of Walsingham)

Lindberg, D. C. *Roger Bacon's Philosophy of Nature.* Oxford: Oxford University Press, 1983. (Roger Bacon)

Little, A. G., and F. Pelster. "The Franciscan School at Oxford in the Thirteenth Century." *Archivum Franciscanum Historicum* 19 (1926): 855–57. (Roger Marston)

Hess, C. R. The *Tract on Holy Orders in the "Summa" of Roland of Cremona.* Rome: Pontificia studiorum universitas a S. Thoma de Aquino, 1969. (Roland of Cremona)

Mews, C. J. "Nominalism and Theology before Abelard: New Light on Roscelin of Compiègne." *Vivarium* 30 (1992): 4–33. (Roscelin)

Van Engen, J. H. *Rupert of Deutz*. Berkeley: University of California Press, 1983. (Rupert of Deutz)

De Paepe, N. *Jan van Ruusbroec: The Sources, Content and Sequels of His Mysticism*. Leuven: Peeters, 1984. (Ruysbroeck, Jan van)

Fox, M. "On the Rational Commandments in Saadia: A Re-Examination." *Modern Jewish Ethics: Theory and Practice*, 174–87. Columbus: Ohio State University Press, 1975. (Saadiah Gaon)

Harvey, S. "The Quality of Philosophy according to Averroes and Falaquera: A Muslim and His Jewish Interpreter." *Miscellanea Mediaevalia* 26 (1998): 910–31. (Shem Tov Ibn Falaquera)

Nielsen, L. O. "Parisian Discussions of the Beatific Vision after the Council of Vienne: Thomas Wylton, Sibert of Beka, Peter Auriol and Raymundus Bequini." In *Philosophical Debates at Paris in the Early Fourteenth Century*, ed. S. F. Brown, T. Dewender, and T. Kobusch, 179–86. Leiden: Brill, 2009. (Siger of Beka)

Bukovsky, T. P. "Siger of Brabant vs. Thomas Aquinas on Theology." *New Scholasticism* 61 (1987): 25–32. (Siger of Brabant)

Bursill-Hall, G. L. *Speculative Grammars of the Middle Ages*. The Hague: Moutun, 1971. (Siger of Courtrai)

Ebbensen, S. Introduction to *Simon of Faversham: Quaestiones super libro Elenchorum*, 1–22. Toronto: Pontifical Institute of Medieval Studies, 1984. (Simon of Faversham)

Smalley, B. "The '*quaestiones*' of Simon of Hinton." In *Studies in Medieval History Presented to F. M. Powicke*, 209–22. Oxford: Clarendon Press, 1948. (Simon of Hinton)

Häring, N. "Simon of Tournai and Gilbert of Poitiers." *Mediaeval Studies* 27 (1965): 325–30. (Simon of Tournai)

Kanarfogel, E., and M. Sokolow. *Between Rashi and Maimonides: Themes in Medieval Jewish Thought, Literature and Exegesis*. New York: Yeshiva University Press, 2010. (Solomon ben Isaac *or* Rashi)

Wiesel, E. *Rashi*. Schocken: Knopf Doubleday, 2009. (Solomon Ben Isaac *or* Rashi)

Huenemann, C., ed. *Interpreting Spinoza: Critical Essays*. Cambridge: Cambridge University Press, 2008. (Spinoza)

Salas, V., ed. *Collected Studies on Francisco Suarez, S.J. (1548–1617)*. Leuven: Leuven University Press, 2011. (Suárez, Francisco)

Wilenius, R. *The Social and Political Theory of Francisco Suarez*. Helsinki: Societas Philosophica Fennica, 1963. (Suárez, Francisco)

Clark, J. M. Introduction to *Little Book of Eternal Wisdom and Little Book of Truth*, 9–39. London: Faber and Faber, 1953. (Suso, Heinrich)

Sturlese, L. *Homo divinus: Philosophische Projekte in Deutschland zwischen Meiser Eckhart und Heinrich Seuse*. Stuttgart: Kohlmanner, 2007. (Suso, Heinrich)

―――. *Eckhart, Tauler, Suso. Filosofi e mistici nella Germania medievale*. Firenze: Le Lettere, 2010. (Suso, Heinrich and Tauler, Johannes)

Ozment, S. E. *Homo Spiritualis: A Comparative Study of the Anthropology of Johannes Tauler, Jean Gerson and Martin Luther (1509–1516) in the Context of Their Theological Thought*, 13–46. Leiden: Brill, 1969. (Tauler, Johannes)

Sturlese, L. *Eckhart, Tauler, Suso. Filosofi e mistici nella Germania medievale*. Firenze: Le Lettere, 2010. (Tauler, Johannes)

McLaughlin, M. M. *Intellectual Freedom and Its Limitations in the University of Paris in the Thirteenth and Fourteenth Centuries*, passim. New York: Macmillan, 1977. (Tempier, Étienne)

Piron, S. "Le plan de l'évêque. Pour une critique interne de la condemnation du 7 mars 1277." *Recherches de Théologie et Philosophie médiévales* 78 (2011): 383–415. (Tempier, Étienne)

Fredborg, K. M. Introduction to *The Latin Rhetorical Commentaries of Thierry of Chartres*, 1–43. Toronto: Pontifical Institute of Mediaeval Studies, 1988. (Thierry of Chartres)

De Young, R. K., McCluskey, C., and Van Dyke, C. *Aquinas's Ethics: Metaphysical Foundations, Moral Theory and Theological Context*. Notre Dame, Ind.: University of Notre Dame Press, 2009 (Thomas Aquinas)

Jensen, S. *Good and Evil Actions: A Journey through Saint Thomas Aquinas*. Notre Dame, Ind.: University of Notre Dame Press, 2011. (Thomas Aquinas)

Torrell, J.-P. *Saint Thomas Aquinas: The Person and His Work*. Vol. 1. Trans. R. Royal. Washington, D.C.: Catholic University of America Press, 1996. (Thomas Aquinas)

―――. *Saint Thomas Aquinas: Spiritual Master*. Vol. 2. Trans. R. Royal. Washington, D.C.: Catholic University of America Press, 2003. (Thomas Aquinas)

McGinn, B. "Thomas Gallus and Dionysian Mysticism." *Studies in Spirituality* 8 (1998): 81–96. (Thomas Gallus)

Bursill-Hall, G. L. *Grammatica Speculativa of Thomas of Erfurt*. London: Longman, 1972. (Thomas of Erfurt)

Kennedy, L. A. "Two Augustinians and Nominalism." *Augustiniana* 38 (1988): 118–28. (Thomas of Strasbourg)

Trapp, A. D. "Augustinian Theology in the 14th Century." *Augustiniana* 6 (1956): 175–82. (Thomas of Strasbourg)

Scully, E. "The Power of Physical Bodies according to Thomas of York." *Sciences ecclésiastiques* 14 (1962): 109–34. (Thomas of York)

Klima, G. "Thomas of Sutton on the Nature of the Intellective Soul and the Thomistic Theory of Being." In *Nach der Verurteilung von 1277*, ed. J. Aertsen, K. Emery Jr., and A. Speer, 436–55. Berlin: De Gruyter, 2000. (Thomas Sutton)

Dumont, S. D. "New Questions by Thomas Wylton." *Documenti e Studi sulla Tradizione Filosofica Medievale* 9 (1998): 341–81. (Thomas Wylton *or* Wilton)

Lescoe, F. J. *God as First Principle in Ulrich of Strasbourg: Critical Text of "Summa de bono," IV, 1, based on Hitherto Unpublished Mediaeval Manuscripts and Philosophical Study*. New York: Alba House, 1979. (Ulrich of Strasbourg)

Lynch, J. E. *The Theory of Knowledge of Vital du Four*. St. Bonaventure, N.Y.: Franciscan Institute Publications, 1972. (Vitalis of Furno)

Duckett, E. S. "Walafrid Strabo." In *Carolingian Portraits: A Study in the Ninth Century*, 121–60. Ann Arbor: University of Michigan Press, 1962. (Walafrid Strabo)

Brown, S. F. "Walter Chatton's 'Lectura' and William of Ockham's 'Quaestiones in libros Physicorum Aristotelis.'" In *Essays Honoring Allan B. Wolter*, ed. W. A. Frank and G. J. Etzkorn, 81–93. St. Bonaventure, N.Y.: Franciscan Institute, 1985. (Walter Chatton)

Friedman, R. L. "The 'Sentences' Commentary, 1250–1320." In *Mediaeval Commentaries on the "Sentences" of Peter Lombard*, ed. G. R. Evans, 1:50–52. Leiden: Brill, 2002. (Walter of Bruges)

Häring, N. M. *Life and Works of Clarembald of Arras*, passim. Toronto: Pontifical Institute of Medieval Studies, 1965. (Walter of Mortagne)

Glorieux, P. "Mauvaise action et mauvais travail: le 'Contra quatuor layrinthos Franciae.'" *Recherches de Théologie ancienne et médiévale* 21 (1954): 179–93. (Walter of Saint-Victor)

Studeny, R. F. "Walter of Saint-Victor and the 'Apologia de Verbo incarnato.'" *Gregorianum* 18 (1937): 579–85. (Walter of Saint-Victor)

Kraml, H. Introduction to *Guillelmus de la Mare: Scriptum in librum primum Sententiarum*. Munich: Bayerische Akademie der Wissenschaften, Bd. 29, 1989. (William de la Mare)

Dumont, S. D. "The Univocity of the Concept of Being in the Fourteenth Century: John Duns Scotus and William of Alnwick." *Mediaeval Studies* 49 (1987): 1–75. (William of Alnwick)

Teske, R. J. Introduction to *William of Auvergne: The Trinity, or the First Principles*, 1–60. Mediaeval Philosophical Texts in Translation 28. Milwaukee, Wisc.: Marquette University Press, 1995. (William of Auvergne)

Principe, W. H. Introduction to *William of Auxerre's Theology of the Hypostatic Union*, 9–16. Toronto: Pontifical Institute of Mediaeval Studies, 1963. (William of Auxerre)

Dronke, P. *A History of Twelfth-Century Western Philosophy*, 231–16, passim. Cambridge: Cambridge University Press, 1988. (William of Champeaux)

Fredborg, K. M. "Some Notes on the Grammar of William of Conches." *Cahiers de l'Institut du Moyen-Age Grec et Latin* 37 (1981): 21–41. (William of Conches)

Ronca, I., and M. Curr. Introduction to *William of Conches: A Dialogue on Natural Philosophy (Dogmaticon Philosophiae)*, xv–xxvi. Notre Dame, Ind.: University of Notre Dame Press, 1997. (William of Conches)

Crowley, T. "John Peckham OFM, Archbishop of Canterbury, versus the New Aristotelianism." *Bulletin of the John Rylands Library* 31 (1951): 242–55. (William of Hothum)

Hinnebusch, W. A. *The Early English Friars Preachers*, 410–12. Rome: S. Sabina, 1951. (William of Macclesfield)

Clagett, M. *Archimedes in the Middle Ages*. Vol. 2, part 1, *The Translations from the Greek by William of Moerbeke*, introduction. Philadelphia: University of Pennsylvania Press, 1976. (William of Moerbeke)

Little, A. G. *The Grey Friars in Oxford*, 182–85. Oxford: Oxford University Press, 1892. (William of Nottingham)

Adams, M. M. *William Ockham*. 2 vols. Notre Dame, Ind.: University of Notre Dame Press, 1987. (William of Ockham)

Brower-Towland, S. *Ockham and Ockhamism: Studies in the Dissemination and Impact of His Thought*. Leiden: Brill, 2008. (William of Ockham)

Maurer, A. *The Philosophy of William of Ockham in Light of Its Principles*. Toronto: Pontifical Institute of Mediaeval Studies, 1999. (William of Ockham)

Dawson, J. D. "William of Saint-Amour and the Apostolic Tradition." *Mediaeval Studies* 40 (1978): 223–38. (William of Saint-Amour)

Bell, D. N. *The Image and Likeness: The Augustinian Spirituality of William of Saint-Thierry*. Kalamazoo, Mich.: Cistercian Fathers Publications, 1984. (William of Saint-Thierry)

Stump, E. "William of Sherwood's Treatise on Obligations." *Historiographia Linguistica* 7 (1980): 249–61. (William of Sherwood)

Brown, S. F. "Henry of Ghent on Aquinas's Subalternation Theory." In *Knowledge and the Sciences in Medieval Philosophy (Proceedings of the Eighth International Congress of Medieval Philosophy)*, ed. R. Tyoerinoja, A. I. Lehtinen, and D. Foellesdal, 3:337–45. Helsinki: Annals of the Finnish Society for Missiology and Ecumenics, 1990. (William Peter of Godino)

Kenny, A. *Wyclif in His Times*. Oxford: Oxford University Press, 1986. (Wycliffe, John)

Lahey, S. E. *John Wyclif*. Oxford; Oxford University Press. 2009. (Wycliffe, John)

Levy, I. C. *A Companion to John Wyclif: Late Medieval Theologian.* Leiden: Brill, 2006. (Wycliffe, John)

# About the Authors

Although we are from different cultural backgrounds (one from Philadelphia and the other from San Salvador), we have a number of resources in common. Both of us pursued our doctoral studies at the University of Louvain, in Belgium. We are both officially doctors of philosophy but nonetheless have extensive theological backgrounds. We are also the editors of numerous medieval Latin philosophical and theological texts. In brief, the world of medieval thought is and has been the center of our teaching and research.

**Stephen F. Brown**, who did his undergraduate studies at St. Bonaventure University, has spent more than forty years teaching undergraduate and graduate students in the Theology Department at Boston College. He was recently honored by the Festschrift *Philosophy and Theology in the Long Middle Ages*, edited by professors Kent Emery Jr. (Notre Dame), Andreas Speer (Köln), and Russell L. Friedman (Leuven).

**Juan Carlos Flores**, who studied as an undergraduate at Connecticut College and received his master's degree from Boston College before doing his doctoral studies at Leuven, is professor at the University of Detroit Mercy. His doctoral dissertation focused on the doctrine of the Trinity in the writings of one of the outstanding late 13th-century theologians, Henry of Ghent. An updated version of this dissertation was published under the title *Henry of Ghent: Metaphysics of the Trinity*.

CPSIA information can be obtained
at www.ICGtesting.com
Printed in the USA
BVHW03*0745120718
520930BV00008B/2/P